Freekanr

The Complete Reference

About the Author

Roderick W. Smith is a professional
computer book author and consultant based
in Woonsocket, Rhode Island. He has been
a user of UNIX systems since 1987, and has
administered UNIX-like systems, including
FreeBSD, since 1994. *FreeBSD: The Complete
Reference* is his tenth book. His other titles
include *Advanced Linux Networking*
(Addison-Wesley, 2002) and *The Multi-Boot
Configuration Handbook* (Que, 2000).

FreeBSD:
The Complete Reference

Roderick W. Smith

McGraw-Hill/Osborne

New York   Chicago   San Francisco
Lisbon   London   Madrid   Mexico City
Milan   New Delhi   San Juan
Seoul   Singapore   Sydney   Toronto

The McGraw·Hill Companies

McGraw-Hill/Osborne
2600 Tenth Street
Berkeley, California 94710
U.S.A.

To arrange bulk purchase discounts for sales promotions, premiums, or fund-raisers, please contact **McGraw-Hill/**Osborne at the above address. For information on translations or book distributors outside the U.S.A., please see the International Contact Information page immediately following the index of this book.

FreeBSD: The Complete Reference

1234567890 DOC DOC 019876543

Book p/n 0-07-222674-9 and CD p/n 0-07-222675-7
parts of
ISBN 0-07-222409-6

Publisher
Brandon A. Nordin

Vice President & Associate Publisher
Scott Rogers

Acquisitions Editor
Franny Kelly

Project Editor
Laura Stone

Acquisitions Coordinators
Emma Acker, Martin Przybyla

Technical Editor
Glenn Becker

Copy Editor
Marti Paul

Proofreader
Emily Hsuan

Indexer
David Heiret

Computer Designers
Apollo Publishing Services
Michelle Galicia

Illustrators
Michael Mueller, Lyssa Wald

Series Design
Peter F. Hancik

This book was composed with Corel VENTURA™ Publisher.

This book is for Bethany and Tarl,
friends who moved too far away too soon after they'd moved to Boston.

Contents at a Glance

Contents

Part I

FreeBSD Installation

Part II

Basic System Administration

Part III

Network Configuration

Part IV

Servers

Part V

Common User Programs

Part VI

System Maintenance

Acknowledgments

Although books have authors whose names go on their books' covers, authors cannot do the job alone. In the case of this book, I'd like to thank the publishing team at McGraw-Hill/Osborne—Franny Kelly, Acquisitions Editor, who provided valuable direction and feedback; Emma Acker and Martin Przybyla, who helped organize everything; Laura Stone, Project Editor, who dealt with many pesky details during the revision process; and Marti Paul, the Copy Editor, who corrected grammatical errors and pointed out awkward phrasings so you wouldn't have to see them. Glenn Becker served as the book's Technical Editor, which means he kept me on the technical straight-and-narrow path, although any errors that remain are of course my own. Vicki Harding and Sherry Rogelberg at Studio B Productions were invaluable in connecting me with McGraw-Hill/Osborne and helping this book get off to a good start. I'd like to thank David King for helpful discussions about FreeBSD. Last but far from least, the entire FreeBSD community deserves great thanks—without their dedication, FreeBSD would not exist.

Introduction

Certain operating systems (OSs) dominate the desktop and small server computer landscape. The most omnipresent of these are Microsoft's products, Windows 2000 and Windows XP. On its own hardware, Mac OS is important. Challenging these OSs are a collection of *open source* operating systems. These OSs are developed by individuals and organizations who give their work freely to the community. The resulting products are powerful derivatives of UNIX, an extraordinarily influential OS that dates back to the late 1960s but has managed to keep up with the times. Many of the features we take for granted in computers generally, such as TCP/IP networking, originated on UNIX. Two families of open source UNIX-like OSs are popular. One is the open source BSD family, and the other is the Linux family. This book is about the most popular member of this first family, FreeBSD. This book focuses upon what is in early 2003 the latest version of FreeBSD, version 5.0.

FreeBSD is sometimes mistaken for a version of Linux, but it's not—although FreeBSD and Linux do share many important features and even programs. Linux is built around an OS *kernel* (the core of an OS, which serves as a bridge between ordinary programs and hardware) that was developed as a from-the-ground-up re-implementation of the UNIX kernel. FreeBSD, by contrast, originated in an effort to rewrite the UNIX kernel on a file-by-file basis, as described in more detail in Chapter 1. At least as important in some ways, FreeBSD uses a different mix of low-level utilities and configuration files than does Linux. There are differences of a similar nature between FreeBSD and commercial UNIX OSs, such as IBM's AIX, Sun's Solaris, and HP's HPUX. Thus, even if you're familiar with Linux or a commercial UNIX, FreeBSD requires some explanation. If you're unfamiliar with Linux or a commercial UNIX and want to learn FreeBSD, a guide written for FreeBSD is far superior to one written for another OS, even a related OS. That's where this book comes in—it's a guide to FreeBSD, written from the ground up for FreeBSD.

Who Should Buy This Book

FreeBSD is a complex OS with many possible uses. You can run FreeBSD as an OS at home for browsing the Web, writing letters, playing games, and so on. You can use it as a business desktop OS, running word processors, spreadsheets, and so on. You can use it as a scientific or engineering workstation OS, running sophisticated data analysis tools, and writing new tools yourself with any of FreeBSD's many development languages. You can run FreeBSD on a network server computer, using Apache, Samba, sendmail, and other popular server programs to deliver information to clients around the office or around the world. You can even use FreeBSD as a dedicated router and firewall computer to protect a local network from the outside world and vice-versa. This range of potential uses for FreeBSD makes for a large book—especially one daring to call itself *FreeBSD: The Complete Reference*. To a greater or lesser extent, this book covers all of the FreeBSD uses just mentioned.

The range of uses for FreeBSD also means that this book is written for a wide audience. As a general rule, I've tried not to make too many assumptions about you in writing this book. In particular, I don't assume prior knowledge of or experience with FreeBSD or any other UNIX-like OS—although such experience certainly won't hurt. You might be a professional system administrator who's less than perfectly familiar with FreeBSD, or even with UNIX—for instance, you might be a Windows administrator who wants or needs to give FreeBSD a try. On the other hand, you might be a home user who's interested in trying out FreeBSD. Your FreeBSD system might have just one user (you) or hundreds of users. The wide range of applicability of FreeBSD makes it impossible for me to predict what your needs will be. Individual chapters may emphasize one set of possibilities or another, though, because these chapters' topics may fit better with one type of use than another.

One assumption I do make is that you're familiar with computers in general. If you've never touched a computer before in your life, this book is probably not for you—at least, not by itself. In fact, administering a FreeBSD system may not be the best introduction to computers you can have. Using a FreeBSD system that's administered by somebody else may be a better starting point; or you could start out on a non-UNIX OS, such as Windows or Mac OS (the most recent versions of which are actually based on UNIX, but hide it well), then move up to FreeBSD once you're familiar with computers generally.

One more point deserves elaboration: This book emphasizes FreeBSD system administration, not ordinary use. This distinction between administration and use is a clear one in FreeBSD, but it's blurry in many OSs, including the Windows $9x$/ Me line, Mac OS Classic, and even the latest from Microsoft and Apple, Windows NT/ 2000/XP and Mac OS X. In FreeBSD (or UNIX generally), the system administrator handles configuring the computer—setting up networking, installing and removing programs, and setting up accounts for use by ordinary users. These ordinary users are the ones who do productive work with the computer—writing programs, calculating spreadsheets, creating graphics, and so on. (On a server, the system administrator may be the only user with a normal account; other users access the computer remotely, and sometimes anonymously, via network connections.) If you have an account on a FreeBSD computer but aren't that computer's system administrator, this book will be of limited use to you, although some information, particularly in Part V, may be helpful. This book's emphasis is on the system administration side. This fact makes this book a good choice for somebody administering a FreeBSD system for other users. It's also a good starting point if you're an individual who's setting up a FreeBSD system for your own use. FreeBSD differs most from the likes of Windows or Mac OS in its administration. Clicking on icons to launch programs or selecting text in a word processor works much the same way in any OS, so even if you're setting up a single-user FreeBSD system to use as a workstation, this book will provide you with the information you need to accomplish this goal.

How This Book Is Organized

This book is organized into six parts, each of which contains between four and nine chapters, for a total of 32 chapters. The parts of the book are

- **Part I: FreeBSD Installation**   This part contains four chapters and covers preliminary issues—FreeBSD's requirements, installing the OS, a quick tour of an installed OS, and using FreeBSD on a multi-OS computer. These chapters are of most interest if you're installing FreeBSD from scratch. If you're sitting at a computer on which FreeBSD already exists, they're probably of less interest, although Chapter 3 can be a good starting point if you've never used a UNIX-like OS before, and some information in Chapter 4 can be helpful when dealing with removable disks from other computers or when running programs in an emulator.

- **Part II: Basic System Administration**   At nine chapters, this part is the longest in the book. It covers all the most basic tasks of FreeBSD system administration—the tools you use to do the job, how FreeBSD starts up and runs programs, partition management, file management, printer configuration, user account management, software installation, configuring the kernel, and the X Window System (FreeBSD's GUI environment; *X* for short). Sooner or later, most FreeBSD system administrators must deal with most or all of these topics, although you may be able to skip one or two of these chapters on some systems. For instance, you don't need to run X on most servers.

- **Part III: Network Configuration**   TCP/IP networking was developed on UNIX systems, so FreeBSD's network configuration tools are tightly integrated into the OS as a whole. As such, network configuration is really just a particular type of basic system administration, but I've created a four-chapter part of the book to cover this topic because it can be fairly complex. Chapters cover basic network configuration, dial-up network configuration, basic principles of clients and servers, and firewall configuration.

- **Part IV: Servers**   This part of the book consists of five chapters that cover some of the most important server programs you can run on FreeBSD—file servers, mail servers, web servers, login servers, and miscellaneous servers. (This last chapter actually covers several mostly unrelated small servers, so more than five server types are covered in this part of the book.) Because FreeBSD systems are often employed as server computers, this part of the book is very important to many FreeBSD administrators. If you want to use FreeBSD as a dedicated server computer, though, you may want to supplement this book with another on the specific server type, such as the Apache web server or the Samba file sharing server. Each chapter provides pointers to appropriate books and other documentation sources.

- **Part V: Common User Programs**   This part of the book diverges from the book's overall focus on administrative tasks and instead focuses upon user programs. Nonetheless, some of the information in this part is on installing and configuring user programs. The five chapters of this part cover GUI environments, networking tools, office tools, graphics tools, and multimedia applications (including games).

- **Part VI: System Maintenance**   Like most man-made things, FreeBSD requires maintenance to continue operating at its best. This part is devoted to this topic. The five chapters cover automated and non-automated routine maintenance, security issues, software compilation, writing scripts, and troubleshooting.

You can read this book straight through if you like, but chances are you won't want or need to do this. For the most part, each chapter stands on its own. Some chapters, though, rely upon information presented in other chapters. If you're already familiar with FreeBSD or even UNIX-like OSs generally, you may be able to skip some of these prerequisites. If not, each chapter includes references to material covered in more depth elsewhere in the book in case you need it. You can also use the book's index and glossary to help out if you need to quickly find more information or run across an unfamiliar term.

Conventions Used in This Book

This book uses certain conventions to help aid comprehension and break up the page into blocks that can be easy to scan. Conventions include fonts applied to specific words and lines, special text elements applied to paragraphs, and uses of IP addresses and hostnames used in networking examples.

Text and Font Conventions

Writing about computers presents certain pitfalls. Certain words can be rendered ambiguous by the fact that they may be program names, command names, computer names, and so on. When presenting a text-mode interaction between a human and a computer, it may not be clear what the human types and what the computer displays on the screen. For these reasons, this book uses certain typographical conventions to help clarify matters. These include:

- A normal proportionally spaced font like this one is the default font; normal text appears in this font.

- **Bold text** is used at the start of certain bulleted and numbered lists to summarize information contained in the item.

- *Italic text* denotes a new technical term that's being described for the first time in the chapter. Italics are also used for emphasis.

- `Monospaced text` is used for filenames, computer hostnames, uniform resource locators (URLs), the syntax used by a command, complete or partial configuration file contents, and text displayed by a computer in a text-mode display, such as when running a text-mode program. Program names sometimes appear in this font, when the program is most commonly known by the filename used to launch the program.

- **`Bold monospaced text`** denotes text that a user types, usually at a shell command prompt (described shortly). Sometimes you might type this text when interacting with a non-shell program, though.

- *`Italic monospaced text`* indicates a variable—information that's likely to vary from one system to another or from one situation to another. For instance, a file might be referred to as *`file.txt`*, meaning any file or a file with a name that I can't know.

- ***`Bold italic monospaced text`*** has the same meaning as italic monospaced text, but for something you type into the computer.

When you use FreeBSD in text mode, you do so by running a *shell*, which is a program that accepts your commands. FreeBSD launches the shell automatically when you log in. When I present long commands or extended series of interactions, I place these commands on separate lines from the bulk of the text. In these cases, I present a *shell prompt*—a character that the shell uses to tell you it's ready to receive input. I use a pound sign (#) as the shell prompt for the administrative account (`root`) and a dollar sign ($) as the shell prompt for ordinary user accounts. Thus, you might see something like this:

```
$ ifconfig | grep vr0
```

This line indicates that the command can be issued from an ordinary user account. (In most cases, `root` can also issue the same command, but you don't need to be `root` to issue the command.) If the line had begun with a pound sign, it would work properly only from the `root` account. For commands specified in the body of the text, I don't use this convention because it's potentially more confusing in that context. For instance, I might write "type `ifconfig` to see information on your network interfaces."

Some example lines are, in reality, longer than can be presented on a single line in this book. In such cases, the first line in this book ends with a special arrow as a line continuation character, thus:

```
/usr/src -network 172.17.2 -netmask 255.255.255.0 nova nebula ↵
blackhole browndwarf
```

If you see this symbol, it means that the text should be considered one line. Many FreeBSD configuration files enable you to use a backslash character (\) as a line continuation character, so in the case of configuration files, you may be able to enter long lines on multiple lines and use a backslash in place of the line continuation character used in this book. This feature isn't universal, though, so if in doubt it's best to stick with a long line.

Special Text Elements

Another set of text conventions highlights information that's important or unusual in some way. These elements are:

A Note provides information that's interesting or useful, but somewhat peripheral to the main thrust of the discussion. For instance, a Note might point out how a command differs from similar commands in other OSs.

A Tip describes a practice, procedure, or command that can help save you time or that can achieve a goal in some unusual or non-obvious but desirable way.

A *Caution warns you of potential danger. This danger might be a type of misconfiguration that can lead to trouble, typos that could cause problems, or even potential legal difficulties associated with a course of action. Pay attention to Cautions!*

Sidebar

A Sidebar is normally longer than Notes, Tips, and Cautions; these other elements are short paragraphs, whereas Sidebars contain two or more paragraphs. You can think of a Sidebar as an extended Note.

IP Address and Hostname Conventions

If you're familiar with TCP/IP networking, you may know that certain IP addresses are reserved for *private* networks—those that aren't connected to the Internet at large. Specifically, the ranges 10.0.0.0–10.255.255.255, 172.16.0.0–172.31.255.255, and 192.168.0.0–192.168.255.255 are so reserved. In order to avoid accidentally using somebody's real IP address, I use these ranges in most examples that require real IP addresses, even for systems that, in these examples, would be on the Internet.

If you've moved in networking circles for a while, you may know that the Internet standards document known as RFC 2606 describes domains whose names are reserved, much as the private network IP address ranges are reserved. In particular, example.com, example.net, and example.org are all reserved for use in documentation. Although I use these domain names in a few examples, they are—well—*boring!* Also, many examples require the use of multiple domain names, and these three reserved names are too similar to one another to stand out in most peoples' minds. Thus, I mix things up by using various domains that are not currently registered and probably never will be, such as luna.edu, pangaea.edu, and threeroomco.com. My apologies if any of these domains ever comes into use and causes confusion. Some examples require the use of real domains because the examples rely upon those specific domains. In such cases, I use the appropriate domain.

About the CD-ROM

This book includes with it a CD-ROM of FreeBSD 5.0. FreeBSD is a very large OS, so a single CD-ROM doesn't contain the entire OS. The CD-ROM included with this book is enough to get you started, though; it includes the core OS and the most important tools and utilities. You can boot the CD-ROM (or create a boot floppy from files on the CD-ROM, as described in Chapter 2) and install FreeBSD using nothing but the CD-ROM included with this book. Because FreeBSD is open source software, you may install it on as many computers as you like.

If you want to install software described in this book that's not on the CD-ROM, you can obtain it from the Internet. The easiest way to do so is to specify installation of the additional packages from an FTP site, as described in Chapter 11. In fact, you can also boot the CD-ROM but install FreeBSD itself from an FTP site, which may enable you to install programs initially that aren't on the included CD-ROM. Network installations of FreeBSD work best when you have a fast network connection; if you have only a 56Kbps dial-up modem, it may take hours to download all the packages you choose to install, so using the CD-ROM and then adding more packages from the Internet will be much faster.

Contacting Me

If you have comments or questions about the book, feel free to contact me at `rodsmith@rodsbooks.com`. I maintain a web page about this book at `http://www.rodsbooks.com/freebsd/`.

The
Complete
Reference

Part I

FreeBSD Installation

Chapter 1

FreeBSD Requirements

This book is your guide to the FreeBSD operating system. Before you embark too far on the FreeBSD journey, though, it's important that you understand some basics: why you might want to run FreeBSD, how it fits into the software world, and how it fits into the hardware world. This chapter addresses these issues. Understanding them can help you avoid costly mistakes, such as attempting to run FreeBSD on inadequate hardware or attempting to use FreeBSD in an inappropriate environment. If you're new to FreeBSD, this chapter is vitally important. Even if you're already familiar with FreeBSD (or some other UNIX variant), this chapter can help you plan your FreeBSD installation. (Chapter 2 continues the description of installation planning and execution.)

Why Run FreeBSD?

Using the right tool for the job is critically important to any undertaking, and your choice of OS is no exception to this rule. FreeBSD is a very capable and flexible OS, and as such, you can use it in many different ways. Despite this fact, though, FreeBSD isn't the perfect choice for all situations. For this reason, this book begins with a look at the circumstances in which you may want to run FreeBSD.

As a general rule, FreeBSD is used in one of two ways: as a workstation or as a server. This section describes these roles and covers FreeBSD's strengths and weaknesses with each. FreeBSD is one of a family of OSs that are derived from or modeled after the UNIX OS. In deciding on an OS to use, it's therefore important that you understand both how FreeBSD (or UNIX generally) compares to non-UNIX OSs and where FreeBSD fits in the family of UNIX-like OSs. This section therefore covers these relationships.

FreeBSD as a Workstation OS

In this book, the word *workstation* is used primarily to refer to any computer at which a user sits to perform day-to-day work, such as word processing, programming, graphic design, or web development. (Workstations can also be used for playing games.) Some people like to restrict the word *workstation* to high-powered computers used for these functions, or to systems with permanent network connections. When *workstation* is used in this way, the term *desktop computer* is used to refer to lower-powered or non-networked computers that otherwise resemble workstations. Distinctions based on computer power must constantly change with the technology, though, and networking distinctions can be blurry because of the popularity of dial-up network links on low-end systems. Therefore, this book uses the word *workstation* in reference to computers fulfilling the entire range of end-user functions.

The ability of any computer to function as a workstation depends upon two main factors:

- **A sophisticated user interface**   Today's users expect a computer to be easy to use. This ease of use factor has many aspects, the most obvious of which is a graphical user interface (GUI). In FreeBSD, the *X Window System* (or *X* for short), which is described in Chapter 13, provides the GUI. The core of X is very primitive as GUIs go, so various elements are built upon it, such as a *window manager* (which controls the borders around windows) and a programming *widget set* (which provides programmers with tools to display menus, dialog boxes, and the like). This modular approach makes X (and FreeBSD) very flexible from a user interface perspective, but this flexibility creates inconsistency between applications and can cause confusion for some users.

- **Available workstation applications**   A workstation runs end-user applications, such as word processors, spreadsheets, e-mail readers, compilers, graphics programs, and even games. Any OS that lacks a good selection of workstation tools makes a poor workstation OS. Furthermore, the quality of workstation tools must be high. FreeBSD supports a good selection of workstation applications. FreeBSD, though, lacks some of the more common workstation application titles; for instance, Microsoft's popular Office package isn't available for FreeBSD. There are alternatives, such as OpenOffice.org (described in Chapter 25), but if you need 100 percent perfect file compatibility, these alternatives may not be quite good enough. FreeBSD's selection of workstation application categories is deficient in some areas, such as games, but it's excellent in others, such as scientific tools.

Overall, FreeBSD can function as a workstation OS, but its suitability for this role is highly dependent upon your specific needs. FreeBSD's strengths as a workstation OS include its low cost, ability to function on older hardware, stability, flexible user interface, and its similarity to other UNIX-like OSs. Its weaknesses include a user interface that's less consistent than those of Windows or Mac OS and a user interface that's unfamiliar to those accustomed to Windows or Mac OS. The availability of specific applications can swing either way, depending upon your needs. If you aren't tied to specific non-UNIX programs or file formats, and if the applications you need are available for FreeBSD, it can be a good choice. On the other hand, if you need to use applications such as Microsoft Office that aren't available for FreeBSD, you may find another OS to be a better choice.

Tip   *If you want to run a UNIX-like OS as a workstation OS (say, because your local support personnel are trained on UNIX), but need to run Microsoft Office or other consumer-oriented packages that aren't available for FreeBSD, Mac OS X may be a good compromise. This OS is built around the Mach microkernel and many FreeBSD components. Mac OS X is* not *FreeBSD, but because it borrows heavily from FreeBSD and other UNIX-like OSs, Mac OS X should be familiar in many ways to UNIX administrators—more so than Microsoft Windows or earlier versions of Mac OS. Mac OS X supports many consumer-oriented applications, including Microsoft Office.*

If you choose to run FreeBSD as a workstation OS, pay particular attention to Part V of this book. If you're configuring a network for the use of many employees, students, or the like, you also should attend to issues surrounding the default GUI configuration, as described in Chapter 23. These environments have matured substantially since the mid-1990s, and are still improving at a rapid rate.

FreeBSD as a Server OS

A *server* is the second major role for FreeBSD. Servers are computers that have network connections and that respond to requests from other networked computers for data exchanges. This rather dry definition hides the fact that servers underlie the utility of networks. Examples of servers include

- **File servers** These computers enable other computers to read files from or upload files to the file server system. They can be used to distribute publicly available files (such as those that make up FreeBSD itself) or as centralized holding areas for files on a local network.

- **Web servers** In some sense, web servers are just a specialized form of file server. The popularity of web servers means that they deserve special attention, though. They typically deliver files from the server for display in a web client program, better known as a *web browser*.

- **Mail servers** A mail server is a computer that exchanges e-mail messages with other mail servers or with end-user mail programs. Most e-mail exchanges on the Internet at large involve at least two mail server computers, but local mail exchanges can use just one mail server.

- **Login servers** You can configure a FreeBSD system to accept logins from remote locations. When so configured, the system can be used in a workstation-like way, but from a distance. In some sense, this configuration blurs the line between workstation and server because the networking functions make the system a server, but it's often used as if it were a workstation. (In some cases, these features may be used on a server computer to enable remote administration, as well.)

- **Miscellaneous servers** There are server computers that provide many network support functions, such as the *Dynamic Host Configuration Protocol (DHCP)*, used to let one computer configure another's network settings; and font servers, which deliver font information to workstations.

These server functions are described in more detail in Part IV of this book. As you might guess by this coverage, FreeBSD makes an excellent server OS. Part of the reason for this is that many popular server programs were developed first for UNIX, and FreeBSD runs these UNIX servers very well. Coupled with the inexpensive *x*86 hardware on which FreeBSD runs, FreeBSD can be a very cost-effective way to run many of the world's most popular server programs.

> **Note**   *The word* server *can refer to either the entire computer or to a specific program that runs on the computer to provide the specific server functionality. One consequence of this fact is that a single computer can provide multiple network server functions. For instance, a single system might run a web server and a mail server. In most cases, the meaning of the term* server *(in reference to a computer or a program) should be clear from context. When the meaning might not be clear, I elaborate by referring to a* server computer *or a* server program.

Another advantage of FreeBSD as a server OS is FreeBSD's excellent reliability. Despite the fact that *x*86 hardware is quite varied and sometimes not as reliable as the hardware used in traditional server computers, such as those made by Sun or Silicon Graphics (SGI), FreeBSD is quite stable. It's not uncommon to find a FreeBSD server that's been running continually for months without problems. Reboots are often done to perform hardware upgrades rather than to upgrade an individual software package or to work around a problem that's causing flaky behavior. Because many computers rely upon a server computer, this high reliability is very important in a server OS.

Server computers need efficient and reliable networking subsystems. These include the individual server packages that they run, as well as core OS features, such as drivers for network cards and the *Transmission Control Protocol/Internet Protocol (TCP/IP) stack*, which is the part of the OS's kernel that's responsible for managing network functions. The FreeBSD TCP/IP stack is well respected and efficient. It also includes security features that enable you to implement a *packet-filter firewall* with FreeBSD. This topic is covered in Chapter 17. A packet-filter firewall enables you to block individual network packets based on features such as the source and destination IP addresses. Such features, which are increasingly common and sophisticated in modern OSs, are vital for servers, which often come under attack. Many individual FreeBSD server programs also include important security features aside from FreeBSD's packet filtering capabilities.

FreeBSD vs. Non-UNIX OSs

In deciding which OS to run, you're faced with specific choices. If FreeBSD is one of your choices (as presumably it is if you're reading this book), then you can classify other potential choices in two groups: non-UNIX-like and UNIX-like. This section describes the options in the first group, and summarizes FreeBSD's strengths and weaknesses compared to each. FreeBSD is a UNIX-like OS. If you're casting your OS net widely at first, you may want to first decide whether or not to run a UNIX-like OS, and then settle on the specific UNIX-like OS if you decide to take that route.

The range of OSs available today is quite broad—so broad that this section can't cover all of them. Instead, this section focuses on the most popular (and some not-so-popular) OSs that run on common low-end hardware (*x*86 and PowerPC CPUs):

- **DOS**   The *Disk Operating System (DOS)* was the original OS for the IBM PC, and it's still available today in various forms. All of these forms are primitive and limited compared to modern OSs. Their main advantages are their small sizes (both in disk space and memory usage) and the fact that they can very easily run *real-time* applications—those that require very precise and accurate timing, such as some types of scientific data collection software.

■ **Windows 9x/Me** This OS family is no longer current. It's built upon a DOS core, but with a heavily integrated GUI and preemptive multitasking extensions. Windows 9x/Me suffers from limited reliability and general quirkiness in many respects. Nonetheless, this OS's popularity and the availability of common workstation programs such as Microsoft Office makes it a good choice if you need these popular Windows-only programs. For new installations, though, something in the Windows NT family may be a better choice.

■ **Windows NT/2000/XP** Windows NT was a from-the-ground-up redesign of the Windows environment. Over successive new releases, this family improved its user interface and became more compatible with popular software. In 2002, Windows 2000 is Microsoft's official business and server OS, whereas Windows XP is marketed to home users. Both are built upon Windows NT, and are much more reliable than the DOS-based Windows 9x/Me line. FreeBSD is often considered more reliable than Windows NT/2000/XP, although there are those who disagree with this assessment. Windows 2000 or XP may be a good choice if you need to run Windows-only software.

■ **OS/2** Although it hasn't seen a new release from IBM since the Warp 4 version in 1996, IBM's OS/2 remains a viable alternative OS in environments that already rely heavily upon it. OS/2's reliability is comparable to Windows 2000/XP, but it can run only older 16-bit Windows applications, DOS programs, and OS/2-specific programs. A great deal of traditional UNIX software has been ported to OS/2. In 2001, Serenity Systems (http://www.serenity-systems.com) licensed OS/2 and released an updated version under the name *eComStation*.

■ **BeOS** BeOS was developed from the ground up to take the computing world into the 21st century. The OS never gained mass popularity, and in 2002 appears to be languishing, although it still has some faithful followers. BeOS is stable and fast, but it's deficient in its software selection. Like OS/2, BeOS is worth considering if you're already using it, but probably not if you're not using it. Be, Incorporated, which developed BeOS, was purchased by Palm (http://www.palm.com) in 2001.

■ **Mac OS** Mac OS has long been the only major competition for Windows on desktop computers, but the two OSs run on different hardware—Windows on x86 and Mac OS on 680x0 and (more recently) PowerPC. (Some versions of Windows NT have run on non-x86 CPUs, but all of these, except the latest IA64 ports, have been abandoned.) Mac OS is best known for its user interface, and it has a faithful following. The latest versions of Mac OS, known as *Mac OS X*, are built around a UNIX core that borrows heavily from FreeBSD, so in some sense Mac OS X is really a UNIX-like OS; but it differs enough, particularly in GUI, that I place it here. Mac OS X may be a good compromise if you want a UNIX-like core but access to popular end-user applications—provided those applications are available for Mac OS X. Because FreeBSD is primarily an *x*86 OS, it doesn't run on the same hardware as Mac OS X. (FreeBSD ports to the PowerPC are under development, though.)

Comparing FreeBSD to these OSs as a group is difficult because there's so much variability among these OSs. The most important of these competing OSs are Windows (particularly Windows 2000 and XP, but also the Windows 9*x*/Me line because of its massive installed base) and Mac OS.

Compared to Windows, FreeBSD's strengths lie mostly in the server arena. Some of the most popular servers, such as the sendmail mail server and Apache web server, are designed primarily for UNIX platforms, and they run very well on FreeBSD. During the late 1990s through early 2002, these FreeBSD servers have attracted less attention from miscreants, and so have been less likely to cause problems than their Windows counterparts. For instance, in 2001, Windows web servers were beset with worms such as Code Red and Nimda. Of course, it's possible that future vulnerabilities could make FreeBSD riskier than it appears to be today.

The popularity of Microsoft Office makes FreeBSD a second or third choice to Windows and Mac OS for common office tasks such as word processing—at least, if you want to exchange files with others who use Microsoft Office. Tools such as OpenOffice.org can read and write Microsoft Office files, but the formatting is sometimes corrupted in the process. If you don't need Microsoft Office compatibility, your choices are more open for workstation use. You may want to evaluate individual workstation software and run whatever OS seems to best support your preferred programs. The flexibility and network-centric features of X are definite plusses for FreeBSD, but the unfamiliarity and slightly cruder nature of the GUI choices are minuses, at least if your users are already familiar with Microsoft Windows or Mac OS.

FreeBSD vs. Other UNIX-Like OSs

If you've decided you want to run a UNIX-like OS rather than some version of Microsoft Windows, Mac OS, or the like, your next choice is *which* UNIX-like OS to run. FreeBSD is one of several choices available to you, and you should understand some of the differences between these UNIX variants. In many cases, any of these OSs will serve quite nicely, but there are situations in which FreeBSD may be better (or worse) suited to a particular task than the alternatives.

For the most part, different UNIX-like OSs can run the same software. Most are capable of running the popular sendmail and Apache servers, for instance, as well as the X Window System and various user-level tools built upon it. UNIX-like OSs vary among themselves in several ways:

- ■ **Kernels** A *kernel* is a software component that lies at the core of most OSs. The kernel serves as an interface between ordinary programs and the computer's hardware, provides features such as filesystems and process management, and generally handles low-level computing tasks. The kernel is therefore very important to the stability of an OS, and determines characteristics such as what hardware an OS supports. (A few devices are supported through nonkernel drivers, though.) Several different kernels are in use in the UNIX world today.

- **Hardware support**   On a broad scale, some UNIX-like OSs run on *x*86 CPUs and others run on other CPUs. The *x*86 CPU is usually considered the bottom rung in performance, at least for current general-purpose CPUs. Some non-*x*86 UNIX variants therefore run on powerful supercomputers with which *x*86 OSs such as FreeBSD can't compete. (You can link together several weaker computers to rival the power of a supercomputer, but this topic is beyond the scope of this book.) On a finer scale, the kernel and a few support programs determine what specific devices (modems, Ethernet cards, sound cards, and so on) a given UNIX variant supports.

- **Distribution policy**   Some UNIX variants are distributed as commercial products, but others are available as *open source*, meaning that anybody may obtain the source code, modify it, and redistribute it. Open source software tends to be less expensive than commercial software. Throughout the 1990s, though, commercial UNIX variants have become less expensive, and today some are even available free for at least some uses.

- **Default software and configuration**   UNIX has existed for about three decades, and in that time many variants of common utilities and configuration methods have emerged. Different UNIX-like OSs have followed different paths. For instance, some use the BSD-style configuration scripts and others use the System V (SysV) configuration scripts. The most common mail server is sendmail, but some UNIX variants ship with other mail servers. These differences combine to form the overall "personality" of a UNIX-like OS. Compared to the differences between any given UNIX-like OS and, say, Windows, these differences are minor; but they're substantial enough that somebody used to one UNIX variant may not be able to handle another without a guide.

FreeBSD uses a kernel that's derived from an open source reimplementation of the original AT&T UNIX kernel, as described in the upcoming section, "The Development of FreeBSD." FreeBSD was originally designed for the Intel *x*86 line of CPUs, and it also works with similar CPUs from AMD, VIA (Cyrix), Transmeta, and others (now defunct, except for rebadgings of AMD and VIA CPUs). Ports are underway to other CPUs, but in 2002, these are mostly immature and experimental. The Alpha CPU port is the most mature of these.

The FreeBSD kernel uses what's known as a *monolithic* design, meaning that the kernel is a single large logical structure that enables its components to interact more-or-less however their designers desire. Monolithic kernels place many tools, such as filesystem drivers, in what's known as *kernel space*, meaning that these systems have extraordinary control over hardware and kernel data structures. A competing design type used by some UNIX variants is known as a *microkernel*. This approach uses a smaller kernel that communicates with separate nonkernel components that handle some traditional kernel tasks, such as accessing filesystems. Microkernels tend to be more rigidly structured. Both monolithic and microkernel designs have their proponents.

FreeBSD is an open source OS. Specifically, most FreeBSD components use what's generally known as the *BSD license* (`http://www.opensource.org/licenses/bsd-license.html`). This license allows modification and redistribution under whatever terms the person doing the redistribution desires. Thus, in theory, somebody could take FreeBSD, modify it, and sell the result under a proprietary commercial license, or under another open source license. Another popular open source license is the *GNU General Public License (GPL)*, which requires that modifications be distributed under the GPL. The Linux kernel uses the GPL, and this difference in licensing drives some of the philosophical differences between FreeBSD and Linux proponents. (To be sure, not everybody has strong opinions on this matter of license terms.) As a general rule, FreeBSD favors using software components that use the BSD license, and Linux distributions tend to rely more upon packages that use the GPL. Although these licenses don't directly affect
the feel of their OSs, many utilities are available in alternate forms that use different licenses; thus, FreeBSD feels different than Linux because the two use a somewhat different mix of utilities.

Some UNIX-like OSs use proprietary (non-open-source) licenses. For instance, Sun's Solaris and IBM's AIX are commercial UNIXes. Sometimes you can use such an OS for free or for a low cost, as in the free Solaris for *x*86. Other times, you must pay for a commercial UNIX license. Just as there are tensions in the open source world between proponents of the GPL and BSD licenses, there are tensions between open source and commercial software proponents. These are philosophical and economic differences, though; FreeBSD works much like its commercial UNIX cousins.

 Note   *Commercial and open source software need not be incompatible. You can run open source programs on a commercial OS, or commercial programs on an open source OS. Nonetheless, most FreeBSD programs use open source licenses.*

Aside from FreeBSD, some popular UNIX-style OSs are

- **NetBSD** NetBSD is one of three OSs derived from 386/BSD (as described later in the section "The Development of FreeBSD"), the other two being FreeBSD and OpenBSD. NetBSD differs from FreeBSD, in part, in that NetBSD has been ported to many more CPUs. Its licensing and overall design are very similar to those of FreeBSD, but FreeBSD remains more popular because it's more heavily promoted and is arguably somewhat easier to install and use.

- **OpenBSD** OpenBSD's claim to fame is security. Its developers have gone to great lengths to create an OS that's not easily compromised. Like NetBSD, OpenBSD is quite similar to FreeBSD in configuration, licensing, and available software.

■ **Linux** You can think of Linux as a family of open source OSs. Technically, Linux is just the kernel; a Linux *distribution* includes the kernel and the software packages that create a useable OS. FreeBSD differs more from Linux than from NetBSD and OpenBSD in overall configuration style and the details of included tools.

Note *Some people unfamiliar with the UNIX world think that FreeBSD is a Linux distribution. It's not. FreeBSD doesn't use the Linux kernel, nor does it follow common Linux practices, such as the use of SysV startup scripts. FreeBSD is best thought of as an OS derived directly from the Berkeley Standard Distribution (BSD), as described later in the section "The Development of FreeBSD;" Linux is a free reimplementation of UNIX with weaker links to the early BSD and AT&T UNIX.*

■ **Solaris** Sun's Solaris is a commercial UNIX variant that's most commonly found on Sun's server hardware. This hardware uses SPARC CPUs, and is often used for heavy-duty servers that compete against high-end *x*86 systems and above. Solaris is also available to run on *x*86 computers, and so can be used on some of the same computers that run FreeBSD. Solaris on *x*86 has a weaker selection of drivers than does FreeBSD, though. If you need to develop programs for Sun computers, running Solaris on an *x*86 may be desirable; but for most other purposes, a BSD or Linux is probably a better choice for *x*86 computers. Sun hardware can make a good high-end server computer, though.

■ **AIX** IBM's commercial UNIX variant is known as AIX, and it runs on proprietary IBM hardware. Like Sun systems, AIX computers are aimed at the high-end server market, so their level of competition against FreeBSD is limited.

■ **IRIX** Most of SGI's workstations run a commercial UNIX variant known as IRIX. SGI's claim to fame in the past has been computers that are optimized for high-end graphics work, such as doing special effects for major motion pictures. Today, less expensive *x*86 computers are eating into this market, but SGI and IRIX are still powerful forces in this arena.

On the whole, FreeBSD competes most directly against its cousin BSDs and against Linux. FreeBSD is the most popular of the BSDs on *x*86 hardware, and so has an advantage when it comes to finding support. FreeBSD was developed with an eye for easy installation and administration; NetBSD and OpenBSD are somewhat weaker in these areas. You might want to consider OpenBSD for enhanced security or NetBSD for support on non-*x*86 CPUs, though. The overall feel of Linux is different from that of any of the BSDs, Linux supports a bit more hardware and commercial software, and the licensing issues are different. If you're just starting out and want a general-purpose open source UNIX-like OS, chances are either FreeBSD or Linux will work quite well. The Linux world tends to be a bit more chaotic, though, and the differences between distributions can be confusing to new users.

For the most part, FreeBSD doesn't compete as directly against the commercial UNIX variants, which run on hardware that's a step or so above typical *x*86 hardware, especially in floating-point math operations. If you have a need for some high-powered systems along with less expensive computers, a mix of FreeBSD on *x*86 systems and more powerful servers running Solaris, AIX, or IRIX can make sense. Although they're not identical in configuration, the skills it takes to administer or use a FreeBSD system are similar to those needed on commercial UNIX variants. In some cases, a high-end *x*86 system can compete directly against low-end Sun, IBM, or SGI hardware. Usually, the *x*86 system running FreeBSD is less expensive, but it may be harder to find service contracts or the like for FreeBSD.

The Software Environment

The preceding sections described where FreeBSD fits in the range of OSs available today. This information can help you decide whether to run FreeBSD or some other OS. If you decide to run FreeBSD, though, you must know how it interacts with other OSs. This interaction includes both other computers on a network and other OSs run on the same computer. It's also helpful to know something about FreeBSD's history, to better understand its design philosophy and its strengths and weaknesses as an OS. This section covers these issues.

The Development of FreeBSD

The history of FreeBSD, and of UNIX generally, is complex. It begins with the development of the first (very primitive) version of UNIX in 1969 at AT&T. From that point on, collaborations with the University of California at Berkeley, contributions by increasing numbers of volunteers, replacement of existing code, and development of "workalike" utilities have all come into play. The original AT&T UNIX has spawned several variants (also known as *forks* in the code base). Good ideas developed in one fork have often found their way into other forks, and there have been periods in UNIX history in which UNIX vendors have worked to reduce the differences caused by code forks. Nonetheless, UNIX today is not a single OS, but rather a family of related OSs.

Note   *Technically, the name* UNIX *applies only to versions of the OS that are officially sanctioned. Some people use* UNIX *(fully capitalized) to refer to such official versions of the OS, and* Unix *(with an initial capital only) to refer to workalike systems. Because this is a very subtle distinction, this book uses* UNIX *to refer to an official UNIX or the family of OSs as a whole, and* UNIX-like systems *or similar phrasings when it's important that the reference be interpreted as referring not just to official UNIX but to similar OSs, such as Linux.*

After the original development of UNIX by Ken Thompson and Dennis Ritchie in 1969, the first important milestone in the branch that led to FreeBSD was the delivery of a copy of Version 4 of UNIX to UC Berkeley in 1974. Over the next several years, the faculty, staff, and students at Berkeley became familiar with UNIX, wrote programs for it, and even modified the OS itself. These programs came together in 1977 in the form of the *Berkeley Software Distribution (BSD)*, which was a set of programs developed at or in cooperation with Berkeley for AT&T's UNIX.

In 1978, the *Second Berkeley Software Distribution (2BSD)* was released; this package improved and expanded the utilities in the original BSD release. Developments continued through several more releases of BSD—2.11BSD, 3BSD, 4BSD, and so on. AT&T objected to the proposed naming of 5BSD because of the potential for confusion with AT&T's own *System V (SysV)* release of UNIX. Thus, subsequent BSD releases took on the names 4.1BSD, 4.2BSD, and so on. Some of these releases pioneered the *Transmission Control Protocol/ Internet Protocol (TCP/IP)*—the basic network stack upon which today's Internet is built.

All of these initial BSD releases were additions to AT&T's UNIX or variants of it; they were not complete OSs in and of themselves. Furthermore, through a variant of the 4.3BSD release, known as 4.3BSD-Tahoe, BSD was available only with a license that required an original AT&T source license—the standard method for UNIX distribution in the 1970s and much of the 1980s. In 1989, this changed; Berkeley created Networking Release 1, which allowed free redistribution of the code, whether or not the recipient had an AT&T source license. This was an early and important step towards today's open source movement and licensing, and modern FreeBSD would not exist without the licensing changes made for Network Release 1.

In 1991, Berkeley made Networking Release 2 available. Despite the similarity in names, Networking Release 2 was far more substantial than was Networking Release 1. Networking Release 2 was nearly a complete operating system; it lacked only six kernel source code files from AT&T UNIX. Within six months, a programmer named Bill Jolitz had rewritten them, and called the resulting package *386/BSD*. This OS is the immediate progenitor of both NetBSD and FreeBSD. (OpenBSD split from NetBSD in the mid-1990s.) The 386/BSD OS was created to run on Intel *x*86 CPUs—or more precisely, the 80386, which at that time was the top-of-the-line *x*86 CPU. As noted earlier, FreeBSD remains largely an *x*86 phenomenon, although ports to other CPUs are becoming available.

Since 1993 (the date of FreeBSD's inception as a distinct project), FreeBSD has remained a single, focused development effort. It has, of course, adopted code from other open source projects and contributed code to others. The version number has increased by a major number every couple of years, on average, with version 4.5 being released in early 2002 and version 5.0 scheduled for release in late 2002. This book focuses on these two versions of FreeBSD.

Interactions with Other Computers on a Network

FreeBSD's history (or perhaps its *pre*history, depending upon your point of view) includes the development of TCP/IP networking, with 4.2BSD. The 4.2BSD networking code has been used as the basis for TCP/IP network stacks in several other OSs. Indeed, even some Microsoft networking utilities still bear copyright notices that indicate they're descended from BSD tools. With a pedigree leading directly back to the original TCP/IP implementation, you might think that FreeBSD would have no problems integrating with other OSs on a network. For some purposes, this is true; but there are caveats and limitations you should consider when using FreeBSD on a network. These include

- **Non-TCP/IP stacks** TCP/IP isn't the only network stack in existence today, but it is the most popular. Some local networks still rely upon other network stacks, such as Apple's AppleTalk, the NetBEUI stack that's used by Windows, or Novell's IPX. FreeBSD's support for such stacks is limited compared to its support for TCP/IP. Fortunately, few networking tools today rely exclusively upon non-TCP/IP network stacks. For instance, the Windows file and printer-sharing tools can work over either NetBIOS or TCP/IP. Samba (described in Chapter 18) relies upon this fact to serve files to Windows systems.

- **Drifting standards** Few vendors who reuse code employ it exactly as they find it. Indeed, even the originators are unlikely to leave code alone. Thus, the original 4.2BSD TCP/IP stack has mutated over the years, with each derivative OS hosting a slightly different implementation. Some have created entirely new TCP/IP implementations. Given this history of change and reimplementation, the remarkable fact is that most OSs *can* communicate with each other via TCP/IP. As a practical matter, FreeBSD is an important enough OS, particularly in the server arena, that TCP/IP compatibility problems between it and other OSs are very rare. You're most likely to encounter problems with specific protocols because of quirks in the client or server you choose to use. For instance, many web pages are designed for Microsoft's Internet Explorer web browser, and some of these don't work well with web browsers available on FreeBSD, such as Mozilla or Konqueror.

- **Security problems** TCP/IP was developed in an environment of trust, so the core features of TCP/IP don't include much in the way of security controls. This fact, combined with the complexity of network software, has led to the routine discovery of security flaws that allow miscreants to gain access to computers of all sorts. Overall, FreeBSD has a good reputation for security, but this doesn't mean you can ignore the issue; poor configuration or neglect can make security breaches almost certain. Many sections of this book describe security concerns, but Chapters 17 and 29 are particularly important in this respect.

Caution *Security is not an all-or-none affair. A statement such as "FreeBSD is a secure OS" should not be taken as an absolute claim that it's impossible to break into a FreeBSD system. At best, you can make a FreeBSD computer so difficult to compromise that none but the best and most diligent attackers can break into it. Security standards are also a moving target; new security-related bugs are constantly being found, so a system that appears to be reasonably secure today may be found to be terribly insecure tomorrow.*

Overall, FreeBSD makes an excellent OS for many networking functions. It has a stable and efficient TCP/IP stack, which is particularly important for network servers. If you pay appropriate attention to security issues, a FreeBSD system can be reasonably secure. Likewise, there are many network server programs available for FreeBSD, which enable FreeBSD users to interact with servers running on other systems.

Interactions with Other OSs on a Single Computer

From fairly early in BSD's development, there was a need for UNIX to coexist with other OSs on a single computer. For instance, the PDP 11/45 system that was Berkeley's first UNIX computer actually ran UNIX only one-third of the time; for two-thirds of each day, the computer ran another OS (known as RSTS). For a time-sharing computer, however, this approach is extremely awkward, so most UNIX systems in the 1970s and 1980s ran just one OS. With the release of 386/BSD, though, the desirability of coexistence with other OSs became acute. Many hobbyist developers had just one computer; like it or not, they often found it necessary to use the more popular DOS (and, later, Windows) OS for some work. This remains true today. If you intend to run a dedicated FreeBSD system (say, a server or dedicated workstation), your task is simpler because FreeBSD need not coexist with other OSs. If you need to occasionally run programs in another OS, though, you must understand something of how FreeBSD uses its hard disk, and how the x86 computer boots an OS, so that you can switch between your OSs effectively.

The first key to understanding and using any multi-OS computer is to understand *partitions.* If a hard disk is like a file cabinet, a partition is like an individual drawer in the file cabinet—a subdivision of the large storage space that you can use to hold related files. You set up partitions on a hard disk when you first prepare it for use. This process is known as *partitioning,* and once partitions are created, they aren't easy to modify. Thus, when you get a new computer, it's important that you set up partitions in a way that you'll find convenient for the foreseeable future.

Note *Some tools enable you to adjust the size of partitions after they've been created. The commercial products Partition Magic (http://www.powerquest.com) and Partition Commander (http://www.v-com.com) are two such products. Open source alternatives include the First Non-Destructive Interactive Partition Splitting Program (FIPS; http://www.igd.fhg.de/~aschaefe/fips/) and GNU Parted (http://www.gnu.org/software/parted). These products tend to be more limited and primitive, but they may be enough to get the job done. These tools can be particularly useful if you want to install FreeBSD on a system that currently runs DOS, Windows, OS/2, Linux, or other OSs.*

Over the years, various partitioning schemes have been developed. For the most part, each of these was developed independently for a particular hardware platform. For x86 computers, the partitioning system supports three different partition types. These partition types exist not because of any compelling need for different partition capabilities, but because a limited partitioning scheme was expanded when it became obvious it was inadequate. The three x86 partition types are

- **Primary** The original x86 partition type is now known as a *primary* partition. The x86 partitioning scheme supports up to four primary partitions. Some OSs, such as DOS and Windows, must boot from a primary partition located on the first physical hard disk. FreeBSD must also reside in a primary partition, but it can exist on a second or subsequent hard disk. Some OSs, such as Linux and

OS/2, can boot from a nonprimary partition. You should consider these limits when planning your system installation.

- **Extended**   An *extended* partition is, in some sense, nothing but a special type of primary partition. It consumes one of the four available primary partition slots and serves as a placeholder for the next *x86* partition type.

- **Logical**   *Logical* partitions reside within extended partitions. The extended partition entry exists to reserve space in the partition table for one or more logical partitions. The number of logical partitions supported by the *x86* partitioning scheme is limited mainly by the size of the disk and the means of addressing partitions in an OS. For instance, DOS and Windows use single drive letters to address partitions, so the theoretical limit is 26 (the number of letters in the alphabet). In practice, A: and B: refer to floppy disks, and a system may need other letters for CD-ROM drives, network shares, and so on. In UNIX-like OSs, device filenames in the /dev directory tree and underlying kernel restrictions serve to limit the number of logical partitions. In either case, few systems even begin to approach these limits. Because logical partitions reside within an extended partition, logical partitions must occupy contiguous sections of the hard disk—they cannot be broken up by primary partitions.

Many DOS and Windows computers use just one primary partition per drive. Some DOS or Windows users partition their drives, though. Furthermore, if you want to install both FreeBSD and some other OS on a single computer, you'll need to do the same. Specifically, you should set aside one primary partition for FreeBSD, along with whatever primary or logical partitions your other OS requires. For instance, Figure 1-1 shows one possible configuration. Both FreeBSD and Windows possess primary boot partitions, and two logical partitions exist within the extended partition to hold additional Windows files.

Note   *Computers based on the new 64-bit IA64 CPUs from Intel may optionally use a new partitioning scheme that's more flexible than the old x86 partitioning scheme.*

Unfortunately, matters are considerably more complex when dealing with FreeBSD. You should first understand that UNIX systems frequently use partitions to separate different types of data. This practice enables you to mount directories with different

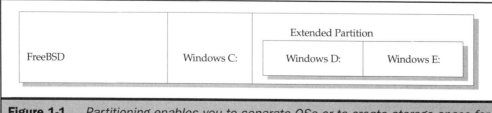

Figure 1-1.   *Partitioning enables you to separate OSs or to create storage space for different types of data.*

options and protect data in one partition against damage should another partition fill up or be damaged. For instance, it's common to separate /home, which holds users' data files, from the root (/) directory. In FreeBSD, as in other UNIX varieties, each partition is *mounted* at a particular directory; there are no drive letters, as there are in DOS or Windows. For these reasons, FreeBSD systems frequently require multiple partitions, even when the computer hosts *only* FreeBSD.

Because of its AT&T and BSD UNIX heritage, FreeBSD relies upon a partitioning scheme that's completely different from the standard *x86* partitioning system. Typically, this BSD partitioning system resides inside a single primary partition. This partition is called a *slice* in FreeBSD, and its subpartitions are analogous to the logical partitions contained within an *x86* extended partition. Only a BSD OS or another OS with support for the BSD partitioning scheme is able to read the BSD subpartitions, though. Chapter 2 describes the types of subpartitions you might want to create for your FreeBSD system, whether or not you're also installing another OS on the computer.

If you want to exchange data between OSs, your best bet is to set aside a partition for this purpose. Unfortunately, different OSs use different *filesystems* for data storage. A filesystem is a data structure that spans an entire partition, keeping track of files, their locations, and associated data such as file creation dates. As a general rule, the DOS *File Allocation Table (FAT)* filesystem is a good choice for cross-OS data transfers because all common *x86* OSs support FAT. Few non-UNIX OSs support the *Fast File System (FFS)* used natively by FreeBSD. Indeed, FFS differs in subtle but important ways across UNIX implementations, so even if you want to dual-boot FreeBSD and some other UNIX, you might need to use FAT as a common exchange medium.

The Hardware Environment

Before you install FreeBSD on any computer, you should take some time to understand FreeBSD's hardware requirements. The *x86* hardware world is extremely varied, so it's not uncommon to find that a computer includes a hardware device that's unsupported by FreeBSD. In most cases, this won't prevent you from installing FreeBSD, but it may prevent you from using the OS to its fullest.

If you want to replace a device that you discover during installation to be unsupported, try to do so before installing FreeBSD. This may eliminate the need to reconfigure FreeBSD after replacing the hardware.

CPU Types and Speed

The core of any computer is its CPU. As has already been described in this chapter, FreeBSD was originally designed to run on Intel's *x86* series of CPUs—or at least the 32-bit versions of the CPU, starting with the 80386. In 2002, FreeBSD supports the Intel 80386, 80486, Pentium, Pentium Pro, Pentium II, Pentium III, Pentium 4, and Celeron lines, including variants of these, such as the Pentium III Xeon. In addition, FreeBSD runs on competing workalike CPUs from AMD, VIA, Transmeta, Cyrix, IDT, and NexGen. (The final three of these companies have gone out of business, but their designs have been incorporated into those of AMD and VIA.) Some companies, such as Evergreen, market combinations of AMD or VIA CPUs and adapter boards to enable older motherboards to work at faster speeds than might otherwise be possible. FreeBSD works with such CPUs, but the CPUs themselves don't always work perfectly in all motherboards.

Projects are underway to port FreeBSD to a variety of non-*x86* platforms (see `http://www.freebsd.org/platforms/` for a description of these projects). These include Intel's IA64 line, AMD's *x86-64* (their answer to Intel's IA64 architecture), Compaq's Alpha, Motorola's PowerPC (PPC), and the UltraSparc used in many Sun servers. In 2002, the *x86* architecture is still very popular, but it seems likely that it will eventually give way to 64-bit platforms. Intel is pushing its IA64 under the names *Itanium, Merced,* and *McKinley*; and AMD is preparing the *x86-64* (aka *K8* or *Hammer*) to compete with IA64. These CPUs will no doubt become very important in the not-too-distant future. Fortunately, most FreeBSD operation details remain identical no matter what platform you use, although you may need to select binary programs with care to be sure they run on your CPU. Partitioning and installation details may differ if you install FreeBSD on a non-*x86* platform. Because of the continued popularity of *x86* hardware, this book focuses on this platform.

As to CPU speed, what you need depends largely upon your needs, rather than FreeBSD's. You can run FreeBSD even on a low-powered 386 CPU, but such a system is unlikely to be adequate for any but very limited uses in today's world. For instance, you might use this system as a dedicated firewall for a small home network or as a DHCP server on a small network; but a 386 won't have enough power to do CPU-intensive graphics rendering or even to run GUI-intensive programs. Most 386 systems are also deficient in terms of RAM, disk space, and so on. If you're assembling a new computer, any *x86* CPU that's sold as new from Intel, AMD, VIA, or Transmeta should be adequate for running FreeBSD and for performing most common tasks. If you intend to run CPU-intensive programs, though, you may want to purchase a top-of-the-line CPU, or one close to that point.

Tip   *CPU prices usually drop rapidly from the top-of-the-line model to the next model in line, and then somewhat more slowly with each subsequent speed reduction. Thus, the best CPU value is often found in a mid-range CPU. Precisely what speed this "mid-range" CPU is increases almost weekly, though, so I can't give you a specific speed recommendation to obtain maximum value.*

RAM Requirements

As with CPU speed, FreeBSD's RAM requirements are modest by today's standards. The official documentation states that a minimum of 5MB is required to install FreeBSD, but only 4MB to run it. For all but trivial or extremely specialized applications, though, these amounts are ludicrously small by today's standards. In 2002, even low-end computers ship with at least 128MB of RAM. This amount (or even less—say, 64MB) is more than adequate to install FreeBSD and boot it into a GUI workstation environment, or to run most servers. You should consider more RAM under certain circumstances, including

- **Multiuser environments**   If many users will be employing a system simultaneously (say, via network links), you may need more memory to support their applications and environments.

- **Massive servers**   Although you can run most servers with 64MB or less, server memory requirements grow with server load. If you're putting together a file server, web server, mail server, or the like that's intended to handle hundreds or thousands of users, you'll probably want far more than 128MB of RAM. The details depend upon the server and its expected load, of course.

- **Memory-intensive programs**   Some programs, such as certain scientific simulations or animation tools, require large amounts of memory to run acceptably, even with just a single person using them. Chances are you know if you're running such tools. If in doubt, check the memory requirements in your program's documentation.

For the most part, the same conditions that require large amounts of RAM also require fast CPUs, but there are exceptions—for instance, some scientific simulations may need a lot of RAM but not much CPU power, or vice-versa.

Hard Disks

Disk space is always a concern when installing an OS. A previous section, "Interactions with Other OSs on a Single Computer," outlined some of the partitioning needs of FreeBSD, and Chapter 2 provides more specific information. You should consider two issues before you begin installing FreeBSD, though: the type of hard disk you intend to use and the total amount of space you intend to devote to the OS.

SCSI and EIDE Disks

Most *x86* computers sold today use *Enhanced Integrated Drive Electronics (EIDE)* hard disks. Modern motherboards invariably include EIDE controllers, so connecting these disks is easy from a system assembly point of view. There is a competing type of hard disk, though: *Small Computer System Interface (SCSI)*. Few motherboards include SCSI connectors, so to use a SCSI hard disk, you must add a SCSI *host adapter*—typically a plug-in PCI card. FreeBSD supports both EIDE and SCSI hard disks, but there are caveats for each type, and each technology has its advantages and disadvantages.

EIDE's primary strength is its cost. Because EIDE controllers are built into modern motherboards, there's no cost associated with adding a host adapter, as there is for SCSI devices. (You can add PCI EIDE controllers to improve performance or host more than four devices, though, as described shortly.) EIDE hard drives are also inexpensive compared to similar SCSI drives. All told, using EIDE rather than SCSI can save $100 to $500 on the cost of a system, or sometimes more. All EIDE controllers also support a single lowest-common-denominator hardware standard, so a single driver works for all of them, at least to get minimal operation. To get the best speed, though, FreeBSD needs a driver for the specific EIDE controller you use.

EIDE's primary weaknesses lie in its inflexibility. You can connect only two EIDE devices to a single *chain* (that is, a cable that connects to the motherboard or EIDE controller card). Most motherboards support just two chains, for a total of four EIDE devices. Because CD-ROM drives, removable media drives, tape backup drives, and so on frequently use EIDE or SCSI, this 4-device limit can be awkward. You can expand the limit by adding an extra EIDE controller card, but this consumes a PCI slot and an interrupt (a limited hardware resource). Also, EIDE permits simultaneous access to just one device per chain, so in a heavily multitasking system, EIDE can become a bottleneck if it's desirable to perform simultaneous access to more than one device on a chain.

Note   *In the past, EIDE controllers supported only* Programmed Input/Output (PIO) *access modes, which require intervention by the CPU for all data transfers. This made EIDE a poor choice for a multitasking OS such as FreeBSD. Today's EIDE controllers, though, support the more advanced* Direct Memory Access (DMA) *transfer modes, in which the controller can send data directly to memory. DMA operation requires explicit driver support for the EIDE chipset in use, though.*

SCSI is very flexible compared to EIDE. Depending upon the SCSI variant in use, you can attach seven or fifteen devices per chain, so SCSI is an excellent choice if you want to build a computer with many physical disks. SCSI also supports simultaneous access to multiple devices per chain, which is very useful for multitasking purposes. SCSI hard disks of a given capacity are also usually faster than EIDE hard disks of the same capacity, although this factor varies from one drive to another. You can find a wider range of device types for SCSI, and in some cases higher-end devices. For instance, SCSI scanners are available, and high-end tape backup devices almost always use SCSI interfaces. Most SCSI host adapters always use DMA mode, although some very cheap ones use only PIO mode.

SCSI's drawbacks boil down to cost. The SCSI host adapter costs money (typically $50 to $250), and SCSI devices are usually more expensive than their EIDE counterparts. SCSI also has no lowest-common-denominator hardware standard, so FreeBSD *must* support whatever SCSI host adapter your system uses.

Overall, EIDE's cost advantages make it a good choice for low-end and midrange systems. If you build a computer using an EIDE controller for which FreeBSD includes DMA support, you can get good performance from a one-disk EIDE system. If you're building a big server or something else that needs exceptional disk performance, though, the extra cost of SCSI may be justified. Be sure to research the capabilities and needs of each SCSI component, including your hard disks and the SCSI host adapter itself.

Note   *You can build a computer that uses both EIDE and SCSI. For instance, you might want to use SCSI for its superior disk performance and for a high-end tape backup unit, but use EIDE for inexpensive CD-ROM and Zip drives.*

In the future, other interfaces are likely to play an increasingly important role. In particular, IEEE-1394 (aka FireWire) may become the successor to SCSI for at least some purposes. IEEE-1394 hard disks are already available. Support for FireWire in FreeBSD 5.0 is very limited.

To learn which EIDE controllers and SCSI host adapters are supported, consult the HARDWARE.TXT file that comes with FreeBSD. Note that this file focuses on *chipsets*; the specific brand and model device in your computer may not be listed, even if it's supported. Check the names of the chips on a PCI card to learn what you have. If Windows is currently installed on your system, you can use the Windows System control panel to learn something about it. Click the Device Manager tab and expand the Hard Disk Controllers item. For instance, Figure 1-2 shows a computer that uses a VIA EIDE controller (*IDE* is an older standard that evolved into EIDE, and some utilities continue to use the older term, as in Figure 1-2).

Note　*You don't need drivers for specific EIDE or SCSI devices. For instance, if you change your EIDE CD-ROM drive for another EIDE CD-ROM drive, you don't need to update your FreeBSD CD-ROM drivers because these devices use standardized command sets. You do need drivers for most specific EIDE or SCSI device* types, *such as hard disk or CD-ROM drivers. These drivers are included in the standard FreeBSD kernel, so their use is usually transparent.*

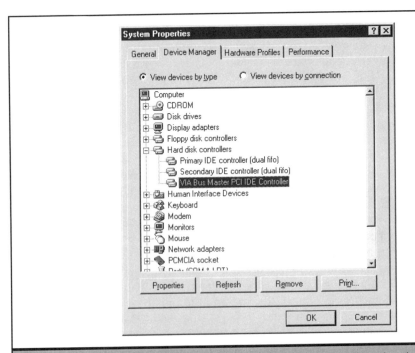

Figure 1-2.　*Windows can be a useful tool for discovering what hardware a computer has.*

Total Disk Space Requirements

Researching the EIDE controller or SCSI host adapter in your system is critically important for avoiding or resolving disk-related problems with FreeBSD. Independent of the choice of EIDE or SCSI, though, is the question of total disk space. Officially, FreeBSD requires 100MB of disk space. A 100MB installation, though, will be extremely limited. A serious installation requires at least several hundred megabytes, and probably 1GB or more. If you want to install and try out lots of software, setting aside 2GB or even 3GB for FreeBSD may not be excessive. You may need still more space if your system will handle very many or very large user data files, or if it will be a server that needs to support very many or very large files. You have to decide just how much disk space to allocate for site-specific functions.

In 2002, it's difficult to find a new hard disk that's smaller than 20GB, so meeting FreeBSD's basic disk space requirements isn't much of a challenge. If you're adding FreeBSD to an existing system, you have two choices for how to proceed:

- **Repartition and share a drive**   You can use utilities such as the commercial PartitionMagic or the open source FIPS to shrink an existing partition and create space for a FreeBSD slice. This approach can be effective and frugal if you have sufficient free space on your existing hard disk, but it's not without risk. Dynamic partition resizing tools occasionally fail, and the result can be lost data. For this reason, you should back up your existing data before using such a utility.

- **Add a new drive**   You can add a new hard drive for the exclusive use of FreeBSD, or to be shared between FreeBSD and the current OS. This approach is safer than shrinking existing partitions and adding new ones on a single drive, but it may not be practical if you've already reached the limits on the number of devices supported by your system.

In either case, when you install FreeBSD, you must also install a *boot loader*. This is a very simple program that boots one or more OSs. FreeBSD comes with a boot loader that enables you to choose which OS you want to boot when the system powers up. You can use this tool alone or in conjunction with a third-party boot loader, such as PowerQuest's BootMagic (`http://www.powerquest.com/partitionmagic/`), V-Com's System Commander (`http://www.v-com.com/product/sc7_ind.html`), or Linux's LILO. Chapter 4 provides further information on installing and configuring a FreeBSD boot loader.

Video Hardware

In order to create a display on your screen, FreeBSD must support your video hardware. The monitor itself is seldom a problem, and requires no explicit drivers (although you may need to adjust certain settings to match your monitor, as described in Chapter 13). Instead, you should focus your research on your video adapter card.

All modern video cards support certain basic modes that FreeBSD can use. In particular, FreeBSD can operate in text mode and in low-resolution *Video Graphics Adapter (VGA)* 640×480 mode. Sometimes higher resolution generic graphics modes also work. Although text mode may be adequate for some uses, such as servers, most workstation users want to use a GUI environment, and this requires a graphics mode. The VGA modes work, but just barely—for serious use, you need to use a video card that FreeBSD (or, more precisely, X) supports, and in better than basic VGA modes.

The video support you need to be concerned with, although included as a standard part of a FreeBSD package, is technically part of an independent project: XFree86 (`http://www.xfree86.org`). XFree86 is also used by other open source UNIX-like OSs, such as NetBSD, OpenBSD, and Linux. It's also available on various commercial UNIX implementations (although these often include their own proprietary X servers, as well) and even for many non-UNIX systems, including Windows, Mac OS, and OS/2.

In FreeBSD, XFree86 talks more-or-less directly to video hardware, so XFree86 needs to support your video card. If XFree86's support of your video hardware is weak, your video performance will suffer. This could mean lower resolutions than you could achieve in Windows or slow speed. (All modern video chipsets include features designed to speed up common video operations, such as moving objects on-screen. If drivers are immature, they may not support all of these features, resulting in poor video performance.) You can find information on the chipsets supported by XFree86 at `http://www.xfree86 .org/current/Status.html`.

This web page provides information on the latest drivers available. Depending upon how old your FreeBSD package is, it may include an older set of XFree86 drivers, so the XFree86 web page may indicate that drivers exist, but they may not be present in your FreeBSD installation. If this is the case, you can upgrade XFree86, or at least the driver for your video card alone.

As with EIDE and SCSI hardware, the list of supported video hardware is built around chipsets and chipset manufacturers, but some video card makers don't publicize these details. You may therefore need to examine the chips on your video card, or the Display Adapters item in the Windows System control panel, if Windows is installed on the computer. Some of the most popular video card manufacturers, though, such as ATI and Matrox, also produce their own chipsets, so locating support for these should not be too difficult.

Tip　*If you buy a new video card, be cautious about the latest models. XFree86 development often lags a few months behind the most recent chipsets, so the latest models may be supported poorly, if at all. Information on the XFree86 web page should help you locate appropriate hardware.*

The FreeBSD installation routines attempt to detect and configure your video hardware, as described in Chapter 2. If this process doesn't work correctly, or if you need to change your configuration, you can edit the XFree86 configuration files, as described in Chapter 13.

Network Hardware

Many FreeBSD systems operate as network servers, or at least as networked workstations. Such systems invariably require some form of network hardware. In 2002, the most common type of local network hardware is Ethernet. Many forms of Ethernet are available, and they differ in two main ways:

- **Speed** The lowest Ethernet speed is 10 megabits per second (Mbps). The fastest that's readily available is 1000 Mbps (or 1 Gbps—often called *gigabit Ethernet*). In 2002, 100 Mbps is the most common speed for new installations, although gigabit speeds are becoming more popular.

- **Media** Ethernet works over cables of some sort. In the past, two varieties of coaxial cabling were common—*thick* and *thin* coax. Both forms resembled the cables used by cable TV, but varied in thickness. Both used a *bus topology*, in which the cable connected one device to another, and so on, in a single line. Coaxial cabling is now rare on new installations, having been supplanted by *twisted-pair* cabling, which resembles telephone wiring, but with wider heads. Twisted-pair cabling uses a central device, known as a *hub* or *switch*, to connect devices; each computer's cable links to the hub or switch to create a *star topology*, as depicted in Figure 1-3. Most recently, optical cabling is emerging as an alternative to twisted-pair cabling on gigabit Ethernet networks. Optical cabling generally uses a star topology.

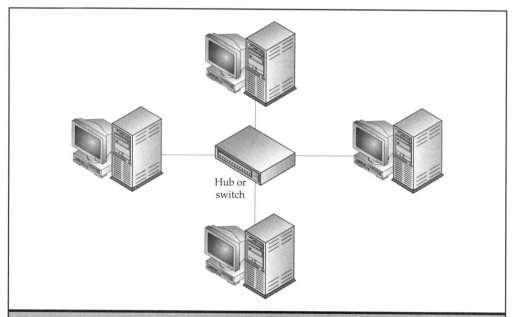

Hub or
switch

Figure 1-3. *A star topology makes diagnosing cable failures relatively straight-forward because the failure is isolated to just one computer.*

Most new networks use 100 Mbps twisted-pair hardware, but you may need to connect a computer to an older 10 Mbps twisted-pair or coaxial network. If you need the fastest hardware, you may want to consider building a new gigabit Ethernet network with twisted-pair or optical cabling.

Fortunately, FreeBSD doesn't care what sort of Ethernet cabling or topology you use; you need only ensure that your Ethernet adapter card is supported. (A few high-end motherboards include Ethernet support built-in, but this is rare.) The HARDWARE.TXT file that comes with FreeBSD describes the Ethernet adapters that FreeBSD supports. As with EIDE, SCSI, and video hardware, this compatibility is usually specified in terms of the chipset used on the board, so you may need to examine markings on the largest chips on your Ethernet card, or consult the Windows System Properties dialog box. (When opening a computer, be sure to turn the computer off first, and ground yourself by wearing an antistatic wrist strap, or at least touching a radiator or water faucet frequently. Don't wear rubber-soled shoes or shuffle across a carpet in dry weather. These measures protect both you and your computer.)

> **Note** *FreeBSD must support the Ethernet card in your computer, but you don't need FreeBSD support for the hub or switch you use, or for most other network devices, such as broadband routers. You may need FreeBSD support for specific types of servers that run on other computers or dedicated network appliances, though, such as file servers or print servers.*

In addition to Ethernet, various wireless networking products are becoming popular, particularly in home and small office environments. FreeBSD includes support for many of these devices, and from a logical point of view they work much like Ethernet cards. The same HARDWARE.TXT file that describes supported Ethernet cards also includes information on supported wireless networking hardware.

You can configure many networking properties during FreeBSD installation, as described in Chapter 2. If you need to fine-tune these settings or change them after installing the OS, Chapter 14 describes the process.

One other type of networking hardware deserves mention: modems. On a stand-alone system, and sometimes even on a system connected to a local network, modems are a means of linking a computer to the Internet via a dial-up ISP. FreeBSD supports all external RS-232 modems and some internal modems. Many internal modems, though, are *software modems*. These devices rely upon special software drivers to handle some functions that are implemented in hardware in conventional modem designs, and these drivers are rare for FreeBSD. You should avoid software modems at all costs.

> **Note** *Modems designed to provide broadband Internet access (such as cable and DSL modems) often use Ethernet interfaces. To FreeBSD, these devices function as ordinary parts of an Ethernet network, and so require no special drivers. This rule has two exceptions, though. First, if the modem is internal or uses a Universal Serial Bus (USB) interface, it requires special drivers, and these are very rare for FreeBSD, as of 2002. Second, some broadband providers use a protocol called PPP over Ethernet (PPPoE) to assign IP addresses. PPPoE isn't strictly a requirement of the broadband modem, though. You can use PPPoE with a FreeBSD system.*

Printers

Most of the hardware devices described so far are internal—they reside inside the computer. Some hardware devices, though, are external. The most common of these are printers. Unfortunately, printer hardware is quite varied, so FreeBSD requires an extensive library of drivers for the many printer models that are available.

Printer drivers are independent of the printing technology (laser, inkjet, and so on) and of the printer interface (parallel port, RS-232 serial, USB, or networked). Although some driver types are more common with certain printing technologies than others, the FreeBSD printer drivers don't really care how the image is formed on the paper. The printer interface is more important, in the sense that FreeBSD must include support for the interface hardware. Parallel, RS-232 serial, and various networking protocols are well supported, but USB support is weak. Assuming the interface works, though, the actual printer drivers don't care about this detail.

In fact, the FreeBSD printer drivers share something in common with the XFree86 video drivers: They're part of a package that extends beyond FreeBSD. That package is known as *Ghostscript* (http://www.cs.wisc.edu/~ghost/), and is a program that converts PostScript files into any of several printer formats. Chapter 9 describes the FreeBSD printing philosophy and the reasons for using PostScript as a common printing language. For now, you should simply know that UNIX (and hence FreeBSD) programs that print usually produce either plain text or PostScript output, which is fed into a print queue. This queue can then feed PostScript files through Ghostscript, which produces a binary file that a printer can handle. Thus, the best printers for FreeBSD understand PostScript natively because they obviate the need for Ghostscript. PostScript printers tend to be pricier than non-PostScript models, though. If you have a non-PostScript printer or if you plan to buy a new one but don't want to spend the extra money for a PostScript model, you should be sure that your printer is supported by Ghostscript. The Linux Printing Support Database (http://www.linuxprinting.org/printer_list.cgi) hosts a database of printers and their level of support in Ghostscript. (Despite the web page's name, it's as applicable to FreeBSD as to Linux.)

Caution	*Some printers are advertised as supporting PostScript, but in fact they don't. These printers rely upon Windows software that's similar to Ghostscript for their PostScript functionality. Such software is useless in FreeBSD. Some other printers have PostScript interpreters that were not designed by PostScript's creator, Adobe. Such PostScript-compatible printers are usually fine, although some very early models (from the late 1980s) have problems with some files.*

If your printer isn't PostScript-capable and isn't supported by Ghostscript, your ability to use it will be severely limited. In some cases, you may be able to run Ghostscript (or some other PostScript interpreter) on a Windows computer, connect the printer to the Windows system, and print by using a Windows printer share. If you need more direct access, though, you'll need to replace the old printer with one that's better supported by Ghostscript. Fortunately, Ghostscript supports most of the printers that are available today; it's mostly a few very low-end printers that cause problems.

Miscellaneous Hardware

Many additional hardware devices are available today. Many of these require explicit support in FreeBSD to be useful. The HARDWARE.TXT file that comes with FreeBSD describes FreeBSD's support for many of these devices. Some key features and devices you may want to consider include the following:

- **Sound cards**   The sound card marketplace is very broad. Although FreeBSD supports many of the most popular sound cards, FreeBSD lacks support for many of the newest and less popular models. You should check the "Audio Devices" section of HARDWARE.TXT to find out if your sound card is supported. If it's not, you can either do without sound or replace your sound card with a supported model. Leaving an unsupported card in the computer is unlikely to cause problems.

- **USB ports and devices**   All modern computers include USB ports. FreeBSD's USB support is still fairly new, but FreeBSD does include support for the two major USB chipsets (known as UHCI and OHCI) and for a handful of USB devices. Unlike some external devices, USB requires that the FreeBSD kernel include explicit support for particular USB devices, or at least device classes (such as printers or modems). You can learn the current status of FreeBSD USB support at http://www.etla.net/~n_hibma/usb/. Because USB support is evolving, you may need to update your kernel to use the latest USB drivers. Chapter 12 covers this topic.

- **Removable media devices**   FreeBSD support for floppy disks and CD-ROM drives is very mature. You can use removable disk devices, such as Zip, LS-120, or Jaz drives, much like floppies. (Some of these devices are normally partitioned like a hard disk. This doesn't pose a problem.) USB-interfaced removable devices have problems with limited USB support, though. Recordable CD and DVD devices are unusual in that they aren't treated like other removable-media drives. Instead, you need to use a special package to prepare a disc image and "burn" it to the removable medium.

- **Scanners**   Scanners can interface through the parallel, SCSI, or USB port. Support for SCSI scanners is strongest, but there's some limited support for parallel and USB scanners. Aside from the basic interface support, scanners need model-specific drivers, which reside in the *Scanner Access Now Easy (SANE)* package (http://www.mostang.com/sane/). This package, like XFree86 and Ghostscript, provides support for specific models outside of the FreeBSD kernel.

- ■ **Human input** People interact with computers by entering information via keyboards, mice, and occasionally other devices. For years, *x*86 keyboards have been standardized, so FreeBSD's keyboard drivers are stable and transparent. XFree86 supports many different types of mice, including all the popular software protocols. In 2002, the most common of these is the PS/2 mouse protocol or variants of it. Since the late 1990s, the rise in popularity of USB has begun making USB mice and keyboards more common. FreeBSD includes support for these, but it's not as mature as support for conventional keyboard and mouse interfaces.

More exotic devices, such as cameras, video input cards, scientific data acquisition cards, and so on, are supported on a spottier basis. You should research your specific device if such support is important to you. FreeBSD supports common devices such as standard RS-232 serial ports and standard parallel ports. If you have questions about a device, consult the `HARDWARE.TXT` file or do a web search using your favorite search engine.

Summary

Before you install FreeBSD, you should know something about its capabilities and requirements. FreeBSD can function as either a workstation or a server, and in fact it's a popular platform for Internet servers. FreeBSD can interact in various ways with other OSs, both on a network and on the same computer. In fact, a multiboot environment can be very useful, but poses certain challenges in terms of coexistence and data sharing. FreeBSD's hardware requirements are lower than those of modern versions of Windows, which means that modern hardware is more than adequate for a basic FreeBSD system, in terms of CPU speed and memory. You may need to pick other components with care, though, because FreeBSD's support for certain ancillary components, such as sound cards or even printers, is weaker than that in more popular OSs such as Windows.

The
Complete
Reference

Chapter 2

System Installation

C hapter 1 summarized the history of FreeBSD and its hardware requirements, and presented an overview of when FreeBSD is a good choice of OS and how it interacts with other OSs. If you've read Chapter 1 and are still reading this book, you've presumably decided that FreeBSD is worth using. This chapter will get you started on this road by describing the FreeBSD installation process, including some more concrete examples of issues introduced in Chapter 1.

This chapter begins by discussing how to obtain FreeBSD. Because of FreeBSD's open source nature, you can acquire it in several different ways. Next up is preparing a computer to run FreeBSD. The installation process itself is covered next, starting with a look at the installation routines and continuing on to a description of the types of software you might install and the creation of initial user accounts.

Obtaining FreeBSD

If you're impatient to get started, you can do so immediately using the CD-ROM that comes with this book. This CD-ROM includes the latest version of FreeBSD available at press time—5.0. There are other ways to obtain FreeBSD, though, and some of these may have advantages over using this book's CD-ROM. Indeed, depending upon your hardware and requirements, you may *need* to use another source of FreeBSD. Most users need not be too terribly concerned with FreeBSD's licensing terms because they're very simple and liberal, but a basic understanding of these terms is important in some situations. You can obtain the software from many different sources, each of which has its advantages. Once you've obtained a copy of FreeBSD, you may need to take some steps to prepare your system for installing the OS.

FreeBSD Licensing Issues

Many people think of FreeBSD as using the *BSD license*. This license is very short and simple. It explicitly grants everybody the right to use and redistribute the software, in both source code and binary forms, as originally delivered or in a modified form, with the only caveat being that the original copyright notice and (for binary distribution) a no-warranty clause be included. You may obtain a single copy of software that uses the BSD license and install it on as many computers as you like. This is true whether you obtain the software for free over the Internet or pay thousands of dollars to get it from a retailer. (Few vendors can get away with charging thousands of dollars for open source software, but a few open source organizations do sell CD-ROMs with open source software as a way to help fund further development.)

Although many people *think of* FreeBSD as using the BSD license, this is only partly correct. The FreeBSD kernel and many of its support programs do use this license, but some use other licenses. For instance, XFree86 uses the MIT license, which is very similar to the BSD license; and the GNU Compiler Collection (GCC) uses the GNU *General Public License (GPL)*, which is an open source license with somewhat different terms than the BSD license. Because the GPL is so common, it deserves a few additional words. The GPL is a much longer license than the BSD license, and it imposes restrictions on the redistribution of so-called *GPLed software* (software licensed under the GPL). Specifically, the GPL requires that derivative works be distributed under the GPL. The BSD license makes no mention of derivative licenses, thus permitting the distributor to choose any other license for derivative works. GPL advocates claim that the GPL's approach is superior because it ensures that derivative works will remain open source (or *free software*, as some prefer). BSD advocates claim that the BSD license is superior because it permits anybody to do anything with the software, even create proprietary works. Both sides claim that their license offers more "freedom," but each defines this word differently to make this claim. This philosophical debate between adherents of the BSD and GPL licenses is a strong undercurrent in the open source software community, and you're likely to run into debates on this issue if you follow FreeBSD or other open source newsgroups, read web pages devoted to open source OSs, and so on.

Note	*The term* open source *has a precise definition. To learn more about it, consult* `http://www.opensource.org`. *The FreeBSD web site also includes links to several of the more important licenses it uses* (`http://www.freebsd.org/copyright/`).

The GPL, MIT license, and other open source licenses all give you *as a system administrator or user* nearly identical rights. Specifically, you can download or otherwise obtain one copy of an open source program and install it on as many computers as you like. You can make copies of the program's installation medium and give the copies to friends or colleagues, or even sell them for a profit. If you intend to alter a package, though, you may need to further study its licensing terms to be sure you don't run afoul of some clause it contains.

Most FreeBSD software uses one variety or other of open source license. Some programs in the *FreeBSD ports collection* (a set of software that's easily installed on FreeBSD but isn't officially part of the OS as a whole) use licenses that don't conform to the open source definition. Thus, if you use such packages, you may need to consider licensing issues. In most cases, some clause in the license prevents distribution on a for-sale medium, export, or some other use that all open source software permits. Consult `http://www.freebsd.org/copyright/LEGAL` for details. Even a few packages in the main FreeBSD system aren't technically open source, although these do permit free redistribution.

In sum, FreeBSD as a whole uses a mish-mash of licenses, most of which qualify as open source. FreeBSD CD-ROM images obtained from the Internet and most CD-ROMs you buy may be copied and installed on multiple computers, but a handful of specific packages have more limiting terms. Look for a README, LICENSE, or COPYRIGHT file on the CD-ROM if you're in doubt about your specific CD-ROM.

Sources of FreeBSD

Because of its open source nature, FreeBSD can be obtained in any of several different ways. The most common and useful include:

- **FreeBSD boxed set**   Several companies sell one or more FreeBSD CD-ROMs along with manuals, extra software, or the like. In some sense, this book and its accompanying CD-ROM are such a set. This book emphasizes the value of the book's text, though; some other packages include more software but provide only printed and bound documentation you can find online. Whatever the emphasis, these sets can be a good choice if you want to get a traditional package of software plus printed documentation.

> **Note**   *This book includes the "mini" FreeBSD package, which fits on a single CD-ROM. If you want a fuller system, you'll need to download some software from the Internet or obtain a complete multi-CD or DVD-ROM package from another source.*

- **Plain CD-ROM**   You can buy a CD-ROM, CD-ROM set, or DVD-ROM that contains FreeBSD, without any printed documentation. These typically cost much less than FreeBSD boxed sets, but their lack of printed documentation can be a drawback if you want a printed reference or tutorial. Such packages can be a good choice for experienced users or to get the latest software for use in conjunction with a FreeBSD book that ships with older or less complete FreeBSD packages.

- **FTP sites**   FreeBSD is readily available on the Internet, typically from *File Transfer Protocol (FTP)* sites. If you have a fast Internet connection, you can download everything you need and either burn a CD-R or install FreeBSD from your hard disk. Alternatively, you can download just a boot floppy and perform a network install, which installs FreeBSD directly from an FTP site or other repository onto your hard disk. Check `http://www.freebsd.org/doc/ en_US.ISO8859-1/ books/handbook/mirrors-ftp.html` for a list of FTP *mirrors*—sites that hold copies of the official FreeBSD FTP site. These mirrors may be closer to you than the official primary site, and they're often less congested, so you'll probably get better download performance from a mirror than from the primary site.

If you want a physical medium, you can buy FreeBSD from many common software sources. These include local computer stores, local bookstores, and online retailers such as BSD Mall (`http://www.bsdmall.com`), FreeBSD Mall (`http://www.freebsdmall.com`), and CheapBytes (`http://www.cheapbytes.com`). Most of these retailers carry both boxed sets and plain CD-ROMs, although bookstores are unlikely to carry plain CD-ROMs.

If you're adept at burning CD-Rs, you can obtain CD-R *image files* (files that are byte-for-byte copies of the contents of a CD-R) from an FTP site and burn them to a CD-R. You can find these on the official FreeBSD mirror sites. The `http://www.linuxiso.org`

site also includes pointers to these files. The CD-R you create in this way is functionally identical to a store-bought FreeBSD CD-ROM. Alternatively, you can download individual files and install from a hard disk, but with CD-R drives as common as they are today, hard-disk installation is seldom necessary or desirable. Networked installation, in which the install program reads the files from a remote file server, can be very convenient if you have a fast network connection.

If you want to install FreeBSD to several computers on a local network, you can set up your own FreeBSD installation server by copying a FreeBSD CD-ROM or the contents of a FreeBSD site's FreeBSD directory to a server's hard disk. You can then run the network install and point clients to your local file server. (Alternatively, you can directly share a FreeBSD CD-ROM, although this may be slower.) The server holding the FreeBSD files can run any OS, but it must be running an FTP or Network File System (NFS) server.

Preparing Installation Media

If you bought a boxed set, you may have all the installation media you need. In some cases, though, you may need to prepare an installation medium. There are two parts to this: preparing a boot disk and preparing an installation source. The boot disk may be a floppy disk, a CD-ROM disc, or some other type of medium. The installation source today is often the same CD-ROM that functions as a boot medium, but in the case of a floppy boot it's usually a separate CD-ROM, a local hard disk, or a network installation medium.

Boot Disks

Most FreeBSD CD-ROMs sold today are bootable, meaning that a modern computer can boot directly from the CD-ROM into the FreeBSD installation routines. As described in the upcoming section, "Booting an Installer," you may need to adjust some BIOS settings to do this, though. If you created a CD-R from an image file, your CD-R should be bootable. If you created a CD-R from individual files, though, this may not be true unless you set up your CD-R software to create a bootable disc. In this case, or if you're using an older computer (from the mid-1990s or earlier) that lacks the ability to boot from a CD-ROM, you'll have to create another boot medium to run the FreeBSD installer.

The typical choice is a floppy disk. FreeBSD includes floppy disk images on its CD-ROM or FTP site. The images you need are called `kern.flp` and `mfsroot.flp`, and they're in the `floppies` directory. If you're running DOS or Windows, you can write these files to floppy disks by changing to the CD-ROM's `floppies` directory, inserting a blank formatted disk in the `A:` drive, and typing the following commands (inserting a fresh floppy before issuing the second command):

```
E:> ..\TOOLS\FDIMAGE KERN.FLP A:
E:> ..\TOOLS\FDIMAGE MFSROOT.FLP A:
```

These commands run the `fdimage.exe` program, which is a DOS program to create a floppy disk from a disk image. When it's done, your floppy disks should contain a FreeBSD installation boot system. The first disk (`kern.flp`) boots the system, and the second contains the installation utilities. If you have access to another computer that's currently running FreeBSD or some other UNIX-like OS, you can achieve the same results by using the standard UNIX `dd` command. For instance, if the FreeBSD CD-ROM is mounted at `/cdrom`, you could type the following commands (again, inserting a fresh floppy between commands):

```
# dd if=/cdrom/floppies/kern.flp of=/dev/fd0
# dd if=/cdrom/floppies/mfsroot.flp of=/dev/fd0
```

You might need to change the floppy disk identifier (`/dev/fd0`) or the CD-ROM mount point on some OSs, but this basic form should work on most UNIX-like OSs.

Installation Sources

If you're installing from a store-bought CD-ROM or an official FreeBSD FTP site mirror, you don't need to do anything to prepare your installation medium. If you download a CD-R image file, though, you must burn it to a CD-R using the appropriate image file mode. Precisely how you do this depends on your CD-R software. If you use a FreeBSD or other UNIX-like system, you can use the `cdrecord` program to send the file to a CD-R:

```
# cdrecord dev=6,0 speed=4 freebsd.iso
```

You'll need to adjust the device (`dev=6,0`), the speed, and the image filename to suit your system. If you're using a Windows or Mac OS CD-R package, you should look for an option called *burn CD-R from image file*, *create CD from ISO image*, or something similar. This tells the package to burn the CD-R from a file without creating a filesystem around it, which is the usual procedure for Windows and Mac OS CD-R programs.

If you burn the image file to a CD-R using the same options you normally use, you'll end up with an unbootable CD-R that contains just one file—whatever the image file is called. This CD-R will be useless for installing FreeBSD. A correctly burned FreeBSD CD-R contains several files and directories in its root directory, including the tools *and* floppies *directories described earlier in "Boot Disks."*

Preparing a Computer to Run FreeBSD

Before you actually install FreeBSD, you must take some steps to prepare your computer to hold the OS. The first of these steps is to check that your hardware is compatible with FreeBSD. If it's not, you must replace the hardware or obtain updated FreeBSD software to use the hardware. The second step is to clear disk space for use by FreeBSD. This second step is simplest if you intend to use *only* FreeBSD on the computer. If the system currently runs other OSs, you may need to add a hard disk, shrink existing partitions, or re-allocate partitions for FreeBSD's use.

Checking Hardware Compatibility

Chapter 1 included a description of some of the major concerns in hardware compatibility. Of the core system components, you should check on the compatibility of SCSI host adapters, network cards, and video cards. All of these components require special FreeBSD drivers (or drivers in tools within FreeBSD, such as XFree86). Most instances of these devices are well supported by FreeBSD, but a few are not. Less critical systems, such as sound cards, video capture cards, internal modems, scanners, and printers also require drivers. Support for these is spottier, but still good for some device types, such as printers and sound cards. For all of these devices, consult the `HARDWARE.TXT` file that comes with FreeBSD to learn about support for specific devices. (This file is also available at `ftp://ftp.FreeBSD.org/pub/FreeBSD/releases/i386/5.0-RELEASE/`.)

Some devices are very well standardized, so FreeBSD supports them using its normal drivers, and you don't need to be too concerned about compatibility. These devices include CPUs (within the *x*86 family, as described in Chapter 1), motherboards, RS-232 serial ports, parallel ports, keyboard ports, PS/2 mouse ports, floppy ports and drives, specific models of hard disk and CD-ROM drives, and to some extent EIDE controllers. EIDE controllers all work alike in their most basic and low-performance modes, but to get better performance, FreeBSD needs special controller-specific drivers. Because EIDE controllers are integrated on modern motherboards, this issue is sometimes discussed as if it were a motherboard (or motherboard chipset) issue. In a worst-case scenario, you can add a separate EIDE controller card to work around lack of support for the accelerated modes of an EIDE controller on a motherboard.

If the computer is currently running Windows, you can learn a lot about its devices from the Windows Control Panel. Specifically, the System object's Device Manager window (shown in Figure 2-1, from Windows 2000), which is accessible as an option from the Hardware tab, lets you browse through various devices. You may be able to learn the device's manufacturer, the name of the chipset, or the name of the driver. These can be important clues, but they can sometimes be deceptive. For instance, the device manufacturer's name may not be what's important because most FreeBSD drivers are written for the *chipsets* used by the device. (A chipset is one or more chips that provide most of the device's functionality. Many manufacturers use chipsets from other manufacturers.)

Another way to learn about your computer's hardware is to examine the chips yourself. Look at the largest chip. This probably bears a manufacturer's name or logo and a model number, as shown in Figure 2-2. This figure shows the main chip on a Matrox Millennium video card, clearly identifying it as using a Matrox MGA 2064W

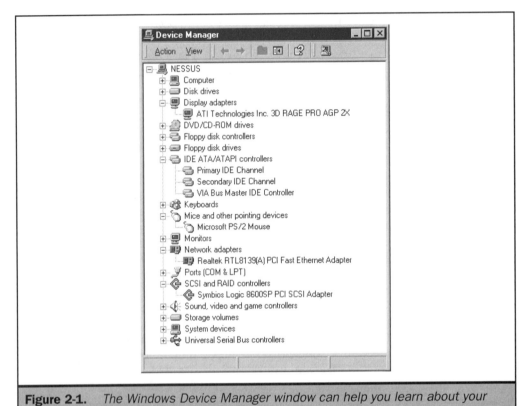

Figure 2-1.   *The Windows Device Manager window can help you learn about your computer prior to installing FreeBSD.*

chipset. Even if the information appears cryptic, it may match an option you'll find when you install FreeBSD or configure it after installation.

Caution   *Some chips, such as many recent video card and motherboard chipsets, generate so much heat that they're covered with heat sinks, which obscure chipset identification markings. Do not attempt to remove such heat sinks because you may damage the chip, and even if you don't, you'll have a hard time re-attaching the heat sink so that it does its job.*

If you can't find mention of a device in HARDWARE.TXT, that doesn't necessarily mean that it won't work. The device might be known by multiple names, and you simply haven't found the one by which it's listed in the file. Try doing a Usenet search using http://groups.google.com or a web search using your favorite search engine using *FreeBSD* and the name you've discovered. You could also try simply installing FreeBSD; the OS automatically detects many devices, so you may learn if it works quickly enough.

Figure 2-2.   *Device chipsets are usually labeled for easy identification.*

If the device doesn't work, you have three choices:

- **Replacement**   You can replace the nonfunctional device with a supported model. This is often the most effective and simplest course of action, particularly with inexpensive devices such as Ethernet or sound cards. Many motherboard components, although they can't be removed, can be circumvented by adding a card that duplicates the motherboard component's function. You may need to disable the motherboard component in the computer's BIOS, though.

- **Workaround**   It may be possible to work around an incompatibility in some way. In some cases, this may mean using a device in some sort of compatibility mode that provides limited functionality. For instance, some printers work with a lower resolution using a common protocol that FreeBSD (or, more precisely, Ghostscript) supports, while their higher-resolution modes remain inaccessible from FreeBSD. In other cases, you can do without the device entirely. For instance, you might not really need a sound card in FreeBSD, if you use the sound card mainly for games in Windows.

- **Driver development**   If you have the programming skill or are willing to hire somebody with such skills, you can write a driver yourself or have it written for you. This task is well beyond the scope of this book, and it's useful mainly if you're a hobbyist programmer yourself or if the cost of replacing a component would be huge (for instance, replacing hundreds of expensive cards at a large site).

In a few cases, there may be support for a hardware device, but only in an experimental form or in software that doesn't ship with FreeBSD. If the device is critical to the computer's functioning, such as a SCSI host adapter that handles the computer's hard disks, using the updated driver may be tricky. You may have to prepare and use a custom FreeBSD installation floppy, for instance. Consult the documentation for the new driver for details. In the case of more peripheral devices, such as sound cards or printers, you may be able to install FreeBSD and then add the new driver later. Again, consult the driver's documentation for details.

Clearing Disk Space

FreeBSD needs disk space in which to operate. If you're installing FreeBSD to a new computer or replacing an existing OS, setting aside disk space requires no special preparation. As described in the upcoming section, "Partitioning the System," you can simply tell the installer to use all your disk space, and it will replace any existing data on the disk.

A more complex situation involves adding FreeBSD to an existing OS. In this case, you must set aside a dedicated primary partition for FreeBSD's use, as described in Chapter 1. Many FreeBSD CD-ROMs include an open source utility known as the First Non-Destructive Interactive Partition Splitting Program (FIPS; `http://www` `.igd.fhg.de/~aschaefe/fips/`). You can use this program to split an existing primary FAT partition into two parts. You can then use the FreeBSD installation program to delete the second partition and use its space. Another option is to use a third-party utility such as PowerQuests's (`http://www.powerquest.com`) PartitionMagic. Such tools are often more flexible and easier to use than FIPS. One potentially very important advantage of PartitionMagic over FIPS is that PartitionMagic can shrink the New Technology File System (NTFS) partitions that are common with Windows NT, 2000, and XP installations. (Some of these systems use FAT, though, so don't assume FIPS is inadequate; check the filesystem type using the Windows Properties dialog box for the disk.)

FIPS, PartitionMagic, and other dynamic partitioning tools are inherently dangerous. Bugs, power outages, and other problems can cause data loss—potentially even destroying critical filesystem data structures, thus rendering access to all files on the disk impossible without difficult and potentially expensive repairs. For this reason, you should back up all your data before proceeding with such an operation.

Using FIPS

To use FIPS to shrink an existing FAT partition, follow these steps:

1. In DOS or Windows, run a disk defragmenter on the C: partition. You can use the disk defragmentation options available from the Windows disk Properties dialog box, as shown in Figure 2-3. The idea is to ensure that all the files are in

the early part of the disk, leaving nothing but empty space at the end, in the area you want to devote to FreeBSD. It's also a very good idea to perform a check of the partition's integrity (by clicking Check Now in Figure 2-3). Note that some disk utilities place files that cannot be moved at the end of the disk. You may need to temporarily disable such utilities and delete their data files before proceeding.

2. Boot to DOS. Ensure that you have CD-ROM drivers available on your DOS floppy, or copy the `FIPS.EXE` program from the FreeBSD CD-ROM's `TOOLS` directory to a floppy disk or hard disk partition you can read from DOS. If you don't have a DOS boot floppy, you can use FreeDOS (`http://www.freedos.org`), an open source re-implementation of DOS.

Do not *run FIPS from a multitasking OS such as OS/2 or Windows. (The Windows 9x DOS boot works, but don't run FIPS from a DOS window in the Windows desktop.) Doing so can confuse the OS and cause file corruption.*

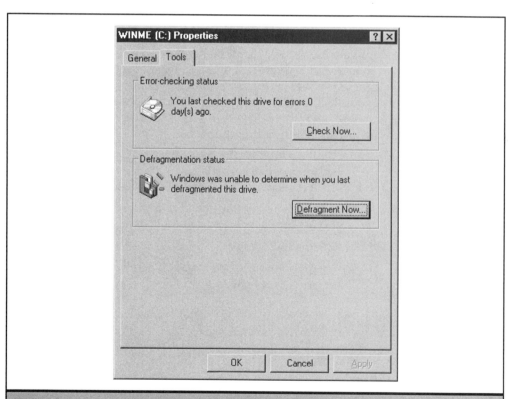

Figure 2-3. *Click Defragment Now to defragment a hard disk in Windows.*

3. Change to the directory in which FIPS resides and type **FIPS** to run the program. The program displays some introductory text.

4. Press a key. FIPS displays information on the hard disk's partition table. This information applies *only* to primary partitions; FIPS can't operate on logical partitions, and so displays no information on them. Partitions are defined in terms of their starting and ending cylinders, heads, and sectors. These so-called *CHS numbers* are used by the BIOS for addressing the disk, and you'll subsequently modify the ending cylinder number to shrink the DOS or Windows partition.

5. Press a key. FIPS displays information on your C: partition. If you're familiar with FAT data structures, you can check that this information is correct, or at least reasonable; otherwise you can ignore it. FIPS also asks if you want to make a backup copy of the root and boot sectors. I recommend you respond **y** to do so, allowing you to back out of the operation if something goes wrong.

6. FIPS asks if a bootable floppy disk is in the A: drive. If necessary, insert a floppy disk and type **y**. FIPS will then save the root and boot sectors to the floppy disk.

7. FIPS computes the minimum size it can make the existing C: partition and displays this size, along with the size of the new primary partition it will create. If you want to make a larger C: partition (which is advisable in most cases, so you have room for new files on your DOS or Windows installation), use the right arrow key to increase the size of C: at the expense of the new FreeBSD slice. FIPS modifies partition sizes by one cylinder at a time; so, depending upon the size of your disk, you may see your partitions change in size by several megabytes with each arrow keypress. When the system displays the division you want, press Enter to continue.

8. FIPS displays summary information on the new partition layout similar to what it showed in Step 4. If you approve of the new layout, type **c** to have FIPS continue with the changes. If not, type **r** to redo the changes (going back to Step 7).

9. FIPS displays summary information on the new C: partition's FAT filesystem, similar to what it showed in Step 5. Type **y** to continue, and FIPS writes its changes to the disk.

At this point, you'll have two partitions in place of one. When you install FreeBSD, you can tell the installer to delete the second partition and create a new FreeBSD slice in its place.

Unfortunately, FIPS is limited in its features. If you want to resize logical or NTFS partitions, move partitions, or perform other actions, FIPS won't do. For that, you'll need a more sophisticated tool, such as the commercial PartitionMagic.

Using PartitionMagic

PartitionMagic is a much more flexible tool than FIPS. Using PartitionMagic, you can create, delete, move, or resize FAT, NTFS, High-Performance File System (HPFS), or

Second Extended File System (ext2fs) partitions. (HPFS support was removed from version 7.0 of the software, however, so if you need HPFS support you should get version 6.0 or earlier. Versions prior to 4.0 didn't support Linux's ext2fs.) You also need not defragment a hard disk before running PartitionMagic, although checking the disk integrity beforehand is a good idea.

PartitionMagic can run from either a DOS boot floppy or from a fully booted Windows system. The user interface is similar in either case, although the DOS version lacks some features, such as the ability to automatically design layouts for various combinations of OSs. Once the system is booted, it presents a graphical view of the disk, including both a bar chart showing your partitions and a textual partition list. You can click on a partition in either area and select Partitions | Resize to resize the partition. The result is a dialog box like the one shown in Figure 2-4, in which you can enter the new partition size by dragging the right end of the existing partition or entering a new size in the numeric data entry fields.

For FreeBSD use, it's simplest if you leave the space for FreeBSD unallocated; PartitionMagic can't create a FreeBSD slice, so you'll have to create that within the FreeBSD installer. Be sure this unallocated FreeBSD space is *not* within an extended partition; FreeBSD needs to create a primary partition for itself, and if the only free space is within an extended partition, FreeBSD won't be able to use it. (PartitionMagic displays extended partitions as light blue boxes within which logical partitions reside. If necessary, you can shrink an extended partition just as you would any other partition type.)

When you're done with entering changes, click the Apply button in the main PartitionMagic window. The program will then commit the changes you've entered, ultimately making space available for FreeBSD.

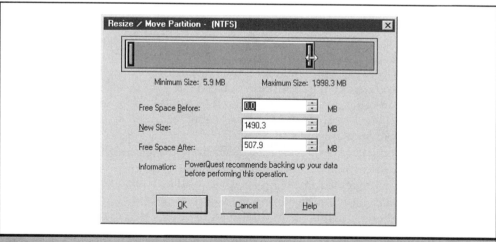

Figure 2-4.   *PartitionMagic lets you resize partitions using GUI controls.*

Beginning the Installation

Once you've cleared away space for FreeBSD, you can begin the installation process. This involves booting a FreeBSD installer, setting some initial configuration options, and creating a FreeBSD slice and partitions within that slice for your FreeBSD installation.

Booting an Installer

To install FreeBSD, you must boot its installer. This is a special stripped-down FreeBSD system that includes software to copy FreeBSD files from an installation medium to your hard disk. The two types of FreeBSD boot media are

- **CD-ROMs** Most FreeBSD installation CD-ROMs, including the one that comes with this book, are bootable. To boot, you must configure your BIOS to try to boot from the CD-ROM drive before booting from the hard disk, insert the FreeBSD CD-ROM in the computer, and exit from the BIOS utility. If you can't find a boot-from-CD-ROM option in your BIOS, if it doesn't work, or if you don't have a FreeBSD CD-ROM, you may need to use a boot floppy.

- **Floppies** The earlier section, "Boot Disks," described how to create FreeBSD installation floppy disks. The first of these is bootable. If your BIOS is configured to try to boot from a floppy disk before trying the hard disk (as most are by default), you can insert the FreeBSD boot floppy and start the computer. It will eventually ask for the second disk, which you should insert when prompted, and load up the FreeBSD installation program.

The FreeBSD installation procedure is the same whether you boot from a CD-ROM or a floppy disk. Indeed, even the boot process is very similar. In both cases, you'll see a large number of messages scroll by on the screen. These relate to internal kernel checks and hardware driver installation. Some of these messages may scroll past so quickly that you won't be able to read them. Don't worry about this unless you have problems using some vital hardware component. In such a case, you may need to temporarily work around the problem and then perform troubleshooting, as described in Chapter 32. For instance, if the installer doesn't recognize your CD-ROM drive, you may need to perform a network installation or temporarily use another CD-ROM drive, then work on fixing the problem once FreeBSD is fully installed.

Once the installer has booted, it displays a menu similar to the one shown in Figure 2-5. This program is the sysinstall utility, which as the name suggests, installs a FreeBSD system. You can also use it after installing FreeBSD to add or delete software, upgrade the system, and make some modifications to the OS.

You may want to take some time to experiment with the sysinstall user interface, particularly if you're not used to text-based menu systems. The arrow keys move selection points around. In most menus, the up and down arrows move up and down the list of options (such as Usage, Standard, Express, and so on in Figure 2-5), while the left and right arrows select between the action buttons at the bottom of the

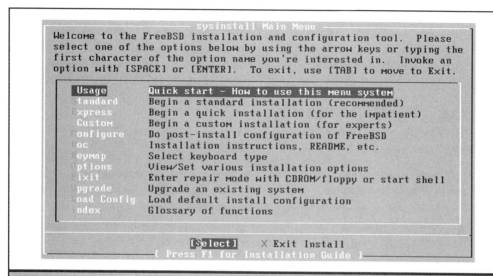

```
────────────────── sysinstall Main Menu ──────────────────
  Welcome to the FreeBSD installation and configuration tool.  Please
  select one of the options below by using the arrow keys or typing the
  first character of the option name you're interested in.  Invoke an
  option with [SPACE] or [ENTER].  To exit, use [TAB] to move to Exit.

        Usage       Quick start - How to use this menu system
        tandard     Begin a standard installation (recommended)
        xpress      Begin a quick installation (for the impatient)
        Custom      Begin a custom installation (for experts)
        onfigure    Do post-install configuration of FreeBSD
        oc          Installation instructions, README, etc.
        eymap       Select keyboard type
        ptions      View/Set various installation options
        ixit        Enter repair mode with CDROM/floppy or start shell
        pgrade      Upgrade an existing system
        oad Config  Load default install configuration
        ndex        Glossary of functions

                    [Select]     X Exit Install
              ── [ Press F1 for Installation Guide ] ──
```

Figure 2-5. *The* `sysinstall` *utility provides basic system installation and configuration tools.*

menu (`Select` and `Exit Install` in Figure 2-5). The Page Up and Page Down keys can be used to scroll through very long lists of options that fill more than one screen. The space bar may toggle an option on or off. No such options are shown in Figure 2-5, but such an option has a box formed from square braces (`[ ]`) to the left of the option, and this box is filled with an X if it's selected. Press ENTER to select the currently active action button. In some menus this action does the same thing as the space bar. In most menus, some options have differently colored leading letters, such as `Standard` and `Express` in Figure 2-5. You can skip directly to these options by typing the appropriate letter along with the ALT key, such as ALT-E to begin an Express installation in Figure 2-5. This procedure isn't perfectly reliable, though, particularly in menus with many options, so if it doesn't work, use the arrow keys to locate the appropriate option.

FreeBSD supports three types of installation: *standard*, *express*, and *custom*. Standard is the best choice for most new installations. Express skips some menus and checks, and so can install a system somewhat quicker if you're in a hurry; but you may need to spend more time later setting it up correctly. Custom can be useful if you're experienced with FreeBSD because it gives you somewhat greater control over certain options. The rest of this chapter assumes that you select the standard installation.

Partitioning the System

Once you select the `Standard` option from the main `sysinstall` menu, the system tells you that you must partition your computer. As described in Chapter 1, this is actually a two-step process. First, you must create an *x86* partition (aka a FreeBSD *slice*). Second, you create BSD-style partitions within the FreeBSD slice. A message appears immediately after you select the `Standard` option telling you that you'll be creating a DOS-style partition; this is the FreeBSD slice. When you select OK to this message, `sysinstall` displays the FDISK Partition Editor screen shown in Figure 2-6.

Creating a FreeBSD Slice

Depending upon how you set aside space for FreeBSD, you may need to do one of two things:

- **Use entire disk**   If you want to use the entire disk for FreeBSD, destroying any existing partitions and data, you can type **A** to do so. This creates a single primary *x86* partition (the BSD slice) in which FreeBSD will reside.

- **Create new partitions**   If you have free space (identified by an `unused` entry in the `Desc` column), you can select it and type **C** to create a FreeBSD slice. The system then asks for a size. In most cases, you'll want to devote all the space to FreeBSD, so just press ENTER to accept the default. Otherwise, type the size in 512-byte blocks, or in megabytes with a trailing M (such as **500M** to create a 500MB slice). If you've created a partition for FreeBSD (say, by using FIPS), you must delete it by selecting it and typing **D**, then use the resulting free space to create a FreeBSD slice.

```
Disk name:     ad0                               FDISK Partition Editor
DISK Geometry:  1015 cyls/64 heads/63 sectors = 4092480 sectors (1998MB)

Offset       Size(ST)       End     Name  PType      Desc  Subtype     Flags

         0         63        62        -      6     unused        0
        63     757953    758015    ad0s1      2        fat        6
    758016    3334464   4092479    ad0s2      2        fat        6
   4092480       3150   4095629        -      6     unused        0




The following commands are supported (in upper or lower case):

A = Use Entire Disk   G = set Drive Geometry   C = Create Slice   F = 'DD' mode
D = Delete Slice      Z = Toggle Size Units    S = Set Bootable   : = Wizard m.
T = Change Type       U = Undo All Changes     Q = Finish

Use F1 or ? to get more help, arrow keys to select.

■
```

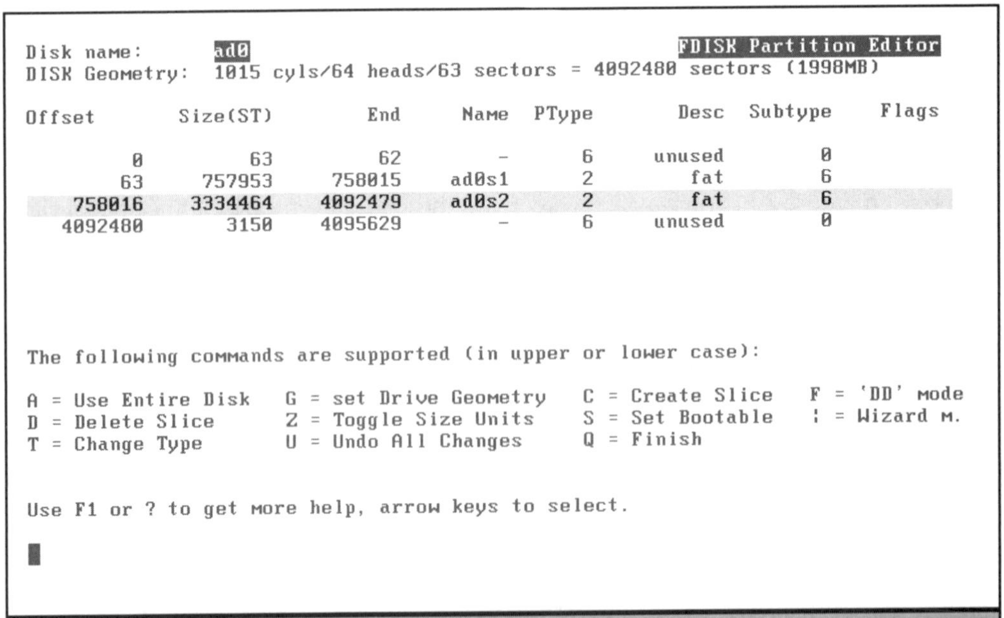

Figure 2-6.   *The FreeBSD FDISK Partition Editor is similar to DOS or Windows'* FDISK *in principle, but the user interface is somewhat different.*

> **Note**
>
> *It's not uncommon to see a disk with a small amount of "unused" space at the start or end; in fact, Figure 2-6 shows both conditions. These tiny areas of free space are artifacts of the CHS method of identifying partitions, and they aren't really useable. If you plan to put a FreeBSD partition next to such space, you may be able to use the space by deleting the partition you intend to use for FreeBSD and then re-creating it with the **c** command.*

In theory, you can create more than one FreeBSD slice, but in practice there's seldom a reason to do so, unless you have two physical hard disks. In this case, you can create FreeBSD slices on multiple hard disks. Creating multiple FreeBSD slices will restrict your options for the sizes of FreeBSD partitions you can create in a subsequent step.

You may want to pay attention to the name of the slice you create for FreeBSD, and perhaps the names used for other OSs' partitions. In Figure 2-6, the ad0s1 partition holds a Windows installation, and the highlighted ad0s2 partition will be deleted and re-created for use by FreeBSD. Although you don't need to manually enter these values during installation, you may need them when performing subsequent administration tasks.

Setting the Boot Loader Option

Once you've made the changes to the *x*86 partition table to add one or more FreeBSD slices, type **Q**. This action writes your changes to the disk and moves on to a question concerning the placement of a boot loader. This topic is discussed in greater detail in Chapter 4. For now, FreeBSD presents three options:

- **BootMgr** This option installs the FreeBSD boot manager on the hard disk's *Master Boot Record (MBR)*, which is the first disk-based code the computer runs when it boots. This option is a good one when FreeBSD is the only OS on the computer or when you have a simple dual-boot configuration (FreeBSD and Windows, for instance). If your system multiboots many OSs and you already have a boot loader, you may want to use another option.

- **Standard** This option overwrites the MBR with a standard one that directly boots only the active partition. You might use this if you plan to subsequently install another boot loader, but even then, the next option should also work.

- **None** This option doesn't touch the MBR. It's the best option if you already have another boot loader, such as System Commander or Linux's LILO, installed. You'll need to reconfigure this other boot loader to boot FreeBSD in addition to your other OSs.

Creating FreeBSD Partitions

After you select an MBR option, FreeBSD enters a second stage of partition creation. In this stage, you create partitions within your FreeBSD slice, using a tool called the *FreeBSD Disklabel Editor* (shown in Figure 2-7). Every FreeBSD system requires at least two partitions: a root (/) partition and a swap partition. If your system also has DOS or Windows, the FreeBSD Disklabel Editor will show a partition for it, as well, as shown in Figure 2-7. On a fresh installation, the initial state of the FreeBSD Disklabel Editor is to show only an existing DOS or Windows partition, if present.

You can create new partitions by ensuring that the Disk line near the top of the screen is highlighted and then pressing the c key. The utility will ask for several pieces of information in turn:

1. The partition's size (in blocks, megabytes, or cylinders).

2. Whether you're creating a filesystem or a swap partition. A filesystem holds files, but FreeBSD needs at least one swap partition. It's a good idea to make this at least as large as your computer's memory because it's theoretically possible for certain types of system crashes to wipe out data in partitions after the swap partition if this isn't the case.

3. The *mount point* for the partition (that is, the directory name under which it will be accessible). Mount points are described in more detail shortly. You need at least one root (/) partition, but you can create more partitions. Swap partitions don't have mount points, so you're not asked about this for swap partitions.

If you have more than a few hundred megabytes of free space, you can type **A** and FreeBSD will set up the free space using some common partitioning rules. This approach can save some time and may be a useful shortcut in some situations, especially if you're

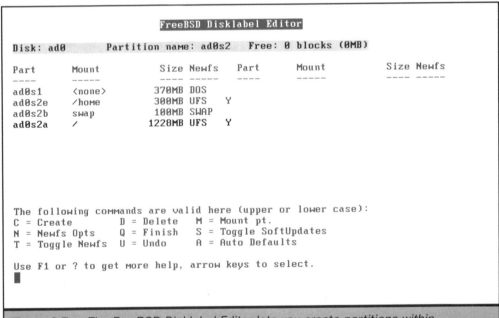

Figure 2-7. *The FreeBSD Disklabel Editor lets you create partitions within a FreeBSD slice and assign them mount points in FreeBSD.*

unfamiliar with FreeBSD. If you're more experienced, though, you may want to set up partitions of your own. Some common partitions, which FreeBSD creates using the A option, include

- ■ **root (/)** This is the base of the FreeBSD directory tree; all files are accessible from the root directory. Thus, this is the only truly required filesystem. The A option makes the root filesystem small because most files go in other partitions with this option. Figure 2-7 shows a larger root filesystem because this installation lacks some of these additional partitions.

- ■ **/home** The /home directory holds users' data files. Its optimum size therefore depends on the number of users your system will support and their disk space requirements. A small single-user system, or a computer that functions as a server with few actual login users, may need just a few megabytes in /home, or it might even be integrated into the root partition. A system with many users who create large files might need gigabytes of /home space.

- ■ **/usr** The /usr directory holds most ordinary program files. It's therefore the largest partition in a default configuration, with the likely exception of /home. For a fully useable FreeBSD installation, you should have at least 1GB in /usr, and preferably more. (A tiny FreeBSD installation can get by with less than 100MB in /usr, though.) If you don't create a separate /usr partition, the root partition should be at least this large.

- ■ **/tmp** This directory holds temporary files. Automatic system tools normally clean it out periodically. FreeBSD puts it in a separate partition so that temporary files don't overwhelm other important partitions, in case some misbehaved process creates too many or too large temporary files.

- ■ **/var** This directory is similar to /tmp in that it holds files that are mostly fleeting. These files are more commonly created by FreeBSD or its processes than by users, though. For instance, this directory holds mail files received by mail servers until they're read by users. Like /tmp, it's often placed on a separate partition to protect other partitions from trouble should too many files be created in /var. A typical install creates a /var partition that's well under 1GB in size, but some systems need much more space than this. For instance, a busy mail server might need a multigigabyte /var.

Getting partition sizes right is one of the most difficult tasks for new FreeBSD administrators. If you intend to use the system as a typical workstation, or for a server that doesn't receive a great deal of data (for instance, for a web or FTP server), the default settings created by the A option work well. If you're in doubt, you might consider simplifying the installation. For instance, rather than using A to create partitions automatically, use C, and create just a root (/), a /home, and a swap partition. Such a configuration poses some risks because runaway processes can fill the root partition by writing to /var or /tmp, but if you're uncertain how much space you'll need in these directories or in /usr, you might have fewer problems with cramped partitions by using a simple configuration. Conversely, if you're experienced and know you'll be putting a lot of files in particular directories, you might want to create additional partitions for directories such as /opt or /usr/X11R6.

Because the swap partition is used fairly heavily on most installations, it's common to place it in the middle of a set of filesystem partitions. This practice reduces the amount of time it takes to seek to the swap partition from other partitions, thus improving overall system performance.

Once you've finished creating partitions, type **Q** to move on to the next stage of the installation, in which you choose an installation medium.

Selecting Software to Install

After you tell the installer what installation medium you want to use, it displays a list of *distribution sets* that you can install, as shown in Figure 2-8. Each distribution set is a collection of related software packages, such as development tools or user applications. You can select one or more distribution sets, or select All to install all of them. After each selection, FreeBSD asks if you want to install the ports collection. This is a set of software "skeletons" that enable you to easily build software from source code. Some ports aren't available as standard precompiled FreeBSD binaries. After making a selection, you may then need to select an Exit option to return to the selection menu shown in Figure 2-8; or you can proceed with the installation.

Note   *If you're familiar with Linux, you know that the word* distribution *refers to an entire installable Linux variant, such as Red Hat or Debian, in the Linux world. FreeBSD distributions are sets of packages* within *the FreeBSD OS, so the word has a very different meaning in FreeBSD than in Linux.*

If you intend to use the computer as an X-based (GUI) workstation, it's important that you select the X-User distribution. As a practical matter, most systems need one or more of the developer distributions. Most UNIX software is available in source code form, so even if you're not a programmer, having software development tools available allows you to use software for which official FreeBSD binaries are not available; you download the source code and compile your own binaries, as described briefly in Chapter 11. An important developer distribution is Kern-Developer (and its variant, X-Kern-Developer), which allows you to modify and recompile the FreeBSD kernel—the heart of the FreeBSD OS. Chapter 12 describes the kernel and its configuration in more detail. If you're in doubt, I recommend you select the X-Developer, X-Kern-Developer, and X-User distributions. (If you don't need the X Window System, you can select the non-X variants of these distributions.) If you fail to select a package and discover you need it later, you can install it by running sysinstall after you install FreeBSD.

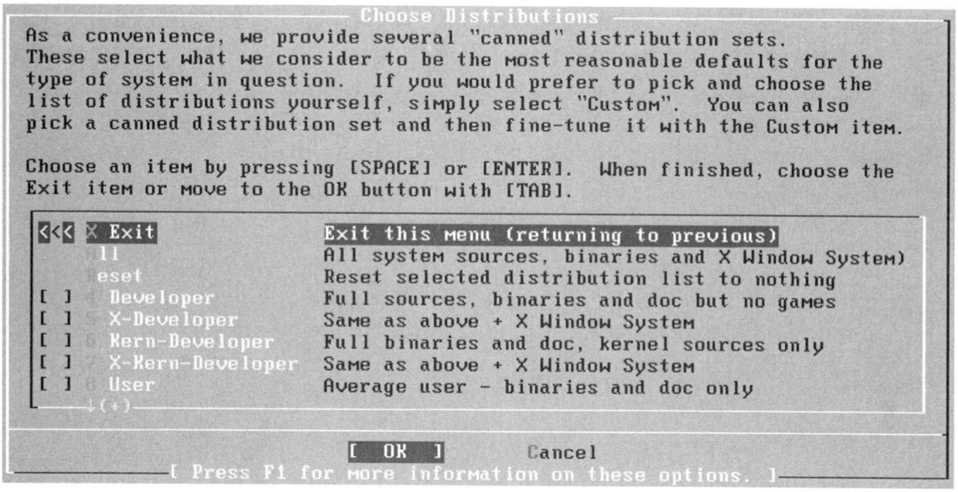

Figure 2-8.   *You can select one or more of several distributions that define what software is installed in FreeBSD by default.*

If you're familiar with FreeBSD software packages, you may want to pick the Custom distribution option, which allows you to select and deselect specific distributions. (The menu shown in Figure 2-8 allows you to select distribution *sets*; the Custom option gives you slightly finer control, allowing you to select individual distributions rather than entire sets of distributions.)

Selecting an Installation Medium

FreeBSD offers many options for installation media. These include

- **CD/DVD**   You can install from a local CD-ROM or DVD-ROM drive by selecting the first option. This is usually the fastest and most convenient installation method if you have access to a FreeBSD CD-ROM or DVD-ROM.

- **FTP options**   There are three FTP options: FTP, which is the most direct option; FTP Passive, which uses FTP's passive mode, which works through some firewalls that block FTP's normal operating mode; and HTTP, which uses an HTTP (Web) proxy to contact an FTP server. All of these options let you install from any of several official FreeBSD sites or from an FTP server you operate locally. (To use a local server, select the URL option in the FTP site list. You can then enter your local FTP site's address and the directory in which the FreeBSD files reside.) FTP installation can be a good option if you have a fast network connection and no FreeBSD CD-ROM.

- **NFS** The *Network File System (NFS)* is a file-sharing tool that's common on UNIX networks. You can place FreeBSD files on a local NFS server and install from that, much as you would from an FTP server.

- **Local filesystems** The DOS and File System options let you install from a local disk. The DOS option prompts you to select a partition from a list, and the File System option requires you to enter a path to a mounted filesystem. Because this option requires that the partition already be mounted, it's not terribly useful for a first-time installation, but it might be useful for an upgrade.

- **Floppy or tape** Two additional options are Floppy and Tape. Although common at one time, these options are seldom used today; FreeBSD consumes too many floppy disks, and tapes are a far less convenient installation medium than are CD-ROMs. Nonetheless, you can still use these methods—if you can find a FreeBSD package distributed on these media.

Most people use CD-ROM or FTP installation options, but NFS can be useful on some local networks, and installing from a DOS partition can be handy in some limited circumstances. The procedure is very similar no matter what medium you use, but of course if you use a removable medium such as a CD-ROM, you'll be prompted to insert it, if it isn't already inserted in its drive when you begin the process. If you opt to use a network installation method, you'll be prompted to enter network configuration information earlier than you would if you use a CD-ROM. (The upcoming section, "Network Configuration," covers entering this information.)

Installing FreeBSD

Once you've selected the installation medium, the installer asks if you want to begin the installation. FreeBSD displays a confirmation request informing you that this is your last chance to make changes or abort the installation. After you select Yes in this screen, there's no going back; the installer creates filesystems on the FreeBSD partitions and copies FreeBSD files to them.

The installation process presents a series of progress notices, beginning with information on filesystem creation and proceeding to screens summarizing the progress when installing major package sets. These may include bin, doc, Xlib, ports, and so on, but the exact details differ depending upon your installation options. How long this takes depends on the speed of your hard disk and your installation medium (CD-ROM drive or network, most likely), as well as how much software you're installing.

Post-Installation Configuration

After sysinstall creates the FreeBSD partitions and copies files to those partitions, it moves on to prompt you with several vital system configuration questions. Most importantly, you set up networking, configure XFree86 (if you've opted to install it), and configure user accounts. There are several other configuration details in addition to these, though.

Network Configuration

The installer asks if you want to configure Ethernet or SLIP/PPP networking. If you don't want to do this, select No; otherwise, select Yes. This description assumes you're setting up Ethernet networking. The exact details of SLIP and PPP networking (used to connect computers via serial cables or to use a telephone modem to connect to the Internet) differ.

The first option you must specify is your network interface, as shown in Figure 2-9. If your system has an Ethernet card installed, the first option corresponds to it, and you should select it; otherwise, you can pick sl0 for a Serial Line Interface Protocol (SLIP) or ppp0 for a Point-to-Point Protocol (PPP) connection. Note that the exact name of the Ethernet interface varies, depending upon the Ethernet chipset used in your Ethernet card. Many systems provide additional options not shown in Figure 2-9, corresponding to additional serial and parallel ports.

Once you select the Ethernet option, sysinstall asks if you want to configure the card to use IPv6 networking, the next-generation networking protocol. In 2002, it's not in common use, but you may want to consult your network administrator to be sure. If you select No, sysinstall asks if you want to use the *Dynamic Host Configuration Protocol (DHCP)* to configure networking. This tool allows a central server to assign IP addresses and other networking options to DHCP client systems. It can greatly

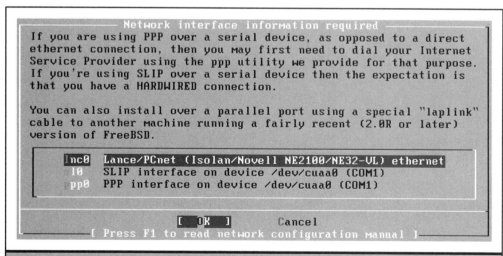

Figure 2-9. *FreeBSD auto-detects your Ethernet card and lets you select it, a SLIP interface, or a PPP interface.*

simplify network configuration, and failing to use it when you should can cause problems for yourself and for other users. Therefore, you should be sure to ask your network administrator if you should use DHCP. If you select Yes, FreeBSD attempts to obtain network information and displays it in a screen like the one shown in Figure 2-10. If you select No, FreeBSD displays the same screen, but you'll need to enter information in it. You'll have to obtain this information from your network administrator. Particularly critical information includes the IP address, netmask (aka network mask or subnet mask), gateway address, and Domain Name System (DNS) server address. Most of these take the form of a four-byte number, each byte separated by a period, as in 192.168.1.27. Your network administrator may provide you with multiple DNS server addresses, but you can enter only one; pick one randomly, or use the one identified as a primary address. Chapter 14 describes how to enter multiple DNS server addresses after FreeBSD is up and running. The hostname and domain name are not technically required for normal operation, but entering them may help your system to function in certain ways, so by all means enter them if you know them.

After you enter this information, sysinstall asks if you want the computer to function as a network gateway. In most cases, the correct answer to this question is No. Only respond Yes if your computer has two network interfaces and is supposed to forward traffic between the two networks. FreeBSD can make a good gateway computer, but such a configuration is beyond the scope of this book.

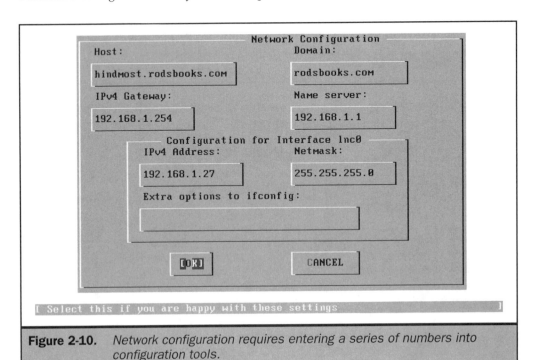

Figure 2-10. *Network configuration requires entering a series of numbers into configuration tools.*

Next, the system asks if you want to configure `inetd`. This is a *super server*—a program that listens for attempts to contact other servers on your computer, and directs traffic appropriately. Not all server programs use `inetd`, but some common ones do, including Telnet and FTP servers. If you're unsure, select `No` here; but if you're certain you want to run Telnet, FTP, or other `inetd`-mediated servers, respond `Yes`. If you do so, `sysinstall` warns you that `inetd` and the servers it handles increase the security risks encountered by your system, and gives you a chance to change your mind. If you still choose `Yes`, the system informs you that it will run an editor to enable you to edit the `inetd` configuration file, `/etc/inetd.conf`. You can locate the line corresponding to any server you want to run and uncomment it—that is, remove the leading hash mark (#). When you're done, press CTRL-[, select option **a** (`leave editor`) from the resulting menu, and select **a** again (`save changes`).

Next, you'll be asked a series of questions concerning specific servers or server configurations:

- **Anonymous FTP**   You'll be asked if you want to enable anonymous FTP access. If you don't know what this means, respond `No`. Note that you do *not* need to enable this option to use other anonymous FTP sites, just to run your own anonymous FTP site.

- **NFS server**   Running an NFS server allows other FreeBSD, UNIX, or UNIX-like systems to access files on your computer as if they were local. If you're uncertain, respond `No`. If you respond `Yes`, you'll have to edit the NFS server configuration file, `/etc/exports`. Chapter 18 describes this file in more detail.

- **NFS client**   You can mount other UNIX-like systems' NFS exports if you respond `Yes` to this option, but you don't need to further configure it at this time.

- **Security profile**   FreeBSD supports many security features. You can set many options to either moderate or restrictive settings by choosing `Yes` to the security profile question. If you select `No`, it's the same as choosing `Yes` and then picking the `Medium` security profile.

If in doubt, leave networking options disabled. You can enable them after the fact, as described in Part III of this book. Leaving network features disabled is usually safer than enabling the features because enabled network servers are potential security holes.

System Console Settings

If you plan to do much work in text mode, you may want to adjust the console settings. You can set several different options from this menu:

- **Font**   The default font works well in most cases, but you can select several different character sets, which are mostly useful for displaying non-Roman alphabets or extensions to the Roman alphabet.

- **Keymap**   Keymap settings are mostly useful for use outside of the United States. You can tell FreeBSD that you have a French or Russian keyboard, for instance.

- **Repeat rate**   You can choose any of four keyboard repeat rates. Unfortunately, there's no way to test them during installation.

- **Screensaver**   The Saver option lets you enable a text-mode screensaver, which may display a pattern or blank the screen when you've not used the computer in text mode for a time. The Green screen saver may be of particular interest if you want to save power; modern monitors will go into a low power mode when this screen saver activates.

- **Screen map**   You can select any of several methods of mapping UNIX-style characters to PC-style fonts with this option. This option is most useful if you need to use a non-Roman font.

- **Settings for ttys**   *Terminal types (ttys)* are protocols that programs use for addressing the screen. Like the screen map and font settings, these are most useful if you're using a non-US computer.

Time Zone

Time zone configuration is very important, particularly for UNIX-like OSs. Although you can skip this configuration option, doing so isn't a good idea. The first question you're asked is whether the clock is set to *Universal Coordinated Time (UTC)*, which is closely related to Greenwich Mean Time (GMT). Traditionally, UNIX has stored all times in UTC and converted to local time on the fly, based on the time zone. Most *x86* systems, though, use local time internally and convert to UTC for protocols that require it. Tell FreeBSD whether your hardware clock is set to UTC or to local time.

> **Tip**   *If your computer runs only FreeBSD, or FreeBSD and some other UNIX-like OS such as Solaris or Linux, set the hardware clock to UTC. Doing so will result in a reduced likelihood of problems if you live in an area in which clocks must be changed for daylight savings time. If your FreeBSD system dual-boots with DOS, Windows, OS/2, or some other OS that assumes the hardware clock is set to local time, use the local time setting. You may need to reset your system clock at least once each spring or fall, but rebooting to another OS won't cause clock problems.*

Setting the actual time zone is a three-step process. First, you must select your region, such as America. Second, you select your country within the area, such as United States. Finally, you select the time zone within your country, such as Eastern Time. (In some cases, one of the last two steps may not be required.) The system then presents a three-letter abbreviation for your time zone, such as EST, and asks if it looks reasonable. If you know this code is wrong, select No to repeat the process; otherwise, select Yes.

Linux Binary Compatibility

FreeBSD has the ability to run Linux binaries. Although most Linux programs are available in native FreeBSD forms, the Linux binary compatibility can still be convenient when FreeBSD binaries aren't available and source code either isn't available or compiling it is difficult. For instance, if you want to run a commercial game, such as *Civilization: Call to Power*, you can do so, but you need the Linux binary compatibility to run the Linux version.

Some OSs include the ability to run other OSs' binaries, but at a huge cost. For instance, the Win-OS/2 component of OS/2 allows OS/2 to run 16-bit Windows programs, but Win-OS/2 takes a long time to load, and Windows programs don't run as well as native OS/2 programs. Such problems don't plague FreeBSD's Linux compatibility module because Linux and FreeBSD are so similar that just a few libraries and kernel support features are needed to get Linux binaries running under FreeBSD. For these reasons, you should probably opt to include the Linux binary compatibility. When you do so, `sysinstall` will attempt to load the module from the installation medium. Chapter 4 includes information on using FreeBSD's Linux binary compatibility mode.

Mouse Configuration

FreeBSD supports a text-based mouse tool that lets you cut and paste text in text mode. The first question `sysinstall` asks to determine whether and how to configure this tool is whether you've got a USB mouse. If you do, choose `Yes`; otherwise, pick `No`. If you select `No`, `sysinstall` next presents a menu (shown in Figure 2-11) in which you configure and test your mouse.

You can configure the mouse by setting several options:

1. **Mouse type**   Select the mouse type by choosing the `Type` option, which sets the software protocol used by the mouse. Most mice today use the PS/2 protocol, which is set by picking the `Auto` type. FreeBSD also gives you the option of picking any of several protocols that are common with older RS-232 serial mice, such as `Logitech` and `Microsoft`.

2. **Mouse port**   Use the `Port` option to choose the hardware port to which the mouse connects. Options include `PS/2`, `COM1` through `COM4` (for RS-232 serial mice), and `BusMouse` (for old-style bus mice). Note that the PS/2 *protocol* (set in the `Type` menu) is separate from the PS/2 *hardware port*, although PS/2 mice generally use both.

3. **Additional options**   If you're familiar with the mouse daemon, you can enter additional options by using the `Flags` option. Chances are you won't need to use this, though.

4. **Test and enable**   Pick the `Enable` option to test the mouse daemon. You should see a mouse pointer appear on the screen and respond to your mouse movements. (The buttons won't have any effect, though.) Answer the question about whether it works. If it doesn't, try other settings until you find one that works.

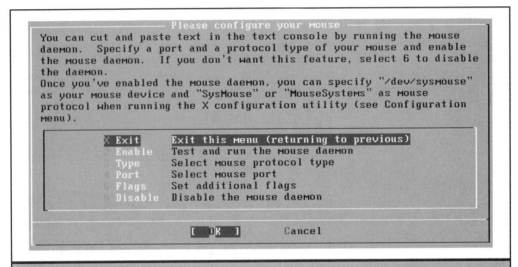

┌─ Please configure your mouse ─┐
You can cut and paste text in the text console by running the mouse
daemon. Specify a port and a protocol type of your mouse and enable
the mouse daemon. If you don't want this feature, select 6 to disable
the daemon.
Once you've enabled the mouse daemon, you can specify "/dev/sysmouse"
as your mouse device and "SysMouse" or "MouseSystems" as mouse
protocol when running the X configuration utility (see Configuration
menu).

```
X Exit      Exit this menu (returning to previous)
  Enable    Test and run the mouse daemon
  Type      Select mouse protocol type
  Port      Select mouse port
  Flags     Set additional flags
  Disable   Disable the mouse daemon
```

[OK]   Cancel

Figure 2-11.   At a minimum, you need to use the `Type` and `Port` options to
configure most mice.

If you can't seem to get the mouse working, you can select the `Disable` option
to disable the mouse daemon. You may then need to address the mouse directly in
XFree86, or leave both mouse and XFree86 configuration until later. In the meantime,
you can still use FreeBSD in text mode.

When you're finished with mouse configuration, select the `Exit` option to move on
with the basic system setup options. The system asks if you want to configure the X server.
Doing so now can reduce your work later, but certain rare problems can cause the system
to hang during configuration. Thus, if you have particularly new or exotic video hardware,
you might prefer skipping X configuration and doing it later by running `sysinstall`
from a normal FreeBSD boot after everything else is configured. Most people will select
`Yes` to perform initial X configuration, though.

XFree86 Configuration

The main XFree86 configuration menu presents four options, in addition to the
ubiquitous `Exit` option:

- **xf86cfg**   This program is a GUI X configuration tool. It will work correctly
  only if your video card works with the standard X VGA drivers, which most
  but not all cards do. Using this minimal support, you can pick your hardware
  for more optimal support once FreeBSD is fully installed.

- **xf86cfg -textmode** This option is a variant on the first; it runs `xf86cfg` in text mode so that you can configure your system even if X's VGA driver doesn't work on your video card.

- **xf86config** This program is another text-based X configuration tool. It asks a series of questions concerning your video hardware, mouse, and so on. This tool is definitely cruder than `xf86cfg`, and it's unforgiving of errors; if you make a mistake, you have to re-run the entire program. I recommend trying it only if you have problems with `xf86cfg`.

- **XDesktop** This option doesn't configure the X server proper, just the X desktop environment—that is, it tells the system what types of windows, desktop icons, and so on to present by default. You can use this option if your system is already configured to use an appropriate X server and you just need to modify this one feature of X configuration.

Most users will select the `xf86cfg` option or its text-mode variant. If you've previously configured your mouse, `sysinstall` presents a note informing you of the mouse settings you should use. When you select OK, the system tells you to press ENTER again to switch into graphics mode. The screen will clear and show a gray background with an X-shaped cursor; then the `xf86cfg` main window appears (shown in Figure 2-12), including a summary of the configuration options. To configure your X server, you need to select each of the icons along the top or in the body of the window in turn. To select an option, point at it and click the right mouse button. A pop-up menu appears with an option called Configure. Select that option to see a new window with a new set of device-specific options. Each of the devices must be named, with a default name based on the device type, such as `Keyboard1` for the keyboard. These default names are fine in most cases.

| Tip | *If you try to use `xf86cfg` and your screen goes blank or you can't move the mouse, press CTRL-ALT-BACKSPACE. This option kills the X server and gives you the chance to try again. This time, pick the `xf86cfg -textmode` option, which gives the same features as `xf86cfg`, but in text mode and using keyboard commands.* |

The devices you must configure are:

- **Mouse** If you enabled the mouse earlier, pick the `SysMouse` protocol from the list of protocols, and type **/dev/sysmouse** in the Select Mouse Device entry field. (The mouse daemon reads the actual mouse hardware and echoes its input to the `/dev/sysmouse` pseudo-device for X's benefit.) If you did *not* enable the mouse earlier, you'll have to pick the appropriate mouse protocol and physical device. Likely physical devices are `/dev/psm0` for PS/2 mice, `/dev/ums0` for USB mice, and `/dev/cuaa0` through `/dev/cuaa3` for RS-232 serial ports 1–4 (`COM1:` through `COM4:` in DOS or Windows). You must also select the mouse protocol, which for all PS/2 and USB mice is `PS/2`. If you have

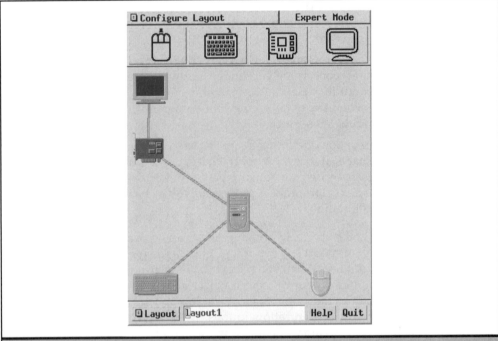

Figure 2-12. *The* xf86cfg *program runs a minimal VGA X server to allow GUI configuration of the X server FreeBSD will ultimately run.*

a two-button mouse, be sure to pick the Emulate 3 Buttons option, which lets you click both buttons simultaneously to emulate pressing the middle mouse button.

Many X programs assume you have a three-button mouse. If your mouse has just two buttons, you should consider replacing it with a three-button model, because the middle-button emulation is awkward to use.

- **Keyboard** The keyboard configuration settings let you change the keyboard model you use. In the United States, 101-key and 104-key models are common. (The 104-key models have Windows logo keys near the space bar.) Non-U.S. keyboards also have slightly different layouts. When you pick a keyboard, you see a diagram of it, so you can compare it to what you're using.

- **Card** The video card configuration is extremely important. It lets you select your video card, which determines the video driver XFree86 uses. If your video card model is listed, select it. If not, you may be able to spot the chipset that your video card uses. If you can't find that, you may have to select a generic video mode, which you can do by clicking the Driver button and clicking the VGA or VESA option. The `fbdev` device also works with some cards, but typically with reduced performance. An incorrect choice at this point will cause X to fail at startup.

■ **Monitor** The monitor configuration area lists several common monitor types, such as High Frequency SVGA, 1024×768 @ 70 Hz. If one of these describes your monitor, select it. If you have your monitor's manual, you can use it to locate the precise horizontal and vertical frequency ranges that your monitor accepts and enter those values in the appropriate fields. This will let X take the best advantage of your monitor's capabilities.

Caution *Older monitors can be damaged if run at a higher resolution or refresh rate than their designs permit. Therefore, you should be very careful in entering your monitor information. Do not select a monitor type that supports a higher resolution or refresh rate than you know yours does. Fortunately, most monitors made since the late 1990s ignore out-of-range signals and so can't be damaged by them, but you'll see no display (or a message to the effect that the monitor can't handle the signal) if you try to use such a setting.*

■ **Screen** In X configuration parlance, the screen is a specific collection of settings for a video card and monitor. You set the video mode, such as 800×600 or 1280×1024, as a screen. Near the top of the `xf86cfg` display is a bar that reads Configure Layout (see Figure 2-12). Click it and select Configure Screen. A large monitor graphic appears; right click it and pick Configure. You can then add and delete resolutions and color depths to the list on the right; the ones in this list are resolutions that X will attempt to use. As a practical matter, 800×600 is the minimum useable display size for X because many programs assume the display is at least this large. A still better size is 1024×768 if your monitor can handle it. Larger displays are usually better, of course, if your hardware can comfortably accommodate the size.

You can move back and forth between the various options as you see fit, so complete them in whatever order is convenient. When you're finished, click the Quit button at the bottom of the screen. You then have the option to return to configuring or to test your settings. When you're done with all of this, X exits.

X Desktop Configuration

After configuring XFree86, `sysinstall` lets you configure your X desktop environment. You have several choices:

■ **KDE** The *K Desktop Environment* is one of two major integrated desktop environments that are common on FreeBSD. Most KDE files are missing from one-CD FreeBSD packages, though, so you may want to forego this option unless you have a multi-CD pack or are performing a network installation.

- **GNOME + Sawfish and GNOME + Enlightenment**   The *GNU Network Object Model Environment (GNOME)* is the second major integrated desktop environment for FreeBSD. There are two GNOME options available, which differ in the *window manager* that's used by default—Sawfish or Enlightenment. (The window manager controls window positioning, drag bars, and similar tools.) The Sawfish window manager is slimmer than Enlightenment, and so is a better choice on low-memory systems or if you want a slightly snappier desktop environment. Enlightenment has more in the way of appearance customization options, and so may be a good choice if you like a lot of "eye candy."

- **Afterstep**   Afterstep is a window manager that's modeled after the windowing environment used by the old NeXT OS.

- **Windowmaker**   This window manager borrows ideas from many others. It's also the core of GNUStep (`http://gnustep.org`), which aims to implement the OpenStep specification used by NeXT. The Windowmaker option provided in the FreeBSD installation doesn't install all of GNUStep, but you can add it later if you like.

- **fvwm**   One of the oldest traditional window managers is `fvwm`, and you can pick it as an option for your X desktop.

The final three options are "bare" window managers. They impose little in the way of memory requirements when run, and so can be a good choice for slim systems. KDE and GNOME are both huge environments that consume several megabytes of memory all by themselves, but they include much fuller desktop environments, including file managers, configuration tools, and so on. Either of these is a good choice if you or your users are used to Windows or Mac OS and want similar functionality.

It's important to note that what you're setting here is the *default* environment. You can install multiple window managers and desktop environments, subject only to disk space limitations. Users can then configure their accounts to launch any installed window manager or desktop environment, even if it's not the same as the system's default environment. Such options are described in Chapter 13. Of course, to use an environment, it must be installed first. You can use `sysinstall` to do this after you've installed the rest of the system.

Another important point to know is that various tools and utilities, including many of those that come with the GNOME and KDE environments, can be run from any environment; you're not restricted to running just KDE programs within KDE, for instance. Each of these environments has collected a wide assortment of programs, though, some of which work best with other programs from the matching environment. For instance, you may be able to set a default font set for your environment's programs, and all the programs for that environment use that font set. Programs written for another environment may not honor these font settings.

Which environment should you choose? That's a matter of personal preference. For new users with lots of RAM (128MB or more), GNOME is a good starting point, but you might prefer KDE. If you have less RAM or prefer a more Spartan environment, any of the three stand-alone window managers should work well. Ultimately, window managers and desktop environments are choices dominated by personal preference. You can select one randomly; then explore other options as you learn more about FreeBSD.

FreeBSD Package Configuration

After you configure your X environment, `sysinstall` lets you browse the FreeBSD package collection. Several categories are available, such as `afterstep` and `audio`. Each of these contains some number of programs that you might want to install. If you don't want to take the time to browse these options now, you don't need to do so; you can launch `sysinstall` later to install programs. You might want to browse the collection now, though, particularly if there are certain programs you know you want to install.

One particularly important class of programs is the `editors` group. FreeBSD installs only a couple of very basic editors, such as `ee` and `vi`, by default. (The `ee` editor is the one you use to edit a few configuration files, such as `/etc/inetd.conf`, during installation. The `vi` editor is popular among some users, but is very strange if you're new to it.) The `emacs` editor is popular and extremely powerful, but is huge and can be intimidating. Smaller `emacs`-like editors include `uemacs`, `jed`, and `pico`. Two X-based editors you might want to consider installing are `gxedit` and `nedit`. Not all of these editors are available on a single-CD installation, though.

User Configuration

After installing additional packages, FreeBSD allows you to set up initial user accounts. Before describing precisely how this is done, though, I present a brief description of why FreeBSD uses accounts and how you might want to configure them.

The Role of User Accounts

Older *x*86 PC OSs, such as DOS and Windows 9*x*/Me, are designed primarily as single-user OSs. The assumption is that a single person uses the computer from its keyboard and monitor, or possibly a small group of people who know and trust one another share the computer. Any user can easily view or modify any file on the computer, including personal data files belonging to other individuals (if more than one person uses the computer) or system files such as fonts, driver files, program files, and so on.

There are ways to get Windows 9x/Me, or even DOS, to display a login screen to acquire a username and password. In a network environment, these can be used to restrict a user's access to certain network resources, but the local computer is still wide open to any user. The Windows 9x/Me login prompts include Cancel buttons that allow anybody to use the computer, even without a username or password.

UNIX, by contrast, has long supported multiuser operation. In the 1970s and 1980s, UNIX systems were typically minicomputers and mainframes used primarily from remote terminals, and many users could be logged in simultaneously. In many cases, UNIX developers and administrators could not make the sort of assumptions of trust that were common in the PC world. Therefore, UNIX has long supported tools to limit users' access to each others' and the system's resources. FreeBSD has inherited these tools, which are centered on the concept of an *account*.

An account is a set of data structures maintained by the OS for a single user or purpose. Features associated with an account include:

- **Username**   The *username* is a name that's linked to the account, such as `bjolitz`. The user enters this username to gain access to the computer, and the username can be used or displayed in various other contexts, such as to identify processes run by the user or to send e-mail to the user.

- **Password**   The *password* lies at the core of security on a FreeBSD system. This topic is so important that it merits its own section in Chapter 29, which discusses system security. For now, know that passwords should not be actual words or names, although they might be corruptions of words. Ideally, passwords should be random collections of letters, numbers, and punctuation. Users must enter their passwords to log into the computer.

- **Group**   UNIX and FreeBSD security uses the concept of a *group* to make its setup more flexible. Groups are collections of users who may be granted access to particular files or programs. For instance, you might use groups that correspond to collaborative workgroups, to permit these users to more easily read the same set of files related to their projects.

- **UID and GID**   The *user ID (UID)* and *group ID (GID)* are numbers that underlie the username and group name. FreeBSD uses these internally, converting to the alphanumeric username or group name when interacting with users. For instance, you might type **bjolitz** as a username, and FreeBSD might convert this to a UID, such as 1098, which it uses to do whatever you indicated with the username, such as log in or send e-mail.

- **Home directory**   Most systems set aside disk space for users to store their files. In order to avoid confusion and keep the directory structure organized, most users have their own unique *home directories* in which most of their files reside. The default location for home directories is /home, and most users' home directories are named after their usernames, as in /home/bjolitz. You can alter the default location, or the home directory location for a specific user, as described in Chapter 10.

■ **Shell**   A *shell* is a program that accepts user commands and processes them. FreeBSD supports several text-based shell programs, such as `tcsh` and `bash`, but the default is usually `sh`. Text-based shell information is part of the main account configuration. The equivalent for X operation is the choice of window manager or desktop environment, which can be set in configuration files stored in the user's home directory.

In addition to accounts for ordinary users, FreeBSD maintains several accounts that the OS uses for its own internal purposes. These include `root`, `daemon`, `bin`, and `nobody`. Certain programs require specific dedicated accounts, which you may need to add. Most of these *system accounts* have UIDs of 100 or below, whereas accounts used by ordinary users have UIDs of 1000 or above, by default. Similarly, there are several standard system groups, such as `root`, `wheel`, and `nobody`.

Note   *Not all UNIX-like OSs give ordinary users UIDs starting at 1000. Some Linux distributions, for instance, begin assigning UIDs to ordinary users starting at 500, or even 100. Because the OS uses UIDs to identify users, this discrepancy can be important in a few situations. For instance, when an NFS server makes files available, it identifies users by UID. If they don't match on the server and client, users may not have access to the proper files. There are ways to correct this problem, but on a network with few users, you should try giving users the same UIDs on all computers.*

Some system accounts have privileged access to certain files or other system resources. Others, such as `nobody`, have very limited access. FreeBSD uses these differences as a security measure, to grant certain processes access to files or hardware that should not be generally accessible, or to limit access for other processes.

One particularly important system account is `root`. This account has a UID of 0, a GID of 0, and complete access to the entire FreeBSD system. The system administrator (also known as the *superuser*) uses the `root` account to maintain the computer. This account is therefore extremely important. Only a limited number of authorized personnel should have access to the `root` account, and its password should be very secure. If you're setting up a FreeBSD system, chances are you'll be the superuser and therefore have access to the `root` account, although it's possible you'll hand this responsibility off to somebody else in the future.

Normally, the superuser also has a regular user account on the computer. You'll use this account for day-to-day work—sending e-mail, browsing the Web, compiling software, and so on. You'll use the `su` utility to acquire `root` privileges when you need to, as described in Chapter 3.

Caution   Do not *use the* `root` *account for ordinary tasks such as web browsing or word processing. Because* `root` *has full read/write access to the entire computer, it's easy to accidentally do serious damage when you're logged in as* `root`. *For instance, a simple typo can cause you to delete all the files on the computer. FreeBSD includes few protections against such goofs; instead, it relies upon the limited access granted ordinary users to prevent disasters.*

With this background information in mind, it's time to proceed with the FreeBSD installation, which presents an opportunity to create initial user accounts. The installer asks if you'd like to create such accounts. I strongly recommend you respond Yes to this query.

Creating an Initial Group

You can create both users and groups during installation. If you know the types of users who'll be using the computer and how they'll be organized, you may want to create some groups from the beginning, using the Group option in the User and Group Management menu. When you select this option, sysinstall presents a screen in which you can enter the group name, the GID, and initial group members (you'll leave this last field blank unless you've already created users). Using an initial GID of 1000 or above is usually a good starting point.

One common default configuration on some versions of UNIX is to support a group called users that holds ordinary user accounts. This can be a good approach if your computer holds just a few users who should have uniform access to certain files or directories. Another common approach is to create a unique group for each user. You can then add other users to each user's group to grant specific individuals special access rights to the first user's files.

Note *Users can belong to more than one group. Therefore, a* users *group can be augmented by other groups to restrict access to particular files or directories.*

You don't need to create any special groups if you don't want to. If you're unfamiliar with UNIX-style permissions, ownership, and groups, you can begin with no special groups, but pay attention to the Tip in the next section concerning the wheel group; or create a users group and make it the default for new users.

Creating an Initial User Account

The User option on the User and Group Management screen displays a menu similar to the one shown in Figure 2-13. You should enter information in most of the fields, as shown in Figure 2-13 (some fields will display default values after you fill out other fields). Most of these fields are described in the preceding section, "The Role of User Accounts." A few deserve special attention, though.

The Login ID is the username, and must be unique on the computer, but may be the same as a username on another computer. (It's usually best to assign one individual the same username on multiple computers, if possible, to reduce the chance of confusion.) FreeBSD uses case-sensitive usernames, and most FreeBSD users have all-lowercase usernames—the utilities make it difficult to add usernames with mixed case. The Full Name field holds freeform information on the user—conventionally the user's full name, but it could be something else, such as the user's office number.

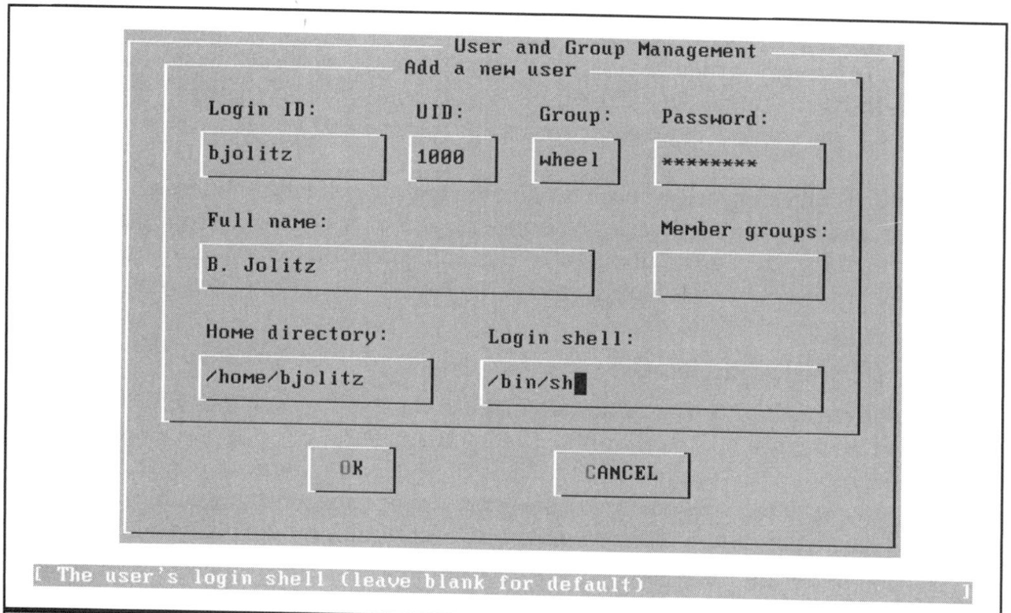

```
┌─────────────── User and Group Management ───────────────┐
│                  Add a new user                          │
│                                                          │
│   Login ID:      UID:      Group:     Password:          │
│  ┌──────────┐  ┌──────┐  ┌───────┐  ┌───────────┐        │
│  │ bjolitz  │  │ 1000 │  │ wheel │  │ ********  │        │
│  └──────────┘  └──────┘  └───────┘  └───────────┘        │
│                                                          │
│   Full name:                        Member groups:       │
│  ┌─────────────────────────────┐  ┌───────────────┐      │
│  │ B. Jolitz                   │  │               │      │
│  └─────────────────────────────┘  └───────────────┘      │
│                                                          │
│   Home directory:        Login shell:                    │
│  ┌─────────────────────┐ ┌──────────────────────┐        │
│  │ /home/bjolitz       │ │ /bin/sh█             │        │
│  └─────────────────────┘ └──────────────────────┘        │
│                                                          │
│        ┌─────────┐          ┌──────────┐                 │
│        │   OK    │          │  CANCEL  │                 │
│        └─────────┘          └──────────┘                 │
│                                                          │
└──────────────────────────────────────────────────────────┘
[ The user's login shell (leave blank for default)         ]
```

Figure 2-13.   *FreeBSD lets you enter critical account information for as many accounts as you'd like when you install the OS.*

The Group field holds the user's initial group—the group that will be assigned to files the user creates, used for programs the user runs, and so on. The Member Groups field holds the names of other groups to which the user belongs. The user will be able to access files that are accessible to these groups, and if the user creates a file in a directory owned by the group, that file will be accessible to members of the group. It's possible you won't need to enter anything in the Member Groups field, as shown in Figure 2-13.

Tip   *The wheel group is one of the special groups maintained by FreeBSD. Members of this group may use the su command to acquire the privileges associated with another user, including root. When you create accounts for yourself and any other administrators of the computer, these users should belong to the wheel group, either via the Group field or the Member Groups field. Users who should not have such access should not belong to the wheel group.*

If you're unfamiliar with FreeBSD, you should leave the Home Directory and Login Shell fields at their default values. If you're an experienced administrator, you may want to adjust these values.

If you or your users like the bash shell, you should be aware that it's not installed by default; you may need to install it as a separate package before you can specify it. When it is installed, it resides in /usr/local/bin, rather than /bin, where most shells exist. If you try to specify a nonexistent shell, sysinstall notifies you of this fact.

I recommend creating at least one user account for yourself when you install FreeBSD. If you're unfamiliar with UNIX-style accounts, or if you must create many accounts, you may want to put off creating additional accounts until later. You can access this same utility after installing FreeBSD, or use tools such as adduser or even a text editor to do the job.

Finishing the Installation

After you've created all your user accounts, select the Exit option. FreeBSD then informs you that it's about to ask for the system manager's (root's) password. Once this is done, FreeBSD asks if you want to view the system configuration menu. You can use this menu to change various options. When you're done, or if you don't want to check this menu, the system returns you to the sysinstall main menu (Figure 2-5). You can change various options, particularly from the Configure option, or select Exit Install to finish the installation. When you do this, sysinstall informs you that it will reboot the computer. You should remove your boot floppy or CD-ROM, and the system will reboot.

Soon after the system reboots, you'll see a boot loader prompt. If you used the default boot loader options described earlier, in "Setting the Boot Loader Option," and if you have DOS or Windows installed in addition to FreeBSD, this will probably include F1 DOS and F2 FreeBSD options. Press F1 to boot to DOS or F2 to boot to FreeBSD. After you've booted one OS, that choice becomes the default for the next boot, so the default can change often if you frequently boot to the different OSs. If you've only installed FreeBSD on the system, that will be the only boot option. If you've used a third-party boot loader, you'll see its menu instead of or in addition to the FreeBSD boot loader's prompt. If you need to reconfigure your boot loader options, consult Chapter 4, which includes a discussion of this issue.

Summary

Installing FreeBSD involves obtaining the OS, preparing the computer, and running the installation. During installation, you'll have to tell FreeBSD where to reside, how to arrange its partitions, and what specific components you want to install. You'll also have to configure various devices and packages, such as your mouse, video card, and possibly a few servers. Unfortunately, some of the decisions you must make are difficult for first-time FreeBSD users, but the default values are usually reasonable, so you can start with these and then change your configuration, or even reinstall from scratch, once you're more familiar with the OS. Much of the rest of this book is devoted to making such changes, to help you use FreeBSD for a variety of tasks.

Chapter 3

An Overview of the System

With FreeBSD installed on your computer, it's time to begin using the OS. This chapter provides a quick overview of FreeBSD, including the boot process, logging in, running programs, starting and using X, logging off, and shutting down. If you use FreeBSD as a desktop workstation, chances are you'll need to know how to perform most of these tasks on a fairly regular basis. FreeBSD systems often go for days or even months without rebooting, though, so the booting and shutdown actions, although important, may be infrequent. If your FreeBSD system is a server, you might not run X on it, but the remaining topics are important.

Booting the Computer

In one sense, booting a FreeBSD computer is a simple matter—you turn on the power and wait for the system to come up. You may need to deal with an option or two, though, and the boot process provides a great deal of information that you may find useful later, particularly if you need to debug a problem. This section therefore describes the boot process from a practical perspective.

Selecting FreeBSD

The early stages of an x86 computer's boot process are controlled by the Basic Input/ Output System (BIOS) installed in the system. Once the BIOS finishes its self-tests and other startup procedures, it hands control over to a boot loader that's stored on disk— typically the hard disk when booting an installed OS, although floppies, CD-ROMs, and other removable media devices can contain boot code as well.

If you installed FreeBSD alongside another OS, chances are you'll see a boot prompt that resembles the following (the FreeBSD *Stage 0* boot prompt):

```
F1    DOS
F2    FreeBSD

Default: F2
```

FreeBSD labels Windows partitions *DOS*, so don't be concerned if this is what you see and your non-FreeBSD partition holds Windows. Press the key (F1, F2, or some other key if there are more than two options) that corresponds to the OS you intend to boot—FreeBSD in the case of this example. The default value corresponds to the OS you booted last. If you regularly boot one OS, you can wait for the system to boot this default OS, but for a quicker boot, press the appropriate function key.

If you've installed a boot loader other than FreeBSD's default, you see it rather than the FreeBSD boot loader. Chapter 4 includes a discussion of third-party boot loaders.

Once FreeBSD starts to boot, it begins displaying status messages. The first of these relates to the bootstrap loader, which is a secondary boot loader (also known as the *Stage 1* and *Stage 2* boot loaders, in FreeBSD parlance; the two are distinct programs, but function as one). The Stage 0 boot loader is very small and simple; it merely redirects the boot process to the appropriate partition. The Stage 1/Stage 2 boot loader is more complex and more FreeBSD-specific. It displays a message similar to the following:

```
Hit [Enter] to boot immediately, or any other key for command prompt.
Booting [/boot/kernel/kernel] in 9 seconds...
```

The time in the second line counts down. Ordinarily, you can wait for it to time out to boot FreeBSD, or press ENTER to speed up the process slightly. In some rare circumstances, though, you may need to load special kernel modules (that is, hardware drivers) or otherwise configure the kernel. If so, press any other key and the bootstrap loader allows you to enter commands. Some of them are described in Chapter 4.

You may enter any special parameters for the bootstrap loader, or let it time out, or press ENTER to have it move on without special options. Once this happens, the bootstrap loader loads the FreeBSD kernel into memory, from the file `/boot/kernel/kernel` or from another file that you specify as an option. The kernel then displays status information and runs FreeBSD startup scripts.

Interpreting Boot Messages

Unlike Windows, which displays little in the way of startup messages, FreeBSD is quite verbose as it starts up. In fact, it's so verbose that much of the information it presents scrolls off the screen before you have a chance to read it. Fortunately, the kernel messages are stored for a time after you boot, and you can view them by typing **dmesg**. You may want to redirect these messages into a file for perusal with a text editor (as in **dmesg > dmesg.txt**) or pipe the result through a text viewer such as `less`, as in **dmesg | less**. You won't be able to do these things until after you've logged in, though, as described later in this chapter in the section "Logging Into an Account."

Note   *Redirection and piping, which are the techniques used in the preceding commands to send the output of* dmesg *to a file or through a text viewer, are common methods of getting programs to work together or to capture program output in FreeBSD. These topics are covered in Chapter 5.*

Whether you're quickly scanning the boot messages as they're displayed or studying them in more depth after you log in, these messages can be a useful source of information about your system. They begin with a series of copyright messages and information on the version of FreeBSD you have installed. Subsequent lines identify your CPU, including its make, model, and clock speed. The system also reports the amount of memory you have installed. This includes both the *real memory* (the amount on the SIMMs, DIMMs, or other memory chips you've installed in the computer) and the *available memory* (the real memory minus that used by the kernel, BIOS caches, and so on).

The bulk of the information that the kernel displays consists of reports on various hardware devices. These reports typically begin with a device name (which usually bears little resemblance to any name you might use for the device), a colon (:), and a more descriptive expansion or report of details. Some devices consume more than one line. For instance, the following is a report that's likely to appear very early:

```
npx0: <math processor> on motherboard
npx0: INT 16 interface
```

This identifies the computer as supporting a math coprocessor, which is a component that performs floating-point arithmetic. All CPUs since the 486DX series include a math coprocessor as part of the main CPU, but 386, 486SX, and some NexGen CPUs lacked this feature. Such systems often supported math coprocessors as add-on chips that fit into motherboard sockets, hence FreeBSD's claim that the math coprocessor is on the motherboard.

Other devices that you're likely to see mentioned include:

- **PCI and ISA busses** The `pcib0`, `pci0`, `isab0`, and `isa0` devices relate to the PCI and ISA *busses*—that is, the slots in which you insert expansion cards.

- **ATA controllers** The *Advanced Technology Attachment (ATA)* interface is another name for the Enhanced Integrated Drive Electronics (EIDE) hard disk interface. Modern computers are likely to have three ATA devices: `atapci0` (the ATA controller, which is built into modern motherboards) and the devices associated with the two ATA busses, `ata0` and `ata1`. Some systems may have more or fewer ATA devices than this, though.

- **SCSI host adapters** If your system has a SCSI host adapter, you're likely to see a device for it. The name varies depending upon the type of chipset used on your SCSI adapter.

- **USB controllers and devices** You may see several devices whose names begin with *u* that relate to USB support. Most systems have a `uhci0` or `ohci0` device that corresponds to the USB controller itself, a `usb0` device that serves as an abstraction of the USB controller, and a `uhub0` device that grants access to the USB ports on the computer. You may have additional USB devices, such as `umass0` for a mass-storage device such as a Zip disk, or `ums0` for a mouse.

- **Network devices** The names of your network devices, if any, vary depending upon the chipsets used. There's usually a core device, whose description includes the name of the chipset used, and several additional devices related to specific component parts of the network device.

- **Keyboard and mouse** If you're using a standard keyboard, FreeBSD reports it as `atkbdc0` and `atkbd0`. The mouse may be `psm0` (for a PS/2 mouse), `ums0` (for a USB mouse), or something else, depending on its interface type.

- **Parallel and serial devices** The parallel port (ppc0) may support several subdevices for printers (lpt0), generic parallel-port input/output (ppi0), and networking (plip0). The serial ports (sio0 and sio1, typically) might conceivably show a Point-to-Point Protocol (PPP) device (ppp0), but this normally appears only after you've explicitly started a PPP network link.

- **Console** FreeBSD uses a special device to access the console (sc0)—normally the keyboard and monitor attached directly to the computer.

- **Video** Most systems support a vga0 device for the video card.

- **Disk devices** The floppy disk (fd0 and fdc0), EIDE hard disks (ad0 and up), SCSI hard disks (da0 and up), and CD-ROM drive (acd0 for EIDE disks) all have their own devices. You may see an error message about an inability to find the device's capacity for some removable drives, such as Zip drives, unless you boot with a disk in the drive. Don't be concerned about such messages.

If you notice error messages related to any of these devices, it may indicate that FreeBSD has not detected the device correctly or it isn't working. If some important device is missing, it's possible that it's something for which no FreeBSD driver exists, or the device may be damaged or inoperable. Some devices may not show up immediately. For instance, external devices that aren't turned on won't appear. You may also see some devices labeled as unknown. These are probably devices that FreeBSD found but could not configure correctly. This situation sometimes happens with plug-in cards for which no FreeBSD drivers exist.

Understanding Startup Scripts

After starting the kernel, the FreeBSD boot process runs a program called init. This program controls the startup process once the kernel is loaded and running. It does this by running various startup scripts in the /etc directory, starting with /etc/rc. These scripts control the startup process, launching servers and other programs that must run in the background. Many of these actions produce further output on the screen, although this output is not stored for retrieval via dmesg, as are the kernel startup messages.

Some of the tasks performed by init and its startup scripts include:

- **Filesystem checks** When FreeBSD starts, it checks partitions to be sure partitions are *clean*—that is, that they were properly unmounted. If they're not clean, FreeBSD runs the fsck program, which checks the partitions and corrects any problems that might have resulted from a crash or other unclean shutdown.

- **Mounting partitions** FreeBSD mounts its partitions under direction of the /etc/fstab file. This file is described further in Chapter 7. For now, know that it contains information on partitions and mount points, as you defined them when you installed FreeBSD.

- **Miscellaneous configuration** FreeBSD must perform a large number of miscellaneous startup tasks to do things such as configure its network interface, enable PC cards on laptop computers, and initialize serial ports.

- **Running servers and other programs** Some programs must run continuously to do any good. These include, but are not limited to, most servers. They're normally started automatically at boot time.

Most servers run as daemons. *This word derives from the Greek, and means "helper." In FreeBSD (and UNIX generally), daemons typically run unattended in the background, in order to provide some necessary service. Not all daemons are servers, but many are. The similarity of this word to the English word* demon *is what gives rise to the horned red FreeBSD mascot.*

- **Enabling logins** In order to log into a FreeBSD system, that computer must be running some form of login program—a program that accepts a username and password and grants the user access to the system in response. Some login programs are network servers, but others run locally. FreeBSD starts the latter class via entries in the /etc/ttys file.

Chapter 6 describes the system startup scripts in more detail. For the moment, it's important that you know that FreeBSD starts many programs during its startup process, including those that enable you to log onto the system. As described in Chapter 6, you can modify the FreeBSD startup process to add new programs or delete those you don't need.

Logging into an Account

Once the system boots, FreeBSD displays a login prompt of one sort or another. Logging in involves entering your username and password. Before you do this, you should know something of the different login types—text mode vs. GUI, and user vs. root logins. You should also know what to expect once you've logged in, and how to acquire root privileges once you've logged into a user account.

Text-Mode and GUI Logins

The default configuration for FreeBSD is to provide a text-mode login. This means that when you boot the computer, you'll see a text-mode prompt that resembles the following:

```
login:
```

This is FreeBSD's way of asking for your username. Type it, and then press ENTER. FreeBSD responds with another prompt, immediately below the first:

```
Password:
```

Enter your password at this prompt, and then press ENTER again. As a security measure, you won't see your password echoed to the screen. (The security benefit is that nobody lurking nearby sees it, either.) If you enter the correct password, FreeBSD displays a screenful of information about where to find security advisories, FreeBSD documentation, and so on. At the bottom of the screen you'll see a *command prompt*, which is probably a single dollar sign ($). The `root` account's prompt is a pound sign (#), though, to help you identify when you're logged in as `root`. Depending upon your account's configuration, you may see additional information just prior to the prompt, such as your username or the name of your shell.

A text-mode login such as this allows you to run text-based programs and use text-mode commands, as described in the upcoming section, "A Summary of Text-Mode Commands." Sometimes you may want to run multiple text-mode programs. Two common ways to do this are

- **Virtual consoles**   FreeBSD supports a feature known as *virtual consoles*, which enables you to log in several times. After you've logged in once, press F2, or any other function key up to F8. You'll see another `login:` prompt, and you can log in a second time. Press F1 to return to the first virtual console. You can then run different programs in the different screens. You can even log in as different users in the different virtual consoles. (Once you start running X, as described later in this chapter in the section "Starting X," you must press ALT along with the function key to switch to another virtual console. X itself runs in the 9th virtual console, accessed via F9.)

- **Background processing**   You can run one program in the background, meaning that it no longer receives your keyboard input. To do this, append an ampersand (&) to its command name when you run the program, as in **numbercrunch &**. Alternatively, you can suspend a program's operation by pressing CTRL-Z when it's running; this stops the program without killing it and returns you to a command prompt. This step is particularly useful if you want to temporarily exit from a program and then return to it; typing **fg** gets you back into the program, and typing **bg** sets it running in the background, as if it had been started with an ampersand to begin with.

If you log in using text mode, you won't be able to run GUI programs without first starting the X Window System (or X for short), as described in the upcoming section, "Starting X." You can configure a FreeBSD system to automatically start X when the system boots. Such a system uses the *X Display Manager (XDM)* program, or a similar tool, to provide a GUI login screen, as shown in Figure 3-1. When you type your username and password in this screen, FreeBSD automatically starts your X environment. You may prefer this configuration if you do most of your work in X. Properly configuring such a setup requires starting the XDM program in one of the startup scripts, and you may need to adjust users' individualized X configurations, as well. Chapter 21 describes how to configure XDM or similar programs, and Chapter 6 covers users' login control files, including those for use with XDM.

X Window System

Login: bjolitz|
Password:

Figure 3-1.   A GUI login runs in X and logs users directly into their X-based environments.

User vs. root Accounts

As described in Chapter 2, you're likely to use at least two FreeBSD accounts: an ordinary user account and the root account. You employ a user account for day-to-day user tasks, such as reading e-mail, browsing the Web, using a spreadsheet, and manipulating graphics files. The root account is the account used by the system administrator, aka the *superuser*. This account provides more-or-less unlimited control of the computer; root can read, write, move, or delete any file on the computer. For most tasks, you should use an ordinary user account; reserve root logins for the times when you need to administer the system.

In this book, commands you type are shown after a prompt. In most cases, this prompt is either a dollar sign ($) or a pound sign (#), signifying the command's use from a user account or as root, respectively. This mirrors the default prompts displayed on the screen when you're logged in as an ordinary user or as root.

It's not uncommon to find that you've logged in as an ordinary user, but need superuser privileges for some short action. This problem can be overcome in several ways. One is to use FreeBSD's virtual consoles to log in as root, perform whatever action you need to do, and log out again. Such a procedure can be awkward if you're running in X and want to run a program that requires root privileges alongside other programs, though. Even when running in text mode, there's a method that's often simpler: su.

The su program name stands for *substitute user*. It's a method of changing the identity of a user who's already logged in. It can take several options and parameters:

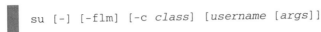

```
su [-] [-flm] [-c class] [username [args]]
```

FreeBSD documentation often lists command syntax as in this example. Square brackets indicate a parameter that's optional. Single-character options within brackets can be added or deleted individually (as in -flm in this example; you can use just -f, just -l, just -m, or any combination you like). Italic indicates variables. Ellipses (not shown here) indicate that an option may be repeated. A vertical bar (|, also not shown here) separates two alternatives that aren't used together.

The simplest use of su is to type it alone, as in **su**. If the user who types it is in the wheel group, su prompts for the root password. If the user types this password correctly, the user acquires superuser privileges. If you enter a username on the su command line, you acquire that user's identity. In either case, typing **exit** ends the identity change. You can further modify su's behavior by adding various optional parameters:

- **-l or a single dash (-)**   Ordinarily, su creates an environment that's not quite identical to a normal login environment. The -l option (or a simple dash by itself) discards most of the user's current environment and creates a new one that should match the target user's normal environment.

- **-f**   If the target user uses csh as a shell, this option causes su to not read the csh configuration file, .cshrc. You can use this to make the target environment *less* like the target user's normal environment.

- **-m**   This option changes your identity without changing your environment at all. For instance, you'll continue to use your normal command shell, even if the target user normally uses a different one.

- **-c** *class*   FreeBSD supports login *classes*, which are similar to groups. You can specify a class whose settings you want to use.

- *args*   If you want to pass arguments (control parameters) to the target user's command prompt shell, you can do so by placing them at the end of the su command.

You'll find that su is an extremely useful tool for administering FreeBSD. Using su, you can log in as an ordinary user and run privileged programs when necessary by first typing **su**. This procedure works both from text-mode logins and from GUI logins once you've started a window in which you can enter commands.

You can log in directly as root at the console, but as a security measure, FreeBSD doesn't accept remote logins via Telnet as root. This restriction means that a remote attacker who knows the root password must also know another user's password to invade the system—a would-be attacker must log in as an ordinary user and then use **su** to acquire root privileges. Of course, the same is true of authorized administrators, which may be an inconvenience. Nonetheless, the increased security is worth this inconvenience. Indeed, even at the console, it's best to not log in directly as root. When you use su, FreeBSD logs the fact, including the user who issued the su command. This logging can help you track who's doing administrative tasks, which may be important if you find that somebody's abusing superuser power.

A Summary of Text-Mode Commands

Because FreeBSD defaults to starting up in text mode, this chapter's first real description of FreeBSD tools focuses on text-mode operations. This topic begins with a description of *shells*—the programs that accept text-mode commands. When running programs from a shell, it's important that you understand a few common standards, such as how the shell interprets filenames and what types of programs you can run. This section then proceeds to cover a few of the more common commands and shell procedures.

| Tip | *If you're used to GUI-oriented OSs such as Windows or Mac OS, you might be tempted to skim this material as quickly as possible. Many FreeBSD administrative tasks are much easier to perform in text mode than in a GUI, though. Although text mode can be intimidating at first, it's very powerful—more so in FreeBSD than in Windows. Thus, learning to use text-mode commands greatly enhances your ability to handle a FreeBSD system.* |

Understanding Shells

When you log into a FreeBSD system in text mode, FreeBSD launches a program—your shell. As described in Chapter 2, the name of your shell is associated with your account. In principle, FreeBSD can use any program as a shell, but by convention only programs designed as shells are used in this capacity for login accounts. The default shell for FreeBSD is sh, but others are available. Common choices include csh (implemented by tcsh in FreeBSD, so these two are equivalent), bash, ksh, and zsh. These shells are ordinary FreeBSD programs. Some reside in /bin, but others live in /usr/local/bin. For the most part, all these shells operate in the same way, although they differ in their advanced features and in a few less advanced ways. For instance, the default prompts presented by these shells differ, and they use different configuration files; sh uses the .shrc file in the user's home directory for configuration, whereas tcsh uses .tcshrc or .cshrc, and bash uses .bashrc. The precise format of these files differs, too, so you can't simply rename, say, .shrc to .tcshrc and expect it to work. Chapter 6 briefly describes some of these files' formats.

In addition to the traditional UNIX shells, FreeBSD supports some nontraditional shells, such as mudsh, which resembles old text-mode adventure games such as Zork in its built-in commands and prompts; and pash, which provides a text-mode file browser interface similar to Norton Commander for DOS, as shown in Figure 3-2.

If you want to experiment with various shells, install them using the FreeBSD sysinstall utility's Configure option, as described in Chapter 11. There's a package area devoted to shells, so you can browse their descriptions and install any that sound interesting. You can then run different shells by typing their names. For instance, if you're in sh as the default login shell but you want to try tcsh, type **tcsh** to launch it. If you decide you want to change your default shell to the one you're trying, you can do so by modifying your account configuration, as described in Chapter 10.

All shells support a combination of built-in and external commands. Most commands you use directly from the shell are external. Most, but not all, of the shell's internal commands are interesting when it comes to scripting: You can write a short program in the shell's

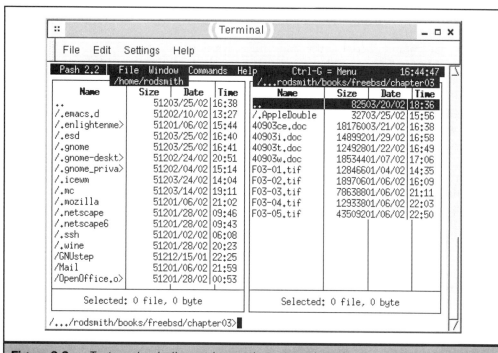

Figure 3-2. *Text-mode shells can be run in text mode or in windows from within X, as shown here.*

command language. These scripts can launch other programs, operate on files, and so on. Chapter 31 covers creating such scripts.

Some shells, including `tcsh` and `bash`, support a useful feature known as *command completion*: If you type a partial command and then press TAB, the shell attempts to complete the command. The shell can do two things in response, depending upon what you've typed:

- If you've typed only part of a program name, the shell tries to find a program that matches what you've typed. For instance, if you type **chm** and then press TAB, chances are the system will respond by filling out your command as **chmod**.

- If you've typed a complete program name and part of a filename to be given to the program as a parameter, the shell tries to locate the file that matches what you've typed so far, much as it tries to find a matching program file in the first case.

In both cases, if the shell finds multiple matches, it either beeps or displays all the possible matches. In some cases, pressing TAB again displays all the matches, if the shell only beeps. If it beeps again, this means there's no match to what you've typed so far.

Note that command completion can't fill out options you give to commands, aside from other files' names. You'll have to know enough about the commands you use to specify the options you want.

Another common shortcut is to use filename *wildcards*. These are a way to specify multiple files at one time. Two common and useful wildcards are the asterisk (*) and the question mark (?). These wildcards work much like their equivalents in a DOS or Windows command line. Use them when you specify a filename, but not a command— to run a command you have to enter the command name precisely. The asterisk matches any character or set of characters, including none at all. For instance, if you specify F*D as a filename, this matches FD, FeD, FreeBSD, or any other filename that begins with *F* and ends with *D*. The question mark, by contrast, matches a single character, so F?D matches FeD and FFD, but not FD or FreeBSD.

More wildcards are available in FreeBSD than just the asterisk and question mark. One common expansion is to place a set of characters to be matched in square brackets ([ ]). If any of the characters in the brackets appear in that position, the wildcard matches. For instance, F[aeu]D matches FaD, FeD, and FuD, but not FoD or FeeD. Instead of listing individual characters, you can specify a range, as in F[a-c]D, which matches FaD, FbD, and FcD.

Running Text-Mode Programs

To run a program, you need only type its name at your shell's command prompt. For instance, to run a program called someprogram, type **someprogram**, and then press ENTER. If the program is in a normal location for programs, the shell loads it and runs it. Depending upon what the program does, it may take over your screen, display some data, ask for input, or create no visible output. Many UNIX programs produce no output when they operate correctly; only when something goes wrong do they produce error messages.

When you type a program's name, shells look in several directories to find the program. These directories constitute the *path*, which is set via an environment variable called PATH in your shell's configuration files (including both your personal configuration file and a system-wide configuration file). Typically, the path includes /bin, /usr/bin, /usr/X11R6/bin, /usr/local/bin, and possibly some other directories. The root account's path usually includes /sbin and /usr/sbin. These directories hold programs that the system administrator may need to run, but that normal users seldom run. Despite these added directories, root's path is often shorter than that of ordinary users. This serves as an incentive to avoid using the root account unnecessarily; without directories for common user tools in root's path, it's awkward to run these programs as root.

If a program isn't on the path, you must type the complete path to the program file. For instance, if someprogram is in /opt/bin, you need to type **/opt/bin/**

someprogram to run it. Alternatively, you can use a *relative* path, in which the file is located relative to the current directory. Relative paths don't begin with a leading slash (/), but take any of several other forms:

- The name may begin with a double dot (. .), which is the indicator for a given directory's parent. For instance, in /home/bjolitz, the . . refers to /home. Thus, from that directory, ../../opt/bin/someprogram is equivalent to /opt/bin/someprogram.

- Another form for a relative path is as a subdirectory of the current directory. For instance, from /opt, you might type just **bin/someprogram** to launch /opt/bin/someprogram.

- A leading ./ indicates that the program file resides in the current directory. Sometimes a current directory (.) entry appears in the path, and if this is the case you can omit the ./ characters.

Caution *Using the current directory (.) entry in the path is risky because it means that FreeBSD executes any program in the current directory as if it were in a standard location for programs, which are normally writable only by* root. *If you decide to place this entry in the path, do so only at the* end *of the path, so that the shell searches for common programs in their normal locations before looking in the current directory. This advice is especially important for* root *because if* root *has a current directory entry in the path, miscreants could trick* root *into running unauthorized programs stored in the miscreants' home directories. Overall, it's best not to place the current directory entry in any user's path.*

- A leading tilde (~) indicates a user's home directory, so ~/someprogram refers to someprogram in the user's home directory.

These conventions apply to any file specification, not just those used to launch programs. For instance, if you have to type the name of a file upon which a program operates on the same line as the command, you can use any of these methods. In addition, you can omit the leading ./ when referring to a data file in the current directory. You may want to experiment with these techniques using cd (to change to a new directory) and ls (to display the contents of the current directory or the one you specify). If you get lost using cd, type **cd** alone to return to your home directory, or **pwd** (short for *print working directory*) to find out where you are.

Many programs accept *options, parameters,* or *arguments,* which are names for additional information fed to a command on the same line as the command itself. For instance, you might pass the name of a file to an editor to have the editor load the file when it loads. Other parameters are program-specific; they change the way the program operates in some way. The upcoming section, "File Manipulation Commands," includes information on the parameters these commands accept.

If you're new to UNIX-like OSs, you should be aware that FreeBSD is a *case-sensitive* OS, meaning that the case of letters in commands and filenames is important. For instance, typing **pwd** tells you what your current directory is, but typing **PWD** is likely to produce a command not found error message. Most commands use case-sensitive options, as well, although there are a few exceptions to this rule.

File Manipulation Commands

This section describes several commands used to manipulate files. You can use these commands to perform basic actions such as listing files in a directory, moving files, and deleting them. Some other actions are quite important, but are covered elsewhere in this book. In particular, Chapter 5 covers using text editors; and Chapter 8 covers ownership, permissions, and additional miscellaneous file manipulation tools.

cd: Change Current Directory

The cd command moves you into another directory. For instance, if you've got a subdirectory called taxes in your home directory, you can move into this directory by typing **cd taxes** (or **cd ~/taxes** if you're not currently in your home directory). Although it's seldom strictly necessary to change your current directory, doing so can reduce the amount of typing you need to do if you plan to operate on several files in a given directory, by eliminating the need to type extended paths to specify these files.

The cd command is built into whatever shell you use; unlike most commands, it's not a separate program.

ls: List Files

If you want to see the files in a directory, use ls. Its basic output resembles this:

```
$ ls
GNUstep          Mail              XF86Config.new  xinit.core
```

Each filename appears without further information. You have several ways to modify the output of ls to provide additional information. One of these is the -1 option, which causes ls to create a *long* listing, thus:

```
$ ls -l
total 406
drwxr-xr-x  5 rodsmith  users       512 Dec 15 22:25 GNUstep
drwx------  2 rodsmith  users       512 Jan  1 20:51 Mail
-rw-r--r--  1 rodsmith  users      3263 Dec 15 21:35 XF86Config.new
-rw-------  1 rodsmith  users    397312 Dec 15 20:50 xinit.core
```

Additional information in this listing includes the permissions on the file (also known as the file's *mode*, signified by the string of ten characters at the start of each line), the username (rodsmith in this example) and group (users) associated with the file, the file's size, and the file's creation date and time (if the file is older than a year, the date format changes to show the year rather than the time).

If you add the name of a directory to the command, it displays information on files in that directory. If you add a partial name with a wildcard, the command displays information on all files or directories that match the wildcard. For instance, typing **ls *.txt** displays all the files with names ending in .txt.

The ls command supports a large number of options. Consult the ls man page (by typing **man ls**) for information on all of them. The more commonly used options include:

- ■ **-a** This option causes ls to display all the files in a directory. Normally, ls doesn't show so-called *dot files*, which are files whose names begin with dots, such as .tcshrc. Dot files are usually configuration files for the programs whose names they otherwise resemble, such as the tcsh shell for .tcshrc.

- ■ **-R** If you want to see all the files in a directory and its subdirectories, use this option, which creates such a recursive listing. Note that this command may create a huge listing, so you may need to pipe the results through a paging tool such as less, as in **ls -R /usr | less**, to make sense of the output.

- ■ **-F** The default short output provides no clues about the type of each file in the listing. Using this option causes FreeBSD to display a character after certain files to indicate their types: a slash (/) for directories, an asterisk (*) for program files, an at-sign (@) for symbolic links, and a few others for more specialized file types.

Note *A symbolic link is a pointer to a file or directory that's stored under another name or in another directory. Symbolic links consume little disk space but enable you to call files or directories by multiple names.*

- ■ **-f** Normally, ls sorts its entries alphabetically. This option disables this sorting.

- ■ **-n** This option is used in conjunction with -l; it causes usernames and group names to be replaced by the underlying user IDs (UIDs) and group IDs (GIDs), respectively.

You can combine multiple options in a single option string. You can also add a path (relative or absolute) to a directory whose contents you want to list. For instance, the following command lists all the files and provides file type information for files in the /tmp directory:

```
$ ls -aF /tmp
./     .X0-lock   .sawfish-rodsmith/   sample-file.txt@  temprog*
../    .X11-unix/  orbit-rodsmith/      sample.txt
```

cp: Copy Files

The cp command copies files. You can use the command in two ways:

```
cp [options] source-file target-file
cp [options] source-file target-directory
```

In the first case, you specify the precise filename to be used for the copy. This name may include a path to the file, or it may be a new filename in your current directory. In the second form, you specify only a directory to which the file will be copied, and cp uses the same filename within that directory as the original file used.

Like ls, cp supports a number of options, enabling it to perform recursive copies (that is, copy an entire directory tree), handle symbolic links, and so on. Chapter 8 covers these advanced cp options.

mv: Move Files

The mv command moves a file from one location or name to another. Its syntax and use are similar to that of cp, and as with cp, you can use either a complete filename for the target or a directory to which the file will be moved with its original name intact.

If you're familiar with DOS or Windows text-mode commands, you should be aware that mv performs the jobs of two separate DOS commands: MOVE and RENAME. When you give mv a target directory, it works much like the DOS MOVE command, moving the file to a new directory. When you provide a target filename, mv renames the file to use the new name. If you give a target directory *and* specify a filename within that directory, mv does both. For instance, consider the following three commands:

```
$ mv file.txt /tmp
$ mv file.txt /tmp/somefile.txt
$ mv file.txt somefile.txt
```

The first command copies file.txt to the /tmp directory, leaving its name unchanged. The second command copies and renames the file, and the third renames it within the current directory. When you specify a target directory without a filename, you can move multiple files by using a wildcard or by listing the files individually, thus:

```
$ mv file.txt morefile?.txt /tmp
```

This command copies file.txt and any file matching the morefile?.txt wildcard to /tmp.

When you move a file between directories on a single partition or removable disk device, the file isn't rewritten. Instead, a directory entry for the file is created in the new location and the old directory entry is deleted. Thus, moves within a partition are very fast. If you move a file between partitions, though, FreeBSD must copy the original and then delete it. Thus, these operations tend to be slower, although you'll notice the difference only on very large files.

rm: Remove Files

If a file is no longer needed, you can delete it with the rm command. You can also use wildcards to delete many files at once. Chapter 8 covers this command's more advanced options, which enable you to perform tasks such as deleting an entire directory tree, requesting confirmation before each deletion, or overwriting the files' contents before deleting them.

 By default, rm *does* not *prompt for confirmation before deleting files. This fact can make* rm *a very dangerous tool, particularly in the hands of the superuser. In combination with the option to delete an entire directory tree,* root *can easily remove all the files on a FreeBSD system with a single* rm *command. Although* rm *is a necessary tool, you should think carefully before issuing an* rm *command, particularly as* root.

mkdir: Make Directory

FreeBSD treats directories much like files. In fact, directories *are* files, but they're files that contain the names of other files and pointers to them. When you want to create a directory, though, you need a special tool, which is known as mkdir. This command's syntax is

```
mkdir [-pv] [-m mode] directory-name...
```

For instance, typing **mkdir textfiles** creates a directory called textfiles in the current directory. Naturally, you can use a path specification as part of the directory name. The options to this command are:

- **-p** Normally, mkdir requires that the immediate parent directory of the specified directory exists. For instance, if you type **mkdir ~/dir1/dir2** and ~/dir1 doesn't exist, mkdir returns an error message. The -p option causes mkdir to create any necessary parent directories instead, so this command would create ~/dir1 before creating ~/dir1/dir2.

- **-v** This option increases the verbosity of the command's output; it reports every directory that it creates.

- **-m** *mode* Every file and directory has a set of permissions, or *mode*. This option allows you to specify the mode of the directory, as described in Chapter 8.

rmdir: Remove Directory

If you want to remove a directory, you can do so with the rmdir command. Type this command followed by the name of the directory you want removed. The directory must be empty, or rmdir won't remove it. If you type the -p option prior to the directory name, though, `rmdir` will remove the entire directory path you specify. For instance, **`rmdir -p dir1/dir2`** removes `dir2` and then `dir1`, provided both directories are empty when `rmdir` gets around to them.

 If you want to remove an entire directory tree, including directories that aren't empty, you can use the `-r` option to `rm`, as described in Chapter 8.

A Quick Tour of the GUI Desktop

You can accomplish a great deal in FreeBSD from a text-mode login. In fact, for some purposes, such as a dedicated server, you might not want or need to run the X Window System (or X for short). Most FreeBSD workstations, though, do run X, so you should become comfortable with it. This section introduces X's GUI environment, including starting X, manipulating files, running programs, and changing the environment's settings.

 X is an unusually flexible GUI environment. Depending upon your installation options and personal settings, you may find an environment that's totally unlike the one described here. Chapter 13 covers X configuration options in more detail.

Starting X

If your FreeBSD system boots up into a GUI login prompt, such as the one shown in Figure 3-1, you needn't do anything explicit to start X; it's already running, and you'll see an X-based interface of some sort when you log in. This mode isn't the default configuration for FreeBSD, though. As described earlier in this chapter, FreeBSD runs in text mode immediately after starting by default. You can change this behavior by running XDM or a similar program, as described in Chapter 21. In the meantime, you can start X from a text-mode login. The usual method of doing this is to type **`startx`**. This action starts X and launches the default GUI environment, which you set when you installed FreeBSD. (You can change this default by editing the `.xinitrc` file, as described in Chapter 13.)

 Some users need to add options to `startx` to get X running in a desirable resolution or color depth. Chapter 13 covers changing your default X configuration so this shouldn't be necessary.

After you type **`startx`**, you may see several lines of text scroll across the screen, or the screen may clear or change to another virtual terminal. If all goes well, the screen will then clear and be replaced by a GUI mode screen. Depending upon the environment you installed, you may see some startup messages, or you may simply see a blank screen or one with a few windows or other widgets on it. If you installed the GNOME desktop environment, your display should resemble that shown in Figure 3-3, although your system may not start the windows or show the icons along the left edge of Figure 3-3. The next few pages provide an overview of GNOME, and so may not apply directly if you've chosen to use KDE or a bare window manager. Many features are common, or at least similar, across different desktop environments, but many details also differ.

Note   *If X doesn't start correctly, examine the last few lines of output for clues about what went wrong, and consult Chapters 13 and 32.*

You should begin your explorations by testing the features of the window manager and desktop environment. Most FreeBSD window managers work much like the GUI

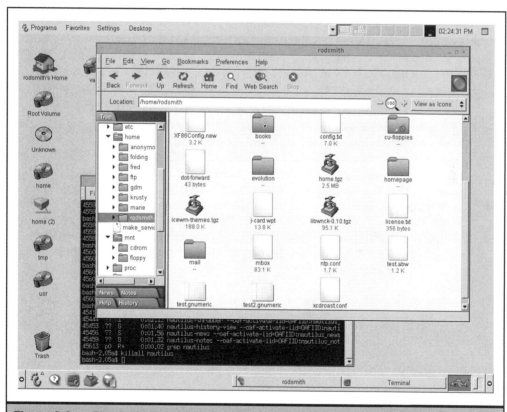

Figure 3-3. *The GNOME environment is similar to that provided by Windows, Mac OS, or other modern GUI OSs.*

in Windows or Mac OS. Here are some important differences between the many FreeBSD window managers and desktop environments:

- **Window focus** A window is said to be *in focus* when it receives input from the keyboard or mouse. Such windows are typically indicated by a different color in their title bars (at the tops of the windows). Usually, the window that's in focus is also the *front* window—the one that's fully exposed. For instance, in Figure 3-3, the file manager window (titled rodsmith) is both in front and in focus. Most window managers shift a window in front and give it focus when you click anywhere in the window, but some shift focus when the mouse moves over the window or only when you click the title bar. Experiment to learn what yours does.

- **Window manager widgets** A *widget* is a GUI tool that lets you interact with a program. Window manager widgets are typically located at the right and left sides of the title bar. Some work much like those in Windows, but others don't.

- **Context menus** Most FreeBSD window managers provide menus with options relating to program launching, exiting from the window manager, and so on. You can often reach these by right-clicking on the desktop. Other environments, including GNOME, provide a menu you can reach by clicking near a corner. In GNOME, the G-shaped foot icon in the lower-left of the screen serves this function.

- **Status bars, menus, docks, and panels** Most desktop environments and some window managers provide some form of menu that's fixed along the top, bottom, or side of the screen. In Figure 3-3, GNOME is configured with menus (which it calls the *Panel*) along both the top and bottom of the screen. In the case of GNOME, menu items at the top enable you to select GNOME options and change between virtual desktops (virtual screens that can hold different programs, reducing clutter, much like virtual terminals in text-mode logins). The bottom panel includes the GNOME Foot, from which you can launch various programs, icons with which you can launch a few particularly important programs, and a button for each program that's running in the current virtual desktop.

Tip *If your experiments damage your working environment, you can shut down X and delete your user-level configuration files for your environment from your home directory. For GNOME, delete any directory whose name begins with* .gnome, *including* .gnome *and* .gnome-desktop. *If you delete these directories and restart X, you'll find your GNOME desktop restored to its defaults.*

Manipulating Files

If you see a file browser window similar to Figure 3-3's rodsmith window open on your screen, you can use it to move, copy, and otherwise manipulate files. If you don't see it, but do see a *user*'s Home icon on the screen for your home directory (such as Figure 3-3's rodsmith's Home icon), you can open the file browser window by double-clicking that icon. If you don't see the icon and are running GNOME, select GNOME Foot | Programs | Applications | Nautilus to launch it, or type **nautilus** in a Terminal window like the one eclipsed by the file manager window in Figure 3-3.

You can move to any directory on the system by clicking Tree in the left-hand side of the window and selecting the desired directory in the resulting directory list. (Figure 3-3 shows this list in its expanded form.) If you want to move to a subdirectory, you can expand a directory by clicking the triangle icon next to the directory's name. Some operations require you to have two windows open. You can do this by selecting File | New Window or by launching a new window using the *user*'s Home icon. Some of the things you can do with GNOME's file manager include the following:

- **Copy files**   You can right-click a file and select Duplicate from the resulting pop-up menu to copy it. The copy has the same name as the original, but with (copy) inserted into the name. Alternatively, you can right-click an icon and drag it to another directory in the same or another window (including in the directory list to the left of the icons). Doing so produces a menu that enables you to move the file, copy the file, create a symbolic link to the original file, or cancel the operation.

- **Move files**   You can move a file by right-clicking it and dragging it, much as with a copy.

- **Delete files**   Right-click a file and select Move to Trash to move the file to the Nautilus trash directory. Alternatively, you can drag the file to the trash can icon (near the lower left of the screen in Figure 3-3). These operations move the file to a special trash directory that you can subsequently "empty" by selecting File | Empty Trash from a Nautilus file browser window. You can move the file back out of the trash before you empty it, however, if you find you need the file after all.

- **Rename files**   Right-click a file and then select Rename from the context menu to rename the file. You can also rename a file by right-clicking it and selecting Show Properties. The resulting dialog box, shown in Figure 3-4, enables you to rename the file or do other things to it.

- **Change permissions**   Right-click the file, select Show Properties, and click the Permissions tab in the Properties dialog box (Figure 3-4) to change the file's permissions. You can use this feature to restrict or loosen access to the file, as described in Chapter 8.

- **Launch programs**   If GNOME associates a file type with an application, you can launch that application and have it load the file by double-clicking a file of the appropriate type in the browser window. To launch some other application to load a file, right-click the file and move your mouse over Open With. Nautilus responds by displaying programs it's configured to associate with the file type. (Chapter 23 describes adding associations for particular file types.) Select a specific program to launch that program and have it load the file.

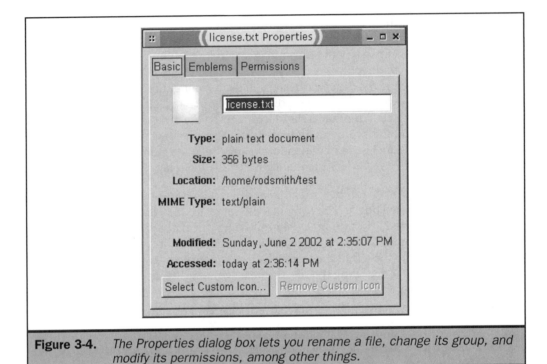

Figure 3-4. *The Properties dialog box lets you rename a file, change its group, and modify its permissions, among other things.*

The KDE environment offers a similar file browser, which doubles as a web browser. FreeBSD supports many more file browsers in addition to these two, and you can use the GNOME or KDE browser even if you're not using the rest of the environment.

Running Programs from a GUI

You can launch programs from a GUI environment in several different ways, including

- **Program icons on the panel** The icons immediately to the right of the GNOME Foot in Figure 3-3 provide quick access to four common programs: The GNOME Help Browser, the GNOME Terminal (which gives you access to a text-mode command line), the GNOME Control Center (described in the next section, "Configuring the Environment"), and the Mozilla web browser.

- **Program menu items** Both the GNOME Foot panel item in the lower-left corner of the screen and the Programs menu item in the upper-left corner of the screen give you access to a variety of common programs, divided into several categories.

- **File browser** As noted earlier, you can launch a program from the file browser, either by locating it in your filesystem and double-clicking it or by double-clicking a file that's associated with the program.

- **Desktop icons** Some desktop icons may launch programs. Most of the default icons shown in Figure 3-3 open Nautilus windows on various hard disk partitions, but you can reconfigure the desktop to include icons for programs you like.

- **Terminal launch** You can open a Terminal session using one of the previous methods and then launch a program by typing its name in the Terminal. The Terminal works much like a text-mode login; it runs within it a copy of your default text-mode shell (`sh`, `tcsh`, `bash`, or whatever you've chosen to use). Thus, you can use the Terminal to run text-mode programs.

Note   *The GNOME Terminal is one of a class of programs that's used to run a text-based shell and other text-based programs within X. The most generic of these programs is called* `xterm`, *and this class of programs is sometimes referred to by that name. Because GNOME's Terminal is only one of several* `xterm`-*like programs, I use the name xterm to refer to them generically in this book.*

When you run X-based programs, they launch into their own windows, although if you launch such a program from an xterm, the X-based program still "owns" the xterm's text display. Thus, the xterm becomes unusable unless you launch the program with a trailing ampersand (`&`) to shunt it into the background, as described earlier in this chapter, in "Text-Mode and GUI Logins." It's possible for text-based programs to be configured to run from menus or the like, but they're usually run by typing their command names in an xterm window.

Because window environments differ so much, this book emphasizes the xterm approach to launching programs. If you find the program in question on one of your menus, of course, you can launch it in this way. You can even customize your desktop environment to add the program to a menu or as a desktop icon.

One quirk of FreeBSD (or X and the programs that have developed around it, to be more precise) is that GUI programs vary greatly in "look and feel." This is because X is composed of layers, from the X server to the desktop environment. Some of these layers are ones that you choose, such as the window manager, but others are elements that the programmer who develops a program chooses. When two programmers select different development kits, their programs often differ in details such as the fonts used in menus and the appearance of buttons in dialog boxes.

Configuring the Environment

Chances are you'll want to reconfigure some elements of your desktop environment almost immediately. For instance, you might find the keyboard repeat rate to be ridiculous, or you might want to add an interesting background image to the desktop. These details are set in different ways in different GUI environments. In GNOME, you set them in the Control Center, which you can launch by clicking the icon that looks like a toolbox in the panel at the bottom of the screen. If you prefer, you can type **gnomecc** in an xterm to launch the Control Center. Figure 3-5 shows the GNOME Control Center with one of its modules loaded.

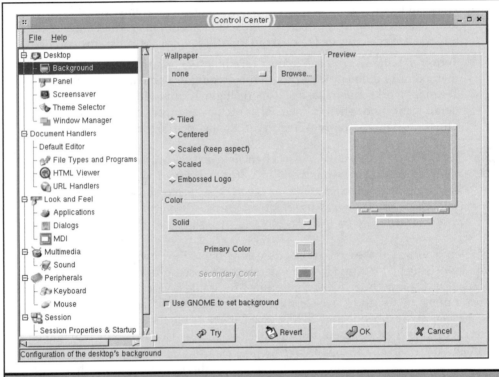

Figure 3-5. *The GNOME Control Center enables you to adjust GNOME's settings and those of affiliated programs.*

To use the Control Center, you select the general type of setting you want to adjust from the list to the left. Figure 3-5 shows the Desktop | Background module, in which you can set the color of your desktop's background or configure it to use a graphics file instead. As you can see from Figure 3-5, these settings are broken into several broad categories, such as

■ **Desktop** This category includes options to set background color or image, adjust the behavior of the Panel, enable a screen saver, load a theme that sets various options in a single operation, and change the window manager that GNOME uses.

■ **Document handlers** You can tell GNOME what text editor you prefer to use, what file types to associate with what programs, how it should display HTML (web) documents, and what programs it should use for particular types of Uniform Resource Locators (URLs).

- **Look and feel**   The modules in this section enable you to set options relating to the user interface of GNOME programs. These options don't apply to most non-GNOME programs, though, so don't be surprised if they don't affect all your programs.

- **Multimedia**   You can configure some sound card settings and associate sounds with particular events, such as logging in, logging out, and receiving e-mail.

- **Peripherals**   You can adjust the keyboard repeat rate, mouse tracking speed, mouse handedness, and similar options with these modules.

- **Session**   You can set assorted login and logout defaults using the items under the Session option, such as programs you want to launch when you log in and whether GNOME should ask you for confirmation when you log out.

One thing that's important to keep in mind about these configuration options is that they're *user* configuration options. They can vary from one user to another, so several people can use the same computer without having to compromise on options. If Sam really likes a bright pink background, but Sally prefers dark blue, they need not compromise on gray or purple.

Because the GNOME Control Center sets only user options, you can't set some options that affect the entire system. For instance, you can't load drivers, install programs, or format disks from the GNOME Control Center. These actions are administrative tasks that affect the entire system, and they're covered in other chapters of this book.

Logging Off and Shutting Down

When you're done using FreeBSD, you should do one or both of two things: log off and/or shut down. Logging off leaves the computer running, including any servers you may be running, but it closes access to your account; to use your account, you'll have to log in again. Shutting down the computer is more drastic; it terminates all programs and sends the system into a state in which it's safe for you to turn the computer off.

You should never turn the computer off without first shutting down FreeBSD. Like most modern OSs, FreeBSD performs many operations in the background, and caches disk accesses—that is, it holds onto data before writing it, in the hope of being able to combine the write into one operation, thus improving performance. These characteristics mean that if you simply shut the computer off, you may lose data, and your filesystems may become corrupted. This can slow the boot process and lose even more data.

Text-Mode and GUI Methods of Logging Off

Logging off prevents people who might wander by from sitting down at the computer and using your account to do things you might not like, such as send offensive e-mail in your name or break into others' computers. Logging off closes all the programs you're running, including those running in the background.

If you've used a text-mode login, you can log off by typing **logout**. This logs you out of the account and displays a new `login:` prompt on the screen. You can log in again at a later time, or somebody else can log in. If you've logged into several virtual terminals, be sure to log out of all of them.

 By default, FreeBSD does not clear the screen as part of the logout process. If any sensitive data appear on your screen, you may want to clear the screen by typing **clear** *before you type* **logout**.

If you're running X, typing **logout** in an xterm window won't work because these windows aren't login sessions. Instead, you must shut down X or log out of your X session. You can accomplish either task by selecting a special logout option on an X menu. Precisely what this option is called varies from one environment to another. In GNOME, it's GNOME Foot | Log Out. In some stand-alone window managers, you can find the logout option in a menu you obtain by right-clicking on the desktop. Sometimes this option is called *Close Window Manager*, *Exit X*, or something similar.

After you select the X-based logout option, you'll either see the XDM login screen (if your system is configured to use XDM) or your original text mode screen, with quite a few messages displayed by the X server. (You can safely ignore these, if your X session worked properly.) You can then type **logout** to log off the computer.

 In some cases, X doesn't terminate correctly after you select the desktop environment or window manager logout option. In such cases, you can press CTRL-ALT-BACKSPACE *to terminate X.*

Text-Mode and GUI Methods of Shutting Down

Shutting down the computer allows you to safely power it off. You have to be logged in as `root` to shut down the computer (an ordinary user login followed by `su` to acquire `root` privileges also works). The command involved is called `shutdown`. You can issue it from a text-mode login or from an xterm inside X. Its syntax is

```
shutdown [options] time [warning-message]
```

The *time* is the time when the system shuts down, and it can take one of three forms:

- **now** The string `now` represents an immediate shutdown. You might use this time specification to shut down a workstation that's being used by a single person.

- **+number** To schedule a shutdown some number of minutes in the future, specify the number of minutes by preceding it with a plus sign. For instance, +30 indicates a shutdown in half an hour.

■ ***yymmddhhmm***   To schedule a shutdown for a particular time, specify it as a ten-digit number, starting with a two-digit year and moving down through the month, day, hour, and minute. (You must use a 24-hour format for the hour.)

The optional *warning-message* is a text message that appears on all users' text-mode login consoles starting at ten hours before the scheduled shutdown time. For instance, you might pass **"Shut down for disk upgrade; up at 7:00 AM"** as the warning message, to let users know why the system is being shut down and when they might expect it to be up again.

Finally, but appearing immediately after the shutdown command when you type it, the program accepts any of several options. These are:

■ **-h**   The system is halted after the shutdown. This form of shutdown enables you to power off or reboot the computer manually.

■ **-p**   The system is halted and powered off after the shutdown. This option requires that your hardware support software-controlled power off, as do most modern computers. (Some older systems don't support this.)

■ **-r**   The system is halted and rebooted after the shutdown. You might use this option to reboot into another OS, or after making changes to the FreeBSD kernel.

■ **-k**   This option kicks all users off the system and disallows further logins, but doesn't actually shut down the system. You might do this if you want to make extensive software changes or perform tests in a controlled environment.

■ **-o**   The shutdown procedure with -h, -p, or -r normally involves the shutdown process calling init, which does the actual work. This option causes shutdown to do the work itself. It's normally not required.

■ **-n**   This option can be used in conjunction with -o, and causes shutdown to skip flushing the filesystem cache. This method can cause disk corruption, so it's not something you'd normally want to use.

■ **- (Dash)**   If you include a single dash as an option, shutdown prompts you for a warning message rather than using one you provide on the same command line.

After you issue a shutdown command, FreeBSD reverses many of the steps it took during startup. FreeBSD terminates any running programs, including X, any servers that are running, and so on. The system unmounts network filesystems and partitions it's mounted, and then performs whatever shutdown action you specified. If you used -h, you'll see a message stating that the system has been halted; at that point, you can power it off or reboot it by pressing the Reset switch on the computer's case. If you used -p or -r, the system automatically powers down (if your hardware supports this option) or reboots, respectively.

An alternative to the shutdown command is to press CTRL-ALT-DELETE at the console's keyboard. This action shuts down and reboots the FreeBSD system, and you may find it easier to remember this keystroke than the details of the shutdown command. This alternative may therefore be a good one if the system is a workstation used by inexperienced users. Of course, if the intent is to shut down rather than reboot the computer, you'll have to hit the power switch before FreeBSD begins booting, or you'll risk file corruption. Some replacements for the XDM GUI login program enable users to shut down the computer from the console. These programs provide a shutdown option from a button or menu item. Both the GDM and KDM programs (parts of the GNOME and KDE environments, respectively) provide this option.

When to Shut Down

If you participate in Usenet newsgroup or mailing list discussions, sooner or later you'll come across a perennial debate: When is it appropriate to shut down a computer? The two schools on this issue are the never-shut-it-down school and the shut-down-to-save-power school.

The argument against shutting down a computer is that component failures are most likely to occur because of the stresses involved in turning devices on and off. The changes in heat and voltage put more wear and tear on a device than does constant operation. Consider light bulbs. They usually fail when you apply power, not when they've been turned on for a while. The same is true of computer components, so the lifetime of a computer may be extended by leaving it on all the time.

An opposing view holds that the extended life you might gain from leaving a computer on at all times is minor, particularly when you consider that the components in question are likely to become obsolete long before they fail. Leaving the computer on continuously consumes power, though, and the power savings is more important (by this argument) than the extension in component life.

Both of these arguments have merit, and you'll have to decide between them for yourself. One further factor, though, lies in the FreeBSD automatic maintenance tools. FreeBSD runs certain programs late at night to handle some routine maintenance issues, such as cleaning old files out of the /tmp directory, as described in Chapter 28. Thus, if you decide to routinely shut down your computer at night, you should leave it running overnight every once in a while.

Of course, all of this assumes that you're running a workstation. Most servers need to run 24 hours a day, 7 days a week, and so are shut down only for hardware upgrades, repairs, or the like.

Summary

FreeBSD is distinguishable from Windows soon after you press the power switch on the computer. The FreeBSD startup sequence produces a great deal of textual output, summarizing the steps it's taking while booting your system. After this, the default FreeBSD configuration presents a text-mode login screen, and logging in lets you run text-mode programs. FreeBSD's UNIX heritage makes it important that you understand at least some of these commands, such as those to view and manipulate files. To run GUI programs, you must start X by typing a single command (**startx**), which loads X and whatever X environment you've chosen as the default or configured for yourself as an individual user. Some FreeBSD GUI environments are very similar to those of Windows or other GUI OSs, so if you're familiar with such tools, you shouldn't have too much trouble adjusting to FreeBSD. When you're done, you should log off of your account to reduce the risk of it being abused by a passer-by. When you need to turn the computer off or reboot it, you should be sure to use a proper shutdown procedure, rather than simply hitting the power switch or Reset button.

The
Complete
Reference

FreeBSD

Chapter 4

Coexistence with Other Operating Systems

A
s described in earlier chapters, and particularly in Chapter 2, FreeBSD can run either as the only OS on a computer or as one of two or more OSs. In the second case, it's important that you know how FreeBSD and your other OS or OSs interact, so that you can make the best use of your available resources and avoid mistakes. (It's possible to completely destroy one OS's installation from another OS, for instance.) This chapter covers these interactions. It begins with a look at the boot process, focusing on the configuration and use of boot loaders. The next topic is partition management—addressing partitions in a way that won't cause problems. Most partitions hold filesystems, and these usually differ from one OS to another. Thus, a large part of this chapter is devoted to this important topic. Finally, the chapter concludes with a look at ways you can run non-FreeBSD programs, such as Linux or Windows applications, in FreeBSD.

Note   *If your computer runs FreeBSD and nothing else, most of this chapter won't interest you. The information on filesystems might be relevant if you need to mount floppy disks, Zip disks, or the like in FreeBSD, though. Likewise, you might want to run non-FreeBSD programs from time to time, even on a FreeBSD-only system.*

Configuring the Boot Process

Chapter 2 included basic information on installing the FreeBSD boot loader. This boot loader works well in most simple configurations, such as FreeBSD with Windows and nothing else on a single hard disk. More advanced configurations, though, may require you to modify the default FreeBSD boot loader configuration, or even use another boot loader. This section covers these topics, as well as using the FreeBSD boot loader to pass special options to the FreeBSD kernel. These options can alter the way FreeBSD treats hardware, thus enabling the OS to boot on some hardware that might cause problems for the default configuration.

Understanding Boot Loaders

When an *x86* computer boots, it looks for code to run in several locations, starting with the computer's *Basic Input/Output System (BIOS)* ROM. The BIOS, in turn, tells the computer to look for a *boot sector* on one or more boot devices. During installation, you may have needed to reconfigure your BIOS to boot from a floppy disk or CD-ROM drive, for instance. Normally, the computer boots from the hard disk, either because the BIOS is configured to check it first or because other potential boot devices don't contain bootable media. The boot sector of a hard disk is more commonly known as the *Master Boot Record (MBR)*. A standard MBR contains code that, in a typical DOS or Windows installation, redirects the boot process to use code in the boot partition's boot sector. This code boots DOS or Windows. This simple one-OS configuration is illustrated in Figure 4-1. (Note that Figure 4-1 shows a FreeBSD partition, but the boot process depicted doesn't boot it.)

In a multi-OS system, some part of this boot process must be modified to support a choice of OSs. The usual approach using the standard FreeBSD tools is to replace the

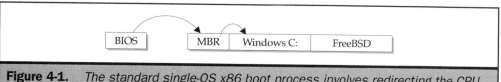

Figure 4-1. *The standard single-OS x86 boot process involves redirecting the CPU to run code from various places.*

MBR's boot code with new code that enables you to choose between FreeBSD and the other OSs on your system. This approach works well in simple configurations, and with a bit of work, in more complex setups. Some OSs support their own boot loaders, though, and third-party boot loaders also exist. These may replace the MBR with their own code, replace the Windows boot sector, intercept the boot process further down the line in the Windows boot process, or install a special partition dedicated to redirecting the boot process. If you want to use such a boot loader, you may, as described in the upcoming section, "Using a Third-Party Boot Loader."

One important complication to understand is the so-called *1024-cylinder limit.* Traditionally, *x86* computers have used *cylinder/head/sector (CHS)* addressing, in which three numbers uniquely identify any given sector on the hard disk. The BIOS was originally written when hard disks were much smaller than they are today, and so it included limits on CHS numbers that today produce a maximum addressable disk size of just under 8GB. (Limits in the old IDE interface further reduced this to 504MB, but BIOS trickery raised this limit to the BIOS maximum of just under 8GB in the mid-1990s.) Because the boot process relies heavily upon the BIOS, these limits, and particularly the limit of 1024 cylinders, have been important ones in booting any OS.

By the late 1990s, BIOSes were shipping with features (known as *extended INT13 calls*) that enabled them to overcome the 1024-cylinder limit, but boot loaders need to support these BIOS features. FreeBSD's boot loader does so, but you may need to add special parameters to get it to boot FreeBSD from above the 1024-cylinder limit. (Note that a disk may be larger than 1024 cylinders but still need no special options, if the FreeBSD boot files reside below this limit.) Third-party boot loaders may also need support for these extended INT13 calls in order to boot FreeBSD (or any other OS) from above the 1024-cylinder limit.

Using the FreeBSD Boot Loader

If you followed the instructions in Chapter 2 and installed the FreeBSD boot loader in the usual way, your system should boot FreeBSD and possibly one or more other OSs, such as DOS or Windows. You may want to modify this configuration, though. For instance, you might want to add another OS to the menu of options that appears when the computer starts. You can do this by reconfiguring the boot loader with the `boot0cfg` command. This command's syntax is

```
boot0cfg [-Bv] [-b boot0] [-d drive] [-f file] [-m mask] ↵
[-o options] [-s slice] [-t ticks] disk
```

In most cases, you won't need more than one or two of these options. In particular, typing **boot0cfg -B /dev/ad0** as root installs the boot loader in the conventional way on the first EIDE disk; the utility searches for all bootable partitions and, at boot time, gives you the option of which to boot. (You would use /dev/da0 instead of /dev/ad0 if your system uses SCSI disks.) In case you need them, the options to this command are

- **-B** This option tells boot0cfg to install MBR code to permit selection of the OS you want to use. Omit this option if you're using another primary boot loader in the MBR, as described in the upcoming section, "Using a Third-Party Boot Loader."

- **-v** Normally, boot0cfg provides little feedback. This option causes it to display additional information (that is, to be verbose), such as the slices it's making bootable.

- **-b *boot0*** To install a boot loader, boot0cfg copies a file from elsewhere into the MBR. This file defaults to /boot/boot0, but you can specify another file if you want to use some other boot loader. You might use this option if you want to try an experimental FreeBSD boot loader, but otherwise you won't use it. (If you use a third-party MBR boot loader, it should have its own way to install in the MBR.)

- **-d *disk*** The BIOS refers to hard disks by a drive number. The first physical disk is normally 0x80 (that is, hexadecimal 80, or decimal 128), the second is 0x81, and so on. If you've configured your BIOS to boot from the second or subsequent disk, you may need to use the -d *disk* option to tell it which one to use. Pass the BIOS drive identifier, such as 0x81, as *disk*. For simplicity, arrange your drives so that the FreeBSD boot loader and any OS that must boot from the first physical disk can reside on that disk; then you don't need this option.

- **-f *file*** This option tells boot0cfg to back up the existing MBR to the specified file. This procedure can be useful in case there are problems; you can restore the original MBR using the dd utility.

- **-m *mask*** Normally, boot0cfg can tell which slices should be listed in the initial boot selections menu. If it guesses wrong, you can use this option to override it. The *mask* variable takes a value from 0 (no slices enabled) to 0xf (decimal 15; all slices enabled). The *mask* is a four-bit binary code, with each bit corresponding to one slice.

- **-o *options*** You can specify any of three special options with this parameter. Precede an option with no to reverse its meaning (for instance, nopacket as opposed to packet). If you want to use multiple options, you can separate them with commas. The options are

  - **packet** The default value is nopacket, which causes the MBR boot loader to use the old CHS addressing modes. This value effectively limits

FreeBSD to booting from the first 8GB of a disk. If you specify `packet`, on the other hand, FreeBSD uses the extended INT13 calls, which enable it to boot an OS from well beyond the 1024th cylinder.

- **setdrv**   Specify this option if you've adjusted your BIOS drive mappings and used the `-d disk` option, otherwise FreeBSD may not boot correctly.

- **update**   Normally, FreeBSD alters the default boot partition whenever you make a selection to boot an OS. The next time you boot, the last OS you booted is the default. Use the `noupdate` option to cause the boot loader to treat the MBR as unchangeable so that you get the same default OS each time you boot.

- **-s *slice***   This option is normally used in conjunction with `-o noupdate`. It specifies the slice number you want to boot by default. (Give a number from 1 to 4 as *slice*.)

- **-t *ticks***   Normally, the system pauses for a few seconds to allow you to select which OS to boot. You can change the delay period with this option, which takes time in *ticks* (1 second contains 18.2 ticks).

- **disk***   This is the disk whose MBR `boot0cfg` modifies. It's normally `/dev/ad0` for EIDE disks or `/dev/da0` for SCSI disks.

You might run `boot0cfg` for several reasons. One is that you might want to change some of the defaults—for instance, to add an OS that was overlooked to begin with, or set it up to use a consistent default boot OS. Another common reason to run the program is to reinstall the FreeBSD boot loader after another OS has wiped it out. Of course, you need an emergency boot floppy to boot FreeBSD if this happens. (The installation CD-ROM or floppy disk can do this job.)

Microsoft OSs usually install a fresh standard x86 MBR on installation. Thus, if you install a copy of Windows after you install FreeBSD, you have to reinstall the FreeBSD boot loader or use a third-party boot loader.

One limitation of the FreeBSD boot loader is that it can redirect the boot process only to OSs that reside on *x86* primary partitions. Some OSs, such as Linux and OS/2, can boot from logical partitions. Thus, if you install such an OS in a logical partition, you must either use another primary boot loader or install a third-party boot loader in another primary partition and use that to boot the OS in the logical partition.

Setting Kernel Options

After the computer executes the MBR code, the boot process moves on to code contained elsewhere. In the case of the FreeBSD boot loader, this is often referred to as *Stage 1* and *Stage 2* of the boot process (the MBR code is *Stage 0*). In FreeBSD, you can use these stages to pass parameters to the kernel to modify its behavior.

If you need to reinstall your Stage 1 and Stage 2 boot loaders, you can do so by typing **disklabel /dev/name**, *where* /dev/name *is the name of your FreeBSD slice, such as* /dev/ad0s2. *Ideally, this command should never be necessary, but it might be necessary if your disk has been damaged.*

From the point of view of somebody booting the computer, this stage of the boot process begins with a prompt such as

```
Hit [Enter] to boot immediately, or any other key for command prompt.
Booting [/boot/kernel/kernel] in 9 seconds...
```

The time in the second message counts down. If you press any key except ENTER before the countdown reaches 0, you can enter boot parameters to modify the way the system boots. These options include

- **autoboot** *seconds*   This option restarts the boot countdown, starting at the specified number of seconds.
- **boot [-***options***] [***kernelname***]**   You can boot the specified kernel and pass it any options you like with this command.
- **load [-t** *type***]** *modulename*   You can load a kernel module with this option. A kernel module is a driver or other kernel extension, so you can use this option to get unusual hardware working. Kernel modules can be loaded after the system has booted, though, so you need this option only if the hardware is required for FreeBSD to boot, such as a driver for an otherwise unsupported disk controller.
- **ls [-l] [***path***]**   This option works much like the ls command once the system has booted; it displays files in a specified directory. You might not have access to all your partitions at this early stage in the boot process, though.
- **lsdev [-v]**   This option lists the devices from which you can load modules. Adding -v creates a more verbose report.
- **lsmod [-v]**   You can see a list of loaded modules with this command. As with lsdev, -v displays more information.
- **more** *filename*   This option displays *filename* a screenful at a time. You may need this feature in order to read documentation on modules you want to install.
- **reboot**   This command reboots the system.
- **unload**   You can unload all loaded modules with this command.

You can use these options to load an alternate kernel—say, for testing purposes after you've compiled a new kernel, as described in Chapter 12. You may also need to load or unload kernel modules to get your system to boot, or pass options to the kernel. (Chapter 12 includes additional information on some of these parameters.)

It's important to realize that you see these boot options whether you use the FreeBSD boot loader in the MBR or a third-party boot loader. Thus, you aren't restricted to using the FreeBSD boot loader if you want to use these features.

Using a Third-Party Boot Loader

Dozens of boot loaders are available today. Most OSs ship with boot loaders capable of handling several OSs, including FreeBSD. If you don't like the FreeBSD primary boot loader or the ones that ship with your other OSs, there are OS-independent boot loaders available. (Usually these install from just one or two OSs, but they don't ship with any OS.) Examples of common boot loaders include

- ■ **LILO**   The *Linux Loader (LILO)* is Linux's traditional boot loader. It can reside in the MBR, in the Linux boot partition, or on a floppy disk. LILO is a very flexible boot loader, but accessing that flexibility requires fairly tedious configuration.

- ■ **GRUB**   The *Grand Unified Bootloader (GRUB)* now ships with many Linux distributions, and can be reconfigured from other OSs, as well as from Linux. It can, of course, be configured to boot FreeBSD.

- ■ **Windows OS Loader**   The *OS Loader* (aka *NTLDR*) is the boot loader for Windows NT/2000/XP. It's fairly inflexible, and is configured through files on the Windows partition. It's almost always better to use the FreeBSD boot loader as your primary boot loader. If you install multiple versions of Windows, you may use OS Loader as a secondary boot loader after you select Windows in the FreeBSD boot loader.

- ■ **OS/2 Boot Manager**   OS/2's *Boot Manager* is a moderately flexible boot loader that occupies its own dedicated slice. It can boot FreeBSD, OS/2, Linux, or just about any other OS.

- ■ **System Commander**   This boot loader, from V-Com (`http://www.v-com.com`), is a very flexible boot loader. It resides on the MBR and on files on a FAT partition, and it can boot just about any OS (including FreeBSD) from primary or (when the OS supports it) logical *x*86 partitions, as well as hide primary partitions from OSs such as Windows.

- ■ **BootMagic**   This boot loader ships with PowerQuest's (`http://www.powerquest.com`) PartitionMagic and is available separately. It's a fairly complete boot loader that's housed in a Windows partition's boot sector and in FAT files. It can boot most OSs (including FreeBSD) from primary or (when the OS supports it) logical *x*86 partitions.

As a general rule, when you use a third-party boot loader, that boot loader replaces the MBR-based FreeBSD boot loader. When you select FreeBSD in this third-party boot loader, it runs the Stage 1 boot loader from the FreeBSD slice, so you're greeted by the boot prompt described earlier, in "Setting Kernel Options."

With most third-party boot loaders, you can make FreeBSD available by using some sort of menu of OSs. LILO deserves special mention as an exception, though. With it, you must create an entry in the Linux /etc/lilo.conf file that resembles the following:

```
other = /dev/hda2
    label = freebsd
    table = /dev/hda
```

This entry boots FreeBSD from Linux's /dev/hda2 (/dev/ad0s2 in FreeBSD parlance), using the partition table stored on /dev/hda (FreeBSD's /dev/ad0) as a reference. More exotic configurations are possible; consult a Linux book or the lilo.conf man page in Linux for details. After you've created this entry, you need to type **lilo** as root in Linux to install LILO. You should then be able to boot FreeBSD by typing **freebsd** at a LILO boot prompt, or possibly by selecting FreeBSD from a menu, if LILO is configured to present one.

Managing FreeBSD and *x*86 Partitions

Partitions are the basic units of disk management. As a first approximation, each OS on a computer should have one or more partitions to itself, and other OSs shouldn't touch these partitions. It's important that you configure your system so that non-FreeBSD OSs don't damage your FreeBSD partitions. On the other hand, it's often useful to have a common partition in which you can exchange files between OSs. This configuration obviously contradicts the original goal, but if you manage your partitions correctly, the risks can be nearly nonexistent.

A Review of Partitioning Systems

Chapter 2 covered partitions, partition type, and FreeBSD's partition management tools. You may want to review this information before proceeding. In brief, an *x*86 computer running FreeBSD may contain several different types of partitions:

- **x86 primary or FreeBSD slice**   The original type of *x*86 partition is most commonly called a *primary partition* today, but in the FreeBSD world, the term *slice* is often used to refer to this partition type. The *x*86 partitioning system is restricted to four primary partitions, and many OSs (including FreeBSD) must boot from this type of partition.

- **x86 extended**   Because four primary partitions is very limiting, a special type of partition was created as a placeholder for a third type of partition. The placeholder partition is known as an *extended* partition. It consumes one of the four available primary partitions, but can stand in for many other partitions.

- ■ **x86 logical**   *Logical* partitions reside "within" an extended partition. In Windows, these partitions are given drive letters of D: or above, depending on the configuration. Most OSs can't boot from a logical partition, although there are exceptions to this rule. FreeBSD doesn't use logical partitions by default, although you can configure FreeBSD to access them.

- ■ **FreeBSD partitions**   FreeBSD normally resides on a single *x86* primary partition, but breaks it down into separate FreeBSD partitions. This arrangement works much like the extended/logical partition distinction; the FreeBSD slice is equivalent to an extended partition, while FreeBSD partitions within that slice are equivalent to logical partitions.

Half the challenge in understanding and configuring partitions is in understanding the distinctions between these partition types. Most Windows-only computers ship with a single primary partition, but installing FreeBSD in addition to Windows requires creating a FreeBSD slice, which contains multiple FreeBSD partitions.

Keeping Other OSs from Damaging FreeBSD Partitions

The *x86* partitioning scheme assigns a partition *type code* to every partition. Some, but not all, OSs use these type codes to avoid damaging other OSs' partitions. In particular, DOS, Windows, and OS/2 all rely upon these codes. Thus, the main trick to keeping your FreeBSD slice safe from damage by one of these OSs is to be sure your FreeBSD slice is marked with the appropriate *x86* partition type code. This should be done automatically when you install FreeBSD, so it shouldn't be an issue. Some disk maintenance tools might change these codes, particularly if the tools are used carelessly. Table 4-1 summarizes some of the more popular partition type codes. Windows uses type codes associated with LBA mode on disks that surpass the 1024-cylinder limit. Older OSs may not recognize these partitions.

Note   *Table 4-1 isn't comprehensive. Many more obscure OSs have their own partition type codes, and there are additional codes used for special purposes by common OSs.*

You can examine the partition types used on your disk with the fdisk command in FreeBSD. Specifically, issue the -s option along with the disk identifier to view the primary partition table, thus:

```
# fdisk -s /dev/ad0
/dev/ad0: 784 cyl 255 hd 63 sec
Part        Start        Size Type Flags
   1:          63     4192902 0x0b 0x00
   2:     4192965     8401995 0x0b 0x80
```

Hexadecimal Type Code	Decimal Type Code	Filesystem	Used by OSs
0x01	1	FAT-12	DOS, most other OSs
0x04	4	FAT-16 (less than 32MB)	DOS, most other OSs
0x05	5	Extended	All x86 OSs
0x06	6	FAT-16	DOS, Windows, most other OSs
0x07	7	HPFS or NTFS	OS/2, Windows NT/2000/XP
0x0a	10	OS/2 Boot Manager	OS/2 Boot Manager
0x0b	11	FAT-32	Windows 95 OSR2 and above
0x0c	12	FAT-32 (LBA mode)	Windows 95 OSR2 and above
0x0e	14	FAT-16 (LBA mode)	Windows 95 OSR2 and above
0x0f	15	extended (LBA mode)	Windows 95 OSR2 and above
0x82	130	Linux swap or Solaris	Linux or Solaris
0x83	131	Linux filesystems (ext2fs, XFS, ReiserFS, etc.)	Linux
0xa5	165	BSD slice	BSD OSs, including FreeBSD
0xeb	235	BeFS	BeOS

Table 4-1. *Partition Type Codes and Their Associated Filesystems and OSs*

This command reveals the disk's size (in CHS values), the size of each partition (in 512-byte sectors), and the partition type codes for all the primary partitions, among other things. If your FreeBSD partition's type code is wrong, it's possible that some other OS will try to access it, possibly damaging it. To correct this problem, you can use the -u option to fdisk. This causes fdisk to prompt you about updating each piece of information. Press ENTER for most of these, and change only the partition type code.

For instance, the following sequence changes the partition type code for the first partition in the preceding output:

```
The data for partition 1 is:
sysid 11,(DOS or Windows 95 with 32 bit FAT)
    start 63, size 4192902 (2047 Meg), flag 0
        beg: cyl 0/ head 1/ sector 1;
        end: cyl 260/ head 254/ sector 63
Do you want to change it? [n] y
Supply a decimal value for "sysid (165=FreeBSD)" [11] 165
```

Note   *Although typing* **fdisk -s /dev/ad0** *produces partition type codes in hexadecimal (base 16), the prompts when you type* **fdisk -u /dev/ad0** *show and expect entry of the partition type codes in decimal (base 10). Table 4-1 shows partition type codes in both formats.*

Some OSs, such as Linux, don't use partition type codes, except possibly during installation. For these OSs, you must configure them to ignore the FreeBSD slice. Most Linux distributions do this by default, so this shouldn't be a problem with Linux. If you want to access your FreeBSD partitions from Linux, though, you have to activate Linux's support for FreeBSD slices and filesystems, as described in the upcoming section, "Accessing FreeBSD Filesystems from Other OSs." Accessing FreeBSD partitions from another BSD OS, such as OpenBSD or NetBSD, is normally fairly straightforward. Typically, each BSD OS has its own slice, but you need only specify the correct slice and partition to mount a foreign BSD filesystem.

Accessing Foreign Partitions from FreeBSD

Under FreeBSD, every partition has a unique identifier in the /dev hierarchy. Disk files in this hierarchy have names built up of several parts:

- **Device type**   Hard disks have two-letter type codes for the device type. EIDE disks use a code of ad, and SCSI disks use a code of da. USB drives are treated like SCSI drives, so use the da code for them.

- **Device number**   Each physical disk has a number. The first disk of a type is normally numbered 0, the second is 1, and so on. For EIDE disks, the device number is tied to the disk controller and position on the chain—the primary controller's master disk is 0, the primary controller's slave disk is 1, the secondary controller's master disk is 2, and so on. SCSI disks are numbered sequentially starting with 0, even if the first disk's SCSI ID is higher than this.

- **Slice number**   The slice number is indicated by the letter s and a number from 1 to 4. These numbers usually start at 1, but some tools create slices in a peculiar order, or enable you to delete a slice, thus creating a gap in the sequence. Logical partitions are treated like slices, but their numbers begin with 5. Thus, a disk with two primary partitions and two logical partitions might have slices numbered 1, 2, 5, and 6.

■ **Partition letter** After the slice number is a letter that identifies the FreeBSD partition within a slice. These partition letters have specific meanings for FreeBSD partitions, as outlined in Table 4-2.

You should omit the partition letter when referring to non-FreeBSD slices or logical partitions, and you should omit the slice number when accessing the disk as a whole (when using fdisk, for instance). Table 4-3 shows some example partition identifiers and their meanings. This table isn't intended to be comprehensive, just illustrative.

If you're not already familiar with FreeBSD partition labels, these naming conventions may seem strange, but they become more familiar as you use them. You may want to examine the contents of your /etc/fstab file. This file lists the partitions that FreeBSD mounts when it boots. Chapter 7 describes this file in more detail.

Note *If you're familiar with Linux, you may realize that the FreeBSD disk identifiers are different from those in Linux. These are simply different conventions used in the two OSs.*

In addition to disk partitions, additional disk identifiers refer to other disk devices. Most importantly, /dev/fd0 is the floppy disk, /dev/acd0 (or /dev/acd0a or /dev/acd0c) is the EIDE CD-ROM drive, and /dev/cd0a is the SCSI CD-ROM drive. If a system has multiple drives of a given type (such as two floppy disks), the number can be incremented to address the second drive (such as /dev/fd1 to use the second floppy drive). Floppy and CD-ROM drives aren't normally partitioned, although some of these drive identifiers imply that they are.

Zip, LS-120, magneto-optical, and other removable media devices are accessed like hard disks. Zip disks usually include *x*86 partition tables with one slice, number 4. For instance, a USB Zip disk on an otherwise all-EIDE system would be addressed as /dev/da0s4. Other types of removable disks may also be partitioned, but they generally use

Partition Letter	Use
a	Root (/) partition
b	Swap space
c	The entire slice (use of this option is not recommended)
d and up	General use partitions

Table 4-2. *FreeBSD Partition Letters and Their Uses*

FreeBSD Partition Identifier	Purpose
/dev/ad0	The entire first EIDE disk
/dev/da0	The entire first SCSI disk
/dev/ad0s1	The fist slice on the first EIDE disk
/dev/da1s3a	The root (/) FreeBSD partition, stored on the third slice on the second SCSI disk
/dev/ad2s6	The second logical partition on the secondary EIDE controller's master disk

Table 4-3. *Example Partition Identifiers*

the first slice (/dev/da0s1 or a similar name adjusted for the hardware type). Some removable disks aren't partitioned, so you use the raw disk identifier, such as /dev/da0.

Understanding Filesystems

Knowing the partition codes to access a partition from FreeBSD isn't enough to actually gain access to the partition's files. For a computer to use a partition, it must normally place a *filesystem* on that partition. This is a data structure that fills the partition and enables an OS to store files in it. Different OSs use different filesystems, so you must know something about filesystems—both those used natively by FreeBSD and those used by other OSs.

The Two Meanings of "Filesystem"

One important consideration is that the word *filesystem* has two meanings. As used in this chapter, the word refers to the data structures that fill a partition (or an entire disk, in some cases). Filesystems in this sense have names and are supported by specific OSs, or sometimes by utilities. For instance, you might refer to "the ISO-9660 filesystem" or say that you want to "mount a filesystem" (meaning to make its files available from a FreeBSD directory).

Another meaning of the word *filesystem* is in reference to the logical directory structure on a computer. For instance, you might say "the FreeBSD filesystem is anchored at its root directory" or "a recursive file search finds a file in any directory on the filesystem." In this sense, a filesystem might conceivably span multiple partitions.

In this book, you should be able to tell from context which meaning is intended. In those cases where it isn't, I use other terms (such as *partition* or *directory tree*) or additional words (such as *FAT filesystem*) to clarify the meaning.

The Roots of the FreeBSD Filesystem

FreeBSD uses the *Fast File System (FFS)* as its native filesystem. This filesystem is sometimes referred to as the *UNIX File System (UFS)*; for instance, Linux's commands for accessing FFS use the UFS acronym. The FFS type code, when you use the `mount` command in FreeBSD, is also `ufs`.

FFS is a remarkably old filesystem, by computing standards; its heritage dates back to some of the early BSD releases developed at Berkeley. As the name implies, FFS was developed with speed in mind. It uses many techniques to achieve this goal, including careful placement of data structures on disks to minimize head movements. Some of these techniques don't work properly on modern EIDE and SCSI hard disks, but FFS remains a good performer, albeit not a great one by early twenty-first century standards.

UNIX systems in general, and FreeBSD in particular, are designed with the assumption that the filesystem provides certain features. Naturally, FFS does so. These features include

- **Ownership** As a multiuser OS, FreeBSD needs to track who created files— that is, their owners. This is done by associating a user ID (UID) number with each file. Similarly, files are associated with a specific group of users through a group ID (GID) number.

- **Permissions** FreeBSD supports a three-tiered permission system based on the file's owner, the file's group, and all other users. For each of these categories, FFS supports the assignment of read, write, and execute permissions. (Execute permissions mark the file as being a program or script that can be run.)

- **Special flags** Certain file types require special handling. For instance, directories are really just files that contain pointers to other files. The device filenames used to access disk partitions are also special, and there are other examples. These flags are stored with files, much like their owners and permissions.

- **Filename characteristics** FFS supports long filenames (up to 255 characters), and these filenames may contain uppercase and lowercase letters, numbers, and most punctuation and even control characters. FreeBSD itself relies upon files being *case-sensitive*—that is, uppercase and lowercase characters are treated differently. Thus, the file `FILE.TXT` is different from `file.txt`, and both can reside in the same directory without problems.

These characteristics are important because many non-FreeBSD filesystems don't provide the same set of features. This means that when FreeBSD accesses these filesystems, it may need to "fake" a feature, or there may be quirks when FreeBSD tries to access the filesystem. For instance, FreeBSD must assign an owner to files on a FAT filesystem because FAT doesn't support this feature. Chapter 7 describes these filesystem features and their use by FreeBSD in more detail.

Important Non-FreeBSD Filesystems

When you need to exchange data with another OS, you may need to work through that other OS's filesystem, or with a filesystem that's not native to either OS. This section provides a quick overview of some of the common options, but doesn't go into detail about any of them. Most of these filesystems use separate mount commands from the normal one used to mount FFS partitions. The upcoming section, "Mounting Foreign Filesystems," covers these commands.

Variants of FreeBSD's Filesystem

Because FFS was developed early in BSD's history, it's found its way into many UNIX-like OSs. FreeBSD's closest cousins, OpenBSD and NetBSD, support FFS. So do Solaris, NeXTStep, Mac OS X, and various other UNIX-like OSs. Many UNIX-like OSs, though, now favor their own proprietary filesystems. If you're familiar with Linux, pay particular attention to the upcoming section, "Ext2fs." Many commercial UNIX variants now favor journaling filesystems, described in the upcoming section, "Journaling Filesystems."

You should have little trouble accessing FFS partitions used by the other open source BSD OSs; they all maintain fundamentally the same structure. This is not necessarily true of other FFS implementations, though. Many commercial UNIX OSs use FFS implementations that deviate enough from the one used by FreeBSD that they're incompatible. If you want to exchange files with such an OS, you may need to use another filesystem, such as FAT, as an exchange area.

FAT

The *File Allocation Table (FAT)* filesystem is named after a data structure it uses to allocate disk space for files. FAT became popular with DOS, but has been the only hard disk file-system supported by the Windows 9x/Me line, as well. Even today, many Windows 2000 and XP systems use FAT, although these OSs also support a more advanced filesystem (NTFS, described next).

As originally designed, FAT supports files with very limited filenames—eight characters with an optional three-character extension (the so-called *8.3 filenames*). These filenames are stored in all-uppercase letters (numbers and some punctuation are also legal), but FreeBSD's FAT drivers convert these to lowercase. With Windows 95, Microsoft introduced a FAT variant known as *VFAT*, which extended the filesystem to support mixed-case long filenames. VFAT is still *case-insensitive*, though, meaning that filenames that differ only in case are treated identically, even though the filesystem records the case of filenames. One important feature of VFAT is that it's compatible with older systems. You can store long filenames on a FAT disk using VFAT and then read those files even on an old DOS computer that supports only 8.3 filenames. The DOS system sees only a truncated 8.3 filename, but the data remains intact.

Independent of the question of filename length, FAT varies in the size of its FAT entries, as measured in bits. There are 12-, 16-, and 32-bit FAT variants, often referred to as *FAT-12*, *FAT-16*, and *FAT-32*. The larger the FAT entries, the larger the disk that can be supported. Today, FAT-12 is used almost exclusively on floppy disks. FAT-16 is used on small disk partitions (up to 2GB, although it's usually beneficial to switch to FAT-32 at about 512MB). Partitions larger than 2GB must use FAT-32, unless the partition will be used only by Windows NT/2000/XP—these OSs can handle 4GB FAT-16 partitions.

FreeBSD's FAT drivers handle both the original 8.3 filename FAT and VFAT, and independently of that support 12-, 16-, and 32-bit FAT variants. The drivers auto-detect the bit size of the FAT, so you need not be concerned with this detail. By default, FreeBSD attempts to auto-detect whether a disk uses VFAT and to mount it appropriately, but you can force either behavior if you like.

FAT doesn't support UNIX-style ownership, permissions, or special flags, so FreeBSD fakes these details. You can adjust how they're manipulated with mount options.

Because FAT is supported by Microsoft's OSs, it's also supported by every other major *x86* OS, and most non-*x86* OSs. Thus, FAT floppies, high-capacity removable disks, and data exchange partitions on multi-OS computers are common, even when neither of the OSs exchanging data is a Microsoft OS.

In addition to regular mounting support, as described in the upcoming section, "Mounting Foreign Filesystems," FreeBSD supports accessing FAT filesystems (particularly floppy disks) using the `mtools` *package. This utility is available in the Emulators package section when installing programs using* `sysinstall`. *You can then use commands whose names begin with m, such as* `mdir` *and* `mcopy`, *to access files on FAT floppies.*

NTFS

Microsoft created the *New Technology File System (NTFS)* as part of its Windows NT product. NTFS supports long filenames (in a case-insensitive way), file ownership, and *access control lists (ACLs)* for security. Because NTFS is the preferred filesystem for Windows NT, 2000, and now XP, it's likely to increase in importance in the future.

Although NTFS supports file ownership and ACLs for access control, these features aren't easily mapped onto FreeBSD's own ownership and permissions model. Therefore, FreeBSD's support for these features in NTFS is essentially nonexistent. As with FAT, you can force FreeBSD to fake these features when you mount an NTFS filesystem, but only for the filesystem as a whole; you can't modify individual files' ownership or permissions.

FreeBSD's NTFS support nominally provides read/write access, but the write options are so restrictive that NTFS is effectively a read-only filesystem. This fact, and the ownership and permissions issues, make NTFS support in FreeBSD limited in value. If you need to exchange data with Windows NT/2000/XP running on the same computer, you're better off using a FAT partition. In a pinch, you can mount an NTFS partition and read files from it.

Ext2fs

Linux's default filesystem is known as the *Second Extended Filesystem (ext2fs)*. This filesystem supports all the same UNIX features as does FFS—ownership, permissions, and so on. Thus, ext2fs can closely resemble FFS from the point of view of a program that must read or write files on it.

Unfortunately, FreeBSD's ext2fs support is not as reliable as it might be. FreeBSD may become unstable when reading ext2fs, or it may corrupt the ext2 filesystem. Linux's FFS support is also imperfect, so if you want to dual-boot FreeBSD and Linux, you may want to include a FAT partition for data exchange.

In 2002, many Linux users are migrating to other filesystems. One of these, the *Third Extended Filesystem (ext3fs)*, is a journaling extension of ext2fs. The FreeBSD ext2fs support should handle these partitions, but I strongly recommend against trying to mount them with full read/write support unless and until this feature has been adequately tested. Linux's ext3fs is an example of a new class of filesystems known as *journaling filesystems*.

Journaling Filesystems

A journaling filesystem maintains a data structure (the *journal*) on the disk in order to track changes before they're made to the disk. The idea is that, should a system crash or power failure occur, the journal can be used to simplify the disk recovery procedure that must otherwise be run. On some filesystems, such as Linux's ext2fs, this recovery process can be very time-consuming, so a journal can greatly reduce system startup times after a crash or power failure.

FFS's recovery process is quicker than that of ext2fs, so there's less incentive to implement a native FreeBSD journaling filesystem than a Linux journaling filesystem. Recent versions of FFS also support a feature known as soft updates. *This is another approach to guaranteeing consistency in case of a crash or power failure, and further obviates the need for a new journaling filesystem for FreeBSD.*

Many journaling filesystems are in use today. In fact, NTFS is one of them. Others include ext3fs (the journaling ext2fs variant), ReiserFS (a new filesystem designed for Linux), XFS (developed by SGI for its IRIX and now also ported to Linux), JFS (developed by IBM for its AIX and OS/2, and also ported to Linux), and BeFS (developed for BeOS). In 2002, there's been talk of porting some of these to FreeBSD, but no working code is as yet available. (Check `http://sourceforge.net/projects/jfs4bsd` for information on a planned JFS implementation for FreeBSD.) The technical challenges are daunting, so it may be some time before FreeBSD supports any of these filesystems. If one or more is ported and made stable, it might eventually replace FFS as the standard FreeBSD filesystem. Before then, the driver could be used to support file transfers between FreeBSD and other OSs.

CD-ROM Filesystems

CD-ROMs are the standard method of exchanging moderately large amounts of data. A standard CD-ROM can hold up to 650MB of data, and some techniques enable this value to be pushed slightly higher, to around 700MB. When CD-ROMs were first developed, they were envisioned as read-only media, and the original CD-ROM filesystems reflected this fact. The most popular of these, ISO-9660, comes in several variants, some of which support filenames even more restrictive than those of DOS—8.3 filename length limits, with a smaller selection of available punctuation characters in filenames.

UNIX-like systems rely heavily upon their unique filesystem features, so many CD-ROMs created for UNIX-like OSs, including FreeBSD, support an ISO-9660 extension known as *Rock Ridge*. A Rock Ridge CD-ROM supports file ownership and permissions, long case-sensitive filenames, and so on. If FreeBSD detects Rock Ridge extensions on a CD-ROM, it automatically uses those extensions when you mount the CD-ROM.

With Windows 95, Microsoft recognized the primitive nature of ISO-9660, and developed its own new CD-ROM filesystem, known as *Joliet*. Like Rock Ridge, Joliet supports long filenames, but it doesn't support UNIX-style ownership or permissions. FreeBSD supports Joliet, but if a CD-ROM includes both Rock Ridge and Joliet extensions, FreeBSD uses the Rock Ridge extensions.

With the development of writable CD drives (CD-R and CD-RW), and larger optical media, such as DVD-ROMs, ISO-9660 and its derivatives and associated filesystems have run into barriers. To address these needs, the *Universal Disk Format (UDF)* has been developed. In 2002, FreeBSD doesn't support UDF, but work is underway to add this support. Check `http://people.freebsd.org/~scottl/udf/` for the latest information on this project.

Accessing Foreign Filesystems from FreeBSD

Understanding what filesystems are and the differences between them is important when planning how to use them. Actually using them, though, requires knowledge of specific FreeBSD commands. This section covers these commands. It also covers the practical quirks and effects of using foreign filesystems in FreeBSD.

Mounting Foreign Filesystems

FreeBSD uses a command called `mount` to mount filesystems. This command links a filesystem to a *mount point*—that is, a directory somewhere in the FreeBSD directory tree. The basic syntax of `mount` is as follows:

```
mount [options] device-file mount-point
```

The *device-file* is the device filename associated with the filesystem, such as `/dev/ad0s4d` or `/dev/fd0`. The *mount-point* is the location where you want the files to be accessible. You can specify many options to modify the behavior of the `mount` command. For instance, `-a` causes `mount` to mount all the filesystems specified in the `/etc/fstab` file, and `-r` causes the filesystem to be mounted read-only. Chapter 7 describes these general-purpose `mount` options in more detail. Two that deserve special attention for foreign filesystems are

- **-t *fstype*** You can tell `mount` what type of filesystem a partition or other disk device holds with this option. In practice, `mount` uses a helper program, called `mount_fstype`, where *fstype* is the argument to `-t`, to mount the filesystem. For instance, **mount -t msdosfs /dev/ad0s3 /windows** causes `mount` to use the `mount_msdosfs` program to mount a FAT filesystem from `/dev/ad0s3` at `/windows`. (Prior to FreeBSD 5.0, `msdosfs` was referred to as `msdos`.)

■ **-o *options*** You can specify various mount options with this option. Some of these apply across all or most filesystems, but others are filesystem-specific. When using filesystem-specific options, you may need to specify the options as a comma-separated list, and use equal signs (=) where you would ordinarily use spaces. (Examples follow shortly.)

If you want to mount a foreign filesystem, you can either use mount with the -t option or call the variant command for your specific filesystem directly. Table 4-4 summarizes the most common foreign-filesystem mount commands, the filesystems they handle, and the more popular filesystem-specific options they use.

Note | *NFS is the* Network File System, *which is a network file-sharing tool common on UNIX networks. It's described in more detail in Chapters 18 and 24.*

Command	Filesystems Handled	Common Options
mount_msdosfs or mount_msdos	FAT (including VFAT)	-u *uid* sets the user ID (UID) of all files; -g *gid* sets the group ID (GID) of all files; -m *mask* sets the maximum file permissions mask for all files; -s causes FreeBSD to ignore and not generate VFAT long filenames; -l causes FreeBSD to create and use VFAT long filenames (if neither -s nor -l is used, FreeBSD looks for VFAT long filenames and, if they're present, uses them)
mount_ntfs	NTFS	-u *uid*, -g *gid*, and -m *mask* all work as with mount_msdosfs
mount_ext2fs	ext2fs	No special options
mount_cd9660	ISO-9660 (including Rock Ridge); Joliet	-j causes FreeBSD to ignore the Joliet filesystem, if present; -r causes FreeBSD to ignore Rock Ridge extensions, if present
mount_nfs	NFS	-2 forces use of NFS version 2; -3 forces use of NFS version 3; -s causes FreeBSD to return failure codes after a number of failed access attempts

Table 4-4. *Foreign Filesystem Mount Commands*

As an example of these commands in operation, consider the following two commands:

```
# mount_msdosfs -u 1002 -s /dev/fd0 /mnt/floppy
# mount_cd9660 -r /dev/acd0 /mnt/cdrom
```

The first of these commands mounts a FAT floppy disk to /mnt/floppy, giving ownership of all files to whoever has UID 1002. (The /mnt/floppy directory must first exist, which it doesn't in a standard FreeBSD installation.) The -s option specifies that FreeBSD is to ignore VFAT long filenames, so if any are present on the floppy, they're ignored; users will see only 8.3 filenames, and if anybody copies files with long names to the floppy, those names will be truncated to fit the 8.3 filename mold.

The second command mounts a CD-ROM on /mnt/cdrom. (Again, you must create /mnt/cdrom or ensure that it already exists.) The -r option tells FreeBSD to ignore Rock Ridge extensions. If the CD-ROM has a Joliet filesystem, you see the Joliet filenames instead. If not, you see raw ISO-9660 filenames, which usually means 8.3 filenames, but some ISO-9660 variants support single-case filenames of up to 32 characters in length.

Equivalent commands that use mount rather than the filesystem-specific commands are:

```
# mount -t msdosfs -o -u=1002,-s /dev/fd0 /mnt/floppy
# mount -t cd9660 -o -r /dev/acd0 /mnt/cdrom
```

Note that -o precedes the filesystem-specific options. In the case of the FAT floppy, an equal sign replaces the space between -u and 1002, and a comma replaces the space between this option and -s. This format enables you to use normal all-filesystem options, such as -r to mount a filesystem read-only, in addition to filesystem-specific options.

If you want to make a non-FreeBSD partition available at all times, you can create an entry in /etc/fstab for the filesystem, as described in Chapter 7. You can include both filesystem-specific and general options. The result is that FreeBSD will automatically mount the filesystems in question.

Restrictions on the Use of Foreign Filesystems

The preceding sections allude to some of the quirks you encounter when you use a foreign filesystem. The precise effects vary from one filesystem to another, but some of the more common include

- **System instability**   Some filesystem drivers are experimental or poorly debugged, and may cause FreeBSD to crash. There have been such reports for ext2fs, for instance. You should use such filesystems with caution. Note that the popular and important msdosfs and cd9660 filesystems do *not* fall into this category.

■ **Filesystem corruption**   Even if a filesystem doesn't cause FreeBSD to crash, it could corrupt data on the disk or partition in question, particularly if it's used in read/write mode. Once again, FreeBSD's ext2fs support falls into this category, but `msdosfs` doesn't. (The `cd9660` filesystem is read-only, so this problem doesn't apply to it. If you want to create an ISO-9660 filesystem, you can use a special tool called `mkisofs`, in conjunction with another tool called `cdrecord` to write the filesystem to a blank CD-R or CD-RW disc.)

■ **Filename issues**   If you mount a FAT filesystem without VFAT extensions, you won't be able to create files with long names. Neither VFAT nor NTFS is case-sensitive, so you may lose files if you try to copy files whose names differ only in case. You may also access a file if you specify its name in what would be the wrong case on FFS. Joliet works in the same way, but Rock Ridge is much more like FFS.

■ **Ownership and permissions**   These issues can be real bugaboos for new FreeBSD administrators. For a single-user workstation, you may want to include a `-u=`*uid* option in the `/etc/fstab` file for any FAT partitions, floppies, or removable-media disks, so that the workstation's primary user can readily access files. (Substitute the UID of the workstation's primary user for *uid*.) Using `-m=777` gives all files full 0777 permissions (as described in Chapter 8), thus allowing any user to access them. To restrict access to just some users, specify `-g=`*gid*, `-m=770` or something similar, and be sure all the users who should have access to a file are in the specified group (*gid*). Similar options apply to NTFS partitions. For Linux ext2fs partitions, ownership maps by UID and GID, so if your FreeBSD and Linux UIDs and GIDs don't match, you'll see strange ownership effects. There's no easy way around this problem except to synchronize your FreeBSD and Linux UIDs and GIDs.

■ **Speed**   FreeBSD's FFS drivers have been optimized over many years, whereas support for other filesystems is newer and less well optimized. Therefore, access speed for foreign filesystems may not match that for native FFS partitions.

Overall, FreeBSD's foreign filesystem support can be extremely useful in many situations. The ISO-9660 and related extensions support is particularly important on many systems, as is the FAT support. These two foreign filesystems enable FreeBSD to exchange files with most non-FreeBSD systems. Support for other filesystems, such as NTFS and ext2fs, is less well developed, but is still useful in some situations.

Accessing FreeBSD Filesystems from Other OSs

In some cases, you may want to access your FreeBSD filesystems from another OS. This may be handy if you've booted another OS and find you suddenly need to read a file that's stored on a FreeBSD partition, for instance. In some cases, you might even want to use this sort of access to make emergency changes to a FreeBSD configuration if

FreeBSD won't boot. (You can also use a FreeBSD emergency disk to accomplish this goal.) Non-FreeBSD support for FFS is uncommon outside of the UNIX world, though, so your options for such access are limited.

An Overview of Support in Non-FreeBSD OSs

FreeBSD's cousin open source BSD OSs all use FFS, and their implementations are compatible. Thus, you can easily mount FreeBSD partitions in OpenBSD or NetBSD. You need to issue an appropriate `mount` command or add the FreeBSD partition to the `/etc/fstab` file in the OpenBSD or NetBSD OS. These options work much as they do in FreeBSD.

FFS is also supported by many commercial UNIX OSs, such as Solaris. As noted earlier, though, FFS has mutated over the years, so these OSs may not be able to mount the FreeBSD version of FFS.

Although Linux is a reimplementation of UNIX and therefore doesn't share direct descent from BSD, it does include FFS drivers, available under the name *UFS* (using the `-t ufs` parameter to Linux's `mount` command). In fact, Linux's FFS driver includes support for several different FFS variants. You specify which you want to use with the `ufstype` option, which should be set to `44bsd` to access a FreeBSD partition. Thus, you might use a command like the following to mount a FreeBSD partition:

```
# mount -t ufs -o ufstype=44bsd /dev/hda10 /mnt/freebsd
```

One important prerequisite for mounting FreeBSD partitions in Linux is support for the BSD partition scheme. Ordinarily, Linux uses *x86*-style primary, extended, and logical partitions; it doesn't use the BSD-style partitions. To access BSD partitions, therefore, you must enable the Linux kernel option called BSD Disklabel (BSD Partition Tables) Support, which is in the Partition Types submenu of the Filesystems kernel configuration menu. Your Linux distribution may or may not ship with this option enabled. If it's not active, you have to recompile your Linux kernel. Consult a Linux system administration book, such as Richard Petersen's *Linux: The Complete Reference, 4th Edition* (McGraw-Hill/ Osborne, 2000) or Vicki Stanfield's and my *Linux System Administration, 2nd Edition* (Sybex, 2002), for further information on how to do this. Once this feature is added, Linux treats the FreeBSD slice as if it were an extended partition. The FreeBSD partitions within the slice become available using partition numbers of 5 and up, or starting with the number after the last logical partition.

If the BSD slice uses a partition number less than the extended partition, adding or removing BSD partition support to Linux will alter the numbering of logical partitions because Linux numbers logical or FreeBSD partitions according to the order of the extended partition or FreeBSD slice in which they reside. This partition numbering change in turn can render Linux unbootable until you alter your Linux `/etc/fstab` *file to reflect these changes. These problems won't occur if your extended partition has a smaller number than the FreeBSD slice.*

Linux's FFS support is imperfect. In particular, read/write support is compiled separately from read-only support, and the read/write support is considered experimental. Thus, you may not be able to write to FreeBSD partitions, even if you've compiled the basic FFS support into the Linux kernel. If you need to write to an FFS partition, I advise caution because it's possible that Linux will damage the partition.

Caveats Concerning Foreign Access

The same sorts of caveats apply to accessing FreeBSD filesystems from non-BSD OSs as apply to accessing non-BSD filesystems from FreeBSD. In particular, you may not be able to access FreeBSD's filesystems from non-BSD UNIX-like OSs, even if those OSs nominally support FFS, because of FFS divergence over the years. Even when you can mount the filesystems, you may notice discrepancies in the apparent owners and groups of files, if your UIDs and GIDs aren't consistent across installations. Some foresight in creating users and groups can go a long way towards minimizing these problems.

Of more concern is the possibility of file corruption, particularly when using Linux's read/write FFS support. You should back up your FreeBSD files before writing to an FFS partition from Linux. Linux's read-only FFS support is much less dangerous, though, so if you just want to read some FreeBSD files, there should be little problem.

Running Non-BSD Programs in FreeBSD

A wide array of software is available in FreeBSD, but on occasion, you may find you need to run a program that's not available for FreeBSD. Rather than use a second computer or dual-boot into another OS, you may be able to use one of several tools that enable FreeBSD to run programs intended for other OSs. One of the most reliable of these is FreeBSD's Linux emulation, which lets FreeBSD run Linux programs. Other tools let you run Windows programs or run any *x*86 OS within an entire emulated computer.

Running Linux Programs

Despite their different pedigrees, FreeBSD and Linux are very similar OSs. Indeed, in many cases the same source code can compile and run on either OS. For this reason, the vast majority of open source programs that run on one OS also run natively on the other. Not all programs are open source, though, and some commercial programs are available for Linux but not for FreeBSD. For this reason, FreeBSD provides the ability to run Linux programs. This support involves a number of libraries and support packages. After you've installed these, you can run Linux programs almost as if they were FreeBSD programs. Because FreeBSD and Linux use nearly identical system calls, there's no need to use extensive emulation routines when running Linux programs. Linux programs therefore run at roughly the same speed under FreeBSD as they do under Linux. Memory is impacted, though, because the Linux programs require Linux-compatible system libraries, many of which duplicate the functionality in FreeBSD's standard libraries.

Preparing to Run Linux Programs

FreeBSD isn't configured to run Linux programs in a basic installation. To do this, perform these steps:

1. **Install the Linux base port.**   The `linux_base` package includes the core Linux libraries and support tools. Most of these reside in the `/compat/linux` directory tree. You can install this package as you do other packages, as described in Chapter 11.

2. **Configure hostname resolution.**   Some Linux programs have problems resolving hostnames into IP addresses when run with the default configuration. If you have this problem, you should edit the `/compat/linux/etc/host.conf` file so that it contains the following lines:

   ```
   order hosts,bind
   multi on
   ```

3. **Start the Linux compatibility mode.**   Type **linux** to start the Linux compatibility mode. Thereafter you should be able to run Linux programs. If you want your system to enable this mode automatically after you boot, add the following line to your `/etc/rc.conf` file, if it's not already present:

   ```
   linux_enable="YES"
   ```

At this point, FreeBSD should support Linux binaries. To check that it does, you can use the `kldstat` program, which returns information on kernel modules loaded on your system, including FreeBSD's Linux compatibility module. A properly working Linux support layer should produce output that resembles the following:

```
$ kldstat
Id Refs Address    Size     Name
 1    5 0xc0100000 3ef2dc   kernel
 2    1 0xc1cb2000 16000    linux.ko
```

There may be more lines displaying additional modules. The key is that a line referencing the `linux.ko` kernel module should be present, such as the line with an ID of 2 in the preceding example.

Reconfiguring and Running Linux Programs

FreeBSD and Linux use the same basic format for their program files. This format is known as the *Executable and Linking Format (ELF)*. Although the basic format is the same, a few details differ, and these sometimes cause FreeBSD to not recognize Linux binaries as valid. If FreeBSD reports that a Linux binary isn't valid, you must use the `brandelf` program to mark the program file in a way that FreeBSD recognizes. Specifically, you use a command similar to the following:

```
# brandelf -t Linux linux-binary
```

In this example, *linux-binary* is the name of the binary program file you want to run. In some cases, the program should now work as if it were a FreeBSD program; try typing its name and see if it runs. Text-mode programs should create normal output, and X programs should open windows and run. In fact, it is difficult to spot a Linux program as such, judging only by its user interface.

Unfortunately, Linux programs frequently require libraries that aren't installed on your FreeBSD system. To be more precise, Linux programs require *Linux* libraries. Having a native FreeBSD version of a library isn't sufficient; you must install a Linux version of the library. The bulk of the `linux_base` package is just that—libraries upon which many Linux programs rely. This package, however, cannot be comprehensive, so you may need to track down Linux versions of libraries.

One way to do this tracking is to use the `ldd` command, in either Linux or FreeBSD. The result should resemble the following, as applied to the `ls` binary from Caldera OpenLinux 3.1 in a FreeBSD 4.4 system:

```
$ ldd ls
ls:
ls: /lib/libc.so.6: version `GLIBC_2.2' not found (required by ls)
        libc.so.6 => /lib/libc.so.6 (0x28068000)
        /lib/ld-linux.so.2 => /lib/ld-linux.so.2 (0x28053000)
```

Note *This example uses a recent version of Linux and an old version of FreeBSD because it demonstrates the fact that old libraries (in FreeBSD 4.4's Linux compatibility package) may not work with newer binaries (the common `ls` binary in the more recent Caldera 3.1).*

In this particular case, the `ls` program relies upon two libraries: `libc.so.6` and `ld-linux.so.2`. Both exist, but the `libc.so.6` version is too old for the `ls` program in question, hence the message that `GLIBC_2.2` wasn't found. It's also possible that a required library might not exist at all on the FreeBSD system.

In either case, the solution is to copy the required libraries from a Linux system (or from a Linux library package) to the `/compat/linux` directory tree on your FreeBSD system. In this specific case, the Caldera Linux system has a `/lib/libc.so.6` file that's actually a symbolic link to `/lib/libc-2.2.1.so`. To get this working, you should do the following:

1. Copy the actual library file (`/lib/libc-2.2.1.so`) to your `/compat/linux` directory tree—that is, copy `libc-2.2.1.so` to `/compat/linux/lib`.

2. Create a symbolic link that mirrors what's present on the Linux system. For instance, link `libc-2.2.1.so` to `libc.so.6`. If necessary, replace any existing link that points to an older library.

You may need to repeat this procedure for several libraries. In some cases, fixing one problem reveals another. For instance, in the case of Caldera 3.1's ls as run from FreeBSD 4.4, updating libc.so.6 reveals that ld-linux.so.2 also needs updating, so the process must be repeated for that library. When this is all done, the program should run, although some programs produce harmless error messages. For instance, Caldera 3.1's ls as run in FreeBSD 4.4 complains that fstat64 and setup are obsolete system calls.

Rather than upgrade libraries on a case-by-case basis, you may want to look for an updated version of the linux_base package. Installing it may be much simpler than tracking down many updated libraries.

Linux binary compatibility has a few other limits of which you should be aware. Although most facilities available on Linux are also available on FreeBSD, some aren't, or are implemented in different ways in FreeBSD. One important consideration is the /proc filesystem. This filesystem gives programs access to various types of system information. Its details differ between Linux and FreeBSD, so if a Linux program relies upon information obtained from /proc, that program may not function correctly when run in FreeBSD.

On the whole, FreeBSD's Linux binary compatibility is very useful for running commercial (or at least non-open-source) programs such as WordPerfect, StarOffice, Oracle, VMware, and Quake. In most cases, access to the source code makes Linux binary compatibility unimportant for open source programs.

Using WINE to Run Windows Programs

Unfortunately, most programs that aren't available for FreeBSD also aren't available for Linux, so FreeBSD's Linux compatibility, although useful, is of limited applicability. The bulk of the programs you're likely to want to run that aren't for UNIX systems generally are Windows programs. Although Windows has borrowed some concepts and even code from the UNIX world, it's a very different OS, so running Windows programs on FreeBSD isn't as easy as running Linux programs. That said, there are projects underway to add Windows compatibility to FreeBSD's feature list. Arguably the most important of these is *WINE* (which stands for either *Windows Emulator* or *WINE Is Not an Emulator*, depending upon who you ask). WINE is an open source project designed to implement the Windows application programming interface (API) under UNIX-like OSs, including FreeBSD. This means that programs can use Windows calls to open dialog boxes, display text, and so on. WINE also includes a way to load and run Windows executables and to provide various other supports necessary to run Windows programs. The end result is that Windows programs can run under FreeBSD.

WINE is an ambitious project, particularly given that its task is to hit a "moving target"—Microsoft keeps expanding and changing the Windows API, and parts of it aren't publicly documented. Thus, in 2002 WINE is still imperfect, despite having been in existence for close to a decade. Overall, WINE is good enough to run some programs, including some important ones; but it's not good enough to run *all* Windows programs. You may need to experiment with your WINE and application configurations to get programs running. For the latest information on WINE, including the most recent source code and a database of programs that have been tested under WINE, consult the WINE home page, at `http://www.winehq.com`.

Installing and Configuring WINE

The easiest way to install WINE is to use `sysinstall` to download a prebuilt package. WINE is listed in the Emulators category. Alternatively, you can download source code from the WINE web site, an FTP archive site, or a *Concurrent Versioning System (CVS)* site, and compile it yourself. This may yield a more current version of WINE; CVS is always up-to-date, and source code tarballs are released every week or two, whereas the version available as a FreeBSD package may be a few months out of date.

Whatever method you use to install WINE, installing the package alone isn't enough to get it working; you must do some post-installation configuration. This is done mainly through the WINE configuration file, `wine.conf`. In a default configuration, this file resides in `/usr/local/etc`, so look for it there. (A standard installation comes with a `wine.conf.sample` file, which you can copy or rename to `wine.conf`.) WINE itself doesn't always look in this directory, though. It first looks for the `config` file in the `.wine` subdirectory of the user's home directory. You can copy `/usr/local/etc/wine.conf` to `~/.wine/config` or create a symbolic link. Copying the file enables different users to have different WINE configurations.

Whether you copy or link the WINE configuration file, its format resembles that of the old Windows 3.1 `WIN.INI` file. Specifically, the file contains sections, whose names appear in square brackets (`[ ]`). These sections define how WINE maps FreeBSD directories to Windows drives, what serial ports and similar hardware are available to WINE, and so on. The default configuration file is a good starting point, but you'll almost certainly have to make some changes. Important changes you might want to make include

- **Drive C:** Windows normally boots, at least partly, from a partition it identifies as `C:`. In most cases, certain special directories, such as `WINDOWS` and `WINDOWS\SYSTEM`, reside on this partition. If your system includes a Windows installation, you may want to locate the `[Drive C]` section of the WINE configuration file and point it to your mounted Windows partition. For instance, if you've mounted the Windows `C:` drive at `/windows`, set the `Path` option to point to this directory. (In most installations, `Path` defaults to `/c`.) If your FreeBSD system doesn't dual-boot to Windows, you should create an appropriate path and at least create the appropriate directories, even if they're empty. For instance, you might type **mkdir -p /windows/windows/system**. If WINE can't find these directories, it won't run any Windows programs.

- **Drive A:** Windows addresses the floppy disk as A:. WINE's default configuration file maps this to /mnt/fd0, which doesn't exist in most FreeBSD installations. You may need to modify this path to point to whatever mount point you normally use for floppy disks.

- **Data drives** You must point WINE to whatever directories hold your program files. If they reside in your home directory, the standard [Drive F] definition should work; otherwise, you must create a new drive definition with a unique letter label. You should be able to copy the default [Drive C] definition and modify it for your purposes. Be sure to change the drive letter and the Path and Label specifications.

- **DLL options** Windows *dynamic link libraries (DLLs)* are similar to FreeBSD libraries; they contain code that may be used by many programs. Windows ships with many DLLs, and some programs ship with others. WINE can use Windows DLLs, but in some cases it works better with its own reimplementation of the DLL functions. The [DllOverrides] section tells WINE whether to favor native Windows DLLs or its own built-in DLLs. Of course, to use Windows DLLs, you must make them available (typically in the C:\WINDOWS\SYSTEM directory).

- **X options** The [x11drv] section hosts various options relating to how WINE interacts with X. Of particular interest, the Managed option determines whether WINE creates its own window borders (N) or uses your standard X window manager (Y); and Desktop, if uncommented, tells WINE to create a single window in which it launches the application you run.

There are many additional options in the WINE configuration file, but describing them all is beyond the scope of this chapter. Consult the WINE documentation for more detail, or read the comments associated with each option.

Of course, you must make Windows programs available to WINE. Normally, this is handled through the data drives configuration, as just described. You can copy Windows programs to your FreeBSD system, or run programs from a network file server, provided you can mount the file shares in FreeBSD.

You can run both Samba and NFS on a FreeBSD system, as described in Chapter 18, to make programs available to both Windows systems and FreeBSD systems. Of course, you should ensure that your programs' licenses permit this.

Running Windows Programs

You invoke WINE by typing its program name (wine) followed by the name of the program you want to run. For instance, the following command runs the Windows Solitaire program that ships with Windows Me, if the Windows C: partition is mounted at /windows:

```
$ wine /windows/windows/sol.exe
```

The first time you launch WINE, it's likely to take quite some time to start up (possibly well over a minute), while it parses your fonts and creates auto-generated configuration files in your `~/.wine` directory. Subsequent launches of WINE should take less time. The result, if all goes well, is a Windows program running in FreeBSD. For instance, Figure 4-2 shows the result of the preceding command. (This installation used the `Managed X` option to enable the default X window manager to handle the Windows window.).

Some Windows programs run well using a fairly standard WINE configuration. Others don't run at all. In between are the difficult cases—programs that *can* be made to run, but only by setting unusual WINE configuration options. The WINE web site includes information on some of these programs. You may also be able to obtain help from the WINE Usenet newsgroup, `comp.emulators.ms-windows.wine`. As a general rule, the smaller, older, and more common a program is, the more likely it can be made to run well under WINE.

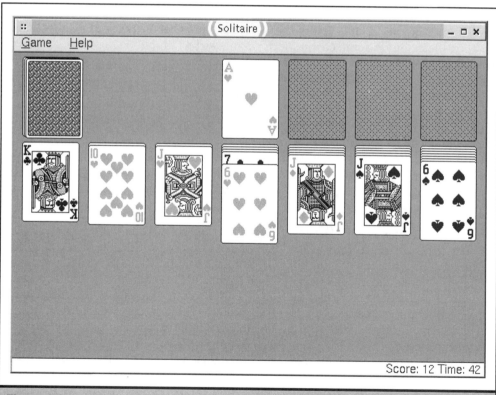

Figure 4-2. *WINE enables you to run Windows programs from FreeBSD's X environment*

Using an Emulator

The acronym WINE, as noted earlier, stands for two contradictory things: *Windows Emulator* and *WINE Is Not an Emulator*. This state of affairs developed because the word *emulator* means different things to different people. To some, an emulator is any program that enables you to run programs for one OS on another. To others, an emulator needs to perform low-level hardware emulation. In most peoples' eyes, FreeBSD's Linux compatibility isn't emulation (although it's grouped with emulators in the FreeBSD package list) and WINE is borderline. However you classify these tools, though, FreeBSD does support packages that are more clearly emulators. Many of these are available from the Emulators package list in `sysinstall`.

Many of the emulators available in FreeBSD serve specialized functions. These tools emulate game consoles or obscure older computers, such as the Commodore 64. If you remember such systems with fondness, you may want to investigate these emulators. You may even have a serious need to run such a tool.

A few other emulators are more serious. These enable you to run an entire modern OS within a simulated computer managed by FreeBSD. For instance, VMware (`http://www.vmware.com`) sets up a simulated *x86* computer in which you can run DOS, most versions of Windows, Linux, FreeBSD, or various other OSs. VMware does an excellent job at this task, but at some cost in performance—the emulated OS seems sluggish, particularly with video operations. Nonetheless, compatibility is much better than with WINE, if your goal is to run Windows programs.

VMware is actually not a FreeBSD program; it's a Linux program. Thus, you must run VMware using FreeBSD's Linux compatibility mode. The VMware package available in the `sysinstall` Emulators package section helps set up VMware to work with this mode, but it sets up only a demonstration version of the program. To continue using it beyond the demonstration period you must buy a license from VMware.

Summary

As a practical matter, FreeBSD systems must often coexist with other OSs. In some cases, you may only need to occasionally read files from a DOS floppy disk, ISO-9660 CD-ROM, or the like. In other cases, FreeBSD dual-boots with another OS, which requires configuring your system to boot either OS on command. You may also require a reliable method for exchanging large files between the OSs. In other cases, you may need to run non-FreeBSD programs on your FreeBSD system. Fortunately, FreeBSD includes mechanisms for doing all these things. FreeBSD includes excellent support for the FAT filesystem used by DOS and Windows, and supported equally well by most non-Microsoft OSs. This support allows for data exchange on both floppies and hard disks. FreeBSD's Linux software compatibility expands your software options to include commercial programs that have been released for Linux but not for FreeBSD. WINE and full-blown emulators let you run Windows programs, or even programs for other OSs, on your FreeBSD system. These tools can help you make the transition from a Windows to a FreeBSD workstation, or run exotic programs that aren't available for FreeBSD.

The
Complete
Reference

Part II

Basic System Administration

The
Complete
Reference

FreeBSD

Chapter 5

System Administration Tools

art II of this book is devoted to *system administration*—tasks that involve changes to the OS as a whole, the software installed on it, or the accounts of ordinary users. Parts III, IV, and VI also describe administrative tasks, while Part II is an introduction to the most fundamental system administration tasks. System administration tasks contrast with ordinary user tasks, such as running a word processor, performing data analysis, or writing ordinary programs. Part V covers these topics.

In this context, this chapter can be considered an introduction to the introduction to system administration. It lays out the fundamental tools and files you use in performing administrative tasks. This chapter begins with a look at the /etc directory tree, which is where most administrative files reside. Because most FreeBSD system administration is done by editing text files stored in /etc, it's vital that you know how to use at least one FreeBSD text editor. This chapter introduces a couple of common ones (vi and gEdit) and points you to many others. You should be familiar with the many basic system administration commands, so this chapter introduces them. These commands tell you important things about your system or let you change general system parameters. Finally, this chapter concludes with a brief look at GUI administrative tools. Such tools have traditionally been disparaged in the UNIX world generally, but they can be useful in certain circumstances, such as when inexperienced people need to be able to perform limited system administration.

The /etc Directory and Its Contents

FreeBSD encourages programs to follow certain conventions in the placement of files, and of course most of the programs that ship with FreeBSD follow these standards. (The section "Understanding the FHS" in Chapter 7 covers these conventions in more detail.) One of the conventions is that system configuration files reside in the /etc directory tree. In many cases, a program names its configuration file after itself, or creates a directory named after itself in which it stores multiple configuration files. Other configuration files in /etc aren't tied to specific programs, though, or are named in peculiar ways. Whatever their names, the files you're likely to find in /etc are covered in this section, at least in broad strokes. You'll find many files in /etc that aren't explicitly mentioned here because you've installed software that's not described in this book or because the files fill relatively minor roles.

Note   *Not all programs place configuration files in /etc. Some don't use configuration files at all. Others place their files in unusual locations. Some configuration files can be found in /usr/local/etc instead of /etc. Still more rely exclusively upon user-specific configuration files, which reside in users' home directories. Such files typically are dot files (their names begin with dots, to hide them from casual use of ls) named after the programs themselves.*

This discussion groups the /etc configuration files into three classes: system startup files, which control FreeBSD's boot process once the kernel has loaded; server configuration files, which control the operation of various servers; and miscellaneous configuration files, which control user programs or general system settings.

System Startup Files

Chapter 3 includes a description of the FreeBSD boot process. As described there, the computer runs through several steps, starting with running code in the BIOS and moving on to the boot loader and booting the FreeBSD kernel. The kernel then kicks off the /sbin/init program, which controls the FreeBSD startup process—meaning the processes that run under FreeBSD, as opposed to those that run before the kernel boots.

In FreeBSD (as in many OSs), a program must be launched by another program. The program that launches the second program is said to be the *parent* of that second program, and the second program is a *child* of the first. A running program is often referred to as a *process*, and each process has a unique *process ID (PID)*, which is a number that's associated with a process. Creating a new process is often called *spawning*.

The relationships between parents, children, PIDs, and so on relates to system startup files because the init process is the parent (or more distant ancestor) of all processes. The kernel runs init when it starts, and init's configuration file is /etc/rc. (Actually, /etc/rc is a shell script—init spawns the /bin/sh shell to run the /etc/rc script.) Thus, /etc/rc controls the boot process. This script controls what processes run when the system starts. If you change /etc/rc or the files upon which it relies, you change how FreeBSD behaves.

Note   *FreeBSD uses a startup scheme that's generally known as the* BSD startup *method. Some other UNIX-like OSs, such as most Linux distributions, use an entirely different startup system known as* SysV startup scripts. *The BSD approach uses a few large scripts, whereas the SysV approach uses many smaller scripts. SysV also supports a feature known as* run levels; *each numbered run level supports a unique set of running servers and other processes. The BSD startup method, and hence FreeBSD, doesn't support this feature.*

The /etc/rc script does many things, such as checking disks if they weren't shut down correctly, cleaning old files out of the /var directory tree, and activating swap space. Many other tasks it delegates, by calling other scripts in /etc whose names begin with rc, such as rc.serial and rc.network. These files collectively control the FreeBSD startup process—they're the main startup configuration files.

These BSD startup scripts are just that—*scripts*. Thus, a knowledge of shell scripting, as described in Chapter 31, can help if you want to make anything more than trivial changes to your system's configuration. Even without understanding shell scripting, though, if you understand the nature of the changes you want to make, you may be able to make those changes by locating the call to whatever program sets the option you want to adjust and changing that call. (In this context, a *call* is a reference to a program that causes that program to run. It might be nothing more than the name of the program on a line in the script.)

 Modifying the FreeBSD startup scripts is a potentially dangerous undertaking. If you err, the computer may not boot at all. What's worse, you may not realize you've made an error until days, weeks, or even months later, if you don't reboot your computer immediately after making a change. I recommend you make a backup of any system startup script before you modify it, and reboot immediately after making the change. If the system then fails to boot, you can use an emergency system to restore the original file or try again.

You might edit two other files or file classes to alter the startup routine: the /etc/rc.local script and scripts in the /usr/local/etc/rc.d directory. Both are designed to accept customizations, but the second is the favored tool in recent versions of FreeBSD. Chapter 6 describes customizing these scripts in more detail.

 Both the /etc/rc.local file and the /usr/local directory names contain the word local. This word refers to the system-specific nature of the programs or files referenced or contained therein, as contrasted with standard tools that can be found on most FreeBSD systems.

Server Configuration Files

A second class of configuration files found in /etc are those related to specific servers. Many of these files are covered in greater detail in subsequent chapters of this book, and particularly in Part IV. As a quick introduction and so that you know what some of these files are, here are several of the more important server configuration files and directories:

■ **X files** The /etc/XF86Config file and /etc/X11 directory control the XFree86 X server and affiliated programs, such as the X Display Manager (XDM) GUI login program. Chapter 13 covers the XF86Config file in more detail.

■ **Apache files** The /usr/local/etc/apache directory contains files for configuring the popular Apache web server. Most importantly, httpd.conf is the main configuration file; other files in the directory are support files. Chapter 20 covers the basics of Apache configuration.

■ **/etc/exports** This file specifies directories that FreeBSD is to make available via the Network File System (NFS) file server, as described in Chapter 18.

■ **TCP Wrappers files** The TCP Wrappers program is an important security package used by many servers. It uses the /etc/hosts.allow and /etc/hosts.deny configuration files. This package is described in Chapter 29.

- **Host access files**   The `/etc/hosts.equiv` file is used by several servers to specify remote computers that can gain access to local servers. The `/etc/hosts.lpd` file serves a similar function, but only for the standard FreeBSD print server.

- **`/etc/inetd.conf`**   This file is extraordinarily important because it controls `inetd`, which is the standard FreeBSD *super server*. This program stands in for several other servers, launching the appropriate target server only when required. This configuration can reduce memory consumption when the computer runs many seldom-used servers, and `inetd` can use TCP Wrappers to provide some uniform access control mechanisms to all the servers it controls. The "Using a Super Server" section of Chapter 16 describes `inetd.conf` configuration.

- **`/etc/mail`**   This directory holds various configuration and control files for sendmail, the standard FreeBSD Simple Mail Transfer Protocol (SMTP) server. The `/etc/mail/sendmail.cf` file is the main sendmail control file, but it's generated from the `/etc/mail/freebsd.mc` file, as described in Chapter 19.

- **`/usr/local/etc/smb.conf`**   This file configures Samba, the file and print server for Microsoft Windows clients. A default Samba installation creates a file called `/usr/local/etc/smb.conf.default`. You should copy this file to `/usr/local/etc/smb.conf` and modify it as described in Chapter 18 if you want to use Samba.

- **SSH files**   The Secure Shell (SSH) package provides encrypted remote login capabilities. The `/etc/ssh` directory contains files for configuring both SSH clients (`ssh_config`) and servers (`sshd_config`).

This list is not complete; there are many servers for FreeBSD, and this book can't even mention more than a fraction of them. If you install a server that's not described in this book, it may have a configuration file in `/etc` or `/usr/local/etc` that's not described here. Consult the server's documentation for details. In addition, this list includes server configuration files that may not be present on your computer because the relevant servers may not be installed. If you want to run such a server, consult Chapter 11 for information on doing so.

In addition to the server configuration files mentioned here, most servers need a way to start up. You can often do this by adding a file to `/usr/local/etc/rc.d`, as described earlier, in "System Startup Files;" or by adding an entry to `/etc/inetd.conf`, as described in Chapter 16.

Miscellaneous Configuration Files

Some configuration files relate to startup scripts or specific servers, as just described. Others set general system parameters or are more loosely affiliated with particular servers or startup procedures. Some of these have already been mentioned, such as the

TCP Wrappers configuration files. This section covers a few other important configuration files. These include

- **/etc/crontab** FreeBSD ships with a utility called crontab that's used to run programs at scheduled times. These *cron jobs*, as they're called, enable you to configure the system to automatically perform routine maintenance tasks, as described in Chapter 28. The /etc/crontab file controls the system cron jobs. Its format is described in Chapter 6.

- **/etc/dhclient.conf** Some computers use the Dynamic Host Configuration Protocol (DHCP) client program, dhclient, to automatically obtain an IP address and associated network information from a DHCP server. The dhclient configuration file is /etc/dhclient.conf. It can usually be left alone, but you may need to set options in this file on some networks. Chapter 14 covers this topic.

- **/etc/fstab** This file is critically important for partition and filesystem management. The name is short for *filesystem table;* the file contains information on partitions, the filesystems they use, and where they should be mounted in FreeBSD's directory tree. Chapter 7 covers this topic in more detail.

- **/etc/printcap** FreeBSD's printer handling relies upon a *printer capabilities* file, called /etc/printcap. This file lists printers, what hardware or remote computers FreeBSD uses to connect to them, what software FreeBSD uses to process files sent to them, and so on. Chapter 9 covers this topic in more detail.

- **/etc/resolv.conf** This file tells FreeBSD what name servers to use to convert Internet hostnames into IP addresses. Chapter 14 describes this file in more detail.

- **User and group files** The /etc/passwd, /etc/master.passwd, and /etc/group files hold information on user accounts and groups. You edit one or more of these files when making changes to user accounts, as described in Chapter 10. (It's often desirable to use specialized tools to make these changes, rather than editing the files directly with a text editor.)

As with other configuration file lists in this chapter, this list is not complete. Some of these files might not be present or might not be used on your system, but most of them are present on most systems. Additional files may be important for particular configurations.

An Overview of FreeBSD Text Editors

Before you can edit configuration files to get your system working the way you want it to work, you must be able to edit files in general. This section therefore describes some of FreeBSD's text editor options, including sample sessions with two editors.

Text editors can be categorized in many different ways. One of the most fundamental is the difference between text-mode text editors and GUI text editors. Even if you prefer to work in a GUI environment, you should be familiar with at least one text-mode text editor because you'll probably have to use such an editor in emergency recovery situations. Some people prefer using text-mode text editors even in a GUI environment.

Note *Text editors are distinct from word processors. The former edit plain text files with minimal formatting and no special fonts. Text editors are most often used to edit configuration files, plain-text documentation files, and so on. Word processors are more often used to generate output that's intended to be printed or that requires special formatting. You can use a text editor in conjunction with a formatting package such as TeX to do the work of a word processor, though, and some people prefer this approach to using a word processor. If you want to know about word processing in FreeBSD, consult Chapter 25.*

Text-Mode Text Editors

In some sense, text-mode text editors are the most flexible variety because they can be run both in a text-only environment and from an xterm window in a GUI environment. Thus, in theory you need only learn one editor to do all your text editing in FreeBSD. In practice, though, you're likely to have to be at least passingly familiar with several editors because one editor or another may be set as the default for certain operations, or may be included on emergency recovery systems.

The range of text-mode text editors is quite broad, but the most popular editors are

- **vi** This editor's history goes back to the early days of UNIX. It uses an unusual three-mode user interface, which some people find confusing. Despite its peculiarities, though, vi is a popular editor. Its simplicity hides a great deal of flexibility, so it's retained a devoted following through the years. vi is also a small editor, which makes it an excellent choice for inclusion on many emergency recovery systems. For these reasons, the upcoming section, "Example: Editing a File with vi," describes the use of vi in greater detail. vi is actually a small family of similar editors, including such variants as Vim and Elvis. At the level they're described in this book, though, these editors are all essentially identical.

- **Emacs** Emacs and vi are, in many respects, diametric opposites. vi's simplicity and small size lie in stark contrast to Emacs' complexity and large size. A standard joke in the UNIX world is that UNIX is a program launcher, and Emacs is the OS—and everything else. In addition to working as a text editor, Emacs can function as an integrated development environment (IDE) for programming, a Usenet news reader, a mail reader, a web browser, and more. Emacs is available both in its original form and as a variant project, XEmacs. Emacs is a very popular editor, but to keep this book's size manageable, it's not covered in any detail here.

- **Small Emacs clones**   Users who like Emacs but who want something slimmer for use on emergency disks or the like have a choice of several different slimmed-down Emacs clones. These programs include jed, joe, jove, and uemacs (aka micro-Emacs). FreeBSD includes many of these tools, so if you don't like vi but need a small text-mode editor, you can load one or more of these instead of or in addition to vi.

- **Easy Editor**   This is a small editor that you use when editing files during the FreeBSD installation process. Chapter 2 includes a brief discussion of the use of this editor. You can run it by typing **ee**, optionally followed by the filename you want to edit.

This list of editors is not meant to be comprehensive. Over the years, many text-mode text editors have been developed. If you don't like any of the editors described here, you may want to browse the Editors package section using the sysinstall utility and try several different editors. Note that this section includes both text-mode and GUI editors, as well as add-on packages and the like, so it may not be obvious which packages are suitable editors for you to try.

Although they're not editors, one additional type of program deserves mention: *pagers*. These programs display a text file one page at a time. The original UNIX pager was known as more, and it's still a standard part of FreeBSD. Indeed, the man program (described in the upcoming section, "man") uses more as its default pager. Over the years, more's limitations have become apparent, and in a twist of humor, an improved version was released under the name less.

To use a pager, type the pager name followed by the name of the file you want to view—**less file.txt**, for example. The file should then appear. Press the SPACEBAR to move through the document a page at a time, or use the ARROW keys to move a line at a time. Pressing ESC followed by the less-than (**<**) key moves to the start of the file, and pressing ESC followed by greater-than (**>**) moves to the end of the file (in the case of more, this action also exits the program). You can search for text by typing a slash (**/**) followed immediately by the text for which you want to search. These pagers, and particularly less, support assorted additional features. You may want to consult their man pages (by typing **man more** and **man less**) to learn more about them.

GUI Text Editors

Particularly if you're coming to FreeBSD from a Windows or Mac OS background, chances are good that you're used to GUI text editors. You'll find plenty of selection in GUI text editors for FreeBSD, too, so if you like GUI text editors, chances are you can find one that suits your working style. Examples of editors in this class include the following:

- **Emacs**   One of Emacs' many features is support for X-based operation. The traditional Emacs includes relatively limited X support, although this support has been increasing with each new release. Emacs can run in a separate X window, and provides a few menus, and so on, but it's not very fully integrated into X. One of the features of XEmacs is increased X integration, so you may want to look into XEmacs if you like Emacs but want an X-based editor. (XEmacs can also function in text mode.)

- **NEdit**   This editor, headquartered at `http://nedit.org`, is designed to be comfortable to users familiar with Windows or Mac OS GUI editors. Although it's not as powerful as Emacs, it includes a lot of features and so is useable as a programmer's editor or for other intensive text-editing tasks.

- **gEdit**   This text editor is a standard part of the GNU Network Object Model Environment (GNOME), and so is easily accessed from the GNOME menus, if you run GNOME as your default environment. It's a capable but fairly basic editor. Because of its ready availability in many default GNOME installations, it's the editor described in more detail in the upcoming section, "Example: Editing a File with gEdit."

- **xedit**   The `xedit` editor is a comparatively simple X-based text editor. It lacks many of the sophisticated features of Emacs or NEdit, but it's relatively small and can be a good choice if you're running on a slimmed-down FreeBSD system that nonetheless includes X.

As with text-based editors, this list is incomplete; it's meant to provide only a few pointers. Some of the text-based editors, including some `vi` and small Emacs clones, include X extensions, but most of these are limited in scope—they may open a separate window and provide a menu bar, but they don't always make full use of X, dialog boxes, fonts, and so on. You can locate a good selection of X-based editors from the Editors packages menu in `sysinstall`, or you can try a web search to locate others.

Example: Editing a File with vi

The `vi` editor is very capable, but as noted earlier, it's also a bit peculiar by today's standards. In particular, `vi` uses three separate operating *modes*. The editor responds differently to the same keystrokes depending upon the mode it's in, so it's important that you understand these modes. That said, `vi` supports the same general types of operations as does any other text editor—entering text, deleting text, pasting text, and so on. This section introduces some of these commands, but it's by no means an exhaustive review of `vi`'s capabilities—particularly its more advanced features. Finally, no text editor is any good unless you can save files, and of course `vi` provides the facility to do this.

Using vi Modes

The three operating modes of `vi` segment the editor's features; most features are available from just one mode. These three modes are

- **Command mode**   This mode enables you to enter commands to manipulate text or perform other actions. Most commands are single characters. For instance, o opens a line immediately below the current line. You can also move around the file in command mode by using your keyboard's ARROW keys.

- **Ex mode** This mode is devoted to extended operations involving outside files. Ultimately, ex mode is the key to vi's flexibility because it enables you to run outside programs to do interesting things with your file, such as perform a spell check or format a source code file in a standard way. You also use ex mode to save your file, as described in the upcoming section, "Saving Your Changes." To use ex mode, type a colon (:) and the ex mode command while in command mode.

- **Edit mode** This is the mode that most closely resembles most other text editors. In this mode, vi enters most characters you type into your document. An important exception to this rule is the ESC key, which returns you to command mode.

If you're not sure which mode you're in, press ESC. Doing so will ensure that you're in command mode.

These descriptions may seem a bit abstract. The distinction between these modes should become clear through an example editing session, which uses all three modes.

Editing a File

Before you can edit a file with vi, you need a file to edit. In principle, you could use any file. This example uses the /etc/fstab file, which FreeBSD uses to map partitions to directories in the FreeBSD directory tree. If you follow along, you'll add a couple of entries and delete another one from this file. In "real life," you might do this to make new filesystems or removable disk devices available or to render current partitions inaccessible. Because this is an example, you should first make a copy of the file so that you can work on the copy. From your home directory, type

```
$ cp /etc/fstab ./fstab-copy
```

Do not edit your real /etc/fstab file for this example. Doing so could render your FreeBSD system unbootable. Copy /etc/fstab to your home directory and edit the copy. You should also do this as an ordinary (non-root) user, to make it less likely that you'll mistakenly edit the real file and save the changes.

With this preliminary taken care of, you can begin your editing session:

1. Start vi and load **fstab-copy** into your vi buffer by typing **vi fstab-copy**. Figure 5-1 shows the result on my system when running vi from a GNOME Terminal window. If you're running in another type of xterm, the borders, fonts, and so on will be different, and if you're running in text mode, you'll see only the text. The tildes (~) running down the left side of the display are vi's way of

indicating the end of the file. The bottom line displays status information. Of course, your /etc/fstab file most likely won't exactly resemble the one in Figure 5-1, which doesn't matter because this procedure is just to show you how to edit text in the file.

2. Suppose you want to delete one of the entries in the file. For purposes of this demonstration, let's say it's the entry for the /windows directory. Move the cursor to this line by pressing DOWN ARROW seven times. The cursor should now rest on the line that begins /dev/ad0s1.

3. The command to delete text is entered in command mode, which is the mode in which vi starts. The command is dd, so type **dd**. You should see the line on which the cursor rests disappear. If you wanted to delete multiple lines, you could precede dd with the number of lines to be deleted, as in **3dd** to delete three lines.

4. Now suppose you want to enter a new line in place of the one you just deleted. Begin by opening up a blank line. Do this by typing **o** in command mode. The line below the one on which the cursor rests should move down, and the cursor should follow.

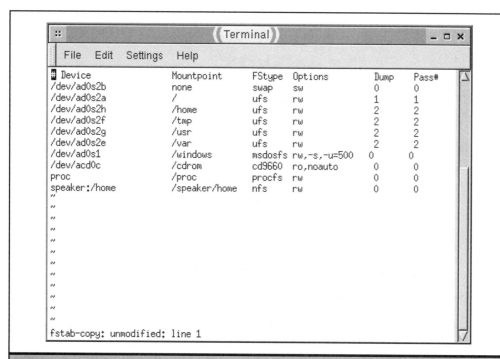

Figure 5-1. vi looks much like any other text-mode editor when running; its unique features relate to the commands you type into it.

5. To enter a new line, you must use edit mode. The o command you typed in the previous step actually placed you in edit mode. If you need to enter edit mode from command mode, you can do so by typing **i**. This command enters edit mode and configures vi to enable you to insert text. If you intended to replace existing text, you might prefer to type **R** instead. Typing **a** would enter edit mode and advance the cursor by one space.

6. Type a new line, such as

    ```
    /dev/da0s4      /zip      msdosfs      rw,noauto      0      0
    ```

7. Press ESC to return to command mode.

8. Now, suppose you want to create a variant of the line you've just entered to enable FreeBSD to mount Zip disks that use FFS rather than FAT. You can begin by typing **yy**. This is the yank command, which copies text to an internal buffer. Typing **yy** yanks one line of text, and preceding that string by a number (as in **4yy**) yanks multiple lines of text.

9. Type **p**. This command pastes text from the yank buffer. You should now have two identical new lines.

10. Use the ARROW keys to position the cursor on the space just after /zip in one of the two lines.

11. Type **R** to enter edit mode with vi configured to replace text.

12. Type **-ffs**, changing /zip to /zip-ffs.

13. Press ESC to return to command mode, and then press the ARROW keys to position the cursor over the m in msdosfs on the line you've just modified.

14. Type **R** to enter edit mode with vi configured to replace text.

15. Type **ufs** and four spaces, replacing msdosfs with ufs.

At this point, you've replaced the original /windows line with two lines for handling Zip disks. The other lines should be unchanged. You may want to experiment further with vi, duplicating, deleting, and editing existing lines and creating new lines. You might also want to experiment with some additional features:

- **Undo**   vi supports an undo feature. In command mode, type **u** to undo the last change you made. vi supports just one level of undo, so typing **u** twice in succession undoes the undo operation.

- **Search**   The slash (/) character in command mode initiates a search. For instance, from near the start of the file in Figure 5-1, you might type **/cd9660** and then press ENTER to position the cursor on the c in cd9660. A question mark (?) initiates a backwards search, rather than a forward search.

- **Replace**   If you want to replace all instances of some text with some other text, you can use the global replace feature. To do this, type **:%s/original/**

replacement in command mode, where *original* is the original text and *replacement* is the new text, and then press ENTER.

For information on still more `vi` commands, consult the `vi` documentation. The Vi IMproved web page at `http://www.vim.org` is a good source of information. If you find yourself using `vi` extensively, you might even consider buying a book on the editor.

Saving Your Changes

Before exiting from `vi`, you should know how it handles saving your changes. You may want to use several ex-mode commands to manipulate files and exit from the program:

- **:w** This command writes changes you've made. If you issue this command without any other option, it writes the changes using the filename from which the file was originally read. If you prefer to write your changes to a new file, though, you can add that filename, as in **:w new-file.txt** to save the changes as `new-file.txt`.

- **:e** If you start `vi` without specifying a filename, or if you want to edit a new file, this command enables you to edit a new file. For instance, **:e /etc/ printcap** loads the **/etc/printcap** file into `vi`. You can edit only one file at a time, though, and you may need to provide an override option, described shortly, to dump a file that you're currently editing in favor of a new one.

- **:r** This command works much like `:e`, but instead of loading a new file in place of an existing one, this command merges the two files under the first one's filename. This command can be very useful if you need to combine two files into one.

- **:q** This command quits from `vi`.

You can combine two or more of these commands into one command. One common example is **:wq**, which saves the current file and then quits.

Sometimes, you need to provide an override switch to get `vi` to abandon changes you've made. This is particularly common with the `:e` and `:q` commands if you've not saved any changes you've made to the current file. The override switch is the exclamation mark (`!`), so for instance, you might type **:q!** to quit without saving the changes you've made. You might do this if you've made a mess of your changes or if you realize you've been editing the wrong file.

Example: Editing a File with gEdit

Although text-mode editors are perfectly capable of editing all text-based FreeBSD configuration files, some people prefer to use GUI text editors. They frequently give you better control over on-screen fonts, colors, and so on, and the menu bar with command options makes it easier to determine how to perform certain tasks. Although every GUI text editor is different, the gEdit program is fairly typical of this breed, and it's readily available on many FreeBSD systems, so I describe its operation here.

Editing a File

As with the preceding example using `vi`, this example edits a copy of the `/etc/fstab` file. You should copy it to your home directory with this command:

```
$ cp /etc/fstab ./fstab-copy
```

Do not *edit your real* `/etc/fstab` *file for this example. Doing so could render your FreeBSD system unbootable. Copy* `/etc/fstab` *to your home directory and edit the copy. You should also do this as an ordinary (non-*`root`*) user, to make it less likely that you'll mistakenly edit the real file and save the changes.*

You must also start X, if it's not already running, as described in Chapter 3. You can then begin the editing process as follows:

1. Open an xterm window and type **gedit fstab-copy** to begin editing the file. The result should be a window resembling the one shown in Figure 5-2. As with the example using `vi`, the exact contents of the file may differ from what's shown in Figure 5-2, but that's unimportant for this example.

2. Suppose you want to delete an entry from this file, such as the `/windows` entry in Figure 5-2. You have several ways to do so. Most involve selecting the line and then deleting it. You can select a line by clicking and dragging with the mouse or by positioning the cursor with the mouse or ARROW keys at the start of the line and then pressing the DOWN ARROW while holding SHIFT.

3. To delete the selected line, click Cut in the button bar, select Edit | Cut from the menu, press CTRL-X, or press DELETE or BACKSPACE on the keyboard. The `/windows` line should disappear. If there's a blank line at this point, you can remove it by positioning the cursor on this line and pressing BACKSPACE.

4. Now suppose you want to add a new line. You can position your cursor at the start of a line you want to modify and type a new line, such as the following, ending it with a press of the ENTER key to separate it from the next line:

   ```
   /dev/da0s4      /zip      msdosfs      rw,noauto      0      0
   ```

5. Now suppose you want to create a variant of this line, which enables FreeBSD to mount Zip disks formatted with FreeBSD's FFS. You can begin by copying the line you've just typed into the gEdit clipboard. Do this by selecting the line (as in Step 2) and clicking Copy, selecting Edit | Copy from the menu bar, or pressing CTRL-C.

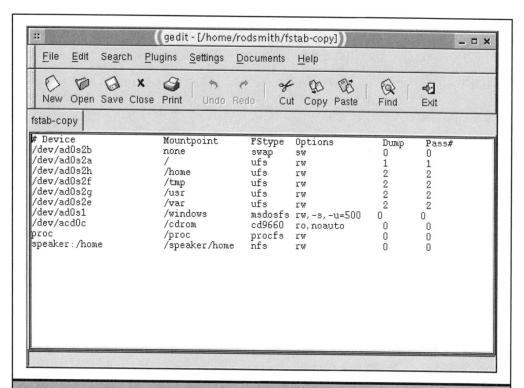

```
gedit - [/home/rodsmith/fstab-copy]                        _ □ ✕

File   Edit   Search   Plugins   Settings   Documents   Help

 New   Open  Save  Close  Print    Undo  Redo    Cut  Copy  Paste    Find    Exit

fstab-copy

# Device              Mountpoint       FStype   Options         Dump   Pass#
/dev/ad0s2b           none             swap     sw               0      0
/dev/ad0s2a           /                ufs      rw               1      1
/dev/ad0s2h           /home            ufs      rw               2      2
/dev/ad0s2f           /tmp             ufs      rw               2      2
/dev/ad0s2g           /usr             ufs      rw               2      2
/dev/ad0s2e           /var             ufs      rw               2      2
/dev/ad0s1            /windows         msdosfs  rw,-s,-u=500     0      0
/dev/acd0c            /cdrom           cd9660   ro,noauto        0      0
proc                  /proc            procfs   rw               0      0
speaker:/home         /speaker/home    nfs      rw               0      0
```

Figure 5-2.   *The gEdit editor is typical of GUI text editors, with its menu bar and other clickable options.*

6. Position the cursor at the start of another line and click the Paste button, select Edit | Paste, or press CTRL-V. The result should be a duplicate of the line you typed in Step 4. Depending upon precisely how you selected the line, you might have to press ENTER to separate it from the line on which you positioned the cursor.

7. Use the mouse or keyboard ARROW keys to position the cursor at the end of /zip.

8. Type **-ffs** to change /zip into /zip-ffs. You may want to press DELETE four times to remove four spaces, keeping columns in line.

9. Double-click the string msdosfs in the new line. Doing so should highlight the string.

10. Type **ufs**, which should replace msdosfs with ufs. You may want to press the space bar four times to keep the remaining columns aligned.

11. To save your changes, click Save, select File | Save from the menu bar, or press CTRL-S. Alternatively, to save the file under a new name, select File | Save As. This action opens a dialog box in which you can enter a new name for the file.

When you're completely finished editing a file, you can exit from the editor by clicking the Exit button, by choosing File | Exit, or by typing CTRL-Q. If gEdit notes any open files with unsaved changes at this point, it asks you if you want to save those changes.

Additional gEdit Features

You may want to experiment further with gEdit. Its options are accessible from the menu bar, and most are clearly labeled. Some specific features you might want to look into include

- **Undo** Selecting Edit | Undo or pressing CTRL-Z activates gEdit's undo feature, so you can back out of an erroneous change. You can perform this action several times, backing out of a string of changes.

- **Search** Clicking Search | Find or pressing F6 produces the Find dialog box shown in Figure 5-3. You can type a search phrase into the Search For field, select from among the various options, and click Find. To repeat a search, select Search | Find Again or press SHIFT-F6.

- **Replace** The gEdit search-and-replace function works much like the search function. Selecting Search | Replace or pressing F7 brings up the Replace dialog box, which looks much like the Search dialog box in Figure 5-3, except that it has an extra Replace With field and two extra buttons: Replace and Replace All.

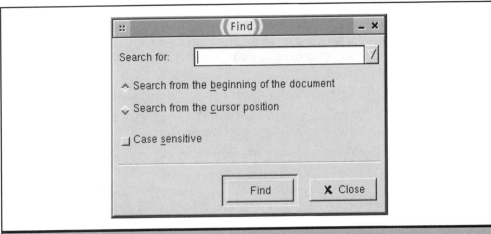

Figure 5-3. *The gEdit Find dialog box enables you to enter text you want to locate in a file.*

These buttons enable you to replace a single occurrence or all occurrences, respectively, of the Search For text with the Replace With text.

■ **Preferences**   Choose Settings | Preferences to open the Preferences dialog box, which includes tabs with various names where you can set assorted default behaviors. For instance, you can set gEdit's fonts and colors, and tell it whether to auto-indent text.

Unlike `vi`, gEdit is able to edit multiple files at once. If you select File | Open or press F3, gEdit displays a file selection dialog box that you can use to locate a new file. When you open it, a tab for the new file appears—Figure 5-2 shows just one tab, `fstab-copy`, but when multiple files are open, each file has its own tab. You can click the tabs to switch between files.

A Summary of Important Administrative Commands

Traditional FreeBSD administration involves both editing text files and issuing text-mode commands. Many upcoming chapters describe specific commands in detail, but this section presents an overview of many basic but important commands. You can type these commands from a text-mode login or in an xterm window. Some require `root` privileges to work, but most don't. These commands fall into two general categories: system information commands (which provide information about the system's current status or configuration) and system manipulation commands (which alter the system's configuration).

Although not technically commands, a topic that's related to basic commands is that of combining commands. This is typically done through a *pipe*, which is a link in which the first program's output is sent to the second program as input. You can create long pipes of simple programs to increase their utility. A related issue is *redirection*, in which a program's output is sent to a file, or the program takes a file's contents as input. Knowing how to use pipes and redirection is vitally important for many administrative tasks.

System Information Commands

These commands provide information on the operation of the computer. Their information can be useful when troubleshooting, in planning how to install software, in determining how many additional users a system can support, and so on.

dmesg

This command replays the kernel's message buffer. Chapter 3 introduced this buffer, as well as the use of `dmesg` to display its contents after booting. The kernel places messages it generates into its message buffer. Immediately after you boot the computer, this buffer is likely to contain information on hardware device detection, low-level hardware error messages, and so on. As a system runs, this buffer is likely to collect additional kernel messages, which may relate to events such as hardware or network timeouts, abnormal program behaviors, and so on. Although this description sounds as if the kernel message buffer collects information on serious problems, many of these messages actually describe harmless events. For instance, if your system is configured to put the hard disk into a low-power mode, the message buffer may fill with timeout messages when the disk spins back up to speed. In any event, these messages may eventually push the original boot messages out of the buffer.

The dmesg command takes few options. Its full syntax is

```
dmesg [-a] [-M core] [-N system]
```

The -a option creates a more verbose report, including console and syslog output. The -M *core* option lets you tell FreeBSD to analyze a kernel *core*, which is a file that's generated in certain types of serious crashes. You're unlikely to use this option. Likewise, -N *system* lets you analyze another system's kernel message buffer.

df

The df command reports on disk free space. This can be extremely useful if you're planning to install new software because it may alert you to a partition that's nearly full. The complete syntax of this command is

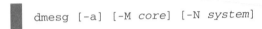
```
df [-b | -h | -H | -k | -m | -P] [-ailn] [-t type] [file | filesystem ...]
```

The meanings of the various options are as follows:

- **Format options** The first block of options controls the units used for reporting disk space. Specifically, -b stands for 512-byte blocks, -h and -H stand for human-readable output (using units of kilobytes, megabytes, and so on, with base 10 or base 2 interpretations, respectively), -k stands for 1,024-byte kilobytes, -m stands for 1,048,576-byte megabytes, and -P creates a POSIX-standard output.

Note *In the computer field, most measurements use base-2 multiples, in which a kilobyte is 1,024 bytes, a megabyte is 1,048,576 bytes, and so on. Hard disk manufacturers use base-10 multiples, in which a kilobyte is 1,000 bytes, a megabyte is 1,000,000 bytes, and so on.*

- **-a** This option causes df to display information on all mount points, even for filesystems that were mounted with options that would otherwise cause df to ignore them.

- **-i** This option causes df to include information on free *inodes*—disk data structures used internally to address files. If a disk runs out of inodes, it can't store more files, even if there's plenty of free space. This can become a problem if you store many small files on a disk.

- **-l** This option limits the display to local filesystems—that is, the computer's own hard disk, CD-ROM drive, and so on, excluding network filesystems.

- **-n** This option displays only information that's already available in memory. Normally, df causes FreeBSD to query each filesystem as to its current state. If a filesystem has become unavailable, though, this won't work. For instance, a network problem might prevent df from obtaining information on a network filesystem.

- **-t** *type* This option displays information only on filesystems of the specified type. You can specify multiple types by separating types with commas, For instance, **df -t ufs,cd9660** causes df to display information only on FFS and ISO-9660 filesystems.

- *file | filesystem* You can limit the output to certain filesystems by listing them, either via their device filenames (such as /dev/ad0s2h) or their filesystem mount points (such as /home).

Information produced by this command includes the filesystem device, the filesystem size, the used space, the available space, the percentage of capacity filled, and the filesystem mount point. For instance, the following command displays information on one system, formatted for easy human consumption:

```
$ df -h
Filesystem     Size   Used  Avail Capacity  Mounted on
/dev/ad0s2a    124M    62M    52M    54%     /
devfs          1.0K   1.0K    0B    100%     /dev
/dev/ad0s2h    1.8G   486M   1.2G    29%     /home
/dev/ad0s2f    145M    31M   103M    23%     /tmp
/dev/ad0s2g    1.6G   1.2G   269M    82%     /usr
/dev/ad0s2e    145M   7.4M   126M     6%     /var
/dev/ad0s1     2.0G   697M   1.3G    34%     /windows
procfs         4.0K   4.0K    0B    100%     /proc
speaker:/home  4.5G   1.7G   2.8G    38%     /speaker/home
```

This output reveals that the root (/) filesystem is 124MB and is 54 percent full, that /home is 29 percent full, and so on. The /speaker/home filesystem is a network mount, as indicated by the speaker:/home device name—this is really an NFS mount specification. The /dev and /proc filesystems are special *virtual filesystems*—they don't correspond to physical partitions or other devices, but are generated on the fly for special purposes. Thus, the fact that they're both reported as having 0 bytes free isn't a problem. The fact that /usr is 82 percent full is potentially more troublesome, should the need arise to add more than 269MB of new programs. In practice, it's usually best to keep a few megabytes free on /usr (or on the root partition, if there's no separate /usr partition).

man

This command enters the FreeBSD manual system—its on-line documentation. To use its simplest form, you can type **man *topic*** to obtain information on *topic*. (The *topic* can be a command, a filename, a system call, or various other options.) You can also use any of several options to modify man's behavior. One you might want to try is -P *pager*, which tells man to use the specified *pager* program to display information. In particular, many people prefer the less pager to the default more, so typing **man -P less *topic*** may be desirable. (You can also set the PAGER environment variable in a shell configuration file, as described in Chapter 6, to change the default man pager.)

uptime

The uptime command takes no arguments. It displays information on how long the computer has been booted, how many users are logged on, and how much of a load they're placing on the CPU. In operation, the command looks like this:

```
$ uptime
 4:38PM up 2 days, 5 mins, 5 users, load averages: 0.00, 0.00, 0.00
```

The number of users reported is really the number of independent logins or xterms running. In this particular example, only one user is logged in, but that user is running five xterms. There's no way to know this from the uptime output alone, though.

The three numbers reported as load averages represent the demands on CPU time during three recent time slices (the last 1, 5, and 15 minutes). The 0.00 values indicate that the system's CPU isn't being heavily taxed. Values of 1.00 would mean that the system's CPU was being demanded for an average of its full capacity. This could be one program performing very CPU-intensive tasks or several programs, all demanding less than the full attention of the CPU. If the load average climbs above 1.0, FreeBSD won't be able to meet all the programs' demands for CPU time. The programs will continue to run, but they won't run as quickly as they would on a system with fewer demands on its time. What represents a reasonable load average varies depending upon your hardware and needs. Note that the load average says nothing about the CPU's speed. A computationally intensive program, running alone, would place a load average of 1.0 on either a 100 MHz Pentium system or a 2 GHz Pentium 4.

ps

This command displays information on running processes. It accepts a very large number of options—more than can be summarized here. For more information, consult the ps man page. Some of the more common options include

- **-a** Displays information about all users' processes. (Normally, ps provides information only on processes owned by the person who issues the ps command.)

- **-h** Repeats the header information that identifies columns of output, to guarantee that a header will be visible in every page of a long output.

- ■ **-j**   Displays additional information on each process.
- ■ **-l**   Displays additional information on each process.
- ■ **-m**   Sorts the output by memory usage.
- ■ **-p** *PID*   Displays information on the specified process ID (PID) only.
- ■ **-r**   Sorts the output by CPU usage.
- ■ **-U** *username*   Displays information on processes owned by the specified *username*.
- ■ **-u**   Displays additional information on each process.
- ■ **-v**   Displays additional information on each process.
- ■ **-w**   Creates wide (132-column) output, rather than the default 80-column display. This may be useful if you have a wide xterm window or if you pipe the output to a file that you'll subsequently process or read in a text editor.
- ■ **-x**   Displays information about processes that aren't associated with terminals, such as daemons.

One piece of information that's included in all the common ps output formats is the process ID (PID) of each process. You can use this number in various other commands, such as renice and kill (described in the upcoming sections "nice and renice" and "kill and killall") to modify a process's behavior. It's common to run ps just to find the PID of a particular process.

Several of these options are described as displaying "additional information." Precisely what additional information this is varies from one option to another. Possibilities include the process's parent process ID (PPID), start time, various measures of memory use, and so on.

One particularly useful variant is **ps -aux**. This command displays information on all running processes, including the username associated with each, the percentage of CPU time and memory each process is consuming, and the command used to launch each process. A common practice is to pipe this command (as described in the upcoming section, "Pipes") through grep, which searches its input for a specified string. Doing so enables you to locate all instances of a running program. For instance, if you want to find all the running instances of the more pager, you might use this command:

```
$ ps -aux | grep more
rodsmith  7445  0.0  0.2   344   55  p3  R+   5:12PM  0:00.02 grep more
rodsmith  7384  0.0  1.1  1372  245  p2  I+   4:57PM  0:00.08 more
```

Note   *This command often catches the* grep *process in addition to the target process (*more, *in this example).*

BASIC SYSTEM ADMINISTRATION

top

In some respects, top is a variant of ps. Like ps, top lists running processes, but it does so in a dynamic way. By default, top sorts processes by CPU time. This makes top an extremely useful tool for spotting runaway processes—those that have locked themselves in infinite loops, consuming CPU time to no useful end. Figure 5-4 shows top in action.

Several top variants are available. For instance, the GNOME project ships with one called gtop, which provides a more GUI-oriented user interface. These GUI variants of top provide functionality similar to that in the standard text-based top, but users more comfortable with GUI tools may find them more intuitive. You can use a GUI top tool even from another environment; for instance, you can use gtop from KDE or when no desktop environment is running, although of course X must be running and you need supporting GNOME libraries.

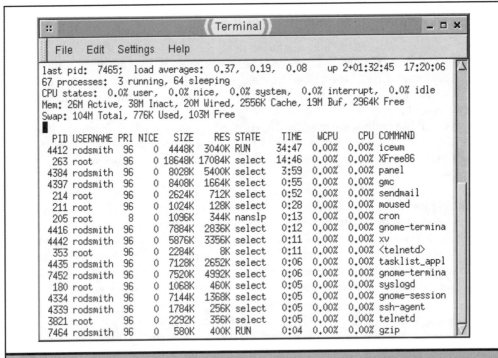

Figure 5-4. *The top command updates its display to show changes in process demands on the system over time.*

System Manipulation Commands

Discovering information about your system can be important in diagnosing problems or planning changes, but to actually fix problems or implement changes, you need to be able to change your system. Various chapters of this book provide information on how to do this, but there are some miscellaneous system manipulation commands that deserve attention here.

nice and renice

The preceding discussion has referred several times to demands on CPU time made by various programs. One of the jobs of the FreeBSD kernel is to mediate such demands when they come into conflict. For instance, if the users `ajones` and `bsmith` both run CPU-intensive programs, who gets CPU time? Ordinarily, FreeBSD splits the CPU time between the two users on a 50/50 basis, so neither user's task is given short shrift. Sometimes, though, you may want to change this behavior, giving one task priority over another. This is the job of the `nice` command, which lets you assign an explicit priority code to a process when you launch it. The `renice` command is related; it lets you adjust a job's priority after it's already started.

The syntax for `nice` is

```
nice [-number] command [arguments]
```

The *command* and *arguments* are the command you want to run and any arguments you want to give to the command. The *number* is the priority number. Ordinarily, FreeBSD gives a process a priority of 0. Confusingly, higher priorities (up to 20) reduce the priority of a task, while lower priorities (to -20) increase the priority of a task. Further confusing the issue, you specify the priority number by preceding it with a dash (–). Thus, to decrease a process's priority, you specify it as what looks like a negative number:

```
$ nice -15 numbercrunch
```

To increase the priority, though, you use a dash followed by a negative number, thus:

```
# nice --15 numbercrunch
```

You may note that these examples used different prompts. This is because any user can reduce a process's priority when launching a program, but only `root` may increase the priority. If you don't specify a priority, `nice` assumes a value of 10.

Although you probably won't use `nice` for many programs, it can be very useful for low-priority processes that nonetheless consume a lot of CPU time. For instance, if you run the SETI@Home program (`http://setiathome.ssl.berkeley.edu`), you probably don't want it consuming CPU time that you want to use for your own work.

Running SETI@Home with a very low priority (say, a `nice` value of 20) will ensure that it uses CPU time only when no other process wants it.

The `renice` program extends the flexibility of `nice` by enabling you to change a running process's priority. Its syntax is

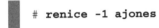

```
renice priority [[-p] pid...] [[-g] pgrp...] [[-u] user...]
```

You can specify processes by their PIDs, as revealed by `ps`, `top`, or various other tools; by the group names of their owners, or by the usernames of their owners. For instance, to give all of the processes owned by `ajones` a boost in priority, you might issue this command:

```
# renice -1 ajones
```

Note that, unlike with `nice`, there's no dash preceding the *priority* value, so an increased priority uses a negative number. In the event of confusion between PIDs, group names, and usernames, you can explicitly include the `-p`, `-g`, and `-u` options. As with `nice`, only `root` may increase a process's priority. Non-root users may use `renice` only on their own processes.

If you're an ordinary user and you use nice *or* renice *to decrease a process's priority, you won't be able to subsequently increase that process's priority, even back to its original level.*

If you notice that your system has become sluggish because of the actions of a few programs, you can reduce their priority through `renice` to restore some zip to the computer. This is likely to be effective if a user is running a very CPU-intensive program, such as a scientific simulation or a ray-tracing graphics package.

kill and killall

The `nice` and `renice` commands can be useful in recovering CPU time for high-priority tasks that might otherwise be wasted on low-priority tasks. In some cases, though, that's not enough. Processes occasionally *hang*—lock themselves in an unproductive loop. Such processes sometimes consume a great deal of CPU time to no good effect. Less serious program hangs and other problems may also make programs unresponsive, or you may not have any easy interactive way to exit from them even if they haven't hung. This is where the `kill` and `killall` commands come in handy: They can terminate arbitrary processes, even if they've hung or you have no way to issue a quit command.

The basic syntax for `kill` is

```
kill [-l] [[-s] signal_name | signal_number] PID...
```

The most basic form of the command omits all the options except for a PID number, which you can obtain from ps, top, or similar commands. For instance, to locate and kill the program called xv, you might use these commands:

```
# ps ax | grep xv
 7672  p2  RN+    0:00.02 grep xv
 4442  p5  I      0:13.40 xv
# kill 4442
```

Normally, kill kills a process by sending it a *signal*—a code that's used to communicate between processes. The default signal that kill sends is number 15, which is also known as *TERM* (for *terminate*). Most processes respond to this signal by shutting down in a controlled way. Unfortunately, some hung processes aren't very responsive. These need a firmer hand, which is provided by signal number 9, *KILL*. For instance, you might type **kill -s 9 4442** to issue this signal to process 4442. This signal tells the kernel to shut down the process without giving it the chance to close open files or follow other routine shutdown procedures. Table 5-1 lists several other signals and their meanings. For a complete list, type **kill -1**.

The killall command serves a similar function, but it kills all the processes that match a given name. For instance, rather than the **ps ax | grep xv** and **kill 4442** commands shown earlier, you could type just **killall xv** to do the same thing. The trouble with this command is that you may unintentionally kill processes other than the ones you want to kill. For instance, if two people were running xv, this command would kill both of them, if issued by root.

Signal Name	Signal Number	Meaning
HUP	1	Hang up
INT	2	Interrupt
QUIT	3	Quit
ABRT	6	Abort
KILL	9	Nonignorable kill
ALRM	14	Alarm
TERM	15	Terminate process

Table 5-1. *Common Signals and Their Meanings*

Some versions of UNIX use a `killall` command that works differently from FreeBSD's. Specifically, this alternate `killall` kills all processes started by the issuing user, except those that are parents of the `killall` process itself. Thus, if you find yourself using a non-FreeBSD system, check the `killall` man page before using this command.

Both `kill` and `killall` can be used by both `root` and ordinary users. As you might expect, though, ordinary users are restricted to killing only their own processes.

Redirection

The subject of redirection has popped up once or twice in earlier chapters. This tool is extremely important for text-based FreeBSD administration, and even for ordinary users. Redirection enables you to redirect a program's input or output, connecting it to a file rather than to the keyboard or screen.

To understand redirection, you should first understand that many text-mode programs accept input from and send output to multiple sources (which are often called *streams*). Normally, all a program's input sources are tied to the keyboard at which the user sits, and all the output sources are tied to the screen, xterm, or remote login process the user is using. The usual input and output streams are known as *standard input* and *standard output* (often abbreviated `stdin` and `stdout`, respectively). An important second output stream is known as *standard error* (or `stderr`). This secondary output source handles important error messages. Although it normally links to the same console as `stdout`, `stderr` is separate so that it may be redirected in a different way.

Redirection involves connecting these input or output streams to some other source or destination. For instance, rather than read output on your screen, you might want to direct it into a file. You can then include this file in a document you're writing with a word processor, or search through the output and study it at your leisure. You can redirect `stdout` by using the greater than symbol (>) and following it with the name of the file to which you want to send the output. For instance, to save a long file listing to a file, you might use this command:

```
$ ls -l > listing.txt
```

After issuing this command, you could use a paging tool such as `less` to view the output, load the file into a text editor, or manipulate it in any way you could manipulate any text file. Some programs tend to use `stderr` more than `stdout`, the idea being that the user should really read the "error" output immediately. Unfortunately, sometimes this output is copious, so redirecting it to a file for later perusal is often desirable. You can do so by using a minor variant of the `stdout` redirection: Use 2> rather than >. For instance, if you run a program called `bigerr` that produces lots of `stderr` output, you might redirect it this way:

```
$ bigerr 2> bigerr-error-output.txt
```

If you want to redirect both `stdout` and `stderr`, you could do so like this:

```
$ bigerr > bigerr-output.txt 2> bigerr-error-output.txt
```

All of these commands cause FreeBSD to overwrite any existing file with the redirection file's name. If you want to append a command's output to a file, rather than overwrite the file, you can use a double greater than sign:

```
$ ls -l >> listing.txt
```

Many programs accept input from the keyboard. If the program is very well structured—for example, a script that accepts information such as a person's name, address, and telephone number—you can use input redirection to pass the contents of a file to the program instead of keyboard input. Input redirection uses a less than symbol (<). For instance, if this script were called `getinfo`, you could pass it the contents of `address.txt` this way:

```
$ getinfo < address.txt
```

You can combine both input and output redirection:

```
$ getinfo < address.txt > get-out.txt
```

This command passes the contents of `address.txt` as input and sends output to `get-out.txt`. Redirection of this form is common in automated scripts, as described in Chapter 31.

Pipes

Pipes, or pipelines as they're sometimes called, are closely related to redirection. Essentially, a pipe is a way to link two programs so that the first program sends its output to the second program as input. You can extend a pipeline to include more than two programs, as well; the second passes its output to the third, and so on. Using this process, you can link together many small and simple programs so that they collectively do something much more complex.

Pipes made an appearance earlier in this chapter, in examples involving the use of ps and grep in the "ps" and "kill and killall" sections. The ps command creates a potentially large amount of output—one line for each process that the command finds, which could amount to dozens or hundreds of lines of output, even on a fairly modest FreeBSD system. You may often want to run such a command but be interested in just a few lines of output. That's where the pipe through grep comes in—grep is a tool that looks for lines matching a specified pattern in its input, so if you can specify a pattern that you know will appear in your ps output, you can pipe the two together to filter the ps output. You do this by using the vertical bar (|) as a pipe operator, thus:

```
$ ps -aux | grep xv
```

This command finds any line in the ps output that contains the string xv and displays the result. This particular technique is very useful in sifting through the output of verbose commands. Of course, you can use pipes to do other things, as well. For instance, you might pipe the output of a file-location command such as find into a backup utility, or link together several audio-processing tools to produce unusual sound effects. Another common approach is to pipe a large output through a pager such as more or less:

```
$ ps -aux | less
```

| Note | *Chapter 8 includes more information on the* grep *and* find *commands.* |

GUI Administrative Tools

Although this chapter focuses upon text-based administrative tools, there are tools available that enable you to administer FreeBSD using GUI interfaces. Most FreeBSD administrators rely primarily upon text-mode tools because that's the way FreeBSD administration has traditionally been done and because the system's standard configuration doesn't emphasize GUI tools (with one partial exception, mentioned shortly). In certain situations you might want to investigate GUI alternatives, though. These include if you're unfamiliar with a particular area of administration and need to get that subsystem working quickly or if somebody with less experience needs to be able to perform at least some minimal administrative tasks. In these situations, GUI tools can provide clues that can help an inexperienced administrator get the job done. GUI tools are usually more limited than their underlying text-mode counterparts, though, so it's best not to rely upon them as a long-term administrative option.

This section can't cover all the GUI tools that are available, or even describe any of them in any detail; instead, I provide pointers to these tools and give a basic overview of their capabilities. These tools include

- **sysinstall**   This tool is not really a GUI one, but it's a standard part of a FreeBSD installation, and it serves some of the same functions as GUI tools. This program is what directs the FreeBSD install process, as described in Chapter 2. You can run it from a text-mode login or an xterm by typing **sysinstall**. Thereafter, you can use this tool to install software, reconfigure X, set your time zone, and so on. Certain chapters of this book refer to sysinstall, beyond Chapter 2.

- **Webmin**   This tool, which is available from http://www.webmin.net, is a web-based administrative package for FreeBSD and many other UNIX-like OSs. This tool is unusually complete in the range of administrative tasks it supports. It works through a wide array of administrative modules, which handle specific servers or configuration tasks.

- **SWAT**   The *Samba Web Administration Tool (SWAT)* comes with Samba (described in Chapter 18). Like Webmin, SWAT is a web-based tool. It handles only Samba, but provides access to almost all of Samba's features, so it can be a good way to get quickly up to speed on relatively sophisticated Samba configurations.

- **CUPS**   The *Common Unix Printing System (CUPS)* is an alternative to the standard FreeBSD printing tools described in Chapter 9. I mention it here because part of the standard CUPS installation is yet another web-based administrative tool, which handles printer configuration. You can learn more about CUPS, including its web-based printer administration, at http://www.cups.org.

- **Miscellaneous tools**   Some other programs ship with web-based or GUI administrative tools, or make them available as add-ons. Most of these apply to relatively esoteric packages such as fetchmail (http://www.tuxedo.org/~esr/fetchmail/) or Leafnode (http://www.leafnode.org; check http://www.vision25.demon.co.uk/oss/leafwa/intro.html for the Leafwa GUI administration add-on).

Web-based tools are fairly popular for GUI administration. Such tools enable you to administer a FreeBSD computer from any computer that supports a web browser, no matter what OS it runs. Used beyond a local network, though, such tools are potentially quite dangerous because of the risk of an interloper intercepting your administrative password, and because the availability of a server devoted to system administration poses a risk in the event of a security problem with the administrative server. Indeed, even on a local network such tools can be risky, if your local network's internal security is compromised. On the whole, it's best to use such tools with caution.

Summary

FreeBSD system administration involves running tools that are targeted at specific tasks and editing text files that contain the system's default configuration. Understanding the commands and files involved is therefore critically important to administering a FreeBSD system. So is the ability to edit a text file using any of the many text editors available for FreeBSD.

This chapter is only an introduction to FreeBSD system administration. Although a few commands and files are introduced here, the bulk of what you need to know to administer a FreeBSD system resides in subsequent chapters.

The Complete Reference

FreeBSD

Chapter 6

System Startup and Control Processes

One of the most important administrative tasks is controlling a FreeBSD system's boot and login processes. If these processes don't work correctly, you won't be able to use the system—at least, not in the usual way. (You should be able to use an emergency boot system, as described in Chapter 32, to fix such problems.) Previous chapters have covered several aspects of the FreeBSD boot process. This chapter covers a few more aspects of these processes, and looks at how FreeBSD enables users to log in.

Even when nobody's logged in, FreeBSD runs programs. Many of these are launched during the system startup process, but one class of programs isn't. These are scheduled tasks, which you can set up using a tool called `cron`. This chapter concludes with a look at `cron`, including how to set up user or system cron jobs.

This chapter describes a wide assortment of processes that are related in various ways, and Figure 6-1 summarizes these processes. It's far from a complete picture of all the processes that run on a FreeBSD system, but you may find it useful in understanding the relationships between common FreeBSD processes.

Understanding the Kernel's Control

The FreeBSD kernel is the core of the operating system. It plays many roles in a running system, and it's so important that several chapters of this book devote sections to the kernel. This section provides an overview of the role that the kernel plays in a normal FreeBSD system, which is vitally important in understanding other kernel-related topics.

Loading the Kernel

Chapter 4 describes how the kernel is booted. In brief, it's loaded by the FreeBSD boot loader. Specifically, the Stage 0 boot loader in the MBR loads the Stage 1 boot loader in the FreeBSD slice, which runs the Stage 2 boot loader as an extension of itself. The Stage 1/Stage 2 boot loader is responsible for starting the kernel. In a default configuration, the boot loader reads the kernel from the file `/boot/kernel/kernel`, but you can change the kernel file that you load by using the `boot` command in the Stage 1/Stage 2 boot loader, as described in Chapter 4.

Once the boot loader runs the kernel, the kernel is in control of the computer. Any program that attempts to bypass the kernel to directly address the computer's hardware fails. Instead, the kernel provides high-level interfaces to the computer's hardware. The kernel also provides various important services to running programs, as described in the upcoming section, "The Kernel's Role in a Running System."

Kernel Control of Subsequent Startup Steps

As described in Chapter 5, the kernel controls the startup process by running the first nonkernel program: `init`. This program in turn uses the `sh` shell to run several startup scripts, as described in Chapter 5 and the upcoming section, "Customizing Startup Scripts."

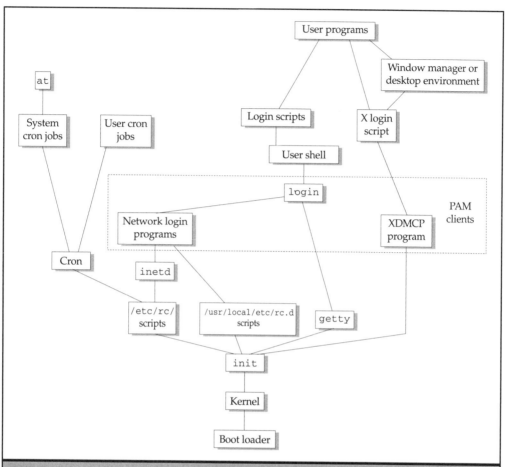

Figure 6-1. *The FreeBSD startup and control process is a somewhat tangled tree of interdependencies.*

The kernel doesn't really control these startup steps, but it's important for two reasons. First, the kernel controls what program controls the startup sequence. In principle, you could change the kernel to run some program other than init as the first program, thus changing the system's behavior. Second, the kernel provides critical support features to init, the startup scripts init calls, and the programs launched from those startup scripts. This support comes in the form of the same underlying support provided to all running programs.

The Kernel's Role in a Running System

Although users are seldom consciously aware of the kernel, it underlies everything users do on the system. The services provided by the kernel are said to run in *kernel mode*. These services have privileged access to the hardware and to other kernel-mode processes. This contrasts with *user mode* programs, which rely upon the kernel for hardware access and other kernel-mode services. You should realize that even programs run by `root` are user-mode processes.

Some of the important services provided by the kernel include

- **Hardware interfaces**   The kernel includes vital device drivers for most hardware components. If a program needs to send data to a serial port, read a keystroke from the keyboard, display data on the screen, or use any other hardware, it does so through the kernel, at one level or another. Some accesses may be buffered through other kernel or nonkernel services, such as filesystems or XFree86, but sooner or later the kernel gets involved. In practice, most user-mode programs access the kernel's hardware interfaces through *device files*, which are special files conventionally located in the `/dev` directory.

> **Note**   *Some devices, such as modems and printers, don't have direct support in the kernel. Instead, they're controlled by user-mode programs. These programs access such hardware through devices that are managed by the kernel, such as serial or parallel ports. XFree86 deserves special mention because of its unusual status. Although it's a user-mode process, it has unusually direct access to a video card's hardware.*

- **Memory access**   All programs need memory, and to ensure that programs don't overwrite each others' memory, the kernel is in charge of allocating available memory. The FreeBSD kernel does this in such a way that every program believes it's running by itself; no program can access another program's memory. (Some earlier OSs, such as Mac OS Classic and DOS with Windows 3.1, used more primitive memory allocation methods, which is one reason application programs could so easily crash these OSs.)

- **CPU time**   FreeBSD is a *preemptive multitasking* OS, meaning that the kernel controls how much CPU time each process receives. This feature contrasts with *cooperative multitasking*, in which processes use however much CPU time they need and then relinquish control to other processes. Cooperative multitasking tends to produce systems that are less responsive to individual processes' CPU needs because one program can hog an inordinate amount of CPU time. You can control how much CPU time different processes take in FreeBSD with the `nice` or `renice` commands, described in Chapter 5.

- **Filesystems**   Whenever you access a file, the kernel serves as an intermediary. Your application program asks the kernel to deliver data from a file or to write data to the file. The kernel must therefore understand all the filesystems you might want to use. This topic is covered in Chapters 4 and 7. Filesystems must also interact with the hardware interfaces to disk devices. Thus, filesystem access involves two kernel components: the filesystems themselves and the hardware on which the filesystems reside.

■ **Networking**   In addition to controlling the network hardware, the kernel provides higher-level networking constructs, such as support for the Transmission Control Protocol/Internet Protocol (TCP/IP) *network stack*—a collection of protocols that give user-mode programs easy access to a network. FreeBSD includes many user-mode programs that enable you to control and interface with these network features. Parts III and IV of this book, as well as parts of various other chapters, cover these tools.

With so many responsibilities, the kernel is an unusually important component of any OS. The FreeBSD kernel is related to the kernel in other open source BSDs (OpenBSD and NetBSD), but isn't identical to either. The FreeBSD kernel is completely unrelated to the Linux kernel, which is why FreeBSD is not a version of Linux, despite the fact that FreeBSD and Linux support many of the same higher-level programs, such as XFree86 and Emacs.

Fortunately, the FreeBSD kernel is well tested and very robust, which accounts for much of FreeBSD's reliability. Even if a user-mode program is poorly behaved, there's little that such a program can do to disrupt kernel-level operations or other programs. One important exception is that user-level programs can interact with each other and, depending upon the permissions and ownership involved, such programs can disrupt one another. For instance, a program run by `root` can terminate or otherwise interfere with programs run by any other user—but even a program run by `root` must go through the kernel to access a computer's hardware, acquire memory for itself, and so on. This level of insulation is critically important in providing a stable system on which potentially hundreds of users may be simultaneously working.

Customizing Startup Scripts

Chapter 5 introduced startup scripts. On a FreeBSD system, these scripts take two forms:

■ **System startup scripts**   These scripts reside in `/etc` and have filenames that begin with `rc`. The `/etc/rc` script is the master of these scripts, and it's the one that's first run by `init`. These scripts create the standard working configuration for a FreeBSD system, including its basic operation and the running of many standard servers.

■ **Local startup scripts**   These scripts reside in `/usr/local/etc/rc.d`. They provide startup support for miscellaneous servers and other programs that you might add to a standard system. These scripts should respond to at least two commands: `start` and `stop`, which should start and stop, respectively, the programs launched by these scripts. (The system startup process normally starts these scripts automatically at boot time, but you can start or stop them manually later.)

If you want to modify the computer's startup procedure, you can alter either the system startup scripts or the local startup scripts. Whenever possible, it's best to work with the local startup scripts. This approach works well when you want to add support for some new server you've installed, or some other package that must be run at boot time. If you need to change the way a system works, though, you may have no choice but to work on the system startup scripts.

Editing System Startup Scripts

Editing system startup scripts can be a tricky proposition—a mistake can render a system unbootable. Thus, I recommend that you undertake such a change only as a last resort—if you can't get the system to do what you want without editing these scripts. There are two exceptions to this rule, though.

First, you can edit the /etc/rc.conf file with relative impunity. This file sets several variables that are used by other files to control the startup process. These variables are named fairly obvious things, such as hostname, sendmail_enable, and sshd_enable. Some chapters of this book tell you to edit certain of these items in particular situations.

The /etc/rc.conf *file sets values that override those set in* /etc/defaults/ rc.conf. *You can study the latter file to learn what sorts of defaults you can set in* /etc/rc.conf.

Second, you can edit the /etc/rc.local file to have the system start servers you add yourself. This script actually doesn't exist in a default configuration, but the /etc/ rc script does look for it, and runs it if it's present. You might use this approach if you've compiled a new server and want FreeBSD to start it when it boots. For instance, Listing 6-1 shows an /etc/rc.local script that starts the /usr/local/bin/servera server, passes it the -a parameter, and launches the /usr/local/bin/startcheck script.

Listing 6-1.
A Simple
/etc/rc
.local
Startup Script

```
#!/bin/sh
/usr/local/bin/servera -a &
/usr/local/bin/startcheck
```

Listing 6-1 begins with the string #!/bin/sh. This string identifies the file as a *shell script*—a program that's run with the help of a shell (/bin/sh in the case of Listing 6-1). Most scripts also have their execute bits set, which you can do for this script by typing **chmod a+x /etc/rc.local**, but this isn't strictly necessary for this script. Subsequent lines can be as simple as commands typed on a command line. The ampersand (&) after the servera call may or may not be necessary, depending upon the server; it launches the program in the background, so that subsequent items in the script, and subsequent scripts, run correctly. Some servers are designed to run in this way even if they're launched without the ampersand.

Although `/etc/rc.local` can be a quick and convenient way to start local servers, this method is deprecated, meaning that its use is discouraged, and the ability to use this method may disappear in future versions of FreeBSD. Instead, the current administrative recommendation is to use local startup scripts, described next.

Creating New Local Startup Scripts

Instead of creating a single monolithic `/etc/rc.local` script, you can create one or more scripts in `/usr/local/etc/rc.d`. These scripts are typically more complex than an `/etc/rc.local` script because they need to handle both `start` and `stop` parameters sent to the script. Listing 6-2 is an example.

Listing 6-2.
An Example
`/usr/
local/
etc/rc.d`
Startup Script

```
#!/bin/sh

case "$1" in
start)
    /usr/local/bin/servera -a
stop)
    /usr/bin/killall servera
```

Listing 6-2 is extremely simple as local startup scripts go; it merely launches `servera` if the script receives the `start` option, and issues a `killall` command if the script receives the `stop` option. More sophisticated scripts may record the program's PID in a file so that the script kills only the instance that the script launched when it's given the `stop` command, may check that the program file exists before attempting to launch it, and so on. You should set any local startup script's execute bit, by typing **chmod a+x /usr/local/etc/rc.d/*scriptname***, where *scriptname* is the script's name.

Many server packages compiled for FreeBSD include local startup scripts to start and stop the server, so you may not need to explicitly create such scripts yourself. Using an existing script as a model can sometimes help you get a new script up and running, but some scripts use moderately sophisticated shell scripting techniques, so they may be hard to understand if you're not familiar with shell scripting.

Inside the Login Process

Once the computer has booted, it presents a login prompt, as described in Chapter 3. What happens at this point depends largely upon the login method chosen, but there are some common features used by many login methods. In a standard FreeBSD configuration, the login process should go smoothly, assuming the user types the correct password. You may want to change the default behavior for all system accounts, or alter what happens to individual users' logins, though, so this section describes these options, as well as the processes that underlie the login procedure.

BASIC SYSTEM ADMINISTRATION

Methods of Logging In

FreeBSD supports several different login methods. These methods are accessed in different ways, may present different user interfaces, and may produce different actions, but most use the same authentication tools at their core. Knowing about these methods helps you configure access to your FreeBSD system.

Text-Mode Console Logins

This is the login method that was emphasized in Chapter 3. In such a login, the user sees a text-mode `login:` prompt, types a username, sees a text-mode `password:` prompt, types a password, and is rewarded with a text-based shell. A standard FreeBSD installation uses this procedure as the primary login method.

This method of login is controlled through the `/etc/ttys` file, which contains a series of lines like this:

```
ttyv0    "/usr/libexec/getty Pc"          cons25   on   secure
```

This line links the `/usr/libexec/getty` program to `ttyv0`, which is FreeBSD's name for the first virtual console. Subsequent lines in the file link the same program to `ttyv1` through `ttyv7`. These virtual consoles can be accessed by pressing ALT-F*n*, where *n* is a number from 1 to 8. (F1 links to `ttyv0`, and so on.) Thus, you can log into FreeBSD multiple times.

When the `getty` program runs, it links to the console and runs the `login` program, which handles the actual login process. Specifically, `login` presents the `login:` and `password:` prompts, processes the user's input, and calls the *Pluggable Authentication Module (PAM)*, which is FreeBSD's authentication tool, as described shortly in "Authenticating Users via PAM." If PAM authenticates the user, `login` checks the `/etc/passwd` file to find what the user's default shell is, and runs that shell, linking it to the console. At this point, the user is logged in, but the shell may run further scripts to set up the user's desired environment, as described in the upcoming sections, "Adjusting User Login Defaults" and "User Login Control Files."

GUI Console and Remote Logins

FreeBSD relies on a program that uses the *X Display Manager Control Protocol (XDMCP)* to handle GUI logins. An XDMCP program ties itself to an X session, or accepts access from remote X servers. In either case, it uses X to present a GUI login prompt. When the user enters a username and password, the XDMCP program passes this information to PAM. If PAM authorizes the user, the XDMCP program starts the user's default X environment on the X session it used, as described in "Adjusting User Login Defaults" and "User Login Control Files."

Several different XDMCP programs are available for FreeBSD, including the original XDM, the GDM program that's part of the GNOME desktop environment, and the KDM tool that's part of KDE. These tools are launched from `/etc/ttys`, just as are `getty`s for text-mode logins. Chapter 21 covers the configuration of these tools in more detail.

If you want to use such a tool, a quick method is to locate the following line in /etc/ttys:

```
ttyv8    "/usr/X11R6/bin/xdm -nodaemon"  xterm   off  secure
```

Change `off` to `on` in this line, and then shut down X (if it's running) and type **kill –HUP 1** as `root`. This action tells `init` (which always has PID 1) to reread its configuration files, including /etc/ttys, and to implement any changes, such as the one you've just made. After a brief delay, X should start and you should be greeted by a GUI login prompt like the one shown in Figure 6-2. If you use GDM or KDM, or if you alter your XDM configuration, your prompt may include extra graphics, a logo, or even tools to change various login details.

Remote Text-Mode Logins

If you configure your computer to accept remote text-mode logins, as described in Chapter 21, the login servers may operate much like the `getty` programs for local logins, or they may be a bit different. In particular, a Telnet server listens for network connections. When such a connection occurs, the Telnet server launches `login`, which functions much as it does for a login on a local virtual console, except that it passes data back and forth over the network, rather than using the local keyboard and display.

The *Secure Shell (SSH)* remote login protocol works a bit differently. Instead of calling `login` for authentication, SSH calls PAM directly, or may be configured to bypass PAM and use its own authentication procedures. This feature provides greater flexibility. Whether or not SSH uses PAM, its actions after a login has been authenticated are similar to those of a Telnet server or of `getty`. Specifically, the SSH server links the user's default shell to the remote SSH client, thus giving the user remote access to the system.

The `rlogin` tool is an old UNIX remote-login standby. By default, it tries to use a remote system's IP address for authentication, so it doesn't use PAM. When `rlogin` detects a login attempt, it checks the remote system's IP address against addresses authorized in /etc/hosts.allow, /etc/hosts.equiv, or the user's .rhosts file. If the client is authorized and the remote user has an account on the server, access is granted; the `rlogin` server launches the user's default shell.

BASIC SYSTEM ADMINISTRATION

X Window System

Login: bjolitz

Password:

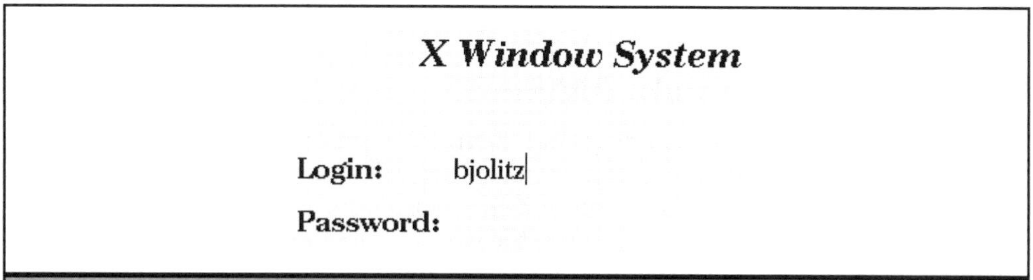

Figure 6-2.   *Many users find GUI login prompts less intimidating than text-mode login prompts.*

Chapter 21 covers configuring Telnet and SSH servers. The rlogin *protocol is generally considered insecure by today's standards, and so is best avoided.*

All of these remote login protocols are handled by servers, and these servers must be launched in some way. Local startup scripts handle some of these, and others (particularly Telnet) are handled via the inetd super server, as described in Chapter 16. The system startup scripts launch this super server (consult Figure 6-1).

Finally, FreeBSD supports logins via serial ports. In years gone by, most UNIX systems had banks of *dumb terminals* attached to their serial ports. These were keyboards and monitors with little CPU power, used only to access the UNIX system. FreeBSD still supports this configuration, so you can use old dumb terminals to give multiple users access to the system. You can also use a regular computer with a terminal program in this capacity. Similarly, you can connect a modem to a serial port and enable remote users to dial into the FreeBSD system. These configurations are handled through the /etc/ttys file. These setups closely resemble those for local virtual consoles. For instance, the following line configures a FreeBSD system to accept logins from a modem:

```
ttyd0    "/usr/libexec/getty std.9600"   dialup   on secure
```

This line tells init to launch a getty attached to /dev/ttyd0, which is a device associated with the first serial port (COM1 under Windows). The std.9600 string tells the system to run the modem at 9600 bps. The dialup string identifies the terminal as a dial-up modem connection. If you used a terminal hard-wired to the computer, use a code from /etc/termcap for its terminal type, such as vt100 for a DEC VT-100 terminal.

Miscellaneous Servers

Some servers provide a sort of remote login access. For instance, File Transfer Protocol (FTP) servers and Samba both give users access to files on the computer. Remote mail-transfer protocols also give users access to the computer, but in a still more limited way. Many of these servers can be configured to use passwords to do so. Some of these servers rely on PAM to do their work, but others don't. In all cases, the login process is highly server-specific. Some use system-wide configuration files, whereas others use user configuration files. You should consult the server's documentation to learn more about what it does. Part IV of this book covers several of these servers.

Authenticating Users via PAM

PAM is an important part of the FreeBSD authentication process because it provides a centralized method of authentication. Prior to PAM, UNIX systems relied upon the ability of each program to read an encrypted password from a password file, encrypt the password the user typed, and compare the two. This method worked, but it had several drawbacks. For instance, to implement extended authentication checks, it would be necessary to do so in each program that would have to use them. Similarly, if the encryption method used by the password file ever changed, every program would have to be rewritten to use the updated encryption method. By having login programs rely upon PAM, these problems are eliminated. Special authentication methods and changes to the password format can be implemented once, in PAM. Programs that rely upon PAM (known as *PAM clients*) need not even realize that the changes have occurred.

To provide authentication support, PAM uses its own configuration files. In FreeBSD 5.0, these are located in the /etc/pam.d directory, with a file named after each program that uses PAM. Earlier versions of FreeBSD used a single configuration file, /etc/pam.conf. The format and options of this file are the same as in the program-specific files in /etc/pam.d, with one exception that's described shortly.

PAM provides four types of authentication support:

- **User authentication**   This method is of most interest to this discussion; it enables a server to grant or deny access to the computer based on a username and password. The module type name for this feature is auth.

- **Account management**   PAM can tell a server whether the user's current account is valid, which is an important concern for login protocols, potentially independent of authentication. For instance, this module can deny access if the user's password has expired or if there are time-of-day restrictions on access to an account. The module type name for this support is account.

- **Password management**   This method enables a program to change a user's password. It's not normally used in login processes, but is used by tools such as passwd (described in Chapter 10). The module type name for this support is password.

- **Session management**   This method helps programs set up and terminate user sessions. The module type name for this support is session.

For the most part, you won't have to adjust your PAM configuration. If you want to alter the system's authentication behavior, though, you may need to modify the PAM files for one or more login methods. To do this, configure PAM to use (or to stop using) one or more authentication *modules*. These are PAM libraries, each of which provides some method of authentication. You can configure PAM to use a library with a line of the following form in the PAM configuration file:

```
[service_name]  module_type  control_flag  module  [options]
```

The *service_name* field is the name of the service, such as login for the login program or su for the su program. It's omitted from PAM configuration files in the /etc/pam.d directory, but it's included in entries in the /etc/pam.conf file. (This is the single file format difference mentioned earlier.) The *module_type* field lists the type of service provided by the module. The preceding descriptions of PAM services included the names you use for the `module_type` field in the PAM configuration file. The `control_flag` can be any of the following:

- **required** This module must succeed. If it doesn't, PAM returns an authentication failure code, but it first runs other modules to mask where the failure occurred.

- **requisite** This module must succeed. If it doesn't, PAM returns a failure code immediately.

- **sufficient** This module is sufficient to succeed, so long as no preceding *required* or *requisite* module failed. If this module succeeds, PAM immediately returns a success code.

- **optional** This module is ignored unless the other modules for the service return PAM_IGNORE.

Most configurations use the `required` flag because it makes for a more secure system—an attacker can't try variant methods of logging in to discover why a login failed, and thus work out a way around that failure.

Finally, the `module` field contains the name (possibly including a path) to the PAM module for the type of support. Some modules take options, which you can pass as a final field in the PAM configuration file. An example of a complete set of PAM configuration lines is as follows:

```
auth     required  pam_nologin.so  no_warn
auth     required  pam_unix.so     no_warn try_first_pass
account  required  pam_unix.so
session  required  pam_unix.so
password required  pam_unix.so     no_warn try_first_pass
```

Note   *This example extracts lines from an /etc/pam.d-format file. An /etc/pam.conf file would include a service name, such as login, at the start of each line. Actual PAM configuration files also usually include comment lines, which begin with pound signs (#). These lines frequently hold alternative configurations that may be activated by uncommenting the comment lines.*

In this example, two PAM modules (pam_nologin.so and pam_unix.so) are required for authentication, and one module (pam_unix.so) is used for account management, session management, and password management. In practice, pam_unix.so is the workhorse PAM authentication module in most configurations. You might want to add or change your PAM configuration to use some tool that's not part of the standard configuration. For instance, you could add support for Kerberos authentication by adding an appropriate line. (Samples are commented out in the standard FreeBSD PAM configuration.)

Note	*Kerberos is a network authentication system that's used on many large networks. It permits centralized maintenance of password databases and provides various encryption services. Its configuration and use is beyond the scope of this book. Check the Kerberos web page,* `http://web.mit.edu/kerberos/www/`, *for more information.*

Adjusting User Login Defaults

As noted earlier, text-mode login processes involve running special scripts or reading special configuration files that set up a user's environment. Two levels of configuration are involved: system-wide defaults and user-specific files. This section describes some common system-wide login configuration files, and the next section describes user login files.

For text-mode logins, the most important configuration file is the file for the user's default shell, which differs from one shell to another. Some common shells and their default configuration files are

- **sh**   This is the default shell for FreeBSD; if you don't specify otherwise, users have `sh` as their default shells. Its global configuration file is `/etc/profile`.

- **tcsh**   Although not the default shell, `tcsh` is a popular one. It uses both `/etc/csh.cshrc` and `/etc/csh.login` as global configuration files. This shell also executes `/etc/csh.logout` when a user logs out.

- **bash**   The `bash` shell is popular with some users, but it's not installed in FreeBSD by default. If you install it, it uses the same `/etc/profile` file used by `sh` as its global configuration file.

The default FreeBSD configuration uses empty configuration files for all of these shells. You may want to modify these configurations in certain ways, though. These configuration files are shell scripts, so you can program them to do just about anything, as described in Chapter 31. One common modification is to set *environment variables*. These are settings that programs can access by name. For instance, the shell itself uses the PATH environment variable to determine in which directories to search for programs whose names you type. Many programs rely upon program-specific environment variables to locate configuration files or to set default options. For instance, some programs use the EDITOR environment variable to determine which editor to launch when a file should be edited.

For `sh` or `bash`, you can set an environment variable as follows:

```
export VARNAME=value
```

You can include other variables as part of the *value*, by preceding the variable name with a dollar sign ($). For instance, the following line adds `/opt/bin` to the PATH environment variable:

```
export PATH=$PATH:/opt/bin
```

For `tcsh`, the same goal can be achieved by using `setenv` rather than `export` and omitting the equal sign. When referring to another variable, it may be necessary to enclose it in quotes. For instance, the following `tcsh` line adds `/opt/bin` to the PATH environment variable:

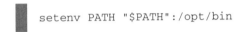

```
setenv PATH "$PATH":/opt/bin
```

Another useful command is `alias`, which sets up one command to work like another. For instance, suppose your system has users who are familiar with DOS or Windows command-line tools. They might expect a long directory listing when they type **dir**, so you could use a line like the following in `/etc/profile`:

```
alias dir='ls -l'
```

For `tcsh`, the command is the same, except that you should replace the equal sign with a space. Thereafter, any user who types **dir** receives a long directory listing, just as if the user had actually typed **ls -l**.

As a general rule, it's best to make few modifications to global configuration files. Such changes can be confusing to users if they're familiar with a more standard default setup. Instead, users can modify their own configuration files in much the same way as you can modify the global file. This means that users can customize their configurations with environment variables and aliases that they find useful, without potentially confusing or causing problems for other users.

User Login Control Files

The user login control files work much like the system-wide files. In addition to text-mode login files, you can configure GUI login files to adjust your default environment.

Text-Mode Login Control Files

The shell runs user-specific control files after running any system-wide control files. In particular, these files are:

- **sh**   The user-level configuration file for sh is called `.profile`. Most configurations include a call to `.shrc` in the user's home directory, as well. The `.profile` script is run only at login, but `.shrc` is run every time a shell is invoked (for instance, if you launch an xterm in X).

- **tcsh**   The tcsh shell tries to read, in order, `.tcshrc`, `.cshrc`, `.history`, `.login`, and finally `.cshdirs`. Non-login shells don't try to read the last three of these.

- **bash**   This shell tries to read `.bash_profile`, `.bash_login`, and then `.profile` when the session is a login session. Upon logout, bash tries to run `.bash_logout`. For non-login sessions such as xterm sessions, bash tries to use `.bashrc` on startup.

These files can be modified just like their global counterparts—you can add aliases, set environment variables, and so on. Because they're user-specific, they also enable users to customize their environments. If one user wants to be able to type **dir** and get a long directory listing, but another wants this command to play a sound file, both can be pleased. These files should be set with full execute permission, as described in Chapter 8. As a quick introduction, type **chmod a+x *login-script***, where *login-script* is the name of the login script.

FreeBSD stores default login files for some shells in the /usr/share/skel directory. Instead of being dot files, these files' names begin with dot, as in dot.cshrc. These files can optionally be copied to new users' directories and renamed appropriately when you create user accounts. They can be a good starting point for further customizations.

GUI Login Control Files

The GUI login process, like the text-mode login process, involves the reading and processing of configuration files. In a traditional setup, one of two files is used, both in the user's home directory:

- **.xinitrc**   This is the X startup script that's run when a user types **startx** in a text-mode login.

- **.xsession**   This script is the equivalent of .xinitrc, but for GUI logins via the XDM program.

Note   *If you use the KDM or GDM programs instead of XDM, they may or may not use .xsession, depending upon what type of session you opt to use. Typically, these XDMCP packages give you a choice of running a conventional XDM-style login or executing one of several desktop environments (typically one or two options for KDE and GNOME, and perhaps one or two others).*

As with text-mode login scripts, GUI login scripts should be executable, so type **chmod a+x .xinitrc** or **chmod a+x .xsession** in your home directory to set these permissions. Also as with text-mode login scripts, these scripts can set environment variables or launch programs. Most frequently, they're used to launch a window manager or desktop environment and a handful of useful programs. For instance, Listing 6-3 shows a script that starts the IceWM window manager and an xterm window.

Listing 6-3. A Sample .xinitrc or .xsession Login Script

```
#!/bin/sh
/usr/X11R6/bin/xterm &
/usr/X11R6/bin/icewm
```

Because these scripts generally run one or more programs, it's vital that you attend to the use of ampersands (&) as a means of launching programs in the background. In the preceding example, the line that launches the xterm uses an ampersand, so that the xterm runs in the background. Execution of the login script then continues on the next line, which launches IceWM. This line, though, lacks the ampersand. Execution of the login script stops at this point, until IceWM exits. This configuration is typical, and has two important consequences:

- *No program listed after IceWM executes until after IceWM exits (by selecting the log out option).* Thus, you might want to place cleanup programs, a command to play a logout sound, or the like after the call to `icewm`, but you should include all programs you want run automatically *before* the call to `icewm`.

- *IceWM controls the X session.* When IceWM exits, the script continues executing. These scripts typically contain few or no commands after the call to the window manager, and, when the script stops executing, X shuts down or you're returned to the XDMCP login program.

You should ensure that any program that doesn't terminate quickly, such as the xterm in Listing 6-3, is followed by an ampersand so that it doesn't delay or suspend execution of the rest of the script. Typically, the window manager itself is used as the program whose termination triggers the end of the X session. You can use another program for that purpose, though. For instance, if you were to reverse the order of the `xterm` and `icewm` calls in Listing 6-3, add an ampersand to the `icewm` call, and omit the ampersand from the `xterm` call, your X session would end when you closed the xterm window.

When you start X by typing **startx**, if your account lacks an `.xinitrc` file, the system uses the file `/etc/X11/xinit/xinitrc` instead. If an XDM-based login lacks an `.xsession` file, XDM launches `/usr/X11R6/lib/X11/xdm/Xsession` instead. This script in turn launches the `twm` window manager and a program called `xsm` as an X session manager—when you select the Shutdown option in `xsm`, you log out of the X session. As with text-mode login files, default `.xinitrc` and `.xsession` files exist in the `/usr/share/skel` directory, and FreeBSD can copy these to new accounts when you create them. Both these default files start GNOME as the default GUI environment.

Running Programs at Scheduled Times: Cron

We typically think of computers as being things that are fairly passive except under human control. Computers don't just decide to go do something for no reason— although when you're debugging a problem, you may think otherwise! Aside from such mysterious problems, there is an important exception to this model of computers as passive tools: scheduled jobs. You may have cause to run a program at a specified time when you're not present. You might also want the system to perform tasks repeatedly and automatically. FreeBSD supports two main tools for doing this: at and cron. Of the two, cron is the more complex. You can use at to schedule a one-time operation, such as a single run of a CPU-intensive task late at night. You can use cron to run jobs on a repeated basis, such as retrieving your mail from an ISP's mail system once an hour. In fact, FreeBSD comes configured to use cron to perform routine maintenance, so it's in use on your system even if you're unaware of it.

Using at

The at command gives you the ability to run a program once, at a specified time. A variant program, batch, lets you tell the system to run a program when the system load drops low enough (specifically, below 1.5). The syntax for these commands is

```
at [-V] [-q queue] [-f file] [-mldbv] time
batch [-V] [-q queue] [-f file] [-mv] [time]
```

The options to these commands are

- **-V**   Displays the version number of the program.

- **-q queue**   The at command supports multiple queues, each of which is identified with a letter (a to z and A to Z). Normally, at uses queues with lowercase letters, and batch uses queues with uppercase letters. The default queues for at and batch are c and E, respectively. Queues with later letters run with lower priority.

- **-f file**   Normally, you type the command you want to run after you type the at or batch command, then press CTRL-D, which is a standard FreeBSD end-of-file indicator. Alternatively, you can enter the command in a file and pass the filename to at or batch. This method is especially useful if you want to run a script as the command; you can simply pass at the name of the script.

- **-m**   This option sends mail to the user who runs the job when the job finishes.

- **-l**   Causes at to display jobs that are currently queued. This option is equivalent to typing **atq**.

- **-d**   Deletes a job from the queue. The atrm command does the same thing.

- **-b**   Causes at to work like batch.

- **-v**   When used with -l, displays jobs that are completed but that haven't yet been removed from the queue.

- **time**   The time for the job to be run. You can use several formats for this specification, including *HHMM* or *HH:MM* to run a job at a given time in the next 24 hours, with an optional AM or PM suffix. The strings noon, midnight, and teatime (4:00 P.M.) also work. To specify a run time more than 24 hours in the future, you can provide a date after the time specification. The date can take the form *MMDDYY*, *MM.DD.YY*, *MM/DD/YY*, or *month-name day year*. You can also give the time in a relative form by giving a plus sign (+), a value, and units, such as +30 minutes.

In a default FreeBSD installation, only root may run at or its related commands. You can change this restriction by adding the files /var/at/at.allow or /var/at/at.deny. To give only a few specific users permission to use these commands, create at.allow and place those users' usernames in the file. To enable everybody but specific users to use at, create at.deny and place the restricted users' names in the file.

As an example of at in action, consider the following command:

```
$ at -m +2 minutes
/bin/ls > ~/listing.txt
```

You can type this command, terminate it by pressing ENTER and then pressing CTRL-D. A short time later, a file called listing.txt should appear in your home directory, containing the output of the ls command, and you should receive e-mail telling you that the command has completed.

The at command queue is processed by a cron job, as described in the next section. The default FreeBSD configuration runs this job every five minutes, so it may take more than two minutes for this example command to run.

An Overview of Cron's Operation

Often, scheduling a single job isn't enough; you must schedule a job to repeat on a regular basis. For instance, you might want to use the fetchmail program (described in Chapter 19) to check your ISP for mail once an hour or use a time server (described in Chapter 22) to set your system's time once a day. These are situations in which cron comes into play; it tells your system to run specific scripts, often called *cron jobs*, at regular intervals.

Cron provides substantial flexibility in scheduling cron job execution. You can tell it to run a job as frequently as once a minute, although in practice you're unlikely to do this. You can also schedule a job to execute at different intervals on different days or times of day—for instance, more frequently during working hours than late at night or on weekends.

The two basic types of cron jobs are *system cron jobs*, which only root can create; and *user cron jobs*, which ordinary users can create. These two types of cron jobs offer similar functionality. You create or edit system cron jobs as root by editing files in /etc, but you create or edit user cron jobs as root or as an ordinary user by using the crontab utility.

Once created, system and user cron jobs have essentially identical capabilities. FreeBSD ships with a standard set of system cron jobs that handle functions like rotating log files so that they don't grow to consume all disk space. If you want to add new administrative cron jobs, you can do so using either system cron jobs or user cron jobs. Normally, tasks that don't require root or some other system account privileges are handled by user cron jobs.

FreeBSD's cron functionality is provided by a daemon called `cron`. This is one of many daemons started in the BSD startup scripts (specifically, in /etc/rc; consult Figure 6-1). This daemon runs constantly and checks its queue every minute to see if any cron jobs should be executed. If so, it runs these jobs; if not, it sleeps for another minute.

Creating System Cron Jobs

The main system cron job control file is /etc/crontab. This file begins with some variable assignments, like this:

```
PATH=/etc:/bin:/sbin:/usr/bin:/usr/sbin
```

These set up the cron environment, so that you don't need to type the full path to programs and so that programs can use environment variables upon which they rely. The file can also include comment lines, which begin with pound signs (#) and are ignored. The most important `crontab` entries take the form

```
minute   hour   day-of-month   month   day-of-week   user   command
```

The first five columns contain codes for the time a command should be run. You can specify a time in several different forms:

- **Every time**   An asterisk (*) means that the job executes for any value of the specified time unit. For instance, if a job should run every day, include an asterisk in the *day-of-month* and *day-of-week* columns.

> **Note**
>
> *If you provide nonasterisk values for both the* day-of-month *and* day-of-week *fields, cron executes the command when* either *field matches the current day. Providing a nonasterisk value for just one means that the command executes only on the specified day, overriding the asterisk for the other field.*

- **Simple numeric**   A single number, such as 7 or 23, is interpreted as you might expect. In the case of the *day-of-week* column, 0 and 7 both correspond to Sunday. The *hour* is specified in 24-hour format.

- **Names**   The *month* and *day-of-week* columns accept names. Use the first three letters of the month or day name, such as Nov for November or Tue for Tuesday. Case is unimportant.

- **Ranges**   If you want an action to repeat during a particular range, you can specify a range by using a dash (-), as in Mon-Fri in the *day-of-week* column or 8-17 in the *hour* column.

■ **Lists**   You can list specific values by separating them with commas, as in 0,20,40 in the *minute* column to have a job run three times an hour.

■ **Stepped values**   You can follow an asterisk or a range with a slash (/) and a number to have it skip values. For instance, an *hour* value of */3 causes the job to run every third hour.

The *user* column lists the user under whose name the job is to run. For system cron jobs, most run with root authority, but you can specify another user if a job doesn't require root privileges. Finally, the *command* column lists the command that's to be run. This may be a shell script that's stored somewhere on the disk, or an ordinary command. For instance, consider the following /etc/crontab entry:

```
04,34 8-17 * * mon-fri mailnull fetchmail
```

This entry causes cron to run the fetchmail command twice an hour (at 4 and 34 minutes past the hour), every hour from 8:04 A.M. to 5:34 P.M. Monday through Friday, using the mailnull account. (This account is a standard low-privilege account for mail operations.) Such an entry is a fairly typical system cron job.

> **Tip**   *This example illustrates a principle that you may want to employ. You might be tempted to schedule cron jobs for "logical" times, such as on the hour and half-hour. If many people do this for network operations, though, the load on the network servers may spike at these times, causing problems. Thus, using a more peculiar time, such as four minutes after the hour or half hour, can help reduce the load on the network server. Of course, this principle may be unimportant for purely local cron jobs, but useful for tasks like retrieving e-mail or setting your clock from an external time server.*

Many cron tasks are handled through the following standard lines in /etc/crontab:

```
# do daily/weekly/monthly maintenance
1       3       *       *       *       root    periodic daily
15      4       *       *       6       root    periodic weekly
30      5       1       *       *       root    periodic monthly
```

These lines invoke the periodic utility, which runs scripts stored in subdirectories of /etc/periodic—specifically, /etc/periodic/daily, /etc/periodic/weekly, and /etc/periodic/monthly. One quick way to add a system cron job is therefore to add a script to perform your task to one of these directories. In FreeBSD, these scripts are named *sequence.name*, where *sequence* is a three-digit sequence number and *name* is a name describing the task. The tasks are run in the order indicated by their sequence numbers.

Creating User Cron Jobs

Ordinary users can create cron jobs by using the `crontab` command. This command's syntax is:

```
crontab [-u user] [-l | -r | -e] [cronfile]
```

Ordinarily, you type **crontab *cronfile***, where *cronfile* is the name of the crontab file you want to install. This file's format is almost identical to that of the system `/etc/crontab` file. The only difference is that you do *not* specify a username for the cron jobs. Using `crontab` in this way installs the specified file, replacing whatever file might have been in use for the user's crontab file before.

The `-l`, `-r`, and `-e` options cause the system to display the current crontab file, remove the crontab file, or edit the crontab file, respectively. In the final case, the system uses the editor specified by the `EDITOR` environment variable, which defaults to `vi` on a standard installation. If you use one of these options, you do *not* list a `cronfile`; the system works on the crontab file that's already installed for the user.

The `root` user can use the `-u user` option to `crontab`, in order to replace, view, delete, or edit a user's crontab file. Ordinary users can't use the `-u user` option. One use of this function is to set up cron jobs in the name of a system account, such as `daemon` or `nullmail`. These accounts normally can't be used as login accounts, so only `root` can create cron jobs in their names. Of course, you can also use this option to debug an ordinary login user's crontab file.

Summary

Most of the time, when you use a FreeBSD system, you use it to run programs. Ordinarily, you do this by typing the program name at a command prompt or by launching the program from a GUI environment. Some critically important programs run in other ways, though. Most importantly, the FreeBSD kernel itself is launched by a boot loader program, and the kernel in turn runs the `init` process, which runs various startup scripts. These scripts launch assorted daemons and configuration programs, which define how the FreeBSD system operates immediately after it's booted. Being able to tweak this process is important, so that you can customize your system. The FreeBSD login process also involves running various programs. Which programs run depend upon the login method chosen, and altering these programs enables you to alter the environment that you or your users see upon login. Finally, FreeBSD provides methods of running programs at scheduled times, either once (via `at` or `batch`) or at regular intervals (via cron). These timed methods can enable you to schedule tasks so that they don't impose an undue burden on system resources or to schedule tasks that should be performed on a regular basis.

Chapter 7

Managing Partitions

hapter 2 included an introduction to the FreeBSD partitioning system—enough
to get you up and running. This chapter covers FreeBSD partitions in more detail,
including the reasoning behind the use of partitions; tools you use to create,
manipulate, and use partitions; and the layout of FreeBSD partitions and directories.
After you read this chapter, you should have a better idea of why the FreeBSD installation
routines created partitions the way they did, and you may begin to understand why
that system is or is not a good match to your needs. On subsequent FreeBSD installations,
you might consider creating a new partitioning scheme.

Partitions: Containers for Data Files

A disk partition is something like a file cabinet drawer: You can store a limited number
of files and folders (or directories) in a partition. If a file cabinet drawer or partition fills
up, you must place additional files in another drawer or partition. Unlike a file cabinet
drawer, partitions can vary substantially in size—one partition on a disk might be just
a few hundred kilobytes, and another might consume several gigabytes. Although your
FreeBSD installation created partitions, you may want to change that configuration (a
difficult task) or add a new hard disk to expand your storage capacity.

Reasons for Partitioning a Disk

As described in Chapter 2, hard disks are normally partitioned to provide different OSs
with different data storage areas, to create data storage areas with different characteristics
for a single OS, or to separate data within an OS to reduce problems caused by runaway
disk processes or the like. Ordinarily, you'll create a partitioning scheme when you
install FreeBSD, and then leave it alone. There are reasons you might need to partition
disks after this point, though:

- **Adding a disk**   If your current disk fills up, you may want to add another one.
  When you do this, you must partition the new disk and add its partitions to your
  current directory tree.

- **Replacing a disk**   If your current disk is too small and you can't easily add a
  new disk, you may want to move your system over to a replacement. As when
  installing your system from scratch or adding a new disk, you must partition
  the replacement disk. You must then copy your old system to the new disk,
  which can be a tricky task. In brief, it can be accomplished by using tar to copy
  the data through a pipe, if you can temporarily connect both drives. You may
  then need to use an emergency boot system to install a boot loader on the new
  disk. For instance, if the new drive is mounted at /mnt, you can copy a system
  that's stored on root (/), /usr, and /home with a command like the following:

  ```
  # tar cplf - / /usr /home | (cd /mnt; tar xvpf -)
  ```

- **Repartitioning**   The trickiest partitioning task is *repartitioning*, in which you re-work an existing partitioning scheme because you've found you made incorrect initial guesses about the partition sizes you'd need. Commercial and open source tools exist to help do this in a non-destructive way for some filesystems, but options for FreeBSD's native Fast File System (FFS) are limited. Specifically, the standard FreeBSD `growfs` tool can increase the size of an FFS filesystem. This tool requires that you first modify the partition size with `disklabel`, and it requires that you have free space after the partition you intend to grow. In many cases, instead of using a partition resizer program, you must find a temporary home for the data on any partitions you want to resize. This location can be on another hard disk, on a removable disk, on a network file server, or on a tape backup drive. You can then re-work your partitioning scheme and restore your data.

- **Using removable media**   Some removable media, such as floppy disks, are not partitioned. Others, such as Zip disks, usually are partitioned. These disks usually come in a prepartitioned form, but you may need to redo this scheme, particularly if you want to use FFS for data storage.

Disk partitioning is an inherently destructive process, except when using nondestructive partitioning tools such as PartitionMagic (`http://www.powerquest.com`), GNU Parted (`http://www.gnu.org/software/parted/`), and `growfs`. Thus, partitioning is a task that's best done once and then not changed for a long time.

 Whenever you perform any type of partitioning or filesystem creation task, be very careful to use the correct device filename. It's very easy to mistype device filenames, thus wiping out all the data on a partition or even on an entire hard disk.

Creating Partitions

Many tools exist to help you create partitions, and some of these have already been discussed in Chapter 2. Nonetheless, it's useful to review how these tools fit together, and to introduce some new ways to get the job done.

Using Third-Party Tools

One approach to partitioning is to use third-party tools. Most OSs include a utility called `fdisk` or `FDISK` to partition a disk. FreeBSD's `fdisk` is described shortly, in "Using Command-Line Tools." Other disk partitioning tools are most useful when preparing a disk for use in a multi-OS environment, or if you want to use a filesystem other than FFS on a removable disk. Such tools are usually simpler to use than FreeBSD's `fdisk`, although FreeBSD's `sysinstall` interface simplifies use of `fdisk`.

In addition to the tools included with most OSs, there are partitioning tools that don't come with any OS. PartitionMagic and GNU Parted are two examples in this category. Most such tools are far more powerful than the average OS's partitioning tool because they support nondestructive repartitioning of supported OSs' filesystems or other advanced features.

Third-party tools are useful for creating *x*86 partitions, but not for creating BSD partitions within the BSD slice. Thus, if you use this approach, you can go only so far, at least if you want to use FFS. You have two choices when creating a partition for use by FreeBSD. First, you can create a primary partition and give it a partition type code of 165 (hexadecimal 0xA5). FreeBSD will recognize this as a FreeBSD slice, and you can then use other tools to create BSD partitions within the slice. Second, you can leave blank space on the disk, and use FreeBSD tools to create both the FreeBSD slice and the partitions within it.

Using sysinstall

The "Partitioning the System" section of Chapter 2 describes using `sysinstall` during system installation to create a FreeBSD slice and the partitions within it. As a general rule, this is the simplest way to create FreeBSD partitions on a second hard disk, removable disk, or the like.

After you've installed FreeBSD, you can reach the `sysinstall` partitioning tools as follows:

1. As `root`, type **/stand/sysinstall**. This command launches the `sysinstall` utility and displays the main `sysinstall` menu, shown in the following illustration.

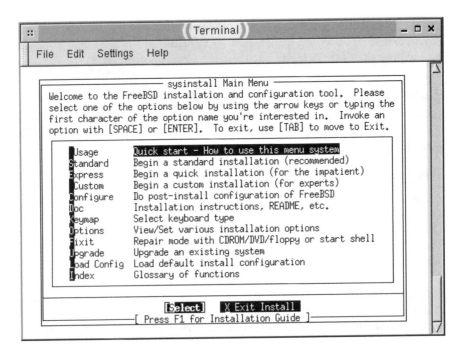

2. Use the ARROW keys to scroll down to the Configure option and press ENTER. The FreeBSD Configuration Menu opens, as shown next.

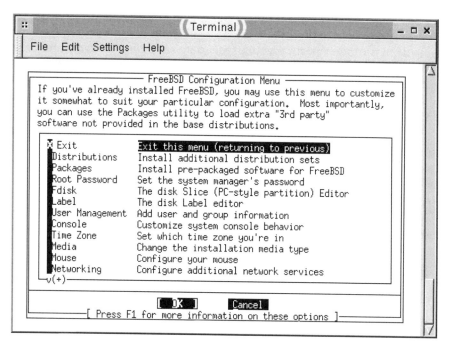

```
┌─────────────── FreeBSD Configuration Menu ───────────────┐
│ If you've already installed FreeBSD, you may use this menu to customize  │
│ it somewhat to suit your particular configuration.  Most importantly,    │
│ you can use the Packages utility to load extra "3rd party"               │
│ software not provided in the base distributions.                         │
│ ┌─────────────────────────────────────────────────────────┐             │
│ │ Exit            Exit this menu (returning to previous)    │             │
│ │ Distributions   Install additional distribution sets      │             │
│ │ Packages        Install pre-packaged software for FreeBSD │             │
│ │ Root Password   Set the system manager's password         │             │
│ │ Fdisk           The disk Slice (PC-style partition) Editor│             │
│ │ Label           The disk Label editor                     │             │
│ │ User Management Add user and group information             │             │
│ │ Console         Customize system console behavior         │             │
│ │ Time Zone       Set which time zone you're in             │             │
│ │ Media           Change the installation media type        │             │
│ │ Mouse           Configure your mouse                      │             │
│ │ Networking      Configure additional network services     │             │
│ └v(+)─────────────────────────────────────────────────────┘             │
│                                                                          │
│                    [  OK  ]        [ Cancel ]                            │
│         ─[ Press F1 for more information on these options ]─            │
└──────────────────────────────────────────────────────────────────────────┘
```

3. The Fdisk option enables you to edit the *x*86 partition table, much as you can with the fdisk utilities in other OSs. If you use this option, you'll be automatically moved to the next option when you finish.

4. The Label option enables you to edit the FreeBSD partition table (also known as the *disk label*) within the FreeBSD slice. Editing the disk label enables you to set up FreeBSD partitions.

The details of the last two steps are described in Chapter 2, so consult it when you create new partitions using sysinstall. When you finish using the FreeBSD Disklabel Editor tool, use the w option to save your changes. At this point, sysinstall runs the newfs utility, which creates filesystems on your new FreeBSD partitions. Thus, sysinstall can control the entire partition-creation process—creating a FreeBSD slice, creating BSD partitions within that slice, and creating filesystems on the partitions.

Using Command-Line Tools

The sysinstall utility is a convenient way to create partitions, but sometimes you need to dig into the underlying tools that it uses. There are three of these, as far as partition creation is concerned: fdisk, disklabel, and newfs. Variants of this last one create filesystems other than FFS. These tools control the creation of the *x*86 primary partition

BASIC SYSTEM ADMINISTRATION

table, the BSD disk label within the FreeBSD slice, and the filesystem within the BSD partitions.

Using fdisk Like the disk partitioning programs in other OSs, FreeBSD's fdisk lets you examine or edit the *x86* partition table. This program can display information on a partition table, write a new partition table from data stored in a configuration file, or write data based on information it collects from you using a rigid prompting order. If you want to alter partitions in a more arbitrary manner, you should use sysinstall or a non-FreeBSD partitioning tool.

The fdisk command can be used with one of two syntax forms:

```
fdisk -f configfile [-itv] [disk]
fdisk [-BIaistu] [-b bootcode] [-1234] [disk]
```

The first form collects data from a configuration file stored on disk (*configfile*). If you routinely partition disks that are identical in capacity, you might consider creating a file describing the layout of these disks and using this format of the command. The result can be quicker and less error-prone partitioning. The format of this file is described in the fdisk man page, so consult it if you want to use this option.

The second form of the command either displays information on the disk or enables you to edit the partition table. If you specify only the target *disk* (such as /dev/ad0 for the first EIDE disk or /dev/da1 for the second SCSI disk), fdisk displays the partition table information, thus:

```
# fdisk /dev/ad0
******* Working on device /dev/ad0 *******
parameters extracted from in-core disklabel are:
cylinders=784 heads=255 sectors/track=63 (16065 blks/cyl)

parameters to be used for BIOS calculations are:
cylinders=784 heads=255 sectors/track=63 (16065 blks/cyl)

Media sector size is 512
Warning: BIOS sector numbering starts with sector 1
Information from DOS bootblock is:
The data for partition 1 is:
sysid 12,(DOS or Windows 95 with 32 bit FAT, LBA)
    start 63, size 4192902 (2047 Meg), flag 0
        beg: cyl 0/ head 1/ sector 1;
        end: cyl 260/ head 254/ sector 63
The data for partition 2 is:
sysid 165,(FreeBSD/NetBSD/386BSD)
    start 4192965, size 8401995 (4102 Meg), flag 80 (active)
```

```
        beg: cyl 261/ head 0/ sector 1;
        end: cyl 783/ head 254/ sector 63
The data for partition 3 is:
<UNUSED>
The data for partition 4 is:
<UNUSED>
```

This output includes information on the disk's cylinder/head/sector (CHS) geometry, sector size, and the four primary partitions. In particular, partition 1 in this example is a 2047MB DOS or Windows FAT partition, and partition 2 is a 4102MB FreeBSD slice. Partitions 3 and 4 are undefined.

Note *FreeBSD's* fdisk *does* not *present information on logical partitions, nor does it let you create or otherwise manipulate such partitions.*

Options you can use with fdisk are

- **-B** Reinitializes the boot loader in the MBR, which can help fix some boot problems.
- **-b *bootcode*** Writes the boot loader in the MBR from the specified file, which defaults to /boot/mbr.
- **-u** Updates the MBR. The program prompts you for changes to disk geometry and all partitions, enabling you to add, delete, or edit partition information.
- **-I** Creates a partition table that contains a single BSD slice that covers the entire hard disk. This is a quick way to set up a disk if you want to dedicate it to FreeBSD.
- **-i** Initializes the MBR and prompts for changes, much as does -u.
- **-f *configfile*** Reads partition information from a configuration file.
- **-a** Changes only the active partition.
- **-s** Prints summary information and exits.
- **-t** Test mode; performs all the usual actions, but doesn't write data.
- **-v** In conjunction with -f, causes fdisk to print the partition table information.
- **-1 through -4** Operates only on the specified partition.

In practice, you'll probably use **fdisk -i /dev/*diskid*** or **fdisk -u /dev/ *diskid*** to make most changes. Using one of these commands produces output similar to that shown earlier, except that fdisk prompts you about whether to change each piece of information. At the end of the process, the program asks if you want to save the changes, so you can back out of a change if you make a mistake. You may want to experiment with this command (adding -t or using a spare disk for extra safety) to see what you can do with it.

If you have a spare Zip disk or the like, it can make an excellent test platform. Be sure to specify the correct device identifier, though.

Using disklabel   The `disklabel` command lets you view or modify the partition table that's stored within the FreeBSD slice—the disk label. This command can be called in many ways, each having its own effects. A simplified syntax for the command is as follows (consult the `disklabel` man page for more options):

```
disklabel [-wenWN] disk [disk-type | auto]
```

The options available in this simplified syntax are

- **-w**   Writes a new disk label to the disk. The new disk label contains no partitions. You must normally specify a `disk-type` or use the `auto` keyword.

- **-e**   Edits an existing disk label using the editor specified by the `EDITOR` environment variable. When you exit from the editor, your changes will be saved.

- **-n**   Prevents changes from being written to the disk; instead, a summary is displayed on the screen.

- **-W**   Enables writing to the disk label area. FreeBSD often disallows writing to the disk label, so you may need to use this option to enable such alterations.

- **-N**   Disables writing to the disk label area. This option undoes the effect of the `-W` option.

- **_disk_**   The disk that's to be modified. Normally, this is an *x86* partition identifier, such as `/dev/ad0s2` or `/dev/da0s1`. You can omit the `/dev/` portion of the identifier, and in fact doing so is sometimes necessary, as when you use the `auto` disk type.

- **_disk-type_ | auto**   The `/etc/disktab` file contains a set of disk geometry and partition settings for some common disk types. You can specify a disk from this set, or pass `auto` as a parameter to have the system auto-generate the disk information. Some of the disks in `disktab` are regular hard disks, but others are common removable media types, such as `zip100` and `orb2200`.

Typically, when you're preparing a new disk, you'll issue at least two `disklabel` commands: one to create a new FreeBSD partition table and another to edit it. You may need to surround these by commands that use the `-W` and `-N` options if you find your changes aren't having any effect. For instance, the following sequence sets up a new Zip disk on `/dev/da0s4`:

```
# disklabel -w da0s4 auto
# disklabel -e /dev/da0s4
```

These commands look simple, but the second hides substantial complexity because you must manually edit the disk label information. The file you'll see in your editor begins with several lines of information such as the CHS geometry and number of sectors. Towards the end of the file are the partition definitions. On a fresh system, there'll be only one, with a filesystem type (`fstype`) of `unused`. A more complete layout resembles the following:

```
8 partitions:
#        size    offset    fstype   [fsize bsize bps/cpg]
  a:   262144         0    4.2BSD    1024  8192    22    # (Cyl.   0 -  16*)
  b:   213163    262144    swap                          # (Cyl.  16*-  29*)
  c:  8401995         0    unused       0     0          # (Cyl.   0 - 522)
  e:   307200    475307    4.2BSD    1024  8192    23    # (Cyl.  29*-  48*)
  f:   307200    782507    4.2BSD    1024  8192    23    # (Cyl.      48*-  67*)
  g:  3407872   1089707    4.2BSD    1024  8192    22    # (Cyl.      67*- 279*)
  h:  3904416   4497579    4.2BSD    1024  8192    22    # (Cyl.     279*- 522*)
```

The first column is the partition identifying number. The second is the partition's size in blocks (normally 512 bytes; you can double-check by looking for the line earlier in the file that's labeled `bytes/sector`). The `offset` column is the partition's starting point. The `fstype` column is the filesystem type—set this to `4.2BSD` for normal FFS partitions. The `fsize`, `bsize`, and `bps/cpg` columns specify filesystem-specific values. Try using the defaults shown here (the `bps/cpg` value isn't critically important). The information following the pound sign on each line is a comment that describes the cylinder numbers the partition occupies; you can ignore this information.

The partition identifiers have particular meanings. Partition a is reserved for the root (/) partition, b is reserved for swap space, and c refers to the entire disk. Although it's no longer used today, d used to be reserved, as well, and some utilities behave poorly if you use the d partition. The remaining partition letters through h are available for normal filesystems.

Creating partitions in this way is normally quite tricky because you must be very careful not to create overlapping partitions. You must check and double-check the `size` and `offset` columns; a new partition's `offset` value should exactly equal the sum of the preceding partition's `offset` and `size` values. (An exception is that partition c essentially does not exist, as far as these calculations are concerned.)

Editing the BSD disk label with the `disklabel` utility is a very powerful capability, but the potential for doing harm is extremely great. For this reason, you should probably use `sysinstall` and its interactive `disklabel` interface, rather than use `disklabel` directly. If you need to make unusual changes for some reason, access to `disklabel` can prove useful, though.

Using newfs   The `newfs` command enables you to create a new FFS filesystem. Its syntax is as follows:

```
newfs [-NOU] [-S sector-size] [-b block-size] [-f frag-size] ⏎
[-g file-size] [-i bytes-per-inode] [-m percent] [-o space|time] ⏎
[-s size] [-v] device
```

This syntax presents a subset of available `newfs` *options. Most of the remaining options relate to optimizations based on disk geometry information that's meaningless for modern hard disks.*

The meanings of the options for this command are

- **-N**   Displays filesystem parameters without actually creating the filesystem.

- **-O**   Creates a 4.3BSD-format filesystem. This option is most often used when a system must be booted using an older BIOS.

- **-U**   Enables *soft updates,* an optimization strategy that speeds recovery after a power failure or system crash.

- **-S *sector-size***   Sets the size of sectors in bytes. This value defaults to 512, and should almost never be changed.

- **-b *block-size***   Sets the block size used by the filesystem. This is the minimum amount of disk space that FreeBSD can allocate to a file. This value must be a power of 2, and the minimum allowable value is 4096. The default is 16384. Larger values can produce modest performance improvements on large partitions at the cost of wasted disk space.

- **-f *frag-size***   Sets the fragment size in bytes. This value must be a power of 2 between *block-size*/8 and *block-size*. The default value is 2048.

- **-g *file-size***   Sets the expected average file size.

- **-i *bytes-per-inode***   Sets the number of bytes per inode. Each file is associated with an inode, so this effectively sets the limit on the number of files the filesystem can support. The default is to create one inode per $4 \times$ *frag-size* bytes of disk space, which is usually sufficient.

- **-m *percent***   Sets the percentage of disk space that's reserved for `root`. The default value is 8, which gives `root` some room for recovering in case a disk fills up. Without this option, `root` might not even be able to log on to fix problems.

- **-o space|time**   Optimizes FFS for space (to fit the most files on the partition) or time (to produce the best possible disk speed). The default is to optimize for time if *percent* is 8 or more, or space if *percent* is less than 8.

- **-s *size***   Sets the filesystem size in sectors. This value is normally determined by the partition size.

- **-v** Forces `newfs` to create a filesystem on a partitionless device. You might use this to create an FFS floppy disk, for instance.
- **device** Sets the name of the device, such as `/dev/da0s4e` or `/dev/ad1s2a`.

In most cases, you won't need most of these options; `newfs` picks reasonable defaults. Instead, you can type a command like the following:

```
# newfs /dev/da0s4e
```

This command creates a new filesystem on `/dev/da0s4e`. In some cases, you may want or need to add some options.

For removable-media devices such as Zip disks, you can usually set −m 0 because these devices aren't usually needed for basic system operations. Using −m 0 gives you more space for data storage, which is usually the best configuration for a removable-media device.

FreeBSD includes another tool that's related to `newfs`: `newfs_msdos`. This command creates a FAT filesystem. Its operation is similar to that of `newfs`, but its options differ. The most important `newfs_msdos` options are `-F FAT-type` (which takes values of `12`, `16`, or `32` as `FAT-type`, for the bit size of the FAT) and `-L label` (which lets you set the FAT filesystem's disk label). Neither option is strictly necessary; `newfs_msdos` computes a default FAT size based on the partition or device size, and the label can be left blank, although it may be useful in helping to identify a disk in Windows.

Ordinarily, you'll use `newfs_msdos` to put FAT filesystems on floppy disks or other removable-media devices. It can also be useful if you want to add space for Windows on a new disk, or in some emergency recovery situations, if you're using FreeBSD to restore a DOS or Windows system. You don't ordinarily create FAT filesystems on FreeBSD partitions, but on primary or logical *x*86 partitions, or on raw floppy disk devices.

*When used on a floppy disk, the DOS and Windows FORMAT command combines a low-level format (which prepares the disk to receive data) and a high-level format (writing the filesystem). In FreeBSD, these are two separate operations. If a floppy disk has never been formatted, you can perform a low-level format on it by typing **fdformat /dev/fd0**. You can then use newfs or newfs_msdos to write an FFS or FAT filesystem to the disk, respectively. You don't have to perform a low-level format on a hard disk because hard disks are low-level formatted at the factory.*

Mounting Partitions

After you've created a partition and created a filesystem on it, you must mount it to use it. Mounting can be done in one of two ways: You can temporarily mount a partition by using the `mount` command, or you can configure FreeBSD to automatically mount a partition by creating an entry for the partition in the `/etc/fstab` file.

Note

In some circumstances, it's possible to access a filesystem without mounting it. In particular, the Mtools (`http://mtools.linux.lu`) and HFS Utilities (`http://www.mars.org/home/rob/proj/hfs/`) packages give you access to DOS/Windows FAT and Macintosh HFS filesystems, respectively, without mounting them. These tools are most often used to access floppy disks, or occasionally Zip disks or similar removable-media devices. Some CD-ROMs for Macintoshes use HFS, so HFS Utilities can be useful for retrieving files from these CD-ROMs.

The mount Command

If you want to mount a partition temporarily, for testing purposes, or to access a removable media device, the usual approach is to use the `mount` command. This command attaches a filesystem to a *mount point*, which is a directory somewhere in your directory tree. The files on the filesystem then become available under that mount point. The syntax of this command is

```
mount [-adfpruvw] [-o options] [-t fs-type] [device] [mount-point]
```

The meanings of these parameters are

- **-a** This option mounts all the filesystems described in `/etc/fstab` (covered in the next section), except those marked as `noauto` in `/etc/fstab`, those that are already mounted, or those excluded by use of `-t`.

- **-d** This option does all the work of mounting a filesystem except for the actual mounting operation. It's useful for debugging, particularly in conjunction with `-v`.

- **-f** This option can have two effects. First, it forces mounting an unclean filesystem (that is, one that wasn't properly unmounted the last time it was used) in read/write mode, which is potentially dangerous. Second, it forces the revocation of read/write access to any open files when a filesystem is remounted in read-only mode using `-u`.

- **-p** This option displays information on mounted filesystems in the format used by `/etc/fstab`.

- **-r** This option causes the filesystem to be mounted read-only.

- **-u** Use this option to change the status of an already-mounted filesystem. For instance, **mount -ru /floppy** remounts the already-mounted `/floppy` as a read-only filesystem.

- **-v** This option displays verbose information on the mount process.

- **-w** This option causes a read/write mount of the filesystem. It is the default for most filesystems.

- **-o *options*** You can pass a variety of options to modify the way the filesystem is handled with this parameter. Common options include `nodev` (ignore device files), `noexec` (don't allow execution of executable files), `nosuid` (don't honor the set user ID bit on executable files), `nosymfollow` (don't follow symbolic links), and `union` (add files to existing files at the mount point rather than rendering existing files inaccessible). The `mount` man page describes more options, and there are also filesystem-specific options, some of which are covered in Chapter 4.

■ **-t *fs-type*** You can specify the filesystem type (*fs-type*) with this option. The default is `ufs`, which mounts FreeBSD's native FFS. Other possible options include `cd9660` (for ISO-9660, Joliet, and Rock Ridge CD-ROMs), `msdosfs` or `msdos` (for DOS or Windows FAT floppies or partitions), `ext2fs` (for Linux ext2fs), `ntfs` (for Windows NT/2000/XP NTFS), and `nfs` (for Network File System, or NFS, network file sharing exports).

■ ***device*** The *device* is the device filename associated with the partition or removable disk device. In the case of NFS, this is the network specification for the export, which consists of a server hostname, a colon, and the path to the exported directory, such as `nfsserver:/home`.

■ **mount-point** This is the location where you want files to be made accessible. It's normally an empty directory.

If a filesystem is listed in `/etc/fstab`, you can get by with an abbreviated `mount` command that includes either a device name or a mount point but no options. The system recovers options from the `/etc/fstab` file. This approach is often used for removable media devices such as floppy disks and CD-ROMs. For instance, the following command mounts a CD-ROM on a standard FreeBSD installation:

```
# mount /cdrom
```

If you want to specify extra options or mount a device that's not listed in `/etc/fstab`, you must add more information—at a minimum, both the device file and the mount point. For instance, suppose you're installing a new hard disk for use as a larger `/home` directory. If you've prepared it as described earlier in this section, and created a filesystem on `/dev/ad2s1e`, you could mount it temporarily on `/mnt` as follows:

```
# mount /dev/ad2s1e /mnt
```

You could then copy your existing `/home` directory tree to the new partition, delete the original files, and edit `/etc/fstab` to mount the new partition at `/home`.

Caution *When copying files to a new disk, it's best to preserve the original files for a period while you test the new configuration. If some files weren't copied correctly, you can then go back to the original directory to retrieve them. You can use the mv command to rename a directory, or unmount an old partition and not convert it for other uses for a few hours or days.*

When mounting non-FFS partitions or disks, you can use the `mount` command as described here, in conjunction with the `-t` option. Alternatively, you can use commands dedicated to each filesystem, such as `mount_cd9660` and `mount_msdosfs`. These commands are described in Chapter 4, along with their options.

Using /etc/fstab

The `/etc/fstab` file controls what partitions are mounted when FreeBSD boots and what partitions and disks may be mounted with truncated options, as just described. Listing 7-1 shows a simple `/etc/fstab` file. This listing includes a comment as the first line (indicated by the leading pound sign, #), which provides labels for each of the fields in the file. On each line, one or more spaces or tabs separate each field.

Listing 7-1.
Sample
`/etc/fstab`
File

```
# Device          Mountpoint      FStype   Options        Dump   Pass#
/dev/ad0s2b        none            swap     sw               0    0
/dev/ad0s2a        /               ufs      rw               1    1
/dev/ad0s2f        /home           ufs      rw               2    2
/dev/ad0s1         /windows        msdosfs  rw,-s,-u=1000    0    0
/dev/acd0c         /mnt/cdrom      cd9660   ro,noauto        0    0
proc               /proc           procfs   rw               0    0
speaker:/home      /speaker/home   nfs      rw               0    0
```

Most of the information in the `/etc/fstab` file is the same as information provided on a `mount` command line. In particular, the `Device` field specifies the device filename associated with the partition or disk, the `Mountpoint` field lists the mount point, and the `FStype` field specifies the filesystem type. The `Dump` field provides information on the dump frequency—the frequency with which the `dump` utility backs up a partition, if you use `dump` for backups. The `Pass#` field is the order in which `fsck` checks filesystems when the system boots—normally, the root (`/`) filesystem uses an order of 1, and other FFS partitions have an order of 2.

The `Options` field deserves more explanation. It lists options that can be passed via the `-o` parameter to `mount`. Some of these options duplicate the action of `mount` parameters that don't use `-o`, others are unique to `-o` or are used only in `/etc/fstab`, and a few are filesystem-specific. Some common options include

- **ro and rw**   These options specify a read-only or a read/write mount, respectively. An initial FreeBSD configuration specifies one or the other for every filesystem.

- **noauto**   By default, FreeBSD mounts the filesystem when it boots. Some devices, such as a CD-ROM, might be better configured with `noauto`, which makes FreeBSD ignore them at boot time. This setting enables you to issue a shorthand `mount` command, such as **mount /mnt/cdrom**, to mount the CD-ROM device specified in Listing 7-1.

■ **Filesystem-specific options** Listing 7-1 illustrates the use of some filesystem-specific options for the /windows mount point. Specifically, the -s and -u=1000 options cause FreeBSD to ignore VFAT long filenames and assign ownership of all files to the user with a user ID (UID) of 1000, respectively. Chapter 4 describes such options, and you can obtain information for more from the man pages for specific mounting subcommands, such as mount_msdosfs.

When you create an /etc/fstab file, the changes don't take effect immediately; you must type **mount -a** or reboot before you'll see new filesystems added, and any filesystems you delete won't disappear unless you reboot or unmount them manually, as described in the upcoming section, "Unmounting Partitions."

Listing 7-1 shows the use of a special filesystem known as the proc filesystem, which is mounted at /proc. This isn't a filesystem in the usual sense. Instead, it's a hardware interface method, which gives programs access to information on your hardware. Like disk filesystems, it must be mounted. You should be careful not to delete this entry because it's required by an increasing number of FreeBSD programs.

The final line in Listing 7-1 demonstrates access to an NFS export. Just as with mounting such a filesystem with mount, you specify the server name and the path on the server. Chapter 18 covers configuring an NFS server.

Unmounting Partitions

When you finish using a floppy disk, CD-ROM, or other removable-media device, you must *unmount* it before you can safely eject the device. Unmounting the filesystem tells FreeBSD to finish any pending operations and mark the partition as being in a stable state. You may also want to unmount a hard disk partition if you want to make it inaccessible.

 The floppy drives used on x86 computers have eject buttons that let you eject a floppy disk without first unmounting it. Doing so may damage the data on the disk! *Be sure to unmount a floppy disk before ejecting it!*

The command to unmount a device is umount (that's not a typo; the command does not include the first *n*.) This command's syntax is

```
umount [-fv] [-a | -A] [-h host] [-t type] device | mount-point
```

The meanings of these options are

■ **-f** This option forces the unmount operation, even if files are open on the device. It can be useful in some situations, but it's usually best to avoid this option.

■ **-v** This option displays additional information as a filesystem is unmounted.

■ **-a** This option unmounts all the filesystems described in /etc/fstab, except for the root (/) filesystem.

- **-A** This option unmounts all the currently mounted filesystems except for the root (/) filesystem.

- **-h** *host* This option is normally used to unmount NFS exports from the specified server. If used in conjunction with -t, though, you can use it to unmount local filesystems.

- **-t** *type* You can restrict umount's actions to filesystems of a specified type with this option.

In most cases, typing **umount** followed by either the device name or mount point will unmount a single filesystem. For instance, you might type the following to unmount a CD-ROM mounted as specified in Listing 7-1:

```
# umount /mnt/cdrom
```

In some cases, you may need to add more options. For instance, -f can be handy if users are currently using a device—but employing this option can cause files to disappear mid-use, which can cause unpredictable problems with many applications, so you should apply this option only as a last resort.

Using Traditional UNIX Partitioning Schemes

The preceding description of partitioning tells you how to use partitioning tools, in the sense that it gives you information on the commands. Another matter is how to *apply* these tools—that is, what sorts of partitions you should create, where they should be mounted, and so on. To some extent, the types of files that reside in particular locations determine these matters. There are also conventions that are common in FreeBSD (or in UNIX more generally), and practical limits.

You will have created a partitioning scheme when you installed FreeBSD. I present the information in this section so that you can use it on subsequent installations or to help if and when you add or replace a hard disk.

Which Directories Can Be Partitions?

The first question you should consider is which directories can be partitions. Most can be. FreeBSD bases its directory layout on the root (/) partition, which contains both ordinary directories and mount points. Naturally, the root directory needs its own partition. Most of the directories that fall directly off of root can also reside on their own partitions. The main exceptions are /etc, /sbin, /bin, and /boot. (The /dev and /proc filesystems are also separate, but they don't occupy partitions on the disk.) These directories all hold utilities that the system needs when booting.

In addition to partitions that fall directly off of the root partition, you can place subdirectories in their own partitions. For instance, you might want to put /usr/ local or /usr/X11R6 in their own partitions. This configuration will work whether the /usr directory is in a partition of its own or it's an ordinary subdirectory on the root partition.

Common Partitioning Schemes

The FreeBSD installation routines can automatically create common partitioning layouts. In particular, the system may automatically set up separate root (/), /home, /usr, /tmp, /var, and swap partitions, using sizes that are designed for the average system. Chapter 2 describes this arrangement. The /home directory holds user files, /usr holds most program files, /tmp holds user temporary data, /var holds various queues and other system-level temporary data, and swap functions as an extension to your system's RAM. If you like, you can use as few as two partitions: a root partition and a swap partition. If you want to increase your use of partitions, you can do so. Common additions to the five-partition FreeBSD split include /usr/X11R6, /usr/ local, /opt, and expansion directories for additional user space (users' home directories can be split across multiple directories or partitions, such as separate /home and /home2 directories, if you need to add space).

Using separate partitions for these functions offers several advantages over trying to use very few partitions:

- **Variable filesystem and mount options**   You can use different filesystem and mount options on each partition, thus optimizing system performance and improving security. For instance, /usr can be mounted read-only, reducing the risk that a miscreant could modify important system files; or you could mount /var with options to optimize disk speed if it's used heavily.

- **Filesystem layout**   With some careful planning, you can place partitions on the disk in an order that can optimize performance. Heavily-accessed partitions should go near the center of the disk, to reduce disk head seek times. To do this, create partitions using fdisk or disklabel in the desired order. If you have two physical disks, you can place partitions such that two heavily-used partitions reside one per disk, again improving performance.

- **Improved robustness**   Disks sometimes lose data after a power failure or system crash. If your partitions are small, chances are you'll lose less data, thereby greatly simplifying recovery efforts.

These advantages are at least partly offset by an advantage of using few partitions: Using separate partitions means that each individual partition is more likely to fill up quickly, particularly if you misjudge the partition sizes. You can generally work around this limitation by using symbolic links to place subdirectories on other partitions, but this configuration requires extra effort to set up, and it reduces the benefits of using multiple partitions.

Mounting Non-FreeBSD Partitions

In addition to the standard FreeBSD partitions, you may need to mount non-FreeBSD filesystems. These may be partitions for other OSs, such as Windows, or they may be removable-media devices such as floppy disks or CD-ROMs. There are two common approaches to mounting such filesystems:

- **Off the root** You can mount non-FreeBSD filesystems directly off the root directory. For instance, the default configuration includes a /cdrom mount point for CD-ROM devices. You might create a /c or /windows mount point to hold a Windows partition's contents.

- **Off /mnt** The /mnt directory traditionally holds removable-media or other temporary filesystems. In a default configuration, /mnt contains no subdirectories, but you may prefer creating subdirectories for specific purposes, such as /mnt/ floppy for floppy disks or /mnt/cdrom for CD-ROMs.

Listing 7-1 shows examples of both types of placement. In particular, that listing includes a /windows directory for Windows files, a /speaker directory and /speaker/ home subdirectory for holding exports from the speaker file server, and a /mnt/ cdrom directory for CD-ROMs. This final item is at variance with the standard FreeBSD configuration.

Understanding the FHS

As described in Chapter 1, the history of UNIX includes quite a few splits of UNIX into competing branches, as well as cross-pollination of ideas across branches. One consequence of this wild past has been a proliferation of schemes for the location of files. This situation is generally viewed as a disadvantage of UNIX as a whole because it means that somebody trained on one UNIX variant may have problems administering another simply because the administrator may not know where the relevant files reside. A partial solution to this problem is the Filesystem Hierarchy Standard (FHS), which was developed in the mid-1990s as a formalization of standards for directory uses and even the placement of critical system files. This section provides an overview of the FHS. Understanding it will help you understand why FreeBSD places configuration, program, and user files where it does.

The Role of the FHS

The FHS is fully described in documents available from its web site, http:// www.pathname.com/fhs/. The latest version as I write these words is 2.2, which was released in May of 2001. Work is underway on FHS 2.3, but chances are the basic features described here will remain relevant in this and subsequent versions.

The FHS sets up two major distinctions that are used to describe directories:

- **Static vs. variable files**   *Static* files don't change very often, but *variable* files do. For instance, program binary files are considered static, whereas user data files are variable.
- **Shareable vs. unshareable files**   It makes sense, under at least some circumstances, to share certain files with other computers, but other files are inherently local in nature and should never be shared. For instance, user data files and program files are both potentially shareable, but local configuration files are not shareable.

Note   *You can configure an NFS server to share an unshareable directory, but doing so provides no advantage and may pose a security risk.*

Taken together, these criteria create a 2×2 matrix. The FHS attempts to place every directory within one cell of this matrix. In some cases, the directories that fall directly off of the root directory can't be placed in a single cell, in which case the FHS places sub-directories in a cell. This scheme is illustrated in Figure 7-1, which presents this 2×2 matrix and a sampling of directories placed in appropriate cells in this matrix. The goal is to be able to classify directories so that it's possible to place data on partitions that can be mounted read-only whenever possible (for static files), and to isolate directories that might be shared via NFS from those that shouldn't be so shared.

Note   *The static/variable and shareable/unshareable distinctions aren't absolute. For instance, although /home is shown as being shareable in Figure 7-1, you might not want to share your /home directory.*

Within this hierarchy, the FHS lays out a series of required and optional directories. To be FHS-compliant, an OS must include the required directories or links of the same name that point elsewhere. The standard also includes extra information about certain directories; for instance, it states that /bin should have no subdirectories, and it provides information on a minimum set of files that should exist in some directories.

	Shareable	Unshareable
Static	/usr /opt	/etc /boot
Variable	/home /var/mail	/var/run /var/log

Figure 7-1.   *Every directory should contain files that fall in only one cell of the static/variable × shareable/unshareable matrix.*

An Overview of FHS Directories

The complete FHS is a 41-page document, so it's impossible to describe it fully in this chapter. Highlights of the FHS directories are

- **Root (/) filesystem** This directory is the base of the filesystem tree. The FHS specifies that this directory must contain subdirectories or mount points called /bin, /boot, /dev, /etc, /lib, /mnt, /opt, /sbin, /tmp, /usr, and /var. The FHS also lays out three optional directories, which are present on many systems: /home, /lib<qual>, and /root.

- **/bin** This static directory is shareable, although because of its importance, few systems will mount it as a client. The most basic user-accessible binary files (programs) reside here, such as ls, cp, and sh. The idea is that these commands should be accessible even if non-root partitions cannot be mounted, as might happen in some emergency situations.

- **/boot** This static and unshareable directory holds basic boot files, such as the FreeBSD kernel and boot loader support files.

- **/dev** This static and unshareable directory holds device files for accessing a computer's hardware. In FreeBSD 5.0, this is implemented via a special filesystem, devfs, which generates device files based on the hardware that's actually installed in the computer.

- **/etc** The /etc directory is static and unshareable; its contents are described further in Chapter 5. This directory holds system configuration files.

- **/lib** This static and shareable directory holds vital system libraries— program code that supports other programs. (Like /bin, /lib is technically shareable, although it is seldom shared.) Specifically, any libraries needed by programs stored in /bin or /sbin must reside here. FreeBSD lacks a /lib directory because the programs in /bin and /sbin are compiled *statically*, meaning that they don't require libraries to function.

- **/mnt** This is a mount point for temporary filesystems. In a default FreeBSD installation, it's a single directory with no subdirectories, but some administrators create subdirectories for mounting different specific media under this directory, such as /mnt/floppy and /mnt/cdrom.

- **/opt** Add-on software packages reside in this static and shareable directory. In practice, /usr/local picks up most such packages in a FreeBSD system, so /opt usually goes little used. When it is used, it contains subdirectories named after the programs it contains, such as /opt/OpenOffice.org for OpenOffice.org.

- **/sbin** This static and shareable directory is much like /bin, but it holds programs, such as shutdown and fsck, that are likely to be used by only the system administrator.

■ **/tmp** This variable and unshareable directory holds temporary files. It must be accessible (for both reading and writing) to all users and programs. Programs cannot assume that files stored in /tmp will be accessible between program invocations, although in practice they often are.

■ **/usr** This shareable and static directory is very large because it holds most of the system's program files. It contains a series of subdirectories that mirror some of the directories that fall off of the root directory, such as /usr/bin, /usr/sbin, and /usr/lib. Rather than critical system files, though, these directories hold ordinary programs that the system doesn't require for minimal functionality. There are also several subdirectories that themselves contain important filesystem hierarchies, two of which are described next.

■ **/usr/local** This subdirectory holds *local* files—that is, those that were created or installed specifically for the system on which they reside, as distinct from files that are a standard part of the basic OS. For example, you may have compiled source code from scratch rather than installed a program from a precompiled package. Such files should be safe from automatic updates by OS update processes. In practice, FreeBSD relies heavily upon this directory tree because FreeBSD installs many packages here, including most programs installed through the ports system. (Methods of installing programs, including the ports system, are described in Chapter 11.)

■ **/usr/X11R6** This directory tree holds files related to the X Window System, including both X servers and X-based applications.

■ **/var** This directory holds variable data files. As shown by Figure 7-1, this directory holds both shareable and unshareable subdirectories. Examples include run files (/var/run, used to communicate when a program is running, possibly including its process ID number), mail spool files (/var/mail), and system log files (/var/log).

■ **/home** This optional directory holds variable and shareable data—specifically, user data files. In practice, few systems will do without a /home directory, although some may call it something else or split it across multiple directories. Typically, each user has one /home subdirectory. There may also be /home subdirectories that house data that's shared between users.

■ **/lib<qual>** The FHS specifies this as the name for an optional directory that's shareable and static. The <qual> portion of the name is a stand-in for a specification of a library type. The idea is that systems can have two or more library directories, each of which supports some set of system features. This feature is most commonly used for 32- and 64-bit binary support on 64-bit architectures. As such, FreeBSD on *x*86 systems doesn't use this directory.

■ **/root** This optional unshareable and variable directory functions as root's home directory; it contains root's configuration files and any files root may generate or need to store in an out-of-the-way location. If this directory doesn't exist, the default is to use the root (/) directory as root's home.

Although they're pronounced the same way, the /root directory and the root (/) directory are different directories. Don't confuse them.

You can learn more about the FHS directories by reading documentation available from the FHS web site (http://www.pathname.com/fhs/). This documentation overlaps substantially with information on FreeBSD's own partition layout, available by typing **man hier**.

In sum, the FHS provides a structure for UNIX-like OSs, specifying locations for important file types such as library files, user program files, system administration program files, configuration files, temporary files, and user data files. In many of these cases, the FHS further subdivides the file types, as in the /usr directory and even subdirectories of /usr, holding program files that aren't critical for system operation. Understanding this structure can help you locate files when you need to do so.

FreeBSD's Level of FHS Compliance

Overall, FreeBSD might be described as being mostly FHS compliant. Although FreeBSD includes all the required directories and follows the overall spirit of the guidelines, it doesn't conform to all the FHS details. For instance, the FHS specifies that the login and mount programs reside in /bin, but FreeBSD places these programs in /usr/bin and /sbin, respectively. FreeBSD also relies heavily upon directories that aren't included in the FHS (such directories don't *violate* the FHS, but they aren't explicitly covered by it). For instance, the FHS doesn't mention /usr/local/etc, where many FreeBSD packages place configuration files. Thus, the FHS is a good guideline for understanding the FreeBSD directory tree, but it's not the final authority on what goes where.

Summary

Managing partitions is critically important to FreeBSD system administration. Although your partitions are defined at system installation, you may need to modify or create new partitions when you add or replace a hard disk or if you find your original partitioning layout to be inadequate. Some removable media devices, such as Zip disks, also use partitions. In FreeBSD, the sysinstall utility provides a fairly straightforward interactive interface for managing partitions and filesystems. If you eschew such tools, or if you need to do something particularly exotic or unusual, you can run the underlying programs (fdisk, disklabel, and newfs) directly.

Once you've created partitions, you normally mount them to access them, which means you issue a mount command to add the filesystem to a point in your directory tree. Although you can mount some partitions just about anywhere, FreeBSD's directory structure requires certain files reside in certain locations, and understanding this structure can help you mount new partitions or removable media devices at appropriate locations.

The Complete Reference

Chapter 8

Managing Files

Both the FreeBSD system administrator and ordinary FreeBSD users need to know how to manage files—after all, most of what you do with a computer involves manipulating files in one way or another. This chapter therefore covers FreeBSD's general file manipulation model and tools. It begins with a look at file ownership and permissions. These issues have come up in previous chapters, but this discussion is more in depth. The chapter continues with a look at many commands that are used in manipulating files, including commands to copy, delete, and find files, as well as to change their ownership or permissions. Finally, this chapter concludes with information on backing up a computer or a subset of its data.

> **Note** *This chapter focuses on text-mode tools. You can use GUI file managers to do many of the things described in this chapter using their point-and-click interfaces. These tools are not as well standardized, though—there are many competing GUI file managers. Chapter 3 includes an introduction to the file manipulation tools available in the GNU Object Network Model Environment (GNOME), one of the more popular GUI desktop environments in FreeBSD.*

Understanding Ownership and Permissions

FreeBSD, with its UNIX heritage, relies heavily upon the concepts of file ownership and permissions. Implementations of these two concepts lie at the core of many FreeBSD security measures and make it possible for many users to use a single computer while keeping their files secure from accidental or intentional snooping or destruction. Every file has both an owner and a set of permissions that grant or deny access to the file. Understanding how these features work and interact is critical to effective file management. This knowledge is particularly important for the system administrator, who must ensure that permissions on system files and directories are set in a way that's appropriate for the system.

The Relationship Between Accounts and Ownership

Chapters 2 and 3 introduced the concept of a FreeBSD account. Chapter 10 provides much greater detail on accounts and account management. For now, recall that an account is a set of interrelated data structures that enable one person to use a computer. Accounts can also be used for internal purposes, such as accounts dedicated to a particular server. More than one person can share a single account, but such a practice is discouraged because it makes abuse difficult to track and because using separate accounts is usually preferable for the convenience of all users.

Every account is linked to one or more *groups*. Each group is a collection of accounts. For instance, suppose your computer hosts four users: dana, fox, walter, and monica. This system might have two groups, research and development. The users dana and walter might be in the research group, while dana, fox, and monica are in the development group. In addition, every system supports several standard system groups, which are used by system accounts.

In some sense, every file is owned by both one user and one group, although the user's ownership is far more important. The ownership is recorded in terms of a *user ID (UID)* and *group ID (GID)*. These are numbers that are associated with both an account (or a group) and a file. For instance, a file might be recorded as having a UID of 1021 and a GID of 1003. These numbers might be equivalent to the user `dana` and the `development` group. (In fact, FreeBSD uses the UID and GID internally; it uses names such as `dana` or `development` primarily when interacting with users.)

When a user creates a file, the user owns the file. A new file's group is normally set by the group of the directory in which the file is created. For instance, if the `/home/dana` directory belongs to the `research` group, then when `dana` creates new files in this directory, they'll also belong to the `research` group. If `dana` wants to create files that belong to the `development` group, she can use the `chgrp` command, described in the upcoming section, "Changing Ownership;" or she can create a subdirectory, change its group ownership with `chgrp`, and create new files in the subdirectory.

The nature of these relationships has several consequences that can be important in certain situations:

- **Independence of file owner and group**   The user who owns the file and the group to which the file belongs are independent. A file could be owned by `walter` but belong to the `development` group, despite the fact that `walter` isn't a member of that group.

- **Owner/ID number correspondence across systems or OSs**   If an individual has accounts on multiple systems, that user may or may not have the same UID number on both systems. This mismatch can cause a file to appear to have the wrong owner when it's transferred in some ways, such as via a floppy disk that uses FFS or via a Network File System (NFS) network file transfer. Similarly, if a computer runs multiple UNIX-like OSs, you may want to take measures to ensure that all the OSs use the same UID/account name mappings to avoid mismatches when reading each others' filesystems.

- **Changes in UID**   If you change an account's UID (say, to work around problems like those just mentioned), you'll need to adjust the ownership of all files owned by the user.

- **Changes in username**   You can change the username associated with an account without touching the files. Such changes are uncommon, though. A potential trouble related to this action is that if you reuse UIDs for now inactive accounts, the new users may find existing files in their names, which can be confusing and potentially lead to false accusations of impropriety if the new user shouldn't have access to information in the leftover files.

Accounts are associated with more than just files. Running programs are linked to accounts and groups via UIDs and GIDs. Indeed, it is technically these processes whose UIDs must match the permissions and UID of a file in order to access the file. When you log on, FreeBSD starts your shell with an appropriate UID, based on information it finds in its account files.

Using Permissions to Control Access to Files

From a text-mode shell, type **ls -l**. In any nonempty directory, you should see one or more lines like the following in response:

```
-rw-r--r--  1 fox       users    517 Jan 31 21:23 file.txt
```

This line is a long directory listing of the file. It includes information such as the file's name (file.txt), its creation date and time (Jan 31 21:23), size (517 bytes), group (users), owner (fox), number of hard links (1; links are described later in this chapter in "Creating and Using Links"), and permissions (-rw-r--r--). The permissions, owner, and group collectively control access to the file. You can change the owner and group using the chown and chgrp commands, as described in "Changing Ownership." The permission string produced by an ls -l command requires further elaboration. This string consists of ten characters. The first character is a code that represents the file's type, as shown in Table 8-1. Most files are normal data files, but other file types are very important for certain purposes. Ordinary users are most likely to be concerned

Character	Meaning
–	Normal data file; most files use this code.
d	File is a directory; directories are actually normal files, but they contain filenames and pointers to files on disk.
l	File is a symbolic link; this is a pointer to another file by name. When a program accesses the symbolic link, it reads data in the pointed-to file.
p	File is a named pipe; these enable two programs to communicate, by opening the file simultaneously, one for reading and one for writing.
s	File is a socket; these are like named pipes, but they enable network and bidirectional communication.
b	File is a block special device; this is one of two types of device files, and is used for devices that accept data transfers in blocks, such as hard disks.
c	File is a character special device; this is the second type of device file, and is used for devices that accept data a character at a time, such as serial or parallel ports.

Table 8-1. *File Type Codes and Their Meanings*

with directories and perhaps symbolic links. The other file types are used in relatively limited, but important, ways. Some of these are covered elsewhere in this book.

The final nine characters of the permission string are the most important with regard to permissions. They're broken into three groups of three characters each. These groups represent permissions for the file's owner, the file's group, and all other users (sometimes called *world* permissions). Each group represents the presence or absence of read (r), write (w), and execute (x) permission—when the character is a dash (-), the permission is absent, and when the character is present, the permission is present. A few special permission types, described shortly, place different values in the execute position.

Note *FreeBSD uses the execute permission bit to identify program files—both binary files and scripts. (It is possible to execute scripts that lack the execute bit, but the usual practice is to set this bit.) This feature contrasts with Windows, which identifies program files by their filename extensions, such as .EXE and .COM for executable files. FreeBSD binaries usually lack such extensions, although they* can *have them.*

Another method of representing the final nine characters of the permission string is to use an *octal* (base-8) code. Each of the three permissions is considered a bit in a three-bit number, so the entire permissions string is a three-digit octal number. Read permission is the high bit (octal 4), write permission is the middle bit (octal 2), and execute permission is the low bit (octal 1). You can add these bits together to obtain the octal code for each of the owner, group, and world permissions. For instance, rwxr-x--- has all three owner permissions, and so is 4+2+1=7; group read and execute, but not write, permissions, and so is 4+1=5; and no world permissions (0). Thus, rwxr-x--- can also be expressed as 750. Table 8-2 shows several permission strings, octal permission codes, and their meanings

Permission String	Octal Code	Meaning
rwxrwxrwx	777	The file's owner, the file's group, and the world have full read, write, and execute access to the file.
rwxr-xr-x	755	The file's owner has full access to the file, and the file's group and all other users may read and execute the file, but not write to it.
rwxr-x---	750	The file's owner has full access to it, and the file's group can read or execute the file, but not write to it. Others cannot access the file at all.

Table 8-2. *Permission Codes and Their Meanings*

Permission String	Octal Code	Meaning
rwx--x--x	711	The file's owner has full access to it. The file's group and all others can execute the file, but not read or write to it.
rw-rw-rw-	666	The file's owner, the file's group, and all other users can read and write to the file, but cannot execute it.
rw-r--r--	644	The file's owner can read or write to the file. The file's group and the world can read the file but not write to it. Nobody can execute the file.
r--------	400	The file's owner can read the file but not write to it or execute it. The file's group and all other users have no access to the file.

Table 8-2.   *Permission Codes and Their Meanings* (continued)

Note   *Table 8-2 is a sampling of possible permissions, but it's by no means exhaustive. There are 2^9, or 512, possible combinations in the 9-bit permission string.*

You can grant world access to a file that's greater than the group access. For instance, rw----r-- (604) gives world read access but no group access. In practice, this works just like rw-r--r-- (644) access because users in a given group also fall into the world category. This is usually the case with owner and group permissions, but it's possible for a file's owner to not belong to the file's group. In such a case, if the group permissions are greater than the owner's permissions, the group may be able to do things with the file that the owner can't do. Such configurations are very strange and have few practical applications.

Symbolic links normally have rwxr-xr-x (755) permissions. These grant every user the right to see the name of the file or directory to which the link points. Permissions on the linked-to file control access to the file itself.

One important exception to the permissions rules is the root account. The superuser can read and write any file on the computer, no matter who the owner is or what the permissions are—root can even read or write a file with 000 (---------) permissions! The superuser can also change the ownership or permissions of any file on the computer. The system administrator needs this sort of access to be able to effectively police the system.

In some relatively new configurations, `root` does not have absolute access to all files. Such configurations can be a security boon because some servers ordinarily run as `root`, which gives them—and their bugs—free reign over the system. Another limit to `root`'s power is in non-FreeBSD filesystems. When FreeBSD mounts a FAT partition or floppy disk, for instance, all the files acquire the same owner and permissions (although the FAT read-only bit is mapped as the inverse of the FreeBSD write bit). Even `root` cannot change permissions or ownership on a FAT partition on a file-by-file basis, except for write permissions, because FAT doesn't support this feature. You can use `mount_msdosfs` options to change ownership or permissions on FAT partitions, though, as described in Chapter 4.

In addition to these common permissions, there are three special permission bits that you can set on a file:

- **Set User ID (SUID)**   This permission is used in conjunction with executable files. Normally, a program runs with the UID code of the user who launches the program. You can use this bit to tell FreeBSD to use the UID of the program file, instead. This feature is used by some programs that require `root` privileges to operate normally (called *SUID `root`* programs). SUID `root` programs are potentially dangerous, but this technique is sometimes necessary when a program needs to access privileged files or data but be run by ordinary users. SUID programs can be identified by an s rather than an x in their owner execute permission position, as in `rwsr-xr-x`.

- **Set Group ID (SGID)**   This feature works much like the SUID bit, but as its name implies, it sets the program to run using its own GID rather than the user's GID. Such programs are identified by an s rather than an x in their group execute permission position, as in `rwxr-sr-x`.

- **Sticky bit**   In modern FreeBSD, the *sticky bit* is used on directories to indicate that only a file's owner may delete a file. (As described in the next section, file deletion rules often permit nonowners to delete a file.) This bit is routinely set on `/tmp` and `/var/tmp`. The sticky bit is indicated by a t rather than an x in the world execute permission position, as in `drwxr-xr-t`.

As a general rule, you shouldn't try setting these bits on any file or directory. If a program's documentation indicates that it needs to run with the SUID or SGID bit set, or that it requires a directory to have its sticky bit set, you can do so with the `chmod` command, described in the upcoming section, "Changing Permissions."

Special Considerations for Directories

Directories are a bit odd when it comes to permissions. The overarching principle in understanding directory permissions is that a directory is a file. The contents of this file happen to be filenames and pointers to disk inodes, which in turn point to the sectors on the disk that hold files. Like any file, a directory's contents are protected by the ownership and permissions associated with the directory. Thus, if a user has write access to a directory, that user can add files to or delete files from the directory—*even if the user doesn't own the file being deleted!* This feature means that users' home directories almost always deny group and world write access. It's also the reason for the use of the sticky bit on public directories such as /tmp. Without it, any directory that could be used as a common temporary or file-exchange area wouldn't be safe from accidental or malicious damage caused by users issuing rm commands.

Because directories can't be executable programs, the execute permission bits take on new meanings with directories. Specifically, these bits control the ability to search for information in the directory. You can still take a simple directory listing (using ls) on a directory for which you lack execute permission, but any attempt to find a file with a tool such as find (described in the upcoming section, "Using find") will fail. Even some ls options, such as -l (which displays permissions, file creation times, and so on), fail when the directory lacks execute permission.

Designing a System Permissions Policy

One of the most important tasks of a FreeBSD system administrator is designing a permissions policy that's appropriate for a system. When you first install FreeBSD, it's set up to give ordinary users full read access to most directories. Indeed, this access is required for directories that house ordinary programs, such as /bin and /usr/bin. Some directories, such as /root, are off-limits to ordinary users. Others, such as /tmp, are wide open to both read and write operations from ordinary users. Several types of changes you might want to make to the default configuration include

- **Reduced access to system directories** In some very high-security environments, you might want to deny ordinary users access to certain directories. For instance, you might create an xusers group, change the /usr/X11R6 directory's group ownership to that group, and deny world access to that directory. You can then control who may run X-based programs by controlling who belongs to the xusers group. You can do the same on a program-by-program basis by granting or denying read and execute permission to an individual program. One major caveat with this approach is that because most FreeBSD programs are readily available on the Internet, users can easily overcome many of these restrictions by placing duplicate programs in their home directories.

- **Shared directories** If your computer hosts multiple users who collaborate on projects, you may want to create a shared directory for common files. Indeed, you can create several such directories, and by assigning them to different groups, you can control who has access to each directory. For instance, if /home/ projects/research and /home/projects/development are owned by the research and development groups, respectively, and if both have rwxrwx--- (770) permissions, only users in the specified groups will be able to read from or write to those directories. Any user who belongs to both groups (such as dana, from the users described earlier) can access both directories.

■ **Home directory permissions**   You should adjust your users' home directory permissions in a way that's appropriate for your site. The default permissions are `rwxr-xr-x` (755), which gives all users read access to all other users' home directories. In many cases, `rwxr-x---` (750) or even `rwx------` (700) is a more appropriate choice. Your options in this respect are closely tied to your decisions concerning what type of groups you maintain on the system, as described in Chapter 10.

> **Caution**   *Users can change the permissions on their own home directories. Thus, if you run a very high-security system, you may need to perform regular security audits, or use some creative measure to prevent users from accidentally or intentionally compromising their own directories' security. For instance, you might implement a user private group security policy (described in Chapter 10), give ownership of home directories to* root, *and use* rwxrwx--- *(770) ownership on home directories.*

File Manipulation Commands

The preceding discussion of file ownership and permissions is necessary to understand some of the subtleties of FreeBSD's commands for file manipulation. This section covers these commands, beginning with the commands that change ownership and permissions. Copying and deleting files are two common file manipulations that work only when file (or directory) permissions allow. Because links are very important tools, their creation and use is covered next. Although not technically file manipulation commands, tools to find files based on names, contents, or other characteristics are important in dealing with files. Finally, directories have their own special commands, although some file-centric commands also apply to directories.

Changing Ownership

Ordinarily, a file is owned by the user who created the file. In some circumstances, though, you may want to change this ownership. For instance, you might create or copy a configuration file as `root` for an ordinary user. Users should own their own local configuration files, so you should change the ownership of the file so that the user owns it . You can do this with the `chown` command, which has this syntax:

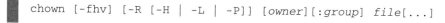

```
chown [-fhv] [-R [-H | -L | -P]] [owner][:group] file[...]
```

The options for this command are

■ **-f**   Normally, `chown` reports failures (due to read-only filesystems, insufficient permissions, or the like). This option causes `chown` to not report such problems.

■ **-h**   Normally, when `chown` is used on a symbolic link, it modifies the ownership of the linked-to file. This option causes `chown` to modify the link instead.

■ **-v**   This option causes chown to display each filename as it's modified.

■ **-R**   This option causes a *recursive* change in ownership; when the specified file is a directory, not only does chown change the directory's ownership, but the ownership of every file and directory in it, every file in every subdirectory, and so on. The -H, -L, and -P options modify the way this command works with symbolic links to directories. -H causes chown to recurse into a symbolic link specified as *file*, -L causes chown to recurse into symbolic links within the specified directory tree, and -P causes chown not to recurse into symbolic links. -P is the default.

Ordinarily, chown is used with an *owner* specification. Instead of or in addition to this, you can specify a *group*, whose name must be preceded by a colon (:). Both the *owner* and the *group* may be specified by name or by number (UID or GID). You *must* specify an *owner*, a *group*, or both; there is no default value.

Examples of this command in use are

```
# chown walter csm.sxw
# chown dana:research *.tex
# chown -R :development /home/development
```

The first command gives ownership of a single file (csm.sxw) to walter. The second changes ownership of all files ending in .tex in the current directory to dana and the research group. The final example changes the group of all files in the /home/development directory to development, but does not follow symbolic links or modify the owner associated with any file. This final example could also have been handled with the chgrp command, which works very much like chown, except that you cannot specify an *owner*, and the *group* is not preceded by a colon. For instance, the following command is equivalent to the final one of the previous three:

```
# chgrp -R development /home/development
```

Although root can issue both the chown and chgrp commands to change ownership of any file to any valid user or group, ordinary users' use of these commands is more limited. Specifically, a user can change the group of a file to any group to which the user belongs, but not to other groups; and a user cannot give the ownership of a file to another user.

Changing Permissions

Both root and the file's owner may change the permissions of a file using the chmod command. This command's syntax is very similar to that of chown:

```
chmod [-fhv] [-R [-H | -L | -P]] mode file[...]
```

Most of these options have the same meanings in chmod as they do in chown. The exception is the chmod-specific option, *mode*. This is a specification of the permissions of the file. It may be specified in one of two forms: *absolute* or *symbolic*.

An absolute mode is the octal representation, as described earlier. For instance, 644 sets the permissions to rw-r--r--. You may optionally turn this three-digit octal number into a four-digit form by preceding it with another number. A 0 is equivalent to omitting this number, a 1 activates the sticky bit, a 2 activates the SGID bit, and a 4 activates the SUID bit. You can add these values together to activate more than one of these bits; for instance, 6 activates the SUID and SGID bits. Thus, 6755 sets rwsr-sr-x permissions. Absolute modes are very useful when you know the exact permissions value you want to set, and especially if you want to both add and subtract permissions compared to the current value.

A symbolic mode uses a variant of the permission string representation. Instead of providing the complete permission string, though, this method relies upon your specifying whose permissions should be changed, whether the permission should be added, deleted, or set equal to a value, and the permissions to be set or changed. Table 8-3 summarizes the possible values.

Whose Permissions	Meaning	Change Type	Meaning	Permissions Set or Changed	Meaning
		=	Set equal to		
a	All permission groups	+	Add	r	Read
u	Owner (User)	–	Remove	w	Write
g	Group			x	Execute
o	World (Other)			X	Execute on directory or if execute bit is already set
				s	SUID or SGID
				t	Sticky bit
				u	Existing owner permissions
				g	Existing group permissions
				o	Existing world permissions

Table 8-3.   *Symbolic Mode Components*

To use a symbolic mode, you combine one or more of Table 8-3's Whose Permissions values, one symbol from the Change Type column, and one or more Permissions Set or Changed values. You can create more complex changes by constructing multiple change modes and separating them with commas. Because the effects of symbolic modes depend upon the file's original mode, you must consider that mode when constructing a symbolic mode. (An exception is if you use the = operator for all permissions.) Table 8-4 presents some examples, including the initial permissions, symbolic mode, and end permissions.

Symbolic modes can be tricky to use, particularly if you have a hard time remembering the correct codes. They have their advantages, though. For instance, you can use them to change the permissions of certain features of groups of files of various types or if you don't know the current mode and don't want to modify certain characteristics of it. For instance, typing **chmod -R a+rX somedir** makes the directory called somedir readable to all, and gives all users read access to all files in the directory, without modifying the files' write permissions. This command also sets the execute bit only on subdirectories or files whose execute bit is already set. An equivalent command using absolute modes doesn't exist.

In addition to using chmod, you can change the default permissions assigned to new files by using the umask command. This command is built into most shells, and it sets a feature that's known as the *user mask* (or *umask* for short). This is a number that represents the permission bits that are *not* set. For instance, the default umask is 022, which means that the owner is denied no permissions, but the group and world are denied write access to new files. (In practice, execute permission is also removed from ordinary files, but not from directories.) You can change the umask value by using the umask command:

```
$ umask 027
```

This example denies non-owner and nongroup users any access to new files. You can enter this command in a user's login scripts or in global login scripts, as described in Chapter 6.

Initial Permissions	Mode	End Permissions
rw-r--r--	a+x	rwxr-xr-x
rw-r--r--	og-r	rw-------
rw-r-----	gu=rwx	rwxrwx---
rw-r--r--	g=u,o-r	rw-rw----

Table 8-4. *Examples of Symbolic Modes and Their Effects*

Copying and Moving Files

Chapter 3 introduced some basic file manipulation commands, including cp and mv. This section expands on this earlier coverage, and adds two more commands—cat and dd. All of these commands are useful tools for copying files or otherwise moving data.

Using cp

The cp command is FreeBSD's workhorse file copying command. Its syntax is best described using two formats:

```
cp [-R [-H | -L | -P]] [-f | -i] [-pv] source target
cp [-R [-H | -L | -P]] [-f | -i] [-pv] source[...] target-dir
```

The first form of the command is used to copy a single file to another name in the same directory or to the same or another name in a different directory. The second form of the command copies one or more files to another directory, using the files' original names. The cp options are

- **-R** This option sets up a recursive copy, in which an entire directory's contents are copied. The -H, -L, and -P suboptions work just like their counterparts in chown, described earlier in the section "Changing Ownership."

- **-f** This option causes cp to overwrite existing files without prompting, in the event of a name conflict.

- **-i** This option causes cp to prompt you (via stderr) if a copy would overwrite any existing files.

- **-p** Normally, certain characteristics of the copy, such as the owner, file creation time, and permissions, are not copied from the original. This option causes cp to copy as many of these elements as it can, given your own permissions (for instance, only root can set the copy's owner to another user).

- **-v** When this option is given, cp displays the name of each file as it's copied.

As examples of cp in action, consider these commands:

```
$ cp file-2139.tex insects.tex
$ cp -Rp important-cases /mnt/zip
```

The first command creates a copy of the file-2139.tex file in the current directory under the name insects.tex. (This copy could be created in another directory by adding a directory specification, such as /home/research/insects.tex.) The second command copies the entire contents of the important-cases directory to /mnt/zip. If important-cases were a file, only that one file would be copied.

BASIC SYSTEM ADMINISTRATION

Mass file copying can also be accomplished with tar, *which is described in the upcoming section, "Backing Up." In fact,* tar *is more reliable at duplicating certain file characteristics, and so is preferred if you need the best possible copy of a directory, as when you're moving files to a new hard disk.*

Using mv

The mv command is similar in syntax and operation to cp, but it lacks a recursive function. This command moves, rather than copies, files. In practice, it's also used to rename files—"moving" a file from a directory to the same directory but under another name serves as FreeBSD's renaming command. The syntax for this command can be described as follows:

```
mv [-f | -i] [-v] source target
mv [-f | -i] [-v] source[...] target-dir
```

The options to this command are the same as those for cp. In practice, mv sometimes works much as does cp, by copying files, but it then deletes the originals. This happens when the target directory is on another filesystem, such as a mounted floppy or Zip disk. When moving files within a single filesystem, though, FreeBSD can create a new directory entry in the target location and then delete the original directory entry, without moving the file's contents. This process can make moves within a filesystem very fast, even when the files are very large.

Using cat

The cat command name is short for *concatenate*, and it's a tool that's used to combine multiple files into one. In practice, it's also often used to view the contents of a single text file. The command's syntax is

```
cat [-bnvtesu] [file [...]]
```

Ordinarily, cat writes to standard output (stdout), so to use it for file copying, you must use redirection, as described in Chapter 5. The options to cat are

- **-b** This option adds line numbers to the output. (Blank lines are not numbered.)
- **-n** This option adds line numbers to the output. (Blank lines are numbered.)
- **-v** This option displays nonprinting characters using printable codes, such as ^X for CTRL-X.
- **-t** This option is the same as -v, but TAB characters are displayed as ^|.
- **-e** This option is the same as -v, but the ends of lines are marked with dollar signs ($).

- ■ **-s** This option omits blank lines from the output.

- ■ **-u** This option produces unbuffered output. Buffering can improve performance in some situations, such as copying disk files, but it can also cause reliability problems when dealing with some text-oriented output devices, such as terminals. Ordinarily this option won't cause much of an effect either way.

One common use of cat is to view the contents of a file. For instance, typing **cat somefile.txt** causes the entirety of somefile.txt to be displayed. This command works well for short files or if you're using an xterm or similar tool that lets you scroll back to see the entire file's contents. For long files, you're better off using a pager such as less (described in Chapter 5).

When you pass cat multiple filenames, the program displays all files in succession. You can use this feature with redirection to copy multiple files into a single file. For instance:

```
$ cat file1.txt file2.txt > combined-file.txt
```

The resulting file, combined-file.txt, contains the text of file1.txt followed immediately by the text of file2.txt. You can, of course, add options to number lines, display unprintable characters, and so on, if you like.

Using dd

You can think of dd as cp on steroids. The dd command offers many options that enable you to perform unusual transformations on the copied material, such as copying only part of a file or converting a file's contents from lowercase to uppercase. The command's basic syntax is

```
dd [operand[...]]
```

The power of the command lies in its operands. For a complete description of these, consult the dd man page. Some of the more useful operands include

- ■ **if=*file*** You can specify an input file with this operand. If you omit this, dd attempts to read from standard input (stdin).

- ■ **of=*file*** You can specify an output file with this operand. If you omit this, dd attempts to write to standard output (stdout).

- ■ **bs=*size*** This option sets the block size. This number is often unimportant, but it may be helpful for your computations when copying part of a file or a specific number of bytes. For instance, if you know you want to copy 23KB, you can set bs=1024 and count=23.

- ■ **count=*number-of-blocks*** This option, used in conjunction with bs, tells dd how much data to copy.

■ **seek=*skip-blocks*** This option tells dd to skip the specified number of blocks before writing the first data to the output file. You can use this option to overwrite part of a file or if you want to modify a targeted area on a hard disk or the like.

■ **skip=*skip-blocks*** This option tells dd to skip the specified number of blocks when reading from a file. You can use it to omit the start of a file from a copy.

■ **conv=*value*** You can have dd perform various conversions on data with this option. For instance, conv=lcase converts all text to lowercase, conv=ucase converts all text to uppercase, and conv=swab swaps byte pairs (which is sometimes useful when transferring binary data files between machines with different byte-order requirements). The dd man page includes information on other possible conversions.

In practice, dd is frequently used in conjunction with various device files. For instance, consider the following commands:

```
$ dd if=/dev/zero of=blank.img bs=1024 count=1440
$ dd if=floppy.img of=/dev/fd0
```

The first command copies 1440KB from /dev/zero to blank.img. Because /dev/zero is a special file that produces nothing but 0 values when read, this command effectively creates a 1440KB blank file. You could then use utilities to create a disk image or use it for some program that requires empty files of a particular size. The second command copies in the other direction—it takes the floppy.img file and copies it to /dev/fd0 (the floppy disk device). You might use this command to write a floppy image file, like the ones that come with FreeBSD to enable you to boot the installer, to a floppy disk. In practice, you can use cp or even cat for this second job, but dd has the advantage that it reports on the success of the operation, which can be reassuring, particularly when you're dealing with media that tend to be unreliable, such as floppy disks.

Deleting Files

The rm command handles file deletion. In its most basic form, it deletes individual files, but it supports several options, some of which let it do more, such as delete an entire directory tree. Its command syntax is

```
rm [-dfiPRrvW] file[...]
```

The meanings of the rm options are

■ **-d** Normally, rm won't delete directories. This option tells it to do this job, but even with this option, rm won't delete a directory that contains files or subdirectories.

Tip

If you try to delete a directory that you believe to be empty but rm *responds that the directory is not empty, use* **ls -a** *to check for dot files. These are easy to miss, but prevent deletion of directories.*

- **-f**   Causes rm to delete files without prompting for confirmation. This option is useful when you want to delete a lot of files, but is potentially dangerous when used with wildcards.

- **-i**   Causes rm to request confirmation before deleting files.

- **-P**   Normally, rm deletes files by removing their directory entries and modifying their inodes to indicate that the disk space they occupied is unused. The files' data still exist on the disk. This option causes the files to be overwritten three times before the disk space is marked as unused, once with binary 1 values, and then with binary 0s, and then with binary 1s again. This process slows the deletion, but makes it much harder to recover the data, which may be desirable if you're deleting a sensitive file.

- **-R or -r**   Causes rm to perform a recursive deletion of a directory tree. This option implies -d.

- **-v**   Causes rm to display filenames as files are deleted.

- **-W**   Causes rm to attempt to undelete a file. This option is unlikely to work with current software and filesystems, but its functionality may improve in the future.

Caution

The rm *command is potentially very destructive, particularly in the hands of* root *and when used with the* -R *option. For instance, suppose you want to delete* monica's *home directory. You might try to type* **rm -R /home/monica***, which should do the job. If you mistakenly insert a stray space between* / *and* home/monica*, though, the result will be a deletion of all files on the computer. Also, FreeBSD's tools for recovering deleted files are limited compared to those for some OSs, such as Windows. A deleted file may be recoverable only from a backup.*

A variant of rm is rmdir. This command is designed specifically for deleting a directory. The rmdir syntax is much simpler than that of rm:

```
rmdir [-p] directory[...]
```

The lone option, -p, causes rmdir to delete an entire directory tree, provided that no regular files exist within that tree, just directories. Like rm, rmdir won't delete a directory that contains files. In practice, it's often easier to use rm -R to delete a directory tree—but as noted earlier, this approach isn't without its risks.

Creating and Using Links

A *link* is a pointer that enables one file to have two directory entries. Similar concepts in other OSs include the Windows *shortcut*, the OS/2 *shadow*, and the Mac OS *alias*. Implementation details differ from one OS to another, and in fact FreeBSD supports two different types of links: *hard links* and *symbolic* (or *soft*) *links*. Figure 8-1 illustrates how each of these types of links works.

A hard link is really just two directory entries that point to the same file data, via the same *inode*. (An inode is a data structure that tells FreeBSD where to find the file's data on the disk, when the file was created, and so on.) If you delete one directory entry (by using rm, for instance), the inode and file remain intact and useable. Accessing a file through either of its hard link names is equally fast, but the fact that the directory entries need to point directly at the inode means that hard links work only within a single filesystem (that is, a partition or removable disk). Also, some backup programs, such as tar, back up hard links twice when they exist, but handle symbolic links more sensibly. FreeBSD doesn't permit directories to be hard links.

A symbolic link, by contrast, is a higher-level pointer. Figure 8-1's Symbolic Link Directory Entry 1 is a link to Directory Entry 2. In order to read data in the file, the symbolic link file stores the name of the linked-to file as ordinary file data, and FreeBSD knows how to parse this data to reach the target file. This lookup takes more time than a hard link reference, although you're not likely to notice the difference unless it's multiplied (say, by a script that accesses many files in quick succession). Symbolic links can point across filesystems, which makes them the preferred form of link in many situations. You can delete the link without damaging the file data, but if you delete or move the linked-to file, that file will become inaccessible and the link will be *broken*—it won't be useable unless a new file with the old linked-to file's name is created. Moving a symbolic link works if the link uses an absolute path, but if it uses a relative path, moving the symbolic link is likely to break the link.

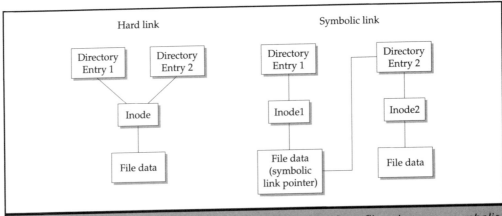

Figure 8-1. *A hard link is an alternative directory entry for a file, whereas a symbolic link connects one file to another via the symbolic link's own file data.*

A default FreeBSD installation uses links in various roles. A few files in /etc are actually symbolic links to the real configuration files stored elsewhere, for instance. As you use your system, you may find that you need to create links in order to better use your available disk space. For instance, if you run out of space in the root (/) filesystem because you've installed large packages that use /opt, you could create a /usr/opt directory (if /usr is on a separate partition), move the contents of /opt to that directory, delete the original /opt, and re-create it as a symbolic link to /usr/opt. You can also use links as an ordinary user, to make it easier to reach particular directories in your own home directory or to more easily reach mounted removable or network filesystems.

You create links with the ln command, whose syntax is

```
ln [-fhinsv] source-file[...] [target-file | target-dir]
```

When you specify a filename as the target, ln creates a link in that name. When you specify an existing directory, ln creates a link in that directory that's named after the source file. Some of this command's options are similar to those of cp or mv. Specifically, -f, -i, and -v have the same function in ln as in cp. The remaining options' meanings are

- **–h or –n**   This option causes ln to not follow a symbolic link as a target. This option is generally used in conjunction with -f and -s, which causes ln to replace an existing link to a directory with another one.

- **–s**   The default ln behavior is to create a hard link. This option causes it to create a symbolic link instead.

As an example of ln in action, consider these commands:

```
$ ln deeply/buried/directory/tree/file.txt ./
$ ln -s /mnt/zip/instructions.ps use-instructions.ps
# ln -s /opt/newprogram/bin/newprog /usr/local/bin
```

The first of these commands creates a hard link so that a file that's deeply buried in a directory tree can be more readily accessed. Because only a directory name (./) is provided as a target, the link will have the same name as the original file (file.txt). You could subsequently delete the original file's directory entry and the new one would remain accessible.

The next two examples create symbolic links. The first of these links a file located in /mnt/zip to another filename in the current directory. The second example links a program executable file to a directory that's likely to be on most users' paths, thus making it more readily accessible. This last example is likely to be useable only by root, although the basic form of this command is useable by ordinary users—it's only the fact that most users lack write access to /usr/local/bin that makes this command require root privilege.

BASIC SYSTEM ADMINISTRATION

Finding Files

Being able to manipulate files is very important, but sometimes the challenge is in finding them so that you can manipulate them. Fortunately, FreeBSD provides several tools that can help you locate files. Two of the most powerful of these are `find` and `grep`, which let you search for files based on their *metadata* (filename, file creation time, and so on) or their contents, respectively.

Using find

The `find` command enables you to search for files based on their names, creation dates, last access times, and so on. As such, it can be a useful way to locate a file if you don't recall where it's stored but you do know enough details about such metadata to be able to create a useful search rule. The basic `find` syntax is

```
find [-f] pathname[...] expression
```

 The `find` *command supports several options not described here. Consult the* `find` *man page for more details.*

The `-f pathname` option enables you to specify where you want `find` to begin looking for files. For instance, if you know a file is somewhere in `/usr/local`, you could pass `-f /usr/local` to `find` as part of the command. This is an extremely useful technique to limit the scope of a search—without such a limiting factor, `find` is likely to take several minutes to return, as it searches every file in your FreeBSD directory tree. In practice, you need to provide a search path, even if it starts at the root (/) directory, but the `-f` specification is optional.

Much of the complexity of `find` lies in the innocuous-looking *expression* component of the syntax. This can take any of several forms that enable you to search for various types of data. A sample of the options you can pass as the *expression* include

- **-atime *time*** This option causes `find` to return a file if it was last accessed within *time* period. For instance, `-atime -12h` means that the file was accessed within the last twelve hours. The *time* specification is provided as a negative number, and can be specified in seconds (s), minutes (m), hours (h), days (d), or weeks (w).

- **-ctime *time*** This option works like `atime`, but it locates files based on their creation times, rather than their access times.

- **-delete** This option, when used with others, causes `find` to delete the found files. I recommend you try a `find` without this option before using it, to be sure you don't delete the wrong files.

- **-group *group-name*** This option searches for files based on their group. For instance, `-group research` finds files belonging to the `research` group. You can specify *group-name* as either a group name or a GID.

- **-links *num***   This option searches for files that have *num* hard links.

- **-maxdepth *depth***   This option causes `find` to terminate its search after reaching *depth* directory levels, which can be useful to limit the search if you know the file wasn't buried too deeply in the directory tree.

- **-mtime *time***   This option works like `-atime`, but it uses the files' modification times.

- **-name *pattern***   This option searches for files based on the filename. The specified *pattern* may be a simple filename or it may contain various wildcards, such as asterisks (`*`) and question marks (`?`). You may need to enclose the *pattern* in quotation marks to keep the shell from expanding it, if you use wildcards.

- **-newer *filename***   You can find files that are newer than a specified other file with this option.

- **-perm [+|-]*mode***   Use this option if you want to find files that have a particular set of permissions. You can specify the *mode* as you would with `chmod`. If used without a plus or minus sign, this mode must be matched exactly. If you precede it with a plus sign, then `find` matches any file that includes any of the permission bits specified, even if others are also present. If you precede the *mode* with a minus sign, then all of the specified bits must be present, and others may be as well.

- **-size *n*[c]**   You can find files based on their sizes with this option. Follow the size by a c character to find a file of a specific size in bytes, otherwise `find` locates files whose sizes match a number of 512-byte blocks.

- **-type *file-type***   This option locates files of a specified type. The *type-code* is the code listed in Table 8-1, with the addition of f for a regular file.

- **-user *username***   You can find files owned by a particular user with this option. The *username* can be specified as either a username or a UID.

These expressions are only some of the most useful for `find`. Consult the program's man page for more exotic options. Some examples of `find` in action include

```
$ find ./ -name "*txt"
$ find /usr/local -perm +u+s
# find /etc -mtime -24h -name "*rc"
```

The first example finds all files in the current directory whose names end in txt. This is the sort of action that an ordinary user is likely to perform. The second example finds all the files in /usr/local that have their SUID bits set. Although an ordinary user can perform such a search, a system administrator is more likely to find this type of search useful, to help locate files that are set SUID root. The final example locates all files in the /etc directory tree whose names end in rc and that have been modified in the past 24 hours. An ordinary user can run such a command, but this example shows it as requiring root privileges because some directories in /etc aren't readable to ordinary users, and so won't be searched. Thus, find may return incomplete results in such cases.

As output, find returns the names of all the files that match the search. If find locates no matching files, it returns no output, so it may look like it's not done anything.

Using grep and egrep

You can use find to locate files based on filenames, modification dates, file types, and so on, but sometimes that's not enough. You may need to locate files based on their contents. For instance, you might need to locate an important letter you wrote to a person named Byers, but you might not see any file with an obvious name. This is where grep comes in handy—it searches through the contents of files in a directory (or a directory tree) and returns the names of the files that contain the specified strings. When grep finds such information, it has a *match*. In the case of text files, grep returns any line of text in which the match appears. This command's syntax is

```
grep [options] [pattern | -e pattern | -f file] [file[...]]
```

The egrep command is related, but it uses a slightly different syntax for its *pattern*. Like find, grep supports a large number of options, only some of which are covered here. Consult the grep man page for details. Some of the more common options include

- **-A** *num*   This option causes grep to display *num* lines of text following each match.

- **-B** *num*   This option causes grep to display *num* lines of text preceding each match.

- **-c or --count**   This option causes grep to display a count of the number of matching lines, rather than the matching lines themselves.

- **-F**   Normally, grep interprets *pattern* as a regular expression, as described shortly. This option causes it to interpret *pattern* literally, which can make searching for certain strings easier.

- **-i or --ignore-case**   Normally, grep matches patterns in a case-sensitive manner. This option causes grep to match in a case-insensitive way.

- **-r or --recursive**   This option causes a recursive search of a directory tree, rather than a search of specified files or a single directory and not its subdirectories.

- **-v or --invert-match**   This option causes grep to invert the sense of its operation; it reports lines that *don't* include the specified pattern.

You can specify a match pattern as a string following the options, optionally preceded by -e. (The -e can be useful to distinguish matches that begin with a dash, which would otherwise be interpreted as grep options.) If you routinely perform a complex match, you may want to place the pattern in a file and call it with the -f *file* option. In any event, the matching pattern is a *regular expression*, which is a way to specify a string of characters, possibly including variables. Regular expressions can be quite complex, and this chapter can only scratch the surface of this topic. Sometimes you need to enclose regular expressions in quotes, particularly if they include asterisks or question marks, to prevent the shell from trying to interpret them as filenames and expand them. A few things you might find useful in `grep` regular expressions include

- **Literal strings**   Most characters are interpreted literally, meaning they match themselves. For instance, the string `trust` matches the word `trust` in any file.

- **Character sets**   A string enclosed by square brackets, such as `[aeiou]`, matches any one character from the set within the brackets, such as any of the vowels in this example. If the first character of this list is a carat (`^`), then the string matches any character that's *not* in the list. A range of characters can be specified by square brackets with a dash separating the start and end points, such as `[0-9]` to match any digit.

- **Single characters**   The period (`.`) matches any single character. The string `\w` matches any single alphanumeric character (any number, uppercase letter, or lowercase letter), and the string `\W` matches any single nonalphanumeric character (punctuation, nonprintable characters, and so on).

- **Repetition codes**   Certain codes tell `grep` that a preceding item may be repeated some number of times. Most importantly, a backslashed question mark (`\?`) means that the preceding item is repeated zero or one time, an asterisk (`*`) means that the preceding item is repeated zero or more times, and a backslashed plus (`\+`) means that the preceding item is repeated one or more times. When using `egrep`, the backslashes are omitted from the `?` and `+` codes.

- **Two options**   If a vertical bar (`|`) separates two regular expressions, a match to either satisfies `grep`.

Some of these special codes mean that you can't search for the characters used for the codes without taking an extra step. This step is to add a backslash (`\`) immediately prior to the character to be searched. For instance, you'd use `\?` to search for a question mark. This is known as *escaping* the character. You can also escape the backslash if you need to search for it. Alternatively, you can use the `-F` option to have `grep` interpret the entire *pattern* literally.

By default, `grep` takes its input from stdin. This makes `grep` very easy to use in a pipe, as described in Chapter 5. If you're using it to find files, though, chances are you'll pass it a filename, a directory name, or a wildcard that matches many file or directory names.

Some examples of `grep` in action include

```
$ grep Byers *.tex
$ grep trust.*one gullible/* paranoid/*
$ grep "Chapter.*\.\+[0-9]" *.txt
$ egrep "Chapter.*\.+[0-9]" *.txt
$ grep -r "copyright 200[12]" ./
```

The first example locates any files whose names end in `.tex` in the current directory that contain the string `Byers`. This command is a relatively straightforward application of `grep`. The second example locates any file in the `gullible` or `paranoid` directories that include the words `trust` and `one` on the same line. For instance, this search will find files that match the strings `trust everyone` and `trust no one`. Note that the asterisk in this search is being used in two ways—in `trust.*one`, it's part of the regular expression that indicates a potential blank space, and in `gullible/*` and `paranoid/*`, it's a wildcard in the filename specifications. The third example searches for any file ending in `.txt` that includes the string `Chapter` followed by zero or more spaces (`.*`), followed by one or more periods (`\.\+`) followed by a digit. This command might be used to match a file with a table of contents for a book, which is likely to have lines like the following:

```
Chapter 23......479
```

The fourth example is an alternative way of doing the same thing as the third, but it uses `egrep` and omits the backslash preceding the + operator. Finally, the fifth example matches any file in an entire directory tree that includes the strings `copyright 2001` or `copyright 2002`. Ordinarily, `grep` takes a file specification as its final argument, but when doing a recursive search, you can list a directory name instead, as in this final example.

When `grep` finds a match in a text file, it displays the name of the file and the matching line of text. (If many lines match, they're all displayed.) When `grep` finds a match in a binary file, it displays only the message `binary file <filename> matches`, where `<filename>` is the filename in question.

Backing Up

Manipulating files on your computer is critically important to using a FreeBSD system. In some situations you need to move files off of your computer, though. Sometimes you may just need to copy a few files to another location, in which case normal file copying commands used with floppy disks, Zip disks, or other removable media will probably suffice. Another common use for copying files off of a computer is backup. This is the practice of storing files off of the computer so that they're accessible in case of emergency. In this context, "emergency" could mean anything from a user accidentally deleting a single file to the destruction or theft of the computer. For most purposes, storing backed-up files in a safe or the like near the computer will suffice, but for best protection, it's important that you store a copy in another location. Such *off-site backups* can be invaluable in the event of a major disaster such as a fire or hurricane.

No matter what backup medium you use, be alert to the security requirements of the media. Files that are inaccessible to normal users become readily accessible to anybody if your backup media can be easily "borrowed," because common backup tools don't enforce FreeBSD ownership and permissions restrictions. If a system contains sensitive data, you should be sure to store backups in a safe.

Backup Media

The most common form of backup medium is magnetic tape. Tape drives cost between a hundred and several thousand dollars, depending upon their capacity, speed, and reliability. Tape drives you might use for a FreeBSD workstation or small server typically cost between $200 and $1500. The less expensive units in this range are *Travan* drives, which use expensive (roughly $40) tapes, and the more expensive units are *Digital Audio Tape (DAT)* units or various other midrange devices, which typically use less expensive ($5 to $20) tapes. In the end, therefore, the cost of the units plus tapes varies by less than it first appears.

Tapes have the advantages of high capacity (modern units store tens of gigabytes per tape), reasonably high speed, and moderate cost per gigabyte backed up. Potential rival media types, such as removable disks, tend to be lower in capacity or much higher in cost. For instance, you'd need dozens of 100MB Zip disks to back up a modern computer, but you might be able to do the job with just one or two tapes.

One media type deserves special mention: optical discs. *Compact Disc Recordable (CD-R)* media store 650MB on a standard disc, which is enough (particularly when data are compressed) to hold a basic FreeBSD installation. If your installation is not too large, you may be able to back up a newly-installed system to CD-R for emergency recovery, and rely upon tapes for restoring user data. CD-R media are inexpensive, and they have the advantage of being readable on any computer, so in a networked environment, you can use them to restore clients even if those clients lack tape drives. CD-R media are also very reliable and have long expected shelf lives (between 20 and 100 years, by most estimates), so they make good archival media. Newer recordable *Digital Versatile Disc (DVD)* drives can record several gigabytes, and so can be even better backup devices, but in 2002 these drives are still more expensive than CD-Rs, and even read-only DVD drives still aren't universal.

A Sample of Backup Tools

FreeBSD supports several backup programs. Most of these are designed for use with tapes, but they can be used with other backup media, as well. The more popular backup tools include

- **tar** The `tar` program is an old standard in the UNIX and FreeBSD world. Its name stands for *tape archiver*, and that's what it does—create archives of data on tape. It's also become a popular way to package files for distribution on the Internet and for storage on nontape removable media devices; `tar` can create files (sometimes called *tarballs*) that are conglomerations of many other files, thus simplifying the distribution of software. Chapter 11 covers this aspect of tar's use.

■ **dump** The dump program, like tar, is an old standard backup tool. One unusual feature of dump is that it's strongly tied to the filesystem data structures. This means that you may not be able to dump some filesystems, such as FAT partitions. You may also be unable to recover data to another filesystem type. For instance, if you create a dump backup on FreeBSD, you might not be able to recover it using Linux to its native ext2. Unlike most backup tools, dump uses a separate restore program, appropriately called restore.

■ **cpio** The cpio program is roughly equivalent to tar in features and capabilities, but certain details differ, such as the command syntax and the details of the archive format.

■ **CD-R tools** If you choose to use CD-R media for backup, you must use special tools. Ordinarily, this process involves two steps: You use a program called mkisofs to create an *image file* of an ISO-9660 filesystem containing your files; then you use cdrecord to copy that image file to a blank CD-R. For backup purposes, recording your files directly in an image file is probably not a good idea because the image file will lose some information—for instance, the files will be stripped of their write permission bits. Instead, you can use tar, dump, or cpio to create a tarball and record that to disc, either directly or after placing it in an image file.

All of these programs are a standard part of a FreeBSD installation. Because tar is very popular and is commonly used for non-backup purposes, this chapter's discussion of tar focuses upon its use for backups. The basic principles described here work for other tools, but of course the command details differ.

Using Backup Tools

The tar program supports a huge number of options, so only a few of them can be described here. Consult the tar man page for more details. The basic syntax for tar is

```
tar function [function-modifier[...]] [file[...]]
```

The *function* is one function to be performed, such as --extract (e for short), to extract files from the archive. A *function-modifier* is an option that fine-tunes the way tar behaves. Tables 8-5 and 8-6 summarize the most important functions and function modifiers. The *file* that ends the command is a list of one or more files or directories (listing directories is usually simpler than listing files).

Function	Abbreviation	Effect
--create	c	Creates a new archive.
--concatenate or --catenate	A	Adds the contents of one archive to another one.
--append	r	Adds new files to an existing archive.
--update	u	Adds changed files to an existing archive. (Doesn't work with tapes.)
--diff or --compare	d	Compares archive to files and displays differences.
--list	t	Displays the contents (filenames) of an archive.
--extract or --get	x	Extracts files from an archive.
--delete	(none)	Deletes files from an archive. (Doesn't work with tapes.)

Table 8-5. *Important `tar` Functions*

Function Modifier	Abbreviation	Effect
--file [*host*:] *file*	f	Uses the specified *file* as the archive file. If a *host* is specified, uses network operations to access the file on the remote computer.
--listed-incremental *file*	g	Performs an incremental backup, in which only files modified since a previous backup are backed up. Uses data in *file* to determine what files have been previously backed up.
--bunzip2, --bunzip, or --bzip	y or j	Compresses archive through the `bzip2` package.
--one-file-system	l	Processes files on just one filesystem (partition).

Table 8-6. *Important `tar` Function Modifiers*

Function Modifier	Abbreviation	Effect
`--tape-length N`	L	Creates an archive of N kilobytes, then pauses to allow you to change tapes.
`--multi-volume`	M	Processes a multivolume archive.
`--same-permissions` or `--preserve-permissions`	p	Processes all permissions information.
`--absolute-paths`	P	Records the leading slash (/) in absolute filenames.
`--verbose`	v	Lists files processed with `--create` or `--extract`, and displays more permissions information with `-list`.
`--exclude pattern`	(none)	Excludes files matching the *pattern* from the backup.
`--gzip` or `--gunzip`	z	Compresses archive through the `gzip` program.

Table 8-6.   *Important* `tar` *Function Modifiers* (continued)

To use `tar`, combine one function with one or more function modifiers. For instance, to create a backup of the `/home` and `/var` partitions to a SCSI tape drive, use a command like this:

```
# tar --create --verbose --file /dev/sa0 /home /var
```

This same command can be listed more succinctly using abbreviations:

```
# tar cvf /dev/sa0 /home /var
```

This command illustrates a principle that's common to `tar` and other backup programs that work with tapes: The tape drive is treated as an ordinary file. Specifically, `/dev/sa0` is a SCSI tape drive, and `/dev/ast0` is an EIDE (ATAPI) tape drive. (On systems with multiple tape drives, they can be accessed by incrementing the number, such as `/dev/sa1` for the second SCSI tape drive.)

> **Note**
>
> *The first time you use a tape, you may receive an error message. Typing **mt fsf 1**, ejecting the tape, and using it again should then work. The mt program can be used for various other tape operations, such as setting a tape drive's built-in compression features. Consult the mt man page for details.*

> **Caution**
>
> *The tar program compresses data by creating an archive and then compressing it. One consequence of this approach is that if a tape develops a flaw, all data after that flaw will become unusable when you attempt to restore it, so your restoration will fail. For this reason, it's generally best to not use the --bzip2 or --gzip options when creating tape backups. Tape drives' built-in compression features are usually more robust to such problems. Hard disk and CD-R media are usually reliable enough that tar's compression isn't a problem when using these media.*

The --one-file-system function modifier is important for real-world operation because it prevents tar from attempting to back up virtual filesystems, such as /dev and /proc. These filesystems (especially /proc) contain files that FreeBSD generates on the fly and that will needlessly consume disk space. Indeed, attempting to restore such files could conceivably cause problems. If you use --one-file-system, though, you must list each partition you want to back up as a separate file on the tar command line. For instance, suppose you've got a computer with separate root (/), /tmp, /var, /usr, and /home partitions. You could back up this system with a command such as

```
# tar cvplf /dev/sa0 /home /var / /usr /tmp
```

> **Note**
>
> *This example orders partitions according to the likelihood of a need to recover data from a partition (data stored early is more quickly recovered than data stored late). You might reasonably omit the /tmp partition because its data are not guaranteed to survive a reboot.*

Ordinarily, tar strips the leading slash from absolute filename paths, which can help prevent problems on restore. For instance, you might need to use an emergency system to restore data, mounting your ordinary FreeBSD directory tree in an unusual location, such as /mnt. You can then change to /mnt and use --extract to recover your data without overwriting your emergency system's files. Using --absolute-paths tells tar to store the leading slash in filenames. You might do this when creating archive files of programs that must reside in specific directories, but even then it's more common to create a standard relative tar file.

> **Caution**
>
> *If you download a tarball, don't extract it without first examining its contents with --list. A malicious or ignorant individual could create a tarball with absolute paths and load it with files that would overwrite your ordinary system utilities, thus creating a security breach or making your system unusable.*

Restoring Data

A backup is only as useful as your ability to restore data from it. In the case of tar and cpio, restoring data involves the same utilities, and basically the same commands, as backing it up. This restoration process is simplest when your system works and you just need to restore a few files. For instance, suppose the walter user comes to you and says he accidentally deleted a file from his home directory. If walter remembers that the file's name is report78.tex, you might issue commands such as the following to recover the file:

```
# cd /
# tar xvpf /dev/sa0 home/walter/report78.tex
```

Because tar normally stores files without the leading slash, you must change to the root directory, or to the directory from which a backup was made, and give the name of the file to be restored without its leading slash, to successfully restore a file.

If walter doesn't remember the exact name of the file, you may need to use tar's --list function to locate the file before restoring it. You could also restore an entire directory tree by listing the directory tree's name. If you don't provide a file name when restoring data, tar attempts to restore the entire contents of the backup, which is more than you need in most cases.

You can practice making backups using a spare directory. Copy some files to this directory, then restore them to another directory and check that they were restored correctly.

In extreme emergencies, you may need to recover an entire FreeBSD system or files that are needed for basic operation. For instance, your hard drive might have failed, or somebody might have broken into your system and compromised its security. In such situations, a full restore is necessary. You can approach this problem in several ways:

- **Emergency systems**   You can use a FreeBSD emergency boot system, as described in Chapter 32, to boot FreeBSD, prepare new partitions, and restore all your data. This approach takes careful planning *before* disaster strikes.

- **Partial normal install**   You can install a minimal FreeBSD system and use it as if it were an emergency system. For instance, you might install FreeBSD on an old hard disk and use that to restore your regular system to a larger disk, and then reconfigure your disks so that the larger disk is the normal boot disk.

■ **Full install and modification** You can reinstall FreeBSD in the normal way, and then use your backup to restore only key directories that are likely to have changed, such as /home. This approach becomes more difficult the more your system diverges from a standard FreeBSD installation; even with complete notes on your customizations, it can take hours to restore a system to its former normal operating condition.

Emergency full restores can be a nightmare, and that nightmare is all the worse when you're unprepared. For this reason, you should consider what you would do if your hard disk were to stop working or if some other disaster struck. How would you recover your data? If you don't know, you should think the matter through and come up with a recovery plan. If at all possible, you should practice your restoration plan. For instance, you might try recovering a system to a spare computer and try booting that computer. (Hardware differences could cause problems even if the process works, though.) The more critical your FreeBSD system is to yourself or your business, the more time you should invest in preparing for problems.

Summary

Various metadata are associated with FreeBSD files. These include the file's owner, group, and permissions, and this information is critical for using certain file manipulation commands. You can't copy a file if you can't read it, for instance, and you must be able to write to a directory to copy or move a file to that directory. FreeBSD relies upon a handful of file manipulation commands to modify metadata, move files, copy files, delete files, find files, and so on. A good grasp of these commands will help you immensely in both using and administering a FreeBSD system. Managing files also involves protecting them from disaster by backing them up to external media such as CD-Rs or tapes. Thereafter, in the event of a major or minor disaster, you can recover your data quickly.

The Complete Reference

FreeBSD

Chapter 9

Printer Configuration

The paperless office has long been an enticing dream. It has remained just that—a dream—for quite a while, though, and will likely remain so for some time to come. For this reason, printing is an important task for FreeBSD. If you're used to printing in Windows, OS/2, Mac OS, or a similar OS, you may find the FreeBSD printing model odd. Although FreeBSD's printing system bears some similarity to those of other systems, there are also very important differences. Thus, this chapter begins with a look at FreeBSD printing theory. It moves on to the practical tasks of creating a print queue, setting up Ghostscript (which functions as a printer driver), controlling an existing print queue, and controlling network access to the printer.

Understanding the FreeBSD Printing Model

Most modern OSs use a *print queue,* which is a holding area for documents that should be printed. In FreeBSD, various programs exist to submit documents to the print queue; prioritize and otherwise manipulate *print jobs,* as the documents are called once in the queue; process print jobs into a form that a printer can understand; and send print jobs to printers. Understanding how various FreeBSD printing tools fit into this model will help you to configure your print queue when it comes time to dig into the actual configuration files.

The Need for Print Queues

If you remember the days of DOS, you may recall how printers worked in that OS: Programs sent data directly to the printer port hardware. DOS itself did little to control access to the printer, and programs were responsible for delivering data in a format that the printer could understand. With the advent of multitasking OSs, though, a more sophisticated model became necessary. In an OS such as FreeBSD, programs can't be trusted to send data directly to the printer ports. Imagine two programs attempting to send data at once. At best, one program would be denied access to the hardware, and the print job would fail. Multiple users could end up fighting each other for access to the printer, each trying to submit a print job in the brief interval between competing print jobs. At worst, both programs could write data, resulting in output that's a mixture of two jobs or complete gibberish.

Print queues solve this problem by enabling the OS to both accept multiple print jobs and schedule them to be sent to the printer in succession. While FreeBSD sends one job to the printer, the second is stored on disk in an area known as a *print spool* (in a subdirectory of /var/spool/lpd, typically). Because the OS controls the process, it can accept an arbitrary number of print jobs and queue them up for the printer. In practice, of course, the number of jobs is limited by the available disk space in the /var partition or whatever partition houses /var/spool/lpd.

Print queues provide, directly or indirectly, several benefits:

- **Print job scheduling**   By default, FreeBSD print queues process jobs on a first-in-first-out basis, thus preventing problems when multiple users or programs try to access the same limited resource. Indeed, an application that prints can submit a large job and terminate, and the print queue will still print the job. You can also alter the order in which jobs print, as described in the upcoming section, "Reordering Print Jobs."

- **Printer management**   You name your print queues, giving each one a name that users should find easy to remember. In fact, you can give each printer multiple names. Sometimes these are exactly equivalent, but you can configure the same printer to work differently depending upon how it's called—for instance, printing on both sides (*duplexing*) if called by one name, but not by another. If you replace or upgrade a printer, you can attach the new one to an old name, easing the transition for users.

- **Job filtering**   One of the most powerful features of FreeBSD print queues is the ability to apply a *filter* to a queue. This is a program that processes the print job before the printer receives it. In practice, the print filter often calls the Ghostscript program, as described in the upcoming sections, "PostScript as a Standard Printing Language" and "Setting Up Ghostscript."

- **Network access**   The way FreeBSD's printing system works lends itself to network operation. It's easy to configure the system to send files to a printer shared by another print server, and it's equally easy to configure a FreeBSD system to accept print jobs from other computers. (This ease of configuration relates to systems using the BSD printing system or those designed to be compatible with it. Interoperating with Windows, Mac OS, or other types of print clients and servers is more complex.) These topics are covered in the upcoming sections, "Creating a Print Queue" and "Controlling Remote Printer Access."

FreeBSD uses a printing system that's generally known as the *BSD LPD* system, named after the OS that originated it (BSD) and the name of one of its major components, the *Line Printer Daemon (LPD)*. Some competing printing systems are available for FreeBSD. Most notably, *LPRng* aims to be more up-to-date than the BSD LPD system, while maintaining compatibility. Most of this chapter applies to LPRng as well as to BSD LPD. The *Common UNIX Printing System (CUPS)* diverges more from the BSD LPD mold, providing features such as feedback to applications about specific printers' capabilities. The cost is complete incompatibility from a configuration point of view, although CUPS includes programs that work like those in the BSD LPD system for submitting print jobs, so it works in a similar way from a user's perspective. A few programs are beginning to take advantage of CUPS's features, but most don't. Both LPRng and CUPS are available from the standard FreeBSD installation media.

Submitting Jobs to the Queue

Assuming a FreeBSD system is configured to use a printer, as described later in this chapter, the first step in using it as an ordinary user is to submit a print job. In the BSD LPD system, this is done through a program called lpr, as described in the upcoming section, "Submitting Print Jobs." The lpr program can be used either directly by you (if you want to print a file in your directory) or by other programs (for instance, a word processor can submit a print job to the queue by sending a file it creates to lpr).

In practice, lpr works by taking an input file and sending it to the next program in the BSD printing system, the Line Printer Daemon (lpd). Essentially, lpr is just a convenient middleman, enabling you to easily direct a file into whatever print queue you specify.

 The LPRng and CUPS printing systems also use programs called lpr, which work much like the BSD LPD lpr described in this chapter. These alternate printing systems' lpr programs submit jobs to their own printer daemons, though.

Remember that a print job is a file. Even if you don't explicitly create a file, lpr and lpd treat it as if it were a file. In fact, print jobs normally reside on your hard disk as a file at some point in their lives.

The Role of the Line Printer Daemon

The bulk of the FreeBSD printing work is done by the lpd program, after which the BSD LPD printing system as a whole is named. This daemon, like all daemons, is designed to run in the background and wait for input. Part of the key to the FreeBSD printing system is that lpd accepts jobs using network protocols. Thus, when you print locally, lpr passes the job to lpd using the localhost network interface. This means that the print job never sees your network wire, but it's processed as if it were a network access. The lpd program also accepts requests from other computers' lpr programs, assuming it's configured to do so, as described in the upcoming section, "Controlling Remote Printer Access."

When lpd accepts a print job, the daemon stores the file in the spool directory for the printer you specified and makes note of where the file is in the print queue. When print jobs before the one in question are cleared, lpd processes the job. This involves passing the job through any filters you've configured in the queue and then sending them out the printer port or to a remote computer. When the last byte of the job has been sent to its destination, lpd removes the job from the print queue.

PostScript as a Standard Printing Language

One important feature of print queues is that they grant applications some degree of printer independence. In Windows, OS/2, or Mac OS, you install a printer driver for your specific model of printer. Applications can then print to the queue using OS-specific commands, and the OS converts those commands into printer-specific commands.

This interaction can go both ways, so that the OS can tell applications what features a printer supports, such as color or maximum page size. In FreeBSD, the process is somewhat different. Because UNIX systems have historically been powerful computers, they've typically been connected either to high-speed, high-volume printers known as *line printers*, which can't handle complex formatting, or to PostScript laser printers. Thus, UNIX and FreeBSD programs that need to print typically produce plain text or PostScript output, on the assumption that they'll be printing to one of these two types of printers.

The strength of PostScript in the UNIX and FreeBSD world means that Windows-style printer drivers have never caught on. Programs can generate PostScript for printed output, and this works. One negative consequence of this approach, though, is that programs don't know as much about their printers as do Windows programs. For instance, there's no way for a program to know if a printer supports color output, or what resolutions it supports. Thus, FreeBSD programs either make assumptions or require you to enter such information in the application that's printing, often in a print dialog box. Overcoming this limitation is one of the goals of CUPS; it enables you to associate a *PostScript Printer Description (PPD)* file to each queue, and applications can query CUPS for information stored in the PPD file.

Tip *If you need to provide access to printer features that aren't directly supported by PostScript, or by individual programs' PostScript code, you may be able to do it by creating multiple print queues. For instance, you might create two or three print queues to print at different resolutions on an inkjet printer. The upcoming sections, "Creating a Print Queue" and "Setting Up Ghostscript," cover such configurations.*

On desktop computers, plain text output is seldom a problem because most printers can handle plain text; but PostScript can be a problem because PostScript has traditionally added substantially to the cost of the low-end laser and inkjet printers typically associated with *x*86 computers. The solution is to use a filter in the print queue that converts PostScript into whatever format a printer actually accepts. This filter uses a program known as *Ghostscript* (http://www.cs.wisc.edu/~ghost/) to do the conversion. Essentially, Ghostscript serves as a PostScript interpreter that runs on the computer rather than on the printer. The following section, "Creating a Print Queue," describes setting up a print queue *without* a Ghostscript filter, as you might if your printer understands PostScript or if you want to use the printer only for simple text in the printer's default font. The "Setting Up Ghostscript" section describes adding Ghostscript to the mix.

A few FreeBSD applications, such as The GIMP, can generate output designed for specific printers. The results you obtain from such tools may or may not be superior to the results you obtain by generating PostScript and using a conventional print queue. You may want to try both ways to see which works best—but be aware that some filters will misidentify printer-format output and discard it or mangle it, so you may need to create a special queue that uses no filter to print such output.

Selecting a Printer for FreeBSD

If you're buying a new printer for use with FreeBSD, the best choice is probably a PostScript model. Some PostScript printers are equipped with PostScript interpreters licensed from Adobe, but others use PostScript clones. Both work fine in most situations, but some very early PostScript clones (from the late 1980s) do an imperfect job. Some printers today are advertised as PostScript models, but use Ghostscript-like software for Windows. Such models are no better than non-PostScript models in FreeBSD, so be sure a PostScript model ships with PostScript *in the printer.* Many non-PostScript models do work via Ghostscript, though, and the section "Setting Up Ghostscript" includes pointers to find out what specific models should work. For the printer hardware interface, the parallel port is best supported in FreeBSD, but USB printers often work well, too. Some USB hardware is finicky and may not be recognized correctly, though. RS-232 serial printers are slow, and so are best avoided whenever possible. Some high-end models ship with Ethernet interfaces. These work well so long as they understand the BSD LPD protocols, which most such printers do. You can think of them as a combination of a printer and a dedicated print server.

Creating a Print Queue

Creating a print queue involves two configuration steps: Creating a spool directory and editing the `/etc/printcap` file, which is where the BSD LPD system looks for its printer definitions. Before doing these things, though, you should check that your printer device is operating correctly; doing this can obviate the need for a great deal of pointless troubleshooting. This section also covers using a simple print filter. Such a filter might add codes to reset a printer, convert plain text into PostScript, or perform other similar tasks.

Using Printer Device Files

Most printers in 2002 use parallel or USB port interfaces. If you're configuring a workstation to use an existing network printer, you can skip most of this section, but the subsection entitled "Special Comments for Network Printers" is still relevant.

FreeBSD uses the `/dev/lpt0` device file to access parallel-port printers. If your computer has more than one parallel port, the second is accessed as `/dev/lpt1`, and so on. For USB printers, the equivalent device names are `/dev/ulpt0`, `/dev/ulpt1`, and so on. RS-232 serial printer ports are named `/dev/ttyd0`, `/dev/ttyd1`, and so on. Testing and optimizing these ports are important steps in printer configuration.

Testing Printer Device Files

Before proceeding further, you should test your printer port. One way to do this is to copy a short file to the port. For instance, you might try this command:

```
# cat /etc/shells > /dev/lpt0
```

 Be sure to type this command as `root`*. By default, ordinary users lack access to the raw printer port file.*

As a general rule, this command should produce some sort of printer activity. Most inkjet printers will print the file but not eject the final page. Most such printers have a "form feed" or "page eject" button you can press to eject the page. Most laser printers will blink some lights but not print anything until you eject the page. A few PostScript laser printers will discard a plain text file, but you should be able to print a PostScript file. If you've installed Ghostscript on your system, you should be able to find samples in the Ghostscript `examples` directory. For instance, on my system, the following command works:

```
# cat /usr/local/share/ghostscript/6.52/examples/escher.ps
```

 Not all PostScript files produce output. The `escher.ps` *file included with Ghostscript does, so it should work with any PostScript printer. This file also produces color output, and so is a useful test of your printer's color capabilities, particularly when testing a Ghostscript setup, as described in the upcoming sections, "Using Ghostscript as a Translator" and "Setting Up a Smart Filter."*

If you can't get any output from your printer, there are several possible causes:

■ **Text-incapable printer**   A few printers have very limited or no text printing capabilities. These are sometimes called *WinPrinters, GDI printers* (after the Windows GDI interface), or *host-based printers.* These printers often work poorly under FreeBSD. Consult the Linux Printing web page database, `http://www.linuxprinting.org`, for information on your printer and its compatibility with Ghostscript. (Despite the name, this web page is as applicable to FreeBSD as to Linux.) If your printer is listed as a "paperweight," you might as well stop here and replace it.

■ **Format not recognized**   Some printers refuse data unless it's in a particular format. Some PostScript models fall into this category. Some models may require specific prefix codes to tell the printer what format the data takes. Such printers may still work with FreeBSD, but a simple test may fail. One clue that your printer may be in this category is if a data light blinks when you send data to the printer port. If this happens, you may want to proceed with configuring the printer despite the lack of a test printout. If you see no activity light action, you may want to investigate other problems.

■ **No drivers**   If you recompile your kernel, as described in Chapter 12, you must be sure to include drivers for your printer port, or you won't be able to send data to the printer. If you omitted these drivers in FreeBSD 5.0, chances are you won't have a device file in /dev, so this should be easy to spot. Try rebuilding your kernel again or boot from the original FreeBSD kernel. Some USB models may not be properly recognized, so you may need to hunt down a kernel patch for your printer or trade it in for another model.

■ **Parallel port mode**   Some parallel port optimizations, described in the next section, can cause problems with certain printers or parallel ports. You may need to experiment with different settings to find one that works.

■ **Mundane problems**   Finally, I've lumped together in one category a plethora of problems—defective hardware, disconnected cables, lack of power to the printer, and so on. These issues aren't FreeBSD-specific, but some of them are printer-specific, so consult your printer manual's troubleshooting section for advice. If you can print from another OS, your problem does *not* fall into this category.

Optimizing Parallel Port Operation

Once you've verified that the printer port works, you may want to optimize its performance. This is an issue for parallel ports, but not for USB or RS-232 serial ports. You can optimize port performance with the lptcontrol program. This command's syntax is

```
lptcontrol -i | -p | -e | -s [-d device]
```

The -i and -p options set interrupt-driven or polling modes, respectively. Interrupt mode is the default. On most hardware, interrupt mode is faster, but it causes the parallel port hardware to consume an interrupt, which is a limited hardware resource you might need for other purposes. Also, some printers are reported to work poorly with this mode. You may want to try disabling it if you have problems.

The -e and -s options enable or disable, respectively, any extended modes your printer port supports. All motherboards built since the mid-1990s support at least one extended mode, such as EPP or ECP. In most cases, these produce better performance. Check your motherboard manual or BIOS settings to see what extended modes it supports.

The *device* is the printer port device, such as /dev/lpt0 (which is the default if you omit this option).

In most cases, you should delay parallel port optimization until printing is working via a queue. You can then test various options with regular files to see which produces the best results. If you find that you need to deviate from the boot defaults for best printing, you can add the commands to a system startup file, as described in Chapter 6.

Special Comments for Network Printers

If you're trying to configure FreeBSD to use a network printer, you won't be able to perform a raw printer test. You should verify that your network is functioning, though, as described in Chapter 14. If possible, you should also verify that you can print from the print server computer itself and from another network print client computer. If this is the first network print client you set up and you encounter problems, you may have to debug both the client and the server systems. The upcoming section, "Controlling Remote Printer Access," covers configuring a system as a print server.

Creating a Spool Directory

FreeBSD needs to be able to store print jobs somewhere, so the first step in building a print queue is to create an appropriate directory for this purpose. This directory is often called a *spool directory*, and it's traditionally located in /var/spool/lpd. The spool directory is normally owned by the user daemon and the group daemon, and has permissions that allow only daemon to read from or write to it. (The daemon user and group is used by some FreeBSD servers. FreeBSD gives this user and group access to certain directories and files so that the servers can run with non-root privileges.)
You can achieve these effects with commands like this:

```
# mkdir /var/spool/lpd/hp4000
# chown daemon:daemon /var/spool/lpd/hp4000
# chmod 770 /var/spool/lpd/hp4000
```

These commands create a spool directory called hp4000. It's usually best to create spool directories that are easy to associate with the name you intend to use for the print queue. Using the same name works well in most cases, so this spool directory will be used by a queue called hp4000.

The /etc/printcap File Format

The trickiest aspect of FreeBSD printer configuration is setting up Ghostscript and a smart filter, as described in the upcoming section, "Setting Up Ghostscript." The second-trickiest aspect is configuring the /etc/printcap file. This file's name is short for *printer capabilities*, and it tells the lpd program how to process files for a given printer—what filters to use, whether to print separator pages between print jobs, what port or network server to use, and so on. Some programs also refer to this file to obtain a list of available printers.

The BSD LPD and LPRng systems both use /etc/printcap with basically the same format. CUPS doesn't use printcap, but because some programs rely on its contents, systems that use CUPS often implement a stripped-down printcap file for their benefit.

The /etc/printcap file supports a large number of options. To understand them, first consider a sample entry for a single printer, as shown in Listing 9-1. (If your system can print to multiple printers, or uses one printer in multiple ways, you may have several such entries.)

Listing 9-1.
Sample
/etc/
printcap
Entry

```
lp|hp4000:\
        :lp=/dev/lpt0:\
        :br#115200:\
        :sd=/var/spool/lpd/hp4000:\
        :mx#0:\
        :sh:
```

Each entry begins with one or more names for the printer. Many applications use a default printer name of lp, so this entry includes this name as the printer's first name. (If your system supports multiple printers, only one should have the lp name.) If you use multiple names, separate them from one another with a vertical bar (|); in this case, the printer can be accessed as both lp and hp4000 with identical results.

The /etc/printcap file format specifies that each printer definition occupy one line, with colons (:) separating entries. To improve readability, though, most implementations use the common practice of using a backslash (\) as a line continuation character. Note that in Listing 9-1, every line except for the last one ends in a backslash. The second and subsequent lines of each entry are also indented, to make it easier to spot where one entry ends and another begins.

Most options are short codes, often followed by an equal sign (=) or a pound sign (#) to set the option's value. The printcap man page includes descriptions of these options. The most common are

- **lp** This option sets the printer device file, such as /dev/lpt0 or /dev/ulpt1. You should omit this option if you're configuring a network printer (that is, a printer that's connected to another computer or that has a direct network connection; if you intend to share a printer that's connected via a parallel, RS-232 serial, or USB port, you must still make this entry).

- **br** This option sets the baud rate for RS-232 printers. In the case of Listing 9-1, it's not a necessary entry because the printer device is a parallel printer. Thus, it could be omitted from Listing 9-1. Leaving the entry in place does no harm, though. Normally, you should set this value as high as you can. Listing 9-1's 115200 works well in most cases, but sometimes you may need to reduce this to 57600 or lower.

- **rm** This option is used only on network printers. It's the name of the remote print server, such as rm=gutenberg.threeroomco.com. This option must be absent when you're configuring a printer that's attached to a local port.

- **rp** This option is used in conjunction with rm to set the name of the print queue on a remote system. For instance, if the remote system called its printer wgprint, you'd set this value as rp=wgprint. Confusion is reduced if you use the same queue names on all systems when referring to the same printer, so you might want to name your local queue after whatever value you use here. As with rm, you should omit this option if you're configuring a local printer.

- ■ **sd**   You set the spool directory with this option. This directory should be the one you created earlier. If you omit this option, the system uses /var/spool/lpd.

- ■ **mx**   To prevent abuse, you can limit the size of the files that lpd will accept with this option. A value of 0 means there's no limit. Note that the file size may be unrelated to the final print size, so this is a poor way to limit the size of print jobs in pages. This option may be useful to minimize problems should users submit jobs that would otherwise cause /var to run out of space, though.

- ■ **sh**   By default, BSD LPD prints a *header* page between jobs, to identify the user who submitted a job and to make it easier to separate print jobs. This is a good configuration for busy print servers, but for smaller print servers and personal printers, you may want to suppress this header, which is what the sh option does. This option takes no parameters, as shown in Listing 9-1.

- ■ **if**   This option sets the name of the *input filter,* which you can use to process files in various ways, including converting raw text to PostScript or PostScript to a printer-specific format. Listing 9-1 lacks this option, so print jobs go to the printer unchanged. This configuration works well for PostScript printers or if you'll be printing only plain text to a non-PostScript printer, but most configurations will require something else as an if value.

For testing purposes, you may want to create an /etc/printcap file that lacks an if line, even if you need a print filter for normal operation. You can then start lpd if it's not already running. Type **ps ax | grep lpd** to see if it's running, and if it isn't, type **lpd** to start it. If lpd was running before you made your changes, type **killall lpd; lpd** to kill it and restart it. If lpd wasn't running when you booted FreeBSD, you may want to configure the system to do so on subsequent boots. You can use the sysinstall utility's Startup screen in the Configuration menu (shown in Figure 9-1) to start lpd when the system next boots. Alternatively, you can add the following line to /etc/rc.conf, or change it if it's present but is set to NO:

```
lpd_enable="YES"
```

Once lpd is running, you can test it by printing the same file you used earlier. The upcoming section, "Submitting Print Jobs," describes this process in detail, but for now, try a command like this:

```
$ lpr -Php4000 /etc/shells
```

This command prints the file /etc/shells to the printer called hp4000. You should achieve results similar to those you obtained using cat to send the file directly to the printer port. If the file doesn't print, double-check the names of all the /etc/printcap

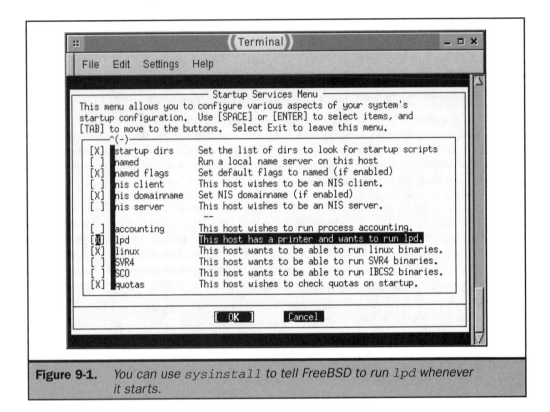

Figure 9-1. *You can use* `sysinstall` *to tell FreeBSD to run* `lpd` *whenever it starts.*

options, and eliminate extraneous ones. For instance, the `rm`, `rp`, and `if` options will all cause problems if they're included but set to null values. You should also try printing as both `root` and an ordinary user; both should work equally well. If you're printing to a remote printer, you may need to adjust that print server's configuration to accept files from your client system. Consult the upcoming section, "Controlling Remote Printer Access" for information on how to do this.

Using a Simple Filter

Much of the power of the BSD LPD system lies in the `if` option, which was omitted from Listing 9-1. The following section, "Setting Up Ghostscript," describes the use of a powerful tool known as a *smart filter* in conjunction with Ghostscript to process a wide variety of file types. In many cases, a simpler filter may do the job. One common example is the need to turn a plain text file into a PostScript file for printing on PostScript printers that don't know how to parse plain text. To do this, you first need a script to function as the filter program. Listing 9-2 shows an example. This script reads a file and looks for the string %!, with which all PostScript files begin. If that string is present, the script passes the file through to the printer unchanged. If the string isn't present, the script uses the `nenscript` program to convert the file to PostScript. (This assumes that the file is plain text; if you try to print a binary file, such as a graphics file, the script will fail.)

Note

Listing 9-2 is useful only if your printer is a PostScript model, although you could adapt it for other printer types by altering it to pass a PostScript file through Ghostscript and not use nenscript *on plain text files.*

Listing 9-2.
A Simple
Input Filter

```
#!/bin/sh
# Check to see if input is PostScript. If not, pass through
# nenscript

read firstline
firstchars=`expr "$firstline" : '\(..\)'`

if [ "$firstchars" = "%!" ]
then
    # PostScript file; pass through $firstline & rest of file
    echo "$firstline" && cat && printf "\004"
    exit 0
else
    # Not PostScript; use nenscript to process
    (echo "$firstline"; cat) | /usr/local/bin/nenscript -p- \
        && printf "\004"
    exit 0
fi
```

BASIC SYSTEM
ADMINISTRATION

Caution

The Listing 9-2 line that begins firstchars= *includes two types of single quotes. The outermost pair are* backquotes, *which are found to the left of the 1 key on most keyboards, sharing the key with the tilde (~). The innermost pair are ordinary single quotes, which appear to the left of the ENTER key on most keyboards. Be sure to use the correct quote type. This line also includes a pair of double quotes, so be sure to use those appropriately, as well.*

Listing 9-2 does several things. Although explaining every line is beyond the scope of this chapter, a basic understanding of this script is useful. The script expects to receive a file on standard input, and sends a file to standard output. The read firstline line reads the first line of the input file into a variable called $firstline. The next line extracts the first two characters of this line into a variable called $firstchars. The if line checks to see if these characters identify the file as a PostScript file. If they do, the script echoes $firstline and the rest of the file, passing it through unchanged. If the first two characters don't identify the file as a PostScript file, the script sends the file through the nenscript program, which converts plain text to PostScript.

To use this script, you should type it in and save it in some convenient location, such as /usr/local/bin. You might call it t2ps-filter. You should then add execute permission, thus:

```
# chmod a+x /usr/local/bin/t2ps-filter
```

You must modify your /etc/printcap entry to point to this script using an if line. For instance, you might change the final line of Listing 9-1 to two lines, thus:

```
:sh:\
:if=/usr/local/bin/t2ps-filter:
```

Caution *Remember to add a backslash to the former last line (sh from Listing 9-1), or the new line will be interpreted as the start of a new printer definition, which won't work. Only the final line in any /etc/printcap entry should lack a backslash.*

When you restart lpd, it will use the input filter. When you try to print a text file, it should print via nenscript, which adds a bold header line with the time and filename (stdin for all files printed in this way). Of course, you must have nenscript installed for this to work. If it's not installed, you can find it in the Print area of the Packages system in sysinstall, as described in Chapter 11.

Setting Up Ghostscript

Although a filter like that shown in Listing 9-2 can be useful on some systems, such simple filters are inherently limited. Listing 9-2, in particular, is limited because it assumes that the printer is a PostScript model, but many FreeBSD systems use non-PostScript printers. This problem is relatively simple to remedy, by altering the script as outlined earlier. A more fundamental problem is that Listing 9-2 handles just two file types: PostScript and plain text. If you want to print some other type of file, Listing 9-2 will create no output at best, or produce pages of complete gibberish at worst. The solution to this problem is to use a smart filter, which is fundamentally like Listing 9-2, but with many more rules for identifying the file type and sending the data through appropriate tools to print them.

Note *If you're configuring a print queue for a network printer that's not PostScript-capable, but that's served by a FreeBSD or similar system that uses Ghostscript to enable the printer to handle PostScript files, treat the printer as if it were a PostScript model. In this configuration, the print server will run Ghostscript; you don't need to do this on the print clients.*

Using Ghostscript as a Translator

Part of the key to smart filters is the use of Ghostscript as a translation program. This package ships with FreeBSD, and serves as a PostScript interpreter on your local computer. When called as part of a BSD LPD printer queue, Ghostscript effectively turns any supported printer into a PostScript printer. For a listing of printers supported by Ghostscript, consult the Linux Printing web site (`http://www.linuxprinting.org/printer_list.cgi`). This site includes more complete information than is available from the official Ghostscript web site (`http://www.cs.wisc.edu/~ghost/`), including information on drivers that aren't included with the main Ghostscript package.

Ghostscript isn't designed to function *only* as a part of the FreeBSD print queue; it can take a PostScript file as input and create an output file that you store on disk. The program's basic syntax is

```
gs [option[...]] [file[...]]
```

The `gs` man page includes a listing of the program's options. Some of the more important include

- **-sDEVICE=*devicename***   This option specifies the output device (that is, the printer driver; this is *not* an indication of the FreeBSD device file). Typing **gs --help** displays help text that includes a list of devices available on your system. Some of these names aren't necessarily obvious, but the Linux Printing site provides pointers to appropriate devices to use for specific printers.

- **-r *xresxyres***   Many devices support multiple resolutions, which you can specify with this option. For instance, `-r 360x720` tells Ghostscript to create output at 360×720 dots per inch (dpi). If you omit the x and *yres*, Ghostscript assumes a *yres* to match the *xres*. When printing, you must specify a resolution that's supported by your printer and by the Ghostscript driver for your printer.

- **-sOutputFile=*filename***   This option specifies the output filename. When used in a print queue, *filename* will be a dash (-), signifying standard output. If you call `gs` outside of a print queue, you'll want to provide an appropriate filename.

Ghostscript normally accepts input from standard input. As an example of Ghostscript in use, suppose you have a Hewlett Packard LaserJet 4 printer. You could use a command like the following to create an appropriate output file from a PostScript file:

```
$ gs -sDEVICE=ljet4 -r600x600 -sOutputFile=escher.pcl escher.ps
```

Aside from printer output formats, Ghostscript also supports some common graphics file output formats. These include TIFF (tiff24nc and others), PNG (png16, png256, png16m, and others), JPEG (jpeg), EPS (epswrite), PostScript (pswrite), and PDF (pdfwrite). Although creating PostScript output from PostScript input sounds strange, it can be useful in some cases, such as if your PostScript printer chokes on the original PostScript file due to lack of memory or other problems.

When you type a Ghostscript command like this one, you'll receive a prompt to press ENTER with each new page; then you'll need to type **quit** at a prompt to exit from the program. You can eliminate these prompts by adding **-dNOPAUSE -dBATCH** to the command prior to the name of the input file. These options can be extremely important if you create a custom filter to handle PostScript files.

Once you create an output file, you can send it to the printer (via cat or lpr—but lpr may not work if you've set up a filter). You should be rewarded with reasonable output. If you don't get output, or if you get page after page of gibberish, you may need to try another driver. If you see no hint of any printer activity, such as blinking lights, you may have to go back and investigate basic printer connectivity issues.

Setting Up a Smart Filter

Several smart filter packages are available for FreeBSD. These are essentially filters like those in Listing 9-2, but more sophisticated. They can identify many different file types and process the files so that they'll print on your printer. Most commonly, the filters call common file conversion programs to convert input files into PostScript. From there the filters use Ghostscript to turn the file into a format that your printer can understand. (If you have a PostScript printer, this last step is skipped.) Once configured, printing any supported file type is a matter of feeding the file to lpr. Two particularly popular smart filter packages are apsfilter and magicfilter, both of which are available from the Print software section of sysinstall. This section describes the configuration of magicfilter.

The normal way of using magicfilter is rather unusual: You call its configuration file as if it were a program. This technique works because the configuration file is marked as executable and begins with a code that FreeBSD uses to launch magicfilter as if it were a shell scripting language. The various magicfilter configuration files reside in /usr/local/libexec/magicfilter, and they're named after the Ghostscript drivers upon which they depend. For instance, the filter for the ljet4 Ghostscript driver is called ljet4-filter. As an example of a magicfilter configuration in action, consider Listing 9-3, which is Listing 9-1 modified to use magicfilter for a LaserJet 4 or compatible printer. As you can see, the only difference is the addition of the call to the magicfilter configuration file.

Listing 9-3.
Sample /etc/
printcap
Entry Using
magicfilter

```
lp|hp4000:\
        :lp=/dev/lpt0:\
        :br#115200:\
        :sd=/var/spool/lpd/hp4000:\
```

```
:mx#0:\
:sh:\
:if=/usr/local/libexec/magicfilter/ljet4-filter:
```

If `magicfilter` happens to come with a filter that's appropriate for your printer, printer setup is straightforward—or at least, little worse than setting up a raw text queue. If the `magicfilter` package lacks an appropriate filter for your printer, though, you must create one yourself.

Note   *Ghostscript—and hence `magicfilter`—provides drivers for classes of printers. For instance, many laser printers use the same Printer Control Language (PCL) used by various Hewlett Packard models, so you're likely to be able to use the `laserjet`, `ljet2p`, `ljet3`, `ljet4`, and similar drivers (and their similarly-named `magicfilter` configuration files) for printers sold by Lexmark, Brother, Okidata, and others. Consult the Linux Printing web site (`http://www.linuxprinting.org/printer_list.cgi`) for information on what Ghostscript driver works well with your printer.*

If you need to create a custom `magicfilter` configuration file, I recommend you begin by copying an existing filter for a similar printer. The most important criterion is that you *not* choose a PostScript file (these begin with `ps` or `cps`) because these send the PostScript output directly to the printer port without invoking Ghostscript. Most of the filter files contain references to Ghostscript early on in the files, like this:

```
# PostScript
0 %!     filter /usr/local/bin/gs -q -dSAFER -dNOPAUSE -r600 ↵
-sDEVICE=ljet4 -sOutputFile=- -
0 \004%! filter /usr/local/bin/gs -q -dSAFER -dNOPAUSE -r600 ↵
-sDEVICE=ljet4 -sOutputFile=- -
```

To modify your copied configuration file, you must alter the Ghostscript driver name specified by the `-sDEVICE` option. Once again, the Linux Printing web site's database can be invaluable in learning what to put there. Many `magicfilter` configurations include lines that enable the filter to recognize files in the printer's native language. This feature enables you to print from the applications that can produce printer-specific output. If you use an unrelated printer's filter as a model, you may want to remove these lines. If you want to print using printer-specific drivers in applications such as The GIMP, you must create new rules for your printer's format, which can be tricky. It's usually easier to print PostScript and use `magicfilter`'s normal PostScript handling rules.

You may also want to create variants of existing configuration files even for printers that `magicfilter` supports. For instance, you might want to create configurations to print at differing resolutions (changing the `-r` value in the call to `gs`) and set up multiple print queues, one for each resolution. For instance, you might have `epson360` and `epson720` queues to print to an Epson inkjet at 360 and 720 dpi, respectively.

Once you've modified your /etc/printcap file to use your new filters, restart lpd. You can then test printing by using lpr to print a variety of files. Try paging through your filter files to learn what file types your filter supports. When you try to print a file that's not supported by magicfilter, the file should quietly disappear from the queue, preventing a possible spew of paper with gibberish. (The root user will receive an e-mail notification of this rejection, though.) If the file type is supported, it should be processed and you should receive reasonable output.

Controlling a Printer

If you've configured your system as you read this chapter, you should now have a functioning print queue on your FreeBSD system. This section describes how to use this print queue, both as an ordinary user and as the system administrator. Topics include submitting print jobs, checking on jobs in the queue, deleting jobs, reordering jobs, and changing the availability of print queues.

Submitting Print Jobs

This chapter has already referred to the lpr utility, which is FreeBSD's tool for submitting print jobs to the queue. This tool is important enough that it deserves an extended description. You should also know how applications interact with lpr to enable you to print directly from a program, rather than generate a PostScript file and then print it manually with lpr.

Using lpr

The lpr program accepts a large number of options, some of which are fairly esoteric. Consult the lpr man page for details. A simplified syntax is

```
lpr [-Pprinter] [-#num] [-U user] [-hmrs] [filename[...]]
```

The meanings of these options are

- **-Pprinter** This option sets the printer queue to be used. It may be the most-used lpr option on systems that support multiple printers. The default is the value of the PRINTER environment variable or lp if that variable doesn't exist. Some versions of lpr require that there be no space between the -P and the queue name, but the BSD LPD included with FreeBSD can tolerate a space.

- **-#num** This option tells lpr to generate *num* copies of the printout. For instance, **lpr -#4 afile.ps** creates four copies of afile.ps.

- **-U user** FreeBSD tracks who submits print jobs. This option, which is accessible to root and daemon only, enables you to specify the user associated with a print job.

- ■ **-h** On sites that print a header page for each job, this option disables the header.

- ■ **-m** If you want to be notified when a job is finished printing, include this option and `lpd` will send you e-mail when the job has printed.

- ■ **-r** If you want `lpr` to delete the original file after printing it, use this option. It's most often used in scripts or by programs that generate temporary files to be printed.

- ■ **-s** Normally, the printing system copies the file to be printed to the spool directory. If you're printing a very large file, though, this practice can temporarily consume a great deal of disk space—potentially enough to keep the print job from succeeding if you're low on disk space. This option tells the system to create a symbolic link rather than copy the file, which reduces temporary disk space requirements.

You can submit one or more files to be printed, and you can use wildcards to submit many files in a directory—but be cautious when doing this, lest you end up with many more print jobs than you had intended. If you don't specify a file to be printed, `lpr` reads from standard input. This feature is most useful for scripting or when using `lpr` in a pipe with other programs. The files must be in a format that's understandable to your print queue. If you've set up a simple queue that uses no filter, this means a format that's acceptable to your printer. If you use a filter, it means a format that's understandable to your filter. Most configurations should be able to handle either plain text or PostScript.

Printing from Applications

Some programs enable you to print directly, without manually invoking `lpr`. In practice, most of these programs generate PostScript output and send it to `lpr`, often using temporary files in `/tmp` or a pipe. Precisely how the application interacts with you varies from one program to another. Some produce a dialog box in which you can enter a printing command, typically with a partial command already displayed. You can then modify the command as you see fit, using the normal `lpr` syntax. For instance, Figure 9-2 shows the print dialog box in the xv graphics program. It uses a default print command of `lpr`, with no options. You can redirect the print job to another printer by adding `-Pprinter`, add other `lpr` options, or even use some entirely different command, such as a custom printing script or Samba's `smbprint` utility.

Other programs provide an interface that may be easier for new users to understand. These programs typically examine `/etc/printcap` or use their own configuration files to identify printers. For instance, Figure 9-3 shows the print dialog box used by OpenOffice.org. In this dialog box, you can select a printer from the *Name* option box, set the number of copies, and so on. Such dialog boxes may have application-specific options, such as the *Print Range* option in Figure 9-3, which enables you to print a subset of the pages in a document.

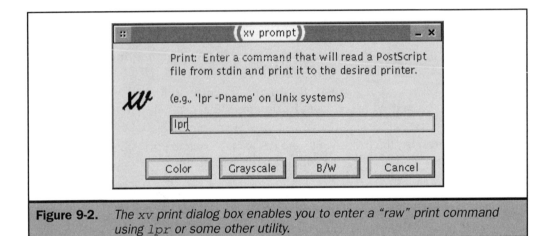

Figure 9-2. The xv print dialog box enables you to enter a "raw" print command using lpr or some other utility.

Checking Print Jobs

No matter how you submit print jobs, you often need to check on their status. You can do this with the lpq command. This command's syntax is

```
lpq [-a] [-l] [-Pprinter] [jobnum[...]] [user[...]]
```

The -Pprinter option has the same meaning as in lpr; it selects the queue you want to examine. The remaining options have the following meanings:

- **-a** If you want to see the status of all the local printers, use this option and omit the -Pprinter option.
- **-l** This option displays additional information about print jobs. The resulting information exceeds one line's length.
- **jobnum** ordinarily, lpq displays information on all the jobs on a printer. If you provide job numbers, though, it displays information on the specified jobs.
- **user** You can obtain information on all the jobs owned by a particular user by providing the username.

If a print queue is empty, typing **lpq** produces a simple no entries response. If the queue isn't empty, though, it produces output similar to the following:

```
$ lpq
waiting for lp to become ready (offline?)
Rank   Owner    Job  Files                                  Total Size
1st    rodsmith 35   fstab-copy                             450 bytes
2nd    rodsmith 37   ...hostscript/6.52/examples/escher.ps 10520 bytes
3rd    rodsmith 38   (standard input)                       1364390 bytes
```

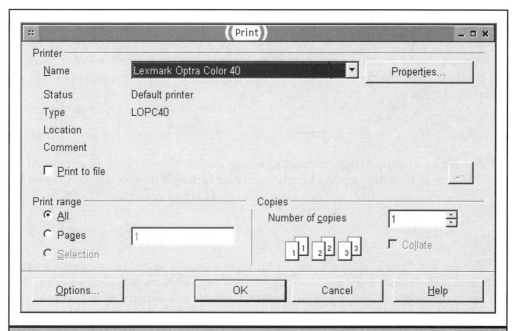

Figure 9-3. *Some applications let you select the printer and other options using drop-down lists, buttons, and so on.*

BASIC SYSTEM ADMINISTRATION

Note   *If you replace the BSD LPD system with LPRng or CUPS, the `lpq` command displays information in a different format than that presented here.*

As you can see, the output includes the job's rank (the order in which it will be printed), the owner, the job ID number, the original file, and the size of the print job. The first line after the command in this example (`waiting for lp to become ready`) indicates that the printer isn't responding. You might see this message if your printer is turned off, is suffering from a paper jam, is out of paper, or has other problems that prevent it from printing. In such a case, `lpd` stops sending jobs to the printer and waits patiently for you to correct the problem. The job ID number is particularly important because you use it in other printer management commands.

The `Total Size` column lists the print job size in bytes. It's important to recognize that this value may not be closely related to final printout size. In this particular case, job 35 (`fstab-copy`) is a short text file, job 37 (`escher.ps`) is a PostScript file that generates one page of output, and job 38 (from standard input) is a one-page graphics printout. Despite their wildly divergent sizes, all three jobs will each produce a single page of output. A multipage job might be just a few bytes, or could be larger than job 38 in the preceding example.

Deleting Print Jobs

If you've submitted a print job and you decide you don't want it to print after all, or if you discover that a user has submitted a job that shouldn't be printed, you can delete the print job from the queue with the lprm command. This command's syntax is relatively simple:

```
lprm [-Pprinter] [-] [jobnum[...]] [user[...]]
```

As with lpr and lpq, the -Pprinter option enables you to specify a printer other than the default one. As you might expect, jobnum is the job ID number, as revealed by lpq. Thus, an ordinary user or root can cancel jobs using a command like this:

```
$ lprm 35 38
```

This command deletes jobs 35 and 38 from the queue. If an ordinary user issues this command, the command will succeed only if the same user owns the specified print jobs, but root can delete any print job, no matter who owns it. The remaining options— a single dash (-) and a username—both enable you to delete many jobs. Only root may specify a username. When root does this, all the jobs belonging to that user will be deleted from the queue. If ordinary users want to delete all their jobs, they can use the dash:

```
$ lprm -
```

This use of lprm has a different meaning when issued by root, though: It deletes all the print jobs in a queue, no matter who owns them.

Reordering Print Jobs

Sometimes you may need to reprioritize jobs in a print queue. For instance, a queue may have a dozen large jobs already, but a newly-submitted job may need to be rushed through quickly. In such situations, the lpc command is useful. This command's syntax is deceptively simple:

```
lpc [command [argument[...]]]
```

If you don't provide a command when you call lpc, it enters an interactive mode in which you enter commands at an lpc> prompt. The lpc program accepts over a dozen commands; consult its man page for more details. (Typing **lpc help** displays a short summary of available commands.) For reordering print jobs, the relevant command is topq, which takes a queue name and one or more job ID numbers or usernames as its argument. When you enter this command, you move the specified jobs, or all jobs owned by the specified user, to the top of the print queue. For instance, to move job 38 in the `hp4000` queue to the top of the queue, you would type

```
# lpc topq hp4000 38
```

This command comes with two important caveats:

■ The `lpc` command is useable only by `root`. Ordinary users can't change the order of jobs in a queue, even if they own all the jobs.

■ The job you move will begin printing *after* whatever job is currently printing. Furthermore, if the queue in question feeds a printer with a large buffer or a remote network printer, you may not be able to reorder jobs because they may have already left the local system's queue.

Changing a Queue's Availability

The `lpc` utility is something of a workhorse program. In addition to changing the order of jobs in a queue, it can completely disable (or re-enable) a queue. Several pairs of `lpc` commands have related effects:

■ **abort/start** The `abort` command disconnects `lpd` from the specified queue and prevents `lpr` from starting a new daemon. This command effectively terminates all printing on the queue, but jobs in the queue are not deleted. You can start printing on a queue by using the `start` command. One variant that's useful in some situations is `restart`, which terminates and then restarts printing. This command can be useful if printing on a queue has hung for some reason, such as a misbehaving filter.

■ **down/up** The `down` command halts printing and enables you to enter a message that will be displayed by `lpq`. For instance, typing **lpc down hp4000 Printer is out of toner** cancels printing and displays the message `Printer is out of toner` to any user who subsequently types **lpq -Php4000**. Jobs in the queue when you issue this command are held and are not printed until you use the `up` command to restore the queue.

■ **disable/enable** The `disable` command keeps `lpr` from accepting new jobs for a queue, but doesn't terminate or delay printing of jobs that are already in the queue. To re-enable printing on the queue, use the `enable` command.

Tip *If you want to bring down a queue that's in use, you might use `disable`, wait for the queue to empty, and then use `down` to give users a message telling them why the queue is inactive. This technique is useful if you need to swap out a printer or perform other maintenance that may take a while. Of course, if a printer is seriously malfunctioning, using `abort` or `down` from the start is a better course of action.*

In all these cases, you specify the `lpc` command followed by the name of the queue you want to affect, or `all` to affect all queues. For instance, to print remaining jobs but refuse new ones on all queues, you'd type

```
# lpc disable all
```

Controlling Remote Printer Access

As noted earlier in this chapter, the BSD LPD system is inherently network enabled. The earlier section, "Creating a Print Queue," included information on configuring a local queue to forward jobs to other computers that accept remote BSD LPD print jobs. (Some workgroup printers are inherently network enabled and accept such jobs directly, as well.) You may want to configure a printer to function as a *print server*—a computer that accepts remote print jobs from other systems. If your remote systems are other FreeBSD systems, other UNIX-like systems, or even non-UNIX systems that understand the BSD LPD protocols, configuring your BSD LPD system to accept print jobs is relatively straightforward: You need to adjust only one configuration file on the print server, after you get it to print locally.

 Note *This section describes the configuration of a computer to accept print jobs using the BSD LPD printing protocols. The LPRng and CUPS packages can use these protocols, as can client packages for various OSs. If you want to configure an LPRng or CUPS system to accept print jobs, though, these instructions don't apply. Also, when dealing with non-UNIX clients, it's often preferable to implement their native printing protocols in FreeBSD. The Samba package (described in Chapter 18) does this for Windows and OS/2, and the Netatalk package (http://netatalk.sourceforge.net) includes a print server for use with Mac OS clients.*

The `lpd` program defaults to running in a fairly restrictive mode—it accepts print jobs from the local system only. To change this restriction, you list the computers from which your local queue should accept jobs in the `/etc/hosts.lpd` file. You can specify hosts by hostname (with or without the domain name; if you omit the domain name, `lpd` assumes you mean the server's own domain) or by IP address. For instance, Listing 9-4 is a `hosts.lpd` file that gives the systems `chaucer` in the server's domain, `shakespeare.threeroomco.com`, and `172.19.45.201` access to the print server.

Listing 9-4.
Sample
`/etc/hosts`
`.lpd` File

```
chaucer
shakespeare.threeroomco.com
172.19.45.201
```

You can also use the /etc/hosts.equiv file to give other systems access to your system, but hosts.equiv has consequences far beyond those of printing—it's used by various other network utilities. In most cases, it's better to configure each server independently because that enables you to fine-tune your system's security policies. You may want to read Chapters 17 and 29 for more information on configuring your system to block unwanted network access.

Summary

Like most modern OSs, FreeBSD uses a print queue system to handle printing. This scheme gives the OS control over scheduling print jobs, which is important in a multitasking OS and critically important in a multiuser OS or print server. Rather than implement printer drivers in the way most OSs do, FreeBSD relies upon programs to generate plain-text or PostScript output, and then uses filters in the print queue to turn that output into a form that the printer can understand. The print queues themselves are controlled through the /etc/printcap file, which lists queue names, printer capabilities, and the filters used by the queues. When printing to non-PostScript printers, these filters normally call Ghostscript, which converts PostScript into a wide variety of file formats suitable for common non-PostScript printers. Whatever the queue does to process data, the queue can be controlled through a handful of commands, including lpr, lpq, lprm, and lpc. Some applications provide GUI interfaces to some of these commands—particularly lpr, which is used to submit jobs to a print queue. The BSD LPD system was designed with network printing in mind, so configuring FreeBSD to accept remote print jobs from other UNIX-like systems is a matter of adding acceptable hosts to a configuration file.

The
Complete
Reference

FreeBSD

Chapter 10

Managing User Accounts

263

A ccounts are central to FreeBSD's user support and security models, so you must understand FreeBSD accounts in order to properly administer these aspects of a FreeBSD system. Typically, every user has precisely one account, although sometimes a single user might merit multiple accounts. Certain system and administrative accounts are either used by nobody or are accessible to one or more system administrators. Previous chapters have described some of these accounts (particularly `root`), but this chapter helps flesh out the details. It also provides practical advice on how to create, modify, and delete user accounts and groups. This chapter concludes with a look at account-related security policies. You may want to change certain system defaults to have FreeBSD function in a way that's better suited to your local needs than the standard defaults allow.

 Account management is closely tied to file management, and particularly settings of ownership and permissions on files. These topics are covered in Chapter 8.

The Importance of Accounts in FreeBSD

Before you begin administering user accounts, you should understand why they exist, how they're used, and how they're implemented. These topics tie into the specific features of FreeBSD accounts, and understanding the hows and whys will help you design a user account structure that's appropriate for your system.

Accounts as a Convenience

One of the most obvious reasons for the existence of accounts is that they function as a convenience for your users. The standard installations of some OSs boot the computer into a single desktop environment by default. Any user may modify desktop defaults and store files in any directory. Examples of such OSs include DOS, Windows 9x/Me, OS/2, Mac OS Classic, and BeOS. (Some of these provide configuration options to support accounts of one sort or another, though.) This type of configuration can be a reasonable one for a single-user system because it minimizes the effort and training required to use the computer; users need only turn on the computer and wait for the desktop to appear before beginning to use it.

One drawback to a single-desktop configuration comes in a multiuser environment. Suppose that two users, Pierre and Marie, share a computer. If Pierre likes a desktop environment with a pale purple background and fast keyboard repeat rate, but Marie prefers a random background image and no keyboard repeat, one or both will have to settle for a nonpreferred environment. Accounts solve this problem by storing preferences separately for each user. Thus, the system uses the preferences of whichever user logs in, satisfying both users.

> **Note**
>
> *User preferences can exist for many FreeBSD programs, not just the generic desktop settings mentioned here. Programs such as mail clients, web browsers, word processors, and even text-mode shells support user-by-user customizations. Previous chapters, such as Chapter 6, described some of these.*

Another account convenience feature is the fact that each FreeBSD account has its own file storage area, known as a *home directory*. This is normally a subdirectory of /home named after the user's username, such as /home/marie or /home/pierre. This feature enables users to store their files in whatever ways they like. If Marie is fastidious and keeps her files in carefully structured directories, but Pierre is more haphazard and uses few directories, neither person's work habits will interfere with the other because neither user needs to deal with the other's home directory. (Depending upon your system's security settings, one user may or may not even be able to read another's home directory.)

Accounts as a Security Tool

Placing user files in separate home directories has security benefits in addition to the convenience factor. Namely, depending upon the permissions granted on users' home directories, subdirectories, and individual files, you and your users can control who may access their files, and in what ways. For instance, if Pierre is working on a project to which Marie should not have access, he can set permissions on related files or directories to exclude Marie from reading those files. This feature is extremely important for any multiuser OS. Chapter 8 and the upcoming section, "Tending to Account Security," cover this topic in greater detail.

In addition to controlling user-to-user access, account security measures help keep the computer as a whole secure. Most of the files that make up FreeBSD itself are readable, and many are executable, by any user; but most files and directories can't be written by any ordinary user. Thus, neither Marie nor Pierre can delete critical system files. In most cases, root (the administrative account) owns these files, and only root can modify or delete them. This characteristic makes FreeBSD useable in relatively public settings by relatively untrained individuals. Using a Windows 9*x*/Me or Mac OS Classic system in a public environment often causes problems because ignorant or malicious individuals can damage the system configuration, but FreeBSD isn't subject to this problem.

> **Caution**
>
> *If you're the only user of a FreeBSD system, you may be tempted to forego an ordinary user account and simply log in as root. Don't do this. It may seem convenient to be able to use the root account's power without using su first, but this is a very dangerous practice. FreeBSD includes few safeguards to prevent root from typing disastrous commands or performing dangerous operations in a GUI environment. If you use root unnecessarily, sooner or later you* will *do serious damage to your installation.*

BASIC SYSTEM ADMINISTRATION

Accounts and Groups

Accounts are powerful tools, but in many environments they don't go far enough. In particular, it's often necessary to provide security based on *groups* of users. FreeBSD implements this capability with its group feature. A group is a collection of accounts. For instance, pierre and marie might belong to the physics group, whereas jane and charles might belong to the biology group. One user can belong to multiple groups, if necessary.

For the most part, groups are used in conjunction with file permissions, as described in Chapter 8, to fine-tune access to files by different groups of users. The upcoming section, "Tending to Account Security," describes some possible configurations for your system.

One group is particularly important: wheel. This group's members have the honor of being able to use the su command to acquire the privileges of another user—including root. This command is described in Chapter 3. Normally, a small number of users (possibly just one) are members of the wheel group and know the root password. This combination allows these users to log on using their regular accounts, type **su** and the root password, and administer the system. Any user who's not a member of the wheel group is denied access to su, and so is less likely to succeed in compromising the system, even if that person is a malicious individual who's somehow acquired the root password. Thus, wheel is a component of the FreeBSD security system.

 If you're administering a FreeBSD system, you should be sure you're a member of the wheel group. When you administer the system, log in using your ordinary account and then use su to become root. This leaves more traces in the system logs concerning your activities than would a direct login as root. Such traces can be important when tracking down abuse, particularly on a system with multiple administrators.

Usernames, Groups, UIDs, and GIDs

At their cores, computers work on numbers. Whenever you read a word or name on a computer screen, that's just a translation of numeric data into a format that's convenient for you as a human. In many cases, such as when using a word processor, this translation occurs at a low enough level that you can almost always ignore it. Such translations involve the conversion controlled by the *American Standard Code for Information Interchange (ASCII)*, which maps numbers to letters and other punctuation, or perhaps some other method of encoding. Other mappings are at work in creating displays of characters on your screen. In the case of usernames and group names, though, this very low-level translation is joined by another one that's more likely to be important in managing user accounts. Specifically, usernames are a convenient human representation of *user IDs (UIDs)*, and group names are a representation of *group IDs (GIDs)*.

Internally, FreeBSD uses UIDs and GIDs almost exclusively. For instance, UIDs and GIDs are stored with other file metadata (data describing a file, as opposed to the file's contents), such as its creation time and size. They're also used to identify the owners of running processes. The usernames and group names that people use are secondary to the UIDs and GIDs, from FreeBSD's internal point of view.

> **Note**
>
> *It's possible to write scripts and programs that refer to usernames and group names rather than UIDs and GIDs. Such scripts and programs could conceivably be used as part of automatic system operation. Thus, this classification of UIDs and GIDs being used internally and names being used only when interacting with humans is not quite perfect.*

Because FreeBSD is a tool for humans, it includes a mechanism to map UIDs and GIDs to usernames and group names, respectively. Thus, when you take a long directory listing, FreeBSD normally displays the username and group name rather than the UID and GID:

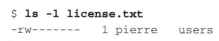

```
$ ls -l license.txt
-rw-------  1 pierre   users      356 Mar  2 2002 license.txt
```

> **Note**
>
> *The −n option to `ls` causes it to display the UID and GID rather than the username and group name.*

Ordinarily, there's a one-to-one mapping of UIDs to usernames and GIDs to group names. It is possible, however, to create an account that has one UID but multiple associated usernames, and likewise for GIDs and groups. Such configurations can be confusing, though, so they're generally not recommended.

> **Caution**
>
> *One trick that computer crackers sometimes use is to create an account with an ordinary sounding username but a UID of 0. This UID is special because it's synonymous with the `root` account. Thus, this cracker's "new" account is just another way to gain `root` access, albeit by another name. You should be alert to this possibility; if you examine your account configuration files and see any account with a UID of 0 other than `root`, your system has almost certainly been compromised.*

By default, FreeBSD begins assigning UIDs with 1000, and GIDs at the same number. Some other OSs use other starting numbers, sometimes as low as 100. Because it is UIDs and GIDs that are associated with files, any file transfer method that involves passing files over a medium that supports UIDs and GIDs requires the user to have the same UID on both systems in order for permissions to work correctly. GIDs must also match to equivalent groups. The user can have different usernames on the two systems, but as long as the user has the same UID, permissions will work. This factor is an issue when transferring floppy or Zip disks using FreeBSD's Fast File System (FFS) or with Network File System (NFS) network transfers. It's not a factor with filesystems that don't support UIDs and GIDs, such as FAT; nor is it a factor with File Transfer Protocol (FTP) network file transfers.

Account and Group Data Structures

Accounts consist of an intertwined set of data structures, as defined in various files and directories. The most important of these are

- **/etc/passwd** This file is the core of all account data structures. It's a text file that contains basic information on all user accounts, including the mapping between UIDs and usernames, the user's default group (specified by GID), the user's home directory, and the user's default shell. Traditionally, this file has held users' passwords, but today this is no longer the case. This file is readable by any user of the computer.

- **/etc/master.passwd** This file holds much of the same information as /etc/passwd, plus a *hash* (a one-way encryption) of users' passwords and a few additional pieces of information. Because of the sensitivity of the password, this file is readable only by root.

- **Binary password files** Although text-based files such as /etc/passwd and /etc/master.passwd are adequate for small systems, searching through thousands of entries in a large system can be quite time consuming. Thus, FreeBSD implements special binary password files, /etc/pwd.db and /etc/spwd.db. These files provide for quicker lookups of user information.

- **Home directory** The user's home directory is an important part of the user's account. Its location is defined in the /etc/passwd and /etc/master.passwd files, and the home directory holds a user's data files.

- **Local configuration files** Users' directories frequently contain files that define many default features of the user's environment. For instance, individualized shell configuration files reside in the home directory, as described in Chapter 6.

- **Server configuration files** Some servers and other system processes include references to particular accounts, typically to grant or deny specific users access to the server or some of its facilities. Calling these files part of the account configuration may be a bit of a stretch, but it's important to remember them if you add, delete, or modify an account. Details vary greatly from one server to another. Examples include features such as Samba's encrypted password file and user-specific delivery rules for mail servers.

Collectively, these files and features define many of the capabilities of individual user accounts. The upcoming sections of this chapter describe how you can modify these files, and hence modify how an account is accessed or how it works. Groups have similar configuration files, but they tend to be simpler. The most important of these group files is /etc/group. It's roughly equivalent to /etc/passwd, except that it defines groups rather than accounts. This similarity includes a mapping of group names to GIDs and lists of users (specified by username). Groups don't have home directories by default, although you could create directories in which group members can share files, if this is appropriate for your system. Some servers may provide differential access based on group, but such configurations are rare compared to user-based access controls.

Creating User Accounts

When you installed FreeBSD, as described in Chapter 2, the system gave you the opportunity to create initial user accounts. The system also created a number of special system accounts (most with UIDs less than 100, although one—nobody—has a UID of 65534). In day-to-day operation, there's a good chance you'll need to add new users. This is particularly likely on systems with many users, such as file servers, mail servers, or systems used with remote-access terminals.

Typically, you'll use a tool such as sysinstall or a more command-oriented tool such as adduser to add users. You can also add users by directly editing the files in question, but this approach is usually too tedious. (It's covered in the upcoming section, "Modifying User Accounts," in conjunction with editing existing accounts.)

Rules for Usernames

Before you begin adding users, you should know what names you can associate with accounts. FreeBSD accepts usernames that consist of lowercase letters, numbers, the underscore (_), and the dash (-). The maximum length for a username is 16 characters, but some programs' displays allocate only 8 characters for usernames, so longer usernames may be truncated or cause alignment problems for columns after the username.

> **Note** *Some UNIX-like systems accept usernames with mixed-case names, names longer than 16 characters, or names that include nonalphanumeric characters (such as punctuation). Although you can create at least some such usernames in FreeBSD by editing /etc/ master.passwd and running pwd_mkdb, as described in the upcoming section, "Modifying User Accounts," doing so might cause problems for utilities that enforce the usual FreeBSD username rules.*

FreeBSD usernames are case-sensitive, so if a username is marie, that user cannot type **Marie** or any other case variant to log in; FreeBSD will respond as if the user typed the wrong password. Likewise, entering a username that differs in case in an account-maintenance tool will fail. One exception to this rule is e-mail; if somebody types **Marie** as the username in a mail message, it will be delivered to marie.

Within the character and length rules, usernames can be just about anything. Most sites base usernames on users' real names by using users' first or last names or initials.

For instance, Marie Curie's username might be marie, curie, mcurie, or something similar. If this system causes a conflict, you may need to resort to using numbers, such as marie2 if somebody named Marie Jones already uses the marie username. You may also need to truncate a name or adapt your system for individuals with particularly long names. Some administrators like to use strictly defined rules for mapping users' real names to usernames, but others are more flexible and allow users to select usernames in whatever way they desire. Whatever the case, these policies are decidedly local; you can use whatever system you like, or even generate usernames that aren't based on users' real names.

Using sysinstall to Create Accounts

The sysinstall package includes a tool that enables you to add users to the system. Chapter 2 includes an introduction to sysinstall for system installation, and part of that process includes creating an ordinary user account. You may need to create a group for new users before you follow this process. The upcoming section, "Using Groups," covers this topic. To use sysinstall to add more users, follow these steps:

1. As root, type **/stand/sysinstall**. This command launches the sysinstall utility.

2. Select the Configure option from the sysinstall main menu. This opens the FreeBSD Configuration Menu.

3. In the FreeBSD Configuration Menu, select User Management. This creates a small User and Group Management menu.

4. In the User and Group Management menu, select User. This produces the User and Group Management form shown in Figure 10-1. Note that some information, such as the UID and Login Shell fields, is already entered into the form.

5. Enter a username in the Login ID field. When you press TAB or ENTER, the cursor moves to the UID field and the Home Directory field acquires a value based on the username you entered, such as /home/marie if you entered marie as the username.

6. If you want to change the UID to make it conform to the UID this user has on another computer, change it. If not, you should leave the UID alone; sysinstall picks the first UID that's available.

 If you need to match UIDs across systems, you should ensure that you don't create conflicts, such as two users with the same UID on one system. You may need to change an existing user's UID to avoid such conflicts.

7. In the Group field, enter the user's default group. This group *must already exist* on the system. If the group doesn't exist, sysinstall won't be able to create

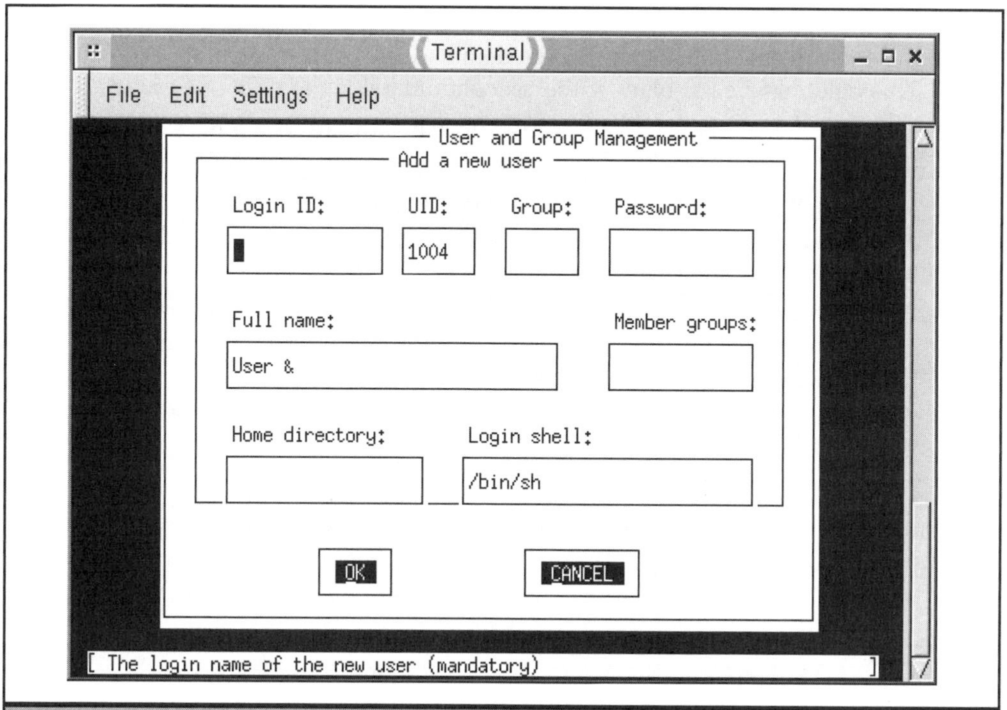

Figure 10-1. *The User and Group Management form is* sysinstall's user addition tool.

the user. If you want this user to have access to the su command, you can enter the wheel group here. If you need to create a new group for the user, back out of the process and consult the upcoming section, "Using sysinstall to Create Groups."

8. Type a password into the Password field. Selection of good passwords is critical to system security. The "Creating Secure Passwords" section of Chapter 29 describes this issue in detail. In brief, passwords should not be words found in a dictionary or proper names (especially names tied to the user, such as the user's spouse's name), they should be mixed-case, and they should contain some letters or punctuation.

9. The Full Name field contains free-form information about the user that's displayed by some utilities. This information is often the user's full name, such as Marie Curie, but the field defaults to User &. Some utilities interpret information separated by commas in a particular way—namely, the user's full name, office location, office telephone number, and home phone number may be entered. Backspace over the default value and type something more meaningful.

10. If the user should belong to more than one group, enter groups in addition to the one you entered in Step 7 in the Member Groups field, separated by commas. This field may be left blank if the user should belong to only one group.

11. You may change the user's home directory by editing the Home Directory field, but in most cases the default based on the username should work fine.

12. Enter a default shell for the user. The system checks this against a list of acceptable shells (stored in /etc/shells). If you enter an invalid shell, sysinstall complains when you select OK.

13. Position your text cursor on OK and press ENTER. FreeBSD now creates a new account using the information you've provided and returns you to the User and Group Management menu (Step 4). You can then repeat Steps 4–13 if you want to add more users, or select Cancel twice and then Exit Install to get out of sysinstall.

This procedure for adding users works well in most cases. It presents prompts for what should go in each field and can quickly add a few users. Like many FreeBSD administration tasks, though, sysinstall presents a menu-based face for other tools.

Using adduser

Sometimes sysinstall isn't adequate. For instance, if you need to add many users, you may prefer to write a script to do the job, and sysinstall doesn't interact well with scripts. You might also prefer not to wade through sysinstall's menus. In such cases, a simpler but more powerful tool exists: adduser. This program prompts you for information in a fairly rigid order using standard input and output, so you can call it from a script using redirection, as described in Chapter 5, if you want to create accounts in a semiautomated way.

The first time you run adduser, the program tries to access its configuration file, /etc/adduser.conf, but this file doesn't exist on a standard installation. The program therefore runs through most of its options, as described shortly, to obtain default values. You can press ENTER to accept the defaults for most of these. If you decide to change them later, you can edit adduser.conf or delete the file and run adduser again to generate new defaults.

After you've generated adduser.conf, or when you run the program, it begins prompting for information. The first information is related to the username and user identity:

```
# adduser
Use option ``-verbose'' if you want to see more warnings and
questions or try to repair bugs.

Enter username [a-z0-9_-]: marie
Enter full name []: Marie Curie
```

As described earlier in the section, "Rules for Usernames," the username should consist of lowercase letters and numbers. The *full name* is normally the user's real name, but you can store other information here as well, if you like. The program then asks questions relating to shells, home directories, the UID, and group affiliation:

```
Enter shell bash csh date ksh no pash sh tcsh zsh [sh]: ksh
Enter home directory (full path) [/home/marie]:
Uid [1003]:
Enter login class: default []:
Login group marie [marie]:
Login group is ``marie''. Invite marie into other groups: guest no
[no]: users
```

You can press ENTER to pick the default for most of these, as was done for most of these responses. In this example, though, `marie` is given the nondefault `ksh` shell, and is added to the `users` group in addition to the `marie` group. This last option deserves special comment. By default, `adduser` creates a special group for each user. At creation, this group is populated only by the user in question, but you can add other users to the group. This can be a useful approach to account security, but it's not the only approach. This and other options are described in the upcoming section, "Deciding Upon a Group Strategy." If you prefer not to use this approach, you can enter an existing group's name at the `Login group` prompt.

The next stage of the account creation process prompts for several password-related options:

```
Use password-based authentication (y/n) [y]:
Use an empty password (y/n) [n]:
Enter password []:
Enter password again []:
Enable account password at creation (y/n) [y]:
```

In this example, the defaults were selected for all options, which is the usual configuration, except for the password (at the `Enter password` and `Enter password again` prompts). Although not shown in this example because the password doesn't echo to the screen, the same password was entered twice. Entering it twice reduces the chance that a typo will render the account unusable, requiring subsequent superuser intervention. After you enter the password information, `adduser` asks you to verify the information you've entered so far:

```
Name:      marie
Password: ****
Fullname: Marie Curie
Uid:      1003
```

```
Gid:       1003 (marie)
Class:
Groups:    marie users
HOME:      /home/marie
Shell:     /usr/local/bin/ksh
OK? (y/n) [y]: y
```

If you type **n**, adduser goes back to collect the information anew. If you type **y**, adduser creates the account. It then prompts you for information concerning an e-mail message that it sends to the newly-created account:

```
Added user ``marie''
Send message to ``marie'' and: no root second_mail_address
[no]: charlesd@pangaea.edu

Marie Curie,

your account ``marie'' was created.
Have fun!

See also chpass(1), finger(1), passwd(1)

Add anything to default message (y/n) [n]: n
Send message (y/n) [y]: y
Add another user? (y/n) [y]: n
```

The system asks if you want to send a copy of the welcoming e-mail to any other address. The default response is no, which causes the mail to not be sent to anybody else. You can instead type **root** to send the mail to the root account, or any other e-mail address (such as **charlesd@pangaea.edu**, shown here). The system displays the message, which by default isn't terribly informative—after all, any user who can read the message presumably knows the account exists. This message is stored in /etc/adduser.message, so you can edit it to something more useful if you like, such as a message that explains local policies. You can also add information to the default message on a user-by-user basis. If you prefer, you can opt to not send the message at all. Finally, adduser asks if you want to add another user. If you respond **n**, it exits; if you respond **y**, it begins the process again.

The adduser command takes various options, which override default values stored in /etc/adduser.conf. For instance, -home *homedir* sets the base of the home directory (usually /home) to something else that you specify. Because these options override items for which you're prompted, there's seldom a need to use them. One exception is -config_create, which creates new default configuration files. You can consult the adduser man page for more information on these options.

Modifying User Accounts

In an ideal world (from a system administration perspective), once you create an account, you can forget about it. Unfortunately, this often isn't the case. You may need to change some of the information you've already entered for an account. One particularly common type of change is to passwords. A good security practice is to change passwords frequently, to minimize the potential for damage should a password fall into the wrong hands. (Just how frequently depends on your environment. Some high-security environments might require one-time-use passwords, which expire as soon as they're used. Low-security environments might get away with a change every few months.) Understanding how passwords work, how to change them, and how to change other account information is important for account management.

Understanding Shadow Passwords

In the early years of UNIX, passwords were stored in the /etc/passwd file along with other information. Various programs needed information in this file—for instance, the finger daemon, which displays information on users of the system, must be able to read the user's real name from this file. Thus, it's readable to the world. This system was considered acceptable because the password was encrypted with a hash, as noted earlier in the section "Account and Group Data Structures." Unfortunately, as computers grew in speed and disk capacity, it became possible to store hashes of entire dictionaries and compare those entries to /etc/passwd file entries. Poor passwords were readily uncovered by this technique.

Part of the solution to this problem is to convince users to pick good passwords, but this task is notoriously difficult. Another partial solution is to move the passwords out of the /etc/passwd file and into another file that's more secure. In FreeBSD, this is the /etc/master.passwd file and its associated database-format variant, /etc/spwd.db. These files contain the same information as their original counterparts, but they're readable only by root. Instead of putting the password in /etc/passwd, the password field contains an asterisk (*), which is an indication that the password is stored in the secure file.

This approach to password security is known as *shadow passwords.* (It's not always implemented in precisely this way in other OSs, but the key point that passwords are stored in files readable only to root is invariant.) Ordinary programs retain access to /etc/passwd, which is required for certain uses, while only programs that run as root can read the password. This approach doesn't provide perfect security, though; if a cracker can obtain even limited root access, the shadow password file is vulnerable to theft. Shadow passwords are an important part of FreeBSD's password security, though.

Using passwd

When you create an account through either sysinstall or adduser, you're prompted to enter a password for the account. Sometimes, though, you or the account's owner must change that password. For instance, you might encourage or require users to change their passwords regularly, to reduce the risk should a password be compromised. The usual tool for changing a password is `passwd`. This command's syntax is fairly straightforward:

```
passwd [-l] [user]
```

Ordinarily, FreeBSD's `passwd` changes the password locally, and if the system is configured as part of a Kerberos realm, it changes the Kerberos password as well. The `-l` option changes this behavior so that only the local password is changed.

Note   *Kerberos is a system of distributed authentication that's becoming popular on networks that host many servers or allow users to log on to any of a number of workstations. Discussion of its features is beyond the scope of this book, though. For more information, consult the Kerberos web page,* `http://web.mit.edu/kerberos/www/`.

Only `root` may use the `user` option, which enables the superuser to specify the user whose password is to be changed. Thus, in most situations, ordinary users can employ `passwd` as follows:

```
$ passwd
Changing local password for marie.
Old password:
New password:
Retype new password:
passwd: updating the database...
passwd: done
```

The program prompts for the old password as a security measure, to be sure it's not been called by an unauthorized individual—for instance, if the account owner left a terminal unattended and a miscreant found the terminal. It then prompts for the new password twice and reports its status. None of these three passwords echo to the screen, to keep them from being read by passersby.

When `root` uses `passwd`, the program doesn't prompt for the old password. This feature allows the superuser to change an ordinary user's password without knowing the old one. This feature is very useful in case a user forgets a password—the user can go to the system administrator, who can enter a new password.

Using chpass

Another tool that's useful in adjusting account behavior is `chpass`. This program lets you change various features of the account, including the password, the account expiration date, and the default shell. Its syntax is

```
chpass [-a list] [-p encpass] [-e expiretime] [-s newshell] [user]
```

The chpass *program also supports a few options related to the maintenance of accounts on* Network Information System (NIS) *databases. NIS is a distributed login database system similar to Kerberos in some respects. Consult the* chpass *man page for more information.*

Most of these options are available only to `root`. The meanings of the `chpass` options are as follows:

- **-a *list*** This option lets `root` provide a complete `/etc/passwd`-format entry for an account. This format is described in the upcoming section, "Editing /etc/master.passwd."

- **-p *encpass*** Only `root` may use this option, which enables changing the password. The password (*encpass*) must be pre-encrypted by the `crypt` program. This option is most likely to be used by scripts that call `crypt` and feed the results to `chpass`.

- **-e *expiretime*** This option, which can be used only by `root`, sets the expiration date for the account. Enter *expiretime* in quotes, in the format "*month day year*", such as "**March 20 2003**". After that date, the system will reject account access attempts.

- **-s *newshell*** This option, which both `root` and ordinary users can employ, changes the default shell.

- **user** Only `root` may use this option, which specifies the account that's to be changed.

Frequently, `chpass` is used with no options, or with only a *user* specification when run by `root`. This usage causes the program to launch an editor that allows dynamic changes to the account, including changes to options that can't be changed through command-line options. Figure 10-2 shows such a session (using the `vi` editor described in Chapter 5). When run as an ordinary user, `chpass` allows editing only a subset of the fields shown in Figure 10-2.

When you run `chpass` in interactive mode, you can fill out or change any of the information provided. Many of these fields have already been described, but some deserve special attention:

- **Password** This field stores the hashed (encrypted) password, so you shouldn't normally touch it.

- **Change and Expire** These fields store the date by which the user must change the password and the expiration date for the account, respectively. Setting a password-change date can be used to enforce password changes, but when the user changes the password, this field clears, so no further changes are required unless you reset this value.

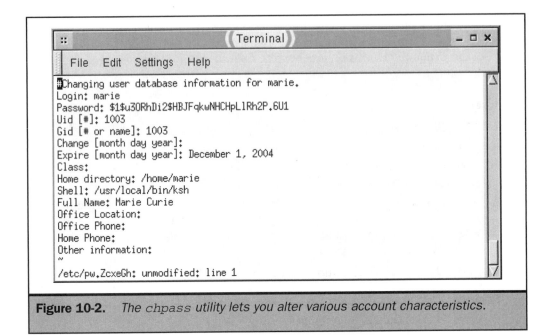

Figure 10-2. The `chpass` utility lets you alter various account characteristics.

- ■ **Full Name through Other Information** This information goes into the `Full Name` /etc/passwd field, as prompted by `sysinstall` or `adduser`. Each of the sub-fields is separated by a comma in the /etc/passwd file. Some utilities read this information and display it with names similar to those `chpass` uses, but others ignore all but the user's name.

Editing /etc/master.passwd

If you want to dig into the files that underlie tools such as `passwd`, `chpass`, and `adduser`, you can do so. Normally, if you do this you'll edit /etc/master.passwd and then run a special utility to propagate your changes to other files. The /etc/master.passwd file consists of a series of lines, one line per user. An example entry resembles the following:

```
marie:$1$u3ORhDi2$HBJFqkwNHCHpLlRh2P.6U1:1003:1003::0:1101877200:↵
Marie Curie:/home/marie:/usr/local/bin/ksh
```

Each entry consists of a series of fields separated by colons (:). The meaning of each field is as follows:

- ■ **Username** The first field (`marie` in the preceding example) is the username.
- ■ **Password** The second field (the 34 characters beginning with `$1$` in the preceding example) is the encrypted password. Ordinarily, you won't touch

this field. This field contains a single asterisk (*) in /etc/passwd, indicating that the true password is stored in /etc/master.passwd. An asterisk in the password field in /etc/master.passwd indicates that the account isn't a login account; any attempt to log in results in an error. A blank password field means there's no password. This configuration is potentially dangerous, but if you forget your root password, you can temporarily remove this password using an emergency system, and then enter a new password when you boot normally.

- **UID**   The third field (the first 1003 in the preceding example) holds the UID associated with the account.

- **GID**   The fourth field (the second 1003 in the preceding example) holds the account's primary GID. If the user belongs to other groups, that information resides in the /etc/group file, as described in the upcoming section, "Using Groups."

- **Class**   The fifth field holds the user's general classification. This field is not used by standard FreeBSD tools, so it's normally blank. This field is absent from the /etc/passwd file.

- **Password change time**   The sixth field (0 in the preceding example) holds the password change time, expressed as seconds since January 1, 1970. This field is absent from the /etc/passwd file.

- **Account expiration time**   This seventh field (1101877200 in the preceding example) holds the account expiration time, expressed as seconds since January 1, 1970. This field is absent from the /etc/passwd file.

- **Full name and information**   The eighth field (Marie Curie in the preceding example) holds the user's full name. In some cases, this field includes comma-delimited entries for the office address, work telephone number, home telephone number, and other information.

- **Home directory**   The ninth field (/home/marie in the preceding example) is the user's home directory.

- **Default shell**   The tenth and final field (/bin/ksh in the preceding example) holds the user's default shell.

You can edit any or all of these fields as you see fit, but in many cases it's simpler to use chpass or passwd. An error in entering information can produce peculiar results, such as an inability to log in because of a corrupt encrypted password or incorrect default shell specification. In some cases, though, the ability to edit, or at least view, this file is important. For instance, you may be able to spot tampering in your account database by viewing the /etc/master.passwd file. If you see accounts defined that should not be defined or passwords entered for accounts that should not be login accounts, your system has probably been compromised.

If you make changes to `/etc/master.passwd`, you must propagate these changes to the other account files. Do this by using the pwd_mkdb command:

```
# pwd_mkdb -p /etc/master.passwd
```

 You may want to check the creation dates on `/etc/passwd`, `/etc/master` `.passwd`, `/etc/pwd.db`, and `/etc/spwd.db`. If the human-readable files (`passwd` and `master.passwd`) have more recent dates than the database files (`pwd.db` and `spwd.db`), then there may be changes in them that have not yet been propagated to the database files. This could also be an indication of a break-in; the intruder may have restored `passwd` and `master.passwd` to preintrusion status to hide the compromise, but if the database files hold new accounts, they'll still be useable.

Changing UIDs

One particularly tricky account modification is changing the account's UID. You might need to do this to coordinate UIDs across systems that use NFS for file sharing, or across OSs on a single computer. You can change the UID easily enough either with chpass or by editing `/etc/master.passwd` and then using pwd_mkdb. Two potential problems with doing this are:

- **UIDs on existing files won't change** Because FreeBSD records ownership based on UIDs, not usernames, changing the UID causes the user's existing files to suddenly appear to be owned by an unknown user. You can correct this problem by locating the files with find, as described in the upcoming section "Removing Stray User Files," and then using chown on the files, as described in Chapter 8. The -R option to chown is particularly likely to be useful when modifying a user's home directory.

- **If the user is logged in, the login session may misbehave** If a user is logged in when you make changes, problems are likely to occur. The session is associated with a number of running processes, and those processes' UIDs won't change. This situation leaves them "orphaned" in the account database, and when you change the UIDs on existing files, the processes may be unable to read and write files in the user's home directory. Thus, it's best to change a UID only when the user isn't logged into the account.

Normally, there's little reason to change a UID on an existing account. If you plan your account creation properly, you can give users the same UIDs on all systems from the beginning, which is less hassle than trying to reassign UIDs after the fact.

Deleting User Accounts

In addition to creating and modifying user accounts, you must sometimes delete accounts. Employees move on to other jobs, students graduate or stop taking courses for which an account is required, and so on. At first glance, the motivation for removing unused accounts may seem slim; after all, it may not be clear what harm an unused account does. There are reasons to delete such accounts, though. One reason is that user files in such accounts consume disk space that might better be devoted to other purposes. On very large systems, the use of a UID (and possibly a GID) may be an issue, as well. Most importantly, though, unused accounts might be broken into and used as a wedge for doing further damage, so such accounts are a security risk. Naturally, FreeBSD provides tools to help you delete unused accounts. Even with these tools, though, you may need to track down stray files that belong to former users.

Using rmuser

The primary tool for deleting user accounts is `rmuser`. This tool's syntax is fairly simple:

```
rmuser [-y] [username]
```

Normally, `rmuser` performs several tasks:

- Removes any cron jobs the user has configured. (These are described in more detail in Chapter 6.)
- Removes any `at` jobs the user has scheduled. (These are also described in Chapter 6.)
- Kills any processes belonging to the user.
- Removes the user's password database entries from `/etc/passwd`, `/etc/master.passwd`, `/etc/pwd.db`, and `/etc/spwd.db`.
- Asks whether you want the user's home directory deleted. If you respond in the affirmative, `rmuser` deletes that directory tree.
- Removes the user's mail queue from `/var/mail`.
- Removes all files owned by the user from `/tmp`, `/var/tmp` and `/var/tmp/vi.recover`.
- Removes the user from all groups in `/etc/group`, and deletes that group if the user was the only member of the group.

In sum, `rmuser` reverses all the normal account-creation effects, including some that occur automatically as an account is used, such as creation of mail queues and temporary files in `/tmp`. On many systems, this command does a complete job of removing a user.

Ordinarily, `rmuser` displays the user's `/etc/master.passwd` entry and asks if you want to delete the account. This prompt helps provide a safeguard against accidental deletion because this entry includes information such as the user's full name, which you can use to verify that you're deleting the correct account. If you include the `-y` option to `rmuser`, though, it skips this query, and assumes a `yes` response to any other questions it might ask, such as whether to delete the user's home directory.

You may want to back up a user's home directory before deleting it. This way, you can restore a user's account if you discover it shouldn't have been deleted, or if the individual comes to you with a request for recovery of files from the account.

If you don't provide a username on the command line with rmuser, the utility prompts you for one when you type the command.

Deleting Users from /etc/master.passwd

On rare occasion, you might want to delete a user from the computer but not perform all of the tasks that rmuser normally performs. For instance, you might want to keep the user's group for use by users you plan to add shortly, or keep a user's temporary files for use by others. In such situations, you can delete a user account by manually performing each of the steps described in "Using rmuser" that you do want to perform. The most important of these is removing the account from the password database files. You can do this by editing /etc/master.passwd and then using the pwd_mkdb utility, described in the previous section, "Editing /etc/master.passwd." Delete the line in this file relating to the user and then run pwd_mkdb:

```
# pwd_mkdb -p /etc/master.passwd
```

This procedure will recreate your password database without the user, effectively removing the account. Several files associated with the now-unused UID will still remain, though, and these could cause confusion in the future. If you reuse the UID, new users might find the old user's mail, for instance, possibly including confidential information.

Removing Stray User Files

Although rmuser makes an effort to remove all the files belonging to a user, it's not always successful. Problems are particularly likely to crop up if your system includes shared file directories in which collaborating users can store files. You can search for such files using the find utility, which was described in Chapter 8. Specifically, you can use the -user *uname* option, where *uname* is a username (if you run the command before deleting the user) or a UID. For instance, consider the following command:

```
# find /home -user 1003
```

This command finds all files in the /home directory tree that belong to UID 1003. You can then delete these files or use chown (also described in Chapter 8) to reassign ownership of those files to other users. Failing to perform this step won't make the files unusable to others, although others might be unable to modify these files or delete files in directories owned by the now-deleted user, depending upon permissions.

If you reuse the old UID for a new user, that new user will appear to own the files, which can be confusing. If the files contain confidential information, the new user might be falsely accused of improper behavior.

The preceding example searches only the /home directory tree because that's likely to reduce search times substantially. Depending upon what directories are writeable by ordinary users, though, you may need to search multiple directories, or even your entire directory tree.

If the user was the last one belonging to a group, you may want to search for files belonging to that group, for similar reasons. Again, you can use find to do this:

```
# find /home -group 1003
```

Using Groups

Most of this chapter has focused upon user creation and management, but using and managing groups can be just as important. FreeBSD's tools for group management are less elaborate than those for user management because there are fewer group-related options. The two most common approaches are using sysinstall to add a group and directly editing the /etc/group file.

> **Note** *As described earlier, in the section "Using adduser," the adduser tool automatically creates a group for each new user it creates.*

Why would you want to create new groups? You might want to create groups to provide an easy way for individuals who are working on a common project to collaborate by sharing common files. You might also want to create a group so that you can give a limited number of users access to some resource or program, such as tools to create a Point-to-Point Protocol (PPP) Internet connection (covered in Chapter 15). The upcoming section, "Deciding Upon a Group Strategy," covers some approaches to using groups on a FreeBSD system.

Using sysinstall to Create Groups

Earlier in this chapter, the section "Using sysinstall to Create Accounts" described creating accounts with this tool. The procedure for creating groups is similar. The differences begin in Step #4 of the procedure outlined in that section. Instead of selecting User to add a new user, you should select Group. Doing so produces the User and Group Management form shown in Figure 10-3. You can enter the group's name, GID, and members of the group using this form.

> **Tip** *If you want to create new users who belong to a new group, create the group first. You can then enter the new group as the users' default group.*

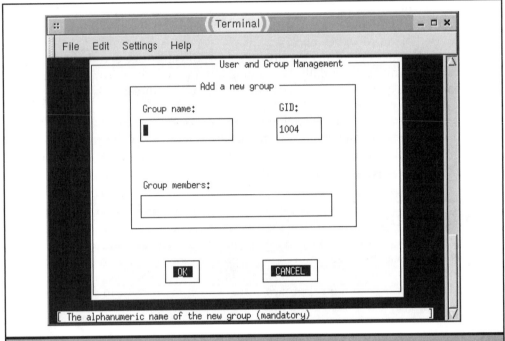

Figure 10-3. *The* sysinstall *utility includes the ability to create new groups.*

Editing /etc/group

Although sysinstall is a quick way to create a new group, directly editing /etc/group is another possibility, and one that enables you to change group configurations. Like /etc/passwd and /etc/master.passwd, /etc/group consists of lines, each of which is a colon-delimited set of fields defining various group characteristics. An example of an /etc/group entry is

```
users:*:1001:marie,charles
```

This entry's four fields are

- **Group name** The first field is the name of the group (users in this example).
- **Password** A rarely-used option is a group password, which is stored in the second field. In this example, it's an asterisk (*), meaning that the password isn't used.
- **GID** The third field holds the GID (1001 in this example).

■ **Members** The fourth and final field holds a comma-delimited list of users in the group. This list normally includes only users for whom the group is a secondary group. For instance, if `pierre`'s account definition specifies `users` as the default group, then the definition of that group in `/etc/group` normally omits `pierre` as a member. For this reason, groups listed in `/etc/group` often contain a blank fourth field because these groups have members who list the group in their `/etc/passwd` entries.

You can create a new group by creating a new entry in `/etc/group` that follows this pattern. You can also edit groups in various ways, such as adding or deleting members.

Tending to Account Security

User accounts and groups are at the core of FreeBSD's security settings. By controlling available groups, assignment of users to groups, default file permissions, and permissions on key directories, you control much of your system's local security. You should realize, though, that users can control the security settings on their own files, so you can't completely control access policies on users' files. You can set defaults to conform to whatever your local policies are, but you'll have to educate your users to keep security at an appropriate level.

Deciding Upon a Group Strategy

As noted earlier, if you use the `adduser` command to add user accounts, that utility automatically creates a special group for each user. This is a defining characteristic of the `user private group` security strategy. Other strategies are possible, though. One of these involves creating separate groups for distinct projects, classes, or other collections of users. I refer to this as the `project groups` strategy. Each strategy has its own unique merits.

User Private Groups

The user private group security strategy begins with a group dedicated to each user. At first glance, this may appear to be pointless because it would seem to make the owner and group permissions on files redundant. Indeed, if left at the default settings, this is the case. All users become islands, from a security point of view, and nonowner permission can be given either to all users or to no users. The beauty of user private groups derives from the possibility of adding users to groups. For instance, suppose a system supports the users `marie`, `pierre`, `charles`, and `jane`, and suppose that this system uses a user private group strategy. If `marie` wishes to share some files with `pierre`, `pierre` can be added to the `marie` group. Any file owned by `marie` (and the `marie` group) can then be given read (and, if necessary, write) group permissions, and `pierre` can access the file.

The user private group strategy is a good way to give access to files on a user-centric basis. That is, each user essentially inherits a list of other users who may or may not be given access to files. If marie wants to give only pierre access to files, but pierre wants to give both marie and charles access to files, this is easy to arrange—the user lists for the marie and pierre groups need only list the appropriate other users.

The main drawback to the user private group approach is that it gives users no ability to provide different access controls to different groups of files. For instance, if marie wants to share some files with pierre and others with jane, the user private group approach is inadequate, at least by itself. You can sometimes get around this problem by creating multiple user private groups, giving each user two or more tiers or sets of access controls. Of course, this limitation doesn't apply to restricting access to group members compared to oneself; group permissions can be granted or denied independent of owner permissions.

Project Groups

The project group approach to security involves creating multiple groups that are not logically tied to any one user, but instead are associated with some collection of users. For instance, your system might have physics and biology groups, with marie and pierre belonging to physics, and charles and jane to biology. Users can then set their group permissions on particular files to let other members of the group access files. If a user belongs to two groups simultaneously, the user can set the group ownership of a file to whichever group should have access to the file, and set permissions appropriately.

Project groups work well in an environment in which users are split into largely distinct groups, which should have relatively unfettered access to at least certain types of work created by any group member. For instance, collaborators on a particular project (hence the strategy name) might benefit from this approach. The approach breaks down when it comes to providing access distinctions to particular members of groups. For instance, if some members of the biology group need access to more files than do other members of the group, complications arise. Sometimes you can overcome this problem by creating multiple hierarchical groups, such as biology, some of whose members also belong to groups called genetics or primatology.

Mixing Approaches

You can mix the user private group and project group approaches to security. Each user can have a user private group, and your system can also implement project groups, thus providing the benefits of both approaches. Creating multiple tiers of either user private groups or project groups can also help. In fact, the two approaches can easily blur together, with the differences becoming a matter of how you think about the groups— as permissions tied to particular users' files or as collections of users.

Setting Default File Permissions

Part of a security policy is setting appropriate default file permissions. This is done through the umask command, which sets a characteristic of the same name. This command is described in Chapter 8. To use it, type the command name followed by an octal representation of the permission bits you want *removed* from any file:

```
$ umask 027
```

This example removes no permissions from the owner, removes write permission for the group, and removes all world permissions. (FreeBSD normally removes execute permission on ordinary files you create, no matter what the umask value.) You can place a umask command in your global shell startup scripts (described in Chapter 6) to have the command apply to all users—but be aware that ordinary users can override your system-wide default umask by resetting the value in their local configuration files.

The default umask value for a freshly-installed FreeBSD system is 022, which produces permissions of 644 (-rw-r--r--) for files, or 755 (drwxr-xr-x) for directories. This configuration works well for many installations with modest between-user security needs; all users can read each others' files, but only the owner may write a file. You may want to tighten your umask value to 027 or even 077 in some environments, thus blocking world access to files and possibly even group access. In an extremely open environment, you might consider loosening the umask to 002, which grants members of the file's group write access. Such a configuration is least risky if you use a user private group strategy and don't add users to each others' groups very often. A umask of 000 is very risky because it gives all users full read/write access to each others' files, effectively disabling FreeBSD's security features.

 Note   *The umask value affects the creation of new files by users. Existing files, such as those that make up FreeBSD as a whole, retain whatever permissions they're given when installed. Most FreeBSD system files are owned by* root *and the* wheel *group, and have 644 (*rw-r--r--*) or 755 (*rwxr-xr-x*) permissions. In most cases, these default permissions for system files are appropriate.*

Summary

User accounts give FreeBSD many important features, including both user convenience and security elements. Although you may be able to set up an account at system installation and not modify this configuration for a single-user workstation, for multiuser systems, account management is an important part of FreeBSD system administration. You can create accounts using tools such as `sysinstall` and `adduser`. Tools such as `passwd` and `chpass` enable you to modify various features of accounts, or you can edit the configuration files directly. You can delete an account by using `rmuser` or by editing the configuration files and performing various cleanup steps. FreeBSD's groups also require creation, maintenance, and deletion through mechanisms that sometimes parallel those used in account operations. However you go through the mechanics of account creation and maintenance, these steps fit into your system's overall security, so you should plan your accounts and groups to fit your site's security policies.

The
Complete
Reference

Chapter 11

Installing Software

When you installed FreeBSD, you configured it with some set of software packages. Chances are good, though, that you'll need to install new software after you've installed the main system. This may be because you forgot or did not know about some package, or because FreeBSD didn't offer an option to install a package during system installation. Whatever the cause, knowing how to locate and install additional software is an important skill for any FreeBSD system administrator. There are several different sources of FreeBSD software, including officially sanctioned packages, semiofficial ports of common packages to FreeBSD, raw source code from program authors, and commercial software. Each of these distribution methods has its merits, and they differ in important ways that you should understand.

In addition to installing new software, you sometimes need to upgrade an existing package. In most cases, you can do this much as you would install a new package, but you should be aware of occasional wrinkles. (Upgrading the entire system is also important, and is described in Chapter 28.) Caveats apply even to installing a previously uninstalled package. Of particular import are issues surrounding the trustworthiness of a program's source. Although most software available on the Internet comes from reputable sources, there are programs floating around from malicious individuals, and you should avoid using such programs.

Forms of Software Packages

Before delving into the details of software installation, or even locating software, it's necessary to understand something of the different forms in which software is available. These forms include both whether the software is distributed in programmer-friendly source code form or as a ready-to-use binary; and the distribution method, which relates to the accessibility of the software. Sometimes these issues are independent of one another, but more often they're correlated; software distributed in certain ways may be available only in source code or only in binary form. These different distribution forms and package types have their unique advantages and disadvantages.

Source Code vs. Binary Code

Programmers almost invariably write software in *high-level computer languages*, such as C, C++, or Perl. These languages provide convenient features such as *variables* (which hold data that may change as the program runs), English-like names for important functions, and access to *libraries* (code to perform common programming tasks). Although even a high-level computer program may look like gibberish to the uninitiated, it's far clearer than the alternative (binary code), described shortly. The high-level computer language files that make up a program are referred to as *source code* files. A programmer can edit these files using an ordinary text editor such as vi or Emacs. Typically, a single program consists of many small source code files.

Although people can understand source code files, computers have a hard time with them; computers work with numbers, and the low-level instructions used by CPUs correspond only loosely to commands in most high-level languages. One common method of bridging this gap is to use a *compiler*, which translates source code files into a *binary* file format. This binary format is ideal for use on a computer because it is the machine language that the CPU was designed to understand. When you run a program such as vi or Mozilla, you're running a binary-format program. Because the compiler converts source code into binary form for a particular CPU, the binary form of a program is useable on only one CPU model or family, such as *x*86 CPUs or PowerPC CPUs.

One other method of dealing with source code is to interpret it directly with a program known as an *interpreter*. A program run via an interpreter runs more slowly than the same program compiled and run in binary form, but because there's no compilation step involved, development using an interpreted language can be quicker. Also, the same interpreted program can be run on many different CPU types. In most cases, a language is usually implemented using either a compiler or an interpreter, but not both. C and C++ are usually compiled, whereas Perl is usually interpreted, for instance. There are exceptions to this rule, though.

Because UNIX has traditionally run on a wide variety of CPUs, it's been common in the UNIX world to distribute software in source code form. This practice enables individual system administrators to compile source code for any computer—at least in theory. The downside to distribution of source code is that compiling the software takes a certain amount of time. This time can be measured in seconds to hours, depending on the program and CPU speed; and large program collections could conceivably take a day or more to compile. At least as important, the theory of being able to compile on any system is often only a theory; problems often crop up that prevent a program from compiling without modification on certain OSs or CPUs. Even moderately skilled programmers can often overcome such problems, but this is sometimes difficult. In practice, therefore, binary programs are usually easier to install—they take less time to install, and, provided they were compiled on a system that's similar enough to the destination system in terms of other software components, the binary package is less likely to cause problems.

Most FreeBSD software is available in both binary and source code forms. Thus, you can use the easy-to-install binary package whenever it's available, but you can still use the source code form if you want to modify it in some way or if you have problems with the binary version that might be overcome by recompiling it. (Such problems are usually caused by trying to install a version of a program that's substantially newer or older than the other software on your system.) Some software is available in only one form or another, though. In particular, some of the more exotic open source packages may not be compiled for FreeBSD, so you may need to install from source code, and commercial packages often ship without source code, so you must install the binary version.

Distribution Method

The software distribution method affects how you acquire a program. In some cases, this also relates to the program's licensing terms. Common distribution methods for FreeBSD software include

■ **FreeBSD packages**   FreeBSD packages are precompiled binary programs, ready for quick and relatively painless installation—provided you're installing a package for the correct version of FreeBSD (packages intended for one version don't always work on another). Packages come with the FreeBSD installation medium and are available on the FreeBSD FTP sites.

■ **FreeBSD ports**   The FreeBSD ports system is a database of links to programs, along with compilation information and FreeBSD-specific modifications, that enables you to compile a program from source code and install it on your system. The great benefit of the ports system is that the modifications and compilation information enables the system to automatically change the source code so that it can compile and install on FreeBSD, thus eliminating one of the problems of source code software. FreeBSD ports exist as pointer files in the /usr/ports directory. When you install a port, as described in the upcoming section "Using FreeBSD Ports," FreeBSD downloads the actual source code from the Internet. Thus, in some sense you obtain a port both from your local system and from the Internet.

■ **Unported general UNIX software**   Some open source UNIX software hasn't been officially ported to FreeBSD, or at least hasn't been turned into a FreeBSD package or port. Such software may compile and run under FreeBSD, but it's generally riskier and more difficult to administer. Chapter 30 describes software compilation in more detail. Typically, you can obtain such software from the program maintainer's web or FTP site.

■ **Commercial software**   Commercial software vendors typically make their products available in binary form only. You may have to buy such software from the vendor's web site, although in a few cases you can find it in computer stores. In some cases, this software installs through the FreeBSD package or ports system, but in other cases the software comes with an installer tool or instructions for manually installing the software.

As a general rule, Internet-based distribution provides for more up-to-date software than does distribution via physical media such as CD-ROMs. In some cases, though, network distribution is tied to local information, which may be out of date. For instance, the FreeBSD ports directory on your system may hold outdated links, so you may end up installing old packages if you use this installation method.

FreeBSD packages come in a format that's particularly useful for system maintenance. The tools used to add these packages also add information about the packages to a database of programs and files on your computer. This database enables you to relatively easily learn what version of a program you have installed, to uninstall the program, or to upgrade the program to a more recent version. These capabilities are extremely important when it comes to maintaining your FreeBSD system. When you build a program from the ports system, it's added through the package system, so the package format's benefits accrue to these programs, as well.

In addition to storing a database of information about installed packages, the package format enables a package to specify other packages upon which it depends (these are sometimes called *dependencies*). The package utilities can use this information to block installation of a package unless its dependencies are met, to automatically download and install depended-upon packages, and to prevent the uninstallation of packages upon which others depend. These features can help keep a FreeBSD system from becoming unusable because of package operations that might break a sensitive chain of dependencies.

Finding FreeBSD Software

A complete FreeBSD system comes on several CD-ROMs, and of course this mass of data represents a large number of software packages. If you're lucky or if your software needs aren't too exotic, there's a good chance that you can find all the FreeBSD software you need on those CD-ROMs. If you're using a single-CD FreeBSD package, though, or if you need some program that doesn't happen to come with FreeBSD, you may need to look elsewhere. In such situations, knowing where to look is imperative. You should also know where to find updated software, particularly as your installation ages. (Although there's nothing wrong with old software *per se*, security flaws and miscellaneous bugs are found and fixed on a daily basis, so an old installation is more likely to harbor packages with security flaws or bugs.)

Using Standard FreeBSD Software

One of the most important sources of FreeBSD software is the FreeBSD collection itself. In particular, the FreeBSD packages collection contains the most popular programs for FreeBSD. The ports collection includes many of the same programs that exist as packages, plus others that are more peripheral to FreeBSD's core programs.

You can find packages on the FreeBSD FTP site and its mirrors or on your FreeBSD installation medium. Packages are distributed as tarballs, with filenames that end in `.tgz`. If you know the name of a package (even an approximate name), you can check your installation CD-ROMs or a FreeBSD FTP site for the file. You can then download the file (if necessary) and install it with `pkg_add`, as described in the upcoming section, "Using Package Tools." If you're not sure of a package's exact filename, you may be able to locate it using `sysinstall`, as described in the upcoming section, "Using sysinstall."

You locate FreeBSD ports in a very different way. Providing you opted to install the ports system when you installed FreeBSD (as described in Chapter 2), the core of the ports system exists in the `/usr/ports` directory of your computer. If you didn't install the ports system, the upcoming section, "Installing and Updating the Ports System," describes how to do this. The `/usr/ports` directory is broken down into subdirectories based on program types, such as `/usr/ports/editors` and `/usr/ports/science`. Each of these subdirectories contains subdirectories devoted to particular programs. Thus, you can probably find the appropriate port by examining one or two directories in the ports directory tree. The ports directory for a given program does not contain the entire program, though, at least not initially; rather, it contains information on where to find source code to the program, patches to the program, and instructions for compiling the program. When you want to install a program available in the ports system, you can issue a command to have FreeBSD download the source code, compile it, and install it. The entry in the `/usr/ports` directory tree is simply a convenient placeholder.

Locating General-Purpose UNIX Software

A vast quantity of software is available via the FreeBSD packages and ports systems. As noted earlier, these packages may be all you'll need. In some cases, though, you may need some other program. Typically, such software is available in only source code form, or in source code and as binaries for one or two platforms that the author favors— which might or might not include FreeBSD.

If you know the name of a program you want to find, you can search for it in several different ways, including

- **A web search** Searching the Web using a search engine such as Google (`http://www.google.com`) can be a good way to start looking for a program. Particularly if a program's name is unusual, a web search is likely to turn up a hit very quickly.

- **Sourceforge** The Sourceforge web site (`http://sourceforge.net`) hosts many open source projects, so there's a good chance you'll find your open source program on this site. It includes a search engine into which you can enter the project's name or keywords.

- **Other OS sites** Sometimes another OS's web site includes links to programs included in that other OS. Although the binary for the other OS may not work with FreeBSD, visiting that site can be a way to track down the program's own site or at least obtain source code.

You can use these same resources if you're looking for a particular *type* of program but don't know the program's name. For instance, you can type **editor** into the search field on Sourceforge to obtain a list of text editors. (In this particular case, you'll also find sound editors, binary editors, and so on.) Of course, the more specific your query is, the more likely you are to obtain useful results.

Finding Commercial Software

Most FreeBSD software is open source and either comes with the OS or can be downloaded from the author's web or FTP site. Sometimes, though, you need to use a commercial package. There's no easy rule to define when a commercial product is better than an open source one—you must decide that on a case-by-case basis. If you've searched the usual open source sites and can't find what you want, though, you may want to begin looking for a commercial alternative. Sometimes a commercial product is the only choice. For instance, the Real Networks (`http://www.real.com`) RealPlayer is a commercial product, and is the only practical way to handle the RealPlayer format multimedia files that are available on some web pages.

Some of the same search techniques that work for open source products also work for commercial products. In particular, a web search may turn up pointers to useful commercial products. One site that's particularly helpful is the FreeBSD commercial software page, `http://www.freebsd.org/commercial/software.html`, which includes pointers to many commercial software vendors for FreeBSD.

Note *Just because a product is commercial doesn't mean that it costs money. Some commercial products are available for free. In some cases, these products are stripped-down versions of more costly programs. Other times, the licensing terms permit free use under certain circumstances, such as for educational or personal use. Some of the vendors listed on the FreeBSD commercial software page sell services for or advanced versions of programs that are otherwise open source.*

Installing Packages

Packages are the simplest software distribution format to handle, especially for new FreeBSD administrators. Packages can be installed by selecting the program from a menu in `sysinstall` or by obtaining the package file and passing it to the `pkg_add` utility. FreeBSD maintains a database of programs you install via packages, so checking a version number or finding out if a program is installed is a relatively straightforward matter. (When you install a program from the ports system, FreeBSD also adds information about the program to the package database, so this benefit accrues to ports, as well.)

Using sysinstall

The sysinstall utility has been described in several earlier chapters of this book. It's FreeBSD's general-purpose system administration tool, and one of its best features is its ability to function as a package installation utility. You can use sysinstall to locate packages (stored either on a CD-ROM you possess or on a network server) and install them. This makes sysinstall a good starting point if you know what type of program you want to install but don't know a precise package name. To use it to install a package, follow these steps:

1. As root, type **/stand/sysinstall** to launch sysinstall.

2. Select the Configure option in the main menu, which brings up the FreeBSD Configuration Menu.

3. Select the Packages option in the FreeBSD Configuration Menu. Doing so brings up the Choose Installation Media menu, in which you select the source of your packages.

4. Select the medium from which you want to install packages. Options include CD/DVD for a local CD-ROM or DVD-ROM; FTP, FTP Passive, or HTTP for a local or remote FTP site; DOS for files stored on a local FAT partition; NFS for a local Network File System (NFS) server; and File System for a local FreeBSD partition. The most likely media are CD/DVD or one of the FTP options. If you use the former, you must insert a CD-ROM or DVD-ROM into your drive. If you use the latter, you must pick an FTP site from the list. (Aside from the primary sites, this list is alphabetical by country, so United States sites are near the bottom of the list.) If you pick the URL FTP site, you can enter any site you like—including one you operate. Once you select the medium, the system reads a list of available packages from the source you've picked. This operation can take anywhere from a few seconds to over a minute. When it's done, sysinstall presents a list of package categories, as shown in Figure 11-1.

Tip

If you maintain a network of FreeBSD systems, you can copy a FreeBSD FTP site to a local FTP server, then use your local server to install and maintain all your network's systems.

Note

The package list can vary from one source to another. In particular, if you pick the CD/DVD option, the list contains only those packages available on the disc you've inserted in your drive. If you have a multi-CD FreeBSD set, you may need to run through this process several times to locate all the available packages. Locating packages on a multi-CD FreeBSD set using sysinstall is often difficult, so if you have problems you may want to try the FTP option instead.

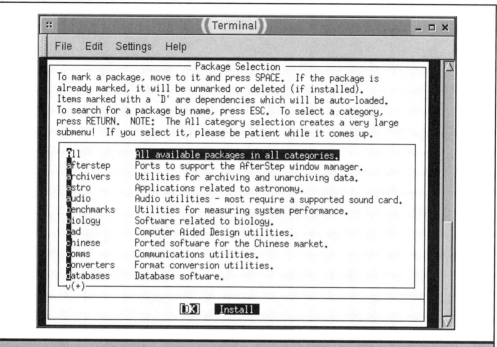

Figure 11-1. *FreeBSD sorts each package into one or more categories.*

5. Pick the category to which the software you want to install belongs. Most packages reside in multiple categories—if nothing else, the All category holds all packages, so you can check there as a last resort, but it can be hard to find what you want in that category because it holds everything. When you select a category, you'll see a list of packages in that category, as shown in Figure 11-2.

6. Some packages are already selected, as indicated by an *X* in the box to the left of the package name. If you want to add a new package, press the SPACEBAR and an *X* will appear in this box.

7. When you're done selecting packages, press TAB to position the cursor on the OK button, and then press ENTER. This step returns you to the Package Selection screen (Figure 11-1).

8. If you want to select packages from other categories, repeat Steps 5–7.

9. Press TAB until the Install button is selected, and then press ENTER to install the selected packages. The sysinstall utility presents a summary of the packages you've opted to install. Select OK. The system downloads the files from the network (if applicable) and installs them, displaying progress information for each package. When this process finishes, you'll see the FreeBSD Configuration Menu screen.

10. Select Cancel and then Exit Install to quit from sysinstall.

When you have some free time, you may want to browse through the packages available via sysinstall. Even if you're familiar with FreeBSD (or with other UNIX-like OSs), chances are good you'll discover a package you hadn't known about before, but that might be useful. Remember to pay attention to the bottom line of the display in the package selection menu (Figure 11-2) because that line contains a brief description of the package, which is often more helpful than the package name alone.

Note *Confusingly, the only way to exit from the Package Selection screen (see Figure 11-1) is to pick Install—even if you've decided not to install any packages. If you pick Install with no packages selected, sysinstall informs you that no packages were selected and returns you to the FreeBSD Configuration Menu screen.*

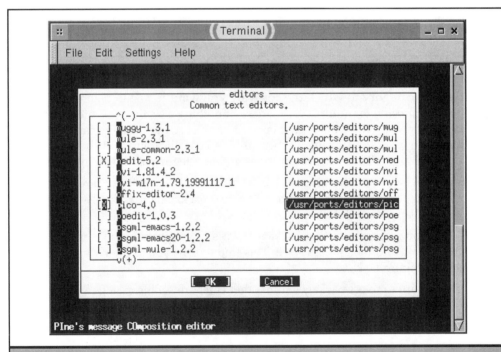

Figure 11-2.   *Each category screen displays package names, and the bottom line holds a description of the package on which the cursor resides.*

Using Package Tools

The `sysinstall` package installation method can be convenient, but it's not without its drawbacks. One of these is that you can install only packages that are available on a FreeBSD medium—typically a CD-ROM, DVD-ROM, or FTP site. (If you control a local FTP site or install from a hard disk, you can modify the `INDEX` file to add other packages, but doing so adds complexity that detracts from the convenience of `sysinstall`.) Another problem with this method is that there's little clue about the sizes of the packages you select. After you begin an installation, `sysinstall` provides information on data transfer rates for each package, but if your available disk space is limited, this information isn't sufficient to judge whether you should try installing a potentially large package.

These problems are overcome by use of the underlying FreeBSD package tools. These programs reside in the `/usr/sbin` directory and have filenames that begin with `pkg_`. The most important of these is `pkg_add`, which adds a package to the system. In fact, `sysinstall` calls `pkg_add` to do its work, and if you watch the messages when you install a package, you'll see a notice that it's waiting for `pkg_add` at one point in the `sysinstall` package installation process.

> **Caution** *Because `pkg_add` can add a package obtained from any source, it's possible to use it to install a package that's not trustworthy. You should pay attention to the advice in the upcoming section, "Verifying Software Authenticity," before using `pkg_add`, particularly on programs obtained from sources other than a FreeBSD CD-ROM, DVD-ROM, or FTP site.*

The `pkg_add` syntax is

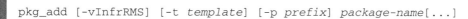

```
pkg_add [-vInfrRMS] [-t template] [-p prefix] package-name[...]
```

The meanings of the options to the command are

- **-v** This option enables verbose output, which may be useful for debugging purposes.

- **-I** Packages often include installation scripts that help customize a program for your system, and `pkg_add` normally runs such scripts. This option disables these scripts.

- **-n** This option causes `pkg_add` to report the steps it would take when installing a package, without actually performing the installation.

- **-f** Normally, `pkg_add` checks that a package's dependencies are met before installing it. This option disables these checks. Normally, this is undesirable, but you might have reason to forego these checks; for instance, you might know that the dependencies are met by programs that were installed without using the package tools.

- **-r** Normally, you provide a package filename or URL to pkg_add, but if you use this option, you provide a package name, and pkg_add attempts to locate the package on the Internet.

- **-R** This option blocks the recording of information about the package in the package database. It's almost never advisable to use this option.

- **-M** You can run pkg_add in *master* mode with this option, which causes it to extract the package contents into a staging area and write the packing list to standard output. You can use this mode in conjunction with custom scripts and slave mode (see the next option) to radically alter how pkg_add works.

- **-S** This option enables *slave* mode, in which pkg_add processes a packing list it obtains from standard input in order to add files it expects to find in a staging area. You might use this mode in a pipe along with another call to pkg_add in master mode and some custom scripts or other text processing commands to alter what pkg_add does.

- **-t template** This option is the name of a temporary holding area for files. The default is /var/tmp/instmp.XXXXXX (pkg_add replaces the XXXXXX with a unique ID number). If your /var partition is too small to handle the temporary files, you can specify a staging area on another partition. Be sure to use a name that ends in six X characters so that pkg_add can replace them with its unique ID number.

- **-p prefix** This option specifies the directory in which pkg_add installs files from the package. This directory is normally specified as part of the package itself, but if you want to store a package in some unusual location, you can do so with this option.

Normally, you'll use pkg_add with few or no parameters, other than the name of a package you want to install. The package name itself can be either a filename on your local disk, or a URL for a file stored on an FTP site. For instance, you might issue either of these commands:

```
# pkg_add ftp://ftp3.freebsd.org/pub/FreeBSD/ports/i386/packages-
5-current/editors/zile-1.6.1.tgz
# pkg_add zile-1.6.1.tgz
```

You may want to use the pkg_info command, described in the next section, before using pkg_add, to be sure an earlier version of a package isn't already installed. If one is, you should consult the upcoming section, "Performing Software Upgrades."

The first of these commands installs the zile editor directly from the ftp3.freebsd.org FTP site. The second installs the same package from the current directory on the hard disk. Of course, this second command requires that the package already exist on the hard disk, so you must obtain it in some way. If you've got a FreeBSD CD-ROM, you can install packages from it by mounting the CD-ROM and specifying the complete path to the file on the CD-ROM.

 Although `pkg_add` *works from tarballs, it doesn't install just any tarball. In particular, FreeBSD packages must include certain special files that* `pkg_add` *uses to help it add information about the package to the package database.*

Before you can use `pkg_add`, you must have packages to add, or know where they can be found on a network. You can mount a FreeBSD CD-ROM and search its directory tree, or browse a FreeBSD FTP site for files. You may also find packages on program authors' sites, on third-party or commercial CD-ROMs, and so on.

Querying Package Information

Sometimes you may want to know something about packages, either before or after you've installed them. You can accomplish this goal with the `pkg_info` command. This command accepts a large number of options that cause it to display various subsets of information about a package or a set of packages. Consult the `pkg_info` man page for details. As a general rule, you'll use this command in one of several ways:

- **Full database query**   You can learn the names of all installed packages and display short descriptions of them by typing **pkg_info** alone.

- **Installed package query**   You can type the name of a package (including its version number) after the `pkg_info` command to see a multiline description of the package. For instance, typing **pkg_info nedit-5.2** produces a full description of the NEdit 5.2 package, provided it's installed on the computer.

- **Locate installed package**   If you're not sure of the exact name or version of a package, you can provide a partial name with the `-x` option. For instance, **pkg_info -x nedit** displays information on the NEdit package, even if you don't know the version number.

- **Uninstalled package query**   Rather than typing the name of an installed package, you can type the name of a package *file* to learn about its contents, whether or not that package is installed. For instance, you might type **pkg_info nedit-5.2.tgz** to learn about the contents of the `nedit-5.2.tgz` file before installing it.

- **Locate files in a package**   If you want to know what files belong to a package, you can use the `-L` option. For instance, **pkg_info -L nedit-5.2** displays a list of the files belonging to the `nedit-5.2` package. (You can also provide a package filename to learn what files it will install before using `pkg_add` on the package.)

- **Locate package for file** If you want to know the name of the package to which a file belongs, you can use the -W option. For instance, **pkg_info -W /usr/X11R6/bin/nedit** causes pkg_info to search the installed package database and return the name of the package from which /usr/X11R6/bin/nedit was installed.

These capabilities can be extremely useful both before and after installing a package. Using these tools, you can learn the name of a package associated with a suspicious or misbehaving program, find out where a package will install files (and thus forestall problems should there be conflicts or insufficient disk space), learn what a package does, and so on. You can also use these commands in sequence, thus:

```
$ pkg_info -W /usr/X11R6/bin/nedit
/usr/X11R6/bin/nedit was installed by package nedit-5.2
$ pkg_info -x nedit-5.2
```

The result of this sequence (not shown here) is extended information on the nedit-5.2 package. This tool can be very useful for learning about your FreeBSD system, particularly if you run across a file whose function is unclear to you.

Tip *If the description returned by the –x option doesn't fully clarify what a program does, use –L to locate the files installed with the package, and check that output for documentation files. These files may include man pages (in directories whose names include* man*) or other documentation (often stored in subdirectories of* /usr/share/doc *or* /usr/local/share/doc*).*

Using FreeBSD Ports

FreeBSD packages are convenient and easy to install. They aren't the perfect software distribution method for all purposes, though. Sometimes a precompiled package simply isn't available, or is available but was built for a newer or older version of FreeBSD than you run. Other times you may want to make modifications to a program. In situations like these, alternative distribution methods are in order. For customizing software, compiling from source code (as described in Chapter 30) is appropriate. Compiling lets you modify the source code as you see fit, but it loses the advantages of the FreeBSD package system. In other cases, using FreeBSD ports is in order. Ports of many programs are available, and you get some of the benefits of compiling your own software when you use ports. At the end of the build process, the ports system uses the FreeBSD package tools, so you get many of the benefits of packages, such as the ability to use pkg_info to learn about a program. On the downside, ports take longer to install than do packages. This is particularly true when the program is large or has many uninstalled dependencies. All in all, FreeBSD ports serve as a good middle ground between packages and compiling "raw" source code.

Note *The word* port *is frequently used to describe the process of converting a program to run on a new platform or the modified program that results. The FreeBSD ports system is a specific type of port. It uses the program's raw source code and a set of code* patches— *changes that enable the code to compile properly on FreeBSD. The ports system automates the process of porting a program to FreeBSD, hence its name. (This automation still relies upon a developer to create the port, though—the process is only automatic for administrators who rely upon the original maintainer's port.)*

In addition to the description presented here, you can learn about various more-advanced ports options from the ports system man page—type **man ports** to read this documentation.

Installing and Updating the Ports System

When you installed FreeBSD, you were given the opportunity to install the ports system. If you did so, you'll find a /usr/ports directory on your computer, and you can begin using the ports system. If you didn't install the ports system, though, /usr/ports will be missing or empty. In such a case, you must first install the ports system to use it. You may also want to periodically update your ports system, particularly if you want to use it to update programs to the latest versions.

The easiest way to install the ports system is to use sysinstall. Follow these steps:

1. As root, type **/stand/sysinstall** to launch sysinstall.

2. Select the Configure option in the sysinstall main menu, which brings up the FreeBSD Configuration Menu.

3. Select the Distributions option in the FreeBSD Configuration Menu. Doing so brings up the distributions menu.

4. Select the Ports distribution and choose OK. The sysinstall utility responds by asking you for a distribution medium.

5. Pick your distribution medium, as described earlier in "Using sysinstall." The program will retrieve the ports system and install it. You can then exit from sysinstall.

At this point, you should have a /usr/ports directory filled with subdirectories containing software belonging to particular categories, such as /usr/ports/x11 and /usr/ports/editors. You can move ahead to the next section, "Compiling and Installing a Port," to learn how to use the system.

One aspect of FreeBSD ports is that the ports files on your hard disk point to specific versions of the target programs. Thus, the ports system may not install the latest version of any given program; if a program has been updated since the ports system on your disk was installed, the ports system will install an older version of the program. If the original program's site has moved, the ports system will fail. Indeed, even if you've installed the latest version of the ports system, you may not get the latest available version of a program because the latest version may not have been ported yet. To minimize this problem, you can periodically update your ports installation by using the *Concurrent Version System (CVS)* to update your ports directory. To do this, follow these steps:

1. If necessary, install the `cvsup-without-gui` package, using either package tools or the ports system itself. (This program was written with the relatively rare Modula-2 compiler, so installing it using ports may involve installing Modula-2 and its dependencies, which can take a long time and require a lot of disk space.)

2. Type **cd /usr/ports/net/cvsupit**.

3. Type **make; make install**. This command installs and configures some updating software and runs an updater (Figure 11-3).

4. Select the version of FreeBSD you're running from the list. This action produces the Source Selection Menu.

Note   *Figure 11-3 shows the process using a beta-test release of FreeBSD 5.0. For the final release version, you'll probably select an option called RELENG_5.*

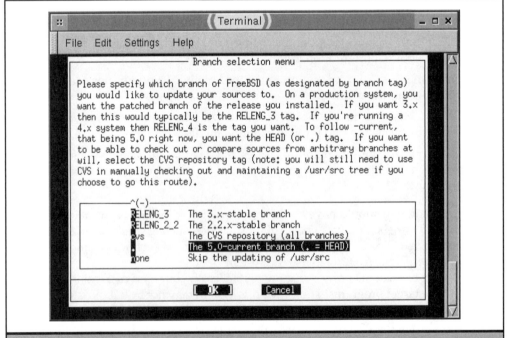

Figure 11-3.   *The CVS updating tools enable you to select which FreeBSD version you want to update.*

5. In the Source Selection Menu, don't select any source packages; just press TAB and then ENTER to update no source packages. (The source packages that can be selected in this menu are unrelated to the ports system.)

6. The system asks if you want to track the FreeBSD ports system. Respond *Yes*.

7. The system asks if you want to track FreeBSD documentation sources. You can respond either *Yes* or *No*, but *No* will be quicker.

8. The system asks for a base directory. Leave this value at its default (/usr).

9. The system presents a list of CVSup servers. Pick one that's close to you.

10. The system asks if you want to run the update now. Respond *No*. You should be returned to your shell prompt.

11. Edit the /etc/cvsupfile file. This file controls the CVSup process. Comment out any line that begins with src- by placing a pound sign (#) at the start of the line. These lines specify core OS source files, which you need not update at this point.

12. Type the following command to update the ports collection:

```
# /usr/local/bin/cvsup -g -L 2 /etc/cvsupfile
```

At this point, the system will update your ports directory tree. You'll see a summary of the retrieved files scroll across your screen, so you can monitor the update's progress. Most updates will happen quickly, but some take more time because the changes are more extensive. Changes to the ports/INDEX/INDEX file are particularly likely to be lengthy because this file contains information on all the ports on the system. The entire process is likely to take several minutes, and could conceivably take over an hour if your ports collection is particularly out of date or your network connection is slow.

Once you've updated the ports system, you'll have pointers to those packages in your ports tree, but if you've previously installed programs from the ports system, your computer will still have old versions installed. Consult the upcoming section, "Deleting and Upgrading Software," for information on upgrading your already-installed programs.

> **Tip** *The Fresh Ports web site (http://www.freshports.org) maintains a summary of information on changes submitted to the ports directory tree. You can check this site periodically to see if there have been any recent changes to important ports. You can also learn what those changes are, so you can evaluate whether it's worth downloading an update.*

Compiling and Installing a Port

The /usr/ports directory contains subdirectories relating to specific categories of programs, much like the sysinstall Package Selection menu (see Figure 11-1). To install a port, follow these steps:

1. Type **pkg_info -x *package-name*** to determine whether a package with the name of the port you're installing already exists. If it does, you may not need

to install the port at all. If you want to upgrade an existing package, read the upcoming section, "Performing Software Upgrades," for advice on how to proceed.

2. Locate the program's directory. You can do this by browsing the directory tree or by using `find` or `grep` (described in Chapter 8).

3. Change to the program's directory.

4. As `root`, type **make** to build the port. This action causes FreeBSD to retrieve the program's source code, apply any patches that are present in the port's `files` subdirectory, and build the program. The system may also automatically retrieve, compile, build, and install other ports, if the one you've chosen depends upon software that's not already installed.

5. As `root`, type **make install** to install the program. This action installs the program files and adds information on the port to the package database. (You can combine Steps 4 and 5 by typing **make install** alone; however, you may want to monitor the output and read summary information at the end of the make process before committing to installing the software.)

Tip   *Before you install any ports, use `sysinstall` or the FreeBSD package tools to install common development software. The GNU Compiler Collection (GCC) is a standard part of FreeBSD and should already be installed, but you might need to install development libraries or other compilers, particularly for X-based programs. The `Makefile` in each port's directory is likely to contain a URL for the program's main site, so you can check there to see what development tools it uses. Check the `devel` section of the `sysinstall` Package Selection menu for the package. If you don't install appropriate development tools in this way, the ports system installs them itself, which can take much longer, as the development tools themselves build from scratch.*

At this point, your system will operate much as if you had installed the port as a package. One important difference is that you'll have complete source code for the package in its ports directory. In some cases this can be a boon because you can then examine and even modify and recompile the source code to fix bugs or change its behavior. One drawback, though, is that this source code consumes space, as do the intermediate (*object code*) files that the compiler produces in the process of building an application. You can eliminate these source code and object code files by typing **make clean** in the port directory devoted to the program. Typing this command in `/usr/ports` cleans *all* the ports subdirectories, which can reclaim many megabytes of disk space if you've built very many or large ports. You can free additional space by deleting the tarballs in `/usr/ports/distfiles`. This directory holds the original program source code files, as obtained from the programs' web or FTP sites. Leaving the files in place allows FreeBSD to forego downloading the program again if you must remake the port, but consumes disk space.

If you're maintaining several FreeBSD systems, one extra option may be of interest: **make package**. Typing this command in a port's directory builds a package from the port and installs that package on the local system if the port isn't already installed. You can then move this package to other FreeBSD systems and install it using `pkg_add`, obviating the need to recompile the program on all your systems.

Deleting and Upgrading Software

In an ideal world, you could install a software package and forget about it. In the real world, sadly, installing a program is only the start of your administrative job with respect to that program. Much of this book is devoted to helping you configure specific programs. Other tasks you're likely to need to do on occasion are removing and upgrading software. You might remove software because you find you no longer need it or because it wasn't the solution you'd hoped it would be. Removing an unused package saves disk space and may be a useful security precaution, particularly for servers or programs that use the set user ID (SUID) bit, as described in Chapter 8. Upgrading software is a necessity to correct bugs and add functionality to your system. Because some bugs are security related, such upgrades can be very important from a security perspective, too.

Deleting Software

If you installed a program through a FreeBSD package, deleting the software is relatively straightforward—you can use the `pkg_delete` command, which has the following syntax:

```
pkg_delete [-dDfGinrvx] [-p prefix] package-name[...]
```

Some of this command's options are similar to those for `package-add`. In particular, the `-v`, `-f`, `-n`, and `-p` options have identical or nearly identical meanings. Other options' meanings are

- **-d** Normally, `pkg_delete` doesn't delete directories unless they're an explicit part of a package. This option causes the program to delete directories that have been emptied as part of the package removal process.

- **-D** Packages can include deinstallation scripts. These may be used to remove users specific to a server, shut down a server, remove configuration files that aren't officially part of the package, and so on. Using this option tells `pkg_delete` not to run these scripts.

- **-G** Normally, using wildcards and similar patterns as part of the `package-name` results in expansion and matching of all packages that match the pattern. This option disables this expansion, so you can delete a package if its name contains a character that would otherwise be misinterpreted.

- **-i** This option causes `pkg_delete` to request confirmation before deleting each package.

- **-r** This option activates a recursive removal, in which packages that depend upon the named package are deleted. Use this option with caution!

BASIC SYSTEM ADMINISTRATION

■ **-x**   This option causes pkg_delete to treat package-name as a regular
expression, so you can delete all packages that match a specified regular expression.

Caution   *The pkg_delete program also supports an option to unconditionally delete all*
packages: –a. This is an extremely dangerous option and should be avoided.

Normally, you'll use package-delete with few or no options, except for the
names of the packages you want to delete. If you want to delete many packages
(especially when using regular expressions or the -r option), I recommend you use
the -i option so that the program queries you before deleting packages. Such an
interaction might resemble the following:

```
# pkg_delete -ir wmcdplay-1.0b1
delete wmcdplay-1.0b1? y
```

In this example, the wmcdplay-1.0b1 package is being deleted, along with all the
installed programs that depend upon it (in fact, none do). Because of the -i option,
package-delete asks for confirmation before deleting the package. If multiple packages
had been listed or selected for deletion because of the -r option, there would have been
one query for each package.

Although the package-delete command will delete a package you installed
through the ports system, a better way to accomplish this task with ports is to cd into
the original ports directory and type **make deinstall**. This command is effectively
similar to package-delete, but takes care of a few subtle differences between the
two program installation methods.

If you installed a package through some other means, such as installing from a nonport
source package (as described in Chapter 30), or installing a commercial program (as per
that software's documentation), the software removal process would be different. Most
typically, you must track down all the installed files and manually delete them. This
process is tedious at best; you may need to use find to locate files with names that are
related to the program in question, then verify that they don't belong to a package or
port by using pkg_info. You might also check any installation script you used to find
clues about the files' names and locations. Some commercial programs ship with
installation programs that can uninstall software, or are installable via FreeBSD's
package system. Such programs are easier to uninstall.

Performing Software Upgrades

Sometimes you need to replace an existing program with a more recent version of the
software. You may need to do this to fix a bug or security flaw, or a newer version may
simply add features or otherwise improve the software's performance. FreeBSD includes
a command to make this replacement with packages: pkg_update. This command's
syntax is

```
pkg_update [-nv] [-r old-package] new-package
```

The -n and -v options have the same meanings as they do with pkg_add. Ordinarily, the -r old-package option isn't required because pkg_update can determine what package the new one is meant to replace. On rare occasion, though, you might want to use this option. For instance, if you've installed multiple versions of a program to different directories, you might want to replace just one of them, in which case you can specify that the new package is to replace just one of the already-installed packages. As an example, you might use the following command, after obtaining the package file itself, to install a new version of Samba:

```
# pkg_update samba-2.2.2_1.tgz
```

If you've installed a port and want to upgrade it, or if you want a more powerful tool for handling package updates, you should look into the portupgrade utility. This can be installed as a package from the sysutils area, or as a port from /usr/ports/sysutils/portupgrade (the port version depends upon several packages that may not be installed, so the package version will be substantially faster to install). The job of portupgrade is to handle upgrades of both packages and ports. The portupgrade man page includes details of its operation, but in general, you'll use it as follows:

```
# portupgrade -P samba
```

This command tells the system to upgrade the Samba package to the latest version available. (You can substitute any other package name, of course, or list several on one line.) The -P option tells portupgrade to attempt the upgrade first using a package, if possible. If portupgrade can't find a package, or if this option is omitted, it uses ports only. A few of the many additional options that may interest you include these:

- **-a** This option tells the system to upgrade all the installed packages. This can take a very long time to complete, particularly if used without -P!

- **-f** This option forces an "upgrade" even if it's to an older version of a program. You might use this if you upgrade to a new version but discover bugs, and so want to downgrade to an older version.

- **-i** Ordinarily, portupgrade doesn't ask for permission before installing a new package, but this option makes it pause and ask before each upgrade.

- **-n** This option tells portupgrade to report on what it would do, but to not actually install any upgraded packages or ports.

- **-N** You can use this option to install a package that's not already installed on the computer.

BASIC SYSTEM ADMINISTRATION

One of the benefits of `portupgrade` is that it monitors dependencies and attempts to upgrade them or fix dependency information in your package database file, when necessary. Another tool that can be helpful is `pkgdb`, and particularly its `-F` option. Typing **pkgdb -F** causes FreeBSD to examine its package database and fix any inconsistencies it finds, asking you for clarifications if required. Typing this command and updating the ports system, as described earlier in "Installing and Updating the Ports System," prior to using `portupgrade` can help keep your system in good working order.

Verifying Software Authenticity

One of the major problems in computing today is *malicious code*. This phrase refers to programs that do nasty things, such as spy on your actions or erase your hard disk. Common means of delivering malicious code include viruses, worms, and Trojan horses. In the Windows world, malicious code can arrive in e-mail messages. Although such delivery methods are theoretically possible with FreeBSD, the FreeBSD user account system helps insulate the computer from harm. A potentially greater threat is bogus software packages. If a miscreant adds malicious code to a popular program and tricks a software repository into stocking the modified software, the potential for damage is great as system administrators download and install the package. Similarly, a miscreant could claim to have developed an interesting-sounding program that's really something else (a Trojan horse).

Here are several steps you can take to help protect yourself from such a possibility:

- **Use trusted sites**   If you download your software only from major sites, such as the main FreeBSD site or official mirrors, you greatly reduce the chance of using a tampered program. Trusting an unofficial mirror is riskier, and installing code from a random web or FTP site is riskiest of all. This measure's weakness is that it's conceivable a site could be hijacked—a cracker might break in and replace files, or alter name server entries to point users at a bogus site rather than the real one.

- **Install only trusted packages**   When you're looking for software to install, use major known packages, such as those available with FreeBSD. If you're looking for a particular type of package, you might be tempted by some interesting-sounding but relatively unknown program. Chances are this is safe, but it could really be a Trojan horse. Major software products, by contrast, have built up reputations of trust over years of development.

- **Check MD5 sums**   Many software authors and repositories today make *Message Digest 5 (MD5)* sums available for their packages. These are 32-byte hexadecimal numbers that are built from the contents of the file. Although it's theoretically possible to create a modified file that produces the same MD5 sum as the original, there's no easy way to do this, so if the software you download has the same

MD5 sum as the author reports, chances are it's not been tampered with. Of course, this leads to the question of whether you can trust the reported MD5 sum. For the security conscious, cryptographic signatures using *Pretty Good Privacy (PGP)* are available to help with this measure, or the MD5 sum may be stored on a site other than the one that houses the program files, but sooner or later you must trust some data.

In the end, there's no way to be 100 percent sure that the software you install is safe. Taking a few precautions can greatly enhance your system's security, though. Notably, the standard FreeBSD tools incorporate these methods. The `sysinstall` tool looks for code from trusted sites (your CD-ROM or a few official FreeBSD mirror sites), and of course installs only packages that are part of FreeBSD. The ports system downloads program source code from official web or FTP sites and uses MD5 sums stored as part of the port information on your hard disk to ensure that the site hasn't been hijacked. The riskiest method of software installation described in this chapter is installing packages from unofficial sites using `pkg_add`, particularly if you don't have an MD5 sum for the package from a more trusted site. If you have an MD5 sum, you can use the `md5` program to check it against the file you have, thus:

```
$ md5 zile-1.6.1.tgz
MD5 (zile-1.6.1.tgz) = c998c146326723f8526ca6701b4bf540
```

You can compare this 32-character output string to the value reported on the program's official web site or some other trusted source. Of course, the MD5 sum will differ across program versions, and possibly even from one build of the program to another, so you should be sure to compare appropriate MD5 sums.

Summary

Installing software is a critical responsibility of FreeBSD system administration, whether you're administering a single-user workstation or a multiuser server. FreeBSD provides several methods of program installation and maintenance. Most of these center around the FreeBSD package database, which maintains information on installed software so that you can quickly check on versions and what software is installed. Both installing raw packages and installing ports use this system, and it's a good idea to use this database so you can track your system's software. If necessary, you can install software without using the package database, either by compiling it yourself from a source that doesn't provide a package or port or by installing a binary version from such a source (most likely a commercial vendor). Once you've installed a package, you can manage it (delete it, upgrade it, check on installed software, and so on) using package tools.

Chapter 12

Kernel Configuration

Y ou can upgrade most FreeBSD programs using the methods described in Chapter 11. One program, however, deserves special consideration: the *kernel*. As described in Chapter 1, the FreeBSD kernel is both unusual and extremely important. The kernel is the core around which an OS is built. It serves as a central control program, giving all other programs access to the computer's hardware resources, resolving conflicts between programs, and so on. These features mean that the kernel must be configured, upgraded, and run differently from other programs, and this chapter describes this important topic.

This chapter begins with an overview of the kernel, so that you can better understand its role in a running FreeBSD system. It continues with a look at methods of modifying the kernel's configuration. Some of these approaches involve fairly straightforward changes, but other changes require recompiling the kernel from source code. Although this task sounds daunting, it's a very useful skill for any FreeBSD system administrator. Sometimes, you may need to upgrade the kernel to a new version. This process often involves compiling the new kernel.

An Overview of the Kernel

To understand the need for unique kernel configuration, installation, and upgrade procedures, it's necessary to understand what the kernel does. The kernel's role in a FreeBSD system is so central that upgrading it often requires rebooting the computer— something that's not true of other software upgrades.

The Kernel's Role in FreeBSD

Chapter 6, and especially its section "Understanding the Kernel's Control," describes the role of the kernel in a FreeBSD system. In brief, the kernel is the lowest-level software that runs on a computer. For most types of hardware, the kernel is the only software that's allowed to directly access the hardware. This is done by hardware *drivers*, which are written for specific hardware components, such as a VIA Rhine Ethernet board or a 16550 RS-232 serial interface. Programs can then call the kernel and tell it that they want to access the Ethernet or RS-232 serial interface, and the kernel translates these calls into ones that work for the specific hardware installed on the computer.

Note *During the boot process, and in some OSs even after the system has booted, code at a lower level than the kernel also runs. This is the* Basic Input/Output System (BIOS), *which was designed to provide an interface between the OS and the hardware. The x86 BIOS, however, is very primitive, and most modern OSs, including FreeBSD, rely on it mainly as a part of the boot procedure because the system runs the BIOS as part of its boot process, but the kernel can do a better job after that point.*

Just as the kernel provides an interface layer between hardware and most programs, it provides similar services for other necessary computer functions. These services include filesystems, so that programs can read and write files without worrying about precisely what sectors on a disk the files occupy; memory management, so that programs can't overwrite each others' memory; and network accesses, so that programs can specify that they want to communicate with some other computer without deciding precisely how to construct data packets to go over a network interface.

There are a few exceptions to the kernel's control of hardware. Most notably, the kernel usually gives certain programs, such as the X server (described in Chapter 13), greater than usual access to the computer's video hardware. Some other hardware, such as modems, printers, and scanners, are also controlled by user-mode programs (that is, those that aren't part of the kernel); but these programs must communicate with their hardware via ports that are controlled by the kernel.

Installing and Modifying the Kernel

FreeBSD installs its standard kernel when you install the system. This kernel resides on your disk in a file called `/boot/kernel/kernel` (`/kernel` in FreeBSD versions prior to 5.0), and it's loaded by the boot loader when you boot the computer, as described in Chapter 6. Installing a new kernel involves adding a new file to that directory and telling the boot loader to boot it, or replacing the existing kernel file. To do either of these things, you normally recompile the kernel from source code, as described in the upcoming section, "Recompiling the Kernel." Sometimes, though, less radical operations can be performed by installing a new kernel module, as described in the upcoming section, "Loading Kernel Modules."

 Don't delete your old kernel and replace it with a new one unless you're sure the new one works. FreeBSD lets you choose which kernel to use at boot time, so you can test a new kernel by calling it something other than `kernel`. *This process is described in more detail in the upcoming section, "Using the New Kernel."*

Why would you want to modify your kernel? Here are several reasons:

- **New drivers**   You may need drivers that aren't included in the standard kernel. These may be hardware drivers (say, for a new EIDE controller) or drivers for a new network protocol, filesystem, or other high-level construct.

- **Updates and bug fixes**   No program of any size is bug-free, although the best programs have few *known* bugs. FreeBSD is no exception, so you may want to upgrade your kernel to obtain bug fixes. Updates may also improve performance or add features.

- **Reduced memory consumption**   The standard FreeBSD kernel includes drivers for many components you don't have. These drivers consume RAM but provide nothing in return. Creating a custom kernel can improve your system's performance by reducing the kernel size (and hence its memory requirements). This reason for modifying the kernel is most relevant on older systems with limited RAM; modern systems with 128MB or more aren't likely to see much effect from shrinking a kernel's size by a megabyte or so.

■ **Adding kernel features and optimizations** Although the standard kernel includes support for most hardware components, a few options may be set nonoptimally in the standard kernel. For instance, the standard kernel lacks support for more than one CPU, so you must compile a new kernel to make the best use of a multiprocessor system.

■ **Hardware conflicts** Although rare, hardware conflicts occasionally crop up. These problems prevent a system from working correctly because one component's driver interferes with the operation of another device. You can eliminate such problems by removing the offending driver for the hardware you don't have.

Any of these goals can be achieved by recompiling the kernel. Resolving hardware conflicts, and sometimes adding new hardware drivers, can be done by modifying kernel boot options, as described in the next section, "Kernel Boot Options." You can sometimes add new drivers or features by loading kernel *modules*, which are kernel components that are stored in files separate from the kernel proper. The upcoming section, "Loading Kernel Modules," describes their use. You can often load kernel modules without rebooting the computer, which is a great convenience if you're testing or debugging a configuration.

Kernel Boot Options

One of the simplest ways to modify your kernel is to pass it boot options as part of the boot process. The "Setting Kernel Options" section of Chapter 4 describes this process in general terms. As described in that section, you can press any key but ENTER to adjust these settings when you're prompted for the kernel to boot. Two parameters are particularly relevant to this discussion:

■ `boot [-options] [kernelname]` You can boot the specified kernel and pass it any options you like with this command.

■ `load [-t type] modulename` You can load a kernel module with this option. This option is particularly likely to be useful if your system relies upon a module for a critical piece of hardware, such as a SCSI host adapter that controls your hard disk. For more peripheral devices, you can use the commands described
in the upcoming section, "Loading Kernel Modules," instead.

The `boot` parameter is interesting because it lets you boot a kernel other than the default `/boot/kernel/kernel`. If you build a new kernel, you can use this parameter to load it instead of the default kernel, or perhaps use this command to load your old kernel if the new one fails, as described in the upcoming section, "Using the New Kernel." You can also pass options to this parameter that affect how the kernel boots. Most of these options don't directly affect what features are available in the kernel, but some are quite important. In particular, -s boots the system into single-user mode, which may be useful for certain emergency recovery operations; and -a causes FreeBSD to ask what device to mount as the root filesystem, which may be useful if your partition layout has changed.

Loading Kernel Modules

If you're basically satisfied with your kernel, but need it to support some feature that it doesn't by default, one potentially simple solution is to load new kernel modules to handle the additional tasks. Sometimes doing this is necessary because FreeBSD doesn't auto-detect the hardware or because you want to use a module that simply isn't part of the default configuration.

To examine the status of your kernel modules, you can use the kldstat command:

```
$ kldstat
Id Refs Address    Size     Name
 1   7 0xc0100000 3ef2dc   kernel
 2   1 0xc1d0d000 16000    linux.ko
```

Normally, this command shows few kernel modules loaded—possibly just the kernel module, which is the main kernel file itself (the preceding example also shows linux.ko, the kernel module to support Linux binary programs, as described in Chapter 4). The fact that modules for other hardware, such as EIDE disks, Ethernet cards, and USB devices, aren't shown isn't a cause for concern; such devices may be compiled into the kernel proper, in which case they don't show up with the kldstat command without additional options. Adding the -v option causes kldstat to display features that are a part of each module. The kernel module, in particular, is likely to contain dozens or hundreds of features. If you want to limit the output of kldstat, you can do so with the -i *id* or -n *name* options. They restrict output based on the ID number (the first column in the preceding example's output) or the name (the final column in the preceding example's output). For instance, to see information on only the linux.ko module using the preceding example, you could type either of two commands:

```
$ kldstat -i 2
$ kldstat -n linux.ko
```

If you want to load a certain kernel module, you can do so with the kldload command, which takes the name of a kernel module as input. For instance, to load the snd_gusc.ko module, you'd type

```
# kldload snd_gusc.ko
```

This command loads support for Gravis UltraSound sound cards. The linkage between the snd_gusc.ko module and the card it supports is partly evident from the name, but sometimes these links can be cryptic, so you may need to consult the kernel release notes for help. Kernel modules normally reside in /boot/kernel or /boot/modules; if you place kernel modules elsewhere, you must specify a complete path to the files. If you add a -v parameter just before the name of the module you want to load, kldload reports what it does and the ID number assigned to the module.

If you want to unload a module, you can do so with the kldunload command, which works much like kldload, but in reverse. You can also specify a module by number by preceding its number with -i:

```
# kldunload -i 7
```

The great advantage to employing kernel modules is that you don't need to go to the bother of recompiling your kernel. You can also load and unload kernel features without rebooting the computer. The downside is that you're restricted to the kernel features that are already available on your system as modules. (In theory, you could drop a new module file into the modules directory, but in practice doing so usually requires recompiling the kernel to get the new module.)

Recompiling the Kernel

The ultimate in kernel configuration is recompiling the kernel, which enables you to fine-tune many kernel options, omit drivers that you'll never use in order to reduce the kernel size, and add features that might not be included in a standard FreeBSD kernel. Although recompiling the kernel may seem intimidating, it's a useful skill to possess because it can produce a better optimized system, and on rare occasion it's the only way FreeBSD can be made to use all of your system's features.

Obtaining the Kernel Source Code

The first step to recompiling your kernel is obtaining the source code. It may already be installed on your system; if so, it resides in /usr/src/sys. If this directory already exists, you shouldn't need to do anything else, unless you want to upgrade to a more recent kernel, in which case you should read the upcoming section, "Upgrading the Kernel." Fortunately, installing the kernel source is a relatively straightforward process. You can use the sysinstall utility to install the kernel source code from a FreeBSD CD-ROM or download it from the Internet. To do so, follow these steps:

1. Launch sysinstall by typing **/stand/sysinstall** as root.

2. Select the Configure option. This brings up the FreeBSD Configuration Menu.

3. Select the `Distributions` option. This brings up a menu in which you select the name of a distribution you want to install. (A distribution is a set of FreeBSD programs or other files, such as the kernel source code.)

4. Select the `src` option. This brings up a subcomponent menu.

5. Select the `sys` option. This is the kernel source code, as indicated by a comment to the right of the option.

6. Select OK in the subcomponent menu and again in the distributions menu. The result is a menu in which you select your distribution medium.

7. Pick the medium from which you want to install the source code (probably your CD-ROM or an FTP site). Depending upon your choice, you may need to make additional choices, such as the exact FTP site. You'll then see a progress indicator as `sysinstall` retrieves the kernel source code and installs it in `/usr/src/sys`. You'll then be returned to the FreeBSD Configuration Menu.

8. Exit from `sysinstall` by selecting Cancel and then Exit Install.

At this point, you should find kernel source code files in the `/usr/src/sys` directory tree. This directory actually contains one file (`Makefile`) and a series of subdirectories that contain specific types of drivers and support features, such as `fs` for filesystems and `pci` for PCI card support. Unless you intend to do kernel development (a topic that's well beyond the scope of this book), you don't need to be too concerned with the exact contents of this directory tree, so long as it exists. The one exception to this rule, though, is the kernel configuration file.

Configuring the Kernel

Recompiling your kernel doesn't automatically configure it for best performance for your system. This task is handled by the kernel configuration file, which is a text-mode file you can edit or, better yet, copy and modify, to tell the system what features you do and do not want included in your new kernel. The standard FreeBSD kernel configuration file is `/usr/src/sys/i386/GENERIC` (the `i386` part will be different if you're using one of the rare non-*x*86 versions of FreeBSD, though). This file specifies a kernel that's configured for use with most options compiled in. The result is a very large `/boot/kernel/kernel` file—close to 4MB for FreeBSD 5.0. (The kernel is `/kernel`, not `/boot/kernel/kernel`, in pre-5.0 releases of FreeBSD.)

It's best not to modify the `GENERIC` kernel configuration file directly; instead, copy it to another name, such as `MYCONFIG` (FreeBSD kernel configuration filenames are traditionally all-uppercase, although they don't need to be). You can then edit your copy with impunity, and if you want to start over from scratch, you can copy the `GENERIC` kernel configuration file again. In fact, you may want to place your modified configuration file in another directory, such as `/root`, and create a symbolic link to it in `/usr/src/sys/i386`. This way, if you decide to completely delete and reinstall the kernel source, you won't wipe out your kernel configuration file.

The kernel configuration file begins with a series of comments—lines that begin with pound signs (#). Below this is a block of lines such as

```
machine        i386
cpu            I486_CPU
cpu            I586_CPU
cpu            I686_CPU
ident          GENERIC
maxusers       0
```

The machine line identifies the general CPU architecture—i386 for *x86* systems. You shouldn't change this. The following three lines identify three possible CPU models or families—486, 586 (Pentium), and 686 (Pentium II and above). You may comment out any of these that don't apply to your system by placing a pound sign at the start of the line. Doing so may modestly improve the kernel's efficiency. The *ident* line identifies the kernel, and you may want to change this to match your new configuration name. The maxusers line is used to tune certain system parameters, such as the total number of running processes FreeBSD supports (this is set to 20 + 16 × maxusers). A value of 0 causes FreeBSD 4.5 and later to auto-tune this value, but you can force it to a specific value if you prefer. Setting it to below 4 (but above 0) usually causes problems. Large servers may need very large maxusers values.

Note   *Despite what you may think, the maxusers value does not explicitly restrict the number of users who may log on, but it does set limits that are related to the number of users on the system.*

Prior to FreeBSD 5.0, various "hints" concerning hardware configuration were included in the kernel configuration file. Configuration lines using hints resembled the following:

```
device         ata0    at isa? port IO_WD1 irq 14
```

The standard procedure in FreeBSD 5.0 is to simplify the kernel configuration file and move hints into a separate file, /boot/device.hints. These hints might resemble the following:

```
hint.ata.0.at="isa"
hint.ata.0.port="0x1F0"
hint.ata.0.irq="14"
```

The simplified kernel configuration file entry lacks the hint information:

```
device         ata
```

If you want to use the old-style configuration, you should uncomment the line that reads as follows:

```
#hints           "GENERIC.hints"
```

Of course, you can tweak the hints themselves in either configuration, if necessary. The default hints work well on most systems, but occasionally you'll need to adjust a setting, particularly if you're using a very old Industry Standard Architecture (ISA) card that's configured in an unusual way. You can set the port and Interrupt Request (IRQ) values using the hints files.

Remaining lines in the configuration file begin with the words `options` or `device`. These indicate kernel features that are not and are directly linked to specific hardware devices, respectively. Sometimes this line can be a bit blurry; for instance, the option to enable Symmetric Multiprocessor (SMP) support for multi-CPU systems is called an option, although of course this relates directly to hardware. Most `options` and `device` lines end in a comment that describes what support the line enables. A few examples include

```
options          INET               #InterNETworking
options          FFS                #Berkeley Fast Filesystem
device           ata
device           atadisk            # ATA disk drives
device           atapicd            # ATAPI CDROM drives
```

These five lines enable TCP/IP networking support, the Fast File System (FFS) that's the default for FreeBSD, Advanced Technology Adapter (ATA; a.k.a. EIDE) interfaces, ATA disk drivers, and ATA CD-ROM drivers, respectively. You should go through this file and place a pound sign before any option you do not want supported—but don't be too enthusiastic about commenting out these options. Sometimes an option may not sound important, but in fact is. As a general rule, if you don't understand an option, leave it alone.

A few options are commented out by default. Sometimes this is because the option provides a duplicate or older driver for a device. Other times the driver can cause problems with other hardware, or degrade the performance of the system if it's not necessary. If you know you need support for such a feature, though, you should uncomment the option. SMP support has already been mentioned as an example of such an option. When you're done, you may have commented out half the lines that had been present initially. Many of these are likely to be in the Small Computer System Interface (SCSI) and Redundant Array of Independent Disks (RAID) areas because most systems have no or at most one SCSI or RAID adapter. Similarly, you can probably disable most of the Ethernet devices because you probably have just one Ethernet card.

For truly meticulous configuration, you should consult the NOTES file. (This file isn't present in pre-5.0 versions of FreeBSD; instead, these versions used a file called LINT that provides similar features.) The NOTES file includes extended commentary on many kernel configuration file options, as well as information on additional options that enable or configure very exotic features or drivers. A few of these features are described elsewhere in this book; for instance, support for the Linux ext2 filesystem (described in Chapter 4) is enabled by a line that's included in NOTES but not in the default GENERIC configuration file.

Performing a Compilation

Compiling a kernel involves running three commands:

```
# cd /usr/src
# make buildkernel KERNCONF=MYCONFIG
# make installkernel KERNCONF=MYCONFIG
```

You should replace *MYCONFIG* with whatever name you gave to your kernel configuration file. The second command will take anywhere from a few minutes to several hours to complete, depending upon your CPU speed and the number of kernel options you've included in the kernel. You'll see the system display information as it compiles a huge number of kernel files and then links them together into a coherent whole. The third command installs the kernel, renaming the old /boot/kernel/kernel to kernel.old. Thus, when you reboot your computer, you'll be using the new kernel. The old kernel will remain available should you need to use it (say, if you accidentally omitted your hard disk's driver from the new kernel), by employing the boot parameter to the boot loader, as described in a previous section, "Kernel Boot Options."

For added safety, back up your original kernel to another directory entirely, such as /root, before you perform your first kernel compilation. This way, you'll have it as a fallback even if you recompile the kernel several times, which might otherwise destroy the original file.

Unfortunately, it's not uncommon for a kernel compilation to fail, particularly if you've never done one before. Typically, the culprit is the lack of some key development tool. Examine the error message and then check the sysinstall development packages for anything that sounds promising and install it. Certain compilation steps also require you to be root, so don't try compiling a new kernel as an ordinary user.

Using the New Kernel

When you reboot your computer, you'll use the new kernel by default. You can check that you're actually using the new kernel by examining the output of dmesg. Try piping this command through less or more so that you can easily examine the first few lines. Look for lines like these:

```
FreeBSD 5.0-20011211-CURRENT #0: Tue Dec 11 10:29:22 GMT 2001
    root@usw2.freebsd.org:/usr/src/sys/i386/compile/GENERIC
```

These lines identify the FreeBSD version (5.0-20011211-CURRENT, a development version leading to the release of FreeBSD 5.0), its compilation date and time (December 11, 2001), the user who compiled it (root@usw2.freebsd.org), and the configuration script (GENERIC). Yours should identify you (or more precisely, root on your system), the time you compiled the kernel, and the kernel configuration file you used. If you see values that seem to point to the original kernel, it's possible that something went wrong in the make installkernel step, or possibly earlier—if the compilation fails, FreeBSD won't be able to install the new kernel.

On versions of FreeBSD prior to 5.0, it's sometimes necessary to take a few additional steps to use all of a new kernel's features. Most importantly, you may need to create new device files for new hardware drivers. Fortunately, this is done fairly easily, by typing these commands:

```
# cd /dev
# ./MAKEDEV
```

The 5.0 and later versions of FreeBSD don't normally require this step because they use a *device filesystem*, which is a special virtual filesystem that's built dynamically to include device files for all the hardware supported by the current kernel.

Upgrading the Kernel

One of the most compelling reasons to recompile a kernel is to upgrade it to a more recent version. For the most part, doing this is much like compiling a kernel as just described; however, there are a few extra steps and considerations involved in the process.

When to Upgrade the Kernel

Upgrading to a more recent kernel may be desirable or even necessary for certain reasons, including:

- **Bug fixes** If your current kernel has bugs, upgrading the kernel may be a practical necessity. Although some bugs may not affect you (for instance, if they're in a driver for hardware you don't own), others may. Kernel bugs are particularly serious because they can affect the stability of the computer as a whole.

- **New drivers** You may want to run a newer kernel because it includes drivers for hardware that's not supported in an older kernel. Similarly, a new kernel may include better features in existing drivers, such as improved speed or better use of a device's features.

■ **New software interfaces** You may find that a newer kernel provides improved features for programs run on the computer. For instance, the device filesystem mentioned in "Using the New Kernel" is a kernel feature.

Upgrading the kernel requires upgrading your kernel source code, which requires some additional work. In many cases, it's simpler to recompile your existing source code. On the other hand, unless you track developments very closely, you can't be sure that the latest kernel source code doesn't fix an important bug, so if you're going to recompile your kernel, you might want to perform the additional steps needed to upgrade to the latest version.

FreeBSD development is broken into two branches: the STABLE branch and the CURRENT branch. Most FreeBSD systems are in the STABLE branch, which means that they're fully released, nonbeta software. The CURRENT branch is devoted to prerelease beta-test software. As a general rule, you shouldn't try to use a CURRENT kernel unless you're desperate for a new feature it implements or you want to contribute to kernel development. The following directions update your kernel to the latest within your system's version and development branch.

Installing a New Kernel

You can obtain a new FreeBSD kernel tree in several different ways. The method described here is closely related to the method described in Chapter 11 for updating the FreeBSD ports tree. In fact, you should review Chapter 11's "Installing and Updating the Ports System" section before proceeding.

To install a new kernel, follow these steps:

1. Follow the directions in Chapter 11 concerning the installation and configuration of the CVSup package, but do *not* type the `cvsup` command to update the system.

2. Edit the `/etc/cvsupfile` file. The directions in Chapter 11 specified commenting out any lines that begin with `src`. To update the kernel source code, though, you must ensure that the file *includes* a line that reads as follows, to update the kernel source code:

   ```
   src-sys
   ```

3. If you don't want to update source code other than the kernel (such as the ports system that's updated in Chapter 11's instructions), comment out the lines in `/etc/cvsupfile` that relate to those items.

4. Type the following command to update the kernel source code:

   ```
   # /usr/local/bin/cvsup -g -L 2 /etc/cvsupfile
   ```

At this point, the system will update your kernel source code. This process may take anywhere from a few seconds (if no update is necessary or if you've got a *very* fast Internet connection) to several minutes, or even over an hour if your network connection is slow. In the end, your kernel source code tree will be updated.

Compiling and Using a New Kernel

You can compile and use a new kernel just as you would the kernel that came with your FreeBSD CD-ROMs. If you've already compiled that kernel, you may want to redo the configuration steps (copying GENERIC to a new file and editing that file) because it's possible that the new kernel has added drivers or changed driver names. Alternatively, you can use diff to obtain a list of lines that differ between your old configuration file and the new GENERIC file. If you see an option listed in the new file that's not present in the old one, you can copy it to your configuration file to enable it. (The output from diff can be tricky to parse if you're not used to it. In brief, the program identifies lines that have changed, and displays the old lines preceded by a less-than symbol and the new lines preceded by a greater-than symbol.)

Summary

The FreeBSD kernel underlies all the other software that runs on a FreeBSD system. For this reason, keeping it updated and tuned to your system's needs can do more than most other steps to keep your system operating at its best. To this end, recompiling your kernel with settings unique to your system can help improve your system's performance and perhaps even contribute to its stability. To recompile the kernel, you must copy a kernel configuration file, edit the copy to reflect your local configuration, and issue a few commands. Because the kernel underlies all other software, you must reboot the computer to use the new kernel.

Chapter 13

The X Window System

Most users today expect a computer to deliver a graphical user interface (GUI) environment, in which applications run in windows and many operations can be accomplished using a mouse. FreeBSD provides such an environment, which has been alluded to in various earlier chapters in this book, especially Chapter 3. This environment is known as *the X Window System*, or *X* for short. Chapter 23 describes many details of user-level day-to-day operation of X and the desktop environments built upon it. This chapter is devoted to more low-level X configuration.

X is an unusual GUI environment, compared to those used in more common desktop OSs such as Windows and Mac OS. Understanding X's model of operation is therefore important to understanding its capabilities; trying to understand X as if it were just like the Windows or Mac OS GUI can cause problems. This chapter therefore begins with a discussion of X's operating model. Most low-level X configuration is accomplished by editing a single file, XF86Config. You can change your video resolution, mouse, fonts, and so on by editing this file. Tools are also available to help you create or edit this file. Some settings, such as mouse speed and keyboard repeat rate, can be adjusted on a per-user basis, typically by editing user startup scripts or using desktop environment tools. This chapter concludes with a look at an unusual feature of X: the ability to run multiple X sessions. Each session can run with unique settings, such as resolution and color depth.

Understanding X

X is a unique GUI environment in many ways. For one thing, X itself is very spare compared to other popular GUI environments. X makes up for its Spartan nature by employing additional tools, such as window managers and widget sets. Another X peculiarity is its network nature. X uses network protocols to link X to X programs, even on a single computer. This characteristic makes X very useful in certain types of network environments, but it also tends to reduce X's speed compared to other GUI environments.

X's GUI Model

One common theme in UNIX applications is that programs tend to be small and modular. These small programs can be combined to perform more advanced tasks. This program design philosophy contrasts with common practice in the Windows and Mac OS worlds, where individual programs frequently grow to accomplish a wide variety of tasks. Of course, there are exceptions to these typical program design philosophies in these OSs, but X isn't one of them. Compared to other popular GUIs, X is a very modular environment. Several individual components, considered as a whole, build a complete working GUI system. Some of these components are part of X, but others aren't.

X Servers

A component known as an *X server* lies at the core of X. The job of the X server is to manage the display, keyboard, mouse, and possibly other human input/output devices. The X server provides a number of routines that programs can use to open windows, display shapes in windows, display text, and so on. (X windows are very simple; they're just rectangular areas on the screen. Another component, described in the upcoming section, "Window Managers," provides elements most people associate with complete windows.) The X server provides at least minimal support for handling fonts, and it's also network-enabled, as described in the upcoming section, "X's Network Nature."

FreeBSD relies upon an X server known as *XFree86* (`http://www.xfree86.org`), which is a very popular X server in the open source world—it's also available for other BSDs, Linux, Mac OS X, and even for non-UNIX systems such as OS/2 and Windows. FreeBSD 5.0 and later ship with XFree86 4.*x*. Previous versions of FreeBSD shipped with earlier versions of XFree86 (in the 3.*x* series for FreeBSD 4.*x*). The transition from XFree86 3.*x* to XFree86 4.*x* saw several changes in how the X server was designed. Most dramatically, XFree86 3.*x* used different X servers for different video card families. For instance, you'd run a server called `XF86_S3` if you had a card based on a chipset from S3, and `XF86_Mach64` if you used a card with an ATI Mach64 chipset. With XFree86 4.*x*, though, there's a single X server executable, called `XFree86`. This single server loads driver modules for specific video card chipsets. This design simplifies configuration and driver development.

Because the X server controls the video card, it's this component (in conjunction with the video hardware itself) that determines how fast your display is, what resolutions it supports, and so on. Some brand-new video card designs have XFree86 drivers that don't yet implement all of the hardware's features, so these cards actually perform worse than older cards. It's also sometimes possible to upgrade the X server alone (or just a driver file) to improve your system's video performance.

Widget Sets

The X server controls access to the video hardware and provides a low-level application programming interface (API) for X programs. This API enables programs to open windows, display information in those windows, and so on. This API is *very* basic, though; unlike the APIs for Windows, Mac OS, and other GUI OSs, the X API doesn't include the ability to display menus, scroll bars, buttons, and similar GUI staples, which are often called *widgets*. This task is handled by an X component known as a *widget set*.

Several competing widget sets exist for X. Each of these creates a slightly different set of GUI components, and has its own unique look and feel. Some of the more popular widget sets include Motif (an early commercial widget set), LessTif (an open source clone of Motif), Qt (a popular open source widget set), and GTK (another popular open source widget set). In 2002, Qt and GTK dominate the widget set arena in FreeBSD, but many programs use other widget sets.

Because programs must be written to take advantage of specific widget sets, programmers make the choice of which widget set to use. As a user or system administrator, you have no choice in the matter, except to use or not use particular programs. In some cases, if you want to use a particular program, you must install libraries that provide the widget set code. This task can be handled automatically by `sysinstall` or the FreeBSD ports system when you install the target program.

Window Managers

X provides low-level window management routines, and widget sets provide tools that enable programmers to present useful information inside windows. Another component of practical X use is the *window manager*. A window manager adds functionality *around* windows. Most noticeably, window managers provide several components that immediately surround a window and enable a user to control its size and placement. Figure 13-1 shows a typical X window, with identified window manager components. These include

■ **Title bar**   The *title bar* or *drag bar* usually resides at the top of a window. It includes a name that identifies the window, and most window managers respond to click-and-drag operations in the title bar by moving the window around the screen.

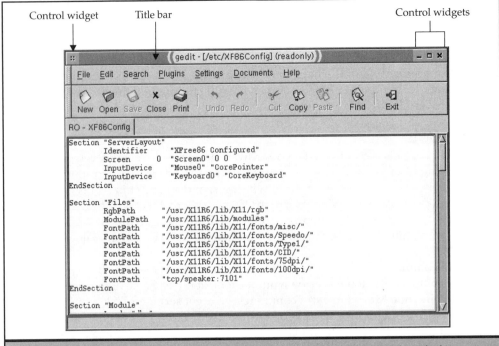

Figure 13-1.   *A window manager creates border decorations around a window, enabling control of window position and size.*

- **Control widgets** Window managers use a small set of widgets to help you control the window. In most cases, these are small squares on one or both ends of the title bar, such as those shown in Figure 13-1. The details of what these widgets do varies from one window manager to another. Most give you the ability to close, shrink, and enlarge a window, and many give additional options, such as the ability to move a window to another virtual desktop, as described shortly.

- **Window borders** Most window managers provide borders that enable you to resize windows. Move the mouse pointer to an edge or corner and the pointer usually changes shape. This is a cue that you can click and drag to change a window's size. Some window managers provide only very limited resize control points, such as the lower-right corner of a window.

In addition to these window components, most window managers provide additional controls located on the desktop (unused space on the screen), and sometimes along the top, bottom, or sides of the screen. Right-clicking on the desktop frequently produces a menu of options to exit from the window manager, launch programs, or perform other tasks. These window manager functions frequently overlap with features provided by desktop environments (described in the next section) and may be overridden by such environments.

One feature of many window managers is the ability to control multiple *virtual desktops*. These are semi-independent workspaces; each one can have a unique set of windows open, and you can switch between virtual desktops by clicking a button or selecting a menu option. Details differ from one window manager to another. This functionality is often provided by the desktop environment, as well.

It's important to recognize that the features provided by a window manager can vary substantially from one window manager to another, as can the look and feel of a window manager. To illustrate this point, consider Figure 13-2, which shows the same application running as the one in Figure 13-1. Figure 13-2 uses the WMX window manager, though, whereas Figure 13-1 shows the IceWM window manager. Note that WMX uses an unusual side-mount location for its title bar, and provides just one window widget, compared to the four used by IceWM. The interior of the window, including the menu bar, scroll bars, and icons, are identical in Figures 13-1 and 13-2 because these elements are controlled by the widget set.

Some differences can't be shown by a screen shot, though. For instance, each window manager supports its own *focus* policy—a way to determine when a window receives input from the keyboard or mouse. The most common default focus policy is often referred to as *click-to-focus*, in which a mouse click anywhere in the window gives it focus. Another common focus policy is *focus-follows-mouse*, in which merely moving the mouse over a window gives it focus. Focus is frequently associated with the front window in a stack, but some window managers can give a window focus when the window is partially obscured by others. This feature is frequently used in conjunction with a focus-follows-mouse policy, and clicking a window is required to bring it to the front of a stack.

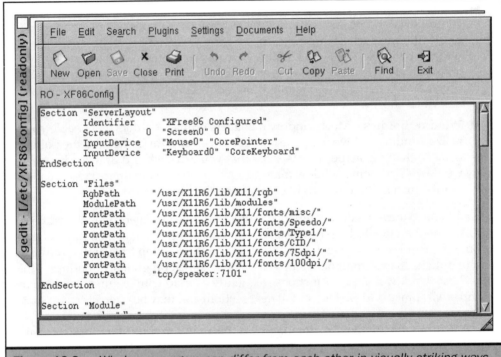

Figure 13-2. *Window managers can differ from each other in visually striking ways.*

Individual users may select their window managers from among all those installed on a system. Doing so is described in the upcoming section, "Changing the Window Manager or Desktop Environment."

Desktop Environments

In years past, FreeBSD users typically ran X and a window manager launched via a startup script, as described in Chapter 6. This combination enables users to launch programs from an xterm or window manager menus, move windows, and so on; but it provides little in the way of integration between applications, and it requires users to place various useful small tools, such as editors, on application menus. (System administrators sometimes perform this last task for default configurations, though.) To combat the perceived awkwardness of such solutions, various *desktop environments* have been developed. These are collections of many small programs, and sometimes fairly major ones, that use the same widget sets and that integrate well with one another. The result is a unified desktop experience, in which you can call useful utilities from a standardized location to edit files, set desktop background images, adjust mouse tracking speed, move files, and so on.

Note *Although desktop environments provide integration and "eye candy" that many inexperienced users expect, they can be huge resource hogs. A FreeBSD system running a slim window manager and traditional UNIX-style programs can perform well with only 64MB of RAM, or possibly less. Add KDE or GNOME and large integrated packages, and 128MB may not be sufficient.*

In some sense, desktop environments are the successors to window managers because they're often launched instead of window managers. In another sense, though, desktop environments are extensions to window managers because they include window managers at their cores. Some desktop environments give you a choice of which window manager to run.

The two most common desktop environments are the GNU Network Object Model Environment (GNOME) and the K Desktop Environment (KDE). FreeBSD favors GNOME, but you can install and use KDE if you prefer. GNOME is built around the GTK widget set, and KDE is built around the Qt widget set. You can run GTK-based programs in KDE or Qt-based programs in GNOME, though. Indeed, you can even run GNOME components in KDE or vice-versa.

Note *Programs are sometimes called "GNOME programs" or "KDE programs" when "GTK programs" or "Qt programs" would be more appropriate terms.*

Miscellaneous Tools

Various additional programs fit into the X hierarchy of tools:

- **X configuration tools**   Various programs exist to help you configure X at a low level (that is, to set its video options, mouse options, and so on). The upcoming section, "Tools to Help Reconfigure X," provides pointers to some of these.

- **Font servers**   No GUI environment is complete without a selection of fonts. X servers include built-in support for delivering fonts to applications, which you can adjust as described in the upcoming section, "Adding or Removing Fonts." In addition, X can use network-enabled *font servers*, which can provide fonts to all the X workstations on a network. Chapter 22 describes font servers.

- **Applications**   X is superfluous without programs to use it. Many standard FreeBSD programs don't rely upon X, but others can or must use X. Large end-user-oriented programs are the most likely to use X.

X's Network Nature

Unlike most GUI environments, X is network-oriented. You can run an X server on one computer and use it to display the output from and send input to a program that runs on another computer. The client/server terminology in this case is confusing to many people because it's common to think of a server as being a big computer that's hidden from sight, and a client as the computer at which a user sits. To better understand the client/server terminology in the case of X (or in any case, really), think of it from the *application's* point of view. To a program such as a word processor, the keyboard, mouse, and display constitute a set of input/output streams, much like a file server on which data files are stored. To the word processor, then, a network server for handling user input may be remote. The fact that a human happens to sit at that server computer is unimportant to the word processor.

X's network-enabled nature makes it possible to set up a powerful FreeBSD system to run applications for many users and employ much less powerful computers as X display terminals. In fact, an entire class of computer, known as *X terminals*, is designed for this purpose. X terminals provide little or no independent computational capacity, but provide a keyboard, mouse, and (typically very large) monitor. You can also use one FreeBSD system as an X server for another—in fact, this practice can be a good way to squeeze more life out of an otherwise outdated computer. Even Windows, OS/2, and other non-UNIX systems can function as X servers, if equipped with appropriate software, such as Hummingbird Exceed (`http://www.hcl.com/products/nc/exceed/`), Netsarang's Xmanager (`http://www.netsarang.com/products/xmanager.html`), or a Windows port of XFree86 (`http://sources.redhat.com/cygwin/xfree/`).

When used over a network, X is slower than when the X server and X client (the application) run on the same computer. Depending upon the type of network and application, though, this difference might be small enough that it's unimportant.

The basic X configuration for FreeBSD sets it up as a local X server only; you can't use a default FreeBSD system to access X applications run from another computer. Chapter 21 describes configuring X to accept remote connections.

Reconfiguring X

When you installed FreeBSD, as described in Chapter 2, the system configured X. Sometimes, though, this configuration goes wrong, either badly (so that X doesn't run at all) or subtly (so that X runs nonoptimally). In other cases you may need to reconfigure a previously working X, such as when you change a mouse or video card. For whatever reason, reconfiguring X is sometimes necessary, and this section describes how to do it, beginning with a look at the structure of the `XF86Config` control file. This section then moves on to some common configuration changes: to video cards, to resolution and color depth, to the mouse, and to fonts. This section concludes with a look at some tools you can use to help make these changes.

Note   *This section describes configuring XFree86 4.x. The older XFree86 3.x configuration file format was somewhat different from what's described here.*

Tips for Making Changes

When editing XF86Config, it's useful to first configure your system to *not* start X automatically at boot time. This configuration enables you to manually start X to test your changes, quickly exit from X, make more changes, and then restart X. A text-mode startup that permits this test cycle is FreeBSD's default configuration, but if you've reconfigured the system to start X automatically, you should undo these changes. One method of starting X automatically, which is described in Chapters 6 and 21, involves running the X Display Manager (XDM) or a similar program from /etc/ttys. By default, this file contains a line like this:

```
ttyv8    "/usr/X11R6/bin/xdm -nodaemon"  xterm    off   secure
```

The off in this line may read on if the system starts X automatically. Change it back to read off, and then type **kill -HUP 1**. This command will reconfigure init so that it doesn't automatically launch XDM, but the current instance may continue to run. You may need to log out of any running X session and type **killall xdm** in a text-mode session to terminate XDM and the X login that it provides.

When you make a change to your X configuration, you can type **startx** to test the new setup. (Try doing this as a regular user, not as root, to be sure that all the necessary files are readable or executable by normal users.) When you select the log out or exit option in your window manager or desktop environment, X should close and you should be returned to your text-mode terminal. If this doesn't happen, try pressing CTRL-ALT-BACKSPACE to kill the X session. In either case, you should see a series of lines with messages from the X server. If all goes well, these will be unimportant; but if something didn't work correctly, one of these messages may contain a vital debugging clue. Unfortunately, the vital message may have scrolled off the top of the screen. To capture these messages, you can use redirection to save them to a file. For instance, instead of typing **startx**, type **startx &> startx**.out to save the X messages to startx.out. You can then examine this file at your leisure for clues to what went wrong.

Basic Structure of XF86Config

The XF86Config file resides in the /etc/X11 directory. Like most other FreeBSD configuration files, XF86Config is a text file, so you can edit it using any text editor you like, as described in Chapter 5. As with other configuration files, it's a good idea to back up the file before changing it; that way, if you make matters worse, you can restore the original and try again. Although editing the file directly gives you the greatest flexibility, you may prefer to use a GUI or automated X configuration tool for at least part of the job. The section, "Tools to Help Reconfigure X," describes such tools.

BASIC SYSTEM
ADMINISTRATION

The `XF86Config` file is divided into several sections, each of which begins with a `Section` keyword and ends with `EndSection`. For instance, the following is the opening section in a typical configuration:

```
Section "ServerLayout"
        Identifier      "XFree86 Configured"
        Screen       0  "MyScreen" 0 0
        InputDevice     "PS2Mouse" "CorePointer"
        InputDevice     "StdKeyboard" "CoreKeyboard"
EndSection
```

This `ServerLayout` section describes the rest of the configuration—it includes an `Identifier` for the configuration as a whole, a `Screen` line to identify the display, and two `InputDevice` lines, one for each input device (the mouse and the keyboard). The `Screen` and `InputDevice` lines point to subsequent sections, which provide more details about the devices in question. Such subsequent sections may optionally refer to still more sections (as the `Screen` section does). Thus, a typical `XF86Config` file describes a hierarchical structure, as illustrated in Figure 13-3. You can trace this structure by reading the identifiers (such as `MyScreen` and `PS2Mouse` in the preceding example) and locating them in `Identifier` lines of subsequent sections. You may want to examine your current `XF86Config` file and create a diagram like Figure 13-3 so you understand its structure. (The diagram you construct will probably closely resemble Figure 13-3.) Some sections in `XF86Config` don't fit in this diagram, though—they apply to the X server as a whole. Sections you're likely to find in `XF86Config` are

- **ServerLayout**   As just described, this section is the top-level configuration; it ties together most of the other sections into a coherent whole.

- **Files**   This section doesn't tie explicitly into the `ServerLayout`, but it's very important. It defines the directories in which important XFree86 files can be found, such as font files (specified by `FontPath` lines) and drivers for specific hardware devices (specified by the `ModulePath` line).

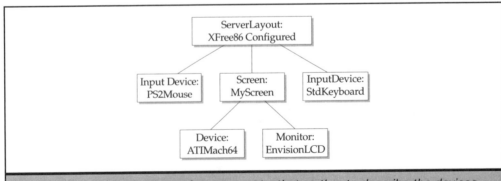

Figure 13-3.   *Most sections of* `XF86Config` *tie together to describe the devices associated with the X server.*

- **Module** XFree86 4.*x* uses a modular approach to drivers, and this section specifies some of the driver modules the server should load. Normally, you leave this section alone unless you want to enable or disable an advanced feature.

- **InputDevice** As shown in Figure 13-3, there are usually two `InputDevice` sections, one for the keyboard and one for the mouse. The keyboard section seldom needs work, but you may need to adjust the mouse section if you specified the wrong mouse when you installed FreeBSD.

- **Monitor** This section provides information about your monitor, such as the range of horizontal and vertical refresh rates it accepts. Properly configuring this section is vitally important—if its options are set incorrectly, your monitor may display no image or display an image at a suboptimal refresh rate or resolution.

Caution

Old monitors can be damaged if you specify a refresh rate that's too high. If your monitor predates the late 1990s, you should be very cautious about adjusting the Monitor *section. Do so only with the monitor's manual at hand so that you can set the correct refresh rate values.*

- **Device** This section defines the video card, including the driver for the board and various other low-level details, including the resolution at which the display operates. It's not uncommon to find multiple `Device` sections in an `XF86Config` file. Typically, one defines an optimized display for your card, and another defines a generic Video Graphics Adapter (VGA) display, which works with most modern video cards, but only at very low resolutions. The VGA definition is likely to go unused once you've created a working optimized configuration.

- **Screen** This section references the `Monitor` and `Device` sections, as shown in Figure 13-3, to create an integrated display. It includes a specification of the default color depth used by the display.

Note

These sections might not appear in your XF86Config *file in the order in which they're described here. Order in the file is largely unimportant, but I've described them here in a logical order for understanding what these sections do.*

Setting the Screen

As shown in Figure 13-3, XFree86 defines a screen in terms of a video card and a monitor. This configuration is handled through a configuration section that most likely appears near the end of the `XF86Config` file:

```
Section "Screen"
        Identifier "MyScreen"
        Device     "ATIMach64"
        Monitor    "EnvisionLCD"
```

```
        DefaultDepth 16
        SubSection "Display"
                Depth       16
                Modes "1024x768" "800x600" "640x480"
        EndSubSection
        SubSection "Display"
                Depth       24
                Modes "800x600" "640x480"
        EndSubSection
EndSection
```

The Identifier line should match the name provided for the screen in the ServerLayout section (MyScreen in this example). The Device and Monitor lines point to definitions for the video card and monitor, respectively, as described in the next two sections, "Changing the Video Card Support" and "Adjusting Monitor Settings."

The Screen section includes one or more subsections labeled Display. These subsections define characteristics of a display, one of which is the color *depth*—that is, the number of bits used to describe a pixel's color. The lowest possible color depth is 1 bit, meaning that a pixel can be one of two colors (usually black or white). More common values include 8 bits (256 colors), 16 bits (65,536 colors), 24 bits (16,777,216 colors), and 32 bits (4,294,967,296 colors). As a practical matter, 16-bit or better displays work best; X programs tend to waste a lot of colors, so 8-bit modes frequently result in color corruption. Greater bit depths slow down displays, so you may want to use the lowest bit depth that produces acceptable results.

Another component of the Display subsection is a specification of supported video *modes*. These settings are named and defined elsewhere (in the Monitor section), but they're usually named after the video resolution in question, such as 1024x768 for a 1024×768 display. Frequently, one Modes line defines multiple modes. These are tried in order until one works, and the user can select from the remaining working modes by pressing CTRL-ALT– or CTRL-ALT-+, using the – or + on the numeric keypad. In XFree86 4.*x*, it's not uncommon to find no mention of video modes, though, because this version of XFree86 can automatically set the maximum resolution the monitor supports. If you want to override this setting, you can do so by specifying a mode in the Screen section and defining that mode in the Monitor section.

One critically important line in the Screen section is the DefaultDepth line, which sets the default color depth from the choices defined in the various Display subsections. Because the resolution is set along with the color depth, this line also defines the resolutions available when XFree86 runs.

Changing the Video Card Support

If you replace a computer's video card, or if you selected the wrong card when you installed FreeBSD, you must update the Device section of the XF86Config file.

A typical `Device` section looks like this:

```
Section "Device"
    Identifier   "ATIMach64"
    VendorName   "ATI"
    BoardName    "XPert 98"
    Driver       "ati"
    Option       "DPMS"
    Option       "OffTime" "20"
EndSection
```

Key points to consider in this section include

- **Identifier**   The `Identifier` must match the name used on the `Device` line in the `Screen` section.

- **VendorName and BoardName**   These options set a name for your use, so that you can easily identify the device. Set them to anything you like.

- **Driver**   The `Driver` line specifies the video driver to be used. FreeBSD stores these drivers in the `/usr/X11R6/lib/modules/drivers/` directory. The driver's filename is the driver name as specified on the `Driver` line plus `_drv.o`. For instance, this example loads the `ati_drv.o` driver file.

- **Option**   You may find one or more `Option` lines. These set assorted options that modify the way the driver operates. This example sets the `DPMS` option, which enables the *Display Power Management System*, so that you can use power management tools to shift the monitor into a low-power state when the computer isn't being used. The `OffTime` option sets one such detail—it sets the monitor to power off after 20 minutes of inactivity. You can also use the `xset` program or tools in desktop environments to adjust many of these settings.

If you need to configure your system to use an entirely new video card, you may want to create a new `Device` section for that card. This way, you can easily reconfigure your system to use the old device should your new configuration not work. Copy a working `Device` section and modify it—the `Identifier` and `Driver` lines are the most important to change. If you're not sure what driver to use, consult `http://www.xfree86.org/current/Status.html`. This page includes information on XFree86 support for various video cards. Remember to change the reference to the video card device in the `Screen` section, too.

Adjusting Monitor Settings

The `Monitor` section defines the monitor's capabilities. A typical example looks like this:

```
Section "Monitor"
        Identifier    "EnvisionLCD"
```

```
        VendorName      "Envision"
        ModelName       "EN-5100e"
        HorizSync       29.0 - 61.0
        VertRefresh     70 - 75.0
EndSection
```

As with other sections, the `Identifier` line uniquely identifies a `Monitor` section. The `VendorName` and `ModelName` lines are like the `VendorName` and `BoardName` lines in the `Device` section—they exist to help you identify the monitor.

From the X server's point of view, a monitor has two critically important characteristics: its *horizontal refresh rate* and its *vertical refresh rate*. These are set by the `HorizSync` and `VertRefresh` lines, respectively. Modern monitors support a range of horizontal and vertical refresh rates, so these values are generally specified as ranges, as shown in this example. The horizontal refresh rate is specified in kilohertz (kHz), and represents how rapidly the monitor can draw a single horizontal line of data. The vertical refresh rate is specified in hertz (Hz), and specifies how rapidly the monitor can display a full screen of data. As a general rule, higher values are better because higher values translate into more displays per second, which is less likely to cause eye strain. You can find the horizontal and vertical refresh rates in your monitor's manual.

Enter these values correctly, and don't make guesses, especially with old monitors. Old monitors can be damaged if driven at too high a refresh rate. (New monitors usually reject such input.)

XFree86 4.*x* supports a feature known as *Data Display Channel (DDC)*, which enables the computer to query the monitor about the resolutions it supports and how to create them. This feature usually works well, but if you've got an older monitor or if the DDC fails for some reason, you may need to add lines like the following to your `Monitor` section:

```
    Mode "1024x768i"
        DotClock        45
        HTimings        1024 1048 1208 1264
        VTimings        768 776 784 817
        Flags           "Interlace"
    EndMode
```

These lines define a *mode*, which provides detailed timing information for a specific resolution—in this case, 1024×768 interlaced. (An interlaced mode takes two passes to display the entire screen.) Creating modes is very tricky, so I recommend you not try doing it yourself. Instead, try copying modes from some source, such as an older XFree86 3.*x* `XF86Config` file, where mode definitions were more common. Don't worry about copying a mode that might drive your monitor at a too-high resolution; XFree86 checks the `HorizSync` and `VertRefresh` values and refuses to apply a mode if it would create a display outside of these limits. In most cases, you don't need to worry about modes because DDC provides them, or XFree86 can use a common mode that works with most monitors. If you try to start X but it complains that it can't find any valid modes, though, you may need to locate a mode definition and insert it in your `Monitor` section. Adjusting the horizontal and vertical refresh rates also sometimes fixes these problems.

Modes are often specified in a single-line form, using the keyword `Modeline` *rather than* `Mode`. *This form includes the numeric information shown in this example, but on one line and without the keywords (*`DotClock`, `HTimings`, *and so on).*

Changing the Mouse Configuration

One common problem in getting X working is in locating and using the mouse. This task is accomplished in an `InputDevice` section, which resembles the following:

```
Section "InputDevice"
        Identifier   "PS2Mouse"
        Driver       "mouse"
        Option       "Protocol" "auto"
        Option       "Device" "/dev/sysmouse"
EndSection
```

An `InputDevice` *section also exists for the keyboard, but because keyboards are standardized, you seldom need to adjust it.*

The `Identifier` line should be the same as the one you used to specify the mouse in the `ServerLayout` section. The `Driver` is normally `mouse`, even if you use a trackball, touchpad, or other alternative pointing device. The tricky part relates to the two `Option` lines, which set two important mouse characteristics:

- **Protocol** The mouse *protocol* is the "language" the mouse uses to communicate its movements. XFree86 4.*x* supports an `auto` protocol, in which XFree86 attempts to determine the protocol automatically. This often works well, but if your mouse doesn't work properly when so configured, you can set the protocol manually. Common values are `PS/2`, `Microsoft`, and `Logitech`. Almost all modern mice that use the USB or PS/2 port use the `PS/2` device type. Most other types apply to RS-232 serial mice.

- **Device** This option specifies the device file that XFree86 uses to access the mouse. In the preceding example, it's set to `/dev/sysmouse`, which is a dummy device created by the `moused` program, which provides limited mouse support in text-mode sessions. (Chapter 2 describes `moused`'s installation.) If you're not running `moused`, you should specify the correct mouse device file, such as `/dev/ums0` for a USB mouse, `/dev/psm0` for a PS/2 mouse, or one of `/dev/cuaa0` through `/dev/cuaa3` for an RS-232 serial mouse.

BASIC SYSTEM ADMINISTRATION

If you select the wrong mouse protocol or device, X may exit as soon as you start it, start with no mouse pointer, or start and show a mouse pointer that doesn't respond in a reasonable way (for instance, it may jump around randomly when you move the mouse). If you get one of these latter cases, type CTRL-ALT-BACKSPACE to exit from X so that you can reconfigure the system and try again.

If you're unsure of what device to use, try using cat *to examine the contents of a device file, as in* **cat /dev/ums0**. *When you move the mouse, you should see gibberish appear on your screen. If nothing happens, press CTRL-C and try again. This procedure may put your terminal into an odd mode, though (for instance, displaying a bizarre character set). Type* **reset** *if this happens to restore a normal display.*

Adding or Removing Fonts

The `Files` section of XF86Config controls the *font path*—a set of directories in which the X server searches for fonts. A `Files` section might look like this:

```
Section "Files"
        RgbPath        "/usr/X11R6/lib/X11/rgb"
        ModulePath     "/usr/X11R6/lib/modules"
        FontPath       "/usr/X11R6/lib/X11/fonts/misc/"
        FontPath       "/usr/X11R6/lib/X11/fonts/Speedo/"
        FontPath       "/usr/X11R6/lib/X11/fonts/Type1/"
        FontPath       "/usr/X11R6/lib/X11/fonts/75dpi/"
        FontPath       "/usr/X11R6/lib/X11/fonts/100dpi/"
        FontPath       "tcp/speaker:7101"
EndSection
```

The first couple of items in this section (`RgbPath` and `ModulePath`) don't set the font path; only the lines labeled `FontPath` do this job. Each of these lines specifies one source for fonts. Most of these are subdirectories of `/usr/X11R6/lib/X11/fonts`— the standard location for fonts on a FreeBSD system. Each of these subdirectories contains a particular type of font. The final `FontPath` entry in this example is unusual. Rather than specifying a directory, this entry identifies a *font server*—a network server that delivers font information to any X server that asks for it. Font server configuration is described in Chapter 22.

XFree86 understands several different types of fonts. Many of the core X fonts (those that programs are likely to assume exist) are delivered in *bitmap* format, which in this context means a font that's defined in terms of particular pixels being light or dark. Bitmap fonts are small and display quickly, but they display properly at only one size and resolution. To increase the size of a font, you need to create a new bitmap font. Another type of font is a *scaleable* (or *outline*) font, which is defined in terms of a mathematical description of its outline. The two most popular outline font formats are Adobe's PostScript Type 1 (also known as Adobe Type Manager, or ATM) and Apple's TrueType. XFree86 4.*x* supports both of these formats, but XFree86 3.*x* and earlier don't support TrueType fonts. If you want to add fonts, your best bet is to use Type 1 or TrueType fonts.

> **Tip** *You can find font collections on CD-ROMs in computer stores. XFree86 expects fonts stored in the same file format that Microsoft Windows uses, so get the Windows version of a font, not the Macintosh version.*

One relatively straightforward way of adding fonts is to create a new subdirectory for your new fonts (a subdirectory of /usr/local should be safe). Placing the fonts in this directory isn't enough, though; you must create a summary file that tells X about the fonts. This file is called fonts.dir, and it's tedious to generate it manually. Fortunately, there are utilities to do this for Type 1 and TrueType fonts: type1inst and ttmkfdir, respectively. Both are available as packages and as part of the FreeBSD ports system. (The FreeBSD package and port name of type1inst is p5-type1inst.) To tell X about the fonts you've installed, follow these steps:

1. Change to the directory in which you've installed the fonts.

2. If the directory contains TrueType fonts, type **ttmkfdir . >fonts.scale**. This command creates an intermediary file called fonts.scale.

3. If the directory contains Type 1 fonts, type **type1inst** to create a fonts.scale intermediary file.

4. Type **mkfontdir -e /usr/X11R6/lib/X11/fonts/encodings**. This action extracts information from fonts.scale and from any bitmap fonts that might be present to create a fonts.dir file.

5. Add a FontPath line to your /etc/XF86Config file pointing to your new font directory.

6. If you want to use the new fonts immediately, shut down X and restart it or type **xset fp rehash** to tell X to use the new font path.

At this point, your new fonts should be available in X applications that let you choose fonts. You can test this with a simple utility called xfontsel (Figure 13-4), which lets you display any of your installed fonts at a variety of sizes and with various attributes set.

> **Tip** *You can forego some of this trouble by installing a prepackaged font set. The FreeBSD ports system provides several in the x11-fonts ports set. Of particular interest is the urwfonts package. This is a set of Type 1 fonts released by URW to duplicate fonts available on PostScript printers.*

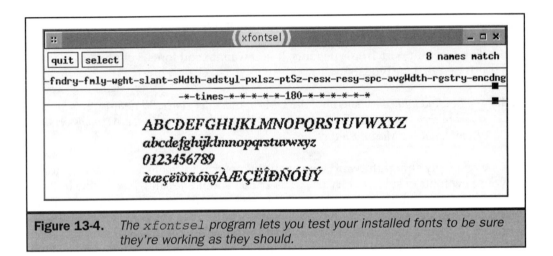

Figure 13-4. *The `xfontsel` program lets you test your installed fonts to be sure they're working as they should.*

Unfortunately, not all programs rely exclusively upon X's font-delivery mechanisms for fonts. The reason is that X's font handling is inadequate for some programs' needs, so some programs require that you install fonts independently of X's fonts. Word processors are particularly likely to have this requirement. If you see your fonts in `xfontsel` but not in a regular program, consult its documentation to determine whether you need to install the font into the program in addition to installing it in X.

If you want to reduce the clutter in your font menus, you can remove fonts. You can either trim entire directories from your font path or trim entries from the `fonts.dir` files. Removing directories from your font path is likely to cause problems unless they're directories you added to begin with. To trim entries from `fonts.dir`, look for the line containing the font's name. A typical entry looks like this:

```
n0210231.pfb -Adobe-Times-medium-i-normal--0-0-0-0-p-0-iso8859-1
```

Some fonts provide multiple entries for font variants such as bold or italic, and bitmapped fonts provide one entry for each font size. Thus, you may need to remove several font entries. When you're done, adjust the first line of the file, which lists the number of entries in the file (the number of lines minus one). It's a good idea to back up the `fonts.dir` file before you work on it.

Caution   *Don't remove fonts that are provided as a standard part of FreeBSD. Some programs assume that some of these fonts are present, so some programs may crash or behave strangely if they're not. You might use this process to trim fonts added from a font package, though.*

Tools to Help Reconfigure X

Reconfiguring X by editing XF86Config provides you with a great deal of flexibility, but it can be a tedious and tricky process, particularly if you're new to FreeBSD. Fortunately, there are some tools that can help you do the job. This section briefly describes two of them: XFree86 itself and the xf86cfg tool.

XFree86 4.x includes the ability to probe your hardware and generate an XF86Config file. To use this feature, type **XFree86 -configure**. This command generates a great deal of status information and creates a file called /root/XF86Config.new, which you can use as the basis for further modifications. You can test this file by typing **XFree86 -xf86config /root/XF86Config.new**, which should launch X using the new configuration file. There's a good chance that this command won't work correctly on the first try, or it may not work as you want it to. The auto-configuration routines frequently miss or misidentify certain types of hardware, such as mice driven through the moused server.

If you generate the XF86Config.new file and find it to be lacking, or if you want to modify an existing file, you may want to try editing it with xf86cfg. This program is included as part of a standard XFree86 4.x installation, and provides a GUI interface to XF86Config editing, as shown in Figure 13-5. Of course, the fact that it uses a GUI interface means that you must already have an X server running on the computer you intend to configure. Thus, xf86cfg is useful for tweaking an already working configuration, or perhaps for creating a new configuration prior to changing a video card. You can call it as follows:

```
# xf86cfg -xf86config /path/to/XF86Config
```

The /path/to/XF86Config could point to /etc/XF86Config or to a test file such as /root/XF86Config.new as created by XFree86 using its -xf86config option. Once the program is running, you can configure a component by right-clicking it and selecting Configure from the pop-up menu. This action creates a dialog box in which you can enter or change information relating to the device, as described in the preceding sections. You can also add devices by clicking the device icons near the top of the window. To add a new device to the layout, right-click it and select Enable from the pop-up menu. For most workstations, there's little need to add components; you're most likely to do this if you want to use multiple monitors to expand your working desktop area, or if you want to define an external USB keyboard or mouse for optional use with a notebook computer.

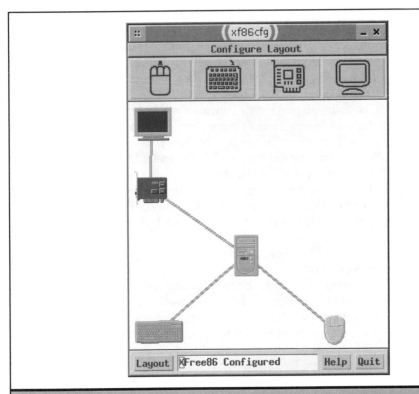

Figure 13-5.   *The* `xf86cfg` *program represents X devices in a graphical hierarchy.*

User-Level X Options

The previous section, "Reconfiguring X," was concerned with global X configuration—features you're likely to set as a system administrator to handle the overall X features. Other X options can be set on a user-by-user basis, though, and this section describes these features. Two major user-configurable changes are picking a window manager and picking a desktop environment. Two more detail-oriented changes are setting the mouse tracking speed and the keyboard repeat rate. All of these are settings that fall squarely in the category of user preferences—users are likely to have very different (and often very strong) preferences concerning these features. As a system administrator, you can set global defaults for all of these items, but individual users may want to override these global defaults.

Changing the Window Manager or Desktop Environment

Chapter 6 describes various system startup scripts, including two that are likely to be used to launch a window manager: .xinitrc and .xsession. These scripts reside in a user's home directory and are run when a user starts X from a text mode login or logs in using the XDM GUI login tool, respectively. To launch a particular window manager or desktop environment, it's necessary to include a reference to the relevant program in the startup script. Chapter 6, and in particular the "GUI Login Control Files" section, provides more details concerning this configuration.

Some replacements for the XDM login program, such as the GNOME Desktop Manager (GDM) and the KDE Display Manager (KDM) provide users with a choice of desktop environments at login. For instance, Figure 13-6 shows the GDM GUI login tool. The Session menu item in this tool provides a number of options, including Xsession (which runs the user's .xsession script), Gnome (which launches GNOME), and Failsafe xterm (which launches a minimal desktop environment). Both GDM and KDM remember the user's last selection on subsequent logins, so they're a good way to enable less experienced users to customize their login options, at least within the parameters of these tools' configurations. Chapter 21 describes the configuration of GUI login programs in more detail.

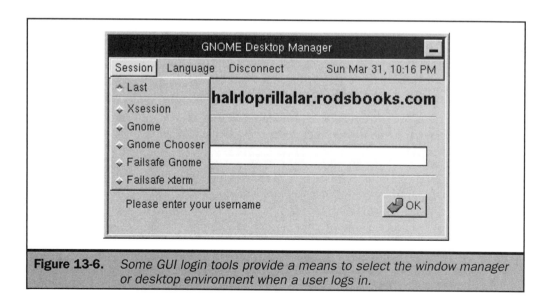

Figure 13-6. *Some GUI login tools provide a means to select the window manager or desktop environment when a user logs in.*

Adjusting Mouse Tracking Speed

Mouse tracking speed refers to the on-screen distance that the mouse moves in response to a given amount of physical movement of the mouse hardware. Some people prefer fast mouse tracking, while others prefer slower tracking. This feature can be adjusted via the xset command, which often appears in the .xsession login script. Specifically, the m *speed* option to xset determines the mouse acceleration. For instance, you might type the following command to adjust the mouse tracking speed:

```
$ xset m 4
```

This command must be typed in an xterm window after X has started; typing it before you launch X produces an error message.

Try experimenting with this command and various acceleration values to see which one you prefer. If you use a login method that uses .xsession or .xinitrc files, you can include this command in these files, prior to the call to your window manager, to set your mouse speed. If the system is a multiuser box, you can instruct your users to do the same.

Desktop environments frequently provide a more GUI-oriented method of setting the mouse tracking speed. For instance, Figure 13-7 shows the GNOME Control Center open to its mouse configuration area (selected from the Peripherals option set in the left pane). If you or your users run such an environment, this feature can be used instead of the xset command, and the desktop environment restores the setting at every login or X startup.

Adjusting the Keyboard Repeat Rate

The keyboard repeat rate is another customizable setting that many users want to personalize. This system characteristic can be adjusted in several ways:

- **XF86Config**   You can set the default keyboard repeat rate in XF86Config's keyboard section. In particular, you can set the AutoRepeat option, which takes two parameters: the delay before a key begins repeating (in milliseconds) and the rate of repeats per second. For instance, the following line sets the key to repeat ten times a second after a delay of 250 ms:

  ```
  Option "AutoRepeat"  250 10
  ```

- **xset**   The xset program can also set the keyboard repeat rate, but you pass it the r rate option along with a delay and repeat rate. For instance, **xset r rate 250 10** sets the keyboard repeat rate at ten per second after a 250 ms delay. Users can place a command like this in their .xinitrc or .xsession files to customize their keyboard repeat rates as they like.

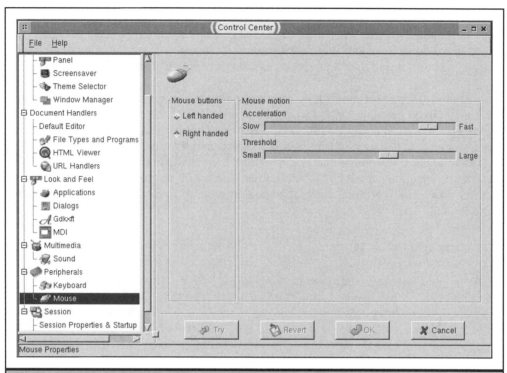

Figure 13-7. Desktop environments provide GUI controls that let you set the mouse tracking speed.

■ **GUI tools** As with mouse settings, GUI tools such as GNOME's Control Center enable you to adjust the keyboard repeat rate using sliders. These tools typically store the repeat rate and restore it after the user logs out and back in again.

You may want to experiment with `xset` *to find a reasonable value, then set it in your* `XF86Config` *file. Individual users can then override this setting, if they like.*

Running Multiple X Sessions

One of X's unusual features is that it enables you to run multiple X sessions on a single computer. Many users can live without this feature, but when it's required, it can be a real boon because it enables you to run sessions in two different resolutions or color depths, or run with two different window managers or desktop environments simultaneously. Such configurations can be particularly handy when you're testing programs for compatibility with different environments, or if you like to run one environment for most uses but need to run another environment for certain programs.

BASIC SYSTEM ADMINISTRATION

The ability to run multiple X sessions is distinct from the multiple virtual desktops maintained by many window managers and desktop environments. Virtual desktops all run at the same resolution and bit depth, and use the same X process, whereas multiple X sessions use multiple X processes and can run using different configurations.

Text-mode virtual terminals let you run multiple programs in text mode and switch between them by pressing ALT-F*n*, where *n* is a number from 1 to 8. Normally, X runs in the 9th virtual terminal, so you can switch to it from a text-mode login by typing ALT-F9. When you're in X, you can switch to a text-mode virtual terminal by typing CTRL-ALT-F*n*.

This model supports more than one X session. If you want to run additional X sessions, they run in virtual terminals of 10 and above. The tricky part is telling the system to launch X in a virtual terminal above the usual number 9. To do so, use a command like the following:

```
$ startx -- :1 vt10
```

You should type this command from a text-mode login. If you're already running X, type CTRL-ALT-F1 to get to a text-mode virtual terminal, login if necessary, and type the command. After a brief delay, you should see a new X session. You can switch between sessions by typing CTRL-ALT-F9 and CTRL-ALT-F10. The first session (number 0) runs on virtual terminal 9, and the new one (number 1, as indicated by the :1 in the launch command) runs on virtual terminal 10. You can extend this principle to launch additional sessions, although after four you'll run out of function keys for switching between them.

The real power of this method comes when you specify different startup options for the sessions. For instance, suppose your normal X session runs at 16-bit color depth. You can specify that a new session run at 32-bit color depth by including the -bpp 32 option in the command, thus:

```
$ startx -- :1 -bpp 32 vt10
```

You can use this trick to set up a session to run at a different resolution, too; define one color depth to run at one resolution (say, 1024×768) and the other color depth to run at another resolution (say, 800×600). You set these options in the XF86Config file's Screen section, as described earlier, in "Setting the Screen." When you select a particular color depth, you therefore also select the associated resolution. Alternatively, you could define multiple XF86Config files and choose between them using the -xf86config option, thus:

```
$ startx -- :1 -xf86config ./XF86Config-lowres vt10
```

Only `root` *may specify an absolute path with the* `-xf86config` *option, so if an ordinary user must use a special* `XF86Config` *file, that file might best reside in the user's home directory and be referenced with a relative path.*

Summary

Although the core of X is simple compared to many competing GUI environments, X is powerful. Indeed, part of X's power comes from its simplicity because higher-level tools, such as widget sets and window managers, can be swapped in and out at will. You can adjust some of these features on a system-wide basis, or even on a user-by-user basis, and individual programs set others.

Much X configuration occurs in the `/etc/XF86Config` file, which controls global features like the resolution of the video display and the device used for accessing the mouse. This file's format appears mysterious at first, but like many FreeBSD configuration files, its key features can be understood through a few keywords and principles. Nonetheless, using a configuration tool can help you get X up and running quickly, or reconfigure the system with minimal pain if necessary. Setting user-level options usually entails editing a user's X login file (`.xsession` or `.xinitrc`, depending upon whether the system is configured to start X automatically or not) or adjusting desktop environment tools.

The Complete Reference

FreeBSD

Part III

Network Configuration

Chapter 14

Basic Network Configuration

This chapter begins Part III, which focuses upon network configuration. FreeBSD is extremely popular as a network server, so this topic is very important to many FreeBSD administrators. Indeed, even hobbyist home users frequently need to know about FreeBSD's network features to tie FreeBSD into a home network or use its dial-up features (described in Chapter 15) to connect to an ISP.

This chapter focuses upon getting basic networking up and running. Subsequent chapters in this section cover dial-up networking, lay out the basics of clients and servers, and describe firewall configuration. Still later chapters (particularly those in Part IV, as well as Chapter 24) cover tools you might want to use with a network-enabled FreeBSD system.

Getting a network up and running may be done in various ways. To understand these, it's helpful to understand the principles upon which networking is built, so this chapter begins with such a discussion. It then proceeds to describe the method that UNIX systems have historically used for network configuration: static IP addresses. A more recent alternative that's common on many networks is to have a central server dynamically assign IP addresses to all other computers. This method is easier to configure, and is described next. Whichever method you use, you should test your configuration with various basic tools. You may need to debug problems, so this chapter provides some pointers to help you do that. Finally, some of the changes described in this chapter are transient, so you may need to make some changes to configuration files to have your system automatically use these settings after you reboot.

Local and Dial-Up Networking Features

Before you embark on a quest to configure FreeBSD to use a network, you should understand some basic networking principles. The most common type of networking hardware today is *Ethernet*, which is available in several different varieties. Most FreeBSD systems use the *Transmission Control Protocol/Internet Protocol (TCP/IP)* to encode data on network hardware. TCP/IP is the most common type of network protocol in use today, and it's the basis for the Internet as a whole. The Internet is built up of many smaller networks linked together by *routers*. With so many linked networks on the Internet, addressing an individual computer can be a tricky affair. This is handled through various naming systems and methods of translating between names. All of these networking features require one level or another of local configuration in order to work correctly.

Understanding Network Hardware

If you want to build an entirely new network, you must purchase all the hardware components that make up a network. If you want to add a computer to an existing network, you need fewer components. In either case, you must ensure that the network components are compatible with one another because various network hardware standards exist. Several types of network hardware are common on local area networks (LANs):

■ **Network interfaces**   Each computer that's connected to a network needs some sort of interface hardware. These often come in the form of *network interface cards (NICs)*, which use the computer's hardware bus (typically ISA or PCI) to add the interface hardware. Some computers, such as Macintoshes and some high-end *x*86 PCs, come with network hardware on the motherboard. Portable computers often use PC Card interfaces, and various other interface methods also exist. The network interface is the only network hardware component that requires a FreeBSD driver.

■ **Network cabling**   Most network hardware requires cables to link computers together. On today's 100 Mbps Ethernet networks, this cabling usually comes in the form of *Category 5* (*Cat5* for short) or better twisted-pair cabling. These cables resemble ordinary telephone cables, except that the plugs are wider. Some more advanced network types, including some varieties of gigabit Ethernet, use optical cables. Wireless technologies are gaining in popularity. These don't require cabling; they use radio frequency transmissions to carry their data.

■ **Hubs or switches**   Some forms of networking, including the common 100Mbps Ethernet, require the use of central devices to link multiple computers. (These devices can sometimes be omitted on two-computer networks, though.) A *hub* is essentially a repeater; when a computer sends data, the hub echoes the data packet to all the other computers attached to the hub. A *switch* is somewhat smarter, and echoes the packet only to the destination computer. In 2002, Ethernet switches cost little more than hubs, and so are preferable. Some types of network hardware, such as the old thin and thick Ethernet varieties, don't use hubs or switches; they tie all the computers together in a single line (known as a *bus topology*, as opposed to the *star topology* created by a hub or switch).

■ **Small routers**   Some installations use simple routers locally, typically for tying together two small LANs or to link a LAN to the Internet. You can configure a FreeBSD system to function as a router, or you can buy a dedicated device to fill this role. In some cases, you don't need a router, either because you're not linking together multiple networks or because your Internet service provider (ISP) provides the router (possibly off your premises).

Most new local networks in 2002 use 100 Mbps Ethernet hardware, which uses Cat5 cabling and hubs or switches to link computers. Older networks often use 10Mbps Ethernet with either Cat5 cabling and hubs or switches, or thin or thick coaxial cabling. Some local networks employ *Token Ring* instead of Ethernet. Token Ring uses hubs and is capable of 16 Mbps (100 Mbps for very recent versions). A very few networks use other types of network hardware. For the very best performance today, you can obtain gigabit Ethernet hardware, which uses Cat5 or optical cabling and gigabit switches. Such hardware is more expensive than 100 Mbps hardware, but prices are dropping fast. In the future, even higher speeds will be commonly available.

If you're connecting FreeBSD to an existing network, it's imperative that you learn what type of network it is. If it's a common type, such as 10 Mbps or 100 Mbps Ethernet, you should have no problem locating a network card that's compatible with FreeBSD. Consult the HARDWARE.TXT file that comes with FreeBSD to determine what cards are compatible (fortunately, most are). You may need to learn what chipset a card uses to determine if it's compatible, though.

TCP/IP Features

TCP/IP is a way for computers to "talk" to each other. It's not restricted to any particular network hardware—it can be implemented atop Ethernet, Token Ring, or various other types of hardware. In fact, you can use the *Point-to-Point Protocol (PPP)* to run TCP/IP over serial ports or modems. (This configuration is unique enough that it's described in its own chapter—Chapter 15.) TCP/IP is one of several *network stacks* that are available today, but TCP/IP is more common than its competitors. A network stack is a set of protocols that enable computers to communicate over a network. These protocols communicate in a hierarchical manner, hence the name, with user applications or servers at the top and low-level drivers and hardware at the bottom. Many of the reasons for TCP/IP's popularity relate to its design features, which include

- **Large address space**   Networked computers need some way to address each other. TCP/IP, like most network stacks, uses a numeric address (called the *IP address*) to do this. The TCP/IP address is 32 bits (4 bytes) in size, meaning that it supports a theoretical maximum of 2^{32}, or 4,294,967,296 addresses. This is large, but in 2002 it's becoming limiting, particularly because current TCP/IP addresses are allocated inefficiently. The next-generation version of the IP portion of TCP/IP, called *IPv6* (the current version is *IPv4*), supports a 128-bit address space—enough for a theoretical maximum of 3.4×10^{38} addresses. This should hold us until we populate the galaxy or nanotechnology becomes *extremely* commonplace.

- **Hostnames**   Although computers work well with numbers, including numeric IP addresses, people don't. Thus, TCP/IP supports a method of linking IP addresses to alphanumeric *hostnames*. The upcoming section, "IP Addresses, Hostnames, and Domains" describes the relationship between IP addresses and hostnames in more detail.

- **Multiport networking**   A computer can run many (potentially thousands of) network-enabled programs. Each program links to one or more network *ports*, which are virtual addresses *within* the computer, much like telephone extension numbers enable many office workers to share one outside telephone number. The benefit of network ports is that many programs can use the network simultaneously, even communicating with the same remote system, and data will find its way to the intended recipient.

- **Routing**   The previous section, "Understanding Network Hardware," mentioned routers. These devices enable you to link networks of computers into networks of networks, or *internets*. The *Internet* (note the capitalization) is the largest internet in existence, and would not be possible without routing. Many competing network stacks have primitive or no support for routing, thus limiting their reach.

- **Cross-platform support**   TCP/IP was originally developed on early UNIX systems, but it was developed in an open manner, so that it could be ported to other OSs. Thus, today TCP/IP is available on everything from palmtop computers to the most high-end UNIX systems. The widespread availability of TCP/IP has also led to the development of a wide range of applications.

Most network stacks, including TCP/IP, break networking tasks into two parts: *client* and *server*. The client initiates a network data transfer, and the server responds to these transfer requests. (The terms *client* and *server* can both be applied either to individual programs or to entire computers. It's usually clear from context which meaning is meant.)

TCP/IP Versus Other Network Stacks

The characteristics of TCP/IP outlined in the previous section are also its strengths over other network stacks. This isn't to say that all other stacks lack all of these features, though. For the most part, the non-TCP/IP network stacks that are still common in 2002 are *local* network stacks—they provide networking functions on LANs, not on internets. Common examples include

- **NetBEUI**   This stack is most strongly associated with Windows file and printer sharing, but these functions also work over TCP/IP. (In FreeBSD, you can use Samba to implement Windows file and printer sharing over TCP/IP, but not over NetBEUI.) NetBEUI is a nonroutable protocol, and it uses a two-tier naming scheme (using only machine names and workgroup or domain names), so it's not useable as an internet stack.

- **AppleTalk**   This stack is to Macintoshes what NetBEUI is to Windows systems— a way to provide file and printer sharing on local networks. AppleTalk uses a 32-bit address broken into two parts, and it supports some routing features, so it's better suited to use on an internet than is NetBEUI. AppleTalk is still limited in its machine naming conventions, though; like NetBEUI, it uses a two-tiered name system, which limits its applicability. Furthermore, AppleTalk never caught on outside of the Apple world. FreeBSD can provide file and printer sharing features over AppleTalk using the Netatalk package, which uses an AppleTalk variant that works over TCP/IP.

- **IPX**   Novell's *Internetwork Packet Exchange (IPX)* protocol stack was designed for internets, but it's not as flexible in naming as TCP/IP. IPX also never developed the range of network applications that TCP/IP supports. It remains a useful protocol for local file and printer sharing, though.

NETWORK CONFIGURATION

This book's networking chapters focus on TCP/IP because it's the most popular network stack and because the close runners-up don't offer greater power, on the whole. In some cases, you can use FreeBSD to provide services over these alternative network stacks, and FreeBSD does support some of them, to at least a limited extent.

Understanding Routing

If you're configuring a FreeBSD system to function on an entirely isolated local network (one that's not connected to the Internet), you may not need to deal with routing. Otherwise, routing is important because it's your network's gateway to the Internet, or even to other networks on a smaller internet.

A router links two or more networks. Frequently, but not always, routers link networks that use different types of network hardware. For instance, a router might link a local network that uses Ethernet to another local network that uses Token Ring, and tie both of these to the outside world using a long-distance routing protocol such as a frame relay connection. This arrangement is illustrated in Figure 14-1. In this case, the router is part of three networks: the local Ethernet network, the local Token Ring network, and the external frame relay network.

Now, suppose that a user on Figure 14-1's Ethernet network wants to access a resource that's located on the Token Ring network. The router enables this access; traffic between the two systems passes through the router. Similarly, access to the

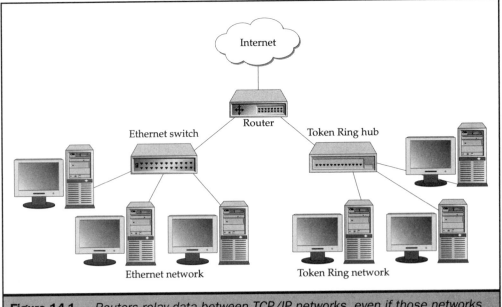

Figure 14-1. *Routers relay data between TCP/IP networks, even if those networks use different physical media.*

Internet from both local networks passes through the router. In fact, there are likely to be many routers because Figure 14-1's Internet "cloud" is really a complex set of interlinking routers and the hosts that they serve.

TCP/IP was designed so that local computers need to know very little about routing details, but there is one detail they need: the local router's IP address. Computers can send data directly to other computers on their local networks (those that can be reached without use of a router); this involves addressing a packet to the target system and sending it out the network interface. The recipient recognizes the packet and processes it. For more distant systems, though, this isn't possible; so when a computer knows that the target system isn't local, the computer sends the packet to the local router, which should know what to do with it. In the case of Figure 14-1's router, it knows about both its local networks and about its frame relay connection, and it knows that data destined for systems on the Internet at large go to another router on the frame relay connection. That router in turn can relay packets further, and so on, until the packet reaches its destination. Thus, internet traffic requires that a client know about one router, and the rest of the work is done in a distributed, piecemeal way by various intervening routers.

One feature that's related to routers and IP addresses is the *network mask* (aka *netmask* or *subnet mask*), which is a number that's applied in conjunction with the IP address to separate the network portion of the address from the machine portion. Typically, all the machines on each subnetwork (such as the Ethernet network in Figure 14-1) share the first few numbers in their IP addresses—this is the network portion of the address. The final few bits of the IP address are unique to each computer. The netmask can be interpreted as a binary number. Any binary 1 in this number represents a network portion of the address, and any binary 0 represents the machine portion. For instance, if the IP address of a computer is 192.168.0.23 and the netmask is 255.255.255.0, this means that the first three bytes of the IP address (192.168.0) are the network address, and the final byte (23) is the machine address. This netmask can also be represented as a decimal value representing the number of 1 bits, typically following the IP address and a slash, as in 192.168.0.23/24. Whoever provides you with an IP address should also give you a netmask. For private networks in the 192.168.*x*.*x* range, a netmask of 255.255.255.0 is typical. Routers work by examining the network portion of an address and using that to decide over what network connection to send the packets.

Netmasks have traditionally been broken up in whole-byte values—that is, each of the four bytes is either 255 or 0. Furthermore, each IP address has traditionally belonged to a *class*, each of which has a different netmask value. Class A addresses are on huge networks (with a netmask of 255.0.0.0), Class B addresses are on medium-sized networks (with a netmask of 255.255.0.0), and Class C addresses are on small networks (with a netmask of 255.255.255.0). Additional classes are reserved for special uses. Today, classes aren't as important as they once were. In order to make the most efficient use of the available IP addresses, they're assigned as is most convenient, in blocks of whatever size is convenient. Nonetheless, you'll still sometimes see a reference to an address belonging to a particular class, and configuration tools make default assumptions about netmasks based on these traditional classes if you don't specify a netmask.

FreeBSD can be configured as a router, but this topic is beyond the scope of this book. (Chapter 17 touches upon a particular type of router configuration, though.) For the most part, you must be concerned with the issue of configuring a FreeBSD client or server to use your local network's existing router. This router may be maintained by a local network administrator, it may be a device that's maintained off-site by your ISP, or it may be a small local device with a simple semiautomated configuration (particularly if you use a broadband Internet connection). You must also have a way to tell the computer which IP addresses are associated with the local network and which must go through the router. The upcoming section "Using a Static IP Address" describes this process.

IP Addresses, Hostnames, and Domains

TCP/IP relies upon two naming systems for its computers, as mentioned in the earlier section, "TCP/IP Features." The first naming system is the IP address, and this is the system upon which most TCP/IP features rely in the most fundamental way. The second naming system is that of the hostname, which is an alphanumeric name that's easy for people to remember—at least, compared to the numeric IP addresses.

> **Note** *The underlying network hardware uses a third type of address. This is called the* Media Access Control (MAC) *address, and for Ethernet, it's a 6-byte number that's assigned to each network card by the manufacturer. The TCP/IP stack includes routines to discover a MAC address when given a local IP address.*

Hostnames are broken down into a hierarchy of names, separated by dots, as in www.osborne.com. The most important distinction is between the *machine name*, which is the first portion of the hostname (www in this example) and the *domain name*, which is the rest of the name (osborne.com in this case). The hostname is linked to a computer—typically just one, although there are some exotic exceptions to this rule. The domain name is assigned to an organization or individual, which allocates machine names within the domain. A domain owner can also create *subdomains*, which are logically distinct sections of a (typically large) domain. For instance, a university might create subdomains for its departments, such as english.pangaea.edu and physics.pangaea.edu. The university could then assign machines within those subdomains, such as byron.english.pangaea.edu and curie.physics.pangaea.edu.

The rightmost portion of a hostname is the *top-level domain (TLD)*, which divides the Internet into sections based on geography or function. For instance, the popular com TLD is intended for commercial uses, whereas educational institutions use edu. Countries use two-letter TLDs, such as us for the United States and jp for Japan.

Hostnames and IP addresses are tied together via the *Domain Name System (DNS)*, which is a distributed database of IP addresses and hostnames. When you enter a hostname in an Internet client, the client calls upon the DNS system to do a translation. This translation occurs in a distributed manner, with your local DNS server querying a hierarchy of DNS servers, starting with those that know about TLDs and concluding with the DNS server that knows the address you typed. (If you make a typo, this process eventually returns a "not found" response.) As with your local router, your FreeBSD client or server must be configured to use a DNS server in order for this process to work. This DNS server might or might not be on your local network, though. If you fail to tell FreeBSD about a suitable DNS server, you can use network tools with IP addresses, but this practice is awkward at best, even for limited local use. Most web sites, e-mail addresses, and so on are specified as hostnames, so DNS is a practical necessity.

Using a Static IP Address

Because every computer requires an IP address to perform TCP/IP networking, you must give your FreeBSD system an IP address. Likewise, you must configure your system to use an appropriate router and DNS server. The conceptually simplest way to provide this information is by explicitly providing it yourself, as described in this section and its subsections. Another method involves using one local server to assign IP addresses to all other local computers. This method is described in the upcoming section, "Using DHCP." If you're attaching a computer to an existing network, find out which method your network uses. If you're creating a new small local network, using static IP addresses is usually simpler, at least at first, unless you're using a broadband router that also functions as a DHCP server.

Obtaining an IP Address

The first step to configuring a static IP address is to obtain one. In most cases, you must consult some outside authority for this data. If you're setting up a FreeBSD system on an existing network, consult your network administrator. If you're installing a system on a broadband connection, your ISP should provide you with the necessary information. If you're setting up a small isolated network, you can use an IP address in one of the ranges of reserved local addresses (192.168.0.0–192.168.255.255, 172.16.0.0–172.31.255.255, and 10.0.0.0–10.255.255.255.255). As a general rule, an IP address should not end in .0 or .255, although there are exceptions to this rule. The 192.168.0.1–192.168.0.254 range is a popular and safe one for private local networks.

In addition to the IP address itself, you need a netmask for your computer. Whoever provides you with an IP address should also give you a netmask. For private networks in the 192.168.*x.x* range, a netmask of 255.255.255.0 is typical. If you set the wrong netmask, some networking functions will work, but you may be unable to contact some computers because your system will think they're not routed when they are, or that they are routed when they aren't.

The router's IP address is another critical piece of information associated with the computer's IP address. (The router's address is sometimes called the *gateway* address.) You'll also need one or more IP addresses for DNS servers (many networks and ISPs provide two DNS server addresses). Once again, whoever provides you with your IP address should give you this information. If you're setting up an isolated local network, you'll have no router address, but if you link to the Internet using a broadband router, use its address. If you want to use DNS on a local network, you'll need to run a DNS server yourself. A simpler alternative in very small networks is to edit the /etc/hosts file on each system to provide the linkage between hostnames and IP addresses.

Configuring Using sysinstall

As with many FreeBSD features, you can configure a static IP address using sysinstall. To do so, follow these steps:

1. As root, type **/stand/sysinstall** to launch sysinstall.

2. Select Configure in the Main Menu.

3. Select Networking in the FreeBSD Configuration Menu.

4. Select Interfaces in the Network Services Menu. FreeBSD displays a menu in which you select the network interface you want to configure, as shown here.

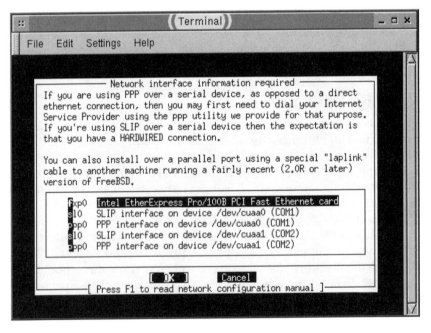

5. Select your network card from the list. Note that the list includes PPP and SLIP interfaces, which are used over serial ports or modems. Chances are your network card is the first item in the list, such as the Intel EtherExpress Pro in the preceding illustration.

6. FreeBSD asks if you want to configure IPv6 networking. Because IPv6 is still rare, it's not described here; select No.

7. The system asks if you want to use DHCP to configure the interface. Select this option only if your network uses DHCP; for static IP address configuration, select No.

8. Now sysinstall displays a form in which you can enter the critical information on your system, as shown in Figure 14-2. The most critical fields are IPv4 Address (your IP address), Netmask, IPv4 Gateway (your router's IP address), and Name Server (your DNS server's address). On small local networks, you might omit one or both of the last two of these, though. The Host field holds your hostname (you can enter just the machine name portion and sysinstall will expand it later), and the Domain field holds your domain name. FreeBSD will function with these fields set incorrectly, but with some Internet software you may encounter problems, such as incorrect return addresses on outgoing e-mail.

Note   *If your ISP or network administrator provides more than one DNS server address, enter either address in the Network Configuration form, or the "primary" address if one is so identified. The upcoming section, "Setting Up Hostname Resolution," describes how to enter additional DNS server addresses. Doing so isn't necessary, but it can improve DNS resolution reliability should one DNS server go down.*

9. The system asks if you want to bring up your interface immediately. You should probably respond Yes.

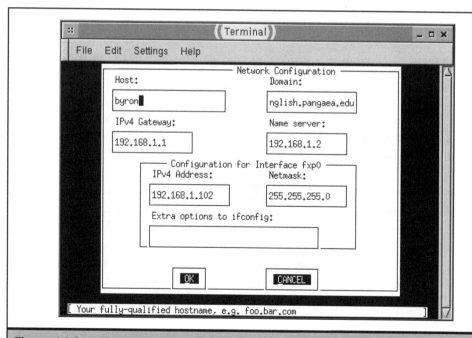

Figure 14-2.   *The Network Configuration form enables you to enter critical TCP/IP configuration options on one screen.*

NETWORK
CONFIGURATION

At this point, your network interface should function normally. To test it, consult the upcoming section, "Testing Your Configuration."

The process just described appends information to the /etc/rc.conf file. You can do this manually, as described in the upcoming section, "Making Your Changes Permanent." The sysinstall tool appends your entries to rc.conf without eliminating old entries, so this file contains a history of network configuration changes you've made. You can delete a new configuration to undo its changes.

Configuring Manually

Sometimes you may not want to use sysinstall. This is often the case if you want to perform some unusual configuration. A manual configuration also gives you greater debugging opportunities, should a sysinstall configuration prove unreliable. Manually configuring networking entails setting network features by using two main utilities and editing configuration files.

Activating an Interface

The first step in manually configuring a network connection is to activate the interface. You can accomplish this task with the ifconfig command, which has a very complex syntax, a simplified version of which is

```
ifconfig [interface] [up | down] [address[/prefixlength]] ⏎
[netmask netmask]]
```

Consult the ifconfig man page for more details. The options to this command are

- *interface* This option is the name of the network interface. Unfortunately, the name varies from one model of network card to another. You can probably learn your interface name by examining your dmesg output shortly after booting. Type **dmesg | less** and browse through this output until you find a line that identifies the Ethernet (or other network hardware) device, such as the following line, which identifies the device as fxp0:

  ```
  fxp0: Ethernet address 00:03:47:b1:ee:b8
  ```

- **up | down** Use up to bring up an interface, and down to take one down. Normally, ifconfig assumes the use of up, so you can probably omit this parameter entirely.

- *address[/prefixlength]* Specify your desired IP address with this option. You can also include the netmask in its number-of-bytes form (*prefixlength*).

■ **netmask** *netmask* If you prefer to specify the netmask in its full four-byte version, you can do so by preceding it with the `netmask` keyword. If you don't provide a netmask at all (through this or the *prefixlength* option), `ifconfig` computes a netmask based on the class of the IP address.

If you don't type any parameters to `ifconfig`, it displays summary information on all the network interfaces. If you provide only the network interface name, the summary is restricted to that interface. For instance:

```
$ ifconfig fxp0
fxp0: flags=8843<UP,BROADCAST,RUNNING,SIMPLEX,MULTICAST> mtu 1500
        inet 192.168.1.6 netmask 0xffffff00 broadcast 192.168.1.255
        ether 00:03:47:b1:ee:b8
        media: Ethernet autoselect (100baseTX)
        status: active
```

The most critical information presented here is the IP address (following `inet` in the second line of output). The mere presence of an IP address indicates that it is associated with the network hardware; the computer responds to traffic directed at that IP address, and sends traffic using that address.

At this point, you should be able to reach other computers on your local network by IP address. For instance, you should be able to use `ping` and get a reply from local systems, as described in the upcoming section, "Testing Your Configuration."

Configuring Routing

Two commands are important for configuring routing. First, `netstat` displays information on current network configurations. In particular, the `-r` option displays the routing table. (You may want to add the `-n` option to display addresses as IP addresses rather than hostnames, particularly if your hostname resolution isn't working.) For instance, you might type the following command to determine how your routing table is configured:

```
$ netstat -rn
Routing tables

Internet:
Destination    Gateway          Flags   Refs      Use   Netif Expire
default        192.168.1.1      UGSc       0       13    fxp0
127.0.0.1      127.0.0.1        UH         0       48    lo0
192.168.1      link#1           UC         2        0    fxp0
192.168.1.1    0:a0:cc:24:ba:2  UHLW       3       44    fxp0   1186
192.168.1.3    0:50:bf:19:7e:99 UHLW       2      719    fxp0    551
```

This command presents a great deal of information. Particularly important features are

- **Local systems** The final two lines in this example specify how to contact two systems that are on the same subnet as the FreeBSD system (192.168.1.1 and 192.168.1.3). These systems are identified by their 6-byte MAC addresses in the `Gateway` column. FreeBSD will eventually remove these entries (after the number of seconds specified in the `Expire` column), but can regenerate them quickly and automatically if they're needed again. Traffic to these addresses is directed over the `fxp0` network interface (specified in the `Netif` column).

- **Local network address** The line labeled `Link#1` in the `Gateway` column identifies the local network addresses. Traffic to those addresses is directed over the `fxp0` network interface. In practice, FreeBSD uses low-level TCP/IP protocols to discover the MAC address of the target system, then adds an entry for that system and uses it to send data to the new system. This type of route should be defined automatically when you use `ifconfig` to bring up an interface.

- **Localhost address** One feature of FreeBSD networking that's not been mentioned so far in this chapter is the *localhost* or *loopback* address—127.0.0.1. This is a special IP address that's reserved for the computer itself. Some low-level tools use it, and it's present in the routing table.

- **Default route** The *default route* directs traffic for which more specific routing table entries don't exist. The default route probably won't exist for a newly defined network interface, but in the preceding example, it's the line that begins `default`. In this case, the default route points to 192.168.1.1 as the router.

To add a default route, you use the `route` command. Like `ifconfig`, `route` supports many options, so consult its man page for details of its operations. Using it to add a route is fairly straightforward; you type a command like this:

```
# route add default 192.168.1.1
```

This command adds 192.168.1.1 as the default route for the computer. If you add an incorrect route, you can delete a route by using `delete` rather than `add` (if the route was not a default route, omit the `default` keyword and specify the identifier from the `Destination` column in the `netstat -rn` output).

At this point, you should be able to use `ping` or other network tools to reach both local and remote systems by IP address. Hostname resolution may not work, though; that's the subject of the upcoming section, "Setting Up Hostname Resolution."

Setting Your Hostname

You can set your computer's hostname with the `hostname` command. When typed without any parameters, this command returns your current hostname; but when you type a hostname after the command, it modifies your hostname. For instance, you might type the following command:

```
# hostname byron.english.pangaea.edu
```

Setting your hostname in this way isn't critical for most network operations, but it is important for a few. For instance, some mail readers use the hostname in outgoing e-mail, or a mail server may accept mail addressed only to users on the specified hostname.

Note *Setting your hostname locally does* not *make your system addressable by that name on the Internet at large. This function is the realm of the Internet's DNS servers. If you want your system to be reachable by a particular name, you must consult with the people who administer the DNS servers for the domain in which that name appears.*

Setting Up Hostname Resolution

Assuming you have access to a DNS server, hostname resolution involves editing a single configuration file: /etc/resolv.conf. This file is typically fairly short, and it should contain the IP addresses of one to three DNS servers. It may also contain the computer's domain name and perhaps a list of other domains that are to be searched. Both of these options enable users to enter short machine names rather than complete hostnames. Listing 14-1 shows a sample /etc/resolv.conf file.

Listing 14-1.
Sample /etc/
resolv.conf
File

```
domain english.pangaea.edu
search classics.pangaea.edu,pangaea.edu
nameserver 192.168.1.2
nameserver 10.40.91.4
```

A computer configured using Listing 14-1 will search for hosts first in the english .pangaea.edu domain, then in the classics.pangaea.edu and pangaea.edu domains, using the 192.168.1.2 and 10.40.91.4 DNS servers. You don't need to use a search line, and in fact entering many domains to search can slow down operations. For instance, suppose a user types **telnet shakspere**, misspelling the name of the computer named after the famous English poet. FreeBSD will query the DNS servers for shakspere.english.pangaea.edu, then for shakspere.classics.pangaea .edu, and finally for shakspere.pangaea.edu, before giving up. Each of these attempts will take some time, so it may be several seconds before the user receives an error message. Furthermore, if for some reason there's a computer called shakspere .pangaea.edu, the user will end up accessing it, probably to no good effect.

If your network is small or if there are some nonstandard mappings you want to maintain, you may want to edit the /etc/hosts file. This file provides an alternative to regular DNS lookups. This file is likely to contain one or two mappings to begin with, particularly one linking 127.0.0.1 to the localhost hostname. Additional mappings take the following form:

```
ip-address   full-hostname   nickname
```

The *nickname* is typically the machine name. For instance, you might include an entry like the following:

```
192.168.1.43  shakespeare.english.pangaea.edu shakespeare
```

This configuration enables your users to reach the named computer even if your DNS servers are unresponsive or if you haven't defined any. This can be an effective means of name resolution on a small network; you need not run your own DNS server if you edit your systems' /etc/hosts files appropriately.

After configuring name resolution (especially by listing DNS servers in the /etc/resolv.conf file), you should be able to perform all normal networking tasks, such as accessing both local and remote computers by both IP address and hostname.

Making Your Changes Permanent

The ifconfig and route commands' effects last only as long as the computer is booted. If you use these commands to configure your system's networking, rebooting the computer requires you to re-enter these commands. Because DNS configuration is done by editing a file, that change survives reboots.

In order to simplify configuration when you reboot, you can enter your configuration commands in a startup script, as described in Chapter 6. In fact, one startup script normally contains information on network configuration: /etc/rc.conf. This file might contain lines like the following:

```
ifconfig_fxp0="inet 192.168.1.102  netmask 255.255.255.0"
defaultrouter="192.168.1.1"
hostname="byron.english.pangaea.edu"
```

These lines aren't absolutely identical to the ifconfig, route, and hostname commands they control, but they contain the same critical information. In fact, this is the file that sysinstall modifies when you use it to configure networking. In normal operation, sysinstall appends entries to this file rather than overwriting existing entries. Later entries take precedence over earlier ones. You may want to follow the same practice, as it allows you to easily back out of a change by removing or commenting out the changed lines.

Using DHCP

Configuring a computer to use a static IP address isn't extraordinarily difficult, especially not if you use tools such as sysinstall to help do the job. Nonetheless, static IP address configuration has certain drawbacks. For instance, it's easy to enter incorrect information. From a network administrator's point of view, handing out IP addresses for every computer can easily become an administrative nightmare, particularly if the rate at which computers are added to and removed from a network is high. For these reasons, various methods of automatically assigning IP addresses have been developed. The most common of these on local networks is the *Dynamic Host Configuration Protocol (DHCP)*.

Note

Digital Subscriber Line (DSL) networks frequently use another method, PPP over Ethernet (PPPoE), to assign IP addresses. This method is closely related to PPP over ordinarily serial lines, and is described in Chapter 15.

Some DHCP configurations require that DHCP clients' MAC addresses be registered in the DHCP server database. If yours is such a network, your network administrator or ISP will ask you for this information. The MAC address (aka the Ethernet address) is a six-byte number that's generally expressed in hexadecimal. Sometimes it's printed on a sticker on the network card. If not, you can obtain it from the ifconfig command, as presented in the previous section, "Activating an Interface." You can also obtain this information from a line in dmesg output soon after booting. Specifically, the following command returns the MAC address:

```
$ dmesg | grep "Ethernet address"
fxp0: Ethernet address 00:03:47:b1:ee:b8
```

A DHCP server computer works by listening for special DHCP request packets on its local network segment. These packets are *broadcasts*, meaning that they're directed at all the computers on a network segment. The DHCP server responds to the DHCP broadcast by returning the client's TCP/IP configuration information, including its IP address, netmask, the gateway system, DNS servers, and perhaps the client's hostname and domain name. DHCP servers may assign a specific computer the same IP address time after time, or the server may assign an address that may change from time to time (typically between boots of the computer; unless the DHCP server's configuration changes or there's a problem, a client's IP address won't change without cause).

If you use sysinstall, configuring a system to use DHCP is similar to configuring the system to use a static IP address. In particular, consult the steps presented earlier, in "Configuring Using sysinstall," but in Step #7, respond Yes to the question about configuring using DHCP. The system will search for a DHCP server on your network and will then display the Network Configuration screen (Figure 14-2). You can leave all the fields blank if you like. If your DHCP server doesn't set your hostname, though, you may want to set this field and the domain name field. (On some networks, the hostname may be set to gibberish, so you may want to correct that detail.)

Using sysinstall configures FreeBSD to obtain an IP address using the dhclient program. This configuration is stored in /etc/rc.conf. Specifically, a DHCP configuration relies upon a line like the following:

```
ifconfig_fxp0="DHCP"
```

If you don't want to use `sysinstall` but do want to use a "plain vanilla" DHCP configuration, you should edit `/etc/rc.conf` so that it includes this line rather than an explicit IP address. When you reboot, your system should obtain its network configuration from your local DHCP server.

Testing Your Configuration

Whether you configure your system using a static IP address or DHCP, you should test your configuration. If you have problems, these tests can help you localize them, so that you can concentrate further diagnostic efforts on the faulty system.

Performing Basic ping Tests

The most basic type of test is a `ping` test, so called because it relies upon the `ping` utility. This program sends a very simple type of packet to the target system, which should respond with an equally simple packet. These transfers rely upon the basic TCP/IP stack, but they don't depend upon correct configuration of more advanced tools, such as web servers or clients. Thus, pinging a remote system is a good way to test your basic TCP/IP configuration and the physical network connections between yourself and the target system.

Despite the simplicity of the task that `ping` performs, the program's syntax is fairly complex. In most cases, though, you can use it by typing its name followed by a hostname or IP address. Your first tests should use the IP addresses of local computers, thus:

```
$ ping 192.168.1.3
PING 192.168.1.3 (192.168.1.3): 56 data bytes
64 bytes from 192.168.1.3: icmp_seq=0 ttl=255 time=0.335 ms
64 bytes from 192.168.1.3: icmp_seq=1 ttl=255 time=0.326 ms
64 bytes from 192.168.1.3: icmp_seq=2 ttl=255 time=0.318 ms
64 bytes from 192.168.1.3: icmp_seq=3 ttl=255 time=0.312 ms
^C
--- 192.168.1.3 ping statistics ---
4 packets transmitted, 4 packets received, 0% packet loss
round-trip min/avg/max/stddev = 0.312/0.323/0.335/0.009 ms
```

Unless you use the `-c count` option to specify the number of pings to send to the target, `ping` continues sending test packets until you press CTRL-C. As you can see from this example, `ping` reports on each packet it receives back from the target system, including the time it took to receive a response (known as the *ping time* or *latency*). At the end of its output, it reports the overall statistics, including the total number of packets sent and received and a summary of latencies. On a local network, you should have very little or no packet loss (occasionally you may interrupt a `ping` test after it's sent a packet but before it's received a reply, though, and a very busy network may experience some packet loss). Local latencies should be very low—typically one millisecond or less.

 Try using your local router as a target for your initial `ping` tests. The router is vital for reaching other networks, so it must *be reachable for optimal functionality. You should also have your router's IP address, either given to you for a static IP configuration or available by typing* **`netstat -nr`**.

If initial ping tests on the local network fail, you should scrutinize your most basic network settings—your IP address and netmask. Chances are one of these is set incorrectly. Type **`ifconfig`** to view your network configuration, as described earlier in "Activating an Interface." If your interface isn't active, review that section. If you're using DHCP, consult your log file (`/var/log/messages`) for errors from `dhclient`. For instance, you might see a message like this:

```
Apr  7 22:02:25 halrloprillalar dhclient: Can't bind to dhcp ↵
address: Address already in use
Apr  7 22:02:25 halrloprillalar dhclient: exiting.
```

The `Address already in use` message indicates that something else is using the network port that DHCP ordinarily occupies. You may see this problem if `dhclient` is already running when you attempt to reconfigure it. Killing `dhclient` and then typing **`dhclient`** should correct this problem.

 Some computers are configured not to respond to `ping` tests. Thus, it's possible that such a test will seem to fail when in fact there is no problem. If one local `ping` test fails, try another system.

Aside from local settings, another possible cause of `ping` test failures is hardware. Issues like bad network cables, unplugged hubs or switches, and so on can cause problems. Try swapping cables, and if possible, test another computer with a known working configuration plugged into the same network hardware used on the system that's not working in order to diagnose such problems.

Testing Hostname Resolution

If your basic `ping` tests work, you can try a more sophisticated use of `ping` to test your hostname resolution mechanisms: Specify a hostname rather than an IP address. If you have a local DHCP server or use `/etc/hosts` to define your local network's machines, this should work for local addresses as well as the use of an IP address with `ping`. In the earlier example of `ping` (in "Performing Basic `ping` Tests"), the first line of `ping`'s output lists the IP address twice. If you use a hostname, the first of these is replaced by the hostname, and the second is the IP address. If your hostname resolution methods don't work, you won't see this line; but if hostname resolution works but you can't reach the target system, you'll see that line and no further output.

 If your DNS server isn't on your local network, a DNS failure could in fact be a routing problem. Consult the next section, "Diagnosing Routing Problems," for further information.

You can also use this method to test resolution of remote hostnames, such as those on the Internet at large. If your DNS server is on your local network segment, it's possible that this name resolution will work even if you can't reach the remote site because your local routing configuration might be incorrect.

The `host` and `nslookup` commands also test name resolution, and in a more direct way than `ping`. These commands are designed expressly to return an IP address when given a hostname, or a hostname when given an IP address.

Diagnosing Routing Problems

You can use `ping` to test basic connectivity between you and a remote system. For instance, you might type the following:

```
$ ping www.osborne.com
PING www.osborne.com (198.45.24.130): 56 data bytes
64 bytes from 198.45.24.130: icmp_seq=0 ttl=238 time=131.518 ms
64 bytes from 198.45.24.130: icmp_seq=1 ttl=238 time=162.523 ms
64 bytes from 198.45.24.130: icmp_seq=2 ttl=238 time=130.061 ms
64 bytes from 198.45.24.130: icmp_seq=3 ttl=238 time=134.463 ms
^C
--- www.osborne.com ping statistics ---
4 packets transmitted, 4 packets received, 0% packet loss
round-trip min/avg/max/stddev = 130.061/139.641/162.523/13.306 ms
```

This test reveals substantially higher latencies than on the local network, but precisely how high depends on your network connection, the distance to the target site, and so on. This example also demonstrates the use of hostname resolution with `ping`, but it's possible for your DNS configuration to be bad but your routing to be good. In such a case, you can try entering the IP address of a remote system, if you know it.

If you can reach some external sites but not others, it's possible that your netmask is set incorrectly, so you should double-check that configuration. Another possibility is that some external router is down or misconfigured, or the problem might reside on the target system. You can help diagnose such problems using `traceroute`, which generates statistics on the path to every router between you and the target system. For instance, you might type the following command:

```
$ traceroute -n 68.1.0.44
traceroute to 68.1.0.44 (68.1.0.44), 64 hops max, 40 byte packets
```

```
1  192.168.1.1  1.299 ms  1.185 ms  1.165 ms
2  10.1.96.1   16.236 ms  46.519 ms  68.663 ms
3  68.9.8.81   41.946 ms  10.701 ms  47.766 ms
4  68.9.14.5   37.191 ms  14.907 ms  45.332 ms
5  68.1.0.44   36.135 ms  *  45.391 ms
```

The -n option causes `traceroute` to omit hostname lookups on the target systems, which can speed up the process. Each router is contacted three times using a packet similar to the packets generated by `ping`, and `traceroute` reports the latencies. In this example, the first router is a local one and generates very low latencies. The second router generates longer and quite variable latencies (16–69 ms), and subsequent routers generate mostly longer latencies, but they're also variable. The target site responded to only two of the three packets it was sent (the asterisk in place of the second time indicates a failure to respond), so any odd behavior reaching that site may be caused by the target system. Intervening routers may exhibit similar problems. For the most part, there's little you can do about such problems except complain to your ISP or to the owner of the afflicted computer.

*The `whois` utility can return information on the person or organization responsible for a computer. Type **whois ip-address**, where ip-address is the IP address in question, to obtain this information. (You can provide a domain name instead of an IP address, if you have this information.) You should get contact information, such as technical contact e-mail addresses or phone numbers.*

Testing More Advanced Protocols

If the preceding `ping` and `traceroute` tests turned up no problems, you should proceed to more advanced protocols. You can use a web browser to browse the Web, an FTP client to log into remote FTP sites, and so on. If basic `ping` tests pass, but more sophisticated protocols fail, the problem is most likely in the configuration of the more sophisticated tools. These issues are very specific to the tools in question, so you should consult their documentation or the relevant chapters of this book (in Part IV and Chapter 24, for the most part).

Summary

In today's world, network configurations are vitally important for most computers. This is particularly true of FreeBSD systems, which are frequently used as network servers or as workstations in heavily network-dependent environments. FreeBSD's `sysinstall` utility provides a fairly straightforward method of configuring a computer to use either a static IP address or an address assigned from a DHCP server. Once you've so configured your computer, a few basic tests, most of which use the `ping` utility, can tell you whether your configuration was correct.

Chapter 15

Dial-Up Networking

Chapter 14 describes configuring a FreeBSD system for a local network using Ethernet, Token Ring, or similar dedicated networking hardware. Not all computers use such connections, though; many small business and home users link to the Internet through a telephone modem, using the *Point-to-Point Protocol (PPP)*, which enables the use of TCP/IP over an RS-232 serial port or modem. Even a computer that resides on an isolated LAN may use a dial-up telephone connection for Internet access; and laptops may use dial-up access when away from their owners' networks. This chapter describes using such a connection with FreeBSD. It also examines a variant of PPP, known as *PPP over Ethernet (PPPoE)*, that's used by many broadband Internet providers, despite the fact that they use Ethernet hardware.

This chapter begins with a couple of mundane but important preliminary steps: Locating an *Internet Service Provider (ISP)* to link you to the Internet and testing your modem hardware. Once you've cleared these hurdles, you can proceed with configuring your connection. This chapter examines two ways to do this: via a GUI dialing utility and via dialing scripts used in conjunction with text-mode utilities. Each method has its advantages and disadvantages. The chapter concludes with a look at PPPoE configuration and use.

Locating an ISP

Open your telephone book to "Internet Providers" and you're likely to find several listings, and probably several *pages* of listings in a large city. If you have Internet access through some alternative source, you can check `http://www.thelist.com` for listings sorted by various criteria. The problem with locating an ISP for use with FreeBSD, therefore, isn't one of a scarcity of choices; it's with knowing which choices work best with FreeBSD. Most ISPs cater first to Microsoft Windows users and second to Mac OS users. Many don't look beyond these two markets, so you may find yourself without support should you run into problems. That said, most ISPs' products can be made to work with FreeBSD. There are a few exceptions, though. Most importantly, any ISP that relies upon heavily customized tools to establish a basic connection, such as the popular America Online (AOL), adds complexity, and so is best avoided.

If possible, ask a potential ISP about their FreeBSD support policies, or at least find out if they have FreeBSD users. As a general rule, you're more likely to find good FreeBSD support from small local ISPs than from huge international companies.

If you already have Internet access through an ISP, or through your employer or school, you can certainly try using it with FreeBSD, and odds are you can get it to work. You might want to use your current connection under another OS to try to locate your ISP's support area; you might be able to find some FreeBSD support notes. Linux support notes may also be valuable, although FreeBSD and Linux do vary in a few details of PPP configuration.

Testing Your Modem Hardware

Before proceeding further, you should test your modem's functionality under FreeBSD. Today's modems fall into three broad classes, each with different requirements under FreeBSD:

- **RS-232 serial modems**   These modems attach to a computer's external RS-232 serial port, or come as plug-in ISA or PCI cards that include serial port hardware on-board. RS-232 serial modems almost always work with FreeBSD, although you may need to reconfigure an internal modem's interrupt request (IRQ) line or disable a motherboard's RS-232 port to get the modem to work. These devices can be accessed as /dev/cuaa0 through /dev/cuaa3.

- **Internal controllerless modems**   Most internal modems sold today are *controllerless*, meaning that they lack much of the hardware traditionally associated with a modem, relying instead upon special drivers. These modems are also sometimes called *soft modems* or *WinModems*. Controllerless modems usually don't work at all with FreeBSD. Drivers for some controllerless modems (particularly the popular Lucent-based modems) exist, but are hard to find— at the time of this writing, the comms/ltmdm port exists, but the files to which it points don't exist. This problem may be remedied by the time you read this.

- **USB modems**   Increasingly, external modems use the Universal Serial Bus (USB) interface rather than the RS-232 interface. Work is underway to support some of these (particularly those built around the Communications Data Class Abstract Control Model, or CDC-ACM, protocol), but it's still primitive, as of FreeBSD 5.0.

As you might gather from the preceding list, your best bet for a modem is an RS-232 serial modem. This usually means an external RS-232 serial model, although older (mid-to-late 1990s and earlier) internal modems also work quite well.

To test your modem, connect it, power it on, and use a terminal program such as the text-based minicom or the X-based Seyon to test basic modem functionality. (Both of these programs can be installed as packages or ports, as described in Chapter 11.) You can launch Seyon by typing **seyon -modem /dev/cuaa0** (substitute your modem device filename, if it's not /dev/cuaa0). You can then type **ATI** or variants of that followed by numbers to obtain status information from the modem, or **ATDT###-####** to dial a number (replace ###-#### with the telephone number you want to dial). Your modem's manual should list other commands you can type, and their effects. Figure 15-1 shows Seyon running, with a successful connection to a modem displayed.

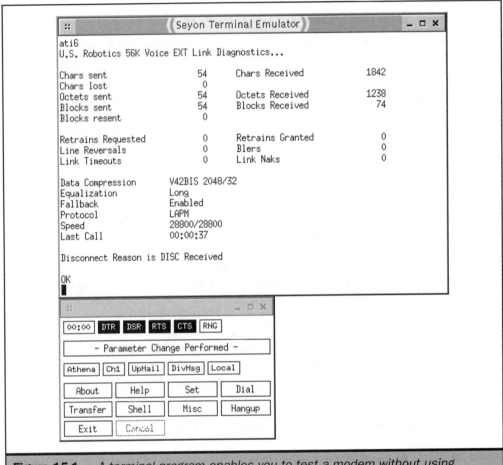

Figure 15-1. A terminal program enables you to test a modem without using PPP tools.

Using a GUI Dialer

If you're new to FreeBSD, the easiest way to initiate a PPP connection is to use a GUI dialing utility. These tools operate much like similar tools in other OSs, such as Windows or Mac OS. You enter critical information, such as your ISP's telephone number, in dialog boxes, and then click a button to initiate a connection. You can usually configure these tools so that ordinary users can initiate connections, so they're good for use on workstations. They can't be controlled through an external script, though, so they aren't so good if you want your system to automatically go online at particular times (say, to exchange e-mail once an hour). For that, a dialing script is superior, as described in the upcoming section, "Using Text-Mode Dialing Tools."

Locating a GUI Dialer

The first hurdle you must overcome in configuring a GUI dialer is in locating one. A wide variety of such dialers are available for FreeBSD. If you've installed KDE, you may have already installed one dialer, called KPPP. The GNOME project provides a similar dialer, GNOME-PPP, but it's not installed in a standard FreeBSD GNOME system, and as of this writing, it's not available in the ports system. For this reason, I describe the X-ISP dialer (http://xisp.hellug.gr). This is a GUI dialer that works from any GUI environment, and is available from the FreeBSD packages system and as a port (consult Chapter 11 for information on installing software).

If you locate and use some other GUI dialer, the details described here won't apply, but the overall needs of the software will be very similar. Consult your GUI dialer's documentation, or just browse its menus and dialog boxes, to learn about its differences from X-ISP.

Creating an ISP Configuration

Configuring X-ISP to connect to an ISP entails two different types of configuration. First, you must create a *secrets* file, which stores your ISP username and password on disk; and second, you must tell X-ISP about your ISP's telephone number, your connect speed, and so on.

 Some GUI dialers enable you to configure your secrets from within the GUI dialer itself, by entering a password in an obvious password field. X-ISP relies upon manual configuration of this critical file, though.

Creating a Secrets File

FreeBSD (or more precisely, the pppd program that's responsible for establishing a PPP link) stores critical authentication information in a file that's called /etc/ppp/pap-secrets. This file stores usernames and passwords for the Password Authentication Protocol (PAP), which most ISPs use in 2002. Another protocol, called the Challenge Handshake Authentication Protocol (CHAP) is still in use by some ISPs, and if your ISP uses CHAP, you should create an /etc/ppp/chap-secrets file, which has precisely the same format and contents as pap-secrets.

 In the past, ISPs frequently used login procedures that required you to create a script that would echo your username and password in response to text-mode prompts. Such configurations are rare today, but you can still configure X-ISP to use this method. If your ISP uses such an antiquated login method, you don't need to create a secrets file.

The secrets file consists of lines that have the following format:

```
client-name   server-name   password   [ip-address[...]]
```

In this context, the *client-name* is usually your username, as issued by the ISP. (This might not be the same as your FreeBSD username.) The *server-name* is the ISP's dial-in server name. Because this name is often unknown, it's common to use an asterisk (*) in this field, to signify that any value is acceptable. The *password* is the password you use to log into the ISP; it's not the same as your FreeBSD login password. Finally, you may conclude a secrets file line with a list of IP addresses you're willing to accept from the ISP. Normally, this final field is missing because most ISPs assign IP addresses dynamically.

Caution *The password you enter in the secrets file is unencrypted. You should ensure that the secrets file is readable only by `root` (it should be owned by `root` and have 0600 permissions), to prevent ordinary users or intruders from reading your ISP password. You should use your ISP password only for logging into the ISP, not for logging into any other computer, including your FreeBSD system. These steps can minimize the risk posed by storing a password in unencrypted form on your hard disk.*

You can create multiple secrets file entries for multiple users or ISPs. When you do this, you'll use GUI dialer or dialing script options to pick which username to use. For instance, the following entries enable a user to log into systems using the agb and alex usernames, each with its own password:

```
agb    *   w8tS4nr6
alex   *   b311gm7
```

Configuring X-ISP

X-ISP, as installed from a FreeBSD package or port, may only be run by `root` or by a member of the `dialer` group. You can use this feature to control who can configure and use X-ISP—add any authorized PPP users to the `dialer` group, as described in Chapter 10, and leave others out of this group.

Once you have created a secrets file, you can launch X-ISP by typing **xisp** in an xterm window. The result is the main X-ISP window, as shown in Figure 15-2. To begin configuring X-ISP to handle your PPP connection, follow these steps:

1. Select Options | Account Information. This action produces the Account Information dialog box shown next:

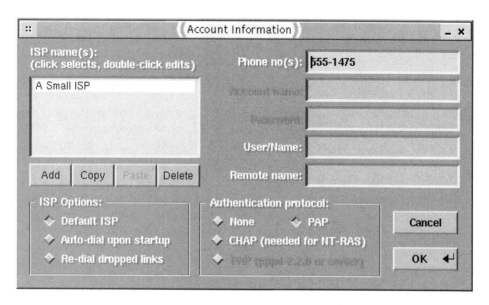

2. Click Add in the Account Information dialog box. X-ISP responds by displaying a small dialog box with the prompt Enter ISP Description.

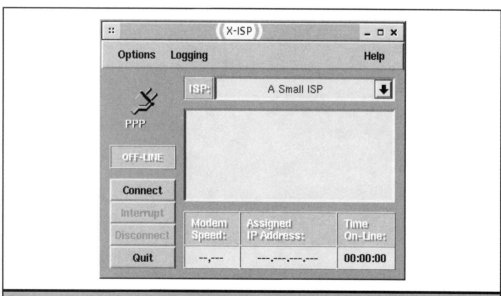

Figure 15-2. *The main X-ISP window lets you control a connection, and you can use dialog boxes from the Options menu item to configure the program.*

3. Type your ISP's name or some other identifying information. This text will later appear as an option in the ISP selection box in the main X-ISP window, such as A Small ISP in Figure 15-2. Click OK when you've entered this information. You should see the new ISP appear in the ISP Name(s) field in the Account Information dialog box.

4. Type the ISP's telephone number into the Phone No(s) field in the Account Information dialog box. Do not include an area code unless you need to dial it to reach your ISP, but do include any codes you need to dial to get an outside line, if applicable. You can use a comma between digits to impose a delay, if you need such a delay at any point in the dialing process.

5. Click PAP or CHAP, if applicable, to use one of these authentication protocols. If you leave None selected in the Authentication Protocol area, you'll need to define a dialing script. Because this need is so rare today, I don't describe it.

6. Type your username in the User/Name and Remote Name fields. Depending upon your ISP's configuration, you may need to enter this information in only one of these fields or in both of them.

7. Click OK in the Account Information dialog box.

8. Select Options | Communications Options from the main X-ISP window (Figure 15-2). This action produces the Communications Options dialog box shown here:

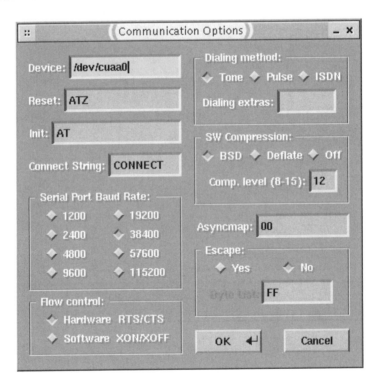

9. You can adjust various serial port options in the Communications Options dialog box. Pay particular attention to the Device field, which should point to your modem device file. This is normally `/dev/cuaa0` or `/dev/cuaa1` for an RS-232 serial modem, but higher numbers are possible if you have more than two serial ports, and if you use an unusual device, it may be something else entirely. The Serial Port Baud Rate section sets the modem speed. Normally, 115200 works best, but the default is 38400, which produces slower-than-optimal speeds.

10. Select Options | TCP/IP Options from the main X-ISP window (Figure 15-2). This action produces the TCP/IP Options dialog box shown here:

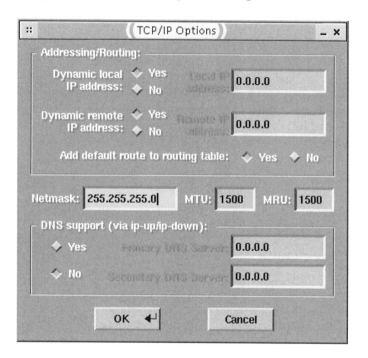

11. The TCP/IP Options dialog box lets you set various options related to TCP/IP configuration. Chapter 14 describes most of these options. You should leave most of them alone, but one possible exception is the DNS Support area. You may need to obtain the IP addresses of one or two DNS servers from your ISP, select Yes to the DNS Support option, and enter the IP addresses in the Primary DNS Server and Secondary DNS Server fields. Your system might obtain its DNS server addresses automatically as part of the PPP configuration process, but this exchange doesn't always go smoothly, so overriding it in this way is sometimes necessary.

X-ISP is now configured to make a PPP connection—at least in theory. Your connection may require tweaking, so you may need to dig into the configuration dialog boxes, including dialog boxes not described here, to tweak settings. Doing this can be a tedious and frustrating process because error messages tend to be cryptic.

X-ISP relies upon pppd *to make the PPP connection, and* pppd *logs information to* /var/ log/messages *as it operates. Thus, if a connection fails, you should check* /var/log/ messages *for clues by typing* **tail -n 20 /var/log/messages**.

Initiating a Connection

Once you've configured X-ISP and created a secrets file for it, you can select your ISP and click Connect in the main window (Figure 15-2). You should then hear your modem dial (if it's set to echo these sounds through its speaker), and you should see some basic progress information appear in the display just below the ISP selection field in the main window. The Modem Speed field will then display your connection speed, and very shortly thereafter, you should be able to use the connection.

To check that your connection is active, you can use any TCP/IP programs, such as ping, as described in Chapter 14. You should be able to use web browsers, e-mail clients, and so on. Some of these may require reconfiguring to use your ISP's servers. Consult Chapter 24 and your ISP's documentation for more information. You can also use ifconfig to check for the presence of a ppp0 interface, thus:

```
# ifconfig ppp0
ppp0: flags=8051<UP,POINTOPOINT,RUNNING,MULTICAST> mtu 1500
        inet 192.168.1.205 --> 192.168.1.2 netmask 0xffffff00
```

If this command doesn't return the final line (which displays the local IP address and that of the computer to which it connects), then something is wrong, or perhaps you've tried it before the computers have negotiated a stable connection.

When you're done using the connection, click Disconnect in the main X-ISP window. You should see PPP Link is Down displayed; and you may hear your modem *click* as it goes off-line and see its lights change, if it's an external model.

Remember to disconnect when you're done using your PPP connection. If you don't, and if your ISP doesn't have an auto-disconnect feature and you pay per-minute connection charges, you may see a huge bill because of a careless failure to disconnect!

Using Text-Mode Dialing Tools

GUI PPP dialers are convenient for individual users, but they aren't always the best method of making a connection. You may want to use text-based Internet tools without running X at all, or you may want to run cron jobs that bring up a connection and perform some automated task, such as retrieving e-mail. You can use the pppd program upon which X-ISP relies more directly to accomplish these goals. To use pppd, your kernel must include PPP support (as it does by default).

 There's a user-mode PPP tool, in addition to the kernel-mode tool described here. The user-mode tool is called ppp, and it's configured using the /etc/ppp/ppp.conf file. The user-mode PPP tool is described in the upcoming section, "Configuring PPPoE," with reference to PPPoE configuration, although its use isn't restricted to PPPoE.

Editing Support Files

Before you begin configuring either kernel- or user-mode PPP, you should see to the status of certain support files. One of these is the secrets file (pap-secrets or chap-secrets, depending upon whether your ISP uses PAP or CHAP). This file is described in the earlier section, "Creating a Secrets File." It's configured the same way for a dialing script as for a GUI dialing tool.

Another important support file is the /etc/resolv.conf file, which lists your ISP's DNS servers. This file is described in the "Setting Up Hostname Resolution" section of Chapter 14, so read it for more information. Some ISPs configure their dial-in systems to give you this information automatically, but this process often doesn't work correctly, so you may need to configure it manually. Ask your ISP for the IP addresses of its DNS servers, if they don't provide you with this information initially.

Configuring Kernel PPP

Kernel PPP configuration requires editing or creating at least two files: a PPP options file and a *chat script*. The latter is a series of strings sent by pppd to the modem and the expected responses from the modem. The chat script enables pppd to dial the modem and, if necessary, issue commands to log into your ISP. Normally, you must also configure a pap-secrets or chap-secrets file, as described earlier, in "Creating a Secrets File." Once you've created the necessary configuration files, you can call pppd with the options required to call your ISP.

Editing /etc/ppp/options

The /etc/ppp/options file controls most pppd options, aside from the secrets used for PAP and CHAP authentication. (It's also possible to pass options as parameters in the call to pppd.) Listing 15-1 shows a typical options file.

Listing 15-1
Sample
/etc/ppp/
options File

```
/dev/cuaa0 115200
crtscts
modem
noipdefault
silent
defaultroute
```

```
user agb
connect "/usr/bin/chat -f /etc/ppp/chat-script"
```

The meanings of the lines in this file, and a few other options you might want to use, are as follows:

- **/dev/cuaa0 *speed*** You must tell pppd which device file to use to initiate a connection. This is normally /dev/cuaa0 or /dev/cuaa1 for one of the first two RS-232 serial ports. You can also set the port speed. For modern 56 Kbps modems, 115200 works well.

- **crtscts** This option configures the system to use *hardware flow control*, which uses lines in the RS-232 serial cable to signal when each side is ready to receive data. This option is normally required to obtain reliable operation from high-speed modems.

- **modem** You can use pppd to initiate a PPP connection with another computer without use of a modem, or to use a modem as an intermediary device. When used in the latter way, you must use the modem option, which tells pppd to wait for a carrier detect signal and to perform other modem-specific operations.

- **noipdefault** Most configurations require this option, which tells pppd to accept the IP address assigned to it by the remote system.

- **silent** This option relates to a detail of PPP negotiation—which side first sends a *Link Control Protocol (LCP)* packet. The silent option is usually required for dial-in operation; it tells pppd that the other system should be the first to send an LCP packet. Some ISPs, though, require callers to send the first LCP, so you must *remove* this option on some systems.

- **defaultroute** This option tells pppd to create a routing table entry to use the ISP as the default route. (Routing basics, including the default route, are described in Chapter 14.) This option is required on most dial-in PPP connections.

- **user *name*** This option specifies the name of the user, as specified in the *client-name* field of the pap-secrets or chap-secrets file, for PAP or CHAP authentication.

- **connect *script*** This option provides a command, enclosed in quotes, that's to be run to begin the connection. Normally, this option points to a program or script that dials the modem and, if necessary, logs into the ISP's system and launches the remote PPP command. The script shown in Listing 15-1 should work on most systems, but requires you to create a chat script, as described in the next section. You can create a more elaborate startup script that in turn calls chat, if you like. Such a script might retrieve e-mail or launch network utilities you want to run whenever a link is active.

- **disconnect *script*** This option works much like the `connect` option, but it specifies a command or script to be run upon termination of the link. You might use this option to terminate programs you start in a connection script that's more elaborate than the one shown in Listing 15-1.

- **connect-max-attempts *n*** You can tell `pppd` to attempt to make a connection some specified number of times (*n*). This option can be useful if your ISP's dial-in lines are frequently busy.

- **debug** This option is useful if you're having problems; it causes more verbose logging of `pppd` activities to `/var/log/messages`.

- **demand** This option creates a dial-on-demand link, in which `pppd` initiates a connection when it detects outgoing network traffic.

- **idle *n*** This option tells `pppd` to disconnect a link if it's idle for *n* seconds or more. This feature can be a useful precaution against accidentally leaving a link active for too long, and it's a practical necessity for use with the `demand` option.

The `pppd` program accepts many additional options; consult the `pppd` man page for more details. In most cases, a configuration file similar to that shown in Listing 15-1 will work well.

Creating a Chat Script

The chat script, referred to as `/etc/ppp/chat-script` in Listing 15-1, controls the initial connection attempt. In most cases, this script resets the modem, dials it, and waits for a modem connection (which is distinct from the PPP connection that relies upon the underlying modem connection). Listing 15-2 shows a typical chat script. This script is parsed by the `/usr/bin/chat` program referenced in Listing 15-1. It consists of both option settings specific to `chat` and a series of *expect-send strings*—strings that `chat` is to look for in its input from the modem and strings that it's to send in response. Nominally, `chat` takes all its options as a single line of input. To make it easier for humans to parse the input, though, it's common to use the backslash (\) line continuation character to break the input into columns. In Listing 15-2, for instance, the first column consists of the expected input and the second column contains the text to send in reply.

Listing 15-2
Sample
`/etc/ppp/`
`chat-`
`script` File

```
TIMEOUT   30 \
ABORT     BUSY \
ABORT     'NO CARRIER' \
' '       ATZ \
OK        ATDT555-1475 \
CONNECT   ' '
```

At the time of writing, a bug in chat *prevents it from correctly interpreting lines broken with backslash characters. Thus, Listing 15-2 won't work unless it's edited to occupy one physical line. With any luck, this bug will be fixed by the time you read this, though.*

The first three lines of Listing 15-2 provide chat options (TIMEOUT and ABORT) to tell chat when to terminate operations. Specifically, chat waits for up to 30 seconds for each command to complete; and if chat receives a reply of BUSY or NO CARRIER, it stops operation because the modem has failed to make a connection. You may want to add new ABORT lines if your modem returns other strings as error conditions.

The final three lines of Listing 15-2 control the modem dialing. The first of these three lines sends ATZ in response to any input. The result is that chat sends the ATZ command, which resets most modems to their defaults, as soon as it starts operation. The next line sends a carriage return and ATDT555-1475 in response to the OK prompt, which most modems generate after the ATZ command. The final line (which is the only one that lacks a trailing backslash) waits for a CONNECT string, and sends nothing in response to it. At this point, the chat script terminates, leaving pppd to begin the connection.

The chat *program normally sends a carriage return after each string. If you need to force it to send an extra carriage return, you can do so by including the string* \r *in the string* chat *sends.*

If your ISP doesn't use PAP or CHAP, you may need to extend Listing 15-2 to look for your ISP's login prompt. For instance, you might add a backslash to the end of the final line in Listing 15-2 and add lines such as these:

```
ogin:      agb \
ssword:    w8tS4nr6 \
rompt:     start-ppp
```

These lines tell chat how to log onto an ISP that presents login: and password: prompts. The system then sends start-ppp in response to a prompt that reads prompt:. Of course, precisely what username, password, and PPP startup command you need varies from one ISP and account to another. The first character or two is missing from each of these expect strings because they're sometimes lost or change in case.

Of course, you must customize your chat script for your own modem and ISP. In fact, this is the trickiest part of pppd configuration. You may want to use a terminal program such as minicom or Seyon to capture a session dialing your ISP to learn what you must include in this script.

Using Your Configuration

Once you've configured all your files, initiating a connection is relatively straightforward: Type **pppd**. The pppd program is owned and executable by root and the dialer group, so you must be root or a member of the dialer group to use the command. Once the link is established, you should see the ppp0 device and information on it in the output of ifconfig:

```
# ifconfig ppp0
ppp0: flags=8051<UP,POINTOPOINT,RUNNING,MULTICAST> mtu 1500
        inet 192.168.1.205 --> 192.168.1.2 netmask 0xffffff00
```

If the second line of output (listing two IP addresses—your local address and that of your ISP's PPP server) doesn't appear, then the link wasn't established. Wait a few seconds and try again; sometimes pppd takes a while to finish its job. If it doesn't come up after a minute or so, you should consult the /var/log/messages file for clues to what went wrong. If necessary, you can enable the debug option in the /etc/ppp/options file to increase the verbosity of pppd's logging.

Once the link is up, you can use normal FreeBSD TCP/IP tools with it, ranging from ping to complex programs such as Mozilla. The "Testing Your Configuration" section of Chapter 14 can be useful in testing your connection. When you're finished using a connection, kill the pppd program to terminate the link:

```
# killall pppd
```

If you initiate multiple PPP sessions, you must determine the process ID (PID) number of the one you want to kill, and use the kill command to terminate that link alone.

Using PPPoE with DSL

One PPP variant is becoming increasingly important, and is configured in a different way than conventional dial-up PPP: PPPoE. This section introduces PPPoE, so you can configure your FreeBSD system to use PPPoE if your broadband ISP uses this protocol.

An alternative to using PPPoE on FreeBSD is to purchase a broadband router, which is a low-end router that "talks" PPPoE to your ISP and uses conventional raw TCP/IP to talk to your local systems. You can then configure FreeBSD as described in Chapter 14. Consult http://www.practicallynetworked.com/reviews/ for reviews of several broadband routers.

What Is PPPoE?

PPPoE is a way for broadband ISPs to assign IP addresses to customers' computers. In 2002, its use is restricted largely to low-end residential Digital Subscriber Line (DSL) accounts, although some business DSL accounts also use PPPoE. Cable modem ISPs generally use DHCP for IP address assignment, and high-end DSL accounts typically use static IP address assignment. PPPoE is a way to use Ethernet as a medium for PPP encapsulation, rather than the more common RS-232 serial line.

Why use PPPoE, though? After all, TCP/IP has been working directly on Ethernet for a long time, so PPPoE complicates matters by adding an extra layer to the Internet connection. The short answer is that PPPoE makes life easier for ISPs, by providing tools that help them manage IP addresses and monitor account usage. PPPoE offers few benefits to subscribers; however, you may have no choice but to use it with some ISPs.

PPPoE Packages for FreeBSD

Two common approaches to using PPPoE with FreeBSD are

- **User-mode PPP**   The same tool that provides user-mode PPP support over RS-232 serial ports also supports PPPoE. (This program is not the same as the kernel PPP daemon described in the earlier section, "Configuring Kernel PPP.")

- **Roaring Penguin**   The Roaring Penguin package (`http://www.roaringpenguin.com/pppoe/`) provides an alternative that originated in the Linux world, but is available through the FreeBSD ports system. Roaring Penguin has the advantage of offering a GUI interface.

The next section, "Configuring PPPoE," describes the standard FreeBSD user-mode PPP tool as applied to PPPoE.

Configuring PPPoE

The main feature you need to adjust to get PPPoE working is the `/etc/ppp/ppp.conf` file. Listing 15-3 shows a typical `ppp.conf` file configured for PPPoE.

Listing 15-3.
Sample
`/etc/ppp/`
`ppp.conf`
File for Use
with PPPoE

```
default:
        set log Phase tun command
        set ifaddr 10.0.0.1/0 10.0.0.2/0

broadband_isp_name:
        set device PPPoE:fxp0
        set authname agb
        set authkey w8tS4nr6
```

```
set dial
set login
add default HISADDR
```

Several of the options in Listing 15-3 require explanation or customization:

- **broadband_isp_name**   This line contains the name of your configuration. It's common to name it after your ISP. If you want to use ppp to initiate both broadband and conventional telephone modem PPP connections, you can create another section for the conventional telephone modem connection. (The default ppp.conf file includes such a section, called papchap.)

- **set device PPPoE:fxp0**   This option tells ppp that you'll be using PPPoE, and identifies your Ethernet device. Change fxp0 to whatever's appropriate for your network hardware. (Type **ifconfig** to see a list of your network devices. Chapter 14 describes identifying your Ethernet device in more detail.) Some ISPs require the use of a *service tag*, which is a name that identifies a particular PPPoE server. If your ISP has given you one, include it after the Ethernet device name and a colon, as in set device PPPoE:*fxp0:service_tag*.

- **Username and password**   The set authname and set authkey lines set your username and password, as assigned by your ISP. They're set to agb and w8tS4nr6, respectively, in Listing 15-3.

- **Default route**   The add default HISADDR line tells ppp to add a default route for the connection. If by some chance the PPPoE connection is a secondary link, you may want to omit this line, but for most configurations, you should leave it.

Using PPPoE

Once PPPoE is configured, you can use it by typing the command:

```
# ppp -ddial broadband_isp_name
```

Naturally, you must change *broadband_isp_name* as appropriate. At this point, ppp "dials" your ISP. The system initiates a PPPoE discovery and connection process to link up to your ISP's PPPoE server. If all goes well, you'll then be able to use your PPPoE connection as you would any other Internet connection. You can do basic tests with ping, use mail clients, and so on. As with a pppd-based serial-line PPP connection, you terminate a PPPoE connection by killing the process that initiated it:

```
# killall ppp
```

If you want FreeBSD to bring up the PPPoE interface whenever it boots, you should add the following lines to /etc/rc.conf:

```
ppp_enable="YES"
    ppp_mode="ddial"
    ppp_nat="NO"
    ppp_profile="broadband_isp_name"
```

Once again, replace *broadband_isp_name* with whatever you called the configuration in your /etc/ppp/ppp.conf file. Also, if you want your FreeBSD system to function as a router that implements *Network Address Translation (NAT)* for other systems on your network, change ppp_nat="NO" to ppp_nat="YES". A NAT router enables many computers to share a single external IP address—the broadband routers mentioned earlier, in "Using PPPoE with DSL," implement NAT. (Chapter 17 describes NAT routing in more detail.)

Summary

Most computers today are networked. FreeBSD systems are frequently linked to the Internet via permanent network connections, as described in Chapter 14; however, dial-up telephone links remain important for many individuals and small businesses. These connections are usually implemented using a protocol known as PPP, and FreeBSD supports PPP. Dial-up links can be initiated through GUI tools such as X-ISP or through text-mode programs such as pppd. One variant of PPP that's growing in importance is PPPoE, which works over Ethernet rather than over RS-232 serial or modem lines. Many low-end DSL providers use PPPoE. You can configure FreeBSD to support PPPoE using the ppp tool or the Roaring Penguin PPPoE client.

The
Complete
Reference

Chapter 16

Principles of Network
Clients and Servers

A
s described briefly in Chapter 14, TCP/IP network operations rely upon the assignment of each program that engages in a network operation into one of two categories: client or server. Clients initiate network operations, and servers respond to requests from clients. This chapter is dedicated to elaborating on this distinction, and to several related networking features, such as port numbers. To help further this understanding, this chapter presents an example of a typical network transaction. It also covers the important topic of how you can run a network server on a FreeBSD system. Finally, this chapter concludes with a brief look at some network diagnostic tools. All of these topics can help you fine-tune your network configuration, particularly if your FreeBSD system runs server programs.

Understanding the Roles of Clients and Servers

In any network transaction, just as in any human conversation, one party must "talk" first. In networking, that party is the client. The client requests a data transfer with the server. Typically, both the client and server transfer many data packets in the subsequent exchange, or even in the prelude to the main transfer, such as in authentication procedures, preliminaries required to establish a secure encrypted connection, and so on. Frequently, the main transfer is of a file, such as a file transferred via FTP or a web page. Even e-mail messages are stored as files on the client or server. Sometimes, the main transfer isn't a complete file. For instance, DNS lookups involve the transfer of just a few pieces of information from much larger files; and remote login sessions transfer information that the user types and programs' output.

The bulk of the data transfer may go in either direction. For instance, in a typical web browser session, the browser (the client) requests that the server send files, so most data travels from the server to the client. This isn't always the case, though; for instance, an FTP user can upload files from the client to the server, and in a Simple Mail Transfer Protocol (SMTP) mail session, the mail is sent from the client to the server.

Both the terms *client* and *server* may apply to either individual programs or to the computers that run those programs. It's usually clear from context which meaning is intended. In this book, I elaborate by using a phrase such as "the server computer" when this might not be the case and the distinction is important. The terms are often clearest in the sense of server programs because an individual computer can run both client and server programs. For instance, a computer might run a Telnet server to enable people to use it remotely, and this same system might also host mail client programs. Such a computer functions as both a client and a server. Indeed, a few programs can assume both roles. For instance, SMTP mail servers often relay mail to other mail servers. Such a program acts as a server when it receives mail, but takes on the client role when it sends the mail to another system. Such programs are generally referred to as servers, despite their dual roles.

Many people think of servers as mysterious and powerful computers that reside in locked rooms, and clients as computers at which individuals sit. This conception is usually not far wrong, but it's not part of the definition of clients and servers, which relates to which side initiates the data transfer. There's one important case where the common conception of servers can lead to confusion: *X servers*. These programs provide the GUI underpinnings for FreeBSD and most other UNIX-like OSs, and they're described in more detail in Chapter 13. An X server, like other servers, responds to data transfer requests from client programs. The X server specializes in human input and output data, though—keyboard and mouse input, windows displayed on the screen, and so on. Thus, the X server runs on the computer that hosts these input and output devices, and the client runs on a computer that could be in another room, or even across the globe, from the user.

Understanding Ports and Their Uses

Suppose you want to design a network stack. You want to arrange matters so that you can run several clients or servers on a single computer. In order to accomplish this goal, you need a way for a client to address a specific server program, and for the server to respond to the client that contacted it. You don't want mail data to be sent to a web server, for instance. Indeed, you don't want mail data from one client to become intermixed with mail data from another client. Keeping these issues straight is the job of TCP/IP *ports*, which are numbers that are linked to specific programs. Ports combine with IP addresses to create a unique identifier of each end-point in the network connection.

 Don't confuse TCP/IP port numbers with the FreeBSD ports system. The latter is a collection of software that's available for easy installation on a FreeBSD system, as described in Chapter 11.

The Role of Port Numbers

Whenever a network-enabled program accesses the TCP/IP stack, it does so by requesting allocation of a port. TCP/IP numbers these ports from 0 to 65,535 (although port 0 isn't of much use), so there are plenty of ports available for programs to use. Some of these ports are allocated to specific server purposes, as described in the next section, "Standard Port Number Assignments." Others are available for use by any program that asks for a port. Programs can request access to a specific port or can have the OS assign whatever port is most convenient. Typically, servers request specific ports, and clients allow the OS to assign a port. Servers run on specific ports so that clients on other computers can reach them, as described in "Standard Port Number Assignments." Clients don't rely on having specific port numbers; they send their port numbers to the servers they contact, and the servers use this information in addressing return packets.

 A TCP/IP port number is distinct from a network hardware port, such as the jack into which you plug an Ethernet cable. TCP/IP ports are virtual, and a single Ethernet connection supports the full range of TCP/IP port numbers.

Only one program may use any given TCP/IP port; for instance, if a web server runs on port 80, no other program may link itself to that port. Thus, the TCP/IP stack sends any data addressed to the computer's port 80 to the web server. When the web server sends data, it's identified as coming from port 80 as part of the standard TCP/IP packet. (Some programs open multiple ports, though. In this case, the program specifies which port it wants to use when sending data.) In many ways, port numbers work like business telephone extension numbers. Individuals working at a large company acquire an extension number with their offices or desks, much like programs running on a computer link to port numbers. In both cases, outsiders can reach individuals by including the port or extension number, and the extensions enable multiple insiders to communicate with the outside simultaneously.

Normally, FreeBSD assigns port numbers above 1024 to programs that don't ask for specific ports. Ports numbered below 1024 are known as *privileged ports,* meaning that only `root` may access these ports. This restriction is done for security purposes. Particular servers normally run on privileged ports, which can help prevent interference with normal server operation by miscreants. For instance, an ordinary user can't hijack the web server's port. Some protocols rely upon this characteristic as a security measure in accepting client accesses; if the client calls out from a privileged port, the client may be granted greater access privileges on the grounds that this outgoing connection must have been made or configured by the system administrator. Unfortunately, this use of port numbers is not foolproof today because it's easy for miscreants to control entire computers and thus control those systems' privileged ports.

Standard Port Number Assignments

When you make a telephone call to an individual who works in an office that uses telephone extensions, you must either know the individual's extension number or risk your sanity navigating the company's voicemail system. Similarly, a network client must know the port number on which a server runs in order to contact that server. Instead of developing a computer equivalent of voicemail, TCP/IP's designers have developed standard port number assignments to help clients locate servers. Few server types are unique to just one computer, so it's possible to assign particular ports to particular server types. For instance, web servers run on port 80, SMTP mail servers run on port 25, and Telnet servers run on port 23. The clients for these servers know these standard assignments and try to make the appropriate connection, even if you don't specify the port number. For instance, if you type **telnet jeeves.threeroomco.com**, your local `telnet` program knows to try contacting port 23. Some clients allow you to override this setting; for instance, you might type **telnet jeeves.threeroomco .com 80** to try to contact the web server's usual port. (This trick can be useful for debugging certain types of network problems because `telnet` enables entering the raw commands used by other protocols.)

Server port number assignments, although largely standardized, can often be overridden. You might want to run a server on an alternate port in order to run two servers of the same type on one computer (such as two different web servers), to overcome network blocks on particular ports, or to run a server as an ordinary user on an unprivileged port.

FreeBSD includes a file, `/etc/services`, that defines standard port numbers. This file consists of lines, each of which includes the name of a network protocol, the port number assigned to it, and the type of port (as described in the next section, "TCP, UDP, and Other Ports"). For instance, here's the entry for the Telnet port:

```
telnet          23/tcp
```

Various server configuration files use the linkage of port numbers to names in `/etc/services`. Most importantly, super servers (described in the upcoming section, "Using a Super Server") use the service name, such as `telnet` from the preceding example. These linkages are agreed-upon standards, although they may be extended in an ad hoc manner for less popular servers. The web site `http://www.iana.org/assignments/port-numbers` provides a listing that may be more complete than the one provided in FreeBSD's `/etc/services`. If necessary, you can edit `/etc/services` to add port assignments. Deleting unused port assignments can have a tiny but beneficial effect on system security because it might foil unauthorized servers that check for `/etc/services` entries.

TCP, UDP, and Other Ports

The TCP/IP stack provides several different methods of transmitting data. Two of the most popular are the Transmission Control Protocol (TCP), after which the stack is partially named, and the User Datagram Protocol (UDP). TCP creates a full two-way link between the two computers with error checking. It's therefore the protocol of choice when a reliable connection is desired and when that connection is likely to be used for transferring more than a handful of packets. TCP's downside is that it imposes substantial overhead; it requires more space in each packet for its error checking and other features. UDP, by contrast, doesn't create a stable two-way link. It's intended for relatively simple protocols that are used for quick transfers of limited amounts of data. DNS resolution, for instance, uses UDP because just a few packets can get the job done. UDP is fast, but if data packets are likely to be lost, it can be unreliable.

The preceding description of port numbers ignored the differences between TCP, UDP, and other packet types. In truth, many of these packet types are associated with a theoretically independent set of port numbers. If you check `/etc/services`, you'll find that it's filled with references to both TCP and UDP ports. In theory, a particular port number might be assigned to one protocol for TCP and another for UDP. In practice, such inconsistency is extremely rare; most protocols are assigned the same number for both TCP and UDP, even if the protocol uses only one. This configuration avoids the potential for confusion that might be caused by one port number supporting two servers, one for TCP and another for UDP.

In addition to TCP and UDP, there are other TCP/IP protocols, such as the Internet Control Message Protocol (ICMP). These don't have assignments in /etc/services, and most don't use port numbers *per se*. ICMP, for instance, is used for low-level network stack messages. There are different types of ICMP messages, but there's no need to create port numbers because few programs use this packet type. (The ping utility described in Chapter 14 is one exception.)

Tracing a Network Connection

To help understand network operations, it may be informative to trace one out, so that you can see some of the variety of computers and protocols involved. Of course, as with many things, the reality is more complex than a brief summary might suggest. There may be more computers and protocols involved than I can describe here. Some of the transactions described here may also involve several back-and-forth data transfers, although this fact may not be apparent to the end user. At the end of this description, in the "Deviations: Firewalls and NAT" section, I cover a couple of important extensions to the standard model.

The following description is best read with Figure 16-1 as a reference. For simplicity's sake, I assume that both the client and server networks use Ethernet locally. Other local network hardware is possible, in which case only the name of the hardware used in the following description changes.

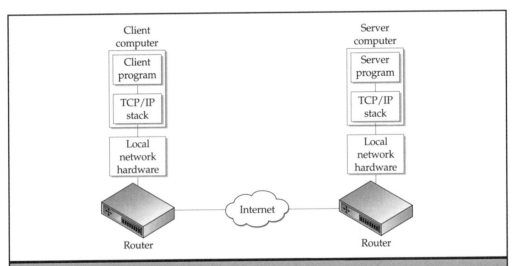

Figure 16-1. *A network transfer involves the interaction of various programs on both client and server computers, as well as assorted network hardware, and possibly hardware and software on the Internet at large.*

Initiating a Connection

The process begins with a client program that's been instructed to transfer data. This instruction may be given in real time by a user, or it could be an automated data transfer process. The client program contacts the TCP/IP stack on its local system with the request, which includes the IP address and port number of the remote server program. The TCP/IP stack bundles up the data into one or more collections of data. Depending upon the level of analysis, these collections may be referred to as *packets*, *frames*, or various other names. Suppose that the transfer under discussion is a web transfer. The initial exchange consists of packets that request the opening of a TCP connection and the transfer of a particular file from the web server computer.

Note   *In most cases, the client program is told to open a connection with a computer with a given hostname. To translate this hostname into an IP address, the client program initiates a data exchange with a DNS server. This data exchange can be as complex as some of the exchanges it serves.*

Some network requests are large enough that they're broken into multiple packets. In such a case, the TCP/IP stack does the job of breaking up the data and marking each outgoing packet so that the recipient system can reassemble the original request, much as you might mark boxes as belonging in particular rooms when you move to a new home.

The TCP/IP stack on the client computer packs data into TCP/IP packets and Ethernet frames, then encodes those frames using the network hardware, such as an Ethernet NIC. At this point, the packets must safely traverse the local network hardware. This hardware may include cables, hubs or switches, bridges, and other devices. Most network hardware at this level doesn't change the data frames; the hardware simply relays the data from one device to another.

The Role of Network Routing

Figure 16-1 shows a network router on the client's network, and another on the server's network. If the client and server happen to be on the same network, a router may not be involved. In this case, the server detects the packets addressed directly to it. When a router is involved, though, it partially decodes the data. Specifically, the router must extract the TCP/IP packet from the Ethernet frame in order to read the IP address. Once the router has extracted the IP address, it re-encapsulates the data in a new frame, typically on a different network interface, and sends it on its way. In some cases, the router may need to break up the data from a single frame into multiple frames on the outgoing connection. When this happens, subsequent routers or the recipient system itself will reassemble the data into a coherent whole.

In an Internet transfer, in fact, many routers are likely to see a packet. For purposes of this description, the Internet cloud in Figure 16-1 is a collection of some number of routers—probably about a dozen—that must handle a data packet in order for it to reach its destination. In each case, the router strips away the layer of "packing" on the data created by the previous router, then repacks the data for delivery to the next router. When the data request reaches the server's local router, it realizes that the addressee is on its local network, so instead of forwarding the data to another router, the server's router encapsulates the data in an Ethernet frame that brings the packet to the server computer itself. Of course, the server system's local network hardware is involved in much the same way as the client system's network hardware.

The Server's Response

The server's TCP/IP stack should notice a packet addressed to it from its local router, then begin unpacking the data. The Ethernet framing is removed, followed by other data for each layer of the network stack. Ultimately, the web server receives the request for initiation of a connection and transfer of data.

Servers may elect to respond to or ignore any given data transfer request. (A server might ignore a request for security reasons—for instance, a request from an external IP address for services that should be available only to local users.) Typically, web servers are configured to ignore few or no requests, so in this example, the web server composes a reply. The web server extracts the origin IP address and port number from the client's request, collects the requested document, and sends it on its way. The data traverse the network in much the same way as the client's request, but in the opposite direction. The reply packets may return via a different set of routers than the original, though. Typically (but not necessarily), the first and last routers are the same, but quirks relating to the business relationships between different Internet providers means that some of the machines in Figure 16-1's Internet cloud are likely to be different for the reply than for the client's initial contact. Indeed, in theory different packets in a single data stream may be routed through different computers, although such an event is fairly rare.

At the client, the server's reply makes its way up the network stack until it reaches the client program. In some cases, this may trigger a follow-on request; for instance, a web page may reference graphics files that the client will request immediately after receiving the main document. In other cases, the client won't initiate further data transfers. In the case of TCP connections, the client must terminate a session—notify the server that no further data transfer requests are pending. If the client needs to contact the server again later, a new connection must be initiated.

Deviations: Firewalls and NAT

One important class of deviations from the process as just described relates to *firewalls*. These are computers (typically routers) that are designed to filter the data they pass. Typically, firewalls block data requests coming to or from certain computers or ports. For instance, the router on the server network in Figure 16-1 might be configured to pass data destined for port 80 on the web server computer because this is the normal port for web servers, but to block requests destined for this computer on most other ports, such as 23 (used for Telnet sessions). Likewise, the router on the client network might be configured to block access to server ports on the client system. Indeed, such a firewall can block access *from* certain servers. For instance, if users of Figure 16-1's client network shouldn't be browsing the Web, the router might be configured to block requests to or from port 80 on external computers, effectively making direct web access from such computers impossible. (Users might be able to get around such a block by using an external *web proxy*, though, which redirects web access requests using an alternate port number.)

Firewalls are an important security measure because they provide a sort of safety net—it's easy to overlook a single server running on an entire network, but if a miscreant locates the server and can exploit a bug or lax configuration settings, that server can become a threat to the computer on which it runs. Once compromised in such a way, that one computer could be used to launch attacks against other computers on your network. Firewalls also provide one means of limiting access to servers that you intend to run—for instance, if you want to run login servers (described in Chapter 21) locally but not make them available to outsiders, you can use a firewall to block outside access to these servers. (You should also use server-specific access restrictions. This redundancy is an important feature of network security; should one restriction fail, another can stop a would-be intruder.)

Some routers are configured to perform *Network Address Translation (NAT)*, which is a technique that allows a router to "hide" several computers behind a single IP address, or to remap IP addresses in an arbitrary manner. NAT is popular on home networks because it allows users to connect multiple systems to a single Internet connection. It's also a useful tool in organizations that have many computers but a limited number of IP addresses because it allows the "stretching" of those IP addresses to all computers.

A NAT router functions by modifying the IP address of the sending computer. In its most common configuration, the router replaces the sending system's IP address and port number with the router's own IP address and a port number it assigns. When the reply arrives, the router can identify the system and port to which the reply should go based on the port number it used when sending the original packet.

In addition to being useful for stretching a limited supply of IP addresses, NAT provides some firewall-like security benefits, at least in the common configuration I've just described. Specifically, because the NAT router assigns external port numbers on an as-needed basis, external attackers can't send packets directly to arbitrary computers on the internal network. Thus, these systems are safe from direct external attack unless the NAT router itself is compromised or configured to permanently link ports on the server to specific internal systems (as you might do to run a server from within a NAT network).

Chapter 17 describes firewalls, including NAT, in more detail.

NETWORK CONFIGURATION

Methods of Starting Servers

One of the most fundamental aspects of server configuration is running the server. This goal can be accomplished in three different ways: You can run the server manually, you can run it automatically in a startup script, or you can use an intermediary server to monitor the target server's port and launch the target server only when its services are needed. Each approach has its unique advantages and disadvantages, not to mention its own configuration files. Thus, understanding these methods is important to administering network servers.

Manually Launching Servers

When you first configure a server, you may want to launch it manually. This process works just like launching any other program: You type the program's name at a command prompt, possibly along with some options. For instance, you can use the following command to launch the smbd server (part of the Samba package, described in Chapter 18):

```
# smbd
```

Many servers automatically detach themselves from your shell when launched in this way, so your shell prompt will return immediately. Others remain attached to your shell, so they can display error messages for debugging purposes. If you want to leave such a program running for an extended period of time, you can follow its name with an ampersand (&) to have it detach from your shell.

The drawback to launching a server manually is that it's a one-time affair. If a computer should always run half a dozen servers, it's inconvenient to have to launch them manually whenever you reboot the computer. Indeed, if the computer reboots automatically (say, because of a power failure), you may not be able to launch the server for some time. Thus, more automatic methods of launching servers exist.

Using Direct Startup Scripts

Chapter 6 describes FreeBSD's main startup scripts. These scripts control programs that FreeBSD runs whenever it starts. Thus, one way to configure a server to run automatically is to add a reference to the server in a startup script. The two main classes of scripts in which such references may appear are

- **/etc/rc.* scripts** These scripts control the standard startup process. The /etc/rc.network script is particularly important because it includes routines to start many common network servers. The /etc/rc.conf file includes configuration options to enable or disable specific servers. For instance, including sshd_enable="YES" in this file enables the Secure Shell (SSH) server (described in Chapter 21).

■ **/usr/local/etc/rc.d scripts**   Scripts in this directory control startup of many servers that are installed in the /usr/local directory tree. Typically, each server has its own startup script. Many packages provide scripts with names that end in .sh.sample. To enable the server, you rename the script so that it ends in .sh. You may also need to edit the startup script in server-specific ways. Consult the relevant chapter of this book or the server's documentation for more details. You can manually start or stop a server by typing the script name followed by **start** or **stop**, respectively.

Note   *Some UNIX and UNIX-like systems use the SysV startup script method to launch many servers. This method resembles the /usr/local/etc/rc.d method, but enables defining different sets of servers to be run on command.*

Whichever class of startup script is used, this method of launching servers leaves them running at all times (short of manual intervention to kill a running server). This fact means that the servers constantly consume a certain amount of system resources—mainly memory, but perhaps a bit of CPU time. The servers bind themselves to their chosen ports, and are ready to respond immediately to requests. The server can maintain information in memory, such as a cache of hostnames for a DNS server, which can improve server performance. The server can perform active tasks on a periodic basis, such as a mail server that attempts to send messages that couldn't be sent on first attempt. This configuration is a good one when the server is large, needs to maintain information across time, or needs to be able to schedule actions. The alternative, described in the next section, provides for a slimmer configuration and the potential for some common security features, but it can result in slower server responses.

Using a Super Server

A *super server* is a special type of server. Rather than process incoming requests itself, a super server stands in for other servers, binding itself to other servers' ports and launching the target server only when an incoming request arrives for that server. This configuration is more complex than one in which the server runs constantly and listens to its own port, but it has certain advantages. One of these is that the super server may consume much less memory than the many servers whose requests it handles. This advantage is important if most of these servers would not be handling connections most of the time; if a server is constantly fielding requests, the memory advantages of a super server are nil. Another advantage of a super server is that it can provide some uniform preliminary security screens for all the servers it handles. This feature can be particularly important for servers that provide limited security checks themselves. One important security feature provided by a super server is the ability to launch a server as a user other than root.

FreeBSD uses the inetd program as its super server. Like many other servers, inetd is launched via the standard startup scripts. You can check whether it's enabled by examining the /etc/rc.conf file, which should have the following line if inetd is enabled:

```
inetd_enable="YES"
```

If you prefer to use sysinstall, you can set this line by activating the inetd option in the Network Services Menu accessible from the FreeBSD Configuration Menu. You can also type **ps ax | grep inetd** in your shell to see if inetd is currently running. If it's not, type **inetd -wW** to run it. (The -wW options enable TCP Wrappers, which is a separate package that inetd uses to provide security for the servers it handles. Chapter 29 describes TCP Wrappers in more detail.)

The inetd configuration file is /etc/inetd.conf. This file consists of a series of lines, each of which takes the following form:

```
service type protocol wait user server options
```

Lines that begin with pound signs (#) are comments and are ignored. The meanings of each of the fields in a noncomment line are as follows:

- **service**   The first field is the service name, as specified in /etc/services. This setting defines the port number to which inetd will listen for this service. For instance, the line that begins with telnet listens to port 23 because /etc/services links port 23 to the telnet name, as described earlier, in "Standard Port Number Assignments."

- **type**   The second field usually consists of one of two words: stream or dgram. These words refer to some low-level details of how the server handles a connection.

- **protocol**   The third field is usually tcp or udp, for TCP or UDP packet types. The standard FreeBSD inetd.conf also includes examples of tcp6, which are TCP services for IPv6 (Chapter 14 briefly describes IPv6, which is rare in 2002). Other values are possible, but unusual.

- **wait**   The fourth field is either wait or nowait, and identifies how a datagram (dgram in the type field) server launches itself—whether it disconnects immediately from the calling program or remains connected until it finishes its work.

- **user**   The fifth field is critically important because it defines the username under which inetd launches a server. If a server doesn't need root privileges to operate, you can reduce the security risks of running the server by running it as some other user, such as nobody (a standard low-privilege account) or an account created specifically for use by a server.

- **_server_** The sixth field is the filename of the server itself, typically specified as a complete pathname, such as /usr/libexec/telnetd for the Telnet server. inetd also supports the keyword internal in this field, meaning that the service is one that inetd itself provides.

- **_options_** The seventh field contains any options you want to pass to the server. Frequently, this field includes the name of the server, such as telnet, in addition to options intended for the server itself.

The default FreeBSD inetd.conf file includes many lines for specific servers, but they're all commented out. You can enable a server by uncommenting the relevant line and then typing **killall -HUP inetd**, which tells the server to reread its configuration file and implement the changes. Some of the servers listed in the default inetd.conf file are normally launched through startup scripts, in which case you should *not* uncomment their lines if they're launched through startup scripts.

As an example, consider the following two inetd.conf lines:

```
telnet   stream   tcp   nowait   root   /usr/libexec/telnetd   telnetd
tftp     dgram    udp   wait     root   /usr/libexec/tftpd     tftpd ⤸
-s /tftpboot
```

The first line is a standard configuration for a FreeBSD Telnet server. This configuration launches the server whenever inetd detects incoming traffic on TCP port 23. The second line configures a Trivial FTP (TFTP) server, which is a fairly rare server type that's typically used to provide boot files for systems that boot from a network server. (TFTP is *not* the same as the more common FTP.) Most of the TFTP options are different from those for the Telnet server. Changing these options randomly is not generally a good idea; in most cases, doing so causes the server to not run correctly. One possible exception is the *user* option—but even then, some servers must be run as root in order to function correctly. This is particularly true of login servers, which must accept logins from many different users. If you install a new server and want to launch it through inetd, consult the server's documentation to learn what settings are appropriate.

Tip

The standard FreeBSD inetd.conf file is reasonably secure; it doesn't launch unnecessary servers. Nonetheless, you should examine it and be sure it's not launching servers unnecessarily. FreeBSD does not rely upon any server started through inetd for basic functionality, so if you see something in inetd.conf that you don't understand, you can comment it out without risking catastrophic failure of your system. Of course, doing so may cause problems for other systems if they rely upon that server on the FreeBSD system.

Using netstat for Network Diagnostics

If you're lucky, your network configuration will pose few problems. Unfortunately, this isn't always the case. Chapters 14 and 15 describe basic configuration and some tools that are useful in debugging problems with these configurations. In particular, ping and traceroute can provide you with information on basic network functionality. More sophisticated tools can help you diagnose problems in higher-level protocols. In particular, netstat provides information on your network connections.

The netstat utility displays information on various network data structures. This command is very complex; it can display a wide variety of information, depending upon the parameters it's given. Some parameters' meanings vary depending upon other parameters; in fact, the netstat man page provides several different syntax statements for these meanings. This section can provide only an overview of some of the more important uses of this flexible command.

Note *Chapter 14 includes an example of the use of netstat for displaying your system's routing table, so consult Chapter 14 for this common use of netstat.*

Basic netstat Use

The most basic netstat command (typing the command with no options) produces a listing that's fairly bewildering at first glance. An edited example is as follows:

```
# netstat
Active Internet connections
Proto Recv-Q Send-Q  Local Address            Foreign Address   (state)
tcp4       0      0  halrloprillalar.telnet nessus.2467       ESTABLISHED
tcp4       0      0  halrloprillalar.1024    speaker.7101      ESTABLISHED
udp4       0      0  halrloprillalar.1019    speaker.nfsd
Active UNIX domain sockets
Address   Type   Recv-Q Send-Q  Inode     Conn Refs Nextref Addr
c928d780 stream      0      0       0 c928d820    0       0 /tmp/.X11-unix/X0
c928d820 stream      0      0       0 c928d780    0       0
```

The first block of output, labeled Active Internet connections, refers to connections between the local computer and other computers. In this example, the first two of these are TCP links (indicated by tcp4 in the Proto column) from the local computer (halrloprillalar) to nessus and speaker, respectively. The third connection is a UDP link to speaker. Each link indicates the port number, or if it appears in /etc/services, the name of the service. Thus, if you can't start a server and the error log indicates that the port is in use, you can use this command to learn something about what's using that port.

The second block of output, labeled `Active UNIX domain sockets`, lists local-to-local connections. Many of these are X-related. The information provided relates to internal network data structures, and can be difficult to interpret.

Normally, `netstat` doesn't display information on servers that are listening for connections but not actually connected to another system. You can have `netstat` display such processes by adding the `-a` parameter. These servers appear with `LISTENING` in the `(state)` column. As shown in this example, `netstat` attempts to resolve IP addresses to domain names. You can disable this resolution and obtain raw IP addresses by adding the `-n` option.

Obtaining Information on Interfaces

Typing **netstat -i** causes the program to display information on all network interfaces, and **netstat -I** *if-name* produces a display of information on the specified interface called *if-name*. For instance, consider this example:

```
# netstat -I fxp0 -n
Name  Mtu Network    Address                  Ipkts Ierrs  Opkts Oerrs  Coll
fxp0 1500 <Link#1>   00:03:47:b1:ee:b8 7239       0   1982     0     0
fxp0 1500 192.168.1  192.168.1.6          7195       -   1944     -     -
```

This output includes two entries for most network interfaces. One (the first in this example) relates to the low-level network hardware interface, and another (the second in this example) shows the TCP/IP stack that's associated with the low-level interface. There may be additional network stacks on some systems, or a stack may be disabled and unlinked from the network hardware. Information in both cases includes input packets (`Ipkts`), input errors (`Ierrs`), output packets (`Opkts`), output errors (`Oerrs`), and collisions (`Coll`). Collisions occur when packets from two systems are sent over a single wire at the same moment, causing both to become unintelligible. They're an inevitable feature of some network hardware, but they degrade performance.

Obtaining Network Use Statistics

The **netstat -s** command displays information on network use (packets sent and received, errors, connection requests, and so on) broken down by protocol (TCP, UDP, and so on). This command can be a good way to see if a system is sending and receiving data, or if some problem such as network errors are impacting performance.

Using netstat in Practice

You can use `netstat` to acquire a lot of data about your network connections. Unfortunately, the power of this tool makes it difficult to interpret its output until you're familiar with it. In addition, you should be familiar with traffic patterns on *your* network. For instance, some networks generate a fair number of collisions, but others generate none. Collisions degrade performance because when a collision occurs, both systems pause a random period of time and retry, so overall throughput drops. Collisions are impossible to eliminate with some network hardware. On such hardware, the number of collisions inevitably rises with network traffic. Old coaxial Ethernet networks and twisted-pair networks that use hubs are particularly prone to collisions. If you see collisions at the rate of a percent or two on such a network, it's not cause for concern; but more than a tiny number of collisions on an Ethernet network that uses a switch rather than a hub is a potential red flag.

If your network uses hubs and suffers from poor performance, upgrading to switches may help. Switches won't suffer from nearly as many collisions, and they can also enable full-duplex transfers, which better utilize network bandwidth.

In the end, you'll have to use `netstat` to learn what sorts of output are typical for your system and your network. Running the tool on a regular basis can help you spot anomalies when they occur.

Summary

Basic network configuration, as described in Chapters 14 and 15, is a necessary prerequisite for running servers or using network clients. In order to do more, especially in the server arena, it's necessary to know more about how a network operates. This knowledge includes the roles of clients and servers and how port numbers are used. As a practical matter, it's also necessary to know how to start servers. Servers may be started directly, in FreeBSD's startup scripts; or indirectly, via a super server. You should also know how to use the `netstat` tool to obtain basic information on the health of your network interface and on specific network connections. This program can be very helpful when it comes time to track down problems with connections.

The
Complete
Reference

Chapter 17

Setting Up a Firewall

Networking is extremely important for many of today's computer functions. Unfortunately, networking brings risks because networks of any size are likely to host malicious individuals. Such people may attack your computer in many different ways, and if their attacks are successful, they may destroy your data, use your system to attack others, or otherwise cause problems. For this reason, understanding network security is critical to operating a computer on a network. Indeed, Chapter 29 is devoted to this topic. This chapter is dedicated to a particular type of network security tool: the *firewall*. This is a tool that can be used to restrict remote access to one computer or group of computers from another computer or group of computers.

To configure a firewall, you must first understand the nature of the security threat that a firewall is designed to counter. This chapter therefore begins with coverage of this topic. It moves on to a description of the types of firewalls that exist, and an overview of the FreeBSD tools that implement these firewall types. Finally, this chapter concludes with information on how to create a particular type of firewall (known as a packet-filter firewall) in FreeBSD. Such a firewall can protect a single computer or (when implemented on a router) an entire network.

Understanding the Threat

At its core, a firewall is a network access control tool; it's designed to block access based on computer names, IP addresses, or other criteria. The premise upon which firewalls are built is that some individuals have ill intentions and may try to abuse the servers that run on your computers. Whenever possible, therefore, you should limit access to your servers. It's also true that individuals on a computer or network you administer may try to launch attacks against others. Firewalls are therefore often configured to block such attacks. Even if no individual who uses a computer you control is a "bad apple," it's possible that a virus or worm could take over one of your computers, leading to such attacks originating on your network.

 Firewalls most frequently block access between networks, but security within a network can be important, as well. Proper configuration of local servers can help reduce the risk of entirely local attacks, as can use of local network security tools such as Kerberos (`http://web.mit.edu/kerberos/www/`).

Outsiders Trying to Get In

When the words "network security" come up, most people tend to think of malicious outsiders attempting to gain access to a network's internal computers. There are a huge number of examples of this sort of abuse, but some common examples include the following:

- **Break-ins of login servers** Login servers (described in Chapter 21) enable users to run programs from a remote site. Crackers sometimes abuse such servers to cause problems for you or others.

- **Exploitation of server bugs**   Crackers frequently learn of bugs in popular servers, and then attempt to exploit these bugs to break into a computer by having the server run unauthorized programs.

- **Open mail relay abuse**   Spammers often seek out mail servers that can relay mail in a promiscuous way, and abuse these servers to deliver spam. Chapter 19 includes more information on this topic.

- **Denial-of-service (DoS) attacks**   These attacks attempt to disrupt your network connectivity by tying up your network bandwidth.

Note   *The media frequently uses the term* hacker *to refer to computer criminals, but this word has an older and more honorable meaning: A person who is skilled at computer programming and enjoys writing software for productive and legal purposes. Many of the people who wrote FreeBSD consider themselves hackers in this positive sense, so I don't use the word in reference to computer miscreants; instead, I use the word* cracker *to refer to these criminals.*

The many possible forms of attack on your network make it impossible to write a general-purpose tool that can reliably block all attacks. A firewall, though, is designed to block *some* types of attack before they reach sensitive internal computers. Consider Figure 17-1, which illustrates a typical use of a firewall. In this configuration, a firewall is a router that's configured to grant or deny outside access to the network it serves based

NETWORK
CONFIGURATION

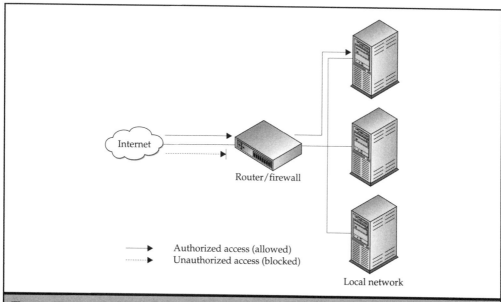

Figure 17-1.   *A firewall selectively grants or denies access based on various criteria.*

on specific criteria. For instance, such a firewall might deny outsiders' access to internal login protocols such as the Secure Shell (SSH) except from certain trusted external IP addresses. Thus, if a cracker attempts to break into a local system, chances are the cracker won't succeed, even if there's a bug in or misconfiguration of your local system's SSH server. The firewall still grants access to legitimate users, though.

One critical feature of security is redundancy. Many servers include controls to limit outside access by IP addresses, much as firewalls can do. Because of the possibility of bugs or misconfiguration, though, it's advisable to use multiple access controls. That way, if one control fails, another may succeed.

In addition to restricting access to known servers, firewalls are frequently configured in such a way that they block access to servers that shouldn't be running. For instance, a firewall can restrict outside access to the Simple Mail Transfer Protocol (SMTP) port (25) to all but the mail server computer. Thus, even if some internal computer is running a poorly configured mail server when it shouldn't be, an outside spammer won't be able to abuse it. Likewise, you can block access to the ports used by protocols intended for purely local consumption, such as file- and printer-sharing protocols (described in Chapters 18 and 9, respectively).

Unfortunately, a firewall isn't a panacea. A cracker might have an account on a system that should be given some types of local access. Indeed, some types of servers *must* be available to a wide variety of outside systems. Your domain's mail server, for instance, must normally be able to accept mail from any system on the Internet. If your mail server is buggy or misconfigured, it can be abused even if a firewall sits between it and the Internet at large. Some networks use multiple firewalls, deployed in layers, to provide minimal security for systems that must process outside requests, and isolating those systems from more sensitive fully internal computers.

Malicious Individuals on the Inside

Although many people think of firewalls as a means of protecting internal computers from the untamed wilds of the Internet, the protection can—and *should*—go both ways. For instance, suppose you're in charge of your employer's firewall machine, which protects a dozen internal systems used by a dozen employees. If one of those employees is actually a cracker, that individual could use your network as a launch pad for attacks on other computers. Seemingly innocent tools such as `telnet` can be abused to attack outside systems. If these attacks are discovered, they might be traced back to you, causing embarrassment at best and criminal charges at worst.

You can configure a firewall to block some types of unauthorized outside access. For instance, suppose that your employees must be able to browse the Web and access random FTP sites. You could let through outgoing requests to ports 80 (web) and 21 (FTP) to any computer. You might also need to permit other requests, such as SMTP (port 25) access from your local mail server, and DNS (port 53) access from your DNS server.

You can then configure your firewall to block all other outgoing data, thus preventing your network from being abused in various ways.

As with incoming data, restricting outgoing access isn't absolutely foolproof. If the hypothetical inside cracker targets systems on one of the ports that's allowed, the firewall won't do much good. Furthermore, the internal cracker could conceivably attack and reconfigure the firewall computer itself. (This possibility also exists for external attacks.) Nonetheless, a firewall to limit outgoing data can be a useful component of an overall network security policy.

Unauthorized Code on the Inside

When more than one person uses a network, there's always the possibility that one of the users isn't trustworthy. In some sense, the same is true even when a network has just one user because of a class of programs that can collectively be called *unauthorized code*. These programs are viruses, worms, and Trojan horses—programs that are unwelcome guests on your computer. In 2002, viruses and worms are running rampant on Windows systems, and Trojans are also moderately popular on these systems and even on UNIX and UNIX-like systems. Viruses invade programs and spread to other programs on the same system. Worms spread on networks, often in e-mail attachments. Trojan horses claim to do one thing but in fact do another. (The lines between these three types of malicious programs can be blurry at times.)

Note	*Viruses and worms are major issues in Windows computing, but a FreeBSD firewall can be a useful tool in restricting their spread. A firewall can protect computers running any OS; a FreeBSD firewall doesn't care if a packet originates from a FreeBSD system, a Windows system, or any other OS.*

A firewall can help prevent the spread of unauthorized code in much the same way that it can frustrate an internal cracker. If a worm is programmed to make an SMTP mail connection to an outside system, for instance, a block on outgoing SMTP connections except from the authorized mail server will prevent the spread of that worm outside of your local network. Just as when controlling malicious individuals on the inside, though, a firewall isn't perfect in blocking worms. For instance, if the worm uses your local mail server to send the mail, a firewall won't prevent the spread of the worm.

Other tools can help fight unauthorized code. One of the most important of these is user education. Don't run programs from untrusted sources, and configure e-mail clients not to execute attachments automatically. Windows antivirus programs, such as Norton AntiVirus (http://www.symantec.com) and McAfee VirusScan (http://www.mcafee.com) can detect and delete unauthorized code on Windows systems.

Because viruses and worms for FreeBSD are virtually nonexistent, tools to detect such problems on FreeBSD are equally rare. That's not to say that FreeBSD is totally immune to such problems, though; they simply take a different form. In particular, in FreeBSD, one must be concerned about the possibility of a cracker breaking into a computer. Much of Chapter 29 is devoted to preventing and detecting such problems.

Types of Firewalls

The previous sections have referred to firewalls as if they were all alike. In fact, there are many different types of firewalls and firewall-like devices, each with its own characteristics. Large networks frequently combine multiple firewalls of different types, but such configurations are beyond the scope of this book. Consult a book such as Zwicky et al's *Building Internet Firewalls, 2nd Edition* (O'Reilly & Associates, 2000) for more information on such complex configurations. This section describes three different types of firewalls or firewall-like configurations, to better help you decide what type of firewall is best for you.

Packet-Filter Firewalls

One common type of firewall, and the type that's emphasized in the upcoming section, "Creating a Firewall Script," is a *packet-filter firewall*. This firewall works by filtering individual TCP/IP packets. For instance, if the firewall is configured to block incoming port-139 (SMB/CIFS file sharing) access to the local network, the firewall does so by looking for packets directed at port 139 and denying or rejecting all such packets. The result is that the computers on the local network never see port-139 traffic except from other local computers.

Packet-filter firewalls are flexible, powerful, and readily implemented with standard FreeBSD tools. This type of filter can restrict traffic based on network interface, source or destination IP address, source or destination port, and various other criteria. A single tool can create a packet-filter firewall that protects a network against attacks on many different servers. For instance, the same tool that sets up a port-139 packet filter can set up a filter on port 22 (used by SSH).

FreeBSD's packet-filter firewall rules can be used on a router to protect an entire network, as depicted in Figure 17-1; or they can be used on a workstation or server to protect just one computer. For instance, you might use these rules to limit which remote computers may access a workstation's SSH server. This feature allows a packet-filter firewall to protect computers against some types of local attacks.

NAT Routers

One special type of configuration is quite popular in small offices and homes: the *Network Address Translation (NAT)* router. A NAT router is not, by itself, a firewall; but it provides many firewall-like features, and it may implement true firewall protections as well. A NAT router's primary function is the ability to transparently convert one IP address to another. That is, a client using one IP address initiates a data transfer, but the NAT router alters the client's packets so that they appear to come from another IP address that the NAT router also serves. When the reply arrives, the NAT router reverses this conversion and sends the packets on to their true destination. A NAT router can also change the destination IP address in a similar manner.

This description raises a basic question: Why bother? The answer is that NAT features allow you to do several things, including

- **Quick network reconfigurations**   If you need to move a server from one address to another on short notice, you can use NAT to redirect traffic to the correct address on a temporary (or even permanent) basis.

- **Load balancing**   It's possible to configure a NAT router to split traffic destined for one address to multiple systems, thus providing a "quick and dirty" method of load balancing. More elegant means exist to do this, but NAT can still be handy for a simple setup.

- **Stretching IP addresses**   A NAT router allows clients to be configured using private IP address ranges (such as 192.168.x.x), yet still access the Internet using a single public IP address (belonging to the NAT router). This feature allows home users and small businesses with dial-up or broadband access that provides a single IP address to link networks to the Internet, and it allows larger businesses to expand their internal networks without consuming huge numbers of new IP addresses.

This final function of NAT may be the most popular, and it's the use that's described in the upcoming section, "Configuring NAT." Even an old 486 computer can function as a NAT router for a private network with a handful, or even dozens, of computers, allowing these computers to share a single external IP address.

Used as a way of "hiding" a private network, NAT provides certain firewall-like protections. Outside systems "see" only the NAT router, and so cannot connect directly to servers that run on the internal network; the result is very much like running a firewall that blocks external access requests. (You can use port forwarding techniques to get around this feature if you so desire.) Connections initiated from internal systems are let through without challenge, unless the NAT router uses separate firewall rules to limit such outgoing requests.

NAT is undeniably a powerful tool, but it's not without its limits. Most importantly, some protocols don't work well with NAT. Some of these require both outgoing and incoming server connections (some teleconferencing tools fall into this category). Others embed IP address information within data packets. NAT implementations sometimes include special rules to overcome such problems, but occasionally this is impossible. For instance, some security protocols encrypt IP address information, so NAT can't decrypt, alter, and re-encrypt the data. Such issues aren't problems for common protocols like those used for e-mail, web browsing, and FTP, but if you use rare protocols, and especially if they use encryption, you should research their compatibility with FreeBSD's NAT tools before attempting to use NAT.

Proxy Servers

A final type of firewall is the *proxy server*. This is a computer that's configured to accept requests from internal systems, partially process them, and send the processed request on to the ultimate destination. When the proxy server receives the reply, it processes the reply and forwards it on to the client. For instance, suppose you implement a web proxy server. When a client initiates an outgoing connection, the client *really* sends the request to your internal web proxy server. This server generates a substantially identical request and sends it on to the external web server. That server then sends the reply to your local proxy server, which forwards it to the local web browser.

Proxy servers need not function as routers; you might situate a proxy server behind a packet-filter firewall and restrict outgoing access for the proxy's protocol to the proxy server computer itself. You can even use proxy servers that reside off your own local network. The proxy server processes data to a greater degree than does a packet-filter firewall, and this fact allows the proxy server to filter data based on higher-level criteria. In addition to blocking data based on IP address, a proxy filter can restrict data based on filenames, or can scan data for viruses or worms.

In addition to or instead of working as access control tools, proxy filters can improve network performance. Some of this advantage may be a side effect of access controls; for instance, a web page may load faster if a proxy strips it of ads. A proxy server may also cache data, so that if it receives another request for the same data, the proxy can deliver the data without making another Internet request.

Proxy servers aren't always marketed as firewalls, but they can be used as part of a firewall strategy. For instance, consider Figure 17-1. The system labeled "Router/Firewall" in that figure might not actually be a router; it might simply run proxy servers for the protocols used for external access. Such a configuration effectively limits access in both directions to the types of access permitted by the proxy servers you run. As noted earlier, too, you can run a proxy server on an internal system and configure a router to restrict access for the proxy's protocol to that proxy server system.

One of the problems with proxy servers is that there are so many of them. Normally, you need a separate proxy server for each protocol you want to use; a web proxy server won't handle SSH access, for instance. Indeed, you might not be able to find a proxy server to handle certain types of protocols. Proxy servers also consume more system resources than do packet-filter firewalls because the proxy servers do much more work in handling their requests. It's often necessary to configure your clients to use a proxy server. An internal cracker might be able to use a proxy server that doesn't log its activities to obscure who within your organization is initiating an attack. For these reasons, this book doesn't describe proxy servers in great detail, although the upcoming section, "Common Proxy Servers," does provide pointers to several proxy server tools.

FreeBSD Firewall Tools

As with many features, FreeBSD supports several tools for building a firewall. This section introduces some of the more popular of these tools, but there are others available as well, particularly in the proxy server arena. A web search on keywords such as *firewall* or *proxy server* should turn up many hits.

Tools for Packet Filtering: ipfw and IP Filter

Ultimately, the FreeBSD kernel must do packet filtering because the handling of packets on the level required of a packet filter firewall is a kernel-level function. Thus, the FreeBSD packet-filter firewall tools are really interfaces—they exist to provide a syntax that enables you to tell the kernel what to do with packets that meet certain criteria. Two tools are commonly used for this purpose:

- **ipfw**   This program is FreeBSD's home-grown packet filter tool. As such, you can find further information about this tool in FreeBSD's own documentation, including the `ipfw` man page.

- **IP Filter**   This package is not as closely linked to FreeBSD as is `ipfw`, but it works well with FreeBSD. It also works with various other UNIX and UNIX-like OSs, including OpenBSD, NetBSD, and Solaris. It comes with FreeBSD, so it's probably already installed on your system. (Look for programs called `ipf` and `ipnat`, among others, in `/sbin`.) You can read more about IP Filter at `http://coombs.anu.edu.au/ipfilter/`.

Both `ipfw` and IP Filter are popular packet-filter firewall tools. Because `ipfw` is more strongly tied to FreeBSD, the upcoming section, "Creating a Firewall Script," focuses upon that tool. If you have access to a ready-made IP Filter script, though, you can use it instead. One advantage of `ipfw` is that it allows you to easily add or delete individual rules, which can make tweaking a running configuration relatively simple; with IP Filter, you must modify your main script and rerun `ipf` to redo the entire configuration.

Both `ipfw` and IP Filter come with associated tools to configure NAT operations. For `ipfw`, that tool is called `natd`; for IP Filter, it's `ipnat`. As with their packet-filter counterparts, these tools differ in details but accomplish largely the same goals. The upcoming section, "Configuring NAT," describes `natd` configuration and use.

Common Proxy Servers

As described earlier, in "Proxy Servers," there are many proxy server programs available. Many of these are designed to handle just one protocol, but some support multiple protocols. Some proxy servers ship with matched clients that are preconfigured to use the proxy server. Others rely upon configuration options in clients such as web browsers, or your ability to use packet-filter firewall rules to redirect outgoing packets to a proxy server system. Figure 17-2 shows the Mozilla configuration tool in which you can tell it to use a proxy server. A sampling of proxy server programs includes the following:

- **Squid**   This is a popular multiprotocol proxy server—it handles HTTP, FTP, and gopher protocols. Squid is highly configurable, but its main design goal is to cache data requests, thus speeding up transfers for local users who frequently access the same pages. You can read more at its home page, `http://www.squid-cache.org`.

- **Privoxy**   This proxy server, headquartered at `http://www.privoxy.org`, is designed to remove ads from web pages and block *cookies* (small pieces of data a web server can give a browser to track your online activities).

- **DNRD**   This program is one of several proxy DNS servers. (In fact, the regular FreeBSD DNS server can be configured as a proxy name server.) Such a program looks just like a normal DNS server to clients, but forwards all requests to an external name server. You can read more about it at `http://dnrd.nevalabs.org`.

- **jftpgw**   This program functions as an FTP proxy server. It can be used to provide a controlled means for users inside a network to access external FTP sites or to give outsiders controlled access to an internal FTP server. Its home page is `http://www.mcknight.de/jftpgw`.

- **Any SMTP server**   Although not usually described in these terms, SMTP mail servers can be considered proxy servers. These programs can accept mail destined for other sites, process it slightly, and relay the mail. You can configure mail servers to filter mail based on various criteria, such as antispam configurations, much as you use more conventional proxy filters to block unwanted data.

Some of these proxy servers, such as sendmail (a popular SMTP server) and Squid, come with FreeBSD. You may need to go to other products' web pages to locate and install them. A web search on keywords such as *FreeBSD proxy server* will turn up many other proxy servers, if you're looking for something specific.

Unfortunately, configuration of these tools is so diverse that I can't present details for most of them in this book (Chapter 19 does cover sendmail, but doesn't describe it in proxy filter terms). Consult the proxy servers' documentation for details. In most cases, the proxy server runs much like any other server, as described in Chapter 16. You may need to modify your clients' configuration using options or dialog boxes such as the Mozilla proxy server options shown in Figure 17-2.

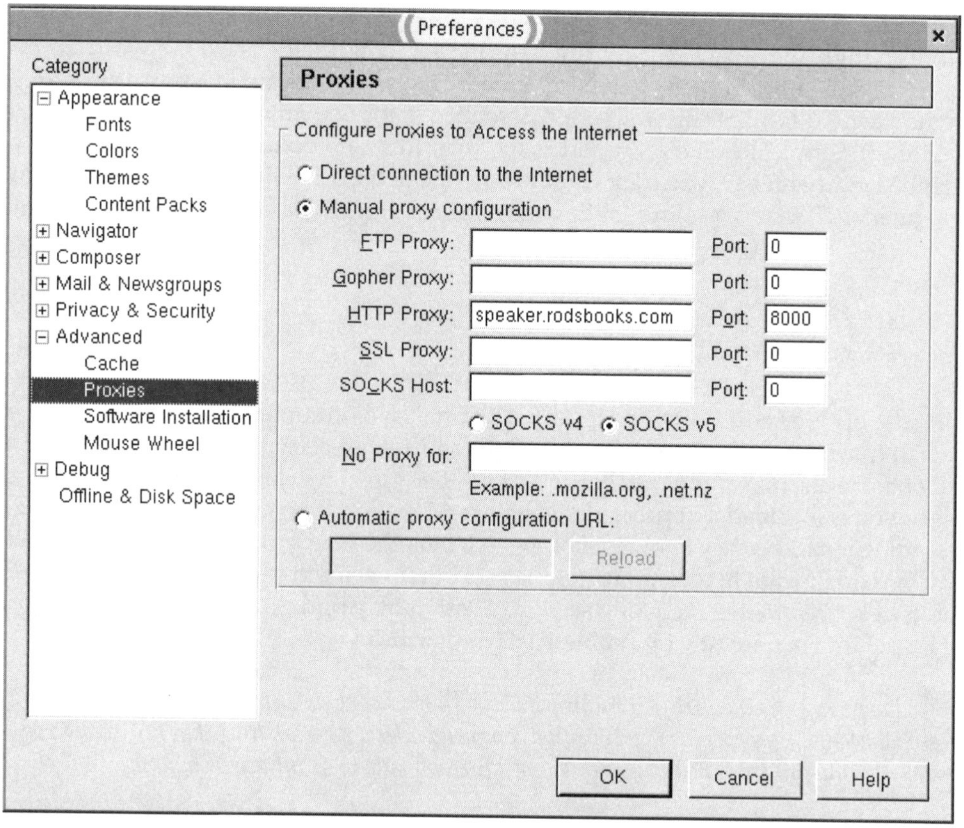

Figure 17-2. *Some Internet clients provide explicit support for proxy servers.*

NETWORK CONFIGURATION

Creating a Firewall Script

To create a proxy-filter firewall, you must run the proxy filter tool, feeding it a configuration file, or create a script that calls the tool multiple times with options to add various specific rules. This section describes this process, beginning with preliminaries such as kernel options and deciding what types of policies you want to implement, and moving on to creating the rules and configuring your system to use them automatically.

Necessary Kernel Options

Before configuring a packet-filter firewall rule set, you must ensure that your kernel supports packet filtering. The generic FreeBSD kernel does *not* support this feature, but the standard FreeBSD firewall script, described in the upcoming section, "Automating the Firewall Script," loads the support in modular form. If you recompile your kernel, as described in Chapter 12, you may want to add one of the following three options to your configuration file (such as /usr/src/sys/i386/GENERIC, the generic configuration file):

```
options IPFIREWALL
options IPFIREWALL_VERBOSE
options IPFIREWALL_VERBOSE_LIMIT=n
```

These options add firewall support. The final two options relate to the logging of firewall traffic. Include them if you want to log firewall activity. The value of n in the final option is the maximum number of packets the system will log before halting logging. This option is included as a precaution against miscreants who might attack your system by sending it packets they know will be logged, thus chewing up CPU time and disk space.

If you don't want to recompile your kernel but do want to experiment with the ipfw tool, as described in the upcoming section, "Designing Appropriate Rules," you can load the kernel firewall module by typing **kldload ipfw**.

 Don't type **kldload ipfw** *over a network login; the default firewall policy is to deny all access, so as soon as you type this command over a network link, that link will go dead. You must unload the module or enter a firewall rule to grant access again.*

The Default Policy

When you reconfigure your kernel to provide packet filtering options, it sets up a *default policy*—a special packet filter rule that applies to all packets that aren't matched by other rules. This default policy is one of denial, so that you must explicitly set up rules to override this one for any traffic your system is to allow, either for itself or to route to other computers.

A default-deny policy like this is the most secure approach because it protects all the ports you might not think about, but that may need protection. For instance, suppose you're configuring a router as a firewall. You might not think to protect port 69 (used by the rare Trivial FTP, or TFTP, server), but if one of the systems your router is to protect is misconfigured to run this server, a default-deny policy is likely to protect it from outside access.

The drawback of a default-deny policy is that it's difficult to configure because you must pay attention to opening access in various ways for both clients and servers. (Some of these issues are described in the next section, "Deciding What to Allow and Deny";

"Designing Appropriate Rules" provides examples.) If you miss some important point, you may spend time pulling your hair out as you try to track down why you can't get a client or server to work. You must also reconfigure your firewall rules whenever you add a new server.

The alternative to a default-deny policy is a default-allow policy. Configured in this way, the computer allows all packets except those that match rules you explicitly enter. This configuration is easy to start with, but provides only those protections you think to create. Thus, as a general rule, default-allow configurations are less secure than are default-deny configurations. If you want to use a default-allow policy, you must enter a rule that overrides the standard default-deny rule. The details of `ipfw` configuration appear in "Designing Appropriate Rules," but for now, here's a command that changes a default-deny policy to a default-allow policy:

```
# ipfw add 65534 allow all from any to any
```

 If you enable packet-filtering in your kernel but can't get around to creating a firewall rule set just yet, you must enter the preceding command to use networking. If you don't, FreeBSD will refuse all network traffic, effectively disabling your network configuration.

Alternatively, if you recompile your kernel, you can reconfigure it to use a default-allow policy by including the following line in your kernel configuration file:

```
options IPFIREWALL_DEFAULT_TO_ACCEPT
```

Deciding What to Allow and Deny

Most packet-filter firewall rules operate on the IP addresses and port numbers of the source and destination systems. You don't need to specify all of this information; for instance, you can tell the system to allow packets destined to port 80 on 172.21.25.101 from any port on any IP address. You must express whatever you want to do in terms such as these, although it's possible to specify ranges of port numbers or IP addresses and to build rules around other criteria, such as the network interface.

One key to remember when configuring a firewall is the difference between *privileged* and *unprivileged* ports. Privileged ports are numbered below 1024. On FreeBSD and other UNIX-like systems, these ports can be opened only by `root`, so servers normally use them. Unprivileged ports, on the other hand, are numbered above 1024. Programs run by ordinary users can open such ports, and servers rarely run on such ports (there are a few exceptions to this rule, though). Some firewall rules may use this distinction, as described shortly.

You needn't build rules for every possible type of traffic—that's what the default policy is for. Nonetheless, you must consider what types of traffic you want to allow and deny, and create rules appropriately, either by letting the default rule do the job or by configuring an exception to that rule. Traffic you might want to allow includes

- **Traffic to legitimate local servers**   If you run servers, you must allow traffic into those servers. Of course, you can limit who you allow in—for instance, you might write a rule to grant access to an SSH server only to computers on your local network.

- **Traffic to legitimate outside servers**   If users should be able to browse the Web, use FTP servers, and so on, you must permit outgoing traffic to such servers. In a very lax configuration, you might permit *any* outgoing traffic, but a tighter rule might limit traffic to specific protocols. You may need to remember to include such mundane protocols as DNS (UDP port 42) and DHCP (UDP port 67). You can limit access to particular internal or external computers by IP address, as well.

- **Return traffic from legitimate servers**   For both internal and external servers, you must permit return traffic from the server. Granting access based solely on an external port number is potentially risky because a miscreant could run an attack program on such a port. Thus, rather than granting return access based on port numbers, it's common to permit packets that are part of an established stream of packets destined to unprivileged ports. This configuration allows clients to establish a connection (if other rules allow it), and it permits the outside server to send return packets.

Whether you use a default-allow or a default-deny configuration, there are certain types of accesses you may want to disallow:

- **Access from unauthorized sites**   Some servers should not be accessible to just anybody. For instance, local file- and printer-sharing servers are normally intended for users on a local network. A packet-filter firewall may restrict such access based on the combination of port number and IP address or (particularly for a router configured as a firewall) the network port.

- **Access to unused or sensitive servers**   Normally, a server that isn't running isn't a threat; however, sometimes a server may be run accidentally. Blocking access to such ports in a firewall can help prevent problems from such an oversight.

- **Bizarre packets**   Some types of packets may be malformed in a way that can cause problems or that might indicate a break-in attempt. For instance, if a router spots a packet coming from its external interface with a source IP address that indicates it comes from the internal network, this is almost certainly an attempt to break in by *spoofing* (forging) an inside IP address. Router firewalls can detect and block such attempts.

Ultimately, the decision of what to allow and what to deny is highly site-specific because it depends upon what types of servers you're running, where the firewall is running (on a router, on a client computer, or on a server computer), what balance between security and user convenience is acceptable, and so on. The next section, "Designing Appropriate Rules," presents some examples, but you *must* evaluate these, and probably modify them for your own needs.

Designing Appropriate Rules

With information on whether you're configuring a router as a firewall or firewall rules on a client or server, knowledge of what protocols you need to pass, and so on, you should now have a general idea of how you want to configure your firewall rules. When you create a set of firewall rules, they're expressed as an ordered list. If a packet matches the criteria specified by a rule, then the rule applies, and the packet is allowed through or rejected, as specified by the rule. Thus, the order of rules is extremely important; if an early rule allows, say, traffic destined to TCP port 80 from any IP address, then a subsequent rule that denies all traffic from a particular IP address won't apply if that address sends data to a system's TCP port 80. Also, early rules entail less processing overhead, so if a rule matches a great deal of traffic (such as return data from external servers), you may want to place it early in the firewall rule set.

ipfw Syntax

Having a general idea of what sorts of rules you want to create is a necessary first step, but it's not enough. The main key that's missing is an understanding of the `ipfw` utility that creates packet filtering rules. This command's syntax is extremely complex; consult its man page for details. A simplified `ipfw` syntax is as follows:

```
ipfw [-N] command [index] [action] [log] protocol addresses ⏎
[options]
```

The meanings of the `ipfw` parameters are

- **-N**   Normally, `ipfw` reports hosts and ports by number. Using this parameter causes it to use DNS and `/etc/services` to convert these numbers into names.

- **command**   This parameter is the command that's to be followed. A summary of important commands follows this list, in the section "`ipfw` Commands."

- **index**   The *index* is a number from 0 to 65535 that indicates the rule's place in the rule set. If you omit this parameter, the system automatically generates an *index* that's 100 higher than the highest rule in the system, excluding the default policy rule (which has an *index* of 65535).

- **action**   The *action* describes what to do with a packet. An *action* of `allow` indicates that the packet is to be accepted. Synonyms for `allow` are `accept` and `pass`. The `deny` and `reject` actions both block delivery of the packet, but in different ways. `deny` causes FreeBSD to ignore the packet, so to the sender, it appears that the packet was lost or the target computer is offline. `reject` causes

FreeBSD to send an error packet back to the sender, just as it would if the host or port was unreachable (as if the router couldn't find the target computer or the target computer exists but had no program running on the target port). Using deny can minimize the impact of certain types of denial-of-service (DoS) attacks, and can make it harder for some cracker scanning tools to find your system; but once you're found, using reject makes it less obvious that you're running a firewall on a port. Which policy is preferable is a matter of some debate, but I generally prefer deny. (One exception is port 113, which is used by the ident server. Using a policy of deny on this port can slow down access to servers that try to log the username of the client's user.) The count action causes FreeBSD to increment counters for a rule, but to take no other action; it tries to match the packet against subsequent rules.

- **log** This parameter causes information on a match to be output to the system console.

- **protocol** This parameter specifies the protocol of the packet. This value is normally tcp, udp, or icmp, for the like-named protocols. A value of ip or all matches packets of any type.

- **address** The address parameter has a moderately complex syntax of its own, as described in the upcoming section, "ipfw Addresses." The address includes information on the source and destination IP addresses and port numbers, as well as the network interface.

- **options** You can provide several options that match particular types of packets. For example, established matches packets that are part of an existing connection, setup matches packets that are an attempt to establish a connection, in matches packets that are coming into the system, and out matches packets that are being sent from the system. The established rule can be particularly helpful in designing a firewall that permits return traffic for network clients, as illustrated in "Examples of ipfw in Action."

ipfw Commands

When you design a firewall rule set, you'll ultimately turn it into a script that your system runs at boot time. Most of these rules will use the add command. During development, though, you'll need to use a wider array of commands, including

- **add** This command adds a rule to the rule set.
- **delete** This command deletes a rule from the rule set.
- **list** This command lists all the rules in the rule set, or a single specified rule.
- **flush** This command deletes all the rules from a rule set, except for the default rule.
- **resetlog** This command resets the counter of matches to a rule. You might create a cron job that periodically resets the rules you want to log, so that if they reach the maximum number of packets you specified when configuring the kernel, you can continue to see matches.

ipfw Addresses

The *address* specification in the `ipfw` command is fairly complex. Its syntax is as follows:

```
from address/mask [port] to address/mask [port] [via interface]
```

Each of these components requires further elaboration:

- Every TCP/IP packet includes a source and destination address. You must specify these in the firewall rule using the `from` and `to` keywords, respectively. (If you don't care about one or another, you can use the `any` keyword for the address, as described shortly.)

- Both the source and destination addresses may be expressed as a single IP address (such as `172.27.145.31`), as a network address with a mask specified as the number of bits (such as `172.27.145.0/24`), or as a network address with a mask specified as a 4-byte number (such as `172.27.145.0:255.255.255.0`; note that a colon separates the address and netmask). You can provide a hostname in place of an IP address if you prefer, but an IP address is more secure because it doesn't rely upon DNS resolution, which can be compromised. Specifying `any` as the address matches any IP address.

- The *port* is the port number for protocols that support them (TCP and UDP). You can omit the port number if you don't care about it. You can also list multiple ports separated by commas (such as `25,80`), or provide a range of ports by using a dash (such as `1-1024`).

- If you want a rule to apply to traffic to or from a particular network interface, you can use the `via` keyword to accomplish this goal. The *interface* in this case is either the computer's IP address on that interface or the name for the interface (such as `fxp0`).

Examples of ipfw in Action

Some examples of `ipfw` rules are now in order, to help you ground the command's fairly complex syntax. First, consider the command presented earlier, in "The Default Policy":

```
# ipfw add 65534 allow all from any to any
```

This command adds a rule, numbered 65534, which is one before the default rule of 65535. The new command tells the system to accept all traffic from any address to any other address. Because this rule is so wide-reaching, and because it occurs just before the default deny rule, it effectively overrides that rule. You can see both rules by using the `list` command just after entering the previous one:

```
# ipfw list
65534 allow ip from any to any
65535 deny ip from any to any
```

The new rule is identical to the default rule, except that it specifies that packets be allowed rather than denied. (In listing the rule, ipfw has converted the all keyword to ip; the two are synonymous, so this change is unimportant in practice.)

Now, suppose you want to create a real firewall on a computer that functions as a client and runs an SMTP (mail) server. If you want to use a default-deny policy, you should clear the default-allow rule that was just created. You can do this with either of the following commands:

```
# ipfw delete 65534
# ipfw flush
```

The first command deletes just the one added rule, whereas the second deletes all the rules except the default rule. Because only one rule has been added, they have equivalent effects in this case. At this point, your system won't accept any incoming or outgoing traffic. You can open incoming traffic to your SMTP server with the following command:

```
# ipfw add allow tcp from any to 172.23.45.67 25
```

This command assumes that the server's IP address is 172.23.45.67; change that detail as required. SMTP servers must normally accept mail from any site, so the source specification is quite lenient. At this point, the system accepts incoming port-25 access, but the mail server can't send replies. To open port 25 to outgoing traffic, a rule like the following does the trick:

```
# ipfw add allow tcp from 172.23.45.67 25 to any
```

Now the computer's mail server should be accessible, assuming it's running. You can verify this configuration by sending mail from another system or by using Telnet on another computer to access port 25. (Consult Chapter 19 for information on configuring a mail server.) Chances are you won't be able to send mail from the system you're configuring, though, because the firewall blocks DNS queries, which go out on UDP port 53. You can rectify this problem with the following rules:

```
# ipfw add allow udp from 172.23.45.1 53 to 172.23.45.67
# ipfw add allow udp from 172.23.45.67 to 172.23.45.1 53
```

These commands permit the system to communicate with UDP port 53 on 172.23.45.1 (the DNS server in this example; this IP address should be changed for your network). If you have multiple DNS servers, you may need to duplicate these lines, with appropriate changes to the DNS server IP address for each DNS server.

The rules presented thus far enable servers to function, but what about clients? Part of the job is permitting outgoing connections. If you want to support particular protocols, you can do so with rules like the following, which permit outgoing HTTP and Telnet connections:

```
# ipfw add allow tcp from 172.23.45.67 1025-65535 to any 23,80
```

This rule explicitly allows outgoing connections from only the unprivileged ports (numbered 1025 and above) to any computer's Telnet (23) and HTTP (80) ports. How can return traffic make it through, though? One trick that's very useful, particularly for protocols that might legitimately be used with many systems, is to allow *established* connections to local unprivileged ports:

```
# ipfw add allow tcp from any 23,80 to 172.23.45.67 1025-65535 ⤸
  established
```

Because the client establishes the connection, all return packets match the `established` option; but an attempt to make an initial connection to any server that runs on a high port will fail. You might also want to create rules to explicitly block undesirable access to servers that run on unprivileged ports. For instance, X servers (described in Chapter 13) run on ports 6000-6063 (the first instance on 6000, the second on 6001, and so on). Thus, you might want to create a rule *earlier* in the sequence to protect these ports.

If you want to permit *any* outgoing requests, you can omit the port numbers (`23,80`) from the preceding two rules. This action will allow access to all network protocols, but it also provides greater opportunity for attack; a miscreant might more easily generate malformed packets that could slip through this rule.

The preceding rules are merely examples. A working firewall is likely to have many more rules than are presented here. Although these rules are aimed at a computer that functions as a client or server, rules designed for a router would be similar. A router's rules would be more likely to include ranges of IP addresses rather than a single IP address, though. A router might also profit from the use of the `via` keyword to protect the system from spoofed addresses.

 The `/etc/rc.firewall` script contains many firewall rules. You can study that script for more ideas about how to create such rules.

Automating the Firewall Script

Naturally, you don't want to have to type a huge number of rules whenever you start your computer. Instead, you should enter your firewall rules in a script. The simplest way to do this is to add lines such as the following to `/etc/rc.conf`:

```
firewall_enable="YES"
firewall_type="client"
```

These options tell the system to run the /etc/rc.firewall script at startup, using the firewall type code client. Possible type codes are open (allowing access to any system), closed (disabling all access, much like the default configuration upon starting firewalling), client (configured in a reasonable way for many network client systems), simple (a good starting point for a router firewall), and unknown (loading no rules except for the default deny rule). In addition, you can specify a filename that contains firewall rules. For instance, firewall_type="/usr/local/etc/firewall" tells the system to load the rules in /usr/local/etc/firewall. This file should contain ipfw commands, minus the call to ipfw. For instance, the file might include lines like this:

```
add allow udp from 172.23.45.1 53 to 172.23.45.67
add allow udp from 172.23.45.67 to 172.23.45.1 53
```

The /etc/rc.firewall script loads the firewall module, as well as whichever rule set you specify. Thus, this approach can be a good way to launch a firewall configuration even without recompiling your kernel. You may want to experiment with the options to learn what they do.

 *You can type **/etc/netstart** to restart the network configuration, including the firewall scripts, without rebooting the computer. If your network uses DHCP to assign IP addresses, you may need to type **killall dhclient; /etc/netstart** instead, or the system will lose its IP address.*

Configuring NAT

If you want your FreeBSD system to function as a NAT router, you must use the natd program to do the job. If you check the natd man page, you'll find a complex syntax for this command. Most of the available options relate to complex NAT configurations, such as using it for load balancing. A simple NAT configuration, in which the NAT router "hides" a network behind its own external IP address, can be implemented by placing the following lines in /etc/rc.conf:

```
gateway_enable="YES"
firewall_enable="YES"
firewall_type="simple"
natd_enable="YES"
natd_interface="fxp0"
natd_flags=""
```

Some of these lines are identical to those used in a firewall configuration, as described in "Automating the Firewall Script." A few additional comments are in order:

- Normally, a NAT router has two or more network interfaces, such as one for a local network and one for a cable modem. The `gateway_enable` option activates routing between these interfaces; all routers use this option or configure the same feature in some other way.

- You can add firewall rules to your NAT router much as you would to any other router. The nature of NAT means that you don't need to be as concerned about direct attacks on the local network, but attacks on the NAT router are still possible, as are attacks originating from behind the NAT router.

- The `natd_interface` option specifies the network interface that's linked to the Internet—that is, your cable modem, DSL connection, or even a conventional dial-up PPP interface. If you specify the wrong interface, NAT will operate backwards—"hiding" the entire Internet behind your router's single IP address!

- If you want to run a server behind the NAT router, you can pass parameters to `natd` using the `natd_flags` option to accomplish this goal. Specifically, the `-redirect_port` parameter does the job, as in `-redirect_port tcp 192.168.1.3:80 80` to redirect traffic addressed to the NAT router's external TCP port 80 to TCP port 80 on 192.168.1.3.

As with packet-filter firewall features, NAT requires support in the kernel, and this support isn't part of a standard kernel. The `natd_enable` option in `/etc/rc.conf` causes the system to load the appropriate support in modular form, but if you recompile your kernel, you may want to add the following options to your configuration file:

```
options IPFIREWALL
options IPDIVERT
```

Summary

Firewalls are extremely important network security tools. In 2002, any system that's permanently connected to the Internet should be protected by a firewall; the number of attacks on systems makes it risky to run an unprotected system. Other security measures, described in Chapter 29, can be used instead of or in addition to some types of firewall configuration in many situations.

Firewalls come in two main varieties: packet filters and proxy servers. The former are implemented in FreeBSD using the `ipfw` or IP Filter tools. The latter are implemented using a wide variety of tools that differ in the types of protections they offer. When using `ipfw`, you must design a set of rules to control access to ports on your system. These rules should pass traffic that you expressly allow and deny all other traffic. In this way, you can protect servers you might not know are running, or protect servers or computers from being abused by external miscreants who have no business attempting to access your systems.

The Complete Reference

FreeBSD

Part IV

Servers

Chapter 18

File Servers

M any network transfers involve the exchange of one or more files. Mail messages are files, web pages are files, Usenet news messages are files, and so on. Thus, servers that handle such protocols deal in file transfers, even if you don't normally think of them in those terms. Some servers, though, deal with files in a way that's more direct from the human perspective. These file servers allow users to upload arbitrary files to or download arbitrary files from the server computer. In some cases, users can do this from within programs that aren't normally network-enabled, such as word processors. This chapter is devoted to the configuration and use of three common file servers: the *File Transfer Protocol (FTP)*, which has long been an Internet standard; the *Network File System (NFS)*, which is a popular file-sharing protocol among UNIX-like systems; and *Samba*, which provides file-sharing support for Windows clients using the Server Message Block (SMB)/Common Internet File System (CIFS) protocol. The chapter begins, though, with a brief overview of what file servers can do and how they differ among themselves.

Types of File Servers

Even when considering only file servers that provide more-or-less direct and arbitrary access to files, the available servers vary substantially in features. Much of this variation is due to differences in the underlying protocols the servers implement. Understanding some of these differences is important when you decide which file server to run. This section describes two broad classes of file servers—file transfer servers and file sharing servers. I also provide an overview of various common servers, including some that aren't covered in greater detail in this chapter.

File Transfer Servers Versus File Sharing Servers

I use the term *file transfer server* to refer to a fairly basic type of file server. Such servers enable a user to run a client program matched to the server. The user can then select files on either the client or the server in order to transfer the files. Such a procedure can be a good way to transfer files from one computer to another, if that's the goal. FTP is an extremely popular file transfer server.

Where file transfer servers fall short is in enabling clients to directly manipulate files on the remote system. For instance, suppose you as a client don't really want or need a local copy of a file; you just want to change the file, or load it directly into a local application. File transfer servers make it difficult to perform such dynamic changes. That's where *file sharing servers* enter the picture. These servers are designed with the intent that the client computer make the server's files available to local applications as if the server were a local hard disk partition. Programs run on the client can then load files directly, save files, or even modify existing files (for instance, by appending data to an existing file). The NFS and Samba servers described in this chapter are two popular file sharing servers.

File sharing servers provide a superset of the functions available in file transfer servers. From the server's point of view, a file-sharing protocol provides additional features, such as the ability to append data to a file. Typically, file sharing protocols also provide features to better enable the server to fit into the client system's filesystem model. For instance, NFS supports UNIX-style permissions and ownership, while SMB/CIFS supports DOS-style hidden, system, and archive attributes. In most respects, though, file transfer and file sharing servers provide similar functionality—namely, the ability to transfer whole files in either direction. (In fact, there are clients to treat FTP as a file-sharing protocol, and Samba ships with a tool called `smbclient` that provides an FTP-like interface on Samba servers.)

Ancillary File Server Features

In addition to basic file-transfer abilities, file servers support a host of peripheral features. Some of these help define the server as falling in the file transfer or file sharing category, and others help determine the precise role that the server can fill in a network. Examples of such features include

- **Filename limits**   Most file server protocols have broad limits on filenames. Many rely upon the host OS for details such as whether filenames are interpreted in a case-sensitive manner.

- **Ancillary file metadata**   Some protocols provide for the transfer of various types of file metadata (data that describe the file), such as ownership and permissions. As just noted, in "File Transfer Servers Versus File Sharing Servers," such metadata can be important in file sharing servers because the available metadata should match the metadata supported by the client OS.

- **File listings**   When transferring files, it's helpful to be able to see a list of available files. The three servers described in this chapter all provide such listings, but a few of the more primitive file servers don't; when using them, you must know the names of the files you want to transfer when making the request.

In addition to file *server* features, *client* features can be very important. In the case of FTP, a wide variety of clients are available, ranging from the original text-mode `ftp` to flashy GUI programs. File sharing servers are typically used from tools that are built into the client OSs, and that make the server look like a local hard disk to local applications. Chapter 24 includes information on some common file transfer clients for FreeBSD.

Common File Servers and Their Uses

Many different file servers exist, and each has its own place in the file server world. Some of the more popular file servers include

- **FTP servers**   As already noted, FTP is an early and still-popular file server protocol. It's implemented in several different servers, such as WU-FTPD, ProFTPd, and BSD FTP. The next section, "Setting Up an FTP Server," describes the operation of BSD FTP in FreeBSD. FTP is useful for general-purpose file-transfer operations when users have accounts on the FTP server system. A special mode, known as *anonymous FTP*, allows users to transfer files when they don't have accounts. (For security reasons, anonymous FTP is usually configured to permit only the retrieval of files from the server.) Although many users today are unaware of FTP, it remains an important protocol because web pages frequently link to binary files stored on FTP servers. One important drawback to FTP is that it's entirely unencrypted, so passwords and data aren't very secure.

- **NFS servers** NFS was developed by Sun Microsystems as a means of file sharing among UNIX systems. NFS supports all the usual UNIX filesystem features, such as ownership and permissions, so it's long been the file sharing protocol of choice on UNIX and UNIX-like systems. NFS relies upon a *trusted hosts* security model, in which the server relies upon the client to authenticate users and control access to files. This model was reasonable in the days when UNIX computers were relatively rare and tightly controlled, but it's riskier in today's environment. Thus, proper control of NFS servers, including very careful access control restrictions, is important.

- **SMB/CIFS servers** SMB/CIFS is most commonly used on Windows-dominated networks for file and printer sharing. The protocol supports DOS and Windows filesystem features, but not UNIX filesystem features. Samba provides elaborate mechanisms to support these features on UNIX-style systems. In fact, in many respects Samba is more flexible than the SMB/CIFS server support built into Windows, which can make a FreeBSD system a valuable addition to a Windows-dominated network. SMB/CIFS uses usernames and passwords for access control. The password may optionally be encrypted, but other data are not.

- **AppleTalk servers** Apple developed a file-sharing protocol called *AppleTalk* for use with its Macintosh computers. You can turn FreeBSD into an AppleTalk server with the Netatalk package (http://netatalk.sourceforge.net). This package is most useful for versions of Mac OS prior to Mac OS X, so I don't describe it in any detail in this book. Mac OS X is built around a UNIX core (including substantial borrowing from FreeBSD), so it can use NFS for file sharing, as well as AppleTalk and SMB/CIFS. Like SMB/CIFS, AppleTalk uses a username/password model for authentication, and the password may or may not be encrypted, depending upon settings on the client and server.

- **rcp servers** The rcp program is a very simple file-transfer tool. It works much like the ordinary cp program for copying files locally, but it's network-enabled. Like NFS, rcp relies upon a trusted-hosts security model, with access controls provided in users' .rhosts files. This tool can be a quick and convenient way to transfer files, but it's not very good for browsing files on a remote server.

- **SSH servers** The Secure Shell (SSH) program is generally considered a remote login server, and is described in Chapter 21. It includes the ability to transfer files, though. This can be done via the scp client program, which works much like rcp. More recently, SSH file-transfer client programs have been acquiring FTP client features, and in some cases the two have merged. The sftp and gFTP clients, for instance, both provide FTP-like interfaces but support encrypted data transfers via an SSH server. (In fact, gFTP was originally an FTP client, and can still function as one.)

■ **Web servers**   Web servers, which use the Hypertext Transfer Protocol (HTTP), are designed primarily for one-way delivery of data files, from the server to the client. They can transfer files in the other direction, though. Web servers typically don't use authentication, although they can. Because web servers typically deliver files that the user reads immediately in the web client program (the web browser), and because web servers are so important, Chapter 20 describes the configuration of the most popular web server, Apache.

Typically, FTP servers are used for cross-platform data transfers or when there's little need for clients to dynamically alter data stored on the server. They can be used with authentication (to give individual users access to their files), but this practice is risky because of the unencrypted nature of the FTP password exchange. You may want to shift to SSH for such functions, if possible. (No special SSH server configuration is required.)

File sharing servers are most commonly used with clients of the target OS types (UNIX or UNIX-like systems for NFS; DOS, Windows, or OS/2 systems for Samba; and Mac OS systems for Netatalk). In a few cases, though, you may want to use a protocol built for another OS, such as NFS with Windows clients. You might do this because a network is dominated by one type of system and you have only one or two clients of another type, thus making it simpler to equip the client computers with appropriate client protocols. You might also do this if the security model of the protocol better fits your network's security policies.

Setting Up an FTP Server

Basic FTP server configuration in FreeBSD is fairly straightforward, but if you want to run something other than the standard BSD FTP server, or if you want to run a more advanced configuration (including an anonymous server), you'll have more work to do. Consult the documentation for the alternative server to learn more about such configurations. Actually running the server requires making changes to your `inetd` super server configuration, as described in Chapter 16. Making changes to the configuration requires altering the options used when launching the server from `inetd`.

Common FTP Server Programs

FTP has been around for long enough that several FTP server programs have cropped up. Some of the options in FreeBSD are

■ **BSD FTP**   The default FTP server in FreeBSD traces its ancestry back to the 4.2 BSD release. This server is fairly simple to configure and is installed by default on most FreeBSD systems.

■ **WU-FTPD**   The Wuarchive FTP Daemon (WU-FTPD; `http://www.wu-ftpd.org`) is a popular FTP server on many platforms, but it's not commonly used in FreeBSD. It has a history of security-related bugs.

- **ProFTPd**   This package, headquartered at `http://proftpd.linux.co.uk`, is designed as a very flexible and extensible FTP server. Its configuration file syntax is based on that used by the Apache web browser.

- **oftpd**   This program is a small FTP server that's designed for security when running an anonymous FTP site. You can learn more about it at `http://www.time-travellers.org/oftpd/`.

- **twoftpd**   This is another FTP server that's designed for simplicity and security. Unlike many FTP servers, it can't run external commands, and it uses the `chroot()` system call to lock itself into the user's home directory once a user logs in.

All of these servers are available as packages or in the ports system, except for BSD FTP, which is installed with the base FreeBSD system. One of the reasons for the large number of available FTP servers is that WU-FTPD, which has long been a popular FTP server, has garnered a reputation for security-related bugs. Thus, many independent projects have cropped up to develop more security-conscious FTP servers. The default FreeBSD FTP server doesn't have a bad reputation in this respect. If you want something with more features, ProFTPd may be worth investigating. Other servers (including some not listed here—check the `ftp` ports directory or package section) may provide features that meet particular unusual needs, such as advanced access control features or the ability to process data as it's transferred.

Running an FTP Server

As described in Chapter 16, servers can be started through startup scripts or run from a super server. FTP servers are frequently, but not universally, run in the latter manner. In the case of FreeBSD, the standard `/etc/inetd.conf` file includes an entry for running the BSD FTP server, but it's commented out by default:

```
#ftp  stream  tcp  nowait  root  /usr/libexec/ftpd  ftpd -l
```

To enable the FTP server, you should:

1. Remove the pound sign (#) that begins the line.
2. Restart `inetd` by typing **killall -SIGHUP inetd**.

At this point, an attempt to access the computer's FTP server from another system should be greeted by an FTP login prompt, assuming no firewall or other access control tool blocks the FTP port. For instance:

```
$ ftp halrloprillalar
Connected to halrloprillalar.rodsbooks.com.
220 halrloprillalar.rodsbooks.com FTP server (Version 6.00LS) ready.
```

```
Name (prill:rodsmith): rodsmith
331 Password required for rodsmith.
Password:
230 User rodsmith logged in.
Remote system type is UNIX.
Using binary mode to transfer files.
ftp>
```

Note *Chapter 24 includes more information on using FTP client packages.*

The default configuration requires the use of a username and password, and gives users access to files in their home directories or to files in other directories that the users are allowed to read, as determined by file ownership and permission (described in Chapters 8 and 10). This configuration is reasonable for many purposes, but one popular use of FTP is not served by this configuration: an anonymous FTP server. To run an anonymous FTP site, you must create an account with a username of ftp. (Chapter 10 covers account creation and maintenance.) This account should have few privileges, and it should probably be configured to disable direct logins. It does need a home directory, though. The FTP server uses the ftp user's home directory as the root directory for all anonymous accesses, so that anonymous users can't access ordinary users' files or system files.

From the client, a user types a username of **anonymous** and any password (traditionally the user's real e-mail address, although the BSD FTP server doesn't enforce this tradition) to access an FTP site anonymously.

Running alternative FTP servers is similar to running BSD FTP, but some details may differ. For instance, most FTP servers can be run from inetd, but you may need to alter the server's name or options. Some of the more sophisticated FTP servers provide configuration files to alter their options (BSD FTP relies upon parameters passed to the server from inetd). Some of these servers may also be run stand-alone (not from inetd), which is a preferable configuration if the site is very busy.

Setting Up an NFS Server

If you need to enable users of UNIX-like systems to read and write files on a server directly from applications, an FTP server isn't the best choice. For such situations, an NFS server is preferable. Configuring such a server requires defining NFS *exports*, which are directories that are to be shared. This definition includes a specification of what computers may access the exports and in what ways—for instance, you can restrict certain clients to read-only access. Once this is done, you can start the NFS server running, at which point NFS clients can use the exported directories. (Chapter 24 includes information on configuring FreeBSD as an NFS client.)

Defining Exported Filesystems

An NFS server needs to define three types of information for exported directories: the directory to be exported, options relating to details of how the server should process access requests, and the names or IP addresses of computers that are to be permitted access to the exports. These three types of information are provided in the NFS server control file, /etc/exports. This file consists of a series of lines, one per exported directory (it's possible to list a single directory on multiple lines in order to export it with different options to different clients). Lines that begin with a pound sign (#) are comments. The syntax of regular export definition lines in this file is as follows:

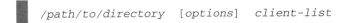

```
/path/to/directory  [options]   client-list
```

The /path/to/directory is the directory that's to be exported, such as /home or /usr/X11R6. This is an absolute path; it cannot contain current directory (.) or parent directory (..) elements. It also cannot contain any elements that are symbolic links.

You don't need to include any options, but they can be very useful in defining certain types of exports. Common options include

- **-alldirs**   This option enables clients to mount any subdirectory of the specified directory. For instance, if you export /home, and if the subdirectory /home/ jennie exists, a client can mount /home/jennie instead of /home.

- **-maproot=user[:group1[:group2[:...]]]**   Ordinarily, the root user on the client is given very limited access to files on the server, as a security precaution in case the client's security has been compromised. This option allows you to specify a user and, optionally, one or more groups, to which the client's root user should be linked. For instance, if you use -maproot=jennie, then the client's root user will be able to read and write files with the permissions of the server's account jennie.

- **-mapall=user[:group1[:group2[:...]]]**   This option works much like the -maproot option, except that it applies the permission change to *all* client users. (Ordinarily, users' permissions are mapped by local and remote user IDs, so somebody with UID 1002 on the client can access the same files that the user with UID 1002 on the server can.)

- **-ro or -o**   Ordinarily, the NFS server gives clients full read/write access to the export, within limits imposed by ordinary file ownership and permissions. These options tell the server to provide read-only access instead.

The final component of an /etc/exports entry is a list of clients that are to be given access to the export. If you list multiple clients, you separate them by spaces. You can specify clients in several different ways:

- **Hostnames**   You can provide a hostname, such as nova.luna.edu (or nova if the server's DNS system looks for hosts in the luna.edu domain).

- **IP addresses**   An IP address, such as 172.17.2.251, works as well as a hostname. In fact, an IP address imposes lower overhead because there's no DNS lookup.

- **Network blocks**   You can specify all the computers on a single network by preceding a shortened IP address by the keyword -network, and optionally following it by -netmask and a network mask. For instance, -network 172.17.2 -netmask 255.255.255.0 tells the server to accept any client in the 172.17.2.0/24 address range.

- **NIS netgroup**   If your network runs a Network Information Service (NIS) server, you can specify an NIS netgroup name. Actually, the system tries to interpret a name as an NIS netgroup name before trying to interpret it as a hostname.

- **No specification**   If you omit any specification of clients, the NFS server accepts connections from anybody.

Caution   *Omitting a client specification is very dangerous! Because a typo or other error could easily result in a missing client specification, and thus a server that's wide-open to anybody who might try to access it, you should be very careful in configuring your /etc/exports file. You should also create a firewall rule (described in Chapter 17) to limit access to the NFS server (port 2049) as a redundant protection.*

As an example of a complete NFS server configuration, consider Listing 18-1. This listing exports two directories: /usr/src and /home. The first directory is exported to the 172.17.2.0/24 network and to the computers nova, nebula, blackhole, and browndwarf.luna.edu. As is common in FreeBSD configuration files, the backslash character indicates a line continuation, which can improve readability of very long lines. The /usr/src directory is exported without any special options. The /home directory is exported with the -alldirs option to 172.17.4.8, nova, and nebula, so that clients can mount individual subdirectories of /home. The /home directory is exported with different options to blackhole. This system's root user may read and write the same files and directories as jennie on the server.

Listing 18-1.
Sample
/etc/exports
File

```
/usr/src -network 172.17.2 -netmask 255.255.255.0 nova nebula \
         blackhole browndwarf.luna.edu
/home   -alldirs  172.17.4.8 nova nebula
/home   -maproot=jennie  blackhole
```

Tending to Security Issues

NFS security can be tricky. The trusted-hosts security model means that the server essentially delegates some of its security duties to the client. If a client computer is compromised, that problem can lead to at least a limited compromise of the NFS server—ideally, not enough to gain `root` access to the server, but enough to access users' files, if the server holds user files. Furthermore, a misconfiguration of the server's list of trusted hosts can be a serious issue, for similar reasons.

NFS server security begins with a careful review of your list of trusted hosts in `/etc/exports`. Be sure you list at least one host for every export, and be sure that every listed host or network should have access to the server. Although Listing 18-1 used hostnames for many entries for illustrative purposes, this practice should be avoided whenever possible. If an intruder compromises the DNS server used by the NFS server, hostname-based security becomes suspect at best. IP addresses are harder to compromise, although even they aren't completely trustworthy, particularly if an intruder has physical access to your network.

Security is best implemented in layers. Restrictions in `/etc/exports` are a good starting point, but they shouldn't be the end. Use a firewall to create redundant restrictions, so that a misconfiguration of `/etc/exports` won't open your system to attack. You should also attend to the ownership and permissions of files on the directories you export. Whenever possible, use `-mapall` to map all accesses to a local low-access user, to make it harder for an intruder to leverage a normal user's access into something greater.

Running the NFS Server

The NFS server is implemented by the `nfsd` program. It's normally run by the system startup scripts, as controlled by the following line in `/etc/rc.conf`:

```
nfs_server_enable="YES"
```

If this line isn't present, or if it's set to NO, you should add or change the line to tell FreeBSD to enable the NFS server when it next boots. You can implement your change immediately by typing **/etc/netstart**. (If your system obtains its IP address via DHCP, type **killall dhclient; /etc/netstart** instead; but servers more commonly use static IP addresses, so that clients can more readily locate them.)

Setting Up Samba

In 2002, most *x86* computers run Microsoft Windows. Thus, FreeBSD systems are often called upon to function as servers for Windows clients. In the file-sharing arena, this goal is best accomplished by equipping FreeBSD to use SMB/CIFS. This task is accomplished by using the Samba server (`http://www.samba.org`). Samba is a very complex server, so this chapter can only get you started using it. For more information, consult its man page, the documentation on the Samba web page, or a book on the subject, such as DeRoest's *Samba UNIX & NT Internetworking* (McGraw-Hill, 2000) or my *Linux Samba Server Administration* (Sybex, 2000).

Samba configuration is handled by editing a file called `smb.conf`, which in FreeBSD's standard Samba installation is stored in `/usr/local/etc`. This file consists of a section called `global`, in which defaults and general settings are stored; and one or more sections named after the *shares* that they create, a share being a resource that can be mounted or used as a printer by the client, much like an NFS export. The `smb.conf` section and share names appear surrounded by square brackets. Conventionally, lines belonging to a share are indented. The pound sign (#) denotes a comment.

Configuring Global Settings

The default FreeBSD `smb.conf` file includes a `global` section that's fairly long and copiously commented, so you can learn a lot about Samba configuration merely by reading this section. A shorter `global` section might resemble the following:

```
[global]
   workgroup = GALAXY
   netbios name = WORMHOLE
   server string = Local file server
   hosts allow = 172.17.2.
   load printers = Yes
   security = User
   encrypt passwords = Yes
```

Each Samba parameter takes the form

```
parameter = Value
```

Case is unimportant, except when the value is case-sensitive, such as a FreeBSD directory name. As you can see from the preceding example, spaces are permitted in both parameters and values. The meanings of the parameters shown in this example are as follows:

■ **workgroup** SMB/CIFS (or, more precisely, NetBIOS, upon which SMB/CIFS is built) collects computers into a *workgroup* or a *domain*. A domain is a workgroup with a central authentication server, known as the *domain controller*. Whether your network uses a workgroup or a domain configuration, you specify its name with this parameter. Failing to do so will cause your Samba server to not appear in Windows systems' Network Neighborhood or Computers Near Me workgroup browsers. This is one of the few settings that you must change from the default in order to enable basic functionality.

■ **netbios name** This parameter is the name to which Samba responds. It may be different from your computer's TCP/IP hostname, but it's usually best if the TCP/IP and NetBIOS names match. If you omit this parameter, Samba uses the TCP/IP hostname, minus the domain portion.

■ **server string** This parameter sets a descriptive string that's visible from Windows workgroup browsers.

Caution	*Some Samba configurations use a default* `server string` *parameter that identifies the computer and its server software in detail. This can be a security risk because it can give a miscreant information on the server version, and hence its vulnerabilities. The standard FreeBSD* `smb.conf` *file sets the* `server string` *to* `Samba server`, *which provides some information on the server, but not enough to identify the server's version number.*

- **hosts allow** SMB/CIFS relies upon a username and password for authentication, but Samba expands this security model by providing a means to limit access based on hostnames, IP addresses, and network blocks. The example limits access to computers on the 172.17.2.0/24 network block (Samba fills out the trailing 0 and netmask when you provide a number of less than three bytes with a final period).

- **load printers** Samba can function as a printer server, as well as a file server. The `load printers = Yes` parameter is part of a configuration in which Samba reads the printer names from `/etc/printcap` and creates printer shares for all the available printers. This configuration also requires a special `printers` share, as described briefly in "Defining File Shares."

- **security** Samba supports several different methods of interpreting usernames and passwords. The most useful is `security = User`, which causes Samba to match usernames to the usual FreeBSD user database and match passwords to normal FreeBSD passwords or to a special Samba password database, depending upon the value of the `encrypt passwords` parameter.

- **encrypt passwords** This option frequently needs attention. The default value, `No`, causes Samba to expect unencrypted passwords from clients. Samba can then match these passwords against the normal FreeBSD password database. The problem with this option is that modern versions of Windows (since Windows 95 OSR2) send only encrypted passwords. To use Samba with recent Windows clients, you must either reconfigure the Windows clients or enable encrypted passwords in Samba, as the example `global` section does. This action requires setting up a separate Samba password database, as described in the next section.

Basic Samba functionality usually requires adjusting the `workgroup` and `encrypt passwords` settings. In most cases, other settings come with reasonable defaults, or at least values that won't cause the server to fail or be invisible to clients. You may want to tweak some of these settings for improved behavior, however. There are also various `global` parameters you might want to change if the computer should function as a domain controller, NetBIOS name server, or in other advanced capacities. Such functions are described in the Samba documentation but are beyond the scope of this book.

Adjusting Passwords

Perhaps the most troublesome aspect of Samba configuration for new Samba administrators is passwords. As described in the previous section, all versions of Windows shipped in recent years are configured to send only encrypted passwords. This is a good feature from a security point of view because it means that the passwords are not as easily compromised by password "sniffers" on the local network. Unfortunately, the encryption method used by SMB/CIFS is incompatible with the one used by FreeBSD for its own local password database. Thus, to use encrypted passwords, you must maintain two FreeBSD password databases: one for normal user logins and one for Samba access.

The tool for creating and manipulating a Samba password database is smbpasswd. To create a new entry in the database, type the following command:

```
# smbpasswd -a jennie
New SMB password:
Retype new SMB password:
unable to open passdb database.
Added user jennie.
```

The -a option to this command adds the specified user to the Samba password database. This user must already exist in the standard FreeBSD user database, so if necessary, you should first add the user, as described in Chapter 10. The message unable to open passdb database may appear the first time you run smbpasswd with the -a option. This message means that the password database file doesn't exist (it's /usr/local/private/smbpasswd). The smbpasswd program creates the file automatically, though.

Caution   *The Samba package includes a default smbpasswd database file that may cause problems. If smbpasswd doesn't work, try deleting the default file. The default file also includes entries for various system accounts, but it's safest not to include such accounts, so if you keep this file, you should delete these entries from the file by using a text editor; delete each line that refers to a system account, such as root or daemon.*

Once you've created user accounts, you can change their passwords using smbpasswd; just run the program without the -a option, much as you'd use the standard FreeBSD passwd utility, as described in Chapter 10. Ordinary users can run this program, as well, in order to change their Samba passwords.

Although encrypted passwords are useful from a security point of view, you may prefer to use cleartext passwords to obviate the need to maintain two password databases if you're confident that your local network is secure. To do so, you must reconfigure recent versions of Windows to provide cleartext passwords. You can do this by using the configuration files in /usr/local/share/doc/samba/Registry. These files have names of the form *WinVer*_PlainPassword.reg, where *WinVer* is the Windows version, such as Win98 or Win2000. Copy the appropriate files for your clients to a FAT floppy disk, insert the floppy in the Windows client system, and double-click the appropriate .reg file. Windows will update its Registry to enable cleartext passwords. Repeat this process with all of your Windows clients. You can then set encrypt passwords = No in smb.conf and forego the smbpasswd database maintenance.

Defining File Shares

Aside from the global section of smb.conf, that file contains definitions of individual file and printer shares. A typical example looks like this:

```
[hubble]
    path = /home/public/hubble-images
    comment = Telescopic Images
    browseable = Yes
    writeable = No
    force user = currie
    write list = grunsveld, linnehan, newman, massimino
```

This example illustrates some common (and not-so-common) parameters:

■ **path**   This parameter is the most important one; it sets the directory that's to be shared. In this case, users who mount the hubble share will see the contents of /home/public/hubble-images. The default value is /tmp, so this parameter is a virtual necessity.

■ **comment**   Like the global section's server string parameter, the share-level comment parameter sets a string that's visible from clients to help describe the share's contents or purpose. This parameter isn't strictly necessary, but it's usually desirable.

■ **browseable**   Windows clients enable users to "browse" the shares on a server to see what's available. This option tells Samba whether or not to enter a share in this browse list. A share that's *not* browseable is still accessible, but a user must know that it's present and enter its name directly in a location field to reach it.

■ **writeable**   This parameter determines whether or not users can write to the share. The default is No, so this example merely reiterates the default. A synonym is write ok, and an antonym is read only, so write ok = No or read only = Yes could be used in place of writeable = No.

■ **force user** Ordinarily, Samba employs the username provided by the client to determine what files a user can read and (for writeable shares) write. This parameter changes this behavior, causing files to be read and written with the specified user's permissions. It's usually not required, but can be handy if a directory should have files owned by only one person or if you want to bypass the normal FreeBSD user-level security.

■ **write list** This parameter creates an exception to the earlier writeable = No parameter; it specifies users who may write to the share even though it's not writeable to most users. (This feature operates independently of the force user parameter; the named users can write to the share, but the files they create will be owned by currie.) The read list parameter has the opposite effect—it enables you to restrict write access for particular users on shares that are normally writeable.

A configuration such as the one presented here is useful for common file areas, such as documents that all users of a network should be able to access or a storage area for program files you want available but don't want to install on every workstation. Another use of Samba is common, though: storing user files. For this purpose, the homes share is perfect. This share works differently than most file shares because the path parameter is set to the user's home directory, dynamically for each login. Thus, you omit the path parameter for the homes share. An example might look like this:

```
[homes]
    comment = Home Directories
    writeable = Yes
    browseable = No
    create mask = 0644
```

This definition is fairly straightforward. It demonstrates one additional parameter, though: create mask. This parameter sets the maximum permissions permitted on files that are created in a writeable share. The default value is 0744, so that files created through Samba may have their owner's execute bit set. If this result is undesirable, setting create mask to 0644 fixes the problem. (Chapter 8 describes FreeBSD permissions in more detail.) Also, homes shares are always browseable under the user's name. The browseable parameter therefore makes the share browseable under the name homes. Ordinarily, this isn't required, so homes shares usually include a browseable = No line.

The result of this homes share is that each user will see a share named after the user's own account, as shown in Figure 18-1, which shows a share called rodsmith. This figure also shows two printer shares, which are created by the load printers = Yes parameter in conjunction with a share called printers, which is part of the default FreeBSD

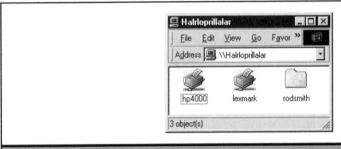

Figure 18-1. *Samba file shares show up in the Windows Network Neighborhood or My Network Places browsers.*

smb.conf file. Samba printer share definitions work just like file share definitions, but they include the printable = Yes parameter to identify them as printer shares. The printers share, like the homes share, can create multiple shares, but one for each printer specified in /etc/printcap.

Running Samba

The Samba server consists of two closely linked daemons: smbd and nmbd. The first of these is the file server itself; it fields requests from clients for actual file transfers. The nmbd program, by contrast, handles browsing and name resolution requests—it's responsible for providing clients information that appears in browsers such as the one shown in Figure 18-1. Both daemons are necessary for normal Samba operation.

The FreeBSD Samba package includes a startup script file, called /usr/local/etc/rc.d/samba.sh.sample, which is designed to start both the Samba servers. This script doesn't run automatically at boot unless you rename it to eliminate the .sample extension, so you should do so if you want to run a Samba server on a regular basis. Once you do this, Samba will run when you next reboot the computer. You can also start it running in a one-time manner by typing the script's name as root. However it starts, you can verify that the server is running by using ps, thus:

```
# ps ax | grep mbd
14925  ??  Is     0:00.01 /usr/local/sbin/smbd -D
14927  ??  Ss     0:00.06 /usr/local/sbin/nmbd -D
14955  p3  R+     0:00.00 grep mbd
```

This example pipes the result through grep to search for the string mbd, which appears in both Samba daemons' names. Such a search may turn up additional processes, such as the grep process itself, as shown here.

If the Samba server doesn't run or doesn't work in the way you expect, consult your `/var/log/messages` file. This file may include error messages that can help point you to a solution. Samba also creates log files called `/var/log/log.nmbd` and `/var/log/log.smbd` for messages from the two Samba daemons, and these can provide useful debugging information as well.

Summary

File servers are critical components of many networks, and FreeBSD is a fine platform for running such servers. FTP is one of the oldest file server protocols, and is still a very popular one, particularly for cross-platform and anonymous Internet file transfers. More sophisticated file sharing protocols such as NFS and SMB/CIFS are often used to serve clients running particular OSs. NFS servers for UNIX-like systems are fairly straightforward to configure. The Samba package provides SMB/CIFS compatibility for FreeBSD and is a very feature-laden server package.

Chapter 19

Mail Servers

From keeping in touch with friends and relatives to exchanging important business documents, e-mail is an important means of communication in today's world. For this reason, the global e-mail network must be reliable. As reliability is a hallmark of FreeBSD (and of UNIX systems generally), it shouldn't be a surprise that most e-mail exchanged today passes through at least one UNIX-like system. FreeBSD makes a fine platform for hosting the mail server programs that process this mail, whether your needs are modest or elaborate.

This chapter begins with an overview of the Internet's mail system, focusing upon the different types of mail server. Next up is information on configuring the major types of mail server. This chapter concludes with a look at an unusual mail tool, Fetchmail. This program isn't technically a server, but it fills a unique role by fitting "between" servers in certain mail delivery scenarios.

Types of Mail Servers

Midsize and large organizations typically set aside at least one computer to function as a mail server. In many cases, these computers run *multiple* mail servers, in order to handle different types of mail protocols. Some mail protocols (known as *push protocols*) require that the sender initiate a mail transfer. Others (known as *pull protocols*) require that the recipient initiate the transfer. Understanding how these two types of protocols interact is critical when planning how to configure a mail server computer.

Push Versus Pull Servers

Mail servers can deliver mail between users of a single computer, but the more interesting (and more difficult to configure) case involves mail sent from one computer to another. The key to this operation is use of a mail server as a *mail relay*—a system that accepts mail from one computer and sends it to another. It's possible to configure a mail delivery system so that several relays handle a message during the course of its delivery.

Most mail relays operate using push protocols: The sender initiates the transfer. For instance, when you compose a message using a mail reader, the mail reader uses a push protocol (most likely the *Simple Mail Transfer Protocol*, or *SMTP*) to send the message to your network's or ISP's outgoing mail server. That server then uses SMTP to send the mail to another mail server, and so on. One critical feature of push protocols is that they require the recipient computer to be accessible at all times. If a sender can't contact the recipient, mail might be lost. (In practice, SMTP relays can hold onto mail and attempt to deliver it in the future in the event of a delivery failure, but sooner or later, they give up.)

Today, the final link in the mail delivery chain is usually a pull protocol, such as the *Post Office Protocol (POP)* or the *Internet Message Access Protocol (IMAP)*. These protocols exist because the ultimate recipient computer is often a workstation that doesn't run a push mail server. Indeed, these workstations often have intermittent PPP Internet connections, so running an SMTP server would be pointless, at least for receiving internal mail.

Figure 19-1 illustrates a typical mail delivery chain. In this example, a user on the `marconi.pangaea.edu` workstation composes a message for delivery to a user in the `threeroomco.com` domain—say, ben@threeroomco.com. The `marconi` workstation's mail reader software must be configured to use the correct outgoing mail server—`morse.pangaea.edu` in this example. This server might be configured to send mail directly to its destination, or it might be configured to use another server as a relay, as shown in Figure 19-1, in which `tesla.pangaea.edu` is the final relay in the `pangaea.edu` domain.

The outgoing mail server must look up the recipient computer's address. This process involves normal DNS resolution, but there's often a twist: DNS supports a special type of address entry designed solely for mail delivery, known as the *mail exchanger (MX) record*. The MX record can be associated with a specific computer, but is more often linked to an entire domain. The MX record points to a specific computer in its own or another domain. Thus, in this example, mail may be addressed to ben@threeroomco.com, so the `tesla.pangaea.edu` computer looks up the MX record for `threeroomco.com`. This record points to a computer called `mail.threeroomco.com`, so `tesla.pangaea.edu` sends the message to that computer. Just as with outgoing mail, though, the server that functions as the point of contact with the outside world might not be the final link in the chain; this computer might be configured to forward mail to another internal mail server, such as `franklin.threeroomco.com` in Figure 19-1. This computer actually runs *two* mail servers: an SMTP push mail server and a POP or IMAP pull mail server. The ultimate recipient (ben) sits at a workstation (`osgood.threeroomco.com`) and uses a mail reader program to access the mail stored on `franklin.threeroomco.com`.

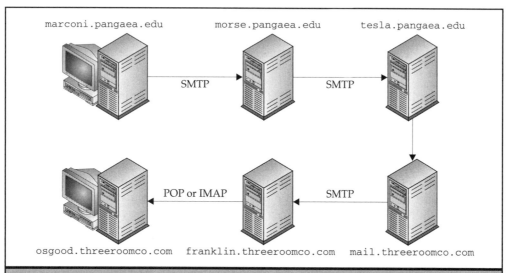

Figure 19-1. *E-mail is frequently relayed through several computers before reaching its final destination.*

It's not necessary to use a pull mail protocol in a mail delivery chain. The recipient might use a mail reader that runs directly on `franklin.threeroomco.com`, *for instance, and access that mail reader through a remote login protocol such as those described in Chapter 21.*

In this example, only the final leg of the delivery relay uses a pull mail protocol. This configuration is typical because pull mail protocols are most appropriate when the recipient system has an intermittent or otherwise restricted Internet connection, such as is common with final mail recipients. The upcoming section, "Setting Up Fetchmail," describes a way to use a pull protocol in the middle of a mail delivery chain rather than in the last step. Using a pull protocol in mid-chain is often desirable when FreeBSD hosts a mail server for local use only or for a small network behind a Network Address Translation (NAT) router, as described in Chapter 17.

It's important to note that Figure 19-1's mail route, although not atypical, is not the only possible route. There might be fewer or more computers involved in either the `pangaea.edu` or `threeroomco.com` domains, or another domain entirely might be involved at some point. Precisely how many computers are involved depends on configuration details for each server, which in turn are based on a domain's specific needs. As a general rule, more servers are involved when firewalls block access except from particular addresses, when there's some need to audit incoming or outgoing mail, when an organization uses multiple servers to distribute the load, or when mail must be converted between incompatible formats.

Examples of Push Servers

Push servers are extremely important components of mail delivery. In 2002, there are many SMTP servers available for FreeBSD. The most popular servers are extremely powerful, and are capable of handling the most demanding mail server tasks for even very large domains. The four most popular of these servers are

- **Sendmail**   This program is the most popular SMTP server in existence; surveys suggest it runs on close to half the Internet's mail servers. It's also the standard FreeBSD mail server, and is installed by default. You can learn more about it at `http://www.sendmail.org`.

- **qmail**   This server, designed in a modular way for efficiency and security, is a popular alternative to sendmail. It uses a different mail file format than sendmail, though, so you may need to replace or reconfigure common mail programs, including pull mail servers. Its home page is `http://www.qmail.org`.

- **Exim**   This program is a moderately popular replacement for sendmail. It uses the same mail file format as sendmail, so it's an easier replacement. It includes unusually strong support for filtering mail by matching patterns in headers or message bodies, which can be useful for filtering spam. The Exim home page is `http://www.exim.org`.

- **Postfix**   Like qmail, Postfix was designed in a modular way for security and speed. Like Exim, Postfix uses the same mail file format as sendmail, so it can replace sendmail with minimal changes to other programs. You can learn more at `http://www.postfix.org`.

All of these mail servers are very capable programs. They all come with the FreeBSD ports system, and sendmail and Exim are available through the packages system, so you can install any of them as described in Chapter 11. Because sendmail is installed by default and because it's the most popular mail server on the Internet at large, the upcoming section, "Setting Up an SMTP Server," covers sendmail.

Examples of Pull Servers

Pull mail servers tend to be much smaller and simpler than push mail servers. They're much less flashy, so they get less attention. Nonetheless, you have options in pull mail servers.

The first choice you face in pull mail server is which protocol to use. POP and IMAP are the most popular protocols. POP is the simpler of the two; it enables users to download mail that the server has accumulated, but provides no means for the user to organize mail on the server. The idea is that the user will implement mail folders using the mail reader on the workstation, if desired, and store mail on the workstation. IMAP, by contrast, is a more complex protocol that supports the use of mail folders on the server, as well as delivery of just parts of messages. Thus, users can store mail permanently on the server, organized into folders. This approach increases storage demands on the mail server, but can simplify life for users who routinely run multiple mail clients (say, using both a desktop and a laptop computer) because mail need not be tied to a single client. POP and IMAP are not mutually exclusive protocols; you can run both, if necessary.

All common FreeBSD pull mail servers support clients that run on just about any OS—Windows, Mac OS, FreeBSD, or anything else. Specific clients may support only certain protocols, but if a client supports a particular protocol, it should work with any server that handles that protocol.

Examples of specific pull mail servers include

- **Cyrus IMAP**   This server supports both POP and IMAP protocols. Cyrus uses its own folder format for IMAP folders. Its home page is `http://asg.web.cmu.edu/cyrus/`.

- **UW IMAP**   The University of Washington IMAP package (`http://www.washington.edu/imap/`) provides both POP and IMAP servers. It stores IMAP folders in users' home directories.

- **dkimap**   This package is a small IMAP-only server. You can read more at `http://freshmeat.net/projects/dkimap/`.

- **QPopper**   This package is a POP-only server. Formerly a commercial product, the latest versions are now open source. The QPopper web page is `http://www.eudora.com/qpopper/`.

- **qmail-pop3d**   This server ships with the qmail SMTP server, and can process the mail file format favored by qmail. It's therefore a good choice if you use qmail as your SMTP server.

For a small site, you'll probably be happy with any of these servers. Most of them are available as FreeBSD packages and in the ports system, but qmail-pop3d is available only in the qmail port, and UW-IMAP is available only as a port (mail/imap-uw).

One further detail that deserves attention is which *version* of your chosen protocol to use. Both POP and IMAP are available in various versions, which are often appended to the protocol name. In 2002, POP-3 and IMAP-4 are the latest versions, and the most popular. If you need to support some particularly old clients, you might need to seek out a server that can handle older protocols, such as POP-2, which runs on a different port than POP-3. There are also secure variants of some of these protocols, which encrypt passwords and data. Using encryption can be a good idea, particularly if your data traverse the Internet at large (say, because traveling employees must access mail remotely) or if pull mail passwords are used for purposes other than mail retrieval (a practice which should be avoided whenever possible).

Setting Up an SMTP Server

SMTP server configuration can be fairly straightforward or extremely complex, depending upon your needs. In a best-case scenario, you may be able to get by with few or no changes to FreeBSD's default sendmail configuration. In other cases, you may need to extensively alter the sendmail configuration or replace sendmail with another server. In such cases, you may want to consult a book on the server in question, such as Vixie and Avolio's *Sendmail: Theory and Practice* (Butterworth-Heinemann, 2001), Sill's *The qmail Handbook* (APress, 2001), or Hazel's *Exim: The Mail Transfer Agent* (O'Reilly, 2001). This chapter can only get you started with this potentially complex topic.

Domain Configuration Issues

The first issue in SMTP server configuration is setting up your domain. As noted earlier, in "Push Versus Pull Servers," DNS provides the means to associate a mail server with a domain. You should consult with whoever manages your DNS servers concerning this matter. If you're doing it yourself, you need to create an entry such as the following in your domain's configuration file:

```
@       IN   MX   10    mail.threeroomco.com.
```

The configuration file is usually located in /var/named, and is named after the domain, such as named.threeroomco.com. Chapter 22 provides more information on DNS configuration, including the meaning of information in the domain configuration file.

It's possible to configure a domain so that a mail server in another domain handles the mail. This configuration is convenient if you use an ISP to host your mail, even as a backup for your main mail server.

Sendmail Configuration Files

Sendmail uses `/etc/mail/sendmail.cf` as its configuration file. Unfortunately, the format of this file reminds most new administrators of gibberish. Indeed, even many experienced administrators are well advised not to touch the file; it's too easy to make a single-character typo that ruins the file and is very difficult to track down. Instead, you should edit the `/etc/mail/freebsd.mc` file. The `freebsd.mc` file uses a format that's substantially more intelligible than the `sendmail.cf` file format. When you're done editing the `freebsd.mc` file, you can convert it into an equivalent `sendmail.cf` file by typing these commands:

```
# cd /usr/share/sendmail/cf/m4
# m4 cf.m4 /etc/mail/freebsd.mc > /etc/mail/sendmail.cf
```

 You should back up the `freebsd.mc` file before changing it, or copy it to another name, edit the copy, and type the copy's name in the preceding command. Likewise, you should back up the `sendmail.cf` file before typing the preceding commands. Both steps ensure that you can return to a known standard configuration if something goes wrong.

Once you've run these commands, you'll have a new `sendmail.cf` file, and you can tell sendmail to read this file and implement its changes by typing the following command:

```
# killall -SIGHUP sendmail
```

Adjusting the Default Configuration

The default sendmail configuration works, at least to a minimal extent. When first installed, sendmail will accept mail addressed to users at the computer's hostname, but not to other hostnames. You may need to alter this configuration, particularly if a computer is to function as a mail server for a domain. In terms of outgoing mail, a default sendmail installation delivers the mail directly. This configuration is probably acceptable for a mail server computer and for some workstations with direct connectivity. In some cases, though, you may want to have sendmail relay its outgoing mail through another server, as `morse.pangaea.edu` does in Figure 19-1. Such a configuration is desirable, or sometimes even necessary, for computers with dial-up or broadband Internet links.

The basic configuration steps described here are the simplest changes that are commonly necessary. Sendmail supports many far more advanced options. A few of these, including some important security features, are described in the upcoming section, "Blocking Spam."

Setting Incoming Hostnames

Consider Figure 19-1 once again. How does any given computer in this delivery chain know when to send a message on to another computer and when to store a message in a local user's mail queue? In a default FreeBSD sendmail configuration, the answer relates exclusively to the hostname in the address. When franklin.threeroomco.com, for instance, receives a message addressed to ben@franklin.threeroomco.com, the server treats the message as destined for the local account called ben. This approach is adequate for most workstations that receive little or no direct outside mail, and even for some mail server computers. In the example of mail delivery that Figure 19-1 illustrates, though, the mail was *not* addressed to ben@franklin.threeroomco.com—it was sent to ben@threeroomco.com. A default FreeBSD sendmail installation will fail on such a message because the computer's name is not threeroomco.com, although the computer is in this domain.

This problem can be overcome by using the /etc/mail/local-host-names file. (This file doesn't exist in a default FreeBSD installation, so you'll have to create it.) This file contains all the hostnames that sendmail is to treat as local, in addition to its standard DNS hostname. For instance, to have sendmail accept mail addressed to users at threeroomco.com, /etc/mail/local-host-names should contain that domain name. You can add more lines in order to support additional hostnames or domains. For instance, if you're configuring a computer to handle the mail for several domains, you might include lines such as the following:

```
tworoomco.com
threeroomco.com
fourroomco.com
luna.edu
```

To do any good, of course, you'd need to configure the DNS servers for these domains to point to your mail server in their MX records. This configuration tells other mail servers to deliver mail to your system, and the domain names in /etc/mail/local-host-names tells your server to accept this mail as local rather than treat it as a relay attempt.

> **Note** *The filename /etc/mail/local-host-names isn't carved in source code; it's set by a define statement in /etc/mail/freebsd.mc. Look for the line that defines confCW_FILE and change it if you want to use another filename. You can also look for such a line if you're using a configuration file other than the standard FreeBSD file, to determine what file to use for this purpose.*

If a sender attempts to send a message through sendmail to a domain that sendmail isn't configured to accept as local, sendmail treats it as a relay attempt. Depending upon sendmail's relay configuration and factors such as the sending machine's IP address, the server may refuse such an attempt, or accept it and send the mail to the ultimate destination itself. The upcoming section, "Restricting Outgoing Spam," describes some of sendmail's relay configuration options.

Configuring an Outgoing Relay

Ordinarily, when sendmail sends mail to a remote system, the program looks up the hostname or MX record and tries to connect directly to the specified computer. Sometimes, though, this procedure isn't practical. Some ISPs, particularly on dial-up and broadband accounts, block direct outgoing SMTP connections as an antispam precaution. Even if you don't have to contend with such a restriction, if you use a dial-up connection, sending mail directly has the drawback that if the recipient is unavailable, sendmail will queue the mail for later delivery. If you don't happen to be online when sendmail tries again, the message may not get through. There are also cases where you might not want sendmail to deliver mail directly because you want to be able to control mail delivery through a central point. For instance, you might want all of a domain's outgoing mail to go through one mail server for accounting and security purposes, even though you have workstations in the domain that can run sendmail themselves.

In such cases, it's possible to configure sendmail on the workstations or dial-up computers to relay mail through another server. Such a system might resemble the `marconi.pangaea.edu` or `morse.pangaea.edu` computers in Figure 19-1. Fortunately, enabling this configuration is fairly straightforward. You need to enter a line resembling the following in your `freebsd.mc` file:

```
define(`SMART_HOST', `tesla.pangaea.edu')
```

  The preceding line uses two types of single quote marks. The first type is a back-quote, which is located to the left of the 1 key on most keyboards. The second type is an ordinary single quote, located to the right of the semicolon (;) key on most keyboards. You must enter these quote marks correctly or the line won't work.

This `define` line tells sendmail to deliver all outgoing mail to `tesla.pangaea.edu`, which is responsible for subsequent delivery. (Figure 19-1's `morse.pangaea.edu` might use this configuration.) A computer configured with this line can still process its own local mail, though. The default `freebsd.mc` file includes a line that's similar to the one in this example, except that it's commented out—that is, the line begins with `dnl`, the comment string for this file type. You can remove the `dnl`, change the relay hostname, and type **killall -SIGHUP sendmail** to use the new configuration.

Blocking Spam

Unsolicited bulk e-mail, or spam as it's more commonly known, is the bane of every mail administrator's existence. Spam chews up system resources and is a general annoyance. Spam often advertises illegal activities or sexually explicit material that users may find offensive or that you might want to block from the eyes of children, if any of your users are underage. All mail servers today support various antispam configurations. Indeed, so many are now available that this chapter can only present a brief overview of what's available. For more information, consult some antispam web sites, such as http://www.mail-abuse.org, http://spam.abuse.net, or http://www.cauce.org.

There are actually two different types of spam block you should be concerned with: incoming and outgoing. You probably think most about incoming spam because it's the type with which you're most personally familiar. You might not want to be bothered with ads for hair-loss seminars in Uzbekistan, for instance. Outgoing spam blocks are at least as important, though; if a sloppy configuration of your mail server makes it a relay for or source of spam, you can find yourself inundated with complaints, or other mail servers may refuse mail from yours, thus impairing legitimate use of your mail server.

 In 2001 and 2002, worms delivered via e-mail have become a serious problem. Some spam-fighting techniques are also effective against worms. In particular, header and content filters can block some worms.

Blocking Incoming Spam

Quite a few techniques exist to filter incoming spam. Some of these methods summarily delete the spam, but others enable you to send the spam into a special mail folder for periodic human review. Common techniques include blackhole lists, header filters, and content filters.

 No antispam technique is perfect. No matter how carefully you design your antispam filters, some spam is likely to get through. Unless you implement no filtering at all, it's likely that some legitimate e-mail will be rejected by your filters. Only experience with various antispam techniques on your site will help you set an appropriate balance to reject spam without undue collateral damage.

Using Blackhole Lists   A *blackhole list* is a service that maintains a list of IP addresses from which you may want to refuse mail. The criteria for inclusion on the list vary from one list to another, so you can fine-tune your own policies by subscribing to particular lists. For instance, one list may include only sites that have sent spam, whereas another list might include sites that are misconfigured in such a way that a spammer *could* abuse the server. Table 19-1 summarizes several common blackhole lists, but is not comprehensive.

To use a blackhole list with sendmail, you must add a line such as the following to your freebsd.mc file:

```
FEATURE(dnsbl, `dialups.mail-abuse.org', `"550 Mail from dial-up ↵
rejected; see http://mail-abuse.org/dul/enduser.htm"')
```

List Name	List URL	Server Address	Description
MAPS Realtime Blackhole List (RBL)	`http://mail-abuse.org/rbl/`	`blackholes.mail-abuse.org`	The RBL lists sites that have spammed, are open relays, or have supported spammers.
MAPS Relay Spam Stopper (RSS)	`http://www.mail-abuse.org/rss/`	`relays.mail-abuse.org`	The RSS lists sites that are open relays that have relayed spam.
MAPS Dial-Up List (DUL)	`http://www.mail-abuse.org/dul/`	`dialups.mail-abuse.org`	The DUL lists IP addresses associated with PPP dial-up or residential broadband accounts, on the grounds that such users should use their ISPs' mail relay servers.
Open Relay Database (ORDB)	`http://www.ordb.org`	`relays.ordb.org`	The ORDB lists open relays, much like the RSS, but the ORDB listing criteria are looser.
RFC Ignorant	`http://www.rfc-ignorant.org`	Various; see web site	These lists identify systems whose owners don't conform to various Internet standards, such as having correct contact information on record.

Table 19-1. *Common Blackhole Lists*

Replace the hostname (`dialups.mail-abuse.org` in this example) with the one specified in the Server Address column of Table 19-1. You should also replace the descriptive text and URL with something appropriate for the list you're using; this information is included in bounced mail messages sent to the sender, which can be important should legitimate e-mail run afoul of the list.

The blackhole lists maintained by the Mail Abuse Prevention System (MAPS)—namely the RBL, RSS, and DUL—are operated on a subscription-only basis, so you may have to pay to use these services. Some of the other blackhole lists are free for anybody to use.

One of the big advantages of blackhole lists is that they operate very early in the process—your mail server can refuse delivery of the message before it's received the bulk of the message. This feature can be important for a high-volume mail server because it can cut the bandwidth requirements, particularly as the average size of spams is increasing rapidly. The main drawback of these methods is that they assign "guilt" based on association with an IP address. If a spammer abuses a system and gets that system into a blackhole list, legitimate users of that system will be negatively impacted.

Tip *One of the reasons for using an outgoing mail relay configuration, as described earlier in "Configuring an Outgoing Relay," is because PPP and broadband accounts often wind up on the DUL and similar lists as a matter of policy, and not because specific users have abused these accounts. Relaying your mail through your ISP's mail server prevents your mail from being blocked on the basis of a DUL listing.*

Implementing Header Filters   Another approach to spam filtering is implementing filters based on the contents of a message's *headers*, which are lines at the start of a message that contain information such as the sender's and recipient's address, the Subject line, and so on. Carefully designed filters can block spam based on header information. For instance, I've found that a very effective spam filter is one that rejects any message with more than five consecutive spaces in the Subject line. (Spammers often use a descriptive subject followed by many spaces and a numeric code, in order to trick filters on relays that block too many messages with the same Subject line from getting through.)

Sendmail supports some very limited forms of header checks—you can reject mail based on the sender's hostname or IP address. More sophisticated header checks are easier to implement using post-sendmail tools, as described next, in "Implementing Content Filters." If you want to use sendmail's header checks, you need to create a file called `/etc/mail/access`. FreeBSD ships with a sample file (`/etc/mail/access.sample`), which you can use as a model. You can fill this file with lines such as the following:

```
badspammer.net              550 No spam allowed
antispam.badspammer.net     OK
spamsrus.com                REJECT
```

The `550` and `REJECT` codes both tell the system to reject mail from the specified domains, but the `550` code allows you to add a customized rejection notice, such as this example's `No spam allowed`. The `OK` code provides a means to explicitly allow messages through. This example uses this feature to provide an exception—`antispam.badspammer.net` can send mail to your system, even though the rest of the `badspammer.net` domain is denied access.

After you create your rules, you must convert the `/etc/mail/access` file into a binary format by typing the following command, then tell sendmail to reload its configuration files, as described earlier in "Sendmail Configuration Files":

```
# makemap hash /etc/mail/access.db < /etc/mail/access
```

Header filters enable a mail server to reject a message fairly early in the process, although not quite as early as blackhole lists. Mail servers that support extensive header filtering, such as Exim and Postfix, can use these filters to block mail on just about any header, thus filtering a lot of spam based on Subject headers or headers inserted by known *spamware* (software that's used only to send spam). Sender-based filters tend to suffer from many of the same problems as blackhole lists. Most importantly, it's easy to block too much legitimate e-mail should you filter a legitimate ISP that happens to be suffering from a spam problem. Maintaining header-based spam filters can also be time-consuming.

Implementing Content Filters   Mail content filters can operate on mail based on their headers or content. For instance, you might write a filter that rejects mail that refers to S.1618 (a failed piece of United States legislation that spammers often cite). Content filters are often implemented using the Procmail package, which sendmail can use to process mail after the server has accepted it for delivery. In this configuration, Procmail places mail messages in individual users' mail folders and can accept, reject, or modify mail based on the mail's contents. Some mail servers, such as Exim, can perform content filtering without the help of an outside package.

A default FreeBSD mail installation doesn't use Procmail for mail delivery. Thus, to use Procmail, you must first install it from the packages or ports system, as described in Chapter 11. An individual user can then use Procmail by editing the `.forward` file in the account's home directory to read as follows:

```
"|exec /usr/local/bin/procmail || exit 75"
```

Be sure to include the quotes surrounding this line; they *are* required. The user's `.procmailrc` file can then be populated with Procmail *recipes*—that is, its rules for how to process mail. Procmail recipes are potentially very complex, but here are two simple examples:

```
:0
*^Subject:.*        .*
/dev/null

:0 B
*^.*mailto:.*subject=3Dremove
/dev/null
```

Both examples begin with a line that starts with : 0. The second example also includes a B on this line, to indicate that it searches the message body, not just the headers. Each recipe includes zero or more lines that begin with asterisks (one line in both these cases). These lines are the recipes' conditions—they describe the data that trigger a rule. For the most part, these lines are ordinary text, but some characters have special meanings. The carat (^), used in both these examples, denotes the start of a line. The two characters . * indicate any string of zero or more characters. Thus, the first rule matches any Subject header that contains five or more consecutive spaces, surrounded by zero or more other characters. The second rule matches any line that contains the string `mailto:` followed by the string `subject=3Dremove`. (A line like this is characteristic of certain "remove" links, which are seldom present in anything but spam.) The final line of each recipe is a filename where the message is to be stored—`/dev/null` in both these cases, which effectively discards the message. Alternatively, you can send the message through another program by preceding the program's name with a vertical bar pipe character (`|`).

Restricting Outgoing Spam

At least as important as controlling incoming spam is restricting outgoing spam. The two main potential sources of spam with which you should be concerned are

- **Internal spam** Your system's users might intentionally send spam, either because they're ignorant of the problem or because they're troublemakers. You should have an explicit antispam policy in place, and you should be sure your users are aware of it, so that you can take appropriate action in case of violations.

- **Relay spam** If your computer is incorrectly configured to accept mail for relay from inappropriate sources, an outsider might use your system to relay spam. Spammers do this both to hide their own location and to offload the work of sending the spam onto a third party.

The first issue is largely a matter of setting and enforcing a local policy. Be sure that your users understand that any unsolicited mail sent to more than a very small number of people is suspect at best. Spam is often commercial in nature, so your users should be especially cautious about sending advertisements or product announcements by e-mail. Even noncommercial messages can be spam, though; users should not send chain letters, pleas to help find lost children, or other messages to many recipients, no matter how noble the cause might seem. Even aside from the issue of these messages potentially being spam, they're often hoaxes.

> **Tip** *There are legitimate uses for bulk e-mail, but the key is that it must be solicited by an opt-in mechanism, preferably with confirmation before a user's e-mail address is added to the list. Do not purchase a list of e-mail addresses from an outsider; such lists are often sold by spammers and misrepresented as being opt-in, when in fact they are not.*

The ability to relay is restricted through any of a number of sendmail configuration options. The default `freebsd.mc` file contains this relay configuration line:

```
FEATURE(relay_based_on_MX)
```

This line tells the system to relay mail from any computer that resides in a domain that lists your server as an MX in its DNS configuration. Such a configuration is convenient when a server must function as a relay for many other domains, but it's potentially easily abused; a spammer need only modify the DNS records of a domain under the spammer's control to be able to relay through your system. In most cases, you're better off replacing the `relay_based_on_MX` option with

```
FEATURE(relay_entire_domain)
```

This option tells sendmail to relay mail for the domain in which it resides, and for no others. This configuration is good for a small network's mail server. Yet another alternative is to remove this option entirely and rely upon the `access` file, described earlier, in "Implementing Header Filters." You can use the `RELAY` target in this file to control the computers that can use your server as a relay, thus:

```
172.29.39      RELAY
pangaea.edu    RELAY
```

These lines configure the computer to relay mail from computers in the `pangaea.edu` domain and from those on the 172.29.39.0/24 network. As a general rule, if you need to do anything remotely complex with relay configuration, doing it with the `access` file is the best approach. Some other sendmail relay options are risky at best.

Caution *One option, FEATURE(`promiscuous_relay`), deserves special attention as one to avoid. If you see this option in a sendmail configuration file, delete it immediately; it opens the server to accept relays from any site to any other site. Such a configuration is very likely to be found and abused.*

For more information on relay configuration and the importance of setting up appropriate antispam relay rules, consult `http://www.mail-abuse.org/tsi/`. This site and the pages it references include a great deal of invaluable information, including tips on configuring sendmail and other servers. You can test your server to be sure it's not an open relay by initiating a Telnet connection *from the mail server you want to test* to `relay-test.mail-abuse.org`. This computer will initiate an SMTP connection to the IP address from which you connected and run through an extensive series of tests.

SERVERS

 # Setting Up a POP or IMAP Server

Sendmail serves the dual function of accepting mail from outside sites and relaying mail from inside your network to outside sites. In many cases, though, you need a pull mail server to deliver mail from the sendmail server computer to the users who read their mail on workstations. Fortunately, such configurations are fairly straightforward, at least for a basic installation. A very large mail server might benefit from configurations that are more sophisticated than those that can be described in this book.

This section describes the configuration of the UW IMAP package (http://www.washington.edu/imap/), which provides both POP and IMAP servers. You can install this server from its ports directory, as described in Chapter 11. If you prefer to use another server, you can do so; most of the installation procedure is the same no matter what server you use, although details such as the server's filename may differ.

Once you install the UW IMAP port, you must reconfigure your /etc/inetd.conf file to call the POP or IMAP server. The default configuration file contains sample lines that have been commented out, but they call different binaries than UW IMAP uses. The following two lines enable the UW IMAP POP-3 and IMAP-4 servers, respectively:

```
pop3   stream  tcp  nowait  root  /usr/local/libexec/ipop3d  ipop3d
imap4  stream  tcp  nowait  root  /usr/local/libexec/imapd   imapd
```

Enter whichever of these lines is appropriate for the protocols you intend to support. UW IMAP, like most other servers that process FreeBSD usernames and passwords for authentication, relies upon the Pluggable Authentication Module (PAM) to interface to the FreeBSD username database. To support this interface, you need to add lines to the /etc/pam.conf file in FreeBSD 4.5 or earlier, or create files called imap and pop3 in the /etc/pam.d directory in FreeBSD 5.0 and later. The /etc/pam.conf file should have lines like the following, or the /etc/pam.d files should look like this minus the first column, as described in Chapter 6:

```
imap  auth     required  pam_unix.so
imap  account  required  pam_unix.so    try_first_pass
imap  session  required  pam_deny.so
pop3  auth     required  pam_unix.so
pop3  account  required  pam_unix.so    try_first_pass
pop3  session  required  pam_deny.so
```

Similar lines already exist in the default file, but are commented out. You should use the lines shown here rather than the default lines with UW IMAP, but another server may require slightly different lines. Consult your server's documentation for details.

After you've created appropriate entries in /etc/inetd.conf and the PAM configuration files, you must tell inetd to reload its configuration file:

```
# killall -SIGHUP inetd
```

At this point, the servers you run should be accessible using mail clients on the same or other computers. You can use any POP- or IMAP-enabled mail client to connect to the server and retrieve mail from it. In the case of IMAP, you should be able to move mail in and out of folders on the mail server computer from the mail client.

 UW IMAP stores mail in the user's home directory. Consequently, if the account is used for anything but mail storage, an IMAP client may take quite some time to scan all the files and directories, and report many of them as mail folders when they aren't. Some other IMAP servers store mail folders elsewhere or provide a way to configure how mail folders are stored.

Setting Up Fetchmail

Ordinarily, a pull protocol such as POP or IMAP is used at the end of a mail delivery chain. These protocols allow mail clients such as Outlook, Eudora, or Sylpheed to retrieve mail from a mail server on which the user has a mail account. There are cases, though, where you might want to extend a mail delivery chain past the pull mail server and its client. For instance, suppose you're setting up the mail system for a small office that uses a broadband Internet connection. This broadband connection comes with an e-mail account, or the office has contracted with another ISP to host its e-mail, because the broadband ISP forbids the use of an SMTP server accessible from the outside. In such a case, you might want to retrieve e-mail from the outside pull mail servers and inject the mail into an internal mail server's mail queue. This approach allows you to combine mail from multiple external servers into a single local mail server. It also allows you to perform various mail manipulation tricks, such as running IMAP locally even if the ISPs support only POP.

To extend the mail delivery chain beyond a pull mail server, you need a special type of pull mail client. Rather than function as a conventional mail reader, this client can automatically inject mail into a local or remote mail queue. The recipient system can forward the mail further through SMTP connections or make it available via its own pull mail server. A popular program for performing this task of retrieving pull mail and re-mailing it is Fetchmail (`http://www.tuxedo.org/~esr/fetchmail/`), which is available as a FreeBSD package and in the ports system.

Fetchmail's Configuration File

Unlike many servers, Fetchmail doesn't need to run with any special permissions; it functions as an ordinary pull mail client, then as a client to a push mail server on its own or another computer. Thus, it's common to run Fetchmail as an ordinary user or as a special low-privilege user devoted to Fetchmail operation.

Fetchmail relies upon a configuration file called `.fetchmailrc` in the Fetchmail user's home directory. This file provides Fetchmail with all the information it needs to operate, including the name of the pull mail server from which it retrieves mail; the username, password, and protocol used to retrieve mail from that server; the push mail server to contact or program to run to deliver retrieved mail; and the e-mail address to which retrieved mail should be sent. Listing 19-1 shows a typical .fetchmailrc file.

Listing 19-1.
Sample
fetchmailrc
File

```
set postmaster "ben"
set bouncemail
set syslog
set properties ""
set daemon 1800

poll franklin.threeroomco.com with proto IMAP4
    user "benny" there with password "beY40u$" is ben here
    options fetchall forcecr smtphost osgood.threeroomco.com
poll pop.abigisp.net with proto POP3
    user "threeroom" there with password "u7(Igq4oO" is sally here
```

There are two main parts to the .fetchmailrc file:

- **Global options** The first five lines of Listing 19-1 set global options. These options include the local user who's to receive Fetchmail errors (`set postmaster`), how to log information (`set syslog`), and how frequently to check the mail when Fetchmail is run as a daemon, as described in the upcoming section, "Running Fetchmail in Daemon Mode" (`set daemon`).

- **Servers to poll** Each sequence of lines that begins with the keyword `poll` describes a server from which Fetchmail is to retrieve mail. A line that begins with one or more spaces is a continuation of a preceding line. Each `poll` sequence must include all the information necessary to retrieve mail from a server.

Fetchmail supports a huge number of options, so this chapter can't hope to describe all of them. You may want to consult the Fetchmail man page, which provides information on the configuration file's options. Listing 19-1 is a reasonable starting point for many systems. Some key points to consider include

- **Postmaster** The Fetchmail postmaster is a local user who is to receive error messages and the like. This user may or may not be the same as the computer's or domain's postmaster, who is responsible for mail configuration generally.

- **Daemon mode** As described in the upcoming section, "Running Fetchmail in Daemon Mode," you can run Fetchmail as a daemon, which means it runs continuously. When so run, the `set daemon` option sets the time in seconds between polls of pull mail servers.

- **Information order in a `poll` line** The structure of `poll` lines is critical. These lines begin with the keyword `poll`, then continue with a description of the server to be polled (its hostname, the protocol to be used, the username, and the password), and then a description of how to dispose of the retrieved messages (a username and perhaps options such as the hostname of the server).

- **Mail disposal options** Listing 19-1's `pop.abigisp.net` configuration is fairly minimal. This configuration sends all mail retrieved from that account to the `sally` account on the local computer. The configuration for `franklin.threeroomco.com` is somewhat more complex. It uses the `smtphost` option to tell Fetchmail to connect to `osgood.threeroomco.com` to send the retrieved mail. The `fetchall` option forces Fetchmail to retrieve messages even if they've already been retrieved. The `forcecr` option alters the use of carriage returns in messages, which is helpful when sending to a qmail server (most other SMTP servers aren't very fussy about this detail).

Most Fetchmail options can be overridden by using command-line switches when you call Fetchmail. One of these that deserves special mention is `--keep` (or `-k` for short). This option tells Fetchmail to leave messages on the remote server (ordinarily Fetchmail deletes these messages when it retrieves them). The `--keep` option is useful in testing; you can run Fetchmail with this option, and if something is wrong with your configuration, you won't lose any e-mail, as might happen if Fetchmail can't send the mail on its way once it's retrieved the mail.

If you have trouble configuring Fetchmail manually, or if you prefer to use GUI configuration files, you may want to use the `fetchmailconf` utility, which provides a GUI interface to the `.fetchmailrc` file. You can also use this tool to browse the many Fetchmail options—but the Fetchmail man page provides this information, as well.

No matter how you create the configuration file, it must be readable *only* to the user who launches Fetchmail (and to `root`). Fetchmail imposes this limitation because the file contains the password to your remote mail account, which is a potentially dangerous piece of information to leave accessible to others.

Running Fetchmail in a Cron Job

To run Fetchmail, you need only type the name of the program:

```
$ fetchmail
```

Fetchmail should then contact the remote server, retrieve any waiting mail, and inject it into the local FreeBSD mail queue or send it on to another computer, if you specified one with the `smtphost` option. You should type this command as the user in whose home directory the `.fetchmailrc` file resides.

You might be tempted to run Fetchmail as `root`*, but there's no need to do so. In fact, running Fetchmail as* `root` *increases the security risk. It's conceivable that a bug in Fetchmail could be exploited by an e-mail sender to cause Fetchmail to do things you'd rather it not do. If the program is run as* `root`*, such a bug could conceivably give a miscreant complete control of your computer.*

Running Fetchmail one time in this way is useful for testing (particularly when paired with the −−keep option), but most people prefer to run Fetchmail in some automated way. For instance, if you use a dial-up PPP connection, you might write a script that makes the connection and immediately calls Fetchmail to retrieve waiting e-mail. Another option is to run Fetchmail in a cron job, so that your system retrieves e-mail on a regular basis—say, once an hour. (Fetchmail's daemon mode provides cron-like scheduling, but has some drawbacks, as described in the upcoming section, "Running Fetchmail in Daemon Mode.")

Chapter 6 describes the use of cron jobs, so you should review it for general information on the subject. Listing 19-2 shows a `crontab` file you might use to run Fetchmail at eight minutes before the hour every hour from 6:52 AM to 6:52 PM. Such a configuration might be useful for retrieving mail for users on a typical office network, who aren't likely to be around before 7:00 AM or after 7:00 PM. The retrieval time is offset from the hour to avoid the possibility of congestion should too many users of the ISP's mail server have the idea of retrieving mail on a regular basis at a "logical" time, such as on the hour exactly. This example also uses redirection to send the output of the Fetchmail command to `/dev/null`; without this option, the user specified by the `MAILTO` line in the `crontab` file will receive a rather boring report of Fetchmail's activities every hour.

Listing 19-2.
Sample
crontab File
for Running
Fetchmail

```
SHELL=/bin/bash
PATH=/sbin:/bin:/usr/sbin:/usr/bin
MAILTO=ben
52 6-18 * * * /usr/local/bin/fetchmail > /dev/null
```

When you run Fetchmail from a cron job or in any other automated way, you should not use the `set daemon` *option. When this option is present in the configuration file, Fetchmail doesn't exit, and runs continuously in the background. When the cron job executes again, the new instance of Fetchmail won't run because Fetchmail will already be running as a daemon.*

Running Fetchmail in Daemon Mode

You can use a cron job to run Fetchmail on a regular basis, but if you don't want to set up a cron job, you can do it using Fetchmail's built-in daemon functionality. You need only include a `set daemon` line in your `.fetchmailrc` file. With this option set, when you run Fetchmail for the first time, it sets itself up to run continuously and poll the specified mail servers at the interval specified by the `set daemon` option. You specify the time in seconds; for example, Listing 19-1 configures the system to poll the server every 1800 seconds, or twice an hour.

To use daemon mode, you must have some way to start Fetchmail, and perhaps stop it. You can use a startup script, as described in Chapter 6, to launch Fetchmail when you start the computer; or on a single-user workstation, you could use a command in the main user's login script to do the same, with a matching command in a logout script to kill Fetchmail.

Unfortunately, Fetchmail's daemon mode isn't always perfectly reliable. On occasion, it gets confused when a server becomes unresponsive, and so stops retrieving mail. For this reason, and because launching (and perhaps stopping) Fetchmail as an ordinary user can be awkward, I recommend using a cron job instead of Fetchmail's daemon mode to get Fetchmail to retrieve mail on a regular basis. Cron jobs are also more flexible; for instance, Listing 19-2 retrieves mail hourly only when it's likely to be read soon. Fetchmail's daemon mode can't provide the gap in retrieval during the night hours that Listing 19-2 provides.

Summary

E-mail is a very important function of many FreeBSD systems. Some such systems operate as mail servers for many users or perhaps even for one or more entire domains. The SMTP push mail protocol that runs on such systems is implemented by many different programs, including the popular sendmail, which is the default for FreeBSD. A default FreeBSD sendmail configuration is functional, but may need some minor tweaking in some cases, or much more work for a large or specialized mail server computer. FreeBSD can also run a wide variety of pull mail servers, which enable Windows, Mac OS, FreeBSD, or other mail client programs to retrieve mail that's been received by the SMTP mail server. Finally, you can run Fetchmail on a FreeBSD system to retrieve mail from a remote pull mail server and inject it into a local or remote mail queue. This operation can be useful on small networks that use outside mail server accounts or when you want to run an internal mail server for any reason.

SERVERS

Chapter 20

Web Servers

To many people, the Internet is synonymous with the World Wide Web (WWW, or Web). In truth, of course, there's much more to the Internet than just the Web—e-mail, FTP, Usenet news, Telnet, SSH, and many other types of data transfer can occur over the Internet and can play critical roles. The Web, however, is highly visible. The Hypertext Markup Language (HTML), from which web pages are built, enables web browsers to provide a more visually complex, appealing, and flexible interface than is possible with most other protocols. Thus, the Web dominates many peoples' thinking about the Internet.

The world's most popular web server is Apache, which hosts 64 percent of the active sites surveyed by Netcraft (`http://www.netcraft.com/survey/`) in April of 2002. Apache is primarily a server for UNIX-like OSs, and FreeBSD runs Apache very well. FreeBSD also runs many other web server programs. Thus, FreeBSD makes an excellent platform for a web server of almost any size; the main limiting factor is the computer's hardware, such as its available RAM and network bandwidth. This chapter describes configuring FreeBSD as a web server, concentrating upon use of Apache in this capacity. This chapter also includes a brief description of the use of HTML to create efficient and portable web pages.

When to Run a Web Server

The first question you should ask yourself before embarking on web server installation is whether you need one. Web servers tend to be fairly high-profile, and so attract more than their fair share of attention from worms and crackers. In most cases, break-in attempts are no more than a nuisance, but sometimes the matter is more serious. Problems can occur in at least two situations:

- If the server you run happens to be vulnerable to an attack, an intruder can gain access to your computer, possibly defacing your web site, using your system as a launch pad for attacks against other systems, stealing your data, or modifying your system in unknown ways.

- An attack might be designed to consume your network bandwidth, thus effectively taking your site offline. Such a *Denial-of-Service (DoS)* attack is most likely to succeed if you run a low-volume site on a low-end connection, such as a Digital Subscriber Line (DSL) account.

In both cases, you'll be faced with the daunting task of correcting the damage, which may require reinstalling FreeBSD or spending hours in consultation with your ISP to block an intruder. You can avoid the possibility of problems by contracting with an ISP to host your web site for you; that way, if the site comes under attack, it's the ISP's problem, not yours. (You may have to restore your site from a backup or even switch ISPs on short notice, though.) Your regular network connection won't be affected. This approach also has the benefit of requiring less time and expertise to configure your own server.

Nonetheless, running your own web server has certain advantages. For one thing, you then have complete control over the site. Many web hosting ISPs restrict what you can do in various ways, ranging from available disk space to limits on the types of web scripting you can perform. When you control the server, you can configure it precisely the way you want. Your own web server may also be more convenient if you want to tie it to other systems—for instance, linking a web site to an internal database. Another advantage of running your own web server is that you can configure it for purely internal use.

Note *Some of the advantages of running your own web server relate to very advanced uses. Such uses are beyond the scope of this book. To learn more, consult a book on Apache, such as Arnold's* Administering Apache *(Osborne, 2000).*

Web Servers for FreeBSD

Although Apache is by far the most popular web server for FreeBSD, it's not the only one. Some of the more popular options include

- **Apache**   As noted, Apache is the most popular web server for UNIX systems generally, and for FreeBSD in particular. Apache is a complex and powerful server, but its basic configuration when first installed is reasonable for small sites. Thus, despite its power and complexity, it's also the easiest web server to use for a simple site. The main Apache web site is `http://httpd.apache.org`.

- **Roxen**   This web server is a strong competitor to Apache in features and overall power. It's designed for large web sites with advanced needs. You can learn more about it at `http://www.roxen.com`.

- **thttpd**   The Tiny/Turbo/Throttling HTTP Server (`http://www.acme.com/software/thttpd/`) is, as its expanded name suggests, designed to be small (about 50KB, versus about 330KB for Apache) and fast. This server's small size helps it handle busy sites on limited hardware.

- **Mathopd**   This server, like `thttpd`, is designed to be small and fast, but its emphasis lies more in efficiently handling a large number of connections. Its main web site is `http://www.mathopd.org`.

- **Boa**   This is yet another small web server. It's especially popular in embedded applications—that is, computers built into devices that aren't traditional workstation or server computers, such as gas pumps or household appliances. You can read more at `http://www.boa.org`.

- **Specialized tools**   Some servers aren't usually thought of as web servers, but they use HTTP on ports reserved for themselves. This feature allows these tools to be used with ordinary web browsers, thus obviating the need to design specialized clients. Examples include the Samba Web Administration Tool (SWAT), which provides GUI administration for Samba; and the Webmin system administration tool (`http://www.webmin.com`).

Because of its popularity and the fact that it ships with FreeBSD, Apache is a good choice for a FreeBSD web server, and it's the one described in this chapter. If you don't need all of Apache's features, though, you might consider a slimmer program, such as thttpd, Mathopd, or Boa. All three of these servers are available as FreeBSD packages or ports, and should work well for a simple web site, even if it's a high-traffic site. If you need sophisticated features such as Secure Sockets Layer (SSL) encryption or support for scripting, a slimmed-down web server may not be adequate. This chapter cannot describe configuring such advanced features, either; consult the server's documentation or a book on your server of choice.

Basic Apache Configuration

This section describes how to get Apache up and running. Despite Apache's power and complexity, running a basic Apache server is not very difficult because the FreeBSD Apache package (or port) installs configuration files that are reasonable for a simple Apache server. Thus, once you start the server running, it will be able to serve files. Nonetheless, there are changes you might want to make. (In fact, one class of changes— setting up web pages customized for your site—is so important that it's covered later in its own section, "Creating Web Pages.") Changes you might want to make include deciding how to run Apache and adjusting the directories used for storing files. If you need to do more than basic Apache operations, you must also know how to load Apache *modules*—code that expands Apache's capabilities. Many of Apache's more advanced features are implemented through modules.

Note   *This chapter describes Apache 2.0. The earlier 1.3.x versions of Apache are still in use as of mid-2002, and both are available in the FreeBSD packages and ports systems. Apache 1.3.x is very similar to 2.0.x at this chapter's level of description, though.*

Starting Apache

As described in Chapter 16, many servers can be run either stand-alone or from a super server. This was true of Apache 1.3.x, but Apache 2 has removed the ability to run from a super server. In the old Apache 1.3.x, a line in the configuration file called ServerType would determine whether the server was configured to run as a super server (ServerType inetd) or stand-alone (ServerType standalone).

Even in the 1.3.x series, Apache's developers discouraged running the server from a super server. Such a configuration degrades Apache's performance, particularly on busy web server computers, and it wasn't as reliable as a stand-alone configuration.

The standard FreeBSD Apache package includes a script called /usr/local/etc/ rc.d/apache.sh. This script starts Apache running when you boot the computer. You can check to see if it's running by using ps and searching for a process called httpd:

```
$ ps ax | grep httpd
  456  ??  Ss     0:00.12 /usr/local/sbin/httpd
```

```
457  ??  I      0:00.01 /usr/local/sbin/httpd
458  ??  I      0:00.03 /usr/local/sbin/httpd
459  ??  I      0:00.02 /usr/local/sbin/httpd
460  ??  I      0:00.02 /usr/local/sbin/httpd
461  ??  I      0:00.02 /usr/local/sbin/httpd
462  ??  I      0:00.03 /usr/local/sbin/httpd
489  p1  R+     0:00.01 grep httpd
```

As this example demonstrates, Apache creates several instances of itself. This approach allows the server to answer a connection and quickly hand it off to one of its processes. Each Apache process handles one client connection. If more clients connect than there are Apache processes, the server spawns more copies of itself to handle the demand.

Immediately after you install Apache, the server won't be running. After you've configured the server as you desire, you can start it by typing its name:

```
# /usr/local/sbin/httpd
```

Note   *You don't need to restart Apache after you change files in your web site, but you must restart it when you change its configuration file. You can do this by typing* **killall -HUP httpd**.

The Apache Configuration File

The Apache 2 configuration file is /usr/local/etc/apache2/httpd.conf. Apache refers to the settings in this file as *directives*, and they take the form

```
Directive value
```

Some directives define a block of values. These directives are surrounded by angle brackets (< >), and the block they define ends with a backslash (/) and the directive name. Intervening lines contain other directives. For instance, the following directives appear in the default configuration file (although in the real file comments intersperse the lines shown here):

```
<Directory "/usr/local/www/data">
    Options Indexes FollowSymLinks
    AllowOverride None
    Order allow,deny
    Allow from all
</Directory>
```

This directive, including all the directives it "contains," specifies how the server is to handle a particular directory. This topic is further described in the upcoming section, "Setting Server Directory Options."

A pound sign (#) denotes a comment; lines that begin with this character are ignored. The default FreeBSD `httpd.conf` file includes many comments, so you can read them to learn something about how the file is structured and what its options do. Some configuration options are commented out; you can remove the comment character to activate these options.

Setting Basic Features

You can leave most (perhaps all) of the directives in the standard `httpd.conf` alone for a simple web server configuration. In some cases, though, you may want to tweak a few settings. Options that are most likely to need adjustment include

- **Spare server options** The `StartServers`, `MinSpareServers`, and `MaxSpareServers` directives control how many Apache processes are kept running. `StartServers` tells Apache how many instances of itself to launch. `MinSpareServers` and `MaxSpareServers` determine how many "spare" instances (those that aren't actively processing requests) are kept running. If connection requests pile in, Apache launches additional instances of itself so it can quickly handle incoming requests—at least `MinSpareServers` copies are kept running and free of connections at all times. As load drops, spare instances are killed to keep the number under `MaxSpareServers`. The default values of 5, 5, and 10 are reasonable for small sites, but busy sites may need to increase these values. `MaxSpareServers` should always exceed `MinSpareServers`. These directives are all contained within an `IfModule` directive. FreeBSD uses the `<IfModule prefork.c>` directive set; others in the default configuration file are designed for Apache run on other platforms.

- **MaxClients** This directive sets the maximum number of clients that Apache will serve at any given moment. The default value of 150 is reasonable for small or even some medium-sized sites, but you may need to increase this value for a large site. Such sites also need better hardware (lots of RAM, a fast CPU, and so on); `MaxClients` serves, in part, to prevent the system from becoming unusable because of too many requests coming in to the server.

- **Listen** This directive defaults to 80, and specifies the port to which Apache binds itself (80 is the traditional port for HTTP). It's sometimes desirable to run a web server on a nonstandard port, such as if you want to run two entirely different web servers on one system. You can also add an IP address to the `Listen` directive to have Apache bind to the specified port on only one interface, which can be handy if a computer has multiple interfaces. For instance, `Listen`

`172.17.2.217:80` binds Apache to port 80 on the network hardware associated with the 172.17.2.217 address.

- **User and Group** These options tell Apache what account to use for running the various Apache subprocesses. The default value of www for each is appropriate for most installations, but if you want to modify your system's security configuration, you might create a new account for this purpose.

 Do not *run Apache as* `root`, *or even as an ordinary user who has normal login privileges. Doing so greatly increases the risks involved in running a web server.*

- **ServerAdmin** This directive sets the e-mail address of the individual responsible for maintaining the web server. This option isn't important in normal operation, but its value is returned to the client in the event of some types of errors, so you should set it to something reasonable for your system.

- **ServerName** This directive sets the name and port of the server, such as `www.threeroomco.com:80`. Apache normally sets it correctly automatically, but specifying it manually can prevent problems if there's a temporary DNS error when Apache starts up.

- **TypesConfig** Files delivered via HTTP include a Multipurpose Internet Mail Extension (MIME) type, which is a code that identifies the file type (plain text, specific graphics formats, and so on). The `TypesConfig` directive specifies a file in which mappings between filename extensions and MIME types reside. The default setting works well, but you may need to edit this file if you add files of an unusual type to your web pages.

- **DefaultType** If Apache can't figure out a file's type, it uses the type specified by this directive, which defaults to `text/plain`. This type causes the browser to interpret the file as plain text.

- **HostnameLookups** This directive can be set to On or Off, and it controls whether Apache logs the hostname of clients or just their IP addresses. Logging hostnames can be convenient if you're interested in knowing who contacts your server, but doing so increases the bandwidth the server uses because it must perform a DNS lookup for each connection.

This list is just a sampling of the directives available in the `httpd.conf` file. Of the directives listed here, `ServerAdmin` is the only one you should definitely change. Modifying others may improve performance, improve security, or enable the server to better interact with clients or deliver web pages.

In addition to the options just described, Apache provides several directives that relate to the delivery of web pages. Most of these center around defining directories that are to be used for storing web pages, and they're described in the next section.

SERVERS

Setting Server Directory Options

When you as a user enter a Uniform Resource Locator (URL) into a web browser, that URL looks something like this:

```
http://www.threeroomco.com/products/fb50.html
```

There can be more or fewer components than are shown here, but this example is typical of a simple web page's URL.

The URL includes information on the protocol used (`http`), the computer to be contacted (`www.threeroomco.com`), and the file to be retrieved from that computer (`products/fb50.html`). This final component is specified as a directory and filename, but you probably don't want to give random clients access to all the files on your computer. Thus, it's common to define one or more directories that are to hold web pages, and define URLs relative to that directory. In the preceding example, the `products` directory is a subdirectory of the web server's document root directory, not the computer's root directory. You can set this option, and several others that affect how Apache treats various types of document access requests, with server directory options. These include

- **DocumentRoot** This directive sets the document root directory, from which most documents are read. The default value is `"/usr/local/www/data"` (the quotes are required). You can change this value to something else if you want to—say, if you have more disk space on another partition.

- **UserDir** If your web server hosts files owned by ordinary users (that is, their personal web pages), Apache can look for these files somewhere other than the server's primary document root directory. You can specify where to look for user files with the `UserDir` directive, which sets the name of a subdirectory within the user's home directory to use for such files. For instance, if `www.threeroomco.com`'s `httpd.conf` file includes `UserDir public_html` (as does the default file), and if a client requests `http://www.threeroomco.com/~amy/mypage.html`, then Apache returns the `public_html/mypage.html` file in amy's home directory (probably `/home/amy/public_html/mypage.html`). The tilde (~) in the URL is a standard indicator that a page is a user's home page, rather than an organizational home page.

- **Directory** This directive begins a directive block, so it appears in angle brackets. It's followed by the name of the directory (relative to the computer's root directory) in which its contents appear. Thus, the line might read `<Directory />` or `<Directory /usr/local/www/data>`. In fact, both of these values appear in the default configuration file, the first to limit access to user directories (which can, in principle, be anywhere), and the second to define access to the main server directory. Be sure to change the second path to match the `DocumentRoot` directive if you change it. A directory directive block ends with a line that reads `</Directory>`.

- **AllowOverride** Apache allows users to create files that contain Apache directives in server directories. These files are called `.htaccess`, and the `AllowOverride` directive determines whether Apache reads them and applies the directives. Specifically, `All` and `None` permit all or no directives; or you can specify a list of directives with more advanced options, described in the Apache documentation. The default setting of `None` is best for a simple site. This directive typically appears within a `<Directory>` directive block.

- **DirectoryIndex** If a URL lacks a filename, Apache returns a file in the specified directory bearing a name indicated by this directive. The name `index.html` is a common default, and FreeBSD's configuration enables this, along with a variant that supports language negotiation. This directive usually appears within a `<Directory>` directive block.

As with global server settings, there are many additional directives you can include within a `<Directory>` directive block. In fact, some of these are the same as global directives, so you can override global settings within particular server directories.

Using Apache Modules

Apache, like the FreeBSD kernel, can be compiled in a modular way. When so compiled, the core Apache server file is relatively compact and can load additional files from separate modules on an as-needed basis. This approach can reduce Apache's memory requirements, particularly on relatively simple sites that don't use more advanced features. This approach can also improve security by keeping potentially buggy code unavailable. Apache's module support also enables developers to more easily extend Apache without recompiling the entire server; a developer can write a module, which interfaces with the Apache core through well-defined methods.

The FreeBSD Apache package ships with many common modules, but you can find many more on the Internet. In particular, the Apache Module Registry (`http://modules.apache.org`) provides links to various Apache module projects and a searchable database of these modules.

Many directives relate to module handling. The three most important are

- **LoadModule** This directive loads a module from a file on disk. It takes a module name and a module filename (normally including the complete path to the file) as options. The default FreeBSD `httpd.conf` file includes a large number of `LoadModule` directives to load common modules.

- **AddModule** This directive activates a module that's built into the Apache binary or that's been loaded. It's often not necessary, and in fact FreeBSD's `httpd.conf` file doesn't use this directive, but you might encounter it in sample configuration files.

■ **IfModule**   This directive begins a directive block that applies only if the named module is present. For instance, `<IfModule prefork.c>` begins a directive block that applies only if the `prefork.c` module is present. (This module is compiled into the main FreeBSD Apache binary.) The directive's meaning can be reversed by preceding the module name with an exclamation mark (`!`), as in `<IfModule !mpm_netware.c>`, which denotes a directive that applies only if the `mpm_netware.c` module is *not* available. The default FreeBSD `httpd.conf` file uses this directive heavily.

You can learn what modules are compiled into the main Apache binary by using the `-l` option to `httpd`, thus:

```
$ /usr/local/sbin/httpd -l
Compiled in modules:
  core.c
  prefork.c
  http_core.c
  mod_so.c
```

Combining this command with the list of `LoadModule` directives in `httpd.conf` provides you with a complete list of the available modules. You can, of course, add more by installing the module (if necessary) and adding a `LoadModule` directive to make it available.

A simple Apache server isn't likely to need any modules except those that it comes preconfigured to use. You may need to adjust your module configuration if you replace your Apache binary with one that includes a different mix of modules or if you need some unusual feature that can be provided by a module, such as the ability to convert text into a graphic on the fly or various types of database interfaces. Detailing all the options is well beyond the scope of this book, however.

In some cases, you may want to comment out modules provided in the standard FreeBSD Apache configuration. For instance, the default configuration includes the following line:

```
LoadModule cgi_module libexec/apache/mod_cgi.so
```

This line enables support for the Common Gateway Interface (CGI), which enables Apache to run scripts to generate web pages dynamically. This advanced feature is very useful on servers that need to customize their output, such as web search engines or e-commerce sites; but it's a potential security threat because a poorly written CGI script could serve as an entry point for crackers. Thus, if your web server doesn't need to serve CGI scripts, you may want to comment out this line. Other modules may also be unnecessary; for instance, the `userdir_module` handles user directories, so if your site lacks these, you can comment out the line that loads this module.

Creating Web Pages

Running a web server is only part of the challenge in putting up a web site. In fact, for a simple site, running Apache is the easy part because its default configuration should suffice. Any real web site, though, requires content—typically, a set of text documents that use HTML encoding. A simple site can consist of just one HTML file, but more complex sites can contain hundreds or even thousands of files.

The basic principles of HTML design and structure are fairly straightforward, so you can create a web site using any text editor. Many people prefer to use special editors that are designed for creating web sites, though; these tools remember all the details and can help you easily produce web pages with tables, graphics, and other elements that can be tedious to implement by hand. Whether you code by hand or by using an HTML editor, though, you should keep accessibility in mind; not all web browsers respond identically to any given HTML file, and the differences can be huge. Finally, CGI scripts enable you to customize your content for each user, but at the cost of complexity and greater potential for security problems.

Note *A standard HTML document can be served by any web server—Apache, thttpd, or even non-UNIX programs such as Internet Information Server (IIS) for Windows. Some extensions, such as CGI scripting, may be available only on some servers, though. Also, different servers may use different filenames for the index file (set by the DirectoryIndex directive in Apache), which may affect your naming conventions.*

Basic Structure of HTML

HTML is fundamentally a plain-text file format, but certain characters have special meaning. In particular, angle brackets (< >) surround HTML *tags*, which are codes that indicate where a special text format begins or ends. Also, the ampersand (&) begins a one-word string that carries special meaning, such as a special symbol (including the angle brackets themselves, if you need to display them). Listing 20-1 shows a typical example of HTML.

Listing 20-1.
Sample
HTML File

```
<!DOCTYPE HTML PUBLIC "-//IETF//DTD HTML 4.01//EN">
<HTML><HEAD>
<TITLE>HTML Sample</TITLE>
</HEAD>
<BODY BGCOLOR="#FFFFFF" TEXT="#000000">
<CENTER><H1 ALIGN="CENTER">Sample Web Page</H1></CENTER>

<P>This is a <strong>sample</strong> web page. Read the
<A HREF="http://www.w3.org/TR/html401/">HTML definition</a>
for more <EM>great</EM> information!</P>
```

```
<P><IMG SRC="logo.jpg" ALT="Our Logo" ALIGN="LEFT" WIDTH="200"
HEIGHT="150"></P>

<BR CLEAR=ALL>

<P>Copyright &copy; 2002.</P>

</BODY>
</HTML>
```

Features in this listing include

- **Document type**   The `<!DOCTYPE>` tag begins most HTML files. Most web browsers work fine if it's omitted, but it's an important component because it identifies the version of the HTML standard that the file contains (4.01 in the case of Listing 20-1).

- **`<HTML>` tag**   This tag identifies the beginning of a block of HTML code. It's mirrored at the very end of the file with a `</HTML>` tag.

- **`<HEAD>` tag**   HTML files typically include two parts: a *header*, which contains meta-information such as the document's title, and a *body*, which contains the bulk of the text that displays in the web browser. The `<HEAD>` and `</HEAD>` tags surround the header.

- **`<TITLE>` tag**   This tag and its closing `</TITLE>` tag surround the document's title. Most web browsers display this title in their title bars.

- **`<BODY>` tag**   This tag begins the body of the document, which ends with the `</BODY>` tag near the end of the file. The `<BODY>` tag includes additional optional parameters, which set the background color (`BGCOLOR="#FFFFFF"`, which sets the background to white) and the text color (`TEXTCOLOR="#000000"`, which sets the color to black). Pages that use background images also set them in the `<BODY>` tag, with the `BACKGROUND="filename.ext"` option.

- **`<CENTER>` tag**   Many tags affect formatting. This tag tells the browser to center the text that ends with the `</CENTER>` tag. Similarly, the `<RIGHT>` and `<LEFT>` tags cause text to appear flush right or flush left, respectively. These tags, and especially `<CENTER>`, are not used or needed by most modern browsers; instead, codes within other tags, such as header tags, accomplish these goals. Listing 20-1 includes a `<CENTER>` tag because it does no harm on modern browsers and makes the document slightly more portable.

- **Header tags**   The `<H1>` tag is a header tag, which denotes a text heading, like the ones in this book. Use these to help organize a web page with more than a few paragraphs. (Its use in Listing 20-1 is unnecessary except as a demonstration of how it *can* be used.) Listing 20-1's `<H1>` tag includes an `ALIGN="CENTER"` option, which is the method most modern browsers use to center an element. Additional levels of heading are possible—<H2>, <H3>, and so on. Most browsers display these headings in varying fonts and font sizes, much as you see in books.

■ **Paragraph tags**   The <P> and </P> tags denote the starts and ends of paragraphs. Web browsers may rewrap text within the paragraphs, so you can place line breaks wherever you like. If you need to place information on a new line, you must surround it in these tags or use another tag, such as
 (described shortly).

■ **Links**   Web page *links* are specified with <A HREF> tags, which list the URL in quotes within the opening tag. (A bare </A> tag closes a link.) The text between the opening and closing tags appears as a link in the web page when viewed by a user, and if the user clicks or otherwise selects that link, an attempt is made to access the specified URL. You can specify any of several different protocols in the URL, such as another web page (http://), an FTP site (ftp://), or an e-mail address (mailto:).

■ **Emphasized text**   The <STRONG> and <EM> tags provide two means of emphasizing text. Most browsers use bold for <STRONG> and italic for <EM>, but this practice isn't universal.

■ **Graphics**   The <IMG> tag specifies a graphic that's to be displayed in the reader's web browser. Listing 20-1 includes several options in this tag, the most important of which is SRC, which specifies the source of the file. This may be a filename alone (possibly including a relative path), in which case the client retrieves the image from the same server that delivered the main page; or a complete URL, in which case the image may reside on a different server entirely. The ALT option provides a brief textual description of the image, which may be important for visually impaired users and those who configure their browsers to not load graphics automatically. The WIDTH and HEIGHT options specify the size of the graphic in pixels, which allows browsers to display text before retrieving the graphic, or to scale the image to another size.

■ **
 tag**   This tag specifies a line break. The CLEAR=ALL option further specifies that the tag is to clear all intervening elements. The net result is that subsequent text appears after the graphic; without this tag, some browsers display the next paragraph to the right of the graphic.

■ **Special symbols**   Listing 20-1 includes only one special symbol, a copyright symbol, which is indicated by ©. You may also want to use < and >, which denote less than (<) and greater than (>) symbols, which can't be used directly because of their special meanings in specifying tags.

Most types of tags may be nested. For instance, you can create text that's both bold and italic (on typical browsers' displays) by using the <STRONG> and <EM> tags simultaneously:

```
<STRONG><EM>A very emphasized point!</EM></STRONG>
```

When doing this, be sure to nest the tags—make sure that the closing tags come in the opposite order of the opening tags. In this example, for instance, <STRONG> and </STRONG> surround the entire line, including the <EM> and </EM> tags.

This description is necessarily incomplete; HTML is a rich markup language, with support for many features beyond the basic formatting covered here. Tables, lists, fonts, forms, and more can all be created using HTML. You can find the complete HTML 4.01 specification at http://www.w3.org/TR/html401/, or more complete tutorials on its use at sites such as the following:

```
http://www.davesite.com/webstation/html/
http://www.w3schools.com/html/
http://www.wdvl.com/Authoring/HTML/
http://hotwired.lycos.com/webmonkey/
```

Another approach to learning HTML is to examine existing HTML documents. Most web browsers include an option to examine or save a web page, so you can peruse it at your leisure. Unfortunately, a lot of web pages today use very sophisticated features or are generated by programs that produce HTML that's difficult for a human to follow. Nonetheless, you can usually learn a lot from examining existing web pages, particularly if you need to figure out how to implement only one specific feature.

Tools for Creating Web Pages

Coding HTML by hand is fine if you're familiar with similar tools and don't mind learning one or two dozen tags. Many people are more familiar with GUI tools such as most modern word processors, though, and prefer to be able to use similar tools for generating web pages. Thus, a small army of GUI web page design tools exists. In fact, there are several different *types* of web page design tools, including

- **Normal editors**   Any editor can be used to code HTML "by hand." Some include features to help with this task, such as *syntax highlighting*, in which key structural elements such as tags appear in special colors.

- **Word processors**   Many GUI word processors now include the ability to export files as HTML. Such programs may include many more features than HTML supports, though, so extra features may be lost, if used. Using a word processor can be very beneficial if you're already familiar with the program or if you want to convert an existing document to HTML format, but it's more likely to produce poor HTML than are dedicated HTML editors.

- **Web browsers**   Some web browsers, such as Netscape, include web page design tools. These tools have the benefit of being built specifically for designing web pages, so they're less likely to suffer from import/export problems than are word processors.

- **HTML converters**   Some programs exist expressly to convert existing file formats to HTML. For instance, `c2html` converts C source code files for display in HTML documents, and `cthumb` creates a "photo album" web page.

- **Dedicated HTML editors**   Many programs exist expressly to support editing HTML. Most of these editors, such as Bluefish, `erwin`, Gnotepad+, Peacock, Quanta, and Screem (all of which are available in the FreeBSD packages and ports systems) are essentially specialized plain-text editors, which show the "raw" HTML with syntax highlighting, and provide menu options to insert HTML tags and other elements. Some of these tools provide "preview" modes in which the HTML is displayed much as it might appear in a web browser. A few programs, such as ASHE (`ftp://ftp.cs.rpi.edu/pub/puninj/ASHE/README.html`), are called what-you-see-is-what-you-get (WYSIWYG) because they display formatting as it's shown in most browsers, much like WYSIWYG word processors.

When using a GUI web design tool, you should remember that these tools' previews or WYSIWYG modes aren't truly WYSIWYG in the sense that most GUI word processors are. Web browsers can and do reformat a page to fit the client system. Fonts, line breaks, colors, color depth, the presence of graphics, and many other elements can vary from one system to another. For this reason, you should test your web page on as many different platforms as possible, as described further in the next section, "Designing Portable Web Pages."

Using an HTML editor is much like using any other editor. In the case of GUI word processors and WYSIWYG HTML editors, you use them just like ordinary word processors, although the mix of features may be different. Most HTML editors provide menu options and even window panes customized to the needs of designing a web site. For instance, Figure 20-1 shows the Bluefish editor. In addition to the main editing pane and typical icons related to saving files, applying text attributes, and so on, there are menus and buttons unique to web design, such as the Tags menu and buttons to insert links. Some HTML editors, including Bluefish, show a list of files in a directory. Because these files typically constitute a complete web site, or at least a logically related subset of one, when you edit one file you're likely to need to edit the others, as well.

Designing Portable Web Pages

One of the problems faced by web page designers is the need to create documents that can be properly viewed on a wide variety of web browsers. Although Microsoft's Internet Explorer accounts for most web browsers in use today, it comes in many different versions, each with a unique set of characteristics. Netscape Navigator, Mozilla, Opera, Konqueror, `lynx`, and other browsers all make up an additional portion of the browser marketplace, and each may interpret pages differently.

What's more, users can set their browsers to behave in different ways. Users may adjust their default colors, default fonts, default font sizes, window sizes, graphics

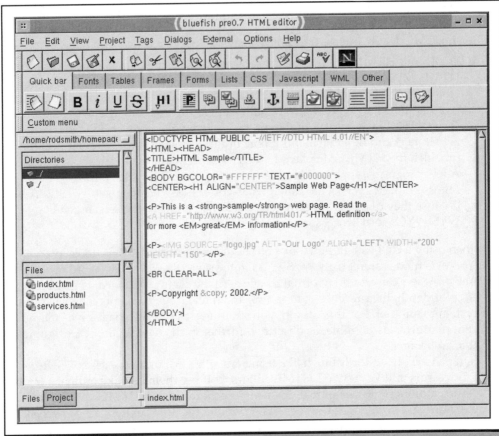

Figure 20-1. *HTML editors work much like ordinary editors, but include additional features to aid in the development of web pages.*

display policies, and so on. Indeed, some browsers lack certain features entirely; for instance, lynx is a text-based browser, and as such cannot display graphics.

Fortunately, HTML was designed as a cross-platform tool. Unfortunately, HTML editors—especially flashy WYSIWYG editors and word processors—often produce HTML that's not very portable. Such documents may include errors (misordered tags, say) that cause some browsers to misbehave. Other problems occur because of a design that makes too many assumptions about the browser's configuration. A page may set the background color but neglect to set the text color, for instance; if a user has set the browser's text color to something too similar to the web designer's chosen background color, the text becomes illegible. For these reasons, it's important that you perform several checks on your web pages, such as

- **Syntax checking programs**   Some programs can check a web page for compliance with the HTML standards. In FreeBSD, the text-based `weblint` does this job; type **`weblint filename.html`** to obtain a report on the compliance of `filename.html` to basic standards. Some HTML editors include similar utilities or can call `weblint` themselves. (The `weblint` program is available as a FreeBSD package or port.)

- **Accessibility checks**   Some programs and services exist to check a web page for common errors that can reduce a page's accessibility. The most popular of these tools is Bobby (`http://www.cast.org/bobby/`), which can check any page on the Web. Bobby flags potential problems such as links that can blur together into one, lack of `ALT` options in `<IMG>` tags, and so on.

- **Manual checks in multiple browsers**   There's nothing like checking a web page in a few actual browsers to see how it works. You should definitely include at least one recent version of Internet Explorer in your tests because it's the most popular browser. I also recommend testing with `lynx`, which is popular on some systems that lack GUI displays. A `lynx` test is also useful in helping to produce a site that will be accessible to the visually impaired, who frequently use speech synthesizers to browse the Web. Testing on two or three other GUI browsers, such as Mozilla and Konqueror, will help as well. You should also test your page on browsers running at various screen resolutions and color depths.

With these tests finished, you can be reasonably certain that your web page won't cause problems for your users. Of course, there's no perfect guarantee—a browser might have a bug that causes it to crash when it receives some particular HTML sequence, even if the code is perfectly legal and acceptable to other browsers. Still, a few checks can greatly reduce the chance of your page displaying incorrectly on some browsers, and thus annoying your readers.

Summary

FreeBSD systems make excellent web servers because the OS is stable and supports a wide variety of web server programs, including the robust and popular Apache. A basic Apache configuration is fairly straightforward because the default Apache configuration file works for a simple web server. More advanced configurations may require changes to assorted Apache options relating to directory locations, modules, and more advanced features.

Once you have a web server running, you need to give it documents to deliver to clients. This task requires creating files, which are typically formatted in HTML. You can create HTML in either an ordinary text editor or an HTML editor designed expressly to create web pages.

SERVERS

Chapter 21

Login Servers

M any server programs run on computers that provide their users with very limited access. For instance, people who browse documents on a web server usually don't even have accounts on the web server computer. Pull mail servers' users may have accounts on the host system, but these accounts may be restricted so that they're useable only for pull mail retrieval. This chapter covers a class of server that gives much greater access to the computer: *login servers*. These servers enable users to log into the computer and run arbitrary programs on the computer. Such servers may be run on large multiuser systems as an alternative to using many workstations; many users can then simultaneously access just one computer using low-powered terminals. Another common use of login servers is to provide users remote access to their workstations.

This chapter begins with a brief overview of the types of login servers, then moves on to a discussion of two examples each of two types of login servers. Specifically, Telnet and SSH are covered as examples of text-mode login servers, and the X Window System and VNC are described as examples of GUI login servers.

Types of Login Servers

In the 1970s, when UNIX was young, most computing was performed using text-mode tools. This tradition remains strong in the UNIX world, including FreeBSD. Thus, remote access protocols that work primarily or exclusively with plain text can be very useful for accessing FreeBSD from a distance. If you can sit at one computer, type a command, and see the output of that command as run on another computer, you can make effective remote use of a FreeBSD system. This is the idea behind a text-mode login server; it enables FreeBSD to treat a remote computer as if it were a local text-mode console, thus extending use of FreeBSD programs to remote users.

Many text-mode login protocols are available, but this chapter focuses on just two: Telnet and Secure Shell (SSH). Telnet is the older and simpler protocol. It's included with all FreeBSD systems and focuses exclusively upon providing text-mode access. Telnet clients come with most OSs, including all UNIX-like OSs, Windows, OS/2, and Mac OS X (earlier versions of Mac OS require add-on software to be used as Telnet clients). Despite its ubiquity, Telnet isn't the best login protocol, because it transfers all data in an unencrypted form, so if the data stream is compromised, information such as passwords or any confidential data accessed during the session is also compromised. There are encrypted variants of Telnet, such as one that ships with the Kerberos security suite (`http://web.mit.edu/kerberos/www/`), but these variants have never gained the popularity of the original Telnet.

SSH is an encrypted text-mode login protocol that can actually do much more. In addition to handling text-mode logins, SSH can *tunnel* other protocols, meaning that the SSH client and server cooperate to send the other protocols' data through the SSH connection. SSH also includes built-in file transfer support. These features make SSH an extremely powerful tool and a superior choice to Telnet when security is an issue. On the down side, SSH's encryption requires some CPU time, and so can degrade performance, particularly when SSH is used to tunnel a high-bandwidth protocol.

As GUIs became popular, text-mode remote access protocols became inadequate for some purposes. For instance, you can't run a graphics editor such as the GIMP over a text-mode protocol. Thus, new protocols emerged to handle this task. One of these is FreeBSD's native GUI environment, the X Window System (X for short). Unlike GUIs for most other OSs, X was designed with network operation in mind, so using it for remote access is straightforward—in theory. In practice, security issues and a plethora of options for how to establish a connection can make using X remotely more complex than using Telnet or SSH for remote text-mode access.

A more recent remote GUI access tool is *Virtual Network Computing (VNC;* http://www.uk.research.att.com/vnc/). Unlike X, VNC is designed to support remote access to many different GUIs, including X, Windows, and Mac OS. When using VNC for remote access to FreeBSD, the system on which your programs run uses X in an entirely local manner, and VNC transfers display data to a remote system. VNC can be simpler to configure than X's native remote access tools in some situations, but this apparent simplicity hides an extra layer of complexity. VNC is also slower than X on many networks, although this problem isn't universal.

FreeBSD comes with support for all of these remote access tools, so you can pick the one that's best for you. In most cases, I recommend SSH when text-mode access is sufficient. For GUI access, both X's native tools and VNC have their advantages and disadvantages. As a general rule, when the system at which the user sits is a UNIX-like OS, X is best used directly; but VNC clients may be easier or less costly to configure on Windows or Mac OS systems, so VNC deserves consideration.

Configuring a Telnet Server

Telnet is among the simplest and most popular text-mode remote-access protocols. For this reason, it's often desirable to run a Telnet server. On the other hand, Telnet is a notoriously insecure protocol; it encrypts no data, so anybody who can "sniff" packets on the source, destination, or any intervening system can easily obtain users' passwords if they use Telnet. For this reason, it's usually better to *not* run Telnet, but to run the more secure SSH protocol instead.

In some cases, Telnet may be unavoidable, though; for instance, you might not be able to assume that users have SSH clients. Telnet's risks may also be acceptable on some small private networks, such as those commonly used in residences. (Wireless residential networks are often very insecure, though, so using Telnet on such networks is inadvisable.) In case you need to run Telnet, this section describes how, beginning with information on how Telnet works, moving on to how to run a Telnet server in FreeBSD, and concluding with a description of restricting access to the Telnet server to minimize its security risks.

Understanding Telnet's Operation

Telnet is a very simple protocol in many respects. The process begins with a Telnet client, such as the `telnet` program in FreeBSD. Such a program initiates a connection to port 23 on the named server computer. For instance, in FreeBSD you might type the following command:

```
$ telnet bunyan.threeroomco.com
```

This command contacts port 23 on the remote system. The client then connects the terminal or window in which the command was typed to bunyan's port 23. On bunyan, the Telnet server notes the incoming request and connects that port to the `login` program, which handles text-mode logins, as described in Chapter 6. (Actually, Telnet is usually run from a super server, so the super server notes the initial request and hands it off to the Telnet server.) The `login` program sends a `login:` prompt to the client, and if the login process succeeds, connects the user's shell to the client program, using the Telnet server and protocol as an intermediary.

The Telnet protocol doesn't modify or interpret data, so it's possible to use a Telnet client as a means of studying other servers. You can add a port number to the `telnet` client command to connect to another port, as in **telnet bunyan.threeroomco.com 80**, *which contacts port 80 on the remote system. This capability is useful to see if a server is running on another computer, and sometimes to help debug it, if you understand its protocol well enough to issue "raw" commands.*

Running a Telnet Server

FreeBSD runs its Telnet server through `inetd`, the default FreeBSD super server. The `/etc/inetd.conf` line that controls the Telnet server looks like this:

```
telnet  stream  tcp  nowait  root  /usr/libexec/telnetd  telnetd
```

In a default `/etc/inetd.conf` file, this line is commented out—that is, it's preceded by a pound sign (#). To activate the Telnet server, you must do two things as `root`:

1. Uncomment the `/etc/inetd.conf` line relating to the Telnet server.
2. Type **killall -HUP inetd** to have `inetd` reexamine the `/etc/inetd.conf` file, and thus activate the Telnet server.

Once you've done these two things, the computer should accept Telnet logins from any computer. Access restrictions such as those described in the next section, "Restricting Telnet Access," can block such logins, though.

Restricting Telnet Access

Because of Telnet's unencrypted nature, its use is best restricted to small local networks with few users. Local networks with many users are more likely to host miscreants who might sniff others' passwords, and using Telnet over the Internet is risky because of the potentially large number of intervening systems that might be compromised. You can do several things to restrict access to a Telnet server to reduce the risk of abuse:

- **Use Telnet behind a NAT router** Network Address Translation (NAT), described in Chapter 17, enables a network of computers to use the Internet through just one IP address. A natural consequence of this arrangement is that outsiders can't directly access internal servers unless the NAT router is explicitly configured to link an internal server to the outside. Internal computers can still access other internal servers, though. You might be able to structure your network so that Telnet programs (both clients and servers) can "hide" behind a NAT router.

- **Use a firewall on a router** A router that's configured with firewall features can protect a network from outside access attempts. In particular, you can configure such a firewall to restrict access to port 23 on internal computers, thus preventing outsiders from accessing the Telnet server. If specific external users need Telnet access to the local network, the firewall can be configured with exceptions to the block. Chapter 17 describes firewalls in more detail.

- **Use local firewall rules** You can implement firewall rules on the local computer, as described in Chapter 17, to permit only authorized systems to contact the Telnet port. This measure can be effective even at limiting internal network access. For instance, perhaps just one computer needs access to the Telnet server. A local firewall can prevent all other systems from reaching the Telnet server.

- **Use TCP Wrappers** The TCP Wrappers program, described in more detail in Chapter 29, provides firewall-like access restrictions. TCP Wrappers is more flexible than a packet-filter firewall in some ways, but less flexible in others. The default FreeBSD configuration applies TCP Wrappers controls to all servers launched through `inetd`, but TCP Wrappers is configured not to restrict access by default.

- **Use care in account maintenance** Be sure that the Telnet server computer has no unused or unnecessary accounts, and do whatever you can to ensure that its passwords are changed frequently. Unused accounts may be targeted for attack, particularly if a former user reuses a password on another system that the cracker has compromised. Frequent password changes can limit the window of opportunity of a cracker who obtains a password.

Most of these tools and procedures restrict Telnet access based on the client's IP address, but some can do more. TCP Wrappers, for instance, includes the capacity to restrict access based on the caller's username, if the Telnet client computer runs an `ident` (aka `auth`) server. Another account-based restriction is on the server side: FreeBSD's default configuration blocks direct `root` logins via Telnet. This practice makes it harder for a would-be intruder who has obtained the `root` password because the intruder must still have the password of an ordinary user in the `wheel` group. An intruder with both passwords can log in as the ordinary user and then use `su` to acquire `root` privileges.

 Using `su` over a Telnet connection, or any other unencrypted connection, is unwise because it exposes the `root` password to any packet sniffers that might be installed on the network. Even a home network might be so compromised by a worm or break-in on a computer other than the one used as a Telnet client or server.

Configuring an SSH Server

Although Telnet is historically important, easy to configure, and even necessary in some situations, it's not the remote login protocol of choice. Telnet's unencrypted data transfer is simply too risky for most installations. There are secure variants of Telnet, such as the client and server provided with the Kerberos security suite; however, another tool, SSH, has become the remote text-mode access tool of choice. SSH has many advantages over Telnet. Obtaining, installing, and configuring SSH is more difficult than obtaining, installing, and configuring Telnet, though, so it takes more explanation.

Understanding SSH Security Advantages

Telnet's simplicity contrasts with SSH's complexity. Telnet delivers data back and forth in an unencrypted and unmodified form. SSH, by contrast, encrypts all data, so that what goes over the network bears no resemblance to the data seen by the users or programs on either side of the client and server programs. This fact alone justifies a strong preference for SSH over Telnet, from a security point of view, because it protects passwords and other sensitive data from being compromised. How does it work, though?

In brief, SSH uses two forms of encryption. The first form is used to initialize the second encryption method. The first encryption type uses *public-key cryptography*, in which two encryption *keys* (large numbers used in scrambling and descrambling data) are used. One system generates both a *public key* and a *private key*. The public key is given to anybody who asks for it. A public key recipient may use the key to encrypt data to be sent to the private key holder; only the private key can decrypt the data. Public-key cryptography also enables the public key holders to verify the authenticity of data "signed" by encrypting it with the private key.

SSH uses public-key cryptography to establish an initial connection, but public-key algorithms are very CPU-intensive. Thus, SSH uses the public-key encryption only to exchange a *shared key*, which is used by another encryption algorithm. This shared-key algorithm uses a single key for both encryption and decryption. Thus, it's critical that the shared key be known to only the SSH client and the SSH server. Such keys can be quickly generated and transmitted securely using public-key cryptography.

All of these details are hidden from the user, at least for the most part. (Many SSH clients inform the user when connecting to a system with which they've never communicated before, as a precaution against a miscreant redirecting incoming requests to another computer.) The user's experience of SSH is very similar to that of using Telnet. (Chapter 24 describes using both Telnet and SSH client programs.) There is one important difference, though: The encryption and decryption operations required of SSH degrade performance slightly. This factor isn't normally very important, and may not even be noticeable on a text-only connection. It can be important when tunneling other protocols, though.

Telnet uses the `login` program to collect a username and password. SSH differs from Telnet in this respect; SSH handles this detail itself. This fact creates some differences in the use of SSH clients, as noted in Chapter 24. It also means that SSH requires its own Pluggable Authentication Module (PAM) configuration. If you change the PAM configuration for `login`, SSH won't be affected, so you must consider this fact when adjusting PAM.

Unlike Telnet, SSH supports tunneling other protocols. This process involves the SSH client or server setting itself up as a server for another protocol. Instead of parsing this protocol, though, SSH sends the data to its counterpart on the other end of the connection. That program then pretends to originate the request for a local server. This feature is most commonly used for tunneling X connections, as described in the upcoming section, "SSH's X Tunneling," but it can be used for other protocols, as well.

SSH Server Software Options

You have a choice of two server programs to implement the SSH protocol in FreeBSD:

- **SSH**   The original SSH program is a commercial product, available from `http://www.ssh.com`. Despite its commercial nature, though, you can install it as a FreeBSD package or port; this is legal for evaluation purposes and for certain educational and noncommercial uses. Consult the SSH license for details.

- **OpenSSH**   The OpenSSH package (`http://www.openssh.com`) is an open source reimplementation of SSH, spearheaded by FreeBSD's cousin OS project, OpenBSD. You can install OpenSSH from either the packages or ports system, but it's installed as part of a base installation with recent versions of FreeBSD.

OpenSSH is the most popular SSH server for FreeBSD systems, and it's installed in a standard FreeBSD 5.0 system. Thus, this chapter focuses upon OpenSSH, although use of the original SSH isn't much different. I use the term *SSH* to refer to the protocol or to either package generically.

To do any good, an SSH server requires that users run SSH clients. FreeBSD's OpenSSH package includes such a client, called ssh. *Clients for other OSs, although not as common as Telnet clients, are readily available. Check* http://www.freessh.org *for information on free SSH clients for many OSs. Commercial terminal programs for Windows and Mac OS often include SSH support.*

Running an SSH Server

One fairly straightforward way to configure FreeBSD to run SSH is to use sysinstall:

1. As root, type **/stand/sysinstall** to launch the configuration utility.
2. From the main sysinstall menu, select the Configure option.
3. From the resulting FreeBSD Configuration Menu screen, select Networking.
4. From the resulting Network Services Menu screen, select the Sshd option, if it's not selected.
5. Select OK, Cancel, and then Exit Install to get out of sysinstall.

Behind the scenes, this procedure adds the following line to the /etc/rc.conf file:

```
sshd_enable="YES"
```

This line controls whether FreeBSD launches sshd, the SSH server, at boot time. If you prefer not to use sysinstall, you can add this line yourself with a text editor. Once this line is added, FreeBSD will launch SSH when it next restarts. In the meantime, you can launch the server manually:

```
# /usr/sbin/sshd
```

Unlike Telnet, SSH usually runs stand-alone rather than via a super server. This configuration improves performance slightly because sshd needs to create cryptographic keys whenever it starts up. Normally, sshd uses configuration options from its configuration file, described in the next section. You can override some of these options with command-line arguments, though. You might do this when debugging the SSH server. Consult the sshd man page for more details on these options.

Configuring SSH Options

The SSH server configuration file is `/etc/ssh/sshd_config`. (There's also an SSH client configuration file called `ssh_config` in the same directory; don't confuse the two!) This file consists of a series of lines, each of which takes the following form:

```
Option value
```

The named *Option* is descriptive, such as `Port` or `PermitRootLogin`. The *value* may be a number, a `yes` or `no` value, a filename, or an arbitrary string, depending upon the option. A line that begins with a pound sign (#) is a comment, and is ignored. For the most part, the default `sshd_config` file works well, but you should examine its contents. Some options you might want to adjust include

- **Port** This option sets the port to which `sshd` listens. The default value is `22`, but you may want to have the server listen to another port if you want to make it less obvious what's running on your system.

- **ListenAddress** You can tell `sshd` to listen for connections on only one network interface by using this option, which takes a hostname or IP address as its *value*, optionally followed by a colon and a port number. For instance, `ListenAddress 172.20.30.40:2222` causes the system to listen on the interface associated with the 172.20.30.40 address, on port 2222 instead of the usual port 22. This option is particularly helpful on systems with multiple network interfaces, such as routers.

- **PermitRootLogin** This option takes `yes` or `no` as its *value*, and controls whether SSH accepts logins directly from `root`. The default value in FreeBSD is `no`, which improves security, as noted earlier in "Restricting Telnet Access."

- **X11Forwarding** SSH can tunnel any protocol, but it includes special support for forwarding X. This support is controlled through the `X11Forwarding` option, which takes `yes` or `no` values. The default is `yes`, but `no` may be preferable if remote users shouldn't have easy access to X programs on the SSH server.

- **RhostsAuthentication** SSH provides the option of using a very old trusted-hosts authentication method used by the `rlogin` tool. This support is normally not necessary and is a potential security risk, so you should ensure that the `RhostsAuthentication` option is set to `no`.

- **Subsystem** You can enable support for additional capabilities with this option, which is unusual in that it takes two items as its *value*: a protocol name and a path to an executable to handle that protocol. FreeBSD's SSH server ships with support for a secure FTP variant (`sftp`). You can disable this support by uncommenting this line, if you don't need or want SFTP support.

The `sshd_config` file includes many additional options, some of which are commented out. Some of these are described in the configuration file itself, and others are described in the `sshd` man page. Consult these sources for more information.

Of the options described in this section, `ListenAddress` is the most likely to be one you might want to adjust. You should seriously consider configuring your system to listen to only one network interface on any computer with more than one interface. For instance, a router might be configured to accept SSH access from a local network, but not from the Internet at large, by using this option.

If you make changes to the `sshd_config` file, you must restart `sshd` for the changes to take effect. You can do this by typing the following commands:

```
# killall sshd
# /usr/sbin/sshd
```

 *The first of these commands terminates any existing SSH connections. If you want to avoid disrupting such connections, you can instead type **ps ax | grep sshd** to learn the process IDs (PIDs) of the `sshd` processes and kill only the parent process, which is easily identified by the fact that it doesn't list a username or tty number in the COMMAND column of the `ps` output.*

Configuring Remote X Access

Remote text-mode access through Telnet or SSH is useful for running many FreeBSD programs, such as text-mode shells, Emacs, `mutt`, and even system administration tools. Many programs for end users, though, now rely upon the X GUI environment. Using these programs remotely is possible because X was designed with remote access in mind. The X client/server relationship is confusing to the uninitiated, though, so you must understand this relationship before you begin configuring such remote access. There are two main ways to access X remotely: through a text-mode login or through a special GUI login tool. This section describes both login methods. The next major section, "Running a VNC Server," describes an alternative method of remote GUI use.

 You should read Chapter 13 before proceeding, if you haven't already. This section assumes basic familiarity with single-computer X server configuration.

Understanding the X Client/Server Relationship

Most people tend to think of server computers as being powerful systems hidden away in air-conditioned rooms and presided over by computer professionals. By this view, clients are less powerful systems at which individuals sit to do work. Although these characteristics aren't part of the definition of servers and clients, this stereotype is often not far wrong. Ordinary users do directly use FTP, web, and e-mail clients, for instance, and the corresponding servers often are powerful systems that reside in machine rooms.

Unfortunately, this conception is *very* wrong in the case of X servers, which are at the core of X. To understand why, try to think of the situation from the point of view of a client program. An FTP client, for instance, initiates a connection to an FTP server in order to request a data transfer. If you use a text-mode FTP client from a FreeBSD system's console, you'll be sitting at the client computer, just as in the stereotype. Consider an X-based FTP client, though. To this program, the display, keyboard, and mouse are network-accessible input/output sources, just like the remote FTP server. The FTP client is therefore also a client to the X server, which provides input from the keyboard and mouse, and enables the FTP client to send data to be displayed on the screen. To the FTP client, the fact that a human sits at the keyboard is irrelevant. This configuration is illustrated in Figure 21-1. Often, the X client computer and X server computer are one and the same, but this need not be the case, and Figure 21-1 separates the two.

In a standard FreeBSD installation, the system is configured so that programs realize that the X server is running on the local system. In remote access, though, these systems are separate, as in Figure 21-1. This configuration means that you must inform your programs of the change, you must configure the X server to accept connections from the X client system, and you must have some way of contacting the X client system to initiate the connection. Several methods have emerged to deal with these needs, as described in "Using X via a Text-Mode Login" and "Using an XDMCP Login."

The description of remote X access in this chapter focuses upon using FreeBSD (or any other computer that runs XFree86) as the X server system. You may want to run FreeBSD programs from a computer that runs another OS, though, such as Windows or Mac OS. You can do so, but you must obtain an X server for the OS in question. Examples include XFree86 (ported to Windows, `http://www.cygwin.com/xfree/`; OS/2, `http://ais.gmd.de/~veit/os2/xf86os2.html`; and Mac OS X, `http://mrcla.com/XonX/`), Xmanager for Windows (`http://www.netsarang.com/products/xmanager.html`), Exceed for Windows (`http://www.hummingbird.com/products/nc/exceed/`), and Xtools for Mac OS X (`http://www.tenon.com/products/xtools/`). The broad outline of using X remotely provided in this chapter

SERVERS

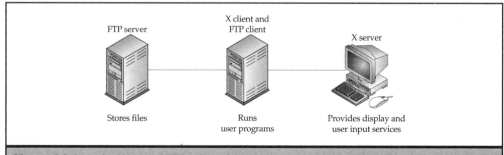

FTP server   X client and
                        FTP client   X server

Stores files   Runs   Provides display and
                      user programs   user input services

Figure 21-1. *An X-based FTP client functions as a client to the FTP server, but it's also a client to the X server, which may run on the same or a different computer than the FTP client program.*

applies to these products, but some of the X server configuration details differ. Consult your X server's documentation for details.

X servers can run in either of two basic ways, with some variants of both possible: *rooted* or *rootless*. A rooted X server provides a complete desktop. This desktop may be a full-screen environment or just a window in which the X server creates subwindows for the client programs. A rootless environment, by contrast, mingles the remote X client's windows with the local system's windows. As a general rule, when you use XFree86 on FreeBSD to access a remote system, you use it in rootless mode, so it can be hard to tell local windows from remote ones, but it may be easier to arrange windows from both systems to your liking. Many Windows and Mac OS X servers offer both rooted and rootless modes, so if you prefer, you can keep your X environment isolated from that of the host operating system. This isolation can be important if you want to run a full desktop environment such as GNOME or KDE without having it interfere with the host OS's desktop environment.

Using X via a Text-Mode Login

Because you sit at the X server, in order to launch a program on the X client computer you must have some way to contact that system to tell it to launch a program. This need means that the X client must run a server of some type to enable remote access. Coincidentally, this need is well served by text-mode remote-access servers, such as Telnet and SSH. Thus, you can use such a server to gain access to the X client system. Some servers, such as SSH, provide options to help with remote X access, as well.

The Basic Procedure

One of the simplest methods of using X applications remotely involves a local X server, a local text-mode login tool, a matching remote text-mode login server, and a handful of commands. To use these methods to run programs on a remote FreeBSD or other UNIX-like system (called bunyan.threeroomco.com in this example) from a FreeBSD or other UNIX-like system (called blueox.threeroomco.com in this example), follow these steps:

1. Log into blueox.threeroomco.com and, if necessary, start X (say, by typing **startx**).

2. In an xterm window, type **xhost +bunyan.threeroomco.com**. This command tells blueox's X server to accept connections from bunyan. You can omit the domain name if both computers are in the same domain, or use an IP address instead of a hostname.

3. Use your preferred remote-access tool, such as Telnet or SSH, to log into bunyan.

4. On bunyan, type a command to set the DISPLAY environment variable to blueox.threeroomco.com:0. In sh or bash, this command is **export DISPLAY=blueox.threeroomco.com:0**; in tcsh, it's **setenv DISPLAY blueox.threeroomco.com:0**. Once again, you can omit the domain name if both systems are in the same domain, or use an IP address instead of a hostname.

5. On `bunyan`, type the name of whatever program you want to use; it should launch and use `blueox`'s display. If you launch an `xterm` on `bunyan`, for instance, you'll see a new `xterm` window, but this one is controlled by `bunyan`. You can launch as many programs as you like in this way.

This procedure works for basic access, and is quite useable in many situations. Ordinarily, this procedure results in a window manager and desktop environment that's controlled by the X server system (`blueox`), although if your method of launching X doesn't launch a window manager, you can launch one that's controlled by the remote system in Step 5.

The security of your username and password is as good as whatever login protocol you use in Step 3. Data passed as part of the X programs isn't secure, though. For instance, if you launch an `xterm` from `bunyan` and use it to run `su`, the password you type traverses the network in an unencrypted form, even if you use SSH in Step 3. If you use the `xterm` window from which you made the initial connection in Step 3, though, the data pass over whatever text-mode protocol you used.

Because this method requires a client and a server on both computers, it may require special configuration if a firewall or NAT router resides between the two computers. For instance, if you want to use a computer on a local network with a NAT router to access a remote system, the NAT router permits the initial text-mode login (Step 3). When you try to launch X programs in Step 5, though, the connection attempt reaches the NAT router. Thus, the NAT router must be configured to forward port 6000 to the X server computer (`blueox`).

These instructions assume that you're running one X session. If you run multiple X sessions on your local computer, you may need to adjust the number after the colon in Step 4. This number identifies the X session number. It's 0 for the first session, 1 for the second session, and so on. If you use an X server running on Windows or some other non-UNIX OS, you can probably omit Step 2 (most such servers configure themselves to accept connections from any system by default). Many Windows X servers provide tools to help streamline this procedure—say, by logging in and launching an `xterm` window controlled by the remote system at the click of a button.

One of the problems with this procedure is that the `xhost` command in Step 2 tells the X server to accept connections from any user on the remote system. Thus, if this remote system has many users, one of those users could display "junk" windows on your X server computer or even intercept your keystrokes, possibly tricking you into divulging a password. The procedures described in the next two sections, "SSH's X Tunneling" and "A Variant with `xauth`," address this problem.

SSH's X Tunneling

A variant of the method presented in the previous section uses SSH to tunnel the X connection. In this configuration, the SSH server on the remote system (`bunyan`) sets itself up as if it were a local X server. This pseudoserver runs as if it were X session number 10 (`bunyan.threeroomco.com:10`), and the SSH server automatically sets the `DISPLAY` environment variable correctly.

SERVERS

When you try to launch an X program, the SSH server accepts X traffic and forwards it to the SSH client. The client then contacts the local X server and echoes the X traffic to it. Replies from your local X server go to the SSH client, which forwards them to the SSH server, which passes them on to the X clients (the programs you launch).

As a practical matter, this configuration means that you can use the method outlined in "The Basic Procedure," but you can skip Steps 2 and 4. Because SSH tunnels the return X connection, you can use this method through a firewall or NAT router, so long as this device permits the outgoing SSH connection.

Using SSH to tunnel an X connection requires that both the SSH server and the SSH client be configured to support this feature. The earlier section, "Configuring SSH Options," described the necessary SSH configuration option, X11Forwarding. The /etc/ssh/ssh_config file on the SSH client system contains a similar option; it should look like this:

```
ForwardX11 yes
```

On the SSH client, this feature can also be enabled or disabled with the -X and -x command-line options, respectively (these options differ only in case). If the server isn't configured to forward X connections, you must use the full procedure described in "The Basic Procedure" or "A Variant with xauth."

In addition to working around some complications related to firewalls and NAT routers, using SSH to forward X connections also adds the benefits of SSH's encryption to all X data. You can type sensitive passwords or display confidential information with little fear that the data will fall into the wrong hands. (In theory, a flaw in SSH security, technological advancements, or a lucky break on the part of a cracker could expose your data, but the risk is very small.) This advantage comes at a price, though: The encryption takes time. Thus, you're likely to experience degraded X performance when it's run over SSH compared to when it's used directly. You can mitigate these effects, and sometimes even improve performance, by using the -C option to ssh, which enables compression in addition to encryption. By compressing data, you can pass more of it over a limited-bandwidth network. Using compression is most likely to be helpful when the X session is over a low-bandwidth network such as a low-end digital subscriber line (DSL) connection and when both computers have fast CPUs.

A Variant with xauth

If you don't want to or can't use SSH, you may be concerned about the security issues noted earlier, in "The Basic Procedure." In particular, the ability of any user of the remote computer to access your X display is a potentially serious concern. You can limit the risk by using a tool other than the xhost command to specify who may connect to your computer. Specifically, the xauth program provides finer-grained X security. This program relies upon keys similar to those used by SSH; but the xauth keys merely authenticate a client program as one that's allowed to use the X server's resources. To use xauth, follow the procedure shown earlier, in "The Basic Procedure," but instead of Step 2 in that procedure, type the following command on the X server computer (`blueox` in this example):

```
$ xauth list blueox:0 | sed -e 's/^/add /' | ssh bunyan -x xauth
```

This command extracts your `xauth` key for `blueox`'s X server, modifies it into a command, and sends that command to `xauth` on the X client system so that the key is available for X client programs. You'll likely be asked for a password to your account on the remote system. The final step is performed by using `ssh`, which means that the X client system must run an SSH server, and the X server system must have an SSH client. In such a situation, it's probably better to tunnel the X connection through SSH, obviating the need to perform this step. If the systems lack SSH, you can transfer the key in some other way. For instance, if the X client system has an `rshd` server running, you could type **rsh bunyan xauth** instead of **ssh bunyan -x xauth** as part of the preceding command. Unfortunately, `rshd` isn't very secure, so this isn't a good alternative. Other options involve more complex means of extracting the key into a file, transferring it to the remote system, and manually adding the key to the X authority file.

Because of the difficulty of transferring the key in a convenient way without SSH, and the improved security possible in tunneling SSH, using `xauth` is of limited appeal; however, it might be useful in some situations, such as if you don't want to take the performance hit of tunneling X through SSH. This tool is also used internally by other methods, such as those described in the next section, "Using an XDMCP Login." Such implementations are hidden from the user and administrator, though; you don't need to take any special steps to configure them.

Using an XDMCP Login

Sometimes gaining access to an X client computer through a text-mode login is inconvenient or impossible. For instance, *X terminals* are dedicated GUI terminals that enable many individuals to use a single more powerful computer, but they usually lack Telnet or SSH clients. You can also configure even a low-end *x*86 system as a dedicated X terminal. In other cases, the five-step procedure described earlier, in "The Basic Procedure," is awkward for ordinary users, who prefer a simpler GUI login method. In any of these cases, one solution is to use the *X Display Manager Control Protocol (XDMCP)*, which is a remote login protocol designed for use with X. An XDMCP server replaces a Telnet or SSH server in the login procedure, in the process automating aspects of that task. To use an XDMCP server, you must configure the X client to run the XDMCP server. Most X servers include XDMCP client functionality. Unfortunately, XDMCP doesn't encrypt usernames or passwords, so it's no more secure than is Telnet.

If you've configured FreeBSD to boot directly into a GUI login mode, as described in Chapter 6, the system is already using XDMCP. You must make some changes to the configuration to enable it to accept logins from remote X servers, though.

Setting Up an XDMCP Server

FreeBSD supports four XDMCP servers:

- **XDM** The original X Display Manager (XDM) program is the simplest of the XDMCP servers. It displays a prompt for a username and password, and gives no other user-selectable options at login time. (XDM uses the .xsession login script in users' home directories, though, so users can set options in that script, as described in Chapter 6.)

- **WDM** The WINGs Display Manager (WDM) is an extension of XDM. It adds various user-selectable options at login time, so that the user can select what desktop environment to run, for instance. The basic WDM configuration file format is similar to that of XDM.

- **KDM** The KDE Display Manager (KDM) is part of the K Desktop Environment (KDE). KDM uses the same configuration file format as XDM, but it uses a supplemental configuration file to set additional options, such as a list of desktop environments that KDM can launch at the user's request.

- **GDM** The GNOME Desktop Manager (GDM) is part of the GNU Network Object Model Environment (GNOME). Like WDM and KDM, it provides additional options at login time, but it uses its own unique configuration file format.

Because the first three of these tools use the same basic configuration file format, I describe them, and particularly XDM. You can enable GDM in basically the same way, but you must consult its documentation to learn how to adjust it to accept remote logins. GDM also ships with a GUI utility called gdmconfig that can help set many GDM options.

The first step in configuring an XDMCP server to accept remote logins is to activate the server. This can be done by editing the /etc/ttys file, which contains a line like the following:

```
ttyv8    "/usr/X11R6/bin/xdm -nodaemon"  xterm    off secure
```

To enable XDM, change off to on. (You can also change /usr/X11R6/bin/xdm to another XDMCP server's complete path, such as /usr/X11R6/bin/wdm, but you may need to install the server first.) When you next restart the computer or type **kill -HUP 1** to tell init to reread its configuration files, the XDM server should start. This act will also start X and display the XDM login screen on the console. It will not, however, enable remote XDMCP logins; for that, you must make more changes.

The XDM configuration file is called xdm-config. In FreeBSD 5.0, this file is stored in /usr/X11R6/lib/X11/xdm, but in some other versions of FreeBSD and in some other OSs, it's located elsewhere, such as /etc/X11/xdm. The default xdm-config file includes the following line near the end:

```
DisplayManager.requestPort:      0
```

This line tells XDM not to request a port on which to listen for remote login requests; the server then manages only the local display. To enable XDM to handle remote logins, this line must be commented out by adding a pound sign (#) to the start of the line; or you can replace 0 with a port number, such as the default XDMCP port of 177.

One further change is necessary: You must edit the Xaccess file, which resides in the same directory as xdm-config. This file controls which remote computers may access the XDM server, and to what types of queries it should respond. To enable the fullest range of remote access, add the following lines to Xaccess:

```
*
* CHOOSER BROADCAST
```

The first line tells XDM that any computer may acquire a login prompt for access to the computer. The second line tells XDM to broadcast a query for other XDMCP servers and to provide a list of the machines found (that is, a *chooser*) if the calling system requests such a list (this type of request is known as an *indirect* query). If your network hosts systems running XFree86 as X terminals, at least one computer should contain the second line because this line enables these computers to obtain a list of XDMCP-enabled computers. Some X servers, including many available for Windows, include the ability to perform their own queries of XDMCP servers, and so don't need to send indirect queries.

The asterisks in both lines in the preceding example denote any computer. To limit access to specific computers, you can list them one per line, or use an asterisk as part of a name. For instance, consider the following lines:

```
*.threeroomco.com
pine.pangaea.edu
pine.pangaea.edu CHOOSER BROADCAST
bunyan.threeroomco.com CHOOSER BROADCAST
```

This example allows any computer in the threeroomco.com domain to obtain an XDMCP login prompt. The pine.pangaea.edu computer is granted the same right, and can obtain a list of other XDMCP servers via an indirect query. Likewise, bunyan.threeroomco.com can perform indirect queries. The indirect queries can be particularly important for remote clients because the broadcasts to discover XDMCP clients may not work over the Internet. In this example, bunyan might lack the ability to perform such a query even locally, but other local clients might support this feature more directly.

Ordinarily, an XDMCP server manages the local display, meaning that the server acts as a client to that X server without first being contacted by the X server. This configuration is controlled through the `Xservers` file in the same directory as `xdm-config` and `Xaccess`. The `Xservers` file contains a line like the following by default:

```
:0 local /usr/X11R6/bin/X
```

This line tells the server to manage the first (`:0`) display on the local computer, and to launch `/usr/X11R6/bin/X` to do so, if X isn't already running. If you want to be able to use X programs from a remote X server, but don't need to run X locally, you can comment out this line by preceding it with a pound sign (#). Once you do this and restart the server, it will respond to remote requests, but will not start X automatically when you boot or start the XDMCP server.

Once you've made the changes to `xdm-config`, `Xaccess`, and `Xservers`, you should tell `init` to reconfigure its running processes by typing **kill -HUP 1**. The system rereads `/etc/ttys` and launches XDM, if it's not already running. If XDM is already running, you may need to kill it by typing **killall xdm**. Once XDM dies, `init` restarts it with the options now specified in `/etc/ttys`, and XDM reads its changed configuration files, thus implementing the changes.

Using an XDMCP Client

XDMCP clients are typically built into X servers or are closely associated with them. Precisely how they're configured and used varies substantially from one server to another, so you may need to consult the server's documentation for details. In the case of Windows X servers, you can usually specify use of XDMCP for remote login in a configuration dialog box, such as the one shown in Figure 21-2, which belongs to Xmanager (`http://www.netsarang.com`). This dialog box illustrates four common XDMCP client options:

- **Passive mode** In passive mode, the X server doesn't attempt to make any XDMCP connections. This mode is useful if you intend to use a text-mode login tool or if the XDMCP server should take the initiative and contact the X server (this mode is used locally when you configure FreeBSD for GUI logins).

- **XDMCP Query** When you configure an X server to query an XDMCP server, you're effectively telling the X server to log directly onto the XDMCP server computer. Users have no choice in what system they'll use.

- **XDMCP Broadcast** This mode causes the X server to send a broadcast to the local network or to a specified set of computers, to find out which ones have XDMCP servers available. The X server then displays a list of available servers, such as the one shown in Figure 21-3. The user can select one system and log into it.

- **XDMCP Indirect** An indirect mode query works much like a broadcast query from the user's point of view. You must configure the X server to use one XDMCP server as an intermediary, though; that system's XDMCP server must be configured to accept indirect queries, as described earlier, in "Setting Up an XDMCP Server." The result is a list of systems similar to the one shown in Figure 21-3, although the fonts, button styles, and so on are likely to be different.

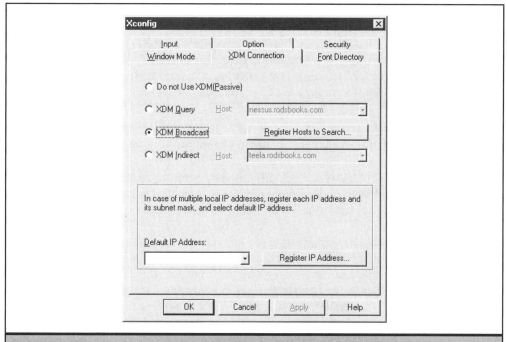

Figure 21-2. *X servers typically provide several options for how to contact and use an XDMCP server.*

Using FreeBSD as a Dedicated X Terminal

If you want to use a FreeBSD system as a dedicated X terminal, you can do so, but you must reconfigure it so that it uses an appropriate XDMCP mode. In fact, odd as it may seem, you must configure FreeBSD so that it does *not* start X automatically in the usual way.

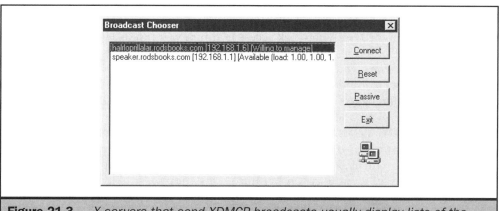

Figure 21-3. *X servers that send XDMCP broadcasts usually display lists of the machines that respond, enabling users to select which system to use.*

SERVERS

As a beginning step and for testing purposes, configure FreeBSD to run without starting its own XDMCP program—change the line that calls xdm in /etc/ttys so that the server is disabled. You can then test XFree86's own XDMCP client options, which you activate with the -query *hostname*, -broadcast, and -indirect *hostname* options, to enable a single-computer login, a broadcast, or an indirect login, respectively. For instance, to obtain a list of available systems via an indirect login, type the command

```
$ /usr/X11R6/bin/X -indirect blueox.threeroomco.com
```

Of course, blueox.threeroomco.com must be running an XDMCP server that's configured to accept indirect queries from the calling system. If it is, and if X is configured correctly on the calling system, you'll see a list of systems similar to the one shown in Figure 21-3.

 Note *One peculiarity of XFree86 compared to many other X servers is that its own -broadcast option causes it to log into the first computer it locates on the local network, rather than present a chooser. Thus, you must use the -indirect option or specify the desired computer with the -query option to choose which remote system you want to use.*

Once you've tested this method of starting X, you may want to make it automatic, rather than requiring users to log in and then launch X manually. To do so, you can create a custom startup script, as described in Chapter 6, to start X late in the system startup process. If you use the -indirect option, the computer will function as a dedicated X terminal; upon startup, it will present a list of available XDMCP servers, enabling users to log into any of them (provided they have accounts on the remote systems, of course).

Running a VNC Server

Because X was designed with network access in mind, you can use it directly from another FreeBSD, UNIX-like, or even entirely non-UNIX system, so long as the remote system has an X server. Using X over a network isn't without its problems, though. As you can tell from reading the earlier section "Configuring Remote X Access," this type of configuration has its share of pitfalls, particularly if a firewall or NAT router sits between the X server and the computer whose programs you want to run. Also, most X servers for Windows and Mac OS are commercial, and many of them are quite pricey, at several hundred dollars a copy. XFree86 on Windows is free, but can be tricky to configure. Finally, XFree86 enables you to run X programs remotely, but it's not much good if you want to run programs on a Windows system from a FreeBSD computer. For all of these reasons, many people prefer using another product for remote GUI access: *Virtual Network Computing (VNC)*, which was developed by AT&T (`http://www.uk.research.att.com/vnc/`) This is an open source program that uses a client on the system at which the user sits to control a special X server on the remote computer. This relationship makes installing, configuring, and using VNC different from installing, configuring, and using a remote X server.

Understanding the VNC Client/Server Relationship

Refer back to Figure 21-1, which depicts the relationship between an X client (that is, an X program) and an X server in a network environment. VNC adds a layer of complexity to this picture by running the X server on the same computer as the X client. This X server doubles as a VNC server. Figure 21-1's X server computer runs a VNC client program. This client program (when run in FreeBSD) communicates with a local X server. Essentially, VNC functions as a local X server that echoes its data across the network so that another X server provides the actual keyboard, mouse, and display.

VNC clients and servers are available for Windows, Mac OS, and other OSs. When you use a non-FreeBSD (or non-X, more precisely) VNC client or server, X obviously isn't involved. Instead, VNC uses native calls to display the data received from the remote system or intercepts the host OS's display.

In adding an extra protocol layer, VNC increases the complexity of the connection. Ironically, this increased complexity can simplify remote access configuration. The key to understanding this peculiarity is that remote X access normally requires both a client and a server on both of the computers involved in the connection. VNC, though, fills both of these roles. The VNC client functions as a login client and replaces (or uses) the local X server; and the VNC server functions as a local X server, obviating the need to initiate a return connection to the computer at which the user sits. SSH's X forwarding feature works in a similar fashion, although it doesn't process the X display data as much. Thus, SSH still requires an X server on the SSH client system, whereas VNC can function without an X server on the VNC client end. VNC needs some sort of display mechanism, though, such as the Windows or Mac OS windowing systems.

In terms of security, VNC encrypts the login password, but doesn't encrypt any other data. Thus, VNC is more secure than Telnet or an XDMCP login, but for the best security, using SSH to tunnel X is the superior solution.

Installing VNC

VNC is available as both a FreeBSD port and as a package (in the `net` section, in both cases). You can install it from either source, as described in Chapter 11. In either case, the resulting installation includes several VNC program files, including `vncpasswd` (which sets the password used by the server), `Xvnc` (the actual X and VNC server program), `vncserver` (a Perl script that starts `Xvnc` with useful default parameters),

SERVERS

and `vncviewer` (the VNC client program). Thus, to access a FreeBSD system from another FreeBSD computer, you install the full VNC package on both computers.

In addition to the main VNC server package, variants are available. For instance, Tight VNC (`http://www.tightvnc.com`) and TridiaVNC (`http://www.developvnc.org`) add data compression techniques that speed up VNC operation. Some of these alternative forms are available as FreeBSD ports or packages, and most are backwards-compatible with the original VNC, so installing TightVNC or TridiaVNC instead of the original VNC is usually the best course of action. This chapter describes configuring the original VNC, but alternative forms work in much the same way.

VNC servers and clients are available on other platforms. Check the main VNC web site for information on VNC for Windows and Mac OS. Others have ported VNC to a wide variety of other platforms, such as OS/2 (`http://www.sra.co.jp/people/akira/os2/vnc-pm/`) and BeOS (`http://www.bebits.com/app/2329`). Try a web search if you want to run a VNC client or server on an exotic platform.

Configuring the VNC Server

Unlike most login servers, a specific instance of a VNC server is tied to a specific user. (The upcoming section, "Using VNC from `inetd`," describes how to run a VNC server as a more conventional login server.) Thus, VNC server configuration is something that ordinary users do. The job is accomplished by editing configuration files in the user's `~/.vnc` directory. As a system administrator, you can modify the `vncserver` startup script to provide default options customized to your system.

User-Level Modifications

The `~/.vnc` directory and its files don't exist until they're created by running the VNC server or other utilities. To begin, follow these steps:

1. Create the `.vnc` subdirectory in the home directory of the user who will run the VNC server. Be sure the correct user owns the directory.

2. *As the user who will run the server*, type **vncpasswd**. Like the ordinary `passwd` command, `vncpasswd` sets a password, which is stored in an encrypted form in the `~/.vnc/passwd` file. The `vncpasswd` utility should create this file with permissions that allow only the owner to read it, but you should double-check this configuration.

At this point, VNC is ready to be run. You should do so *as an ordinary user* (the one who typed **vncpasswd**):

```
$ vncserver

New 'X' desktop is bunyan.threeroomco.com:1
```

```
Creating default startup script /home/rodsmith/.vnc/xstartup
Starting applications specified in /home/rodsmith/.vnc/xstartup
Log file is /home/rodsmith/.vnc/bunyan.threeroomco.com:1.log
```

At this point, the VNC server is active, and you can log into it as described in the section, "Making a VNC Connection." One detail you must note is the VNC session number reported by vncserver. This is the number following the hostname and colon in the first line of output—1 in this example. You use the session number in lieu of a username, and VNC prompts for a password, which is the one you entered using vncpasswd. If two or more people run the VNC server, or if one person runs it multiple times, each session uses a different number.

Note   *You may be wondering how you're supposed to type* **vncserver** *to launch the VNC server when you're not sitting at that computer. You can use a remote login tool such as SSH to do the job—but this means you need two login sessions, the text-mode tool and VNC. If you have physical access to the remote system's console, you can launch the VNC server and leave it running for remote use when you're away. The upcoming section, "Using VNC from* inetd*," provides another solution.*

Because the VNC server includes an X server, it requires an X startup script. When you run vncserver the first time, the script creates a basic VNC X server startup script in ~/.vnc/xstartup. This script starts a fairly basic X session using the twm window manager. Chances are you'll want to edit this script to start some other desktop environment, such as GNOME or KDE. Chapter 6 describes such changes to .xinitrc or .xsession files; the VNC xstartup file works in precisely the same way.

One of VNC's unusual characteristics is that it maintains its state across logins. For instance, suppose you start the VNC server and use it for a while. You can shut down your VNC client and then move to another computer and open a new VNC session with the original VNC server. You'll find your desktop in precisely the state it was in when you closed the original VNC session. Although this feature is useful in some situations, it means that changes you make to xstartup won't take effect until you restart the server. To do this, you must issue the following command to shut it down:

```
$ vncserver -kill :1
```

You may have to change the number that ends this command to match the session number that VNC provided when you started the server. Once this is done, you can restart the server and log back in. You can—and should—shut down the server when you expect not to be using it for some time, particularly when the computer is exposed to the Internet at large. Doing so reduces the risk of a break-in via VNC. Also, if the VNC server (or the computer on which it runs) should crash while you're not using it, you may lose work if you haven't saved it.

Modifying the vncserver Script

The /usr/X11R6/bin/vncserver script sets many variables for the global VNC configuration, much as XF86Config sets global X options for the X server that handles your display. For instance, vncserver controls the size of the virtual VNC desktop, the color depth, and the default user-level startup script. You can modify any of these options by directly editing the vncserver script. Specific options you might want to set include

- **Desktop size**   The $geometry variable sets the size of the virtual desktop that VNC presents to the user. The default value is 1024x768.

Tip   *The virtual VNC desktop appears within a window on the VNC client. Thus, setting the VNC desktop size to something slightly smaller than the client's screen size creates an optimal setting. For instance, if your clients use 1024×768 displays, you might set $geometry to 950x650.*

- **Color depth**   The default color depth is 8 (8 bits, or 256 colors). Assuming the clients support greater depths, 16, 24, or 32 may work better.

- **Font path**   The default font path for the VNC X server is set in the $cmd variable, using the -fp parameter. The default font path is fairly minimal, including only /usr/lib/X11/fonts/misc and /usr/lib/X11/fonts/75dpi. You can easily expand the path by adding directories, separated by commas. Check your /etc/X11/XF86Config file for information on the font path used by the computer's local X server.

- **New users' default script**   The vncserver script contains within it the script that's written to ~/vnc/xstartup when a user first runs the program. Thus, you can change this script by editing it in vncserver. Specifically, look for the variable $defaultXStartup, and compare it to the xstartup script created by vncserver. The vncserver variable specification includes formatting that's not present in the xstartup script, but modifying the original isn't very difficult. For instance, if you want to launch GNOME rather than twm, replace twm with gnome-session.

Caution   *Back up the vncserver script before modifying it; that way, if you make changes that prevent the VNC server from running, you can easily undo them by restoring the original script.*

Some options in the vncserver script can be overridden by parameters passed to the script. Of particular interest, the -geometry and -depth options set the desktop size and bit depth, respectively. Typing **vncserver -help** generates a brief summary of vncserver options.

Making a VNC Connection

Using VNC from a FreeBSD system is fairly straightforward: You type **vncviewer** on the VNC client system, optionally followed by the name of the VNC server computer, a colon, and the VNC session number:

```
$ vncviewer bunyan.threeroomco.com:1
```

This command connects to VNC session 1 on bunyan.threeroomco.com. If you omit the VNC server computer and session number, vncviewer prompts you for this information. If you omit the session number alone, vncviewer assumes you mean session 0. Whether or not you specify a hostname, the program asks for a password, which is the one you created using vncpasswd. There are a few options to the vncviewer command that modify its operation. The more important of these are

- **-shared** Ordinarily, when a user logs into a VNC session, any existing user's connection is terminated. The -shared option tells VNC not to terminate the original connection. You can use this feature if you don't want to disrupt an existing connection you've made or if you want to use VNC as a collaborative tool—say, to help show somebody at a remote site how to use a program. When VNC is used in this way, both users control the mouse and keyboard, which can be confusing if you're not expecting it.

- **-viewonly** This option disables mouse and keyboard control of the session. You can use it to monitor an existing VNC session.

- **-depth** In theory, you can specify a color depth with this option; but in practice it often doesn't work.

The result of a VNC connection is a window in which an entire X desktop is displayed. For instance, Figure 21-4 shows a VNC viewer window open on a VNC server run on another computer. (Note the X window manager border around the entire X desktop.)

VNC viewers for Windows and Mac OS use more GUI-oriented interfaces, but the basic principles of operation are the same—you tell the VNC viewer what computer and session you want to use, you enter a password, and the program opens a window displaying a complete session. If you run a VNC server on a Windows or Mac OS system, you can control it remotely from a FreeBSD system, although this operation tends to be a bit more sluggish because intercepting the Windows and Mac OS X GUI protocols isn't as efficient as translating X to VNC in a custom X server, as the FreeBSD VNC server does.

Using VNC from inetd

One awkward feature of VNC in a multiuser environment is the need for each user who runs the server to launch it manually and remember the session number. For many situations, a far simpler configuration would enable VNC to run like most login servers

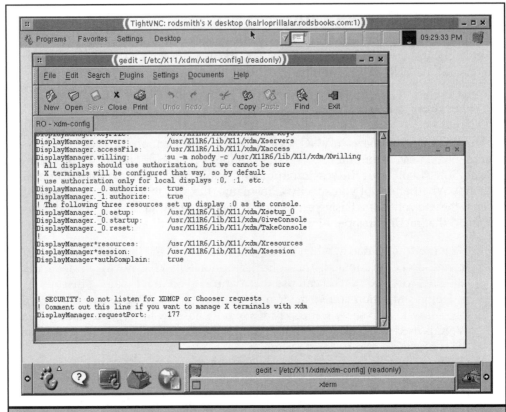

Figure 21-4. *VNC clients use a mode that's akin to a rooted X server interface—the remote system presents a complete desktop within a single window.*

and tap into the FreeBSD user authentication system. This configuration is possible, but it requires taking some unusual steps:

1. Add an entry to `/etc/services` for VNC. Normally, VNC runs on port 5900 and those immediately above it. You only need one entry, so the following line should work well:

   ```
   vnc     5900/tcp
   ```

2. Create an `/etc/inetd.conf` entry for VNC. This entry calls the `Xvnc` program (which is the real server called by `vncserver`):

   ```
   vnc stream tcp nowait nobody /usr/X11R6/bin/Xvnc :1 ↵
   -inetd -query localhost -once
   ```

3. Restart the `inetd` server by typing **killall –HUP inetd**.

4. Configure an XDMCP server on the VNC server computer, as described in Chapter 6 and the earlier section of this chapter, "Using an XDMCP Login."

At this point, the VNC server should respond to queries from other computers to its session 0—for instance, **vncviewer bunyan:0**. When you type such a command, or use the equivalent connection options from a Windows or Mac OS VNC viewer, VNC won't prompt for a password. Instead, you'll see your XDMCP login prompt, just as if you'd used an X server's XDMCP client. You can then use the login session much as you would a local login or a rooted X login.

Some of the details you set in Steps 1 and 2 are extremely important. The port number you choose to specify in /etc/services determines the session number you use to connect to the VNC server. Port 5900 corresponds to session 0, 5901 corresponds to session 1, and so on. The :1 option to Xvnc in the inetd.conf file determines the X session number that VNC occupies. If X is running locally, it probably occupies session 0, which is why this example uses :1. If you don't run X locally, you can omit this option, and VNC will try to use session 0. The -inetd option tells VNC that it's running from inetd, and the -once option tells VNC to stop running when the session terminates, which is necessary in an inetd configuration. The -query localhost option works just like the same option would in an ordinary X server; it links the X server to the XDMCP server running on the local computer.

> **Tip** *If you try this configuration and VNC doesn't respond as you expect, try typing* **telnet vncserver 5900**, *where vncserver is the VNC server computer. This command should show you error messages that may help diagnose the problem. For instance, if VNC is trying to use an X session that's already in use, you'll see an error message to that effect when you use telnet to connect to the VNC port.*

Using inetd to launch VNC changes many of the features that make VNC unique:

- VNC sessions are no longer persistent; if you terminate a VNC session, you must log in again, and if you terminate a session without first logging out, your programs will exit, so you might lose work. Similarly, two users cannot connect to the same VNC desktop.
- The VNC server accepts multiple logins to the same VNC session number.
- There's no need for users to log in and explicitly launch a VNC server; it's always available.
- Logins use whatever login scripts the XDMCP server runs, not the ~/.vnc/ xstartup file.
- Authentication isn't based on the user's VNC password; it's based on the usual FreeBSD username and password. One negative consequence of this feature is that the password isn't encrypted, as it is during VNC's normal password exchange.

On the whole, running VNC from inetd is a good approach for a multiuser computer or if you want a remote-access method that works more like a remote X server, but without the hassles of X server configuration. This approach places the bulk of the configuration work on the VNC server computer; VNC clients can be very simple and easy to install and configure. This feature contrasts with the usual X server configuration, which requires work on both computers.

The `inetd` configuration can be extended by adding support for additional VNC sessions. Repeat Steps 1 through 3, but give the service a new name (such as `vnc2` rather than `vnc`), assign it a new port number (such as `5901`), specify a new X session number (such as `:2`), and pass additional options to `Xvnc` in its `inetd.conf` entry to have it behave differently (such as `-geometry 700x500` to specify a 700×500 desktop). In this way, you can configure VNC to deliver different settings to clients depending upon their needs, such as desktops sized appropriately for a variety of clients. Users will have to remember which VNC session number is associated with each configuration, though.

Summary

UNIX has a long history of multiuser operation and remote access. FreeBSD benefits from this history with text-mode remote-login protocols such as Telnet and SSH, as well as more recent GUI remote-access protocols such as X and VNC. Some of these servers can be configured by changing a line or two in a configuration file, but others require more work, particularly if you want to diverge from the default configuration. Advanced X configurations using `xauth` or XDMCP and certain VNC configurations are particularly likely to require serious configuration effort, but the results are often worthwhile in ease of use for the computer's users. Security concerns with login servers are substantial because these servers enable users to do just about anything and because they usually involve the transfer of passwords. Thus, using an encrypting protocol such as SSH is advisable whenever it's practical.

Chapter 22

Miscellaneous Servers

The last several chapters have described configuring assorted high-profile servers or server types, such as mail and web servers. Many other servers are less conspicuous to end users, but can still be very important. This chapter describes some of these servers:

- **DHCP servers**   These servers deliver network configuration information to other computers
- **DNS servers**   These servers convert between hostnames and IP addresses.
- **Time servers**   These servers enable all the computers on a network to set their clocks to a standard time.
- **Font servers**   These servers deliver a consistent set of fonts to X servers.

DHCP and DNS servers are both very important to the Internet at large and on many individual subnets in particular. They're also both complex enough that this chapter can cover only basic configuration. Time servers and font servers, although relatively simple, can be extremely important in some environments. Time servers, in particular, are important to protocols that rely upon two computers having synchronized clocks, such as the Kerberos security suite (`http://web.mit.edu/kerberos/www/`).

DHCP Servers

The Dynamic Host Configuration Protocol (DHCP) is a popular method of assigning IP addresses and related information to computers on a network. Using DHCP simplifies the configuration of most computers on the network. (Chapter 14 describes basic TCP/IP configuration, including use of DHCP by DHCP clients.) This simplification doesn't come without a cost, though; every network that uses DHCP needs a DHCP server. FreeBSD comes with the popular `dhcpd` DHCP server, and makes a perfectly adequate DHCP server system. This section describes the pros and cons of running a DHCP server, as well as how to configure a DHCP server to deliver both dynamic and static IP addresses.

When to Run a DHCP Server

The question of whether or not to run a DHCP server boils down to one of whether the effort of configuring the server is justified by the effort saved in configuring DHCP clients. Chapter 14's description of static IP addresses and DHCP configuration should give you some idea of the effort involved on the client side. Of course, non-FreeBSD systems require somewhat different setup steps, but the relative effort involved is roughly the same across OSs. Configuring a DHCP server takes more effort than configuring a single computer to use a static IP address. As a general rule, the break-even point comes at half a dozen to a dozen computers. Several factors can modify this estimate, though:

- **Need for static IP addresses**   Configuring DHCP to assign an IP address that's guaranteed not to change takes more effort than configuring the server to assign

IP addresses dynamically. Thus, if your network has many servers that need static IP addresses, using DHCP may not reduce your administrative effort.

■ **Multiboot or variable configurations**   If many computers on the network multiboot between multiple OSs, or if they're used for testing OS installations, DHCP can be particularly beneficial because DHCP saves effort for each OS or installation, not just each physical computer.

■ **Transient computers**   If your network hosts computers that come and go, such as laptops, using DHCP can greatly simplify their configuration. This is particularly true if the laptops routinely connect to several different networks; if all the networks use DHCP, a single configuration on a laptop can work on all the networks to which it connects.

■ **User-configured systems**   If end users configure their own computers, using DHCP can reduce the chance of a misconfiguration.

■ **Too many computers**   If you have more computers than IP addresses, but if not all computers are in use at all times, DHCP can help you get by. The server can assign an IP address to one computer, and then when it shuts down, the address becomes available for reassignment. To work best in such an environment, you need to set a short lease time (described in the upcoming section, "Setting Global Options").

> **Tip** *Network Address Translation (NAT), described in Chapter 17, is another technique for stretching a limited supply of IP addresses. NAT enables use of more computers than you have IP addresses even if all the computers are in use at once.*

On the whole, DHCP is best used on networks with more than half a dozen or a dozen computers, or when the computers on the network change frequently. It's of least value on very small networks or when most of the computers on the network require static IP addresses.

In a standard configuration, a DHCP server responds to *broadcasts* from clients—packets addressed to all computers on a network. DHCP works in this way because a DHCP client doesn't have an IP address when it first boots, nor does it know the address of a DHCP server. Thus, a broadcast will reach the DHCP server if it's on the local subnet. For this reason, if your network is large enough to include routers between multiple subnets, you'll either need a DHCP server on each subnet or a special router configuration to echo such requests between subnets.

Installing a DHCP Server

The most common DHCP server for FreeBSD is the Internet Software Consortium (ISC) DHCP server. You can install this server from either the packages or the ports system, as described in Chapter 11 (it's called `isc-dhcpd`).

Once installed, the ISC DHCP server uses configuration files in /usr/local/etc to control its operation. The most important of these files are

- **/usr/local/etc/rc.d/isc-dhcpd.sh**   This file controls the startup of the server, as described in Chapter 16. The FreeBSD package installs a script called isc-dhcpd.sh.sample, so you must rename this script to have the system start the server automatically. Aside from renaming the file, chances are you won't have to edit it.

- **/usr/local/etc/dhcpd.conf**   This file is the main DHCP configuration file. The operations described in the sections "Basic DHCP Configuration" and "Assigning Static IP Addresses" relate to this file. As with the startup script, the file that appears immediately after installation bears an extra .sample extension; you must copy or rename this file to use the DHCP server.

- **/usr/local/etc/rc.isc-dhcpd.conf**   This file contains startup options you can pass to the server, listed on two lines—dhcpd_options and dhcpd_ifaces. Chances are you won't need to touch this file, but if you want the server to listen to some network interfaces but not others, you can list the interfaces (such as fxp0) on the dhcpd_ifaces line.

The dhcpd.conf file consists of comments, which are lines that begin with pound signs (#); global options, which consist of an option name followed by one or more values; and subnet definitions, which are groupings of options that apply to specific subnets for which the DHCP server is responsible. Most noncomment lines in dhcpd.conf end in semicolons (;). The start and end of option blocks, such as subnet definitions, are exceptions to this rule. These lines use curly braces ({ }) to delineate where a block begins and ends, thus:

```
subnet 10.254.239.0 netmask 255.255.255.224 {
  range 10.254.239.10 10.254.239.20;
  option routers rtr-239-0-1.example.org, rtr-239-0-2.example.org;
}
```

Before starting the DHCP server, you must create a file in which it stores information on the leases it delivers. You can do this by typing **touch /var/db/dhcpd.leases**, which creates an empty file of that name. If you don't create this file, the server won't operate correctly.

Basic DHCP Configuration

The dhcpd.conf.sample file that ships with FreeBSD is functional, but it's virtually certain that you'll have to adjust it to suit your needs. Some of the global options are reasonable defaults, but some need to be changed for your network. The sample file also includes active definitions for several subnets, which you must replace with your own. You can use the definitions included in the file as a model, but in the end, you must create a configuration that's suitable for your own network.

 DHCP delivers IP addresses to other *computers. The DHCP server itself must be configured with a static IP address.*

Setting Global Options

Global options appear at the beginning of `dhcpd.conf`. I recommend you use the `dhcpd.conf.sample` file as a starting point. You can leave most of the global options alone. Some that you're most likely to need to change are

- **`option domain-name "name.tld"`**   This option sets the domain name that's passed to clients.

- **`option domain-name-servers server-list`**   This option tells clients what computers to use as DNS servers. The `server-list` is a comma-separated list of servers, which you can specify as IP addresses or as hostnames. If you use hostnames, `dhcpd` resolves them itself and passes the IP addresses it obtains to clients.

- **`option routers router-list`**   This option enables you to tell clients what their router's (aka gateway's) IP address is. In most cases, `router-list` is a single IP address, but complex networks may host multiple routers, in which case you can list more than one, separated by commas. You can also use hostnames rather than IP addresses.

- **`default-lease-time seconds`**   DHCP operates on the principle of a *lease*. Much like a lease on an apartment, a DHCP lease is time-limited; after it expires, the DHCP server is free to reassign the IP address to another computer. The best lease time varies from one network to another. On a network that sees a lot of changing computers (say, if users frequently plug in laptops for an hour or two and then disconnect), you might want to set the lease time low—say, to `3600` (3,600 seconds, or one hour). On networks that see few changes, a longer lease time reduces DHCP-related network traffic and minimizes the chance of a problem should the DHCP server crash. On such a network, a lease time of a week or more (say, `604800`) may be appropriate. The default lease time in the sample file is `600`, or just ten minutes. This value is reasonable for testing or debugging, but isn't good for a regular installation.

- **`max-lease-time seconds`**   This option works much like `default-lease-time`, but it sets the maximum lease time that the server will accept, should the client request a longer lease.

Chances are you'll adjust all of these global options to suit your network. You may also want to adjust some others, which provide support for more advanced configurations. For instance, there are options to help coordinate DHCP with a DNS

SERVERS

server, or to deliver information relevant to NetBIOS clients. Consult the DHCP documentation for more information.

Creating a Subnet Definition

A minimal subnet definition looks like this:

```
subnet 10.152.187.0 netmask 255.255.255.0 {
}
```

The opening line describes the subnet to which the definition belongs, including the network address (10.152.187.0 in this example) and the netmask (255.255.255.0). This particular example defines a subnet that the server will *not* serve, as indicated by the blank definition block—there are no options between the opening and closing curly braces. You might include a definition such as this one for a subnet to which the DHCP server computer is connected but for which it should not function as a DHCP server. (A router that provides DHCP services to one subnet but not another might be so configured, although for security reasons it's best to run DHCP server software on nonrouter computers.) In most cases, a subnet definition includes at least one additional line. A minimal functional definition looks like this:

```
subnet 172.29.30.0 netmask 255.255.30.0 {
   range 172.29.30.20 172.29.30.254;
}
```

The range keyword specifies the range of IP addresses that the server may deliver to clients. In this example, the server hands out addresses in the 172.29.30.20 to 172.29.30.254 range. In this simple example, the DHCP server delivers addresses to all computers that ask for them, provided the server hasn't exhausted its available addresses. Assuming they aren't listed in another subnet definition, this example also reserves addresses between 172.29.30.1 and 172.29.30.19 for other uses. Typically, you might use such addresses for local servers and routers.

 Be careful not to include the DHCP server's own IP address in the range of addresses it delivers to clients! Duplicate IP addresses on a single subnet are likely to make one or both systems inaccessible.

Subnet definitions may also include options described earlier, in "Setting Global Options." For instance, you might want to override the default lease time for one subnet but not for another. You can also configure specific computers to receive the same IP address time after time, as described in the next section.

Assigning Static IP Addresses

A basic DHCP configuration assigns IP addresses in a haphazard fashion—clients receive whatever IP address the DHCP server happens to deliver. If a client shuts down for a while and comes back online later, the client might or might not receive the same IP address it had originally. This characteristic makes running server programs on DHCP clients tricky at best because other computers can't easily find the server's IP address. There are advanced methods of linking DHCP and DNS servers to overcome this problem, but such techniques are beyond the scope of this book. A simpler approach is to have the DHCP server assign the same IP address to a specific computer every time it boots. Doing so requires creating client-specific entries in the DHCP server's configuration file.

Note   *Although IP addresses may change between boots (or network interface activations) of a computer, they're unlikely to change while a computer is running. The client asks the DHCP server to renew its lease, usually at half the lease interval. At that time, the DHCP server normally complies, extending the lease on the IP address. Thus, if a DHCP client runs continuously, its IP address never changes.*

The simplest way to assign a static IP address via DHCP is to bind the IP address to the Media Access Control (MAC) address of the client's network interface. You can do this with a declaration such as the following, which can appear inside or outside of a subnet block:

```
host teela {
    hardware ethernet 00:05:02:a7:76:da;
    fixed-address 192.168.1.2;
}
```

The `host` keyword is followed by the hostname of the computer in question (without its domain name), then a block of options. The `hardware ethernet` option specifies the MAC address of the Ethernet card. (There's also a `hardware token-ring` option that works in much the same way for Token Ring networks.) The `fixed-address` option specifies the IP address that's associated with the MAC address. When the DHCP server sees a request arrive from the computer with the 00:05:02:A7:76:DA MAC address, the server delivers the 192.168.1.2 IP address. The server also delivers the hostname (`teela` in this example), but many clients ignore this information. No special configuration is required on the client's side, although you must obtain the MAC address from the computer in question.

You can obtain a client's MAC address in many ways. Clients often provide a way to obtain the MAC address. For instance, in FreeBSD, you can type the following command shortly after booting the computer:

```
$ dmesg | grep "Ethernet address"
fxp0: Ethernet address 00:03:47:b1:ee:b8
```

SERVERS

You can also spot MAC addresses from the FreeBSD DHCP server. One way to do so is to use arp, which modifies or displays information on the computer's low-level IP address and MAC address tables. The following command locates the MAC address of another computer, provided you know its IP address or hostname:

```
$ arp 192.168.1.2
teela.rodsbooks.com (192.168.1.2) at 00:05:02:a7:76:da on fxp0 [ethernet]
```

 You may need to contact the target system, say by pinging it, before this command will work.

One drawback to this method is that the computer must already have an IP address. Even a dynamic IP address assigned by the DHCP server will do (you can later reboot the computer to force it to pick up its new custom IP address); or you can temporarily configure the computer to use a static address that you assign manually. Another option is to physically examine the network card; some manufacturers write the MAC address on a sticker affixed to the card.

DNS Servers

DHCP servers run in the background of many networks and go largely unnoticed unless they malfunction. Similarly, Domain Name System (DNS) servers obtrude themselves on users' awareness only when something goes wrong. These servers, as described briefly from the client's perspective in Chapter 14, translate (or *resolve*, as this translation is often called) hostnames to IP addresses and vice versa. When implemented on a small or even mid-sized network, DNS servers can be small computers. In fact, they're often run on the same hardware that hosts DHCP servers. DNS server setup entails configuring two types of files in addition to the server startup script: one file to control the server overall, and one or more files to tell the server about the domains it's to handle.

When to Run a DNS Server

DNS servers provide services to two different types of users:

- **Internal users**   Computers on your own network may call upon a local DNS server to resolve hostnames or IP addresses. The DNS server can then deliver IP addresses associated with local hostnames or contact outside DNS servers to look up an external hostname.

- **External users**   If you operate your own domain, you're required to provide at least two DNS servers that deliver name resolution services for the domain. In practice, it's often desirable to use an outside service for this function, particularly for small domains. If you have static externally-accessible IP addresses, though, you can run your own DNS servers. Doing so gives you direct control over every aspect of the servers' behavior. In a more advanced configuration, you might integrate the DNS server with a DHCP server to dynamically update entries as IP addresses change, but such configurations are beyond the scope of this book.

 If you use a low-end broadband account for Internet access, outside services can link your dynamic IP address to a fixed hostname. Such dynamic DNS providers are common; check `http://www.technopagan.org/dynamic/` or `http://www.othnet.com/dyndns.html` for lists of such providers.

As a general rule, running your own DNS server for local use makes sense only when your network grows to over one or two dozen computers, assuming they need to address each other by name. If you've got just one or two servers and many clients, you might not need a DNS server; instead, you can configure the clients' `/etc/hosts` files (or equivalents in other OSs, such as `C:\WINNT\system32\drivers\etc\hosts` in Windows 2000) to point to the servers.

 Some protocols, such as the NetBIOS upon which Windows file sharing and Samba are built, use their own name resolution methods, so a DNS server may not be necessary if such tools are your primary reason for configuring a name server.

The most common DNS server in FreeBSD is the Berkeley Internet Name Domain (BIND). The server file's name is `named`, and it's installed as part of the base FreeBSD installation. If you prefer, you can run another server, such as `djbdns` or `dns_balance` (the former is available only as a port, but the latter is available as both a package and a port). Because BIND is the most popular DNS server for FreeBSD and because it's installed by default, this chapter describes BIND configuration.

 This chapter emphasizes a basic BIND configuration, as might be suitable for a home or small business network. If your needs are more complex, you should consult a book on BIND, such as Albitz and Liu's DNS and BIND, 4th Edition (O'Reilly, 2001). It's easy to cause serious problems for your domain, and possibly for others, if BIND is misconfigured.

To actually run BIND, you should edit `/etc/rc.conf` so that it includes the following line:

```
named_enable="YES"
```

Adding this line makes BIND run when you next start the computer. You can type **named** as `root` to start it on a one-time basis after you create an initial configuration. If you make configuration changes, you can have `named` reread its configuration files by typing **killall -HUP** named as `root`. Sometimes you may need to type **killall named; named** instead. This command shuts down BIND and restarts it, completely flushing its cache.

SERVERS

Basic Server Setup

The main BIND configuration file is `/etc/namedb/named.conf`. This file defines global options and points BIND to additional files that configure specific *zones* (domains or network blocks that BIND is to handle). The upcoming section, "Configuring a Zone," describes the format of these zone files.

Lines in `named.conf` that begin with two slashes (`//`) or a pound sign (`#`) are comments. Multiline comments sometimes use C-style comment strings—`/*` to open a comment block and `*/` to close it. Other lines are collected into groups surrounded by curly braces, much like subnet or host declarations in the DHCP configuration file. The BIND option blocks end in a curly brace and a semicolon, though. Two types of groups are most important: `options` and `zone`. The first describes overall options for the server, and the second points BIND to an individual zone configuration file. Listing 22-1 presents a complete and functional BIND configuration file. The default file installed by FreeBSD includes comments that explain what various components do, as well as some options that don't appear in Listing 22-1.

Listing 22-1.
Sample `/etc/named/named.conf` File

```
options {
    directory "/etc/namedb";
    pid-file "/var/run/named/pid";
    forward first;
    forwarders {
        10.202.45.108;
        172.20.232.1;
    };
    listen-on {
        192.168.1.4;
    };
};
zone "." {
    type hint;
    file "named.root";
};
zone "threeroomco.com" {
    type master;
    file "named.threeroomco.com";
};
zone "1.168.192.in-addr.arpa" {
    type master;
    file "localhost.rev";
};
zone "0.0.127.in-addr.arpa" {
```

```
    type master;
    file "named.local";
};
```

Features illustrated by Listing 22-1 are

- **directory** The `directory` option specifies the directory in which zone files reside. In a default FreeBSD installation, this directory is the same as the one that holds the `dhcpd.conf` file.

- **DNS forwarding** Ordinarily, a DNS server operates by querying a series of other DNS servers, starting with the *root servers*, which know the addresses of servers that know about machines in the various top-level domains (TLDs), such as `.com` and `.uk`. This mode of operation is known as a *full recursive lookup*. An alternative is to configure BIND as a *forwarding* server, in which it sends its request to just one other DNS server, letting that server do the full recursive lookup. A forwarding configuration makes sense for small networks, such as home or small business networks served by a broadband Internet connection. The `forward first` option tells BIND to try a forwarding lookup, and if that fails, to try a full recursive lookup. A variant is the `forward only` option, which tells BIND to perform only a forwarding lookup. This `forward only` configuration is the default for FreeBSD. In either case, the `forwarders` option block lists one or more outside DNS servers that BIND is to query in its forwarding duties.

- **Interface binding** The `listen-on` option configures BIND to listen on the network interfaces associated with the listed IP addresses. This option can be very useful if the computer has multiple network interfaces and should respond to requests from only one interface.

- **Zone file definitions** Listing 22-1 includes four zone file definitions. The first of these (identified as `zone "."`) is for the *root zone*—in other words, every address on the Internet, except for those handled by more specific zone files. You shouldn't change this entry, except possibly to alter the filename, if for some reason you don't like the default. The `type hint` line tells BIND to perform a full recursive or forwarding lookup for such systems. The remaining zones define specific domains (`threeroomco.com` in Listing 22-1) or IP address blocks (192.168.1.0/24 and 127.0.0.0/24 in Listing 22-1). IP address blocks are listed by zones with their numbers reversed and followed by `in-addr.arpa`, such as `1.168.192.in-addr.arpa` for 192.168.1.0/24. (Only the network portion of the address makes it into the name.) In the case of all zones, the `file` option specifies the name of the file that describes all the names or addresses in the zone.

Recognizing that forward and reverse lookup zones are distinct is important. For instance, consider a small business that runs a handful of computers on a broadband

Internet connection. This business may control its own domain (say, `threeroomco.com`), and so controls forward lookups—in other words, the return of 172.17.202.7 when a remote user wants the IP address of `www.threeroomco.com`. This business's ISP, though, may control the IP addresses themselves. Thus, the ISP controls the reverse lookup zone (`202.17.172.in-addr.arpa`); Three Room Company's BIND server does *not* contain information on that zone. On the other hand, if the company acquired a block of IP addresses directly and contracted with an ISP to connect those fixed IP addresses to the Internet, then the company would be responsible for the reverse lookup. Listing 22-1 is a suitable model if you want to provide DNS services for a small network, particularly if that network is private (say, if it resides behind a NAT router).

If you run multiple DNS servers, one is likely to be a *slave* to the other's *master*. In this configuration, the slave server occasionally synchronizes its zone files to the master by asking the master to send the complete zone files. This is the function of the `zone master` lines in the zone definitions; these lines tell the server that it functions as a master. The slave system's configuration would be similar, but it would include `zone slave` lines, followed by a block that points to the master server:

```
masters {
    192.168.1.1;
};
```

Configuring a Zone

Configuring a zone requires creating a zone file, whose name you specify in the `dhcpd.conf` file's `zone` section for the zone. These files support many options, but the basics can be explained fairly briefly. Forward and reverse zone files share many features, but there are also some important differences between them.

If you contract with an outside party to provide DNS service for your domain, you'll probably have to provide much of the zone file information described in this chapter. DNS providers frequently use web pages that simplify entry of this information.

Configuring Forward Lookups

A forward lookup zone file consists of a series of records describing the domain. The first record describes characteristics of the zone itself, such as how long remote DNS servers should keep information in their local caches. Subsequent records describe individual hostnames within a domain. The comment character for a zone file is a semicolon (`;`), and it may appear at the start of a line or after information on a line. Listing 22-2 shows a short but functional forward zone file.

Listing 22-2.
Sample
Forward Zone
Configuration
File

```
threeroomco.com.  IN  SOA  zeus.threeroomco.com. admin.threeroomco.com. (
                 2002101003 ; serial
                 28800      ; refresh
                 14400      ; retry
```

```
                         3600000   ; expire
                         86400     ; default TTL
                  )
mail              IN  A       172.20.29.101
zeus              IN  A       172.20.29.78
jupiter           IN  CNAME   zeus
@                 IN  MX      10  mail
threeroomco.com.  IN  MX      20  mail.abigisp.net.
@                 IN  NS      zeus.threeroomco.com.
```

The format of a line in a zone file is:

- **Hostname**   The first column is a hostname or domain name, such as `mail` or `zeus` in Listing 22-2. The first line specifies the domain name for the zone. Domain names and fully-qualified domain names (FQDNs) are indicated by trailing periods (`.`); names that don't include trailing periods are interpreted as hostnames within the main domain; for instance, `mail` is expanded to `mail.threeroomco.com`. The at-signs (`@`) used in two entries stand for the domain name specified in the first entry.

- **IN**   The second element is `IN`, which is a code that stands for *Internet*. It's a standard part of all entries.

- **Record type**   A record type code follows the `IN` code. The first record type code in Listing 22-2 is `SOA`, which stands for *start of authority*. An SOA code is the "master" for a zone and defines characteristics of the zone as a whole, as described shortly. The most common record type in most domains is the Address (A) record, denoted by an `A`. This record type ties an IP address to a name. Canonical name (CNAME) records tie a name to another name. In Listing 22-2, the name `jupiter` is tied to `zeus` in this way, so that the same computer can be accessed by either name. Mail exchanger (MX) records tell external mail servers what computers to use when delivering mail addressed to the domain. Finally, name server (NS) records point to the DNS server computers for the zone. Both MX and NS records require a domain name in the hostname field. As Listing 22-2 demonstrates, this can be done by explicitly listing the domain name or by using an at-sign.

- **Record data**   CNAME and A records take just one final element: a hostname or IP address, respectively. MX records take a hostname or IP address preceded by a precedence number; mail servers sending mail to the domain try the MX systems in order, starting with the one with the lowest precedence number. SOA records contain the most record data—so much that it's usually split across multiple lines.

SERVERS

The SOA record is unusually complex, although it follows the same basic form as other records. The record data (following SOA in Listing 22-2) includes several subelements:

- **Name server**   The SOA record includes the name of the DNS server itself— `zeus.threeroomco.com.` in Listing 22-2 (note the trailing period).

- **Administrator e-mail address**   Listing 22-2's `admin.threeroomco.com.` may not look like it, but it's an e-mail address. To send e-mail to the administrator, replace the first period with an at-sign—Listing 22-2 specifies `admin@threeroomco.com` as the e-mail address of the domain's DNS administrator.

- **Cache expiration times**   The block of numbers surrounded by parentheses in Listing 22-2 relate to the expiration of data in remote DNS servers' caches and to how often slave servers should look for updated zone files from their masters. Listing 22-2 uses comments to label each value. The serial number helps slaves know when a zone file has changed; you should increment it whenever you make a change to the file. Some sites use the date in *YYYYMMDD* format followed by a shorter number as the serial number. The remaining values specify intervals in seconds. The refresh, retry, and expire values tell the slave how often to look for updated files, how often to try if an initial attempt fails, and when to drop the zone if a failure is persistent. The final value sets the default time-to-live (TTL) for individual lookups cached by remote DNS servers. If you make frequent changes to your DNS configuration, a short TTL value (a few hours or even less) may be in order; but a value of a day or more, as in Listing 22-2, is more common.

Listing 22-2 is a reasonable starting point for many small domains. You're likely to change many details and add more records, especially A records, to fit your domain's computers. The basic elements shown in Listing 22-2 should account for most or all of the entries you need on a small domain, though.

Configuring Reverse Lookups

Reverse lookup zone files are much like forward lookup zone files, but there are some important differences. Listing 22-3 shows a reverse lookup zone file that might be suitable for use with Listing 22-2's forward lookup file. Like Listing 22-2, this file begins with an SOA record for the zone, but the zone name is in the `in-addr.arpa` pseudodomain. This pseudodomain is used for reverse lookups; whenever a computer needs to do a reverse lookup, it silently reverses the order of the elements in the IP address, adds `.in-addr.arpa`, and submits the query much as it does forward lookups. The result is a hostname associated with the IP address.

Rather than a mix of A, CNAME, and MX records, as in the forward lookup zone file, the reverse lookup file includes PTR records, which tie an IP address to a hostname. (Reverse lookup zone files also include NS records.) There's no reverse DNS equivalent to the forward DNS CNAME record; each IP address is tied to precisely one hostname. It's important that you spell out the complete hostname, including the trailing period; if you specify only a machine name, BIND interprets it as a machine name within the reverse DNS pseudodomain. You can abbreviate the IP addresses, as in the case of the entry for 172.20.29.78 in Listing 22-3 (the final line, with an abbreviated name of 78).

sting 22-3.
Sample
verse Zone
nfiguration
File

```
29.20.172.in-addr.arpa.   IN   SOA   zeus.threeroomco.com. \
                                      admin.threeroomco.com. (
                          2002101003 ; serial
                          28800      ; refresh
                          14400      ; retry
                          3600000    ; expire
                          86400      ; default TTL
                          )
@                         IN   NS    zeus.threeroomco.com.
101.29.20.172.in-addr.arpa.   IN   PTR   mail.threeroomco.com.
78                        IN   PTR   zeus.threeroomco.com.
```

Remember that forward and reverse zone files need not cover equivalent hosts. For instance, an ISP might support users who want their IP addresses to resolve to their own domains rather than to the ISP's domain. This ISP's reverse zone file might include PTR records that point to many different domains. The customer's forward zone files, in turn, might include entries that point to IP addresses on many different networks—say, to support offices located in different cities, or to point callers to a domain hosting service that handles a www hostname.

Time Servers

There's a saying that a person with one clock knows the time, but a person with two clocks can never be sure of the time. Every FreeBSD computer includes a clock, so in a networked environment, you may become annoyed at the drift between the times told by these various timepieces. Worse, some protocols require that computers' clocks have closely synchronized times. Kerberos, for instance, imposes this requirement. A file server that sets a time stamp on a file may cause tools on clients to become confused if these time stamps don't match their own local times. When reporting abuse, it's often helpful to be able to provide logs with time stamps, but of course the value of those time stamps is reduced if your system's time is off by even a few seconds. Thus, keeping your computers' clocks synchronized with each other, and ideally with an outside source, is often important.

Several clock-setting tools are available. One of the most popular and most accurate of these is the *Network Time Protocol (NTP)*. This protocol enables synchronizing two systems' clocks to within well under a second of each other, and a network of publicly-available NTP servers on the Internet is very useful in keeping your systems' clocks set to a veridical outside source.

SERVERS

An Overview of NTP

NTP begins with an accurate time source. This source might be an atomic clock or a clock that's set through the time encoded in GPS signals. Such a time source is known as a *stratum 0* time source. Unless you buy specialized hardware, you won't have direct access to a stratum 0 source. A regular computer can synchronize its clock to a stratum 0 source, though. This computer becomes known as a *stratum 1* time source. Stratum 1 servers are the most accurate time sources available on the Internet, at least in theory. (The quality of the stratum 0 source is an important caveat.) Stratum 1 servers in turn provide a time source for stratum 2 servers, and so on. The next section, "Locating Parent Time Servers," describes how you can locate a time server to which you can synchronize your own system's clock. Typically, you'll run one local time server, then synchronize all the clocks on your network to that time server. This procedure minimizes the load on external time servers, compared to synchronizing all your systems' clocks directly to the outside source.

At each step of the way, the clock synchronization works by exchanging data packets with time information. The problem is that the packets don't arrive instantly, especially when you're using a time server over the Internet. There can be delays and variances in delays. Thus, you can't simply ask a time server for the time and set the clock to the value returned; doing so would result in a time that's behind by a measurable amount—probably less than a second, but possibly more than that. NTP compensates by measuring the time it takes to receive a reply from the server and using that data to estimate the transit time for the packets. The result is that NTP can set your system's clock to a value that's within milliseconds of the server's clock, assuming network congestion isn't too great.

In FreeBSD, NTP is implemented by a program called ntpd. (Earlier versions were called xntpd.) As you might guess by the name, ntpd is a daemon. It functions as both a client and a server, though; ntpd acts as a client to a lower-stratum time server (its parent), and it can function as a server to higher-stratum time servers and clients. It's not uncommon to see a network in which one computer uses ntpd as both a client and a server, and all other computers on the network use ntpd merely as a client to synchronize to the first ntpd server. Why use a complete server if you just need a client, though? The main reason is that ntpd's daemon status means that it can check the time on a regular basis, thus keeping the clock running at a very steady rate. The alternative would be to run an NTP client program from a cron job, or possibly just whenever the computer boots. Although there are programs that function only as NTP clients, using ntpd in its full daemon mode is simple enough that it's the preferred method of keeping a clock set.

Locating Parent Time Servers

NTP servers are arranged in hierarchies based on their distance from a veridical time source. All other things being equal, the ideal situation is to synchronize your server's time to a server of the lowest-available stratum—a stratum 1 server. If everybody did this, though, the Internet's available stratum 1 servers would quickly become overwhelmed by requests, and the entire system would collapse. In practice, therefore, it's best to synchronize small networks' main time servers to stratum 2 servers. The reduction in accuracy is minor for most purposes, and this procedure helps spread the load across more servers. The usual cutoff point between "small" and "large" networks for this purpose is roughly 100 computers.

To locate a suitable stratum 2 server, consult `http://www.eecis.udel.edu/~mills/ntp/clock2.htm`. This site maintains a list of many public stratum 2 servers (157 sites as I write). Locate a server that's near you and make note of its hostname or IP address for the procedure outlined in the upcoming section, "Configuring an NTP Server." Many sites request that you contact them before you synchronize off of them. If your selected site is one of these, be sure to do so as a courtesy to the server's operators.

 Because the measurement error involved in NTP is related to packet latencies, your parent time server should produce low ping times. Try pinging some potential parent servers to discover which ones are best.

In addition to the public stratum 2 servers, you may have access to other servers. For instance, many ISPs operate time servers that are accessible to customers. Such servers are typically close to customers' systems, and so are good choices in terms of producing low latencies.

Unfortunately, NTP servers aren't always accessible. Network paths may go down, or a server may discontinue operation altogether. Potentially worse, the server may be synchronized to a poor clock source. For this reason, a common practice is to synchronize your network's primary NTP server to multiple external NTP servers. Three external servers are typically enough. The `ntpd` program can then detect if one server is bad and automatically disregard its time signals. Using multiple external NTP servers may be overkill for a small network, though. In the event of a transient problem, `ntpd` can keep your clock going with little loss of accuracy because it tracks the deviation of your system's clock from an accurate time source, and can compensate even if access to the accurate time source is lost.

Whether you synchronize your primary time server to one external server or several, you should synchronize all of your network's other systems to your one primary server. If you've got a network of 50 computers, this practice can greatly ease the load on external time servers, with very minor detriment to the accuracy of your local systems' clocks. Large organizations may operate two or more local time servers for redundancy and synchronize local clocks to all local servers.

Configuring NTP

FreeBSD provides two options for NTP use. The first is to use `ntpdate`, an NTP client program, to set the computer's clock whenever you boot the computer. The second option is to use the full `ntpd` package to continuously monitor and adjust the computer's clock, and optionally to serve time to other computers.

SERVERS

Setting the Clock at Boot Time

If you frequently reboot your computer, you can set its clock at boot time and the clock will remain reasonably accurate. You can activate this configuration using `sysinstall`:

1. As `root`, type **/stand/sysinstall** to start the configuration tool.

2. Select `Configure` to get to the `FreeBSD Configuration` Menu.

3. Select `Networking` to get to the `Network Configuration` Menu.

4. Select `Ntpdate` to activate the `ntpdate` option. The system presents the `NTPDATE Server Selection` menu, which lists many NTP server sites, mostly from the list of stratum 2 servers mentioned in "Locating Parent Time Servers."

5. Select a server from the list. (Later, you can change it to one that's not on the list, as described shortly.) `sysinstall` returns to the `Network Configuration` Menu.

6. Pick the `Cancel`, `Cancel`, and `Exit Install` options to quit from `sysinstall`.

These steps add lines such as the following to your `/etc/rc.conf` file:

```
ntpdate_flags="clock-2.cs.cmu.edu"
ntpdate_enable="YES"
```

If you prefer, you can add these lines manually rather than using `sysinstall`. You can also change the server listed in the `ntpdate_flags` option if you prefer to use a server that's not on the preconfigured list. For instance, you would edit this option for a computer other than your primary time server; you would list your local primary time server.

When you next boot the computer, FreeBSD will contact the server you specified and use `ntpdate` to synchronize its time to the server's time. If you're *not* running `ntpd`, you can do the same thing at any time after the system has booted by typing **ntpdate *server-name***, where *server-name* is the hostname of the NTP server. You could put such a command in a cron job (described in Chapter 6) to set the time once a day, for instance, if you can tolerate the potential for a few seconds' drift over a day.

Configuring an NTP Server

To implement more continuous time adjustment, you must activate the `ntpd` server. Two steps are required: You must edit the `/etc/rc.conf` file to have FreeBSD start `ntpd` at boot time and you must edit the `/etc/ntp.conf` file with the options you want to enable, including the time server to be used.

To activate `ntpd` at boot time, add the following line to `/etc/rc.conf`:

```
xntpd_enable="YES"
```

When you reboot the computer, the server will activate, contact its parent servers, and begin adjusting your clock on a fine scale to keep it as accurate as possible. Once you finish configuration, you can activate the server manually by typing **ntpd** as `root`.

Actually configuring `ntpd` requires editing its configuration file, `/etc/ntp.conf`. The most important option appears near the start of the file:

```
server clock-2.cs.cmu.edu
```

This line tells the system what NTP server to use as its parent. You may include several such lines, one for each server, and `ntpd` will contact them all and use the most accurate source from the set. In fact, a default configuration includes a reference to `127.127.1.0`, which is an IP address that `ntpd` associates with the local clock, as a fallback should all other servers be unavailable. (Another line beginning with the keyword `fudge` gives this local clock a stratum of 10, so it won't enter into the picture if a real server is available.)

If you want to configure an entire network to use NTP, you should set up one computer to access one or more external NTP servers. You can then use the same configuration on internal computers, except that they should point to the primary local NTP server *only*. The primary server takes on a stratum one higher than the one to which it synchronizes, and the rest of the systems are one stratum higher. For instance, if your primary computer synchronizes to a stratum 2 server, then it's a stratum 3 server, and the rest of your systems are stratum 4 servers (although they may have no clients).

Unfortunately, it's not always easy to tell if `ntpd` is working as you expect. The server often doesn't adjust the time all at once; instead, it may *slew* the clock, meaning that it adjusts the rate at which it runs until the clock's time is accurate. The server may also abort completely if the clock is off by over an hour. You can check that the server is running by typing **ps ax | grep ntpd**, but to see if it's working correctly, you may need to use a monitoring program called `ntpq`. This program has many advanced options, but the most basic is the `peers` command, which you type at its `ntpq>` prompt. Figure 22-1 shows this program in action. The server whose name is marked with an asterisk in the leftmost column is the one to which `ntpd` has synchronized its clock. Servers marked

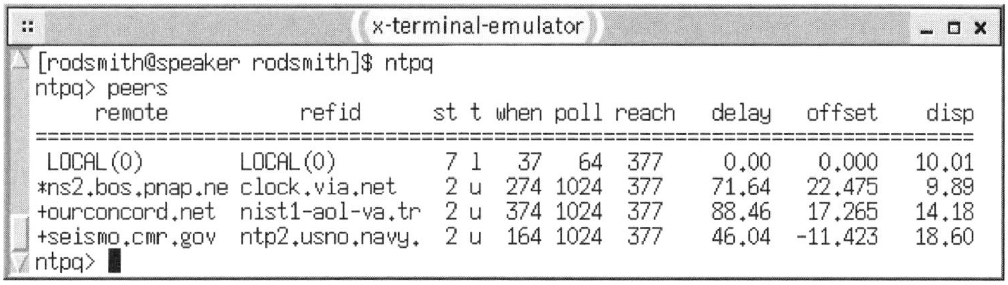

```
[rodsmith@speaker rodsmith]$ ntpq
ntpq> peers
     remote           refid      st t when poll reach   delay   offset    disp
==============================================================================
 LOCAL(0)        LOCAL(0)         7 l   37   64   377    0.00    0.000   10.01
*ns2.bos.pnap.ne clock.via.net    2 u  274 1024   377   71.64   22.475    9.89
+ourconcord.net  nist1-aol-va.tr  2 u  374 1024   377   88.46   17.265   14.18
+seismo.cmr.gov  ntp2.usno.navy.  2 u  164 1024   377   46.04  -11.423   18.60
ntpq>
```

Figure 22-1. *The **ntpq** program provides a way to monitor the behavior of the **ntpd** server.*

with plus signs were considered and have reasonable times, but lost out by one criterion or another (some of these criteria are listed in the last three columns).

Immediately after starting ntpd, *it will take a few minutes for the server to decide with which remote server it should synchronize its time, so* ntpq *may not show any remote servers marked with asterisks. Other values reported by* ntpq *will also fluctuate for a while, and clients might be unable to connect to the server.*

When you run a FreeBSD time server, NTP clients in other OSs can connect to it, as well. Many OSs, including Windows XP and Mac OS X, ship with such clients. For information on more NTP clients and servers, check http://www.eecis.udel.edu/~ntp/software. This page includes links to subpages covering software for over a dozen specific platforms.

Chances are you're running your time server for the benefit of your local network. For this reason, you should use firewall rules, as described in Chapter 17, to block access to port 123 on your time server computer except from authorized clients.

Font Servers

The final class of miscellaneous server in this chapter is the font server. A font server is a program that delivers font data to the same or other computers. Using a font server, you can install a font once, on the font server computer, and it becomes instantly available from all other computers' X servers on your network, provided that those computers are configured to use the first computer's font server. On a large network of workstations that run X, this characteristic can greatly simplify X configuration, particularly if you make regular changes to your local font list. Of course, you must configure the font server, and configure X servers to use the font server, for this capability to do any good.

The legal status of fonts varies around the world. In the United States, fonts cannot be copyrighted, but the TrueType and Adobe Type 1 font file formats are technically computer programs, and so can be copyrighted. In some other countries, fonts can be copyrighted. In any event, you should check with a font's distributor to be sure you may legally make it available via a font server.

An Overview of X Font Handling

To understand font servers, it's necessary to understand how X handles fonts. X dates back to the days when CPUs were weak and memory was severely limited, by today's standards. In those days, fonts typically came in *bitmapped* formats, which means that the font was described in terms of individual pixels. A bitmapped font can be displayed at only one size (at least, without ugly scaling attempts by an artistically-challenged computer program). Thus, to display text in a wide array of sizes, bitmapped fonts were hand-crafted to display in specific sizes at specific resolutions. Some X fonts still ship in bitmap formats, and bitmapped fonts often look better at small sizes than do more advanced formats because they're tuned by a human with better aesthetic judgment than any computer program.

In the past several years, another type of font has come into prominence: *scaleable* (or *outline*) fonts. These fonts are described in mathematical terms, as a series of lines and curves that define the outline of each letter. The computer can fill in the outline with a color and determine what pixels should be on or off to display the font at any size desired. The most common scaleable font formats today are Adobe's PostScript Type 1 (aka Adobe Type Manager, or ATM) and Apple's TrueType. XFree86 4.*x* supports both of these formats, although XFree86 3.3.*x* and earlier didn't support TrueType.

The font server takes font rendering (that is, converting from an outline format to a bitmap for display) out of the hands of the X server. The font server program renders the font and delivers it in bitmap format to the X server. You can run a font server on the same computer as X, but this chapter describes running a font server that can deliver fonts to any number of computers.

 If you're using the old XFree86 3.3.x and can't upgrade to XFree86 4.x, you can use a local font server to add the capability to handle TrueType fonts. You need a font server from the XFree86 4.x package, or a patched or rewritten server, such as the X-TT server (http://x-tt.dsl.gr.jp) or xfsft (http://www.dcs.ed.ac.uk/ home/jec/programs/xfsft/).

Normally, X searches directories in its font path, which is set in the XF86Config file, as described in Chapter 13, for fonts. If you want to use a font server, you can add its name to the font path, as described in the upcoming section, "Using a Font Server."

 It's unwise to delete the core directories from the computer's font path; instead, add a font server to the font path. If the font server becomes unavailable, the computer may still be able to get by on its default fonts, at least enough to shut down X programs.

Font Server Configuration

Configuring a font server is much like configuring X to use new fonts, as described in the section "Adding or Removing Fonts" in Chapter 13. You should read that section before proceeding, if you're not already familiar with the procedure.

The standard FreeBSD font server is installed as part of the XFree86-FontServer package. This package is installed with a default XFree86 installation, so chances are it's present on your system. The font server program itself is /usr/X11R6/bin/xfs, so you can check for this file if you're not sure the server is installed.

Creating Font Directories

To serve fonts, a font server needs access to fonts, and these go in one or more directories dedicated to the function. For instance, you might create a /usr/local/fonts directory, possibly subdivided into categories by font type, much as the standard /usr/X11R6/lib/X11/fonts directory is subdivided by font type (Speedo, Type1, and so on). Alternatively, you can use your existing font directories and make them available via a font server.

Installing fonts in the font directories and configuring them to be served works exactly as it does when preparing a font directory for direct use with XFree86, as described in Chapter 13. You must place the font files in the directory and create a fonts.dir file describing the fonts. If you choose to make your regular XFree86 fonts available via the font server, you don't need to modify the font directories in any way.

Modifying the Configuration File

The font server is controlled through a configuration file called config. In FreeBSD 5.0, this file resides in /usr/X11R6/lib/X11/fs. This file includes lines to set several options, most of which you don't need to adjust. These options set features related to memory use, default font sizes, and so on. One option that you may need to change is the catalogue line. This line specifies the font path used by the font server. It's the equivalent of the series of FontPath lines in the XF86Config file, but xfs's config file combines these options onto a single line, with directories separated by commas. A short example looks like this:

```
catalogue = /usr/X11R6/lib/X11/fonts/TTF,/usr/local/fonts/Type1
```

This example line makes the fonts from two directories available via the font server. The default line lists several common font subdirectories in /usr/X11R6/lib/X11/fonts, so it's suitable for sharing more-or-less the same fonts that FreeBSD uses by default. Such a configuration might be useful if your intent is to access the font server from non-FreeBSD X servers, such as some products for Windows, that provide fewer fonts. Alternatively, you can add or replace font paths with new ones containing more fonts, and use the font server to deliver fonts to X servers running on any platform, including FreeBSD. Because xfs expects an entire font path on a single catalogue line, this line can become quite long; be sure your editor doesn't wrap it onto multiple lines.

Another option you might want to use is port. This option sets the TCP port to which the server listens. The default value is 7100, but there are situations when you might want to use another port. For instance, some programs include specialized font servers that may appropriate port 7100. If you need to run xfs on some other port, include a line like the following in the config file:

```
port = 7101
```

Running the Font Server

When you finish setting up font directories and modifying the font server's configuration file, you must start the font server. You can easily start the server on a one-time basis by typing its name, optionally followed by the -daemon parameter to have it run as a daemon:

```
# /usr/X11R6/bin/xfs -daemon
```

At this point, you should be able to configure your local XFree86 to use the font server, as described in the next section, "Using a Font Server." Assuming there are no obstructing firewalls or other network problems, remote systems should also be able to access and use the font server in the same way.

Your font server should not be accessible to all computers on the Internet. You should use a firewall (on the font server computer or another computer), as described in Chapter 17, to restrict access to the font server.

To run xfs on a regular basis, you must have some way to start it. The regular FreeBSD startup scripts don't provide such an option, so you must create an /etc/rc.local or /usr/local/etc/rc.d/xfs.sh script to do the job (the latter is preferred in recent versions of FreeBSD). At its simplest, such a script needs only the startup command presented earlier, but its execute bit must be set. The "Creating New Local Startup Scripts" section of Chapter 6 describes creating such scripts in more detail.

Using a Font Server

Chapter 13 describes configuring fonts in an X server, and this description includes information on adding a font server to the XF86Config file. Consult Chapter 13 for details; but briefly, you must add a line such as the following to your /etc/X11/XF86Config's Files section:

```
FontPath    "tcp/fontserver:7100"
```

In this example, *fontserver* is the hostname or IP address of the font server computer, and *7100* is the port number on which the server runs. It's best to add this line after your local font directories because local font access is likely to be faster than font server access, and XFree86 tries directories or font servers in the order in which they're listed. After you add this information, the X server will use the font server after you restart X. If you want to use the font server immediately, type the following lines:

```
$ xset fp+ tcp/fontserver:7100
$ xset fp rehash
```

These commands tell X to add the specified font server to its font path and to reread the list of available fonts from the new font path.

If font reconfiguration goes awry, it's possible that the font server will become unresponsive. Thus, you should save any open files and perhaps even close running programs before attempting to reconfigure an X server's font path.

A FreeBSD font server can deliver fonts to X servers other than XFree86. If you're using a Windows or Mac OS X server, chances are you can tell the X server to use a font server. Typically, these programs provide a dialog box in which you can add font directories or font servers. Consult your X server's documentation for details.

Summary

Many servers operate behind the scenes. Users are seldom aware of these servers, but they provide the necessary underpinnings of many network operations. DHCP servers deliver IP addresses and related information to DHCP clients so that they can be easily configured for a network, DNS servers translate hostnames to IP addresses and vice versa, time servers help keep all the computers on a network synchronized to the correct time, and font servers simplify font configuration on a network with many X servers. The default configurations for all of these servers as delivered by FreeBSD is at least close to reasonable, but you must change some settings for each of them to conform to your network. In some cases, you may need to reconfigure your system to launch the server in question.

The Complete Reference

Part V

Common User Programs

Chapter 23

Desktop Environments

T his chapter begins Part V of this book, which focuses upon user programs, as opposed to servers, system administration, and so on. Ultimately, servers and user programs are the reasons computers exist, and servers ultimately serve clients, which are a particular type of user program (described in Chapter 24). Thus, in some sense user programs are the most important type of program a computer can run.

This chapter begins the coverage of user programs with a look at the environments in which they run. On modern workstations today, this environment is typically a GUI, and on FreeBSD, the GUI desktop environment is often a highly integrated set of programs. The range of desktop environments is described in the upcoming section, "An Overview of Available Desktop Environments." The section "Using GNOME" goes into greater depth on the GNOME environment as an example of this type of tool. First, though, it's necessary to describe what a desktop environment is—why should you run a desktop environment?

Note *Chapter 3 includes a brief introduction to desktop environments in the section "A Quick Tour of the GUI Desktop." This chapter assumes you have at least a passing familiarity with these tools; it goes into more detail concerning alternatives and how to perform more advanced tasks.*

The Role of Desktop Environments

As described in Chapter 13, FreeBSD's GUI environment, the X Window System (or *X* for short) is both more and less complex than the GUI environments used by other OSs, such as Windows and Mac OS. X is more complex than these other environments in that it's inherently network-enabled, so you can use X programs from other computers, as described in Chapter 21. X is less complex than competing GUI systems in that X provides very little in the way of GUI tools and support programs. X enables programmers to display windows, draw lines, circles, and other shapes in the windows, receive input from users in the form of keypresses and mouse clicks, and so on. X does not, by itself, support high-level GUI constructs such as sliders, menus, buttons, and so on. These tools are the domain of X *widget sets*—programming libraries that provide user interface tools built atop X and described in Chapter 13. X also does not provide the sort of small support programs that are common in competing GUI systems—programs such as calculators, simple editors, file browsers, and so on. These tools are the domain of desktop environments.

Details differ from one environment to another, but in general, a desktop environment provides several important components:

- **Window manager**   A *window manager* is a GUI element that provides users with control of windows. Most importantly, window managers create the *title bar* or *drag bar* at the top of a window, which enables you to drag the window around the screen. Window managers also provide pop-up menus from which you can launch programs. They're described in more detail in Chapter 13.

- **File manager**   A *file manager* or *file browser* creates windows that display the files in specific directories. You can then double-click a file to launch a program associated with a file, copy files, move files, create new files and directories, and so on.

- **Screen management tools**   Desktop environments typically provide one or more tools for managing the screen as a whole—setting the background color or image, switching between *virtual desktops* (parallel virtual screens that enable you to run many programs without cluttering the screen with too many windows), launching programs, and so on. Some window managers provide screen management tools, but placing them in the desktop environment means that a given desktop environment can provide consistent tools even if you switch window managers.

- **User interface tools**   You can use configuration utilities provided by a desktop environment to set user interface details such as the mouse tracking speed, keyboard repeat rate, and default fonts used by programs associated with the desktop environment.

- **Miscellaneous tools and utilities**   Desktop environments include useful small programs, such as calculators, xterm-like programs, Point-to-Point Protocol (PPP) dialers, simple editors, simple games, and so on.

- **Major affiliated programs**   Desktop environments are expanding to include larger programs such as web browsers, e-mail clients, word processors, spreadsheets, and so on.

Desktop environments don't have a monopoly on any of these program types. Indeed, as described in the upcoming section, "Rolling Your Own Desktop Environment," it's possible to mix and match components from multiple desktop environments or from unaffiliated sources to create a desktop environment that may better suit your needs than any of the prepackaged systems. There are certain advantages to using a complete desktop environment, though. One of these is simplicity—particularly for somebody who's inexperienced with FreeBSD, it's easier to configure the system to use, say, GNOME, than to pick and choose from among the thousands of individual components that are available and to build a working system from those components. Another advantage to an integrated desktop environment is that the tools are designed to work together. Each desktop environment is built upon a single widget set, so all the components have a common look and feel. Furthermore, the individual components often use defaults that can apply to all programs, such as a common default menu bar font or color scheme. In some cases, desktop environment components can share common file formats, such as integrated address books for e-mail and contact manager programs.

Most desktop environments are installed in package sets. These typically include one or more packages for core libraries and support programs, packages for major program groups (networking, games, and so on), and packages for affiliated programs (word processors, web browsers, and so on). Some of the upcoming chapters describe some of the more important peripheral programs in greater detail. Chapter 24 describes networking tools such as e-mail programs and web browsers, Chapter 25 describes office tools such as word processors and spreadsheets, Chapter 26 describes graphics tools, and Chapter 27 describes multimedia programs and games.

It's usually possible to run components designed for or affiliated with one desktop environment in another one. For instance, the GIMP is a popular FreeBSD graphics editor that's affiliated with GNOME, but you don't need to run the GIMP from GNOME; you can run it from KDE, XFce, or a custom-built desktop environment. The same is true even of many more-central tools, such as KDE's Konqueror web browser or GNOME's Terminal xterm program. In some cases, you lose some functionality when you run a program outside of its parent environment; for instance, you might lose drag-and-drop between programs from different environments. In rarer cases, a program won't run at all outside of its parent environment, or won't be useful when so run. This worst-case scenario usually applies to desktop environment configuration tools, so it's not really a problem.

Note *Sometimes a program is referred to as "a GNOME program" or "a KDE program," when what's really meant is that the program uses the same underlying widget set as GNOME or KDE, respectively. Sometimes these programs include features to help them integrate better with the desktop environment, but they can usually run independently of the desktop environment in question.*

An Overview of Available Desktop Environments

Two desktop environments, the GNU Network Object Model Environment (GNOME) and the K Desktop Environment (KDE) are the most popular prepackaged desktop environments for FreeBSD. Both environments provide the full range of desktop environment tools. In 2002, FreeBSD favors GNOME, but you can easily install KDE if you prefer. KDE is a slightly older project, and so is a little bit more polished than GNOME, but both are useable environments. Unfortunately, both also consume tens of megabytes of RAM, so they aren't good choices for low-memory systems. A third desktop environment, XFce, is slimmer than GNOME or KDE, but it provides fewer creature features. It's modeled after the commercial Common Desktop Environment (CDE), which is popular on some commercial UNIX systems. You can also build your own custom desktop environment by combining components from a variety of sources. Such an approach is likely to create a much less memory-hungry desktop environment than either GNOME or KDE, but it requires more effort on your part.

Note *If multiple people use your system, you can install multiple desktop environments and give each person a choice of which environment to use. The "User Login Control Files" section of Chapter 6 and the upcoming section, "Starting GNOME," describe selecting a desktop environment.*

KDE

KDE was the first of the integrated desktop environments for FreeBSD. KDE is built upon the Qt widget set, which is one of fewer than half a dozen major X widget sets. The main KDE web site is `http://www.kde.org`. Major KDE components include

- **Window manager** KDE uses KWin as its window manager. In fact, the two are very tightly integrated; it's difficult to use anything but KWin as a window manager if you use KDE.

- **File manager and web browser** KDE uses Konqueror as both its file manager and its web browser. Konqueror is easily launched from a KDE menu.

- **Desktop tools** KDE includes the usual set of desktop-oriented tools, such as desktop menus for launching programs, a desktop clock, configuration programs, an e-mail client, and so on.

- **Office suite** KDE sponsors the KOffice suite of office tools, which includes a word processor, spreadsheet, and others. Chapter 25 describes KOffice in more detail.

In addition to these obvious user features, KDE provides tools to help programmers develop applications that integrate well with KDE. Developers who use these tools can enable features such as drag-and-drop between their programs and other KDE programs. One KDE developer tool that you may notice as a user is support for *anti-aliased fonts* (aka *font smoothing*). This technique uses gray pixels in curves or diagonal lines in characters to create the illusion of greater resolution than a display can create. Some people like this look, but others don't. You can try it yourself by setting it in the Look & Feel | Fonts area of the Control Center.

KDE version 3.0 was released in 2002, but on the surface, it's very similar to the earlier 2.2.*x* versions of KDE. Figure 23-1 shows a KDE 3.0 session running. This figure demonstrates several features of KDE, many of which are common to other desktop environments. Figure 23-1 shows several open windows, including the KDE Control Center (used to configure KDE features), the Konqueror web browser, and the Konsole xterm program. KDE also provides desktop icons, some of which are visible near the upper-left corner of Figure 23-1. These icons can provide quick access to programs, directories on the computer, or web sites.

Figure 23-1 illustrates the KDE Panel, which is the strip along the bottom of the screen. This tool provides several important features, from left to right:

- **The K menu** The leftmost icon in the Panel provides access to many FreeBSD programs, much like the Windows Start icon.

- **Program launch icons** The next several icons (nine in this case) launch particularly popular or important programs, such as the Konsole, the Control Center, and Konqueror.

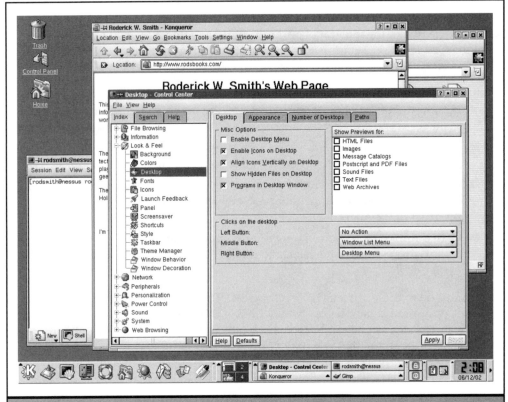

Figure 23-1. *A typical KDE session should look familiar to those used to GNOME, Microsoft Windows, or other desktop environments.*

- **Pager**   KDE provides a *pager*, which is a tool that enables switching between multiple virtual desktops. Figure 23-1 shows a system configured with four virtual desktops; you switch between them by clicking the miniature representation of the desktop you want to use.

- **Program icons**   You can move to any running program that has a window in KDE by clicking its icon in the Panel.

- **Logout and screen lock options**   You can log out of your session or lock the screen by clicking the small icons that resemble power switch icons or padlocks, respectively.

- **Mini-utilities**   KDE ships with some small utilities, such as tools to view the clipboard or display a calendar. Some of these are accessible from the Panel.

- **Clock**   Near the far right of the Panel is a clock. You can click it to see a calendar or right-click it to adjust it in various ways.

- **Panel display options**   By default, the Panel is always displayed. The triangular icon at the very rightmost edge of the Panel hides it, giving you more screen space for your programs. Using the Control Center, you can also reconfigure the Panel to display only when you move your mouse over the bottom part of the screen.

You can reconfigure many of KDE's operational details. You can add or remove icons from the desktop, add or remove Panel elements, alter the appearance and many operational details of KWin, and so on. Some of these features are changed through the Control Center, but others are altered in other ways. The K | Configure Panel menu provides options for altering the Panel's configuration, for instance.

GNOME

GNOME is a very popular desktop environment on FreeBSD, and it's the one that I use as a model for describing desktop environment features in the upcoming section, "Using GNOME." GNOME began life in response to KDE, which uses the Qt widget set. At the time of KDE's beginnings, Qt was distributed under a license that wasn't quite open source, which made many open source advocates wary of Qt and all programs developed from it. (Qt's license has since changed and is now fully open source.) Thus, the GNOME project began, using the GIMP Tool Kit (GTK+) widget set, which was originally developed for the GIMP.

GNOME provides a mix of components that's similar to the ones provided by KDE. Some highlights of GNOME programs include

- **Window manager**   Unlike KDE, GNOME provides substantial choice in window managers. The default configuration uses the Sawfish window manager, but in theory you can use several others. In practice, GNOME works best with window managers that provide "hooks" for GNOME, such as Sawfish, AfterStep, Window Maker, Enlightenment, or IceWM.

- **File manager**   The default GNOME file manager is called Nautilus. Unlike KDE's Konqueror, Nautilus doesn't double as a web browser.

- **Web browser**   GNOME uses Galeon as its native web browser. This program is partially derived from Mozilla, the open source cousin of Netscape Navigator. You can easily run Mozilla (or any other web browser) directly from GNOME, though.

- **Desktop tools**   GNOME includes the usual set of desktop-oriented tools, such as desktop menus for launching programs, a desktop clock, configuration programs, an e-mail client, and so on.

- **Office suite**   GNOME is collecting several previously unrelated office productivity tools into a suite called GNOME Office, with work underway to make them interoperate more easily. Chapter 25 describes GNOME Office in more detail.

In mid-2002, version 2.0 of GNOME was released. This version uses new internal data structures, and doesn't coexist well with earlier versions of GNOME. Thus, you shouldn't try to mix and match GNOME 2.0 or later components with programs from earlier versions of GNOME.

Figure 23-2 shows a GNOME environment. Comparing this screen with the one shown in Figure 23-1, you can see that GNOME is quite similar to KDE, at least on a first pass. Both environments include control bars (called the Panel in both environments) from which you can launch programs, switch between programs, or switch between virtual desktops. Like KDE, GNOME ships with a tool called the Control Center (the front-most window in Figure 23-2), which you can use to configure GNOME features. Both environments support desktop icons for launching programs, opening documents, and so on.

GNOME differs from KDE in many details. GNOME's window manager is more readily configured than is KDE's. (Figure 23-2, and most screen shots in this book, use IceWM and its Helix theme.) Because GNOME is built from GTK+, and KDE is built

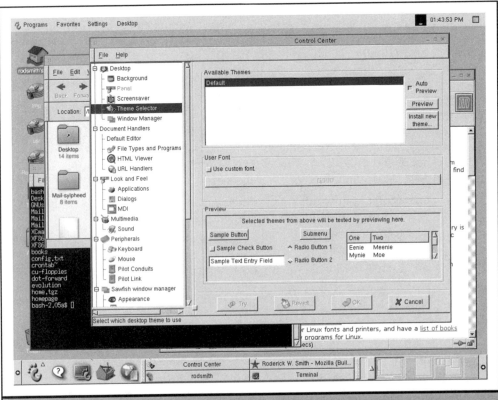

Figure 23-2.   *The GNOME desktop includes elements very similar to those used by KDE (shown in Figure 23-1).*

atop Qt, buttons, menu, and so on look different in the two environments. Individual components such as calculators and editors have different feature mixes. The default GNOME configuration provides a Panel at the bottom of the screen and a menu bar at the top, with some functionality duplicated in both places.

If you want to decide between GNOME and KDE, your best course of action may be to try each environment for a week or two. Which environment works best for you is largely a matter of personal preference based upon the many small differences between the two.

XFce

Compared to KDE and GNOME, XFce is a small desktop environment, both in terms of its absolute size and in terms of its popularity. Like GNOME, XFce is built upon GTK+. GNOME and KDE both take inspiration from GUI desktop environments on non-UNIX platforms, such as Windows, OS/2, and Mac OS Classic. XFce, by contrast, draws heavily from the commercial UNIX CDE package. Features of XFce include

- **Window manager**   XFce uses its own window manager, XFwm. This window manager isn't as configurable as some others, but it is functional.

- **File manager**   XFce provides a file manager called XFTree. Like many other XFce components, XFTree isn't as flashy as its KDE or GNOME counterparts, but it's quite useable.

- **Desktop tools**   XFce provides several desktop tools. Some of these, such as the desktop panel (equivalent to the GNOME or KDE Panel) are XFce-specific. Others, such as the calculator, are unaffiliated but common X programs that XFce is configured to run.

XFce doesn't include any office suite tools, although you can run GNOME Office, KOffice, or other office tools from the program. Likewise, XFce doesn't ship with an XFce-centric web browser, but it does come configured to run Mozilla once installed. XFce ships with substantially less in the way of GUI configuration and support tools than either KDE or GNOME, and many of XFce's tools are less flashy than equivalents in other environments. (Figure 23-3 shows an XFce desktop.) If you find XFce adequate for your needs, its small size can be a great boon, particularly on a low-memory computer.

Rolling Your Own Desktop Environment

One of the strengths of X is that its modular nature enables users to customize their desktops to a degree that's not possible with many other GUI environments. If you try KDE, GNOME, and XFce, and discover that you don't like these environments, even with the customizations they offer, you can reject all of them and start from scratch. This task, although probably not the best choice for a newcomer to X, is not as difficult as it would be on some OSs. You don't need to be able to write any programs to create your own desktop environment; you need only mix and match the components you want.

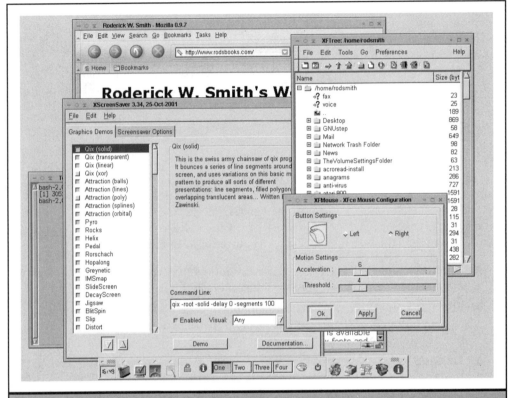

Figure 23-3. *XFce provides fewer features in its configuration and desktop management tools than KDE or GNOME, but it's a less resource-hungry environment.*

You should begin your quest with a window manager. FreeBSD includes many options in the x11-wm packages or ports area. Good options for a lightweight environment include IceWM, WindowMaker, fvwm and its variants, Sawfish, and Black Box. People who want the most configurable and flashy window manager should investigate Enlightenment.

A bare window manager may be all you need if you want a truly austere GUI environment. If not, you can add components by launching them from the same configuration file you use to launch the window manager itself, as described in Chapter 6 and the upcoming section, "Starting GNOME." You can run a file manager from KDE, GNOME, or XFce. Independent file manager projects also exist, such as Desktop File Manager (DFM; http://www.kaisersite.de/dfm/), Gentoo (http://www.obsession.se/gentoo/), and TkDesk (http://tkdesk.sourceforge.net). In fact, the x11-fm ports and packages section is devoted to examples of this class of program.

After collecting a window manager and file manager, the task of developing your own desktop environment becomes one of locating all the little support programs you might want to help make you productive—calculators, e-mail clients, editors, and so on. Many of these tools ship with FreeBSD, so finding them isn't difficult if you take some time to browse the available packages using `sysinstall`. Making them available from your custom desktop environment usually involves editing a window manager or file manager configuration file. As a general rule, window managers use configuration files named after themselves in your home directory, or subdirectories with several configuration files. For instance, IceWM uses `~/.icewm/preferences` for overall preferences and `~/.icewm/menu` for items on its menu. You can edit the latter file to add programs to the IceWM menu. File managers use similar configuration files. For instance, DFM uses the `~/.dfmext` file to associate file types to programs, so that you can launch a program by double-clicking a data file associated with the program. The `~/.dfmdesk` directory contains files associated with icons that appear on the desktop. You can use DFM's own context menus to add a program to the desktop, and that action creates a link or file in the `~/.dfmdesk` directory.

Some tools provided by integrated desktop environment packages, such as programs to set the mouse tracking speed, are best handled in a roll-your-own environment by much simpler tools that you run from your startup script. For instance, you can use `xset` to set X features such as your mouse tracking speed and keyboard repeat rate, and `xsetroot` to set the background color. You might include lines like the following in your `.xinitrc` or `.xsession` file to adjust these values:

```
xset m 4
xset r 250 15
xsetroot -solid SteelBlue
```

The first of these lines sets the mouse acceleration to a value of 4 (the precise effect of this command varies from one mouse and display to another). The second line sets the keyboard to auto-repeat when you hold down a key, beginning 250 milliseconds after the keypress begins, with 15 repeats per second thereafter. The third line sets the desktop background color to blue. Consult the `xset` and `xsetroot` man pages for more information on what these commands can do.

The main advantage to creating your own desktop environment is that you'll get something that's closer to what you want than might be possible with a prepackaged desktop environment, particularly on a low-memory system. KDE and GNOME offer many features, but they might not *exactly* match what you want, and they come at a large price in memory use. Creating your own environment may help you use a system that's low on resources.

Using GNOME

GNOME is a popular FreeBSD desktop environment. It's also very similar to KDE in its overall feature set and operation, although many details differ. This section describes using GNOME, beginning with the question of starting the environment, moving on to operating on files, configuring the desktop, and adding programs to the GNOME menus. Some basic aspects of GNOME operation are covered in greater detail in Chapter 3, and in particular the section entitled "A Quick Tour of the GUI Desktop."

Starting GNOME

GNOME is a FreeBSD program—or more precisely, a set of FreeBSD programs—much like any other. As such, in theory you can start GNOME by typing the name of the main program (`gnome-session`) in an xterm window. In practice, though, starting GNOME—or any other desktop environment or window manager—is something that's done in an X startup script of one sort or another. Such a script starts basic programs that you always want running when X is running. Common X startup scripts include `~/.xinitrc` (used when you log in to a text-based console and then start X by typing **startx**), `~/.xsession` (used by the GUI XDM login program), and `~/.vnc/xstartup` (used by the VNC remote-login server described in Chapter 21). All of these tools work in the same way: They're scripts in which you place commands that you want to run when you start X or log in. Ordinarily, these scripts include commands followed by ampersands (`&`) to launch programs that you want running in the background. The final command is normally the one that launches the window manager or desktop environment. It's not followed by an ampersand, so when you quit from the desktop environment, the script continues executing and the X session terminates. A minimal X login script contains just one line—`gnome-session`, if you want to launch GNOME.

X login scripts occasionally include lines after the window manager or desktop environment call. These commands perform cleanup operations, such as deleting temporary files or playing a sound associated with a logout.

When you first log in or start X, GNOME is likely to present a GNOME Hint dialog box with a tip to help you use GNOME. If you don't want to see these tips in the future, uncheck the Display This Dialog Next Time option and click Close. After you've done this, the system displays a nearly empty screen—it looks like Figure 23-2, but without the open windows, and possibly without the desktop icons. This is a bare GNOME system. You can launch programs by selecting their icons from the Panel at the bottom of the screen or from the Programs menu at the top of the screen.

When you're done, select GNOME Foot | Log Out or Desktop | Log Out. Both actions terminate the GNOME session. Depending upon how you logged in, X will terminate and you'll see your text-mode login, you'll be returned to an XDM login prompt, or your VNC login window will disappear. You can then log in again.

Most programs should do at least minimal cleanup if they're terminated by your logging out of GNOME. A few might not do a very good cleanup job, though. For this reason, you should terminate active programs before logging out. This is especially important for programs that keep files open, such as some word processors.

File Operations

The default FreeBSD GNOME configuration doesn't launch a file manager. There are actually two file managers that are in common use with GNOME. The first is GNU Midnight Commander (part of the `gnomemc` package or port) This program has historically been part of GNOME, but GNOME has been moving away from GNU Midnight Commander in favor of the second file manager, Nautilus. If you install this latter program (from the `nautilus` package or port), it starts automatically when you launch GNOME.

The "Manipulating Files" section of Chapter 3 describes how to use Nautilus to perform common file operations, such as copying files, renaming files, changing files' permissions, and so on. These basic operations should be familiar to those who are used to other GUI environments. One detail that deserves extra attention is linking files to applications. For instance, suppose you use OpenOffice.org for word processing. This program creates files with extensions of `.sxw`. This matter is described in the upcoming section, "Changing Nautilus File Associations."

Configuring the GNOME Desktop

The GNOME desktop is quite complex. You can adjust many details of its operation, including the programs accessible from its menus, programs launched by Nautilus for specific file types, and user interface details such as fonts used in GNOME programs and the response of the keyboard and mouse while GNOME is running. You use the GNOME Control Center to adjust most of these details, so you should take some time to familiarize yourself with it.

Note   *KDE also uses a Control Center, which offers functionality that's roughly equivalent to that of the GNOME Control Center. XFce offers less in the way of configuration options, and what it does offer is spread across several utilities, although all of them are accessible from the XFce tool bar.*

Using the Control Center

To launch the GNOME Control Center, select GNOME Foot | Programs | Settings | GNOME Control Center from the Panel or Settings | GNOME Control Center from the menu bar at the top of the screen. Alternatively, you can type **gnomecc** from an xterm window. The front window in Figure 23-2 is the GNOME Control Center open to one of its modules. You select the module you want to use from the list in the left pane of the program. For instance, to modify the behavior of the mouse, you would select the Peripherals | Mouse option from this list. The right pane then changes to display options relevant to the mouse configuration. If you know the module you want to use before launching the Control Center, you can go directly to the module in question by selecting it from the list under GNOME Foot | Programs | Settings or Settings; these menus contain shortcuts to specific Control Center modules and to a few other configuration tools.

When you make changes to the configuration, you can click the Try button to see what effect those changes will produce without committing to those changes. (Some changes may not have immediately obvious effects, though.) If you don't like the change, click Cancel or Revert to revert to the previous settings. If you like the changes, click OK. Once you've made all the changes you want to make, select File | Exit or press CTRL-Q to close the Control Center.

Changing Nautilus File Associations

You can adjust Nautilus file associations in the GNOME Control Center Document Handlers | File Types and Programs module, shown in Figure 23-4. The cornerstone of this dialog box is the list of document types, each of which includes four components:

- **Description**   The description tells you what type of document the file is, such as *AbiWord document* or *TIFF image*. These descriptions usually begin with the name of the program that creates documents of the specified type or a common name for the document type, if it's commonly created by multiple programs.

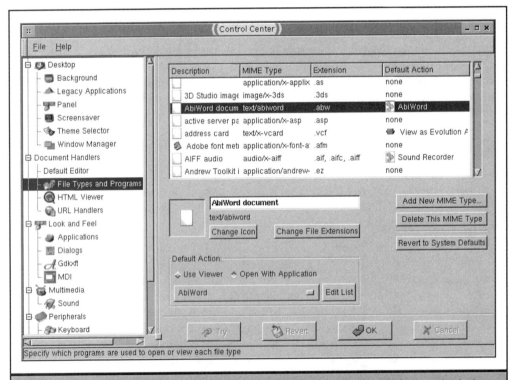

Figure 23-4.   The File Types and Programs module provides tools for manipulating Nautilus file associations.

- **MIME Type** The *Multipurpose Internet Mail Extensions (MIME) type* is a two-part code that describes the file type. The first part of a MIME type describes the general document class, such as *text* or *image*. The second part specifies the program that created the document or its general type, such as *abiword* or *tiff*.

- **Extension** The file extension is in the part of a filename following the final period (.), such as `.abw` or `.tif`. Nautilus enables you to associate one or more filename extensions with a MIME type. Although extensions are frequently three characters in length (not counting the final period), they can be longer or shorter. Not all filenames have extensions.

- **Default Action** You can tell Nautilus to do something when you double-click on a file of a particular type. This is the default action, and much of configuring file associations involves changing the default action for a file type. These actions are associated with specific MIME types.

The simplest case of changing file associations is modifying the default action associated with a specific file type. To do this, follow these steps:

1. Locate and select the file type in the file type list.

2. Click the Open With Application radio button in the Default Action area.

3. Click the application list selector in the Default Action area. (This selector displays None in Figure 23-4.) If you see your target application listed, select it and skip to Step 8.

4. If you didn't see your target application listed in Step 3, click Edit List. This action displays the Edit Applications List dialog box shown in Figure 23-5.

5. If you see your target application in the Edit Applications List dialog box, check it. You can then click OK and return to Step 3.

6. If you didn't see your application in the Edit Applications List dialog box, click Add Application in that dialog box. The result is an Add Applications dialog box.

7. In the Add Applications dialog box, type the name of the application and the complete application program name (that is, what you'd type to launch it from an xterm), then click OK. The application should now appear in the Edit Applications List dialog box (Figure 23-5). Return to Step 5.

8. At this point, you should have selected a new application to be associated with a particular MIME type. If you're done with this Control Center module, click OK. If not, you can adjust more file types.

COMMON USER
PROGRAMS

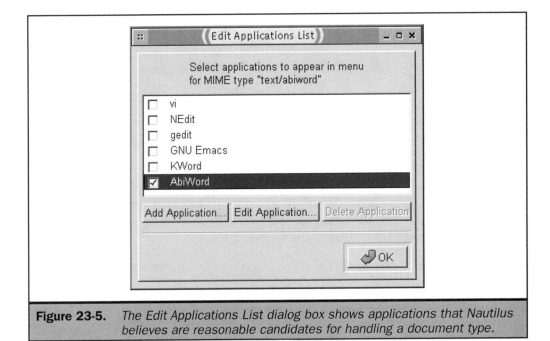

Figure 23-5. *The Edit Applications List dialog box shows applications that Nautilus believes are reasonable candidates for handling a document type.*

You can now test the file association by locating a file of the specified type in a Nautilus file manager and double-clicking it. If everything worked, the application should launch and open the file. If this doesn't happen, try the following debugging tricks:

- In an xterm window, use `ps` to look for the running application. For instance, you might type **ps ax | grep AbiWord** to see if AbiWord is running. You can try running such a command frequently for several seconds after double-clicking a file type to see if the application is starting and then failing. Of course, if it starts and fails very quickly, this test won't be likely to catch it. If the program is launching and then failing, you may want to try the next debugging procedure to help discover the cause.

- Try launching the program from an xterm by typing its name. You might also try passing it the name of a data file, as in **AbiWord myfile.abw**, to test the program's ability to load a file when launched in this way. Launching a program from an xterm may create useful error messages in the xterm window.

- If you see no evidence that the program is launching at all, double-check that it's installed and double-check the filename you typed in Step 7 of the previous procedure.

Editing existing file associations is fairly straightforward. A somewhat more complex task is creating an entirely new file association. You might do this if you've installed an application that creates its own data files that aren't already listed in the Control Center's file list. To do so, follow these steps:

1. Determine what the MIME type should be for the files in question. The documentation may specify a MIME type, or you may be able to find one by doing a web search on keywords such as the file or program type and "MIME type." If all else fails, make one up, such as text/obiewrite for the fictitious Obie Writer word processor.

2. Click Add New MIME Type in the File Types and Programs module (Figure 23-4). The Control Center displays an Add MIME Type dialog box in which you type a MIME type and a file description, as shown here:

3. Click OK in the Add MIME Type dialog box. You should see a new entry for the new file type in the Control Center dialog box (Figure 23-4), and it should be selected. If it's not selected, select it.

4. Click Change File Extensions. The system should display a small dialog box called File Extensions.

5. In the File Extensions dialog box, click Add. The system displays an Add New Extension dialog box.

6. In the Add New Extension dialog box, type the filename extensions (without periods) you want associated with the file type. You can type just one extension or several separated by spaces.

7. Click OK in the Add New Extension and File Extensions dialog boxes. You should now see the extensions you've added in the Control Center's file type list.

8. Follow the procedure earlier in this section to associate an application with the new file type.

At this point, you can test your new file type and association just as you would a new association for an existing file type. One potential complication is that your file type might use an extension that's already in use by another program. If this happens, you might find that double-clicking the document launches the wrong program. If so, you might have to browse through the file type list to locate the unwanted association and edit it. You can remove the extension association from that file type, edit its association to point to your application, or delete the conflicting file type entirely.

Modifying Program Look and Feel

X programs use widget sets to provide consistent sets of GUI controls within windows. To a programmer, these widget sets simplify the programming task considerably; instead of writing line upon line of repetitive code to handle tasks such as displaying buttons, the programmer can call a widget set library that displays a button. Historically, several different widget sets have been popular for X programs, and each widget set has provided its own unique look and feel. This is still true today, but many of today's widget sets provide a great deal of user configurability—you can adjust details such as whether menus can be "torn off" of the main menu bar for easier access to frequently-used options, what colors and button styles are used within windows, and so on. Adjusting these details on a program-by-program basis can be tedious, though, so GNOME provides a way to adjust several user interface details on a global basis. These options are adjusted through several GNOME Control Center modules:

- **Desktop background**   Although it's not a setting that affects individual programs as such, the Desktop | Background module affects all programs in the sense that it adjusts their surroundings. You can set the color of the desktop to a solid or a gradient; or you can set up a background image on the desktop.

- **Widget set themes**   You can tell GTK+ to use any of half a dozen different "themes" for its widgets—mainly buttons, but also dialog box background colors, fonts, and so on. Use the Desktop | Theme Selector module to make these changes.

- **Menus and toolbars**   You can toggle about a dozen features of menus and toolbars on or off using the Look and Feel | Applications module. These features include such options as whether you can detach submenus, whether toolbars provide text labels, and where a status bar appears when a program displays one.

- **Dialog boxes**   GTK+ provides options related to button placement within dialog boxes and placement of dialog boxes on the screen. These options can be accessed from the Look and Feel | Dialogs module.

- **MDI**   Some GTK+ programs make use of a feature known as the Multiple Document Interface, which is a way to handle multiple documents in a single program. You can adjust how you switch between documents in these programs from the Look and Feel | MDI module.

Note   *It's important to remember that none of these options except for the desktop background affects non-GTK+ programs. Thus, if you adjust, say, a widget set theme and then find that a program doesn't use your specified theme, it's likely that the program in question uses another widget set. There may be some way to adjust the appearance of the widgets used by that program, but you won't find it in the GNOME Control Center.*

Modifying the Mouse and Keyboard

You can adjust the mouse and keyboard behavior from the Peripherals | Mouse and Peripherals | Keyboard modules, respectively. Features you're particularly likely to want to adjust include

- **Mouse acceleration**   GNOME provides two sliders to set your mouse's acceleration. One sets the threshold—how far you must move the mouse before X begins accelerating its motion. Using a large threshold may be helpful if you routinely make fine adjustments with the mouse, such as in a graphics program. The acceleration slider adjusts how rapidly the mouse pointer's speed increases with a sustained movement.

- **Mouse handedness**   The Left Handed and Right Handed options adjust the assignment of buttons to actions. If you use your mouse with your left hand, checking the Left Handed option may be desirable.

- **Keyboard repeat rate**   Normally, FreeBSD sets the keyboard to repeat your keypresses when you hold down a key. You can adjust both the delay before your keypresses begin repeating and the rate of repeat.

- **Keyboard click**   Some people like auditory feedback to keypresses. You can turn this option on and off and adjust the volume of the keyclicks.

- **Keyboard bell**   Some programs sound a "bell" at certain times, such as when an error occurs. You can adjust the volume, tone, and duration of this sound.

These options all affect both GTK+ and non-GTK+ programs; they're global in scope. They do not, however, affect text-mode logins (for instance, if you press CTRL-ALT-F1 to switch to a text-mode screen), and they may not have any effect in certain remote login situations, such as using a VNC client to access FreeBSD, as described in Chapter 21. They can all be set using other means, such as the xset program and the XF86Config file; however, GNOME overrides any existing settings when it loads.

Adding Programs to the Panel

Sometimes, installing a program adds entries to the GNOME Panel for the program in question. Other times, though, you must either launch the program by typing its name in an xterm or add the program to the Panel yourself. To do the latter, you must use the GNOME Menu Editor program, which you can launch from GNOME Foot | Panel | Edit Menus or from Program | Settings | Menu Editor. Alternatively, you can type **gmenu** to launch the program from an xterm. The result should resemble Figure 23-6. (Note that this program is *not* part of the GNOME Control Center.)

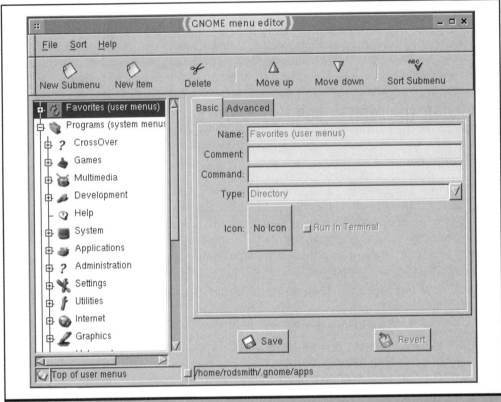

Figure 23-6. *The GNOME Menu Editor enables you to adjust entries on the GNOME desktop menus.*

The GNOME menus appear in an expandable list in the left pane of the program window. There are three main menus: Favorites, Programs, and Applets, each of which may contain submenus, sub-submenus, and so on. Figure 23-6 shows the Programs menu expanded so that you can see its entries and submenus.

Note *Only `root` may edit the Programs and Applets menus. These menus are shared across all accounts, so if you want to make a program easily accessible to all GNOME users, you can, as `root`, add it to one of these menus. If you only want to make private changes for your own personal use, you must make them to the Favorites menu.*

To add a program to a menu, follow these steps:

1. In the list on the left side of the GNOME Menu Editor window, select the menu in which you want your new entry to appear. For instance, to create an item on the Favorites menu, select Favorites, as shown in Figure 23-6.

2. Click New Item or select File | New Item. This action creates a new menu entry, which is initially called Untitled.

3. Type a name for the item in the Name field in the right side of the GNOME Menu Editor window. This is the name that will appear in the menu listing.

4. If you like, type a comment in the Comment field. This comment pops up when you move your mouse over the menu item and leave it for a few seconds, to help further identify what the program does.

5. Type the command that launches the program in the Command field.

6. Select the entry type in the Type field. For a program, this type is Application. You can also create a URL (which launches a web browser) or a Directory (which launches Nautilus on the directory).

7. If the program is a text-mode program, check the Run in Terminal box. If you fail to do this, you won't see the program's display.

8. To add an icon, click the button labeled Icon (which displays No Icon by default, signifying that no icon is associated with the menu entry). GNOME Menu Editor displays a window from which you can select an icon. This window displays the contents of the standard GNOME icons directory by default, but you can browse to another directory to select an icon from anywhere else. Click OK when you've selected an icon.

9. Click Save to save your menu entry.

You should now be able to test the entry. If it doesn't work, review your entry, especially the program command you typed in Step 5. You may also want to try running the program from an xterm to be sure it runs at all; it might not be installed or might have problems even when run in a more traditional way. Using an xterm also displays any text-mode error messages, which may provide clues as to why it's not working correctly.

You can use the GNOME Menu Editor to adjust your menu entries in ways other than adding new programs. You can create a new submenu, delete an entry, move entries up or down in the menu, and sort the entries. These functions all have dedicated buttons in the program's toolbar. Most don't require any further interaction beyond pressing the appropriate button, but the new submenu option requires entering information similar to that for a new program.

Summary

Desktop environments are an important part of modern workstation computing. Two such environments, KDE and GNOME, are in common use on FreeBSD. A sparer desktop environment, XFce, is useful on systems with less RAM or CPU speed, or if you don't like the clutter of KDE or GNOME. Creating your own desktop environment is also an option. FreeBSD enables each user of a multiuser computer to select a different desktop environment, providing more than one is installed. You can also use many components designed for one environment in another one, although sometimes this produces a modest drop in functionality. The details of desktop environment use vary somewhat from one environment to another, but certain features are common across environments, particularly between KDE and GNOME. In particular, KDE and GNOME provide similar file managers and desktop configuration tools.

Chapter 24

Networking Tools

art IV of this book describes network server programs. FreeBSD makes an excellent server platform, but it can also host client programs for most of the servers it supports. For the most part, client programs are easier to configure and use than are servers, so this chapter covers most of the clients that connect to servers described in Part IV. There are also many specific client programs for some protocols, so this chapter tends to cover clients in general terms, using specific servers as examples of a class. This chapter covers e-mail clients, web browsers, FTP clients, file-sharing tools, and remote login clients.

A few clients are described elsewhere in this book. For instance, Chapter 14 covers DHCP and DNS client configuration; NTP clients are covered along with NTP servers in Chapter 22; and GUI login clients are covered along with their servers in Chapter 21.

E-mail Clients

E-mail is an extremely popular use of networking, and FreeBSD supports a wide range of e-mail clients. To use these clients, you must have access to one or more mail servers. You may run these mail servers on your own computer, as described in Chapter 19, or the servers may run on other computers. Either way, you must be able to configure the mail client to use an appropriate server. The most basic e-mail actions are reading, sending, and storing, each of which is done in a way that's unique to the program in question. A specific variant of sending and receiving e-mail that's becoming increasingly common is using attachments, which enable individuals to exchange nontextual documents, such as graphics or sound files. Knowing how to safely handle these documents is important when using an e-mail client.

A Rundown of Common E-mail Clients

To read e-mail in FreeBSD, you must install and use an appropriate e-mail client. Because of its UNIX heritage, FreeBSD supports many popular e-mail clients, ranging from simple text-based e-mail programs to sophisticated modern programs (both text-mode and X-based). A complete listing of e-mail clients is impossible, but some of the more popular options include

- **mail** This program is a simple text-mode mail utility. It's not very popular for regular mail reading, but it is valuable because you can call it in a script to send mail in an automated fashion.

- **pine** This program, headquartered at `http://www.washington.edu/pine/`, is a fairly sophisticated text-mode client. This program was designed to be friendly to new users, but it's still quite powerful.

- ◼ `elm`   This program is similar to `pine` in many respects, although it's not quite as user-friendly. Its home page is `http://www.abo.fi/dc/miniguides/elm-enge.doc.html`.

- ◼ **Mutt**   This text-mode program is newer than its competing programs, and has been gaining in popularity since the late 1990s. You can read more at `http://www.mutt.org`.

- ◼ `rmail`   This package isn't a stand-alone e-mail client; rather, it's a component of Emacs, which is usually considered an editor. You can use `rmail` to read your mail from within Emacs.

- ◼ **Evolution**   This program, headquartered at `http://www.ximian.com/products/ximian_evolution/`, is the UNIX world's answer to Microsoft's Outlook. Evolution is a sophisticated GUI program that includes not just e-mail, but calendar and information management modules.

- ◼ **GNUMail.app**   This program is modeled after the Mail.app program of NeXTStep and Mac OS X. It's available from `http://www.collaboration-world.com/gnumail/`.

- ◼ **KMail**   This program is part of the K Desktop Environment (KDE). It's a capable but fairly small GUI mail reader. Its documentation is at `http://docs.kde.org/2.2.2/kdenetwork/kmail/`.

- ◼ **Mahogany**   This is a sophisticated GUI mail application, headquartered at `http://mahogany.sourceforge.net`.

- ◼ **Spruce**   This program is a GUI mail client that aims to be small and fast. Nonetheless, the program supports the most important mail features, including attachments. You can read more at `http://spruce.sourceforge.net`.

- ◼ **Sylpheed**   Like Spruce, Sylpheed is designed to be a small and fast mail client, despite its GUI nature. It's headquartered at `http://sylpheed.good-day.net`.

- ◼ `xmail`   This program completes the circle; it's an X-based interface for the basic `mail` program.

Most of these programs are available in the `mail` section of the FreeBSD packages and ports systems, so you can install them as described in Chapter 11. The KMail program is installed as part of the `kdenetwork` package in the `net` area of the packages or ports systems. `rmail` is installed as part of Emacs, from the `editors` area.

Which mail client should you use? The answer boils down to personal preference. Some people prefer text-mode mail clients such as `mutt`, even when working in X; others like the point-and-click interfaces of GUI tools. Some mail readers, such as KMail, interface tightly with other components of a desktop environment. Tools such as Evolution provide a plethora of features, whereas others, such as `mail`, are much simpler. Your best bet is to install several mail clients and try them all. If you're administering a system with many users, you should install a range of mail readers for your users.

 Mail readers don't always use compatible mailbox formats. Thus, you may not be able to easily switch between mail readers and maintain your mail spool. I recommend you create a test account for initial mail reader evaluation.

Initial Setup and Configuration

After you install a mail application, it should be more-or-less ready to use. There are, however, several details you may want or need to configure. Most of these features are set on a user-by-user basis, generally in configuration files in the users' home directories named after the program. Some programs create an entire subdirectory in which they store these files. Most programs have default configuration files stored in /etc or in the programs' own directory trees. Examples of these files include

- **pine** This program stores local defaults in /usr/local/etc/pine.conf. Users can override these defaults in the .pinerc files in their home directories.

- **Mutt** The /usr/local/etc/Muttrc file holds global default settings. Users can override these defaults by creating .muttrc files in their home directories.

- **Spruce** This program has no global configuration file; instead, it prompts for configuration values the first time it's run, and stores them in ~/.spruce/spruce.conf.

- **Sylpheed** Like Spruce, Sylpheed prompts for user defaults the first time it's run and stores them in the user's home directory—specifically, in ~/.sylpheed/sylpheedrc.

Some programs—particularly the X-based tools, but also some text-mode programs—enable users to alter their defaults from within the mail program itself. It's generally a good idea to use this feature because it reduces the chance of damaging a configuration with a manual editing error. Figure 24-1 shows an example: the Spruce Configuration Options dialog box. This dialog box appears the first time you launch the program and can be opened again by selecting Settings | Preferences. Most other GUI programs provide a similar dialog box. Options you should be sure to set are

- **Name and address** Many programs fill in your name and e-mail address based on information in the FreeBSD account database and default machine information, such as the hostname. You may want to edit this information—say, to remove the host portion of a hostname if your return mail uses only the domain name. Some programs, including Spruce as shown in Figure 24-1, provide a separate option for a Reply-To address. You can use this feature to have replies sent to another address, if recipients' mail programs honor the field.

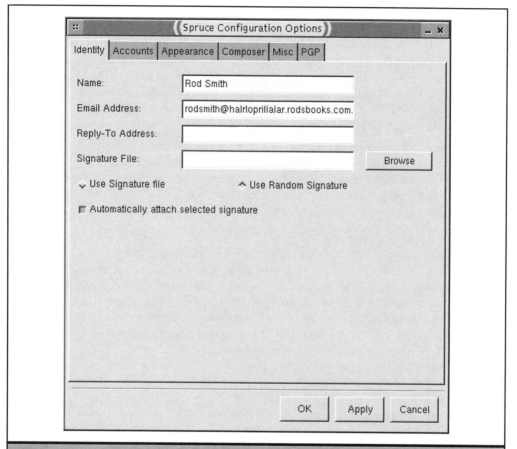

Figure 24-1.   *GUI tools make entering e-mail account information straightforward.*

- **Signature**   An email *signature* is a short element at the end of a message that you can use to list your e-mail address, home page, employer, or other information. Keep your signature under 4–6 lines at most.

- **Outgoing mail server**   Many FreeBSD mail programs (especially text-based programs) default to using sendmail running on the local computer for handling outgoing mail. Others, including many GUI programs, require you to explicitly specify an outgoing mail server. This may be `localhost` if you're running a mail server that can handle the job, as described in Chapter 19; or it can be a mail server on another computer.

- **Incoming mail server**   The mail program must know where to look to find incoming mail. This may be a local mail spool, if your system receives mail directly or if you use fetchmail to retrieve mail and inject it into a local spool, as described in Chapter 19. Alternatively, you can configure most mail readers to access mail on a remote server using protocols such as POP or IMAP. You may be able to configure the mail reader to check for new mail at regular intervals, such as every half hour; or you may need to issue a command or exit and relaunch the program to check for new mail.

- **Editors**   Some mail readers, especially text-based tools, rely upon external programs to edit mail messages you create. For instance, the set_editor option in .muttrc and the editor option in .pinerc set their respective mail readers' editors. Some programs, especially GUI ones, support options to format outgoing mail as HTML or in other sophisticated ways. It's usually best to disable such options unless you need them.

Most mail readers create subdirectories in users' home directories in which they store mail. These subdirectories may be the same as the ones used to store configuration files, or they may be called Mail, mail, or something similar. Typically, the mail reader creates one or more files in the mail directory in which messages are stored. You can use mail reader functions to create *folders* within the mail directory. These folders are usually ordinary files that can contain multiple mail messages, but they might instead be subdirectories that contain mail in a one-message-per-file format. If your mail reader reads the local mail spool, it will also read incoming mail from /var/mail/*username*, where *username* is your username.

Some mail readers automatically transfer mail from your system mail spool into a local mail folder called inbox *or something similar. This behavior can result in some mail that's hard to recover if you test a mail reader that moves mail into its own mail folder but you decide not to use the mail reader.*

Reading and Storing E-mail

Most e-mail programs organize messages into folders. Precisely how you access these folders varies from one program to another. Text-based programs such as Mutt and pine use commands you can type on their main screens to "move into" folders. You can then display messages in the folder, read a message by typing its number or moving a cursor to a message, and so on. X-based programs typically display lists of mail folders in a window or a pane of the main window, or provide a button that opens a list of folders. For instance, Figure 24-2 shows Spruce's main window. The pane in the upper-left corner of the window displays all the available mail folders, broken into three categories: *Local Mailboxes* (those that belong to Spruce and are stored in the ~/.spruce directory), *Remote Mailboxes* (those maintained by an IMAP server you've configured Spruce to use), and *Local Spool* (mailboxes that may be shared with other mail programs, including the main incoming mail spool, if you receive mail in this way). Not all mail readers organize their mailboxes in precisely this way, but such an organization is not uncommon. Within each mail folder category are individual mail folders, such as the *Inbox*, *Drafts*, and other folders shown in Figure 24-2.

You can read mail by clicking a message within the message list pane (near the upper-right corner of Figure 24-2) of a GUI mail reader. Text-mode mail readers typically use message numbers that you type, or highlighting of specific messages. In either case, the message appears, either replacing the message list or in another pane. In Figure 24-2, the message appears below the folder and message list panes.

If you want to save a message for future reference, you can store it in a folder, usually by selecting a menu option or by a drag-and-drop operation. Most mail readers enable you to create new folders. For instance, Figure 24-2's Articles folder is not a standard part of the Spruce mail folder directory; I created it and moved some messages into it.

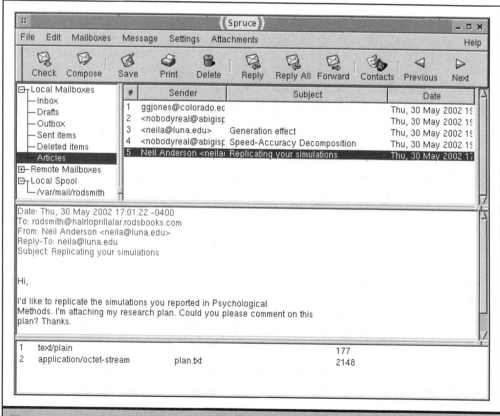

Figure 24-2. *GUI mail programs typically use panes to display different types of information in one window.*

Sometimes it's necessary to store a message in a file. You might do this for archival purposes or to process the message in some way. Most programs include some sort of message save option. Usually, the saved version of the message includes only minimal message *headers* (information used by mail servers to direct a message to its destination and to record information on the systems through which a message has passed). Full headers are necessary when reporting mail abuse, so a mail reader that enables you to save all headers can be a great asset.

You can usually gain access to full headers by creating a new mail folder and moving the message to that folder. The resulting file usually contains the message with all its headers.

Sending E-mail

Sending e-mail involves selecting an option to send a message. The mail reader may then launch an external editor, such as jed, pico, or vi; or it may display its own editor. Unless you specify use of some particularly elaborate editor, the editor you'll see will be fairly simple. Both the default external editors for text-mode tools and the editors included with GUI tools tend to be fairly minimal. In its most basic form, e-mail involves the exchange of plain-text messages, so most e-mail editors don't include options to add formatting features such as bold or italic. In recent years, though, the Hypertext Markup Language (HTML), best known as the file format on which the Web is built, has become popular in e-mail. Thus, HTML-enabled mail readers provide editors that support HTML features, including text effects, tables, and even inline graphics.

Some people object to receiving HTML e-mail. Such messages are usually larger than text-mode messages, so they can take longer to download over slow dial-up links that many recipients still use. (This effect is quite substantial if you include inline graphics.) Recipients whose mail readers can't parse HTML messages end up seeing "raw" HTML markup codes, which reduce message legibility. I recommend you not use HTML e-mail unless the recipient has agreed to accept this format.

When you save a message and exit from an external editor or click a Send button in a built-in e-mail editor, the mail reader attempts to send the message. Some mail readers (particularly text-based ones) default to trying to use the local /usr/sbin/ sendmail program, which works fine with FreeBSD, albeit with some caveats. Specifically, some ISPs block sending mail directly, which is what sendmail attempts to do by default; and if the recipient system doesn't respond immediately, sendmail will try again later, so this approach works best if your Internet connection is up constantly. Chapter 19 describes reconfiguring sendmail to use an outgoing mail relay, which can overcome these problems. Another approach is to configure your mail reader to use your ISP's mail server directly, as described earlier, in "Initial Setup and Configuration."

Using Attachments

Today, *attachments* are extremely common e-mail elements. Attachments are a way to include (or *attach*) ordinary files to an e-mail message using the Multipurpose Internet Mail Extensions (MIME) standard. You can use attachments to send a word processing document, a graphics file, a sound file, a tarball, a plain-text file, or anything else to the recipient. (In fact, HTML e-mail works through attachments; the HTML is sent as an attachment to an empty or plain-text version of the message.) When you read e-mail that includes an attachment, most mail readers provide some indication that an attachment is present. In Spruce (Figure 24-2), this indication appears in the short bottom pane. Clicking, right-clicking, or double-clicking the attachment name typically loads it into an appropriate program or gives you a menu of things you can do with it, such as save it to a file. Text-based mail readers can also process attachments, but you must select them with a keyboard-based command.

Caution   *2001 and 2002 have seen a huge increase in the amount of malicious code that's distributed as e-mail attachments. Most of these attacks have been targeted at Microsoft Windows systems, but in theory, worms or other types of malicious programs could be targeted at FreeBSD systems, UNIX systems generally, or a wide variety of platforms. You should never use an attachment unless it's from a trusted source and you were expecting it.*

If you want to send an attachment, most mail readers enable you to do so. GUI programs typically include a button with an icon of a paper clip or a menu option to attach a file. You can then type in a filename or locate the file you want to attach in a file browser.

Caution   *Be aware of the size of files you attach to messages. Most ISPs limit the size of e-mail messages they'll process, so a message with a large attachment might not arrive at its destination. Even if it does arrive, the recipient might not appreciate receiving a large attachment, particularly if the recipient uses a slow dial-up Internet link. I recommend asking before sending an e-mail with more than about 100KB of attachments.*

One feature of attachments that's not obvious to most users is that the attachments may be larger than the files they deliver. This characteristic is a consequence of the way mail readers encode binary attachments for delivery using a protocol that was designed for text. Plain text requires only six bits per byte to encode, and that's all that e-mail can reliably handle. In binary files, though, all eight bits per byte are significant. MIME attachment standards overcome this problem by adding bytes. For instance, to encode six binary bytes (48 bits) of data, eight 6-bit characters may be used. Additional control characters add to this overhead. Thus, binary attachments consume about 35 percent more bandwidth than would be required to transfer the file in some other way, such as via an FTP server. If connection speeds are low, you may want to use FTP or some other method, rather than e-mail attachments, to transfer files. On the other hand, e-mail attachments are convenient, particularly if neither the sender nor the recipient has easy access to an FTP server.

 If you must send large binary e-mail attachments, first compress the files using gzip *or* zip. *The compressed files will still experience a 35 percent size increase, but the compression may save more space than this, reducing network bandwidth use.*

Web Browsers

Web browsers are ubiquitous and most people know how to use them. For this reason, this chapter doesn't go into great detail about how to browse the Web; instead, it emphasizes available FreeBSD web browsers, quirks of FreeBSD web browser configuration, and web browser security concerns.

A Rundown of Common Web Browsers

In 2002, the most popular web browser is Microsoft's Internet Explorer, but this browser isn't available for FreeBSD. This fact means that a few web pages aren't readily accessible from FreeBSD because some web page designers are inconsiderate enough that they create pages that display *only* on Internet Explorer. Most web pages, though, display just fine on any of the many alternative web browsers available for FreeBSD, such as

- **Netscape Navigator** This browser has historically been the most important competitor to Internet Explorer, but its market share plummeted in the last couple years of the 20th century. Unfortunately, only very old versions of Netscape are available in FreeBSD-native form, and those versions have security problems. You can run more recent versions of Netscape for Linux using FreeBSD's Linux binary compatibility, as described in Chapter 4; or you can use a native FreeBSD build of Mozilla. The official Netscape web page is http://www.netscape.com.

- **Mozilla** In early 1998, Netscape announced plans to release its Navigator browser under an open source license. This plan eventually led to the development of Mozilla, which is Netscape Navigator's open source cousin. In practice, Mozilla works much like Netscape Navigator, but as Mozilla is available in native FreeBSD form, it's preferred to Netscape Navigator under FreeBSD. You can learn more about Mozilla at http://www.mozilla.org.

- **Konqueror** This web browser is part of the KDE project, and doubles as KDE's file manager. Compared to Netscape Navigator and Mozilla, Konqueror is small and agile, but it's less feature-filled. The browser is installed as part of the FreeBSD kdebase package, and its documentation is at http://docs.kde.org/2.2.2/kdebase/konqueror/.

- **Amaya**   This web browser is unusual because it serves as a test bed for many new web technologies. It's not a very popular web browser, though. The browser includes a seamlessly integrated WYSIWYG web page editor. You can learn more at `http://www.w3.org/Amaya/`.

- **Emacs**   Emacs is often called the "kitchen sink editor," because it includes everything, including the proverbial (but metaphorical) kitchen sink. Part of "everything" is a web browser, so if you're an Emacs fan, you can easily browse the Web with this program. The Emacs web browser is installed as a separate add-on package to Emacs, `emacs-w3m-emacs21`, in the www packages or ports area.

- **Galeon**   One of the consequences of Netscape's releasing its Navigator code under an open source license was that others could use the core of that code (the HTML rendering engine) to build new browsers. Galeon is one such program, and is part of the GNU Network Object Model Environment (GNOME) project. You can learn more at `http://galeon.sourceforge.net`.

- **Opera**   This program is one of the few commercial web browsers that runs on FreeBSD. It is not, though, a FreeBSD program; it's a Linux program, so you need the Linux compatibility tools, described in Chapter 4. Outside of the UNIX world, Opera is probably the closest competitor to Internet Explorer and Netscape. You can install it from the `linux-opera` package or port in the www area, or read more at `http://www.opera.com`.

- **Lynx**   This program is important because it's a popular text-based web browser. If you need to browse the Web without using X, Lynx does the job. It's also a useful tool when developing web pages, particularly for evaluating a web page's accessibility; if a page is intelligible in Lynx, chances are the page will work well for visually impaired people who use speech synthesizer technology. The main Lynx web page is `http://lynx.isc.org/current/`.

This list is far from complete. Since Netscape Navigator's source code became available as Mozilla, many projects have sprung up that use its code; sometimes it seems there's a new Mozilla-derived browser announced every week. Most web browsers are not very well developed, though; they're buggy, sluggish, or incomplete. The most mature and useful browsers for FreeBSD are Mozilla, Galeon, Konqueror, and Opera (if you consider Opera "for FreeBSD," given that it's really a Linux program). It's generally best to have at least two of these browsers installed; that way, if you run across a page that doesn't display correctly in your primary browser, you can launch the secondary browser to deal with it. Because Mozilla and Galeon share a rendering engine, I recommend installing Konqueror or Opera. Of course, installing other browsers won't hurt, except insofar as additional browsers will consume disk space and perhaps clutter menus.

Web Browser Configuration

For the most part, web browsers work as soon as they're installed. Some browsers ask you to provide information such as your e-mail address when they're first launched. Such browsers usually include integrated e-mail clients so that you can send mail from them if you click on a `mailto:` link in a web page.

Most web browsers provide a rather large configuration dialog box, such as the one shown in Figure 24-3, for Mozilla. You can open this dialog box from one of the browser's menus (Edit | Preferences, in the case of Mozilla). Most browsers are complex enough that the dialog box's contents are variable. Mozilla uses the pane on the left of the dialog box to display a specific set of controls. Some other browsers use tabbed fields within the dialog box. You may have to check several areas to find the feature you want to adjust. Some features you might want to check include

- **Identity**   You can tell the browser who you are, what your e-mail address is, and so on. This information can be used by an e-mail module, or under some circumstances it might be returned to the server; for instance, a browser might use your e-mail address as a password when accessing an anonymous FTP site.

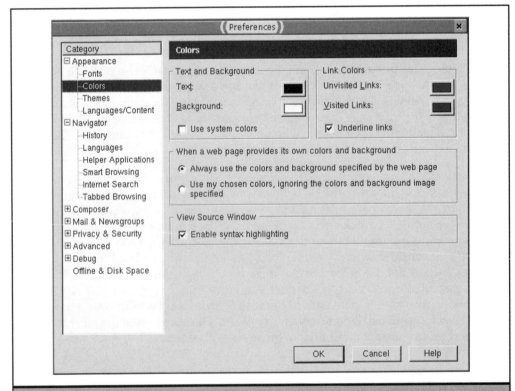

Figure 24-3.   *Web browser configuration tools provide many options that you can set.*

- **Colors**   You can set the default foreground (text) and background colors to suit your tastes. Some browsers also enable you to override document-provided colors, which is sometimes necessary on poorly designed web pages.

- **Fonts**   You can usually set the fonts that the web browser uses for specific types of text. Font size can sometimes be tricky; some methods of setting font size in web pages produce ludicrously large or small fonts in some browsers. Some browsers provide a way to specify minimum or maximum font sizes to help alleviate this problem.

- **Graphics**   Most GUI web browsers default to automatically downloading and displaying all graphics. To speed up web page loading or to avoid clutter, you can usually disable this option.

- **Cookies**   In the context of the Web, a *cookie* is a piece of information that a web page delivers to a web browser, and which the browser returns upon request. Sites use cookies to help track user activities, both for legitimate purposes (such as helping identify a specific customer during an online purchase) and for more questionable purposes (such as building a history of your online activities to advance marketing goals). In most cases, you can adjust how readily your browser accepts cookies, but selecting anything but the "always accept" option can be annoying (if the browser constantly asks you about accepting specific cookies) or can disable functionality of some pages.

- **Proxies**   Some networks require you to browse the Web through a *proxy server*, which is a type of high-level firewall. You can specify a proxy server in most web browsers' configuration tools.

- **Scripting**   Java and JavaScript are tools that enable web designers to extend what a web page can do. Unfortunately, they come with some security risks. This is particularly true of Java. The next section, "Web Browser Security Considerations," describes security issues in more detail.

- **User interface**   Many browsers today feature multiple panes, options for how to display multiple windows, and so on. You can usually set such options in the configuration dialog box.

I recommend you take the time to examine your web browser's configuration options. If you're unsure of what an option does and if it seems important, use the browser's help feature or perform a web search to learn more about the option.

Web Browser Security Considerations

In an ideal world, browsing the Web would pose no risk. Unfortunately, our world is not ideal. The popularity of the Web has made it less than completely safe to use this powerful tool, as miscreants have found ways to exploit security holes in web browsers. A less serious threat (at least in the short term) is the risk of web page owners tracking you and learning more than you might like them to know based on your online activities. Security issues that should concern you include

- **Basic information divulged** With every Hypertext Transfer Protocol (HTTP; the protocol upon which the Web is built) request, your browser provides information about itself—most notably its IP address, the browser name, and the host OS. Some browsers can be configured to lie about their identities, but your IP address cannot be masked except by using a proxy server or network address translation (NAT). If somebody is tracking your online activities through a packet sniffer, that person can learn a lot about you just by examining the web pages you frequent.

- **Browser bugs** Browser bugs can cause a browser to crash, but more importantly, some bugs can disable security settings or enable an outsider to gain access to your files. For this reason, you should keep up to date with security updates on a web browser, just as you would for a server.

- **Scripting** Java and JavaScript, as noted in the previous section, are a potential problem because they allow an untrusted individual to run arbitrary code on your computer. Ideally, you should disable these features, but doing so causes a distressing number of sites to fail, so you may need to enable one or both, at least for some sites.

- **Cookies** As noted in the previous section, cookies can enable web sites to track your activities. In theory, cookies are restricted to one site; however, sites with business relationships may share cookie information, and cookies tied to advertising enable advertisers to track your visits to many web sites. Disabling cookies in the browser or using a proxy server designed to enhance privacy, such as Privoxy (`http://privoxy.org`), can greatly reduce the risk of privacy invasion on the Web.

- **Secure transactions** Whenever you submit information via a web browser, that information might be intercepted by crackers. Thus, protecting sensitive information such as passwords, credit card numbers, and bank account information is critically important. Modern browsers support Secure Socket Layer (SSL) security, which encrypts data so that it will be useless if intercepted. (Future developments might make cracking SSL security practical, but for now it's reasonably secure, especially the 128-bit varieties.) Most browsers include some visual indication, such as a padlock in its closed position, when they're in secure mode. Be sure this indication is present before you submit sensitive information.

- **Passwords** Many sites require passwords to gain access. As just noted, sending such passwords over an insecure connection is risky. Unfortunately, many sites that require passwords for access don't secure those passwords, and the number of sites that require passwords can make it difficult to create and remember separate passwords for each site. Some browsers can remember multiple passwords for you, but that's not without risk because the passwords are then stored on your hard disk, and of course they can still be sniffed. Even if your browser can't remember a host of passwords, I strongly recommend you use unique passwords for particularly sensitive sites, such as online banking services.

- **Untrustworthy files** Although the vast majority of the files you'll find on the Internet are posted by sincere and honest people, it's always possible you'll find an interesting-sounding program that is in fact a *Trojan horse*—a program that claims to do one thing but that does something far more sinister. For this reason, you should be cautious about downloading and running programs you find on web sites unless you have reason to trust that the program is what it claims to be. Try doing a web search or a search of Usenet discussion groups (at `http://groups.google.com`) to see if the program is well respected.

Overall, the most widespread security risks of web browsing are only peripherally security-related—they're the privacy issues associated with cookies and even IP address tracking. The most serious risks, though, relate to malicious code in Java (or to a lesser extent JavaScript), Trojan horses, and browser bugs. Using a privacy-enhancing web proxy tool and fine-tuning a few generic browser options can go a long way towards improving your web browsing security. Being cautious about sending passwords, credit card numbers, and other sensitive data over unencrypted links is also an important security issue, but this is one that requires constant vigilance.

FTP and SFTP Clients

Despite FTP's age and security problems surrounding the unencrypted transfer of passwords, the protocol remains popular. In some cases, such as in anonymous FTP transfers, security issues surrounding passwords are unimportant. In fact, for public distribution of files, FTP has advantages over the more visible HTTP because FTP clients frequently provide the ability to resume an interrupted transfer. For instance, if you've downloaded the first 630MB of a 640MB FreeBSD CD-ROM image file when your Internet connection goes down, you may be stuck downloading most of that file again if you used HTTP. If you use FTP, though, you can reconnect and tell the client to resume the transfer, whereupon you'll have to download only the remaining 10MB.

A wide variety of FTP client programs exist. Some of these are text-mode programs, but others provide GUI interfaces. This section describes some of the popular traditional FTP clients and their commands, so you can use FTP to retrieve files from popular FTP sites or from private sites for which you need a password.

Note *The Secure Shell (SSH) server also provides file-transfer features, including a secure FTP (SFTP) variant. Some FTP clients have absorbed the ability to talk to these SFTP servers. When so connected, they use the same commands as when they connect to traditional FTP sites, so this section applies to SFTP as well as to FTP.*

A Rundown of Common FTP Clients

Given FTP's age and popularity, it shouldn't be surprising that many FTP clients are available for FreeBSD. Some of the more popular of these include

- **ftp** The original `ftp` program is a text-based client, and is installed with the base FreeBSD program set, so it should be installed on your computer with no extra effort on your part. FreeBSD's version of `ftp` includes some extensions from more advanced text-based FTP programs, such as `ncftp`.

- **ncftp** This text-based program is similar to the original `ftp` in many ways, but includes some expanded features, such as a progress display indicator. FreeBSD's `ftp` program has incorporated many of these expansions, though, so on FreeBSD the difference between `ftp` and `ncftp` is smaller than the difference between these programs on many other platforms. You can learn more at `http://www.ncftp.com`.

- **Mftp** This program (installed from the `moxftp` package or port) is an X-based FTP client. Compared to other GUI FTP clients, Mftp's user interface is simple, but it gets the job done.

- **AxY FTP** This program is a GUI FTP client with a user interface that's modeled closely after the popular Windows WS FTP program. You can learn more at `http://www.wxftp.seul.org`.

- **gFTP** This GUI program is a popular one, particularly on systems that use GNOME. It presents a user interface that's similar, but not identical, to the one used by AxY FTP or WS FTP. This program supports SFTP, as implemented by SSH servers. Its web page is `http://gftp.seul.org`.

- **hsftp** This program is not technically an FTP client, but it's a text-mode program that presents an FTP-like command set for accessing files on an SSH server computer. Thus, it can be used as a secure substitute for FTP when the remote system runs SSH instead of or in addition to FTP. You can learn more at `http://la-samhna.de/hsftp/`.

- **Web browsers** All modern web browsers support FTP. You can enter a URL that begins with `ftp://` rather than `http://`, or follow such a link on a web page, to access an FTP site. Web browsers don't give full and easy access to all FTP features, though, so you're usually better off using a dedicated FTP client if you need to do more than retrieve a few small files from an anonymous FTP site.

Aside from `ftp`, which is part of a base FreeBSD installation, and some web browsers, all of these programs are available as both FreeBSD packages and ports. Thus, you can install the programs using any of the methods described in Chapter 11. As with e-mail readers and web browsers, you should probably install multiple FTP clients, particularly on a multiuser system, so that users have a choice of programs to use. Aside from `ftp`, `ncftp` is a good choice for command-line use, and AxY FTP and gFTP are good choices for GUI use.

In addition to these conventional FTP clients, there are some less conventional programs available that use FTP. Some tools are designed to *mirror* an FTP site—that is, to copy all the files from an FTP site (or a subdirectory thereof) to your computer. You might use such a tool to copy a FreeBSD FTP site to a local computer in order to facilitate installing FreeBSD on a network of computers, for instance. Some tools that aren't primarily FTP programs use FTP to accomplish specific goals. For instance, some web page design programs enable direct upload of files to a web server via FTP. You can find some unusual FTP clients in the `ftp` section of the FreeBSD packages or ports systems, but others may reside elsewhere.

Core FTP Commands

FTP supports a specific set of operations—sending a file, receiving a file, and so on. When using a text-mode FTP client, you access these operations by typing commands. In GUI FTP clients, the typed commands are replaced by menu options, button presses, or the like. The full range of FTP commands is greater than can be presented here, but the most important commands, as used by `ftp` and most other text-mode FTP clients, are

- **ascii** One of FTP's strengths is that it supports two transfer modes: *binary*, in which files are transferred without modification; and *ASCII*, in which the file's end-of-line characters, and sometimes other characters, are modified for the receiving system's standards. The `ascii` command enables ASCII transfer mode.

- **binary** As you might expect, this command enables binary transfer mode. This mode is usually, but not always, the default. You should be sure to enable binary mode before transferring nontext data files, or they're likely to be corrupted.

- **bye** or **exit** or **quit** These commands terminate the session and quit from the program.

- **cd** This command works much like its namesake in most FreeBSD shells—it changes the working directory, but on the FTP server system. You specify a path (in absolute or relative form) with this command.

- **delete** You can delete a file on the server with this command, which takes a filename as an option.

- **dir** or **ls** These commands display the contents of a directory on the server. You can optionally add a directory name to see the contents of the directory you specify. On some servers, the `dir` command creates a longer listing (similar to what `ls -l` does in a shell), whereas `ls` creates a more compact listing.

- **ftp** or **open** These commands open a new connection. You specify a hostname after these commands, as in **open ftp.threeroomco.com**.

- **get** This command is one of the most important in FTP; it retrieves a single named file from the server. You can specify a single filename to save the file under that name locally. If you give two names, the client saves the file locally under the second name.

- **help or ?** This command displays a summary of the FTP client's commands. If you follow `help` or `?` with a command name, the program displays a one-sentence summary of what the command does.

- **lcd** Several commands beginning with the letter `l` operate *locally*—that is, on the client system. This command changes the local directory, in which retrieved files are stored and from which files are sent.

- **lpwd** This command displays the name of the current working directory on the client computer.

- **mget** This command retrieves multiple files from the server. You can explicitly list all the files or use wildcards similar to those used in a FreeBSD shell. Depending upon the client and the setting of the `prompt` option, you may be prompted to confirm each retrieval.

- **mkdir** You can create a directory on the server with this command.

- **mput** This command sends several files from the client to the server. As with `mget`, you can list the files individually or use wildcards.

- **prompt** This command enables or disables prompting to confirm each file in a multifile transfer (`mget` or `mput`). Pass `on` or `off` with this command to enable or disable prompting, respectively.

- **put** This command is the opposite of `get`; it transfers a single file from the client to the server.

- **pwd** Use this command to learn the working directory on the server computer.

- **reget** This command is useful if a transfer was interrupted; it tells the system to resume the transfer starting with the last byte of the existing file on the local system, thus eliminating the need to retransfer existing data.

- **rename** You can rename a file on the server with this command, which takes the current and new names as options.

- **rmdir** This command deletes a directory on the server computer.

This list is incomplete, but these commands should get you started using `ftp` or similar text-mode tools, such as `ncftp`. The next section, "FTP in Action: Transferring Files," presents a sample FTP session using some of these commands.

GUI FTP clients provide some method of accessing more-or-less the same functionality that's present in text-mode FTP clients. The GUI tools don't always label actions using precisely the same terms as text-mode clients use, though. Consider Figure 24-4, which shows the main gFTP window. You can select ASCII or binary transfers from the FTP menu item; you can perform various actions on local and remote files from the Local

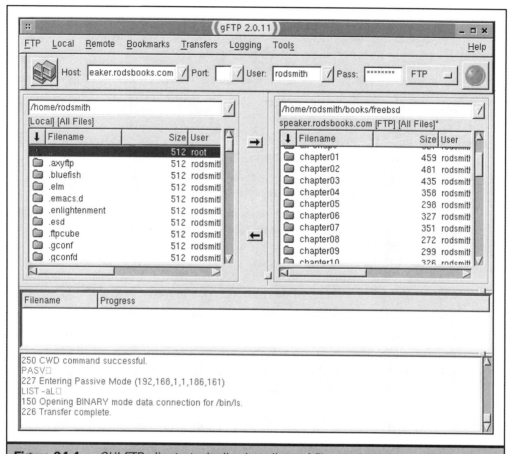

Figure 24-4. GUI FTP clients typically show lists of files on both local and remote systems in scrollable lists.

and Remote menu items, respectively; and you can select individual files for transfer by clicking them in the file lists (the list on the right is for the remote system, and is empty until you establish a connection). You can use the arrow buttons between the two lists to transfer selected files from one system to another.

FTP in Action: Transferring Files

Actually transferring files with FTP involves establishing a connection, locating the files, issuing transfer commands, and then breaking the connection. The exact details differ between programs, but the basic steps remain the same with most programs. This section describes using `ftp` and gFTP to download a binary file (`sample.tgz`) from and upload a text file (`report.txt`) to a fictitious FTP site (`ftp.threeroomco.com`).

Using ftp

Because ftp is a ubiquitous program, this section describes an FTP transfer using this program. To perform the specified transfer, follow these steps:

1. Enter the directory in which you want to store the downloaded file (sample.tgz).

2. Type **ftp ftp.threeroomco.com**. This command initiates a connection with the FTP server.

3. The remote server prompts for a username. Type your username on the remote server, or **anonymous** if you're performing an anonymous transfer.

4. The remote server prompts for a password. Type your password, or your e-mail address if you're performing an anonymous transfer.

5. Use cd to change into the directory in which sample.tgz resides. For instance, you might type **cd tarballs/samples**. If you don't know the exact directory, you may need to hunt for it by using ls to locate promising-sounding directories. Some sites provide files called index, 00index, or something similar. These files contain information on all the files on the FTP site, so you can retrieve and study these files to locate the ones in which you're interested.

6. Type **binary** to be sure ftp is set for binary file transfers.

7. Type **get sample.tgz** to retrieve the file. You should see progress information appear, followed by a summary of transfer information, such as the transfer speed and file size.

8. Use cd to change into the directory on the server in which you want to store report.txt. For instance, you might type **cd ~/uploads**.

9. Use lcd to change into the local directory in which report.txt is stored. For instance, you might type **lcd ~/reports**.

10. Type **ascii** to tell the system you want to perform end-of-line or other necessary conversions for text-only data.

11. Type **put report.txt** to transfer the file. As with the download, you should see a progress bar. This step will not work with most anonymous sites or if you don't have write permissions in the target directory on the server.

12. Type **quit** to close the connection and exit from the ftp program.

Using gFTP

The principles of using a GUI FTP client are the same as the principles of using a text-mode FTP client, but of course the details differ. GUI FTP clients also differ among themselves, although they're similar in many respects. The gFTP program is popular and typical of FreeBSD GUI FTP clients. To use it to perform the transfer of sample.tgz and report.txt, follow these steps:

1. Enter the directory in which you want to store the downloaded file (`sample.tgz`).

2. Type **gftp** to launch gFTP. You should see a window similar to the one shown in Figure 24-4, but some of the fields will be empty, including the file list on the right.

3. Type **ftp.threeroomco.com** in the Host field, your username or **anonymous** in the User field, and your password or e-mail address in the Pass field, and then press ENTER. The file list on the right should fill with whatever files are in the default directory on the server.

4. Use the file list on the right to browse to the directory in which `sample.tgz` resides. You can double-click the parent directory (`..`) entry at the top of the list or the directory name box above the list to move into parent directories, or double click a subdirectory name to move into the subdirectory.

5. Click the FTP menu option to see the menu, and check that the FTP | Binary menu option is selected. If it's not, select it.

6. Click the `sample.tgz` filename in the directory list on the right.

7. Click the arrow button that points to the left. This action transfers the file. You should see a summary of operations, including transfer speed and file size, in the bottom pane of Figure 24-4.

8. Use the file listing panes to change into the directory on the client in which `report.txt` resides, and on the server into which you want to transfer the file. Select FTP | Ascii to enable text-mode transfers that adjust the character set for the target system.

9. Click the `report.txt` file in the left pane.

10. Click the right arrow button between the two file list panes. This action transfers the file. As with Step 7, you should see summary information about the transfer in the bottom pane.

11. Select FTP | Quit or press CTRL-Q to exit from gFTP.

File Sharing Clients

As described in Chapter 18, file transfer servers such as FTP and file sharing servers such as the Network File System (NFS) server and Samba are very similar. Their clients tend to differ more, but this isn't always the case. In particular, a Samba client known as `smbclient` is very similar to `ftp` in operation. Most file sharing clients, though, are components of the OS itself. These clients enable ordinary programs to treat the file server as if it were a local hard disk.

Using NFS Exports

In a network that's dominated by UNIX-like systems, NFS is likely to be in common use. FreeBSD can easily access such NFS servers, providing FreeBSD users with access to the files on the NFS servers.

You can mount an NFS export (that is, the directory that the server makes available) much as you mount a local partition or removable disk. For testing purposes or if you don't want to make the export available at all times, you can use the mount command:

```
# mount -t nfs nfsserver:/export-name /mount/point
```

In this command, *nfsserver* is the NFS server's hostname, *export-name* is the name of the export (that is, its directory name), and */mount/point* is the local directory where you want to mount the export. You can add more standard mount options to this command, such as -r to perform a read-only mount. Chapter 7 describes the mount command in more detail.

Another way to mount an NFS export is to use the mount_nfs command. This command works much like mount, but it gives more direct access to NFS-specific options. The mount_nfs man page describes these options in detail, but the more important options are

- **-2** Normally, FreeBSD tries to use NFS version 3 and then falls back to version 2 if version 3 doesn't work. This option forces use of version 2 of the NFS protocol, which may be faster or less trouble-prone with some version 2 NFS servers.

- **-3** This option forces use of NFS version 3. You might use this option if some NFS version 3 feature is so important that you'd rather not get a connection than do without that feature.

- **-D *threshold*** This option tells FreeBSD to deliver an error message after *threshold* number of timeouts when attempting to contact the server. This option can be useful if the network connection or server isn't 100 percent reliable because it can help prevent local programs from hanging when waiting for file access.

- **-R *retries*** This option is much like the -D *threshold* option in many respects, but -R *retries* sets the number of times FreeBSD will retry an operation before reporting problems.

- **-T** NFS normally uses UDP packets rather than TCP packets. This option, which is useful mainly with other FreeBSD servers, uses TCP rather than UDP. It's most useful when connecting to an NFS server that's on another network segment than the client because it can improve reliability under such circumstances.

- **-U** This option is the opposite of -T; it forces the use of UDP even when the two sides would otherwise negotiate a TCP connection.

- **-i** This option makes the mount *interruptible*, which means that calling programs receive an error message if an operation times out.

- **-s** This option creates a *soft mount*, meaning that filesystem operations will return errors to the calling program after `retries` errors (as set with -R `retries`).

If you try to mount an NFS export and can't, it's possible that the NFS server hasn't been configured to give your FreeBSD client system access to the export. You should contact the server's administrator to resolve this issue. If you're in charge of both systems, consult Chapter 18 for information on configuring a FreeBSD NFS server, or consult documentation appropriate to the server's OS if it's not FreeBSD.

Once you've tested an NFS mount, you may want to make it permanently available. You can do so by adding an entry to /etc/fstab. This entry resembles the entries for local partitions, but you must specify the NFS server's name and export name just as with mount. For instance, the following /etc/fstab line mounts the /opt/Office NFS export from nfsserv on the local computer's /opt/OpenOffice.org directory:

```
nfsserv:/opt/Office   /opt/OpenOffice.org  nfs  r  0  0
```

This line makes the export available in read-only form (even if it was exported with read/write permissions). When you reboot or type **mount -a**, FreeBSD mounts the export. You could then run programs from the export, read data files from it, and so on, much as if the export were a local directory.

Using SMB/CIFS Shares

The *Server Message Block (SMB)*, also known as the *Common Internet File System (CIFS)* is the file-sharing protocol used natively by Microsoft Windows and OS/2. Chapter 18 describes a FreeBSD server package for SMB/CIFS: Samba. This package enables a FreeBSD system to function as a server to Windows clients. Sometimes, though, you may need to work in the opposite direction—access Windows or Samba shares from FreeBSD. Two tools are available to facilitate this operation: smbclient and mount_smbfs. The former is part of the Samba package and provides a user interface and features very similar to that of ftp, and the latter comes with the base FreeBSD system and enables mounting an SMB/CIFS share much as mount_nfs enables mounting an NFS export.

Using smbclient

As a first approximation, you can think of smbclient as being like ftp. You can use it in the same way, in terms of its basic operation and commands. This fact is illustrated by the following exchange:

```
$ smbclient //smbserver/sjones
added interface ip=192.168.1.6 bcast=192.168.1.255 nmask=255.255.255.0
Password:
Domain=[RINGWORLD] OS=[Unix] Server=[Samba 2.2.1a]
smb: \> get license.txt
getting file license.txt of size 356 as license.txt (38.6 kb/s) ⏎
(average 38.6 kb/s)
smb: \> quit
```

The server specification passed to smbclient on the command line
(//smbserver/sjones in the preceding example) contains two parts: the server name (smbserver) and a share name (sjones). The latter is often the same as a username when accessing a Samba server, as described in Chapter 18. Once you've entered a password (which doesn't echo to the screen), you can use common ftp commands, such as cd, lcd, get, put, dir, and help. Some commands differ from those used in ftp, but the basics are very similar.

There are a few parameters you can pass to smbclient after the service name (the machine name and share name) to modify how it operates. The more important of these are

- **password** You can type the password on the command line, but this is usually inadvisable because it echoes the password to the screen, stores it in your command history, and makes it available from a ps command. This feature is useful if you're writing a script to perform automated transfers, though.

- **-s smb.conf** smbclient retrieves many configuration options from the same smb.conf file that controls the Samba server. This file is normally /usr/local/etc/smb.conf in FreeBSD, but you can specify another file with this option, if you prefer.

- **-U username** Ordinarily, smbclient uses your username as the username on the remote system. You can override this setting by passing the –U username command-line option.

- **-I ip-address** Ordinarily, smbclient contacts the computer whose NetBIOS name you specify in the service name. Sometimes this name resolution doesn't work properly, though. In such cases, you can tell smbclient to ignore the NetBIOS name you provided and connect to the computer with the specified IP address.

- **-W workgroup** NetBIOS organizes computers into groups called *workgroups* or *domains*. The smb.conf file specifies a workgroup for your system, but on occasion you may need to override this setting to connect to a computer, such as when the server is in a workgroup other than your local one and is configured to accept connections only from systems on its own local workgroup. You can reset your claimed workgroup with this option.

Overall, smbclient is a good tool if you need to quickly transfer a few files between systems. Because Windows computers often run SMB/CIFS servers for peer-to-peer networking, smbclient enables you to perform file transfers to and from such computers as if they were running FTP servers, without the hassle of installing and configuring FTP servers on the Windows systems. You might even want to use smbclient and Samba instead of FTP between FreeBSD or other UNIX-like systems because SMB/CIFS supports the use of encrypted passwords, which can be more secure than FTP's unencrypted passwords. smbclient is not, however, a full file-sharing client. To gain access to all of the file-sharing features of SMB/CIFS, such as enabling arbitrary programs to directly read and write files on the server, you need another tool: mount_smbfs.

Using mount_smbfs

The mount_smbfs command enables the use of an SMB/CIFS share as if it were a local partition or removable disk. This command's simplified syntax is

```
mount_smbfs [-I host] [-N] [-W workgroup] [-f mode] [-d mode] ⏎
[-u uid] [-g gid] //user@server/share /mount/point
```

The meanings of the options are as follows:

- **-I *host***   This option is similar to the -I option in smbclient, but it takes either an IP address or a hostname as an argument.

- **-N**   Ordinarily, mount_smbfs asks for a password. You can have it look for the password in the user's ~/.nsmbrc file (described shortly) with this option.

- **-W *workgroup***   You may need to specify a workgroup, as described earlier, in "Using smbclient."

- **-f *mode***   SMB/CIFS doesn't support UNIX-style ownership or permissions. This option tells FreeBSD what permissions to assign to files. For instance, -f 0644 assigns 0644 (-rw-r--r--) permissions to all files on the share.

- **-d *mode***   This option works just like -f *mode*, but it applies to directories rather than files.

- **-u *uid***   You can specify the user ID (UID) to be assigned to all the files in the SMB/CIFS share with this option. For instance, -u 1002 makes UID 1002 the owner of all the files in the share. The default is the owner of the mount point directory.

- **-g *gid***   This option works just like -u *uid*, except that it sets the group ID (GID) to be assigned to all the files on the share.

- ■ **//user@server/share** This required option specifies the username to be used to access the share (*user*), the NetBIOS name of the server (*server*), and the share name on the server (*share*).

- ■ **/mount/point** This option is the local mount point to be used to hold the share's files.

As an example, consider the following command:

```
# mount_smbfs -u 65534 -f 0444 -d 0555 //sjones@smbserver/images ⤶
/usr/local/graphics
```

This command mounts the `images` share from `smbserver`, using the `sjones` account, to `/usr/local/graphics`. Files will be owned by `nobody` (who has UID 65534) and be readable to all users (0444 permissions on files and 0555 on directories), but writeable to none.

After you issue the `mount_smbfs` command, you'll be asked for a password, unless you include the -N option. To use this option, you need a `/usr/local/etc/nsmb.conf` file or a `~/.nsmbrc` file in the home directory of the user who runs `mount_smbfs` (normally `root`). This file contains information in groups according to the server. The basic information for mounting the share without a password takes the following form:

```
[servername:username:sharename]
password=pass
```

You can add other options, as well. For instance a `workgroup=wgname` line sets the workgroup, so you can omit the -W command-line option. You can set the IP address of the server with the `addr=ip-address` option.

Caution *If you store passwords in the nsmb.conf or .nsmbrc file, those passwords are potentially accessible to others. Be sure to set 0600 permissions on the file to prevent others from reading it. In the case of nsmb.conf, the file should be owned by root; for .nsmbrc, by the user who runs the mount_smbfs command.*

Ordinarily, only `root` may use `mount_smbfs`. If you want to give ordinary users the ability to mount SMB/CIFS shares, you can make the `mount_smbfs` program SUID `root`, as described in Chapter 8:

```
# chmod a+s /sbin/mount_smbfs
```

Making this change is potentially risky; if a bug exists in `mount_smbfs`, *a miscreant might be able to abuse it in unpredictable ways. Even in the absence of a bug, the ability to mount SMB/CIFS shares might be abused; for instance, a miscreant might mount a share over a standard FreeBSD directory, such as* `/etc`, *thus changing arbitrary security settings or files.*

When you're done using a share mounted with `mount_smbfs`, you can unmount it as you would any mounted partition or share, using `umount`:

```
# umount /usr/local/graphics
```

Remote Login Clients

Remote login clients enable you to access a remote system as if it were local. You can run programs that reside on those systems, review data files stored on those systems, and so on. Chapter 21 describes the login servers that provide this functionality on the remote systems. This section describes two common text-mode remote login clients.

 GUI remote login clients are described along with their matching servers in Chapter 21.

Using Telnet Clients

FreeBSD's Telnet client is fairly straightforward in basic operation—type **telnet** followed by the hostname or IP address to which you want to connect. If all goes well, you'll be greeted with a password prompt, and you'll then be able to log in:

```
$ telnet barsoom.threeroomco.com
Trying 192.168.1.1...
Connected to barsoom.threeroomco.com.
Escape character is '^]'.
Password:
Copyright (c) 1992-2002 The FreeBSD Project.
Copyright (c) 1979, 1980, 1983, 1986, 1988, 1989, 1991, 1992, 1993, 1994
        The Regents of the University of California. All rights reserved

FreeBSD 5.0-DP1 (GENERIC) #0: Sun Apr  7 02:51:42 GMT 2002
bash-2.05$
```

This command attempts to connect to `barsoom.threeroomco.com`'s Telnet server. By default, FreeBSD's `telnet` sends your username transparently to the Telnet server, so you don't need to type it, just your password (which doesn't echo to the screen). If you need to log in as some other user, you can pass your username with the `-l username` option.

After logging in, you can run most text-mode programs—editors, mail readers, compilers, and so on. You can even use su to acquire superuser privileges and administer the system via sysinstall or other text-mode tools. As described in Chapter 21, you can type a few commands and then launch X-based programs from your Telnet login.

Caution *Although you can use su to gain superuser privileges from a Telnet login, doing so is almost always unwise. Telnet doesn't encrypt passwords by default, so if a miscreant has installed a sniffer on your network, using Telnet for system administration exposes your root password for the miscreant to steal. It's better to use SSH to perform remote system administration.*

Because Telnet sends all data, including your password, in an unencrypted form, Telnet is best reserved for use on small isolated networks that are used by few people, such as residential networks that aren't connected to the Internet. On larger networks or when traffic passes over the Internet, it's better to use SSH for remote text-based access.

Using SSH Clients

SSH works much like Telnet, but it provides encryption as a standard part of the protocol. This encryption applies to the username, password, and all data sent over the connection. Like FreeBSD's telnet, the ssh client program sends your username automatically, so you don't need to specify your username on the remote system when making a connection. An SSH login looks like this:

```
$ ssh barsoom.threeroomco.com
The authenticity of host 'barsoom.threeroomco.com (192.168.1.6)'
can't be established.
RSA1 key fingerprint is 48:17:8e:1c:da:ab:81:fe:01:76:bc:a4:f1:90:f5:00.
Are you sure you want to continue connecting (yes/no)? yes
Warning: Permanently added 'barsoom.threeroomco.com' (RSA1) to the list
of known hosts.
jcarter@barsoom.threeroomco.com's password:
Last login: Mon Jun  3 00:26:45 2002 from speaker
Copyright (c) 1980, 1983, 1986, 1988, 1990, 1991, 1993, 1994
        The Regents of the University of California.  All rights reserved
FreeBSD 5.0-DP1 (GENERIC) #0: Sun Apr  7 02:51:42 GMT 2002
bash-2.05$
```

This output is unusually verbose because it's a first connection. The SSH client stores cryptographic identifiers for all the servers to which it has connected in the .ssh/known_hosts and .ssh/known_hosts2 files in the user's home directory. If information on the server can't be found or doesn't match what's already stored, ssh notifies you of that fact and asks for confirmation before it proceeds. This practice is designed to protect against attacks such as a miscreant taking over the IP address of a known SSH server in order to intercept passwords. If you approve the connection or if the server's identity is automatically confirmed, ssh asks for your password, and if that checks out, you're logged in.

At this point, you can do just about anything you can do from a Telnet login—run text-based programs, redirect X to use your local display, and so on. As described in Chapter 21, SSH also supports *tunneling* other protocols—that is, intercepting data that ordinarily use non-SSH protocols and ports and sending the data through the SSH connection, thus encrypting otherwise nonencrypted data. One of the most common uses of tunneling is to tunnel X connections. You can activate this feature by using the -X option on the ssh command line. Alternatively, you can add the following line to /etc/ssh/ssh_config to accomplish the task:

```
ForwardX11 yes
```

Of course, the server must also be configured to forward X connections, as described in Chapter 21. The /etc/ssh/ssh_config file also supports setting various other options, but the standard FreeBSD configuration leaves all options set at their defaults.

Summary

Network clients running on a FreeBSD workstation are very important in many environments. Some clients, such as mail readers and web browsers, help provide connectivity to the outside world, enabling collaboration with colleagues, communication with friends and family, online research, and so on. Other tools, such as file sharing clients, are more often used on local networks, and contribute to office productivity or network efficiency by enabling the sharing of resources. Still other tools, such as FTP clients and remote login clients, can be used exclusively on a local network or more broadly, depending upon your needs. In most cases, FreeBSD offers a choice of network client programs, thus meeting many peoples' needs and preferences.

The Complete Reference

FreeBSD

Chapter 25

Office Tools

Many workstations exist solely to perform a handful of common tasks—word processing, number-crunching with spreadsheets, preparing presentations, and preparing charts or other business graphics. These tasks are important enough that programs to handle them are commonly bundled together in a package known as an *office suite*. In the Windows world, the most common office suite is Microsoft Office, but this package isn't available for FreeBSD. This chapter describes office tools available for FreeBSD, beginning with an overview of the available tools, moving on to a summary of common features and quirks of FreeBSD office tools, and concluding with an example session with one of the most powerful FreeBSD office tools, OpenOffice.org. Of course, office suites are complex enough that this chapter can't do more than introduce these programs. For more information, consult the documentation for the programs in question.

Office Tools Available for FreeBSD

There are quite a few office programs available for FreeBSD. Three suites of programs are popular: GNOME Office, KOffice, and OpenOffice.org. Programs unaffiliated with a particular suite are also available, and you may be able to use these separate programs as effectively as you might use a suite.

GNOME Office

GNOME Office was not conceived as a single unified set of programs; rather, the GNOME Office developers have assimilated programs that began life as independent packages. GNOME Office components use certain common libraries, though, such as the GIMP Tool Kit (GTK+), which was originally developed as the GUI toolkit for the GNU Image Manipulation Program (GIMP) but which was adopted by GNOME and many other programs. Work is underway to provide data sharing and, whenever possible, integrated file formats between the GNOME Office component programs. This isn't to say that these programs make up an exclusive club or must be used as a group; you can install just one GNOME Office component and use it without other GNOME Office components, and perhaps transfer files between it and some unrelated program.

You can find a complete list of GNOME Office components at `http://www`
`.gnome.org/gnome-office/`. The list includes components in fourteen categories: spreadsheet, word processor, communications, browsing, vector graphics, raster graphics, image viewers, e-mail and groupware, plotting, diagramming, project management, finance, presentation, and database tools. Some categories include multiple programs. The most notable GNOME Office components are

- **Gnumeric** This program is a spreadsheet application. Gnumeric developers claim to have implemented 95 percent of the functions available in Microsoft Excel. The program's filename is `gnumeric`.

- **AbiWord**   This program is the GNOME Office word processor. Originally developed as a cross-platform tool, AbiWord is available for UNIX-like systems (including FreeBSD, naturally), Windows, and BeOS. The program's filename is `AbiWord` (with `abiword` as a link).

- **Galeon**   The Galeon web browser, mentioned in Chapter 24, is claimed as part of GNOME Office. The program's filename is `galeon`.

- **The GIMP**   The GNU Image Manipulation Program (GIMP) is the most powerful bitmap graphics editor for FreeBSD, and it's officially part of GNOME Office. Chapter 26 covers the GIMP in more detail. The program's filename is `gimp`.

- **Dia**   This program is designed to create diagrams, such as flowcharts, circuit diagrams, and so on. Its role is roughly analogous to the Windows program Visio, but Dia is not yet as sophisticated as Visio. The program's filename is `dia`.

- **Guppi**   This program is a data plotting program—it takes data generated by other programs and creates graphs and charts from the data. As such, it's potentially quite valuable in scientific and business endeavors. The program's name is `guppi-gnumeric`.

- **Balsa**   This program is an e-mail client similar to some of the programs described in Chapter 24. The program's filename is `balsa`.

- **Evolution**   This program is the second e-mail client that's part of GNOME Office. Evolution supports far more features than does Balsa. The program's filename is `evolution`.

- **Gnucash**   Personal financial management tools have become popular among home users, and Gnucash is probably the most popular such program in the FreeBSD world. The program's filename is `gnucash`.

- **GNOME-DB**   Databases hold critical information on just about everything, and GNOME-DB is the GNOME Office tool for accessing and manipulating databases. The program's filename is `gnomedb-fe`.

- **OpenOffice.org**   The GNOME Office web site claims OpenOffice.org as a not-yet-fully-integrated component. In 2002, I prefer to view OpenOffice.org as a competing office suite, and it's presented as such later in this chapter, in "OpenOffice.org." The main program's filename is `soffice`, but subcomponents can be launched by other names, as well.

Unlike some integrated office suites, the GNOME Office tools are installed independently. Most of them are available as FreeBSD packages or ports in the `gnome` area. Notable exceptions include AbiWord, available from the `editors` area; Sketch, available from the `graphics` area; and Guppi, available from the `math` area.

Strong points of GNOME Office include the GIMP, which is frequently favorably compared to Adobe Photoshop; Gnucash, which approaches Quicken in functionality; Gnumeric, which is a very popular FreeBSD spreadsheet; and (to the extent that it really is a GNOME Office component) OpenOffice.org, which is the closest FreeBSD product to a full replacement for Microsoft Office. Some other programs, such as AbiWord, although they're functional, lack the range of features that users accustomed to Windows applications expect. Of course, this isn't always a bad thing; the UNIX philosophy has traditionally been one of combining many small programs to provide the functionality that's available in larger programs in the Windows world. Furthermore, big office packages can be criticized for their enormous resource requirements.

KOffice

KOffice is to the K Desktop Environment (KDE) what GNOME Office is to GNOME. KOffice, though, was designed from the ground up as KDE's office suite, as opposed to GNOME Office, which has grown from the seeds of many independent projects. The main KOffice web site is http://www.koffice.org, and you can find further information on the project there.

KOffice includes fewer components and component types than does GNOME Office, but the most important component types are represented in both suites. KOffice comprises the following programs:

- ■ **KWord**   This program is the KOffice word processor. KWord is a frame-based word processor that provides more features than AbiWord does.

- ■ **KSpread**   This program is the KOffice spreadsheet. It doesn't implement as many functions as Microsoft Excel or Gnumeric, but it's basically a sound product.

- ■ **KPresenter**   This program handles presentations. An online sample of KPresenter presentations is available at http://www.kde.org/kdeslides/.

- ■ **KVivio**   This program is a flowcharting program similar to the Windows program Visio or GNOME Office's Dia. KVivio provides a plug-in scripting system, which enables you to extend the program in various ways. For instance, you could use this facility to feed KVivio C++ header files to have it generate a class map.

- ■ **Kontour**   Vector drawing programs are common in office suites, and Kontour is KOffice's entry to this field.

- ■ **Krita**   This program is KOffice's bitmap graphics editing program. The KOffice web page compares the program to the GIMP and Adobe Photoshop, but in 2002, Krita is still very new and doesn't come close to matching the GIMP's or Photoshop's features.

- ■ **Kugar**   This program helps automate the creation of business reports. It's the only KOffice component that has no equivalent in GNOME Office.

- ■ **KChart**   This program is another graphics tool, but it generates charts, graphs, and so on from data files.

> **Note**
>
> *Although KOffice has fewer components than does GNOME Office, this fact is somewhat misleading because some GNOME Office applications have KDE counterparts that are not officially part of KOffice. For instance, KMail and Konqueror are KDE's mail reader and web browser, respectively. They aren't part of KOffice, unlike GNOME's equivalents, Balsa and Galeon.*

On the whole, KOffice components are good enough for use in many environments. They lack some of the more advanced features found in some competing programs. For instance, KWord lacks revision tracking and a grammar checker. The KOffice developers aim to provide all the features that users accustomed to Microsoft Windows office suites expect, though, so such shortfalls are likely to shrink in time.

OpenOffice.org

OpenOffice.org (http://www.openoffice.org) is the open-source cousin to Sun's (http://www.sun.com) StarOffice suite. This relationship is very similar to the one between the open-source Mozilla and the commercial Netscape Navigator. In mid-2002, StarOffice 6.0 is equivalent to OpenOffice.org 1.0. Sun supports StarOffice on Windows, Solaris, and Linux, but not on FreeBSD; however, StarOffice can run on FreeBSD using Linux support libraries, as described in Chapter 4. Because OpenOffice.org is open source, developers have been working on compiling the program on FreeBSD, and in 2002, the program now runs natively on FreeBSD 4.6 and later. As of mid-2002, though, the FreeBSD-native versions of OpenOffice.org tend to be very sensitive. If you try OpenOffice.org and find it's unstable or behaves oddly, you may want to try the Linux version running with FreeBSD's Linux support tools.

> **Note**
>
> *The OpenOffice.org developers originally wanted to call their program OpenOffice, but that name is trademarked and belongs to another program. Thus, the developers added the .org to the name.*

Of the three major office suites for FreeBSD, OpenOffice.org is the one that most closely resembles Microsoft Office. OpenOffice.org also has the best Microsoft Office import and export filters, as described in more detail in the upcoming section "File Import and Export." OpenOffice.org components are

- **Writer** As you've no doubt guessed by the name, this program is the OpenOffice.org word processor. It is arguably the most sophisticated word processor available for FreeBSD.
- **Calc** This program is the OpenOffice.org spreadsheet. Like Writer, it's very similar to its Microsoft Office counterpart, Excel, although it's not an exact clone.
- **Draw** Like other office suites, OpenOffice.org includes a graphics tool. In OpenOffice.org, only a vector graphics tool is available.
- **Impress** This program is the OpenOffice.org presentation manager.

StarOffice versions prior to 6.0 included many additional components and used a single executable program for everything. These facts made StarOffice quite sluggish, particularly when starting up. With StarOffice 6.0 and OpenOffice.org 1.0, though, the component count has been trimmed to enable the developers to focus on the suite's core functionality. The programs also start more quickly than did earlier versions. (StarOffice's and OpenOffice.org's programs still start more slowly than many competing programs, though.)

If you want to transition an office of workers who are familiar with Microsoft Office to FreeBSD, using OpenOffice.org can be an important part of this strategy because doing so can minimize confusion and training costs. The OpenOffice.org components, although not identical to Microsoft Office components, are similar enough that users will have to relearn less with OpenOffice.org than with other suites. The fact that the entire suite is available for Windows can also be an important consideration if you operate a mixed-OS environment.

Miscellaneous Tools

Not all office tools fit into the major suites. You can browse the `sysinstall` package listings or the `/usr/ports` subdirectories to learn what else is available. Some highlights include the following:

- **LaTeX**   This package is a publishing tool that doesn't rely upon the what-you-see-is-what-you-get (WYSIWYG) model used by most word processors. To use LaTeX, you edit a file in a text editor and insert formatting commands similar to the HTML tags described in Chapter 20. You then run the file through LaTeX, which creates output in various formats, such as PostScript for printing. LaTeX is popular in certain technical and scientific circles because of its excellent handling of equations.

- **LyX**   This program is a GUI front-end to LaTeX. LyX provides a set of menus similar to those in word processors, but LyX isn't a WYSIWYG program. Nonetheless, it can help users unfamiliar with LaTeX harness its power. You can learn more at `http://www.lyx.org`.

Note   *A modified version of LyX, KLyX, uses the Qt widget set upon which KDE is built. KLyX hasn't been maintained, though, so LyX is the preferred form of this program.*

- **abs**   This program is an X-based spreadsheet that's independent of any office suite. Its main web page is `http://www.ping.be/bertin/abs.shtml`.

- **Oleo**   This program is the GNU project's official spreadsheet. It runs as both a text-mode and an X-based program, and is simpler than Gnumeric.

Numerous tools also exist that fall into other office suite application categories, such as drawing or charting programs, mail programs, and so on. Some of these programs are described in other chapters of this book, but you may have to perform a web search to find others.

 If you're looking for a specific type of program, go to http://www.sourceforge.net and enter the program type in the search box. Not all open source projects register with Sourceforge, but many do, so chances are you'll find something.

You can also mix and match components from full suites. For instance, you might prefer KOffice's KWord to GNOME Office's AbiWord, but prefer GNOME Office's Gnumeric to KOffice's KSpread. If so, you can use KWord along with Gnumeric. There are problems with such an approach, though. The fact that different projects use different development toolkits means that they differ in look and feel, and may consume more memory in total when run. File formats may not be compatible, or you may need to resort to using a third-party file format to exchange data between components. (Even within an office package, though, file formats aren't always completely compatible. For instance, Gnumeric can't import AbiWord files.) Most office suites are installed in an all-or-none way, so using components from multiple suites may require a substantial investment of disk space. GNOME Office is a notable exception to this rule; you install each of its components independently.

FreeBSD Office Tool Quirks

If you're used to office suites in Windows, you may find some aspects of these tools under FreeBSD confusing. This section describes some of the peculiarities and problems you're likely to encounter, along with some of the workarounds and solutions.

Font Handling

One of the biggest problems with text-intensive FreeBSD programs, such as word processors, is that X's font model is primitive by modern GUI standards. X's font system also doesn't integrate well with the printing system, which further complicates matters. For instance, suppose you've installed a font called Oranda in X, as described in Chapter 13. A word processor can then display text in Oranda. Such a capability is plenty for many X-based programs; however, a word processor's needs go further. Most obviously, a word processor must be able to print in the font it displays on-screen. X was designed to deliver fonts as a bitmap, though, and the FreeBSD printing system doesn't tell the program the resolution of the printer, which means that the application can't know what size font bitmap to ask the X server to deliver for printing. X's font-handling shortfalls go further than coordinating the screen and printer fonts, though. To create good-looking text, a word processor needs to be able to precisely control the spacing between letters, but X doesn't give the word processor the data it needs to be able to do this intelligently.

For all of these reasons, office suites and word processors typically provide some unique way of handling fonts. Options include, but are not limited to:

- **Word processor font rendering**   Some programs, such as OpenOffice.org, provide font rendering mechanisms that are independent of X. Thus, you must install your fonts in the word processor independently of X. This approach gives the word processor direct access to the font for delivery to the printer, but requires the word processor to have its own font rendering code for on-screen display.

- **Linking screen and printer fonts**   The word processor may use X to display fonts on-screen and tie those fonts to standard PostScript printer fonts or to font files installed separately in the word processor. AbiWord is one program that uses this approach.

- **Decoupling screen and printer fonts**   LaTeX and LyX both ignore the problem; they don't claim to be WYSIWYG, and so need not display fonts on screen as they'll print. Fonts must still be installed in the program, though.

- **Using an expanded font server**   A commercial program, FontTastic, provides all the features of a normal font server, as described in Chapter 22, but also provides tools designed to help a program integrate X and printer font handling. No major FreeBSD word processor uses this approach, although a couple of commercial suites for Linux (ApplixWare and WordPerfect Office 2000) have followed this route.

If you're dissatisfied with the font selection or quality in your word processor or other text-intensive program, you should consult its documentation or do a web search on your program's name and a word such as *font*. You can perform a similar search at Google Groups, `http://groups.google.com`, to find recent Usenet news group discussions of the topic. Chances are you'll find some useful information on how to install fonts in such a way that you can use them in your program.

Printing

Most FreeBSD office programs rely upon printers having been configured, as described in Chapter 9. These programs typically read the `/etc/printcap` file to determine what printers are available, and present a print dialog box that enables you to choose which of the installed printers you can use. Such dialog boxes are very similar to those used on Windows or Mac OS computers, and so should pose no problems for users familiar with those OSs. Some applications, though, require you to type a printer's name. For instance, Figure 25-1 shows the AbiWord print dialog box. If the user doesn't type a printer name, the print job goes to the default printer. Figure 25-1 illustrates how to direct the job to a specific printer: add `-Pprintername` to the print command, where `printername` is the print queue name in `/etc/printcap`.

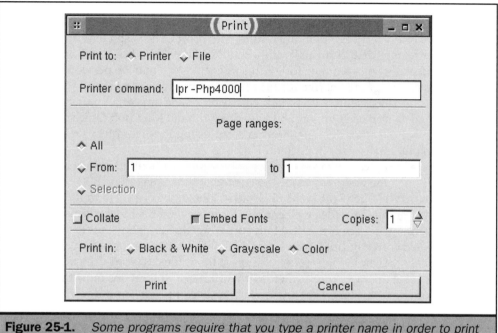

Figure 25-1.   *Some programs require that you type a printer name in order to print to anything but the default printer.*

Some programs provide additional "printer" destinations. The ability to print to a disk file is quite common, for instance. In Figure 25-1, this task can be accomplished by selecting File rather than Printer in the Print To field. The resulting file is usually a PostScript file, so you can manually print it to a PostScript printer, use a PostScript file viewer such as Ghostview, or send it to another system from which it can be printed or viewed. Many office programs now offer the ability to create Adobe Portable Document Format (PDF) files. A few programs support a fax output option, which can be handy if you've got a fax modem. If your preferred program doesn't have such an option, you can add one in the printing system by using a program such as Gfax, which is part of the GNOME Office suite. Gfax sets up a printer queue that in fact calls appropriate tools to ask for a fax number and then send the document as a fax.

Most FreeBSD programs assume that the printer is a PostScript model. As described in Chapter 9, you can configure FreeBSD to convert a PostScript print job generated by an application into a format suitable for most printer models. Thus, the PostScript assumption isn't a problem. A few programs, though, support non-PostScript output. Such programs may produce superior output on some printers when set to use the printers' native drivers, but you'll need to create a "raw" print queue, as described in Chapter 9, so that the print queue doesn't attempt to treat the program's output as PostScript, thus corrupting it.

File Import and Export

Because the world's most popular office suite, Microsoft Office, isn't available for FreeBSD, one feature that's unusually important for FreeBSD office suites is the ability to import and export files suitable for Microsoft Office. You may be perfectly happy to use your chosen programs' native formats for most purposes, but if and when you need to exchange documents with others, Microsoft Office import/export capability is essential. You may also need import ability to deal with old Microsoft Office documents. The ability to handle other document formats, including those for other FreeBSD office suites, is also potentially very important.

As a general rule, word processing files are the most difficult to import and export properly. Although the word processors associated with the major FreeBSD office suites all purport to handle Microsoft Word files, only OpenOffice.org 1.0 (and its near-twin, StarOffice 6.0) handle these files well enough for more than the most basic documents. For example, in my experience with Microsoft Word documents, AbiWord usually retrieves the text correctly, but loses a great deal of formatting information. AbiWord also occasionally crashes when trying to import these files. KWord does better; I've never seen it crash on importing a Microsoft Word file, and it retains most formatting, but it loses or corrupts some characters, such as bullet points, and doesn't retrieve embedded graphics. OpenOffice.org's Writer, by contrast, retrieves files and reproduces almost all aspects of the files' formatting, including fonts, bullet points, revision marks, and graphics. Even OpenOffice.org isn't perfect, though. Particularly when exchanging a file back and forth between OpenOffice.org and Microsoft Word, formatting oddities tend to creep in, such as altered indents on bulleted lists. Imports and exports of other word processor formats, such as Corel WordPerfect or Lotus WordPro, are likely to be imperfect in any of the FreeBSD office suites, but details differ from one product to another.

Overall, if you need perfect word processor file import/export facilities, a FreeBSD product won't work—unless of course the product that created the files can run under FreeBSD. You can run the Linux version of WordPerfect 8 under FreeBSD, for instance, or possibly even run Microsoft Office under WINE, as described in Chapter 4. If you only need very good import/export facilities, particularly for Microsoft Word documents, you may be able to use OpenOffice.org to good effect. The import/export filters on AbiWord and KWord are best applied to simple documents or to recover text as a last resort.

Tip	*If you know you'll need to exchange a document, try saving it in the creating word processor in several formats. For instance, save a Microsoft Word document in Microsoft Word format, in Rich Text Format (RTF), and as plain text. If one import filter fails on the reading word processor, another might have better luck.*

Fortunately, import and export of spreadsheets tends to proceed more smoothly than such operations on word processing documents. Gnumeric and KSpread can both import and export most Microsoft Excel spreadsheets. One potential complication arises when the importing program doesn't support a function used in a given file. In such cases, results may be unpredictable.

Bitmap graphics formats are very well standardized; most graphics programs support file formats such as the Tagged Image File Format (TIFF), the Joint Photographic Experts Group (JPEG), and the Portable Network Graphics (PNG) formats. Thus, loading and saving such files is seldom a problem. Vector graphics file formats, as used by drawing programs, graphing programs, and charting programs, are seldom so portable. Encapsulated PostScript (EPS) is one common file format for exchanging files for such programs, but most programs require their own native formats for full functionality.

Other programs may or may not support file import and export. When the program does support these operations, they may or may not work well. Consult the program's documentation for details. Running some test imports and exports is worthwhile when you need such functionality.

Office Tool Example: OpenOffice.org

As an example of an office suite in action, this section describes the use of OpenOffice.org. Some of the actions described here should be familiar if you're used to office products on other platforms, but others illustrate unusual FreeBSD features, such as font handling. Many details differ between office products, so this section provides only a brief overview. To learn more about your chosen office products, you should consult the programs' documentation.

 As of late 2002, OpenOffice.org is best run in its Linux form, using FreeBSD's Linux support tools, as described in Chapter 4. Chances are good that official and stable FreeBSD OpenOffice.org packages will be available by the time you read this book, though.

Configuring Fonts and Printers

OpenOffice.org uses a utility called `spadmin`, which resides in the `program` subdirectory of the OpenOffice.org installation directory, to manage its font and printer configurations. You may not need to run this program, but if your printers don't appear as options when you try to print or if you want to add fonts, this is the program to use. To launch it, type its name (complete with path, if the `program` subdirectory isn't on your path). The result should resemble Figure 25-2.

 When you first launch `spadmin`, its printer list will most likely be incomplete. OpenOffice.org should detect your regular printers, as listed in `/etc/printcap`, and add them to the available printer list when you run a regular OpenOffice.org program. You may also need to use `spadmin` to tell OpenOffice.org to treat a printer as something other than a generic PostScript model.

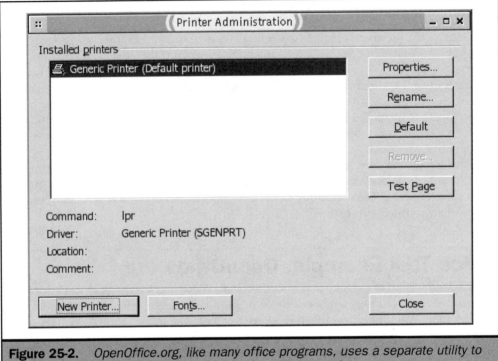

Figure 25-2. *OpenOffice.org, like many office programs, uses a separate utility to help configure certain aspects of its operation.*

Adding Printers

If you need to configure a printer that's not detected automatically or if you want to tell OpenOffice.org to treat a printer as something other than a standard PostScript printer, follow these steps:

1. Click the New Printer button in the Printer Administration dialog box (Figure 25-2). The result is a series of dialog boxes that guide you through the process. The first of these dialog boxes asks you what type of device you want to add— a regular printer, a fax device, or a PDF converter.

2. Click the Add a Printer option and then click Next. The spadmin tool presents a list of printers, most of which are specific PostScript models, but some of which aren't.

3. Select your printer or a compatible model and then click Next. The system responds by displaying a list of commands you can use to print to the printer, as shown here.

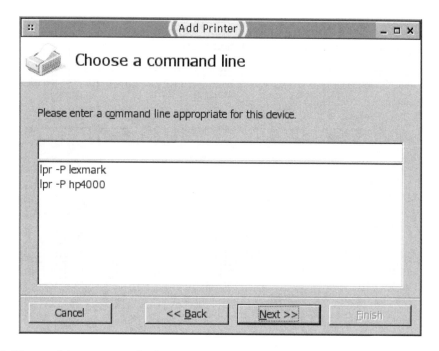

4. If one of the commands shown is appropriate for printing to your printer, select it. If not, type the command in the field above the list of commands. Click Next when you're done.

5. The system asks for a name for the printer. Type a name and click Finish. The printer should appear in the Installed Printers list (Figure 25-2).

At this point, the newly defined printer should be available from within OpenOffice.org when you select File | Print to print a document. (You may need to restart OpenOffice.org to see the new printer definition, though.)

Adding Fonts

Font handling varies substantially from one FreeBSD program to another, as described earlier, in "Font Handling." OpenOffice.org can use X's fonts, but it works better with TrueType or Type 1 fonts that it handles itself. OpenOffice.org can use more characters from such fonts, such as em dashes and "smart" quote marks; and the program can use *anti-aliasing* (aka *font smoothing*) on the fonts it controls to improve the legibility of text. This effect depends upon the presence of XFree86 4.x, though; if you use XFree86 3.3.x or earlier, OpenOffice.org doesn't smooth its fonts.

To add fonts to OpenOffice.org, you use the same `spadmin` tool that you use to add printers. To add fonts, follow this procedure:

1. Place fonts in some convenient directory on your FreeBSD system. This might be a mounted font CD-ROM, a temporary directory, or anywhere else.

2. In the `spadmin` Printer Administration dialog box (Figure 25-2), click Fonts. This action produces a list of installed fonts.

3. In the installed fonts list, click the Add button. This action produces an Add Fonts dialog box that displays the available fonts along with a source directory, as shown here:

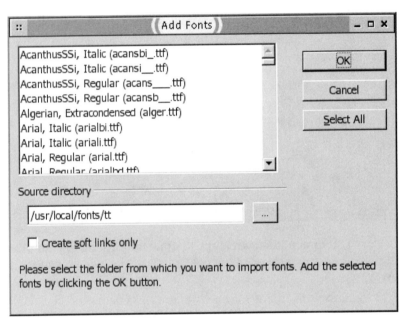

4. Click the ellipsis (...) button next to the Source Directory field to open a file selector dialog box in which you locate the font source directory you set up in Step 1. After a pause as `spadmin` parses font names, the font list should update to show the available fonts.

5. Select all the fonts you want to add by selecting them with your mouse. Holding CTRL while clicking enables you to select multiple fonts, or Shift-clicking enables you to select a range of fonts.

6. Click OK to add the fonts. You should see a progress dialog box and then the font list. Click Close to close this dialog box and return to the `spadmin` Printer Administration dialog box (Figure 25-2).

7. If any OpenOffice.org components are running, you must exit from the programs and restart them to use the new fonts.

OpenOffice.org version 1.0 supports TrueType and Type 1 fonts, which means it works with most font CD-ROMs and fonts available on web and FTP sites. Of course, some fonts work better than others. Version 1.0 of the program is somewhat inconsistent in font display if the same font is installed in OpenOffice.org and in your X server;

sometimes it uses the font delivered by the X server and other times it uses the font you install in OpenOffice.org. This fact can make installing fonts a frustrating experience.

 You can make a font available in X under a name other than the name provided in the font file by editing the font name in the `fonts.dir` *file in the X font directory. You can then install the font in OpenOffice.org, which takes the font name from the font file, thus preventing a conflict.*

Creating a Document

To create a new OpenOffice.org document, you launch the appropriate tool by typing its name, perhaps preceded by the path to the program file—**swriter** for Writer, **sdraw** for Draw, **scalc** for Calc, or **simpress** for Impress. The OpenOffice.org binaries directory also contains a number of programs to launch OpenOffice.org in various special modes. For instance, typing **sweb** launches Writer in its HTML editing mode for editing web pages, and typing **sfax** launches Writer so that it prompts you for fax information such as resolution and cover page elements, so that you can more easily create a fax.

You may find OpenOffice.org elements in your desktop environment's menus after you install the program. If so, you can launch the programs using these menu options.

 If OpenOffice.org doesn't work correctly, launch it from an xterm window. This launch method may produce error messages in the xterm window, so it's preferable to launching the program from a desktop environment's menu because the latter method doesn't display the console error messages.

When you first launch OpenOffice.org, it displays an empty document. You can begin working on it immediately. If you want to create a second new document, you can do so by selecting the document type from the File | New menu. For instance, select File | New | Spreadsheet to create a new Calc document. You can create a document of any type from within any OpenOffice.org component.

To load an existing document, select File | Open. The program displays a typical file selection dialog box. Use it to browse to the location in which the document resides, select the document, and then click Open to load it into OpenOffice.org.

 Before importing a document created by another program, save any unsaved work. Although OpenOffice.org 1.0 is fairly reliable in importing foreign documents, it's conceivable that importing a corrupt or complex document might crash the program.

Editing Text

The OpenOffice.org Writer component looks much like any other word processor, as Figure 25-3 illustrates. The program includes familiar features, such as the menu bar, buttons just below the menu bar and along the left side of the window for selecting

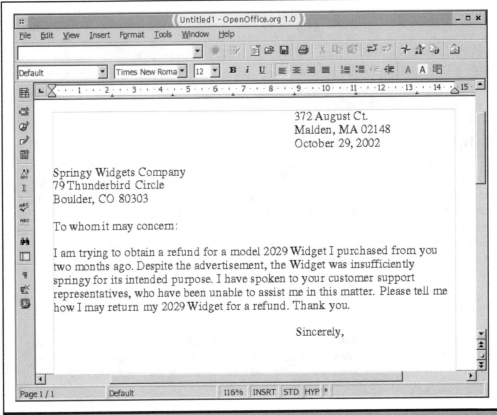

Figure 25-3.   *OpenOffice.org's word processor component should be familiar to those used to other word processors.*

options with a single mouse click, a ruler that displays tab stops and margins, a summary line at the bottom of the window that displays page numbers, and of course the main editing area.

You can edit text as you would with any other word processor or text editor—type to insert text into the document at the cursor, which is a blinking vertical bar. Click the mouse to move the cursor, or click-and-drag to select a block of text. You can format text by selecting it and clicking an appropriate icon, by selecting a menu option, or by typing a keyboard shortcut.

One quirk of OpenOffice.org Writer, at least for users in the United States, is that the word processor defaults to using metric measurements. To change the program to use English measurements, follow these steps:

1. Select Tools | Options. OpenOffice.org displays a large Options dialog box, shown here:

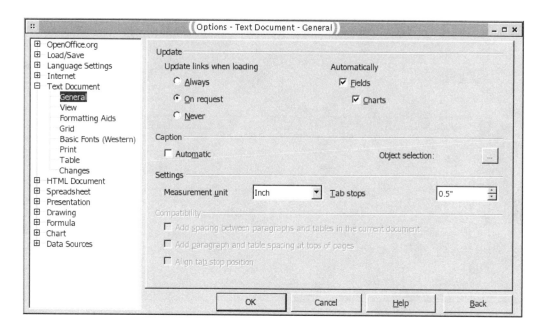

2. In the Options dialog box, select the General option in the Text Document item in the list in the left pane.

3. Select Inch in the Measurement Unit field. You may also want to adjust the Tab Stops field.

4. Click OK to activate your changes.

If you change the tab stops in the preceding procedure, the tabs won't change in any document you're currently editing; this change applies only to new documents. You can manually alter the tab stops by double-clicking the ruler.

The Options dialog box enables you to do much more than set the measurement units used by the program. You may want to peruse its options, some of which apply to OpenOffice.org components other than Writer.

Performing Computations

Just as Writer is a typical word processor in overall look and feel, Calc is a typical spreadsheet in overall look and feel. Figure 25-4 shows a Calc window. If you're familiar with other spreadsheets, you should have little trouble using Calc. If not, read on; the next few paragraphs describe its basic principles of operation.

A spreadsheet is composed of a two-dimensional matrix of *cells*, each of which contains some value. Cells may contain a string, such as *Burns, Sally*; a number, such as *78*; or a formula, such as *=B2/4*. Each cell is referred to by its vertical and horizontal

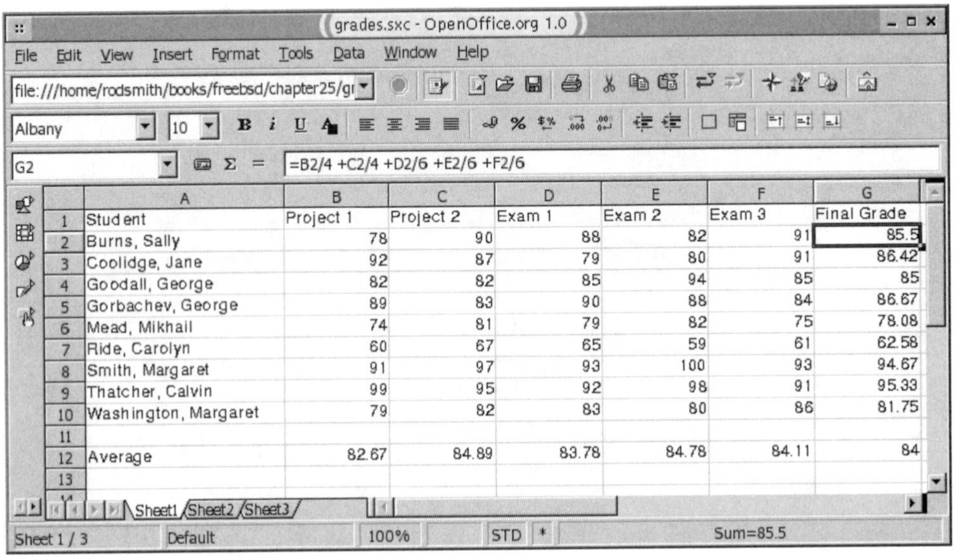

Figure 25-4. *Calc provides the usual matrix of cells and controls used by modern spreadsheets.*

indexes. Vertical indexes are numbers, and horizontal indexes are letters. Thus, *A1* refers to the top-left corner cell, *B1* refers to the next cell to the right, *B2* refers to the cell underneath B1, and so on. Index numbers appear to the top and left of the spreadsheet data area.

As Figure 25-4 illustrates, a spreadsheet is likely to contain a series of strings that identify data in particular rows or columns, or sometimes just individual cells. Many cells then contain numerical data—students' grades, in the case of Figure 25-4. You can enter both strings and numerical data by clicking on the cell in question and entering the data in the data-entry field above the main spreadsheet area. When you're done, press Enter or click the check mark icon to the left of the data-entry field. (The check mark icon appears only when you begin entering data; it doesn't appear in Figure 25-4.)

Formulas are trickier than either strings or numerical data because you must understand the formulas supported by the spreadsheet. Most formulas begin with the equal sign (=) character in order to identify them as formulas as opposed to strings. Formulas typically reference cells by name, such as *A4*, and can use common arithmetic operators, such as addition (+), subtraction (−), multiplication (*), and division (/). You can also include constants and use parentheses to group operators according to the rules of algebra. For instance, the formula =(B2 + C2)/2 takes the average of the values of the B2 and C2 cells.

Formulas can also contain predefined functions. To use a function, click the keypad icon that's two icons to the left of the data entry field, choose Insert | Function, or press F2. These actions produce the dialog box that's shown in Figure 25-5. You can double-click a function name from the list on the left of this dialog box and enter the name of the cell upon which the function is to operate in the fields provided to the right. Alternatively, if you know the function name, you can type it directly in the main window's data entry field. Some functions take a range of cells as input. You can specify a range by separating the cell names by a colon (:). For instance, *B2:G2* refers to every cell between B2 and G2, inclusive.

In some cases, you may want to copy a formula you've created in order to apply it to multiple cells. For instance, in Figure 25-4, the same formula computes every student's final grade, but the formula must reference data on the correct row. Entering that formula, with appropriate row changes, once for each student would be tedious and error-prone. Instead, you can enter the formula once, click in the appropriate cell, choose Edit | Copy or press CTRL-C, select the range of cells to which the formula should apply, and choose Edit | Paste or press CTRL-V. Calc copies the formula into all the new cells, automatically

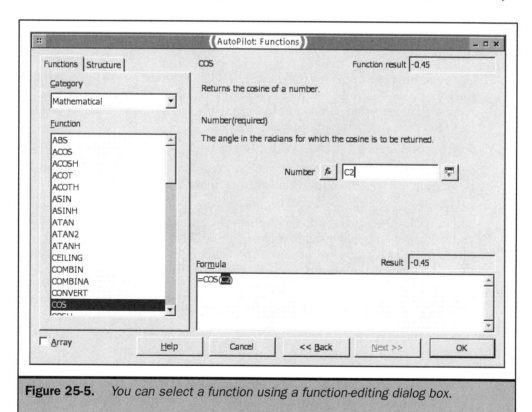

Figure 25-5.   *You can select a function using a function-editing dialog box.*

adjusting for the changed cell numbers. For instance, if you copy Figure 25-4's G2 formula to G3 through G10, each copy references the appropriate row rather than the second row. To force a copied formula to refer to a fixed cell, precede the row or column identifier with a dollar sign ($). For instance, B2 refers to B2 even if the formula in which it's contained is copied to another cell.

Creating Graphics

OpenOffice.org's Draw component can be used to create diagrams, charts, drawings, and so on. It's typically used to create graphics that aren't tied to specific data, such as a flowchart to outline a procedure or a diagram to illustrate a concept. For instance, Figure 25-6 shows Draw with a simple graphic illustrating the path taken by the Apollo spacecraft.

Tip   *If you need to create a chart or graph based on data, you can insert a chart into a Calc spreadsheet and have the chart display data graphically within the spreadsheet.*

The icons along the left side of the Draw window each provide access to a class of tools, such as text manipulation, rectangles, circles, lines, and so on. To create a drawing, follow these steps:

1. Click and hold one of the icons for a specific class of shape on the left edge of the Draw window. You should see a small menu of specific options appear. For instance, the rectangle icon produces a menu of filled and unfilled rectangles and squares with squared or rounded corners.

2. Select a specific shape, such as a filled square with rounded corners.

3. Select any other options you want, such as the color or line width. These can be set from icons on the button bars or from menu items.

4. Be sure the shape you want is selected (the icon should have a sunken appearance), and then click the mouse button in the drawing area. Depending upon the shape you've chosen, you may need to click and drag; click, move the mouse, and double click; or click, move the mouse, and click again. Text items require you to click the mouse button and then type your text. The object you've selected should appear.

5. Repeat Steps 1–4 to place additional shapes in the drawing.

You can fine-tune a drawing by selecting the arrow icon near the top of the tool list along the left edge of the window. Once the arrow is selected, click an object to see its control points. You can click and drag these control points to resize the object. When the cursor becomes a four-pointed arrow, you can click and drag to move the object. You can right-click an object and choose an option from the resulting pop-up menu to change the object in various ways, such as flipping it or editing the text in a text object.

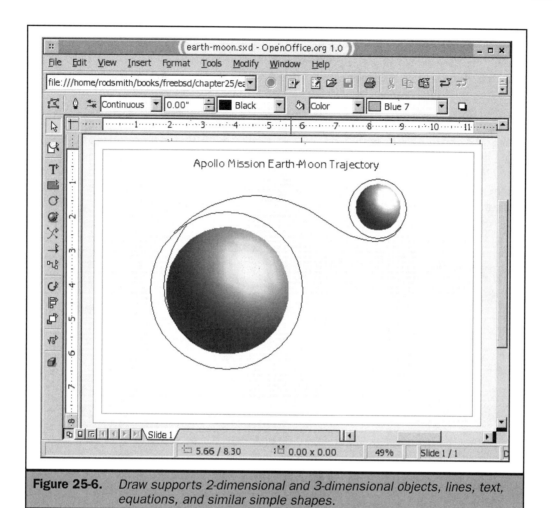

Figure 25-6. *Draw supports 2-dimensional and 3-dimensional objects, lines, text, equations, and similar simple shapes.*

Draw saves its graphics in a vector format, so when you print the image, it will print at your printer's resolution. This characteristic contrasts with bitmap graphics formats, such as those used by the GIMP, which don't scale well; when you print a bitmap graphics file, it may appear jagged because it's been scaled up.

You can insert a bitmapped graphic file in a Draw image. This bitmapped graphic will scale as it would in a bitmapped graphics program.

Creating a Presentation

The OpenOffice.org Impress module resembles the Draw module at first glance, as shown by Figure 25-7. An Impress document, though, is intended to create a series of *slides* (document pages), each of which can be printed onto an overhead transparency or photographic slide, or displayed using a big-screen projection monitor, as part of a talk or presentation. Because of the format of these presentations, individual Impress slides take one of twenty standard forms. Most of these forms include titles at the top along with one or more elements below them. These elements may include outlines, spreadsheets, clip art, free-form text, or generic objects. You can import any other OpenOffice.org document type as a generic object, but of course some objects don't make much sense as generic objects—a book-length Writer document would overwhelm a presentation, for instance.

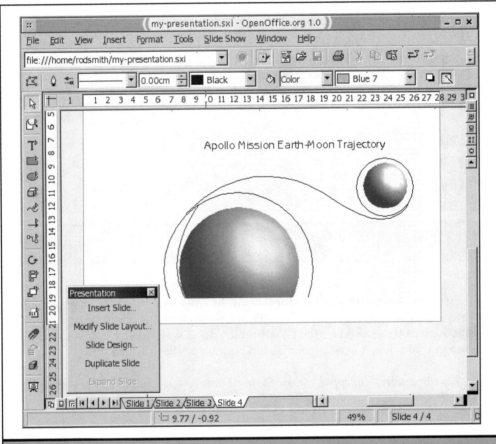

Figure 25-7. *An Impress presentation is a lot like a series of Draw objects.*

When you first create an Impress document, the program presents a series of dialog boxes asking you for information such as whether you want to create a new presentation or edit an existing one, what format the presentation will take (overhead slides, on-screen display, and so on), and what type of effect you want to accompany transitions from one slide to another (which is meaningful for on-screen presentations only). Once you've answered these questions, you'll see the main Impress window (Figure 25-7) and, in front of it, the Modify Slide dialog box (Figure 25-8). You select the type of slide you want to create in this dialog box. When you click OK, you'll see the elements appear in the main Impress window. You can then double-click an object to edit it or insert the object type. You can then edit the object as you would its original type. For instance, if you tell Impress to insert a spreadsheet, you can edit the spreadsheet cells as described earlier, in "Performing Computations." You can cut-and-paste from another document or import another document.

When you're done with the first slide, click Insert Slide in the floating Presentation menu in the main Impress window (near the lower-left corner of Figure 25-7). This action

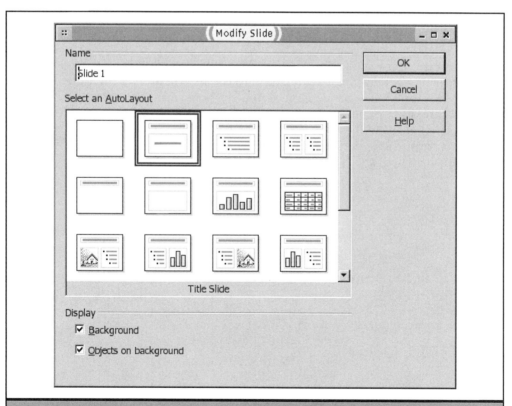

Figure 25-8.   *Impress provides several templates for the layout of individual slides.*

brings up the Modify slide dialog box, in which you select the layout for the next slide in your document. You continue this process until you're done.

To navigate through an existing presentation, click the tabs near the bottom of the window (Slide 1, Slide 2, and so on in Figure 25-7). These tabs will bring you to specific slides, which you can edit to suit your needs. If you want to rearrange your slides, select View | Master View | Slides View. This action creates an overview of all your slides, which you can drag around to change the presentation order.

If you want to create a printout of your presentation, you can print it just as you would any other OpenOffice.org document. If you can run OpenOffice.org on a computer with VGA output that leads to a very large screen or overhead projector adapter, you can run the presentation directly from OpenOffice.org, complete with special effects when moving from one slide to another. Select Slide Show | Slide Show to start the presentation. After a brief delay, the screen will clear and you'll see the first slide. You can use the dialog box obtained from the Slide Show | Slide Show Settings menu to set up the slide show to automatically change slides at particular intervals, or you can click the mouse button to move manually from one slide to the next.

Summary

FreeBSD is often considered a server OS, and it fulfills that role very well. FreeBSD also supports many programs that fall into the most common nonserver computer category, though: office applications for desktop computers. Three major office suites, GNOME Office, KOffice, and OpenOffice.org, are available for FreeBSD, and numerous tools exist that aren't part of any of these three suites. The major FreeBSD office suites should be familiar to users who understand office suites on other platforms, but some details, such as font handling, are different enough that they require special attention.

The
Complete
Reference

To some people, graphics manipulation tools are mere toys; but to others, they're vitally important. Manipulating graphics can be critical in endeavors such as creating a publication, developing a presentation, or preparing a flyer. In fact, graphics preparation and manipulation needs are quite diverse. Two broad classes of graphics manipulation programs exist: those that work on *bitmaps* (images described in terms of individual pixels of specific colors) and those that use *vector graphics* (images built from lines, curves, and other shapes). Both categories, but especially vector graphics programs, include many subtypes, such as programs to create charts from numerical data and programs to create and manipulate circuit diagrams.

This chapter describes several graphics tools, beginning with the most powerful bitmap graphics program on FreeBSD, the GIMP. The chapter then moves on to a few popular vector graphics programs. Finally, the chapter concludes with tools that process PostScript and PDF files, which are commonly used for distributing electronic analogs of printed pages.

The GIMP

The GNU Image Manipulation Program (GIMP) is the premier bitmap graphics program for FreeBSD. The GIMP is officially part of the GNU Network Object Model Environment (GNOME) Office project, described in Chapter 25, but it's more powerful than the bitmap graphics programs in competing office suites. In fact, the GIMP is often compared to Adobe Photoshop in its capabilities. Photoshop includes better tools for printing to Cyan/Magenta/Yellow/Black (CMYK) printers, and the two tools often perform tasks in substantially different ways; but they're very similar in overall power. This chapter can only begin to describe the GIMP's capabilities. For more information, consult its web page, http://www.gimp.org, or consult a book on the program, such as Bunks' *Grokking the GIMP* (New Riders, 2000) or Davis' *The GIMP for Linux and Unix: Visual Quickstart Guide* (Peachpit Press, 2000).

Starting the GIMP

To start the GIMP, type **gimp** in an xterm window. The first time you launch the program, it runs through a series of dialog boxes to provide you with some information and enable you to set some options:

- **Personal GIMP directory**   Like many programs, the GIMP stores personal configuration files in a subdirectory of your home directory. For the GIMP 1.2, this subdirectory is called .gimp-1.2. In the case of the GIMP, this subdirectory contains many subdirectories itself. Although you can't change the .gimp-1.2 directory name, a dialog box appears that displays information on all of the .gimp-1.2 subdirectories. This information might be useful if you want to dig into some of the support files to expand on the GIMP's options.

■ **Installation log**   When the GIMP creates your personal .gimp-1.2 subdirectory tree, it displays the commands it uses to create this tree. If you see any error messages, you can click Cancel to abort the installation, track down the cause of the problems, and correct them.

■ **Performance tuning**   The GIMP uses memory to store image data. You can adjust the amount of memory that the GIMP requests for this storage, known as the *tile cache*. The default is 32MB, which works well on typical single-user workstations with 128MB or more RAM. If you run many other programs or if yours is a multiuser system, you may want to decrease the tile cache size. If your workstation has several hundred megabytes of RAM and you don't run many programs, you may want to increase the tile cache size. You can also set the directory that the GIMP uses to store data that doesn't fit in its tile cache. Normally this is the .gimp-1.2 subdirectory, but you can change it to a system temporary directory (/tmp or /var/tmp) if you prefer.

■ **Monitor resolution**   If creating images of a particular absolute size on the screen (as measured in inches or centimeters, say) is important to you, you must specify the resolution of your monitor in dots per inch (dpi). If you're not sure of this value and exact image size is unimportant, select the defaults. If exact image size is important, measure the portion of your monitor that displays an image, both horizontally and vertically, and divide each value by the horizontal and vertical resolution in pixels. For instance, if an 11.5-inch by 8.7-inch monitor displays a 1024×768 image, then the horizontal resolution is 1024 ÷ 11.5 = 89 dpi, and the vertical resolution is 768 ÷ 8.7 = 88 dpi.

At this point, the GIMP displays its splash window (which merely announces what it is). The first time the program starts, it populates the .gimp-1.2 directory tree with files copied from the main GIMP collection. This process will take a few tens of seconds, depending upon your computer's speed, after which you'll see a collection of windows and dialog boxes, as shown in Figure 26-1.

The next time you start the GIMP, it will start up more quickly because it won't have to copy its standard files.

A Tour of the GIMP

The GIMP Tip of the Day dialog box (the short but wide dialog box in the bottom right of Figure 26-1) provides a tip that changes each time you start the program. If you don't want to be bothered with it, uncheck Show Tip Next Time GIMP Starts and click Close; otherwise, leave that option checked and click Close to get rid of the dialog box, or click Next Tip or Previous Tip to view additional tips.

The GIMP's main window is actually the smallest one that the program displays when first launched. It's the rightmost window above the GIMP Tip of the Day dialog

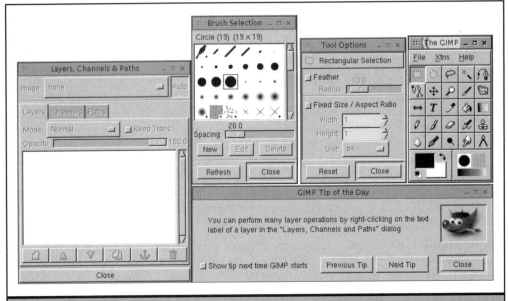

Figure 26-1. *The GIMP uses many small windows and dialog boxes to control its operation.*

box in Figure 26-1. The remaining three windows provide tools that you're likely to need soon after you begin editing a graphic:

- **Layers, channels, and paths** The leftmost window in Figure 26-1 is the Layers, Channels, and Paths tool. This window helps you manipulate graphics elements known as *layers*, *channels*, and *paths*. The GIMP enables you to combine multiple graphics elements in layers, much like drawings on transparent sheets of paper. This organization lets you draw objects independently, then hide one behind another, move them around, and so on. Channels refer to the red, green, and blue color components. Paths provide basic vector-drawing capabilities to the GIMP.

- **Brush selection** The Brush Selection window is the leftmost window above the GIMP Tip of the Day dialog box in Figure 26-1. It enables you to select a *brush*, which is a shape that's used when drawing freehand in the GIMP. Many brushes are simple circles of varying radii, enabling you to draw fat or skinny lines. Other brushes are more complex shapes, enabling you to create various special effects or to place complex shapes in an image by clicking once with a drawing tool.

- **Tool options** The Tool Options window is between the Brush Selection window and the main GIMP window in Figure 26-1. Its contents vary depending upon the GIMP tool that you've selected. In Figure 26-1, a rectangular selection tool is active, so the Tool Options window provides options relevant to selecting areas of an image.

The GIMP's main window is dominated by an array of buttons, each of which corresponds to a specific tool. You can use a tool to perform some operation on an image. Select a tool by clicking it and you'll see the Tool Options window change. Your mouse pointer may also change when you move it over an image's window. You can then click in the window to perform an action unique to the tool in question. Some of these tools are described in the upcoming section, "Entering Text and Drawing;" but the GIMP is complex enough that this chapter can't describe all the available tools.

In addition to the buttons that correspond to tools, the GIMP's main window includes a menu bar. Most of the options available from this menu bar are quite advanced and are not covered in this chapter. For instance, you can use Script-Fu from the menu bar. Script-Fu is an advanced scripting tool that enables you to perform repetitive tasks on graphics files. Much of the GIMP's power comes from Script-Fu.

Many common options are available from a menu you access by right-clicking in a graphic window. You can load and save graphics, apply filters to an existing graphic (to blur it, create simulated lens effects, and so on), manipulate layers, edit the color palette, and so on. The next few sections describe a few of these tools.

Loading and Saving Graphics

When it first starts, the GIMP doesn't load any files unless you pass the graphics filenames on the command line. Thus, to do anything with the program, you must either create a new graphic or load an existing one.

To create a new file, select File | New from the GIMP main window. The result is a dialog box in which you specify the image's size in pixels or in inches. You can also adjust the screen resolution, if you so desire, and specify whether the image will be color (RGB, for red/green/blue) or grayscale. When you click OK, an empty window appears, in which you can begin drawing.

To load an existing graphic, select File | Open. This action displays a file selection dialog box. You can load graphics in any common bitmap format, such as the Tagged Image File Format (TIFF), the Joint Photographic Experts Group (JPEG) format, the Portable Network Graphics (PNG) format, the Graphic Interchange Format (GIF), or the Photoshop Data (PSD) format. Of course, the GIMP can also load its own native file format, XCF. For the most part, the GIMP auto-detects the file type, but you can force it to interpret a file as a particular type by specifying the type in the Determine File Type selector in the Load Image file selector dialog box.

In addition to loading images from disk files, various plug-ins exist that enable you to load an image from a nontraditional source. One such plug-in is standard with the GIMP, and can be accessed from the File | Acquire | Screen Shot menu option. When you select this option, the GIMP displays a dialog box that enables you to select the capture of a single window or of the entire screen, and to specify a delay time. If you select the single-window option, the GIMP captures the first window you click on after the delay time; if you select the full-screen option, the GIMP captures your entire screen after the delay period. Another popular plug-in is a scanner tool, which enables you to use the GIMP to capture graphics using a scanner.

Lossy vs. Lossless Compression

Most graphics file formats today provide for compression to reduce the size (in bytes or kilobytes) of graphics files, which can be quite huge without such compression. For instance, an uncompressed 24-bit 500×500 TIFF is approximately 750KB in size. Compression can shrink these values substantially, which can save disk space. When a file is part of a web page, reducing the file size can make the web page load much faster.

Some graphics file types use lossless compression, meaning that it's possible to recover every bit to its precise original value when loading the file. Such compression is the norm for most compression systems; after all, you don't want corruption in compressed program files in a tarball, to name one example. In the case of graphics, though, lossy compression is often a viable option. Such compression schemes lose a certain amount of data in the service of reducing file size. At their best, lossy compression schemes create files that can't be distinguished from the originals by the human eye at normal viewing magnifications. Lossy schemes often enable a variable rate of compression, though, and if this compression rate is set high enough, visible artifacts result.

Among the common file formats, TIFF, GIF, PNG, and XCF all employ no or lossless compression schemes. JPEG is the most popular lossy format available.

When you're done editing your graphics, you probably want to save them. You can do so by selecting File | Save or File | Save As from the context menu that appears when you right-click in a file's window. The former option saves the file using whatever name and format the file had originally. The latter option enables you to give the file a new name or to change its format. One important feature of the Save Image dialog box is the Determine File Type selector. This selector defaults to By Extension, which means that the GIMP takes its cue for the file format based on the file extension you type—for instance, saving in XCF format if the filename ends in `.xcf`, or in TIFF format if it ends in `.tif` or `.tiff`. You can override this setting if you want to save a file with an atypical filename extension, though.

Note *The GIMP can't save in every file format it can read. The most common problem is with GIF files because the algorithms used to create GIF files are covered by a software patent, so the GIMP can't legally create these files.*

If you want to work on a complex image that includes multiple layers, you must save the file in the GIMP's native XCF format if you expect to preserve the layer information. When you're done editing such a file, you'll probably want to create a file in another format, such as TIFF or JPEG, so that you can most easily view the file from other programs. To do so, you must first flatten the image—that is, reduce it to a single layer. To do this, right-click on the image and select Layers | Flatten Image. This act does the job. If you fail to do this, you'll see only one layer in the exported file.

Some file formats require you to enter additional information when you save them. For instance, JPEG supports variable compression levels, which you set with a Quality slider in a Save as JPEG dialog box. Try experimenting with various Quality settings when saving an image as JPEG to discover their effects. You can also change the Smoothing level in a similar way. This setting affects how sharp edges are handled in the compression routines.

Entering Text and Drawing

You can use the GIMP to create or modify graphics in many different ways. One way is to create new graphics elements—to add text, draw lines, fill empty areas with colors or patterns, and so on. This section covers these types of modifications, which you perform by selecting tools from the buttons on the GIMP's main window. Another class of operation involves modifying existing images, such as cropping the image, changing colors, and applying filters to achieve various special effects. These modifications are described in the upcoming section, "Transformations."

Selecting Colors and Patterns

When you draw an object using the GIMP, the program relies upon two colors: a foreground color and a background color. In most cases, the foreground color is the one that's applied—it's the color in which a line is drawn, or that's used to fill an area, for instance. For a few operations, such as application of gradients, the background color is used, as well.

To set the foreground and background colors, you use the tool in the lower-left corner of the GIMP's main window. In Figure 26-1, this tool shows two rectangles, one black and one white, with the black rectangle partially obscuring the white one. The rectangle that's in "front" represents the foreground color, and the one that's "behind" represents the background color. To change the color, double-click one of the color rectangles. Doing so produces the Color Selection dialog box shown in Figure 26-2. You can specify a color using any of four tools, corresponding to the tabs near the top of the dialog box. Try experimenting with these four tools, and use whichever you prefer.

The tool to the right of the color selector in the GIMP's main window provides access to three options related to colors:

- **Brush selection**   The icon in the upper-left of this tool represents the brush used by many drawing tools. In Figure 26-1, it's a large circle. If you click this portion of the tool, the Brush Selection dialog box (also shown in Figure 26-1) appears or is brought to the front, so you can change the brush style.

- **Pattern selection**   To the right of the brush selection icon is a pattern selection icon. You can perform fill operations using a pattern, and the GIMP provides many standard patterns you can use for this purpose. Clicking the pattern icon brings up a Pattern Selection dialog box in which you select the pattern you want to use. Actually using the pattern requires selecting the Pattern Fill option in the Tool Options window.

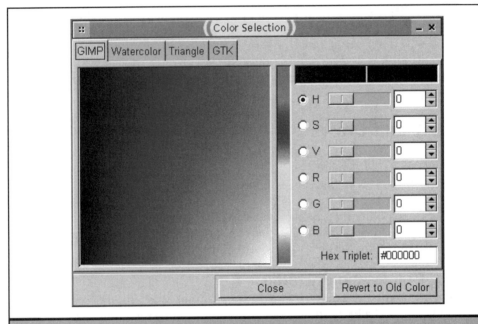

Figure 26-2. *The GIMP provides four means of selecting colors.*

■ **Gradient selection**   Some tools support the use of gradients—a shift from the foreground to the background color. You can set the gradient pattern by clicking the gradient bar below the brush and pattern selector icons. Several options are available that vary from smooth gradients to exotic patterns.

Drawing

The GIMP provides several tools for drawing. Most of these tools are designed to emulate the effects of physical art tools, such as pencils and paint brushes. Move the mouse over the buttons in the GIMP's main window. When you pause, a description of the tool should appear. Click a button and the Tool Options window changes to accommodate options specific to the tool in question. If you're familiar with other paint programs, many of these tools should be familiar to you. If not, experiment with each of them to learn what they can do.

Filling

The main fill tool uses a paint bucket icon in the GIMP's main window. You can opt to fill with the foreground color, the background color, or the current pattern. When you fill, the selected pattern or color replaces the background color in the image area in which you click. For instance, if the image includes an outline of a circle, and if you click within the circle, the circle will be filled, but the area outside the circle will be unaffected.

The GIMP also provides a blend tool, which overlays a gradient on the image. The blend tool's effects aren't limited to a certain area unless you first select that area, as described in the upcoming section "Selecting and Cropping Images." To create a blend, select the blend tool, then select two points on the image. These points represent the two extremes of the blend's color range. Ordinarily, a blend will completely replace everything in the image; but you can use the Opacity slider in the Tool Options window to reduce the blend's opacity, thus letting existing images "show through" the blend.

Entering Text

The GIMP provides a text tool so that you can enter text in an image. To use this tool, select it (it's the "T" icon in the tool buttons). When you click in the graphic window, the GIMP displays the Text Tool (Figure 26-3). You type your text in the Preview field and set the font, font style, and font size using the lists above that field. When you click OK, your text is inserted into the graphic.

Initially, text you insert is in its own layer, in order to facilitate exact placement of the text. Click the Move Layers and Selections tool (the four-headed arrow) in the GIMP's main window to move the text around. You can click the text and position it exactly in this way.

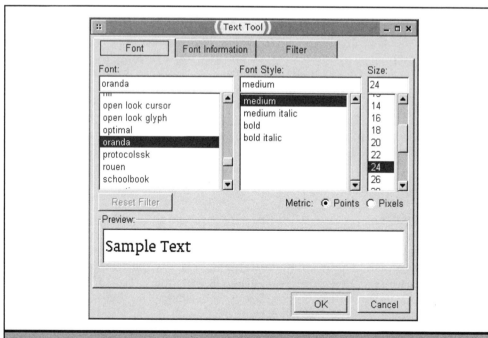

Figure 26-3. *To enter text in the GIMP, you use a separate dialog box that previews the text's appearance.*

Transformations

Adding elements to an image can be quite important, but sometimes you may want to modify an existing image rather than add to it. The GIMP provides many tools that facilitate such operations. Some of the more important of these include selecting and cropping images, altering the color map, and applying filters.

Selecting and Cropping Images

The first row of tools in the GIMP's main window enables you to select regions in various ways—rectangular regions, circular regions, regions defined by freehand drawing, and so on. Once selected, you can perform various operations on the region, such as

- Click within the region and drag to move it.
- Copy the region into the clipboard by pressing CTRL-C.
- Cut the region into the clipboard by pressing CTRL-X.
- Perform drawing operations limited to the region in the normal way— for instance, you can apply a gradient to only the selected area.
- Apply a filter, as described in the upcoming section "Applying Filters," to only the selected region.

For some purposes, the opposite of selecting a region is *cropping* the image— removing all but some central portion of the image. You might crop an image to remove an unaesthetic telephone pole from the edge of a landscape photograph, for instance. To crop an image, right-click in the image and select the Tools | Transform Tools | Crop & Resize option; or select the crop tool from the GIMP's main window (this tool resembles a scalpel). You can then click and hold the mouse button in one corner of the area you want to crop, drag to the opposite corner, and release. The GIMP then displays the Crop & Resize Information dialog box, which enables you to fine-tune the selection area. When you're satisfied, click Crop to remove everything outside of the selected area. You can use the same technique to resize the entire image to fit in the selected area; just click Resize rather than Crop to accomplish this task.

Altering Colors

The GIMP provides several tools for altering colors in an image. These tools are most useful for improving the appearance of digitized photographs; you can change the brightness or contrast, change color saturation levels, and perform more exotic transformations. Most of these options are available from the Image | Colors submenu from the context menu obtained by right-clicking in the image. Try these options to learn what they can do.

One specific color alteration is sometimes necessary and deserves more elaboration: color *indexing*. Some graphics formats support a very limited number of colors, and even formats that support more colors sometimes benefit from using a more limited number of colors because doing so can reduce file sizes. Selecting Image | Mode | Indexed from the GIMP's context menu turns on its indexing tool, which can reduce the number of colors in an image to whatever number you specify (the default is 256 colors, or 8 bits of color information).

Applying Filters

The GIMP provides many *filters*, which are tools that manipulate the image in some predefined way to apply a special effect. These filters are available from the Filters context menu, and are broken into several categories, such as Blur, Noise, Glass Effects, and Artistic. Many of these filters add an element, such as a starburst or background, to an image. Others modify the image to simulate some effect, such as a lens's distortions or particular painting styles.

Vector Drawing Tools

The GIMP is FreeBSD's premiere bitmap graphics program, but sometimes a bitmap program isn't appropriate. You may want to create an image that's built from virtual objects rather than pixels, or that scales well for any output device. Although the GIMP's layers can be used to create independent objects that can be moved around, this technique doesn't address scaling issues. The answer is a vector graphics program, which uses mathematically defined shapes rather than bitmaps at its core. Such programs often define drawings in terms of specific objects, such as circles and lines, that you can move around independently. The range of such programs is quite broad, and this section can describe only a handful of vector drawing tools, and those in limited detail.

 The Draw component of OpenOffice.org, described in Chapter 25, is a vector drawing program. Consult Chapter 25 for information on using this program.

Using Xfig

Xfig (`http://www.xfig.org`) is a fairly basic but functional general-purpose vector drawing program. It's useful for creating many types of simple diagrams and figures. To launch the program, type **xfig** in an xterm window. Figure 26-4 shows xfig in operation. As revealed by this figure, xfig enables you to lay out lines of varying lengths, thicknesses, and styles, as well as an assortment of other shapes (rectangles, circles, polygons, curves, and so on). Xfig, like most vector drawing programs, supports text placement within the figure. You can also group several simple shapes into a more complex shape. In fact, xfig ships with a library of such compound shapes—the computers along the right side of the document shown in Figure 26-4 come from this library. You can use such clip art to easily lend a more professional look to the figures you create with xfig.

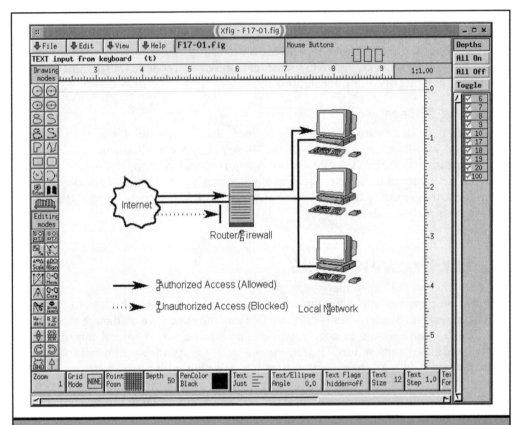

Figure 26-4. *Xfig is a typical general-purpose vector drawing program.*

When you first start xfig, its drawing space is empty. To begin a drawing, click one of the tool buttons along the left side of the window. The top half of this set of buttons provide various shapes—circles, ellipses, curves, polygons, and so on. Buttons for inserting text, bitmap images, and xfig clip art are also present in this area. As a general rule, you place an object by clicking to position one corner, the central point, or a starting point; then moving the mouse and clicking again to position the opposite corner, the outside diameter, or the second point. Some objects, such as polygons, accept an arbitrary number of control points. You click for each one, then click the middle mouse button when you're done. (For some object types, xfig then draws a final line between the last control point and the first in order to close the figure.)

Most object types provide several drawing options, such as line thickness and style (solid, dashed, and so on), line color, fill color, and fill style. Text objects provide font and font size options. In all cases, you can control these options from buttons that appear along the bottom of the xfig window (Figure 26-4 shows the text object options). One of these options is the object's *depth*. This characteristic refers to the position of the object in the "stack" of objects in the image. Objects with lower depth numbers obscure those with higher depth numbers when the two are placed over each other.

It's not uncommon to want to modify objects once you've placed them. You can do so by using the editing tools that comprise the bottom half of the small buttons on the left side of the xfig window. You can use these buttons to group multiple objects into a larger meta-object, break an existing grouping, scale an object, copy an object, delete an object, edit an object's characteristics, rotate or mirror an object, and so on. As a general rule, you must click one of the object's control points (small rectangles placed at an object's edges or vertices) to modify it, but sometimes clicking anywhere in an object works as well. In most cases, an editing action happens immediately, without further prompting; but sometimes xfig displays a dialog box in which you must enter further information.

Tip	*Xfig's dialog boxes sometimes contain text-entry fields. These operate a bit oddly; to enter text into these fields, your mouse cursor must be over the text-entry field. If you click the mouse in the field and then move it out of the way, you won't be able to enter text into the text-entry field.*

Xfig has a small menu bar from which you can select typical file and editing options. You can save your drawing in xfig's native format or export it to PostScript, Encapsulated PostScript (EPS), TIFF, and various other formats. From the Edit menu, you can undo operations, cut or paste objects, and so on. The View menu enables you to zoom in and out, display vertex numbers, and so on. The Help menu, of course, provides access to xfig's help files. Some of these options rely upon external programs, such as a web browser and spell checker. You can adjust the programs upon which xfig relies from the Edit | Global Settings menu.

Using Dia

Xfig is a useful general-purpose vector graphics package, but sometimes a more specialized tool is in order. Dia (http://www.gnome.org/gnome-office/dia.shtml) is one such tool. Dia is part of the GNOME Office suite described in Chapter 25, and is designed to create diagrams. You can launch it by typing **dia** in an xterm window. The result is a small control window. To actually use the program, select File | New Diagram; this action creates a drawing window. Figure 26-5 shows both the control window and the drawing window (including a diagram).

Dia provides fewer object types than does xfig, but some of the Dia objects provide options that enable them to accomplish the same goals as xfig objects. For instance, xfig provides separate objects for rectangles with rounded and squared corners, whereas Dia provides a single rectangle tool with an option to change the corner radius, effectively allowing Dia's single rectangle tool to create both types of rectangle.

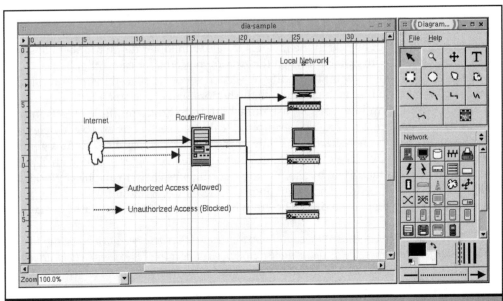

Figure 26-5. *Dia's controls are centered around placement of its predefined objects.*

Tools near the bottom of the main Dia window enable you to set an object's color, line thickness and style (solid, dashed, and so on), and end type (plain, arrow, and so on). The color-setting tool works much like the same tool in the GIMP; click the foreground or background rectangle to set a color.

Dia's strength lies in its range of predefined objects. These objects are collected into various groups, such as Circuit, Flowchart, Logic, and Network. You select an object group by picking it from the selector in the middle of the Dia control window. (This selector is set to Network in Figure 26-5.) When you pick a new object group, the objects available in that group appear below the selector. To place an object, pick it and click in the document window; Dia places the object where you click. You can then right-click the object to obtain a list of actions you can perform on the object, such as viewing the object's properties (line color, text font, and so on). Some actions are available only when you select several objects; for instance, you can align objects when you select several of them.

To save a Dia file, right-click in the file window and pick File | Save or File | Save As from the resulting context menu. The latter always asks you for a filename, but the former does so only if the file's not been saved before. You can also export your creation in various other formats, such as EPS and PNG, by picking File | Export.

Some Dia export formats lose information. For instance, exporting to xfig format is likely to create an xfig file with ugly diagram objects.

Using Gnuplot

The gnuplot (`http://www.gnuplot.info`) program is a text-based tool for plotting data. This description may sound paradoxical, but it's not—the program takes a file that contains numerical data and creates a graphics file that displays the data as a graph. This graphics file may optionally be displayed directly in an X window, or you can create a traditional graphics file that you can print, import into a word processor document, or otherwise manipulate.

Contrary to what you might think by the name, gnuplot is not associated with the GNU Project. In fact, gnuplot isn't even covered by the GNU General Public License (GPL), although it is freeware.

To describe gnuplot use, it may be best to begin with an example. Listing 26-1 shows the data file that's to be plotted. This data file contains raw data in a plain-text format. (Most spreadsheets and other data-analysis tools enable you to export such files, although you may need to manually remove some stray labels.) The first column contains x-axis data points and the second column contains y-axis data points. Listing 26-1 shows the production cost of widgets made by the fictitious Widget Company over time.

:ting 26-1.
Sample
uplot Input
Data File

```
1995 26.34
1996 24.97
1997 25.02
1998 25.67
1999 24.78
2000 23.02
2001 23.69
2002 23.32
```

To create a graph showing these data, follow these steps after installing the `gnuplot` package or port:

1. Type the data from Listing 26-1 into a text file. In actual use, you would use data from some other source.

2. Create a gnuplot control file. This file contains all the options used to control the creation of a graph from the data file. Listing 26-2 shows such a file, referred to as `plot.ctl` in the next step. Its options are described shortly.

COMMON USER
PROGRAMS

3. Type **gnuplot -persist plot.ctl**. This command creates an X window in which the data are plotted, as shown in Figure 26-6.

Listing 26-2.
Sample
Gnuplot
Control File,
plot.ctl

```
set title 'Widget Cost Over Time'
set xlabel "Year"
set ylabel "Cost"
set output
set terminal x11
plot [1995:2002] [22:28] 'data.txt'  with lines
```

If you prefer, you can enter your gnuplot commands (shown in Listing 26-2) interactively. Instead of typing **gnuplot -persist plot.ctl** in Step 3, type **gnuplot**, and then type each of the lines shown in Listing 26-2 at the gnuplot> prompt.

Most of the lines in a gnuplot control file set gnuplot options. In Listing 26-2, the first three lines set labels—the graph's title, the x-axis label, and the y-axis label.

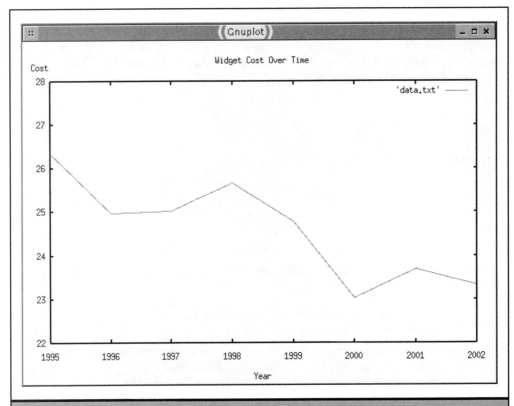

Figure 26-6. *A basic gnuplot graph is not flashy but is quite readable.*

The next two lines set output options. The `set output` line is a dummy line; it's not really necessary when using an X window for output. The `set terminal` option sets the output file type. In the case of Listing 26-2, the output is set for an X window.

If you want to create a graphics file suitable for printing or importing into another application, you can change the `set output` and `set terminal` options. Change the former to specify a filename in quotes, such as `set output "plot.fig"` to save the output to `plot.fig`. You can use several different options in place of `x11` on the `set terminal` line to change the file type, including

- **corel** This option creates an EPS file. It's designed for import into CorelDRAW, though, and may not work with some programs that can load EPS files.

- **fig** You can save a file that xfig can load with this option. Xfig will notify you that the file uses an old file format, but the file loads correctly.

- **hpgl** The Hewlett Packard Graphics Language (HPGL) is a vector graphics format that can be understood directly by many HP and compatible laser printers.

- **pcl5** The Printer Control Language (PCL) is the printer language used by HP and compatible laser printers. This option creates a bitmap output, as opposed to the vector format created with the `hpgl` option.

- **postscript** This option is best if you want to print a file directly because FreeBSD treats all printers as PostScript models, as described in Chapter 9.

- **latex** If you use LaTeX for document preparation, this option is a good one; it creates a file that's easily included in a LaTeX document.

- **png** This option creates a PNG bitmap file, which can be a good format if you want to manipulate the graph using the GIMP or some other bitmap graphics program, or include it in a word processor document.

Many other options are available, most of which are for specific printers or variants on the preceding options. From within gnuplot (at its `gnuplot>` prompt), type **set terminal** to see a complete list of the available output options.

In many respects, the most important command in Listing 26-2 is the final line:

```
plot [1995:2002] [22:28] 'data.txt'  with lines
```

This line tells gnuplot to plot the data from `data.txt`. The two sets of numbers in square brackets (`[ ]`) represent the displayed data ranges for the x- and y-axes. You can check Figure 26-6 to see that these numbers correspond to the displayed ranges. If you omit these values, gnuplot auto-scales, creating a plot that fits all your data. The `with lines` option tells gnuplot to connect the data points with lines. You can replace `lines` with any of several other options:

- **points** Each data point is represented by a single diamond-shaped point on the output.

- **linespoints** You can highlight each point but keep the lines with this option.

- **dots** This option is like `points`, but the points are very small by comparison, which may be useful if your data set consists of a huge number of points.

- **impulses** This option creates lines that spring from the x-axis to the data point, like an anorexic bar graph.

- **boxes** The gnuplot `boxes` type is essentially a bar graph, but there's no space between the bars.

- **steps** You can create a series of "steps" with this option. Think of it as being like `lines`, but the lines can only be horizontal or vertical.

- **xerrorbars and yerrorbars** These options create horizontal and vertical error bars, respectively. Both of these options require a third column in the input data file to specify the size of the error bars.

For a complete list of plot types, type a **plot** command at a `gnuplot>` prompt but specify a bogus `with` option. The program then summarizes all its options.

If you want to plot multiple data files (say, one showing the cost to produce Widgets and the other showing the cost to produce Getwids), you can include both files on a single `plot` line, thus:

```
plot [1995:2002] [22:28] 'data.txt'  with lines, 'data2.txt' with lines
```

Gnuplot offers many options to modify the appearance of its graphs, to create 3-dimensional graphs, and so on. It's an extremely flexible tool for data visualization. For more information, consult its internal help system by typing **help** at a `gnuplot>` command prompt, or read the documentation on the gnuplot web site.

Managing PostScript, EPS, and PDF Files

Chapter 9 describes the FreeBSD printing system, including the fact that FreeBSD programs typically assume that printers are PostScript models. PostScript is more than a printer language, though; it's a full-fledged programming language and a graphics file format. Although PostScript as a programming language is beyond the scope of this book, its use as a graphics file format is important enough that it deserves some elaboration. Many FreeBSD programs that can print can also create PostScript output files. You can manually print such files, view the files with a PostScript viewer, translate the PostScript files into another file format using Ghostscript, or move the files to another computer, where you can do any of these things.

Two common file formats are related to PostScript. The first, Encapsulated PostScript (EPS) is very similar to PostScript, but is designed to describe a small element (typically less than a page) that can be incorporated into a PostScript document. Typically, EPS files contain graphics, although they can contain text. Many programs can create EPS output, and other programs can embed EPS files in their own documents. Ghostscript can process EPS files as easily as it can handle PostScript files. The second related file format is Adobe's *Portable Document Format (PDF)*. PDF files are also often referred to as *Acrobat files* because they can be created and read with an Adobe program of that name. PDF files are more readily handled on non-UNIX systems such as Microsoft Windows, on which Ghostscript or similar PostScript-handling tools are often not installed. PDF files are also usually smaller than their PostScript counterparts.

Using GhostScript

Aside from a PostScript printer, Ghostscript is the most common FreeBSD tool for manipulating PostScript files. The most common use of Ghostscript is as part of a printer queue, as described in Chapter 9. It's possible, however, to use Ghostscript to convert PostScript, EPS, or PDF files into other file formats. Indeed, that's how Ghostscript works as part of a printer queue, but in the printer queue case, the output file format happens to be the format that the printer expects as input, such as PCL for many laser printers.

Suppose that you've created or obtained a PostScript file. This file could be generated by a local program, such as a word processor; or you might have found it on the Web. You can use Ghostscript to translate this file into another format using a command such as the following:

```
$ gs -dNOPAUSE -dBATCH -dSAFER -r72x72 -sDEVICE=jpeg ↵
  -sOutputFile=file.jpg file.ps
```

Options demonstrated in this command are

- **–dNOPAUSE** This option tells Ghostscript not to pause between pages. Ordinarily, the program asks you to accept creation of each new page of output, which can be tedious on long documents.

- **–dBATCH** This option tells Ghostscript to exit once it's finished processing the job. Ordinarily, the program presents a GS> prompt at which you can type commands.

- **–dSAFER** Because PostScript is a computer programming language, it's possible to distribute malicious code as a PostScript file. To minimize the risks associated with this possibility, this option disables Ghostscript's ability to delete or rename files, or to open them except in read-only mode. These restrictions severely limit the damage that a PostScript Trojan horse could do.

- **–r72x72** Most Ghostscript actions convert what is essentially a raster format (PostScript) into a bitmap format. The usual PostScript file defines distances in physical measurements, but bitmap formats' physical sizes depend upon the resolution of the device used to view the bitmap. The -r option enables you to set that resolution, in dots per inch (dpi). A two-value option separated by an x is interpreted as horizontal and vertical resolutions. A single value is interpreted as both horizontal and vertical resolutions, so -r72 is equivalent to -r72x72.

■ **-sDEVICE=jpeg**   This option sets the output format—JPEG in this case. Other options are described shortly.

■ **-sOUTPUTFILE=file.jpg**   This option specifies the output filename. If you omit it, Ghostscript assumes standard output, which is likely to produce either a lot of beeping and a corrupted display or a window in which the output appears as a graphic for x11 and related output formats.

■ **file.ps**   The final option is the input filename. When using Ghostscript in a script, it's common to see a single dash (-) as the input filename, signifying standard input.

You can give Ghostscript input files in the form of PostScript, EPS, or PDF. To obtain a complete list of output file formats, type **gs --help**. The resulting output includes a long list of output devices. These aren't always entirely obvious, but most of the ones relating to other standard graphics file formats (as opposed to printer formats) are fairly obvious. Some of the more noteworthy graphics file options include

■ **BMP files**   The .bmp filename extension is associated with an old but still fairly common bitmap file format. Ghostscript provides several bitmap output options, including bmpmono, bmpgray, bmp16, bmp256, and bmp16m. These options differ in their color depth and type.

■ **PCX files**   The old PC Paintbrush program used files with an extension of .pcx, and Ghostscript can produce such files, using output driver codes of pcxmono, pcxgray, pcx16, pcx256, pcx24b, or pcxcmyk. As with BMP output, the PCX output options create files of varying color depth and encoding methods.

■ **TIFF files**   Ghostscript can create the common TIFF format with its tiff12nc, tiff24nc, tifflzw, and tiffpack options. The last two of these options enable TIFF's compression features.

■ **PNG files**   Ghostscript's pngmono, pnggray, png16, png256, and png16m output options create PNG files of varying color types and depths.

■ **JPEG files**   There are only two JPEG options: jpeg and jpeggray, which create color and gray-scale JPEG files, respectively.

■ **Postscript files**   You can create PostScript output with the psmono, psgray, psrgb, and pswrite options.

■ **EPS files**   The epswrite option creates an EPS file.

■ **PDF files**   The pdfwrite option creates a PDF file.

Creating PostScript or a related format from the same file type may sound odd, but it can be quite useful. The output PostScript file is actually a PostScript bitmap, so if you send it to a printer, the printer will process it differently than it would process the original. This fact can be useful if the original file is complex or contains subtle errors that cause problems for a printer; Ghostscript may be able to "predigest" the file, making it easier for a printer with limited memory or a buggy PostScript interpreter to handle.

Most of the output Ghostscript file types are bitmaps, but PDF files are an exception; PDF files contain fonts and are essentially vector graphics files. PDF is a popular format for distributing text files electronically, and Ghostscript can be a useful tool for creating such files. You can create a document in a word processor, LaTeX, or in some other way, then "print" it to a PostScript file and run the result through Ghostscript to create a PDF file. The resulting file can be read in PDF viewers on any platform.

Using GUI PostScript Viewers

Sometimes it's desirable to view a PostScript file before printing it. For instance, you might want to be sure you're printing the correct file before devoting a hundred pages to the document. Ghostscript enables you to perform this preview operation, either by itself or through a more GUI-oriented front-end. In the simplest case, you can issue a truncated gs command similar to the one presented earlier, in "Using Ghostscript":

```
$ gs -dBATCH -dSAFER -sDEVICE=x11 file.ps
```

The result of issuing this command is an X window that displays the document. Ghostscript displays the following prompt in the xterm window in which you typed the command:

```
>>showpage, press <return> to continue<<
```

Pressing ENTER displays the next page of the document, until you reach the end, at which point Ghostscript exits. This simple method may be acceptable for short documents or if you don't need to page back and forth through a document, but it's not enough for some purposes. If you need to be able to move to arbitrary pages, zoom in and out, or perform other actions, you may want to use a GUI front-end to Ghostscript. Such tools enable these more advanced options. Examples of these programs include

- **Ghostview**   This program is the basic Ghostscript front-end. It can be called by typing **ghostview**, optionally followed by the name of the file you want to view. This program's user interface is quite primitive by modern standards.

- **gv** This program is derived from Ghostview, but adds more options and a more modern user interface. It's used much like Ghostview, but its program name is gv.
- **GNOME Ghostview** As you might guess from the name, this program is part of the GNOME project. It's very similar to gv in operation, aside from differences in widget sets and a few features. The program's filename is ggv.

These programs all ship with FreeBSD and are available in packages or ports named after the programs in question (ghostview, gv, or ggv) in the printing area. Using any of these programs is fairly straightforward; type the program name, optionally followed by the name of the file you want to view. All of these programs use Ghostscript to do the rendering, so they produce very similar results. GNOME Ghostview and gv offer some extra options, though, such as *anti-aliasing* of fonts (aka *font smoothing*), a technique that can improve font legibility in some cases. These programs can all display PostScript, EPS, and PDF files, although some PDF features don't render correctly.

Figure 26-7 shows GNOME Ghostview in operation, displaying a PostScript file. The bulk of the window is dominated by the file being displayed, but there are various GUI controls, as well. Most important, the left side of the window hosts a page list. You can move about in the document by double-clicking a page number. This doesn't work properly in all documents, though; with some, you can only move forward or backward one page at a time. You can also zoom in or out using the magnifying glass icons, change the orientation of the virtual page using options under the Document | Orientation menu, and adjust options such as whether or not to use anti-aliasing from the Settings | Preferences dialog box. These programs also enable you to print the entire document or just a range of pages, which can be a convenient option if you want to print just a few pages from a large document.

Using GUI PDF Viewers

As noted in the previous section, common GUI PostScript viewers support PDF files as well as PostScript and EPS files. There are, however, a few additional options that work only on PDF files. The two most important of these are

- **Xpdf** This program is an open source X-based PDF viewer. Its features are fairly simple; its main window is dominated by a view of the document, it has no menu bar, and it uses a few buttons along its bottom border to page through the document, search for text, or print the file.
- **Acrobat Reader** Adobe's PDF viewer is arguably the standard against which all others must be judged because Adobe originated the PDF format (and PostScript, for that matter). You can install the Acrobat Reader from the acroread4 package or port—but this program is technically not a FreeBSD program; it's a Linux program that relies upon FreeBSD's Linux binary compatibility, as described in Chapter 4.

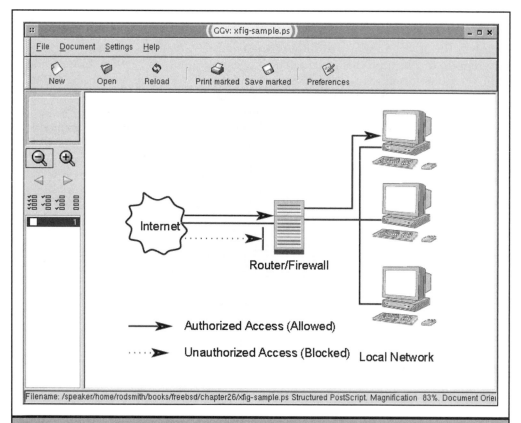

Figure 26-7. GNOME Ghostview displays a document and provides tools for navigating the document and manipulating your view of it.

In broad terms, the PDF-only viewers work much like the PostScript viewers, but some details differ. The most important of these is that Acrobat Reader can display some PDF files that Xpdf and the Ghostscript-based viewers can't handle. These problem files are often created by the latest versions of Adobe's Acrobat Distiller program, which creates PDF files. PDF files created with Ghostscript seldom pose problems for any PDF viewer. Some advanced PDF options, such as tables of contents and some types of embedded elements, also don't display properly (if at all) in anything but Acrobat Reader. For these reasons, if you need to read PDF files very often, and especially if these files come from many sources, you may need to install the `acroread4` package and the Linux compatibility libraries upon which it relies.

Summary

Graphics files come in many different forms and require an associated range of programs to display and manipulate. The biggest difference is between bitmap and vector graphics formats. The former are manipulated by programs such as the GIMP, and encode data as a two-dimensional array of pixels, each of which has an associated color. Bitmap graphics don't scale well, but are good for encoding photographs. Vector graphics represent an image as a series of shapes. They scale very well and are good for creating diagrams, but aren't good for encoding photographic data. A wide array of vector graphics programs exist to create, manipulate, and display general-purpose drawings, data from a data file, mixed text and graphics documents, and so on.

Chapter 27

Multimedia and Games

W alk into a computer store today and you'll be hard pressed to find a computer for sale without a sound card or blazing-fast video hardware. Indeed, these two components are tied directly to two very popular uses of desktop computers today: *multimedia* and *games*. Multimedia applications involve heavy use of at least two media, such as graphics and sound. Movie video clips downloaded from the Internet, videoconferencing, and editing digitally-recorded home movies are all examples of multimedia applications. Games are another example, but they're distinct enough that they're often described separately. Although FreeBSD isn't known as a premier multimedia or games platform, it's not completely lacking in these arenas, and this chapter describes FreeBSD's multimedia and games capabilities.

This chapter begins with a look at audio hardware and tools. Video (in the form of X, as described in Chapter 13) is part of a typical multimedia setup, and is usually configured on a FreeBSD workstation. Audio, though, is less often configured correctly on a random workstation; it's not needed for word processing, graphics editing, or many other common tasks, but is required for multimedia and games. After describing audio setup and tools, this chapter proceeds to look at a few audio/video (AV) tools for FreeBSD, and then some games.

Note *Most of the tools described in this chapter can be installed from the* audio *FreeBSD packages or ports area.*

FreeBSD's Sound Capabilities

Most computer multimedia applications today involve audio and visual data. The X Window System (X for short) handles the visual data, or in some cases it's done through a library known as *SVGAlib*, which enables programs to access various standard *Super Video Graphics Adapter (SVGA)* video modes when X is *not* running. Because Chapter 13 covers X configuration and use, this section covers the hardware required for and configuration of support for the other half of audio/video applications—sound. In most cases, sound support requires FreeBSD kernel drivers for your particular model of sound card. Chapter 12 covers kernel configuration, so you may want to review that chapter before proceeding.

Note *Most x86 computers include primitive sound-generation equipment, consisting of a speaker mounted inside the case and a simple tone generator on the motherboard. Although this hardware can be used to play back sounds, the sound quality is lacking. A conventional sound card and external speakers produce much better sound quality, and permit audio input, which can be important for applications such as teleconferencing or recording voice messages. If your only choice is the internal speaker, you must use the* snd_pca.ko *driver to generate anything but very basic tones from the internal speaker.*

Supported Audio Hardware

To learn if your sound card is supported, check the HARDWARE.TXT file that ships with FreeBSD (it's in the root directory of the installation CD-ROM). The section of this file entitled "Audio Devices" specifies which chipsets are supported. As with many hardware devices, this list appears deceptively short; many of the devices listed are chipsets that are used in many different products. For instance, Crystal Semiconductor, ESS, and OPTi chipsets are used in many sound cards; and the Intel and VIA drivers work with the audio support included on many motherboards.

If your motherboard has built-in audio support that doesn't work with FreeBSD, you can still add a regular sound card and ignore the built-in audio device. Using the BIOS to disable the built-in sound support can help avoid conflicts if you do this.

You can find the kernel sound modules compiled on your FreeBSD 5.0 system in /boot/kernel, or /modules for FreeBSD 4.x. These files have names that begin with snd, so typing **ls /boot/kernel/snd*** (**ls /modules/snd*** on FreeBSD 4.x) should reveal the available sound modules. If you've recompiled your kernel and included your sound support in the new kernel, though, you won't find the module in this location. If you can't seem to find an appropriate kernel module, you may need to recompile your kernel with support for the appropriate device, as described in Chapter 12.

Unfortunately, determining which driver to use isn't always easy. There are two problems you may need to overcome:

- **Determining your audio chipset** You may not be able to tell which chipset a specific sound card uses. You may be able to glean clues from a Windows driver or Windows device listing, if your computer dual-boots to Windows; or you may be able to find the information by inspecting the chips on the board. The FreeBSD dmesg output may also contain clues, if FreeBSD can auto-detect the sound card.

- **Matching the chipset to the driver** The chipset list in the HARDWARE.TXT file specifies the driver name associated with most devices. The names are also usually related; for instance, snd_ess.ko is the driver for ESS chipsets, and snd_via82c686.ko is the driver for VIA chipsets.

If you can't determine with certainty which driver to use, you can try loading modules randomly or semirandomly, as described in the next section, "Starting Sound Support." You'll be able to load an incorrect sound module, but it won't work. Chances are it won't do any harm, although in theory it might cause other devices to malfunction in some rare situations.

If you can't find support for your sound card, you may want to check with 4Front Technologies (http://www.opensound.com). This company provides commercial sound drivers for FreeBSD and other Unix-like OSs. You can download a demo version, and if it works, pay the registration fee, which is probably less than a new sound card would cost.

Starting Sound Support

Soon after you boot your computer, type **dmesg | less** to examine the kernel boot messages. If your kernel was compiled with support for your sound card, you should see one or more messages identifying the card, such as the following for a Gravis UltraSound (GUS) PnP board:

```
gusc0: <Gravis UltraSound Plug & Play PCM> at port 0x32c-0x32f,
0x320-0x327,0x220-0x22f irq 12 drq 7,5 on isa0
pcm0: <GUS CS4231> on gusc0
gusc1: <Gravis UltraSound Plug & Play OPL> at port 0x388-0x389
irq 5 drq 1 on is a0
gusc2: <Gravis UltraSound Plug & Play MIDI> at port 0x330-0x331
on isa0
```

The dmesg command displays the kernel message buffer. This buffer is limited in size, and it's constantly fed new data. Thus, after your computer has been up for some time (a few days or even just a few hours), dmesg won't display information that's useful for identifying your hardware.

These messages may include more than one card driver (gusc0, gusc1, and gusc2 in the preceding example) to handle different parts of the card's hardware. One particularly important driver is the pcm0 driver, which handles *pulse code modulation (PCM)* encoding and decoding. Most digital audio formats use PCM in one way or another.

If you see these messages, your kernel has identified your sound card. You may or may not need to load a sound driver kernel module. If you need to load a driver module, you can do so with the kldload command:

```
# kldload snd_gusc.ko
```

This command is described in Chapter 12. In brief, the preceding example command loads the snd_gusc.ko driver, which supports the GUS PnP and various related cards. As noted in "Supported Audio Hardware," identifying the correct driver for your system isn't always easy.

Tip   *Some sound cards work best with support compiled into the kernel rather than loaded as modules. In fact, some cards' drivers aren't compiled as modules, and so must be compiled into the kernel. You may have to recompile your kernel to use such cards.*

Whether the driver is built into the kernel or loaded as a module, FreeBSD needs device support files for the card. In FreeBSD 5.0, these devices should be created automatically by the device filesystem. In earlier versions of FreeBSD, the files should already exist in the /dev directory, but if you need to rebuild these files for any reason, type the following commands to create the audio devices:

```
# cd /dev
# ./MAKEDEV snd0
```

The second command creates the appropriate device files. One you should check first is /dev/sndstat. You can display the contents of this file to verify that FreeBSD has located your sound card:

```
$ cat /dev/sndstat
FreeBSD Audio Driver (newpcm)
Installed devices:
pcm0: <GUS CS4231> at io 0x32c irq 12 drq 7:5 bufsz 4096 ↵
(1p/1r/0v channels duplex default)
```

If nothing is listed after Installed devices, FreeBSD hasn't found your sound card. In such a case, you should review your device selection in the FreeBSD kernel configuration, as described in Chapter 12, or the kernel modules you've loaded for sound support. It's also possible that your sound card is misconfigured in some way. Older ISA cards frequently use jumpers to set important hardware characteristics, such as the interrupt request (IRQ) used by the card. These must not conflict with other hardware, and you may need to set these characteristics in the /boot/device.hints file, thus:

```
hint.gusc.0.at="isa"
hint.gusc.0.port="0x32c"
hint.gusc.0.irq="12"
```

These lines tell the kernel to look for the `gusc` device on the ISA bus at port 0x32c and IRQ 12.

Once you've performed all these steps and obtained a report of the device's existence from `/dev/sndstat`, you should be able to use the sound card. Of course, you need to have speakers or headphones connected to the sound card, and these sometimes must have power applied. The card is accessed through devices such as `/dev/dsp0` and `/dev/mixer0`, but this detail is usually handled automatically by appropriate sound programs.

 Particularly if you use headphones, it's wise to begin testing with the volume set to the minimum value. If you just play a sound, it might play so loudly that it could damage your speakers, your headphones, or possibly even your hearing. You can set the volume using a mixer, as described in the upcoming section "Audio Mixers," or sometimes by adjusting a volume control on the speakers or headphones themselves.

Audio Tools

FreeBSD supports a large number of basic audio tools. These include mixers, basic audio playback and recording tools, and tools for handling specific types of audio files or media, such as the popular *Moving Picture Experts Group Layer 3 (MP3)* files or audio CDs. Most of these tools come in both command-line and X-based varieties. This chapter provides pointers to several of these tools but limited instruction on their use. For basic operations, most of these tools are fairly straightforward, but some support quite advanced options that are beyond the scope of this book.

 Many audio tools require privileged access to the audio device files. In FreeBSD 5.0, the /dev filesystem grants everybody full read/write access to the audio devices. You can change the permissions on these files, as described in Chapter 8, if you want to limit who can play or record sounds.

Audio Mixers

One of the first types of audio tool you should investigate is audio *mixers*. These programs enable you to adjust the volume of inputs to and outputs from your sound card. The most basic mixer for FreeBSD is called `mixer`, and is installed by default. This program is a command-line tool. A simplified `mixer` syntax is

```
mixer [-s] [[dev] [lvol[:rvol]]]
```

The meanings of these options are

- **-s** Specifying this option creates output that's suitable for input to `mixer` on the command line. You might use this option to save the current settings, which you can then feed back to `mixer` in a startup script.

- *dev* This option is the sound card device. Precisely what devices are available depends upon the sound card, but typical options are `vol` for master volume, `pcm` for PCM playback (that is, most audio playback), `synth` for synthesizer playback, `cd` for CD audio playback, `line` for line input, `mic` for microphone input, `igain` for input gain, and `ogain` for output gain.

- *lvol* and *rvol* These options are the left and right volume levels, which range from `0` to `100`, `0` being no volume and `100` being maximum volume. If you omit *rvol*, it's set to the same value as *lvol*.

More advanced options are available, but they mostly relate to systems that support multiple sound cards. Consult the `mixer` man page for more details.

The most basic use of `mixer` is typing the command alone. This action creates output summarizing the available devices and their current settings. If you want to adjust a setting, you can do so by specifying its name and level:

```
# mixer vol 75
```

Command line tools such as `mixer` are functional and are particularly useful in startup scripts to set your mixer values to something you find comfortable; however, they're not always the easiest tools to use. Some text-mode mixers use text-based menus and sliders that you can control by using the arrow keys, typing highlighted option names, and so on. For instance, Figure 27-1 shows the `aumix` program running in a GNOME Terminal window. (Such programs can be run without X in text-mode logins.)

If you prefer to work with a GUI tool, several are available. These programs present sliders you can adjust to set the various mixer devices. Figure 27-2 shows the GNOME Mixer, which comes with GNOME. You can launch this program by typing **gmix** in an xterm window or by selecting it from the GNOME menus. KDE also comes with a mixer, and there are mixers that aren't closely tied to any desktop environment, such as `xmix`, `xmmix`, and `xmixer`. Although they differ in some details, all work much like the GNOME Mixer shown in Figure 27-2—you click on the sliders and adjust them to the desired values. Buttons near the sliders typically enable you to mute an output or specify which of several input sources will be recorded when you use a recording tool.

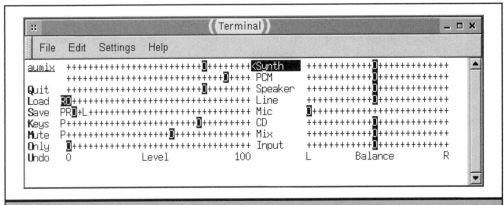

Figure 27-1. *Some text-mode mixers provide visual representations of mixer levels.*

Command-Line Audio Playback and Recording Tools

One of the most basic tasks of audio handling is the ability to record and play back sound files. Among the most basic tools to perform this task is `play`, which plays back or records a sound file, depending upon how it's called. (A symbolic link called `rec` is used to record; the program knows which name you used to call it, and adjusts its actions accordingly.) A syntax for this command is

```
play [options] filename [effect]
```

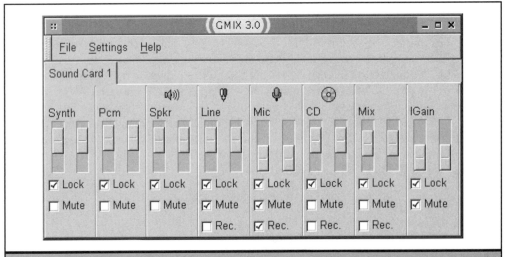

Figure 27-2. *The GNOME Mixer and other X-based mixers provide sliders so you can adjust the volume of various inputs and outputs.*

To use its simplest form, you can type the command followed only by a filename, such as **play zathras.wav** to play the file called zathras.wav. Sometimes, though, you may need to give the program some hints about the file type. You do this by specifying one or more options. These options are frequently required when recording (by using the rec command rather than play) in order to get a file of the desired type. Available options include

- **-c *channels*** or **--channels=*channels*** These options let you set the number of channels of sound in the file. This value is normally either 1 (mono) or 2 (stereo).

- **-f *format*** or **--format=*format*** These options set the recording format—that is, the encoding method used to store the digital data. (This option is separate from the file type, described shortly.) Options for *format* are s (signed linear), u (unsigned linear), U (U-law logarithmic), a (ADPCM), A (A-law logarithmic), and g (GSM). All but the first two of these options enable audio compression, which may degrade sound quality.

- **-r *rate*** or **--rate=*rate*** These options set the recording rate, in samples per second. The higher the rate the higher the sound quality (particularly in reproducing high tones) but the larger the resulting file. Audio CDs are recorded at a rate of 44,100 samples per second, also known as 44,100 *hertz* or 44.1 kilohertz (kHz). Most sound cards can handle at least this high a sample rate. A *rate* of 11250 or even 8000 is adequate for low-quality voice recording, but for music, you should use 44100 or possibly 48000.

- **-s *size*** or **--size=*size*** These options set the sample size in bits—that is, how many bits are used to encode each sample. Options are b (8-bit bytes), w (16-bit words), l (32-bit long words), f (32-bit floats), d (64-bit double floats), and D (80-bit IEEE floats). Most sound files use 8-bit bytes or 16-bit words.

- **-t *type*** or **--type=*type*** These options set the recording file type. The type is usually associated with a particular filename extension, such as .wav for most Windows sound files or .au for Sun-format files.

- **-x** or **--xinu** These options reverse the order of bytes in a word for 16-bit and wider recording formats. They're sometimes required when playing recordings from or making recordings for a platform that uses a different byte order than the system you're using.

As an example of play and rec in action, consider the following two commands:

```
$ rec -t wav -r 44100 -s w -c 2 sample.wav
$ play sample.wav
```

The first command records a file, sample.wav, using whatever input device is specified by your current mixer settings. The file is to be a .wav file and is recorded with CD-quality settings (44.1 kHz, 16-bit, two channels). By default, rec records a file forever; you must terminate it by typing CTRL-C. The second command plays back the file you've just recorded, so you can check to see that it recorded correctly.

 Your mixer's audio gain settings can be extremely important when recording a file. If set too high, loud sounds will reach plateaus at the maximum values you can record, which results in a static-filled distortion. If set too low, the sound may be inaudible unless you adjust your playback volume settings upward. Using GUI tools and editors can sometimes help by providing a visual display of recording levels.

GUI Audio Playback and Recording Tools

The `play` program is a very basic recording program. The program provides little in the way of feedback about a recording in progress, and of course as a text-mode program, it's not appealing to less experienced users. One solution is a simple X-based audio recorder, such as the GNOME Sound Recorder (shown in Figure 27-3). This program has capabilities similar to those of `play`, but it provides a GUI interface. You can launch the program by typing **grecord** at an xterm prompt or by selecting the program from the GNOME menus. KDE provides a similar tool, `krecord`, which you can launch by typing **krecord** at an xterm prompt or selecting the program from the KDE menus. You can record a file by clicking the Record button, play it back by clicking Play, and save it by selecting File | Save As from the menu. You can adjust various recording options, such as the sample rate and number of channels, by selecting Settings | Preferences. This action produces a dialog box in which you can set many of the options you can set in `play/record` via its command-line switches.

More sophisticated GUI audio tools, such as `glame`, `xwave`, and Sweep provide the means to edit an audio file. Figure 27-4 shows a Sweep editing window. This window displays the sound file visually—time runs from left to right, and the volume of the sound is represented by the magnitude of the sound waves in the editing window.

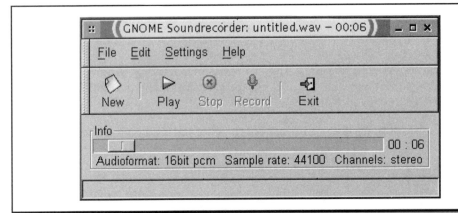

Figure 27-3. *Simple GUI audio playback and recording utilities provide few options, but are adequate for simple playback or recording tasks.*

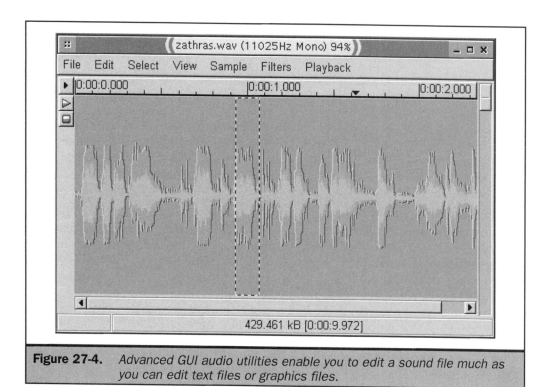

Figure 27-4. *Advanced GUI audio utilities enable you to edit a sound file much as you can edit text files or graphics files.*

You can select blocks of sound and apply various editing tools to them. For instance, you can increase or decrease the sample's volume, reverse the sample, apply echo effects, and so on. Precisely what options are available depends upon the editor, of course.

MP3 Tools

Audio CDs are a popular format for storing music, but for some uses, they're awkward—as physical media, audio CDs can get lost or damaged, and it can be a hassle to juggle them in and out of players. It's possible to extract audio tracks from a CD and store them as audio files, but these files tend to be fairly large. CD-quality recording is 44.1 kHz, 16-bit, with two channels, which works out to about 10MB per minute. Such values are large enough that even a modern 120GB hard disk could hold only about 20 CDs worth of music. To cope with this problem, a compressed format has been developed: MP3. Like the *Joint Photographic Experts Group (JPEG)* graphics file format, the MP3 file format is *lossy*, meaning that it intentionally corrupts data in the interest of saving file size. MP3 is designed to create changes that are difficult for humans to hear, though, so a huge size decrease can be attained with only a modest decrease in quality. High-quality MP3 files are usually about a fifth the size of their uncompressed originals, and lower-quality MP3 files can be even smaller. For this reason, the MP3 format has become a popular one for storing music for playback on computers. Portable MP3 players, similar to portable cassette or CD players, also exist, and they can hold dozens or hundreds of songs. Being able to manipulate and play MP3 files is therefore an important capability.

Most music available today is copyrighted. Although MP3 manipulation programs enable you to copy such music, doing so may be illegal. As a general rule, copying for purely personal use, such as placing a library of MP3 files on your computer or a portable MP3 player, is OK, so long as you possess the original source. Giving MP3 files of copyrighted music to friends is not legal, though. Likewise, downloading MP3 files containing copyrighted music is not legal unless this download is authorized by the copyright holder (say, if you've bought a song in MP3 form on an authorized web site).

Creating MP3 Files

If you want to create MP3 files from an audio CD, the first step is performing *digital audio extraction (DAE)*, often called *ripping*, on the source CD. This step involves retrieving the digital audio data from the CD, using its EIDE or SCSI interface. After you've created uncompressed audio files, you can convert them to MP3 format. Neither of these steps uses your sound card directly. In practice, it's sometimes possible to perform both steps at once. For instance, the text-based cd2mp3 program provides a one-step method for performing this task. After installing the cd2mp3 package or port, type **cd2mp3** to start the process.

To perform DAE, you must have read/write access to your CD-ROM drive (/dev/acd0 for EIDE CD-ROMs). The cd2mp3 software also uses the current directory to store temporary files, so you should launch the program only from a directory to which you have write access, and on a filesystem that has at least enough free space to hold a temporary uncompressed .wav file (about 10MB per minute).

After you start cd2mp3, the program asks you a series of questions:

1. **Encoding option** You can choose to encode an entire CD, just some tracks, or an existing .wav file. You can also use cd2mp3 to extract a track as a .wav file without encoding it as an MP3 file.

2. **Sampling rate** This term is used oddly in reference to MP3 files. Normally, the sampling rate is the number of samples per second, as described earlier, in "Command-Line Audio Playback and Recording Tools." In the case of MP3 files, though, it refers to the rate at which the file must be read to be played back, in kilobits per second. This measurement can be useful if you want to use MP3 files over a streaming medium—that is, delivered in real time via a web server or the like. For personal use, though, it's best thought of as a compression level option. cd2mp3 provides three sampling rate options: 56, 128, and 256. The higher the sampling rate, the better the resulting sound quality, but the larger the file.

3. **Output filename**   You must specify the output filename for the MP3 file. These files normally have names that end in `.mp3`.

4. **CD-ROM drive**   The `cd2mp3` utility defaults to reading files from `/dev/cdrom`, but this file may not be present on your system. You may need to specify the actual CD-ROM device, such as `/dev/acd0` for EIDE CD-ROMs or `/dev/cd0` for SCSI CD-ROMs. Alternatively, you can create a symbolic link from the actual device to `/dev/cdrom`.

5. **Track number**   If you want to encode just one track, the program asks you for the track number.

After you enter this information, `cd2mp3` begins work. The first step is reading the data from the CD-ROM drive. With many CD-ROM drives, this process takes much longer than it would take to play the track on an audio CD player. The reason has to do with the way that music is encoded on the CD, as opposed to data; there's no easy way to reliably seek to a specific point in an audio track, so whenever `cd2mp3` requests audio data, it must compare what it's retrieved to what it retrieved the last time to avoid overlapping or missing data. The retrieved track is stored in a file named `track`*nn*`.wav`, where *nn* is the track number. After `cd2mp3` has retrieved the track, the program converts the `.wav` file into an MP3 file. This process can also take several minutes, depending upon your CPU speed—essentially, `cd2mp3` must compress the multimegabyte `.wav` file, which is a CPU-intensive task. The result should be a file with the name you specified, which you can test with an MP3 player.

Playing MP3 Files

Many MP3 players are available for FreeBSD. A few options include

- **`ksmp3play`**   This program is a text-based MP3 player. It uses the `curses` library to position text elements on the screen.

- **`mp3blaster`**   This program is another `curses`-based text MP3 player.

- **`kmp3`**   This is a KDE-based MP3 player.

- **`replay`**   This is a GNOME-based MP3 player.

- **`x11amp`**   This is a popular X-based MP3 player.

Playing an MP3 file works much like playing a `.wav` or other audio file, as described earlier, in "Command-Line Audio Playback and Recording Tools" and "GUI Audio Playback and Recording Tools." MP3 players are likely to include a somewhat different mix of options, though. One feature that these programs usually include is the ability to handle a *playlist*, which is a list of files that you want to play in one session. You can often save a playlist so that you can easily play the same set of songs without loading them all into a playlist every time you launch the MP3 player. Some MP3 players, such as `x11amp` (shown in Figure 27-5), provide additional options, such as a graphic equalizer.

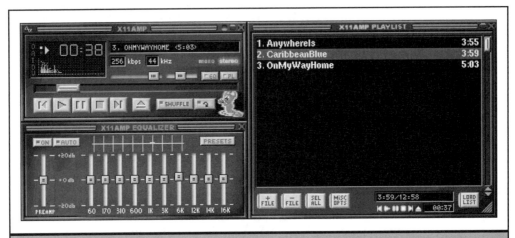

Figure 27-5.   *Some MP3 players borrow features from conventional audio equipment.*

Audio CD Players

Audio CD players work much like MP3 players in many respects; however, there are some important practical differences:

- **Audio path**   When you create MP3 files from an audio CD and then play them, you extract data from a CD-ROM drive via its EIDE or SCSI interface and then play the sound as an ordinary audio file using the PCM hardware on the sound card. When you play an audio CD directly, the CD-ROM drive sends analog audio signals (or occasionally digital audio) to the sound card, which mixes it as a CD input. Thus, playing an audio CD directly leaves your computer's PCM hardware unused, so that you can hear audio tones generated by other programs, such as error tones, new-mail indicators, and so on. Playing an audio CD requires that you connect a wire from your CD-ROM drive to your sound card.

- **Media presence**   You must physically insert an audio CD into your CD-ROM drive to play it. If you'd previously extracted a CD as MP3 files and played those, your CD-ROM drive would remain free for use.

- **Audio quality**   The MP3 format is lossy, so you may notice some degradation of the sound quality if you play from MP3 files rather than directly from the source CD. This degradation is likely to be greater if you select a sampling rate of less than 256 because low sampling rates create greater compression, and hence more data loss.

- **Cross-CD playlists**   You cannot easily create a cross-CD playlist when you play CDs directly, short of extracting tracks and burning a custom mix CD-R.

Cross-CD playlists of MP3 files are no problem, provided you've created the MP3 files.

- **CPU load**   Playing an MP3 file requires a certain amount of CPU time to decompress the MP3 data and send it to the sound card. Playing an audio CD, on the other hand, requires almost no CPU time.

In the end, whether you want to play your audio CDs directly or extract CD tracks into MP3 files and play them indirectly is a matter of personal preference and your specific needs.

Audio/Video Applications

So far, this chapter has described only the audio portion of the multimedia equation. True multimedia tools, though, provide more than audio playback or recording; these tools also provide video playback or recording. In most cases, AV tools require no special hardware, aside from the sound card, because most AV tools exist to deliver content to end users. In a few cases, such as videoconferencing, you need to connect a digital camera to get the full benefit of such tools. Unfortunately, FreeBSD's support for such hardware is still embryonic, so this chapter focuses upon audio/video playback tools. These often exist as stand-alone programs, but AV files are often found on the Web (movie trailers on film sites, for instance), so linking players to a web browser is sometimes an important task to accomplish.

Audio/Video File Formats

As you browse the Web or obtain AV files, you may notice that they come in several different formats. Some of these formats are well supported in FreeBSD, but others aren't. The most popular formats are

- **AC-3, aka ATSC A/52**   This encoding method is used mainly with digital television signals and DVDs. FreeBSD supports it through the liba52 project (`http://liba52.sourceforge.net`).

- **MPEG-1 and MPEG-2**   The *Moving Picture Experts Group (MPEG)* has released several file formats. (In fact, the popular MP3 audio file format originates with this group.) The MPEG-1 and MPEG-2 formats are popular for distributing computer AV files. The libmpeg2 (`http://libmpeg2.sourceforge.net`) and MPEG Audio Decoder (`http://www.mars.org/home/rob/proj/mpeg/`) projects provide support for these file formats in FreeBSD.

- **RealVideo**   This popular format was developed by RealNetworks (`http://www.real.com`) as a video streaming format. It's related to the RealAudio format that's also used by RealNetworks. This file format requires a player (called RealPlayer) from RealNetworks, which doesn't produce a native FreeBSD player; but the Linux player works with FreeBSD's Linux compatibility libraries. You can install it from the `audio/linux-realplayer` port, but the procedure requires retrieving a Linux file after entering information on RealNetwork's web site. (Attempting to install the port produces full directions.)

- **AVI** Microsoft's *Audio/Video Interleave (AVI)* format is a common one for AV files distributed on the Internet or with software packages on CD-ROMs. Although AVI-format files usually have the same `.avi` filename extension, there are actually several different encoding methods, each of which requires explicit support. The FreeBSD `xanim` program supports many, but not all, AVI files.

- **Quicktime** Apple's Quicktime format is moderately popular on the Internet. As you might expect, its strongest presence is on sites catering to Macintosh users. This format was designed as a computer AV format. Like AVI, Quicktime actually comprises several different encoding methods. The FreeBSD `xanim` program supports some Quicktime files.

- **FLIC** Autodesk created the FLIC file format, which is often used for computer-generated animation. Two filename extensions, `.fli` and `.flc`, are associated with specific common subtypes of this encoding method. Once again, `xanim` supports this file type.

- **DivX** This video format is a variant on MPEG-4 that originated with DivX Networks (`http://www.divxnetworks.com`). It's targeted at distributing movie-length files over broadband connections in times measured in tens of minutes. There is some early work on open source DivX players. A more mature Linux DivX player works with FreeBSD's Linux compatibility layer, and can be installed from the `graphics/divx4linux4` port.

FreeBSD AV libraries support some of these file formats. These libraries enable an assortment of programs to play AV files. Other formats require specific programs to run, such as RealPlayer or `xanim`.

AVI file formats have evolved substantially in the decade preceding 2002, and they're likely to continue to evolve in the future. This fact can cause problems because you may download a file that you think you should be able to play, only to find that the file does *not* play. If this happens, you can check for an updated player or libraries, or search for an alternative player for the file type. Sometimes these attempts won't be successful, though.

One common goal is to play video DVDs on a FreeBSD system equipped with a DVD-ROM drive. Various libraries, such as liba52, exist to handle the encoding methods used on DVDs, and tools such as `xine` (`http://xine.sourceforge.net`) are capable of handling the job. Unfortunately, the task is complicated by the encryption technique (*Content Scrambling System*, or *CSS*) used on most commercial video DVDs.

Stand-alone DVD player manufacturers and DVD player software distributors for Windows and Mac OS purchase decryption keys from the DVD Copy Control Association (DVD-CCA), enabling them to play DVDs. The DVD-CCA doesn't make such keys available for open source projects, though, and as of 2002 no commercial DVD playing software is available for FreeBSD. That said, the CSS encryption has been broken, and libraries to decrypt CSS-encoded DVDs are available and can be used in conjunction with `xine` and other programs for FreeBSD; but under the terms of the Digital Millennium Copyright Act (DMCA), distribution of such libraries is illegal in the United States. Several court cases relate to this issue in 2002, though, and it's possible these cases will make playing DVDs on FreeBSD legal in the future.

 Most commercial video DVDs use CSS, but data DVDs don't use CSS. Thus, a DVD-ROM drive can still be used under FreeBSD to read data DVDs. In fact, it's possible to obtain FreeBSD on such a data DVD.

Playing Stand-Alone Files

Suppose that you've obtained an AV file that you want to play using FreeBSD. You can do so, much as you'd play an audio file such as a `.wav` or `.mp3` file. The difference is that you must use an AV file player. Some of these players have already been mentioned. The most common are

- **xanim** This program, headquartered at `http://xanim.va.pubnix.com` and available as a FreeBSD package or port, has long been the standard AV player for FreeBSD and other UNIX-like OSs. It supports a wide range of formats, including many AVI and Quicktime files.

- **xine** This program is rising rapidly in popularity. It supports some of the same file types as `xanim`, but `xine` emphasizes support for higher-quality video formats, including those used on DVDs. `xine` supports plug-ins to extend its capabilities, including some that support CSS decryption (officially available only from sites outside the United States). The main `xine` web page is `http://xine.sourceforge.net`.

- **RealPlayer** This player, mentioned earlier in "Audio/Video File Formats," handles the RealAudio and RealVideo files common on web sites. You can install it using the FreeBSD ports system after downloading a Linux file from the RealNetworks web site, `http://www.realnetworks.com`.

To play a video file, you normally type the player's name followed by the name of the file you want to play. For instance, you might type the following to play an AVI file:

```
$ xanim kinetoscope.avi
```

The result should be a window displaying the file. Some programs provide controls within the playback window, but others (including xanim, shown in Figure 27-6) use separate windows for the playback and control functions.

Linking Players to a Web Browser

Many AV file formats (and audio-only formats, as well) can be found on web pages. Most web browsers enable you to link file types to "helper" programs so that you can load such files directly from the Web, rather than download the file and then manually launch a reader capable of handling them. To accomplish this task, you must associate a Multipurpose Internet Mail Extension (MIME) type with the AV player in your web browser. Details of how to accomplish this task vary from one browser to another, but the basic requirements are the same for all browsers. As an illustration, here's how to do the job with Mozilla:

1. Launch Mozilla by typing **mozilla** in an xterm or selecting it from your window manager or desktop environment menu.

2. Select Edit | Preferences from the Mozilla menu bar. This action produces the Preferences dialog box from which you can configure Mozilla.

3. Select Navigator | Helper Applications from the expandable menu on the left side of the Preferences dialog box. Mozilla displays the Helper Applications tool shown in Figure 27-7.

Figure 27-6. *Video playback tools provide controls similar to those of audio playback tools, but also display a video image to go with the file's sound track.*

4. Click New Type. Mozilla displays the New Type dialog box, in which you enter four pieces of information: A description (for your future reference), a filename extension (such as `.wav` or `.avi`), a MIME type, and the complete path to the application that handles the file type. Table 27-1 summarizes the MIME types for some common AV file formats, as well as the path to a program that can handle them.

5. Click OK in the New Type dialog box. You should see the new type added to the Preferences dialog box.

6. Click OK in the Preferences dialog box.

If you're not sure what the appropriate MIME type is for a file type, and if Apache is installed on your system, check the `/usr/local/etc/apache2/mime.types` file. You can also find MIME type listings on web pages, such as `http://www.december .com/html/spec/mime.html`.

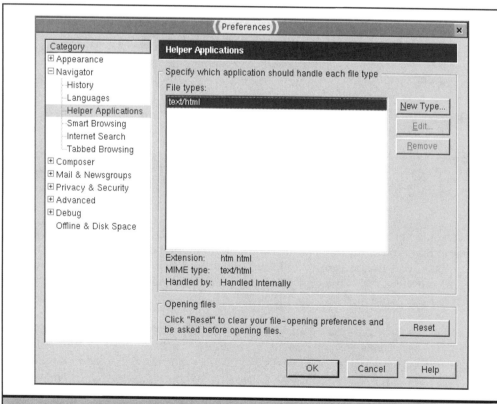

Figure 27-7. *The Mozilla Helper Applications tool in Preferences enables you to associate applications with MIME types.*

File Type	Filename Extension	MIME Type	Possible FreeBSD Helper Application
WAV audio files	.wav	audio/x-wav	/usr/local/bin/play
MP3 audio files	.mp3	audio/mpeg	/usr/local/bin/ x11amp
MPEG video files	.mpg, .mpeg, .mpe	video/mpeg	/usr/X11R6/bin/ xanim
Quicktime video files	.mov, .qt	video/quicktime	/usr/X11R6/bin/ xanim
AVI video files	.avi	video/x-msvideo	/usr/X11R6/bin/ xanim
RealAudio files	.ra	audio/x-realaudio	/usr/local/bin/ realplay
RealAudio files	.rpm	audio/x-pn-realaudio-plugin	/usr/local/bin/ realplay
RealAudio files	.ram	audio/x-pn-realaudio	/usr/local/bin/ realplay
RealVideo files	.rv	audio/vnd.rn-realaudio	/usr/local/bin/ realplay
RealMedia files	.rm	video/vnd.rn-realvideo	/usr/local/bin/ realplay

Table 27-1.   *Common AV File Types, Their Extensions and MIME Types, and Possible FreeBSD Players*

Once you've linked the MIME type to an appropriate player, the next time you click on a link to that type of file, the web browser should launch the player application. It may first ask if you always want to link files of that type to your chosen application, though. If your viewer is a Linux program, you must enable Linux binary compatibility, as described in Chapter 4.

Caution   *In some cases, automatically launching a player is inadvisable—for example, when the file type can contain program code, such as a script or executable program. Also, some file formats may be mistaken for others; for instance, the .rpm extension used by RealPlayer files is also used by Red Hat Package Manager (RPM) package files for Linux programs. Web servers may therefore get the MIME type for such packages wrong.*

Recreation with FreeBSD: Games

Most games are multimedia applications, although there are exceptions—many early text-mode games are available for FreeBSD, and are no more deserving of the moniker "multimedia" than are any other text-mode programs. FreeBSD sports a wide range of games, but most of them are simple by today's standards. Most flashy commercial games are released only for Windows, and sometimes Mac OS, leaving FreeBSD users in the cold. A few are available for Linux, though, and FreeBSD can run many of these programs using its Linux compatibility libraries. You can even run some Windows games using WINE (described in Chapter 4).

Traditional Text-Mode UNIX Games

In the 1970s and 1980s, when UNIX was young, computer games in general were decidedly primitive by today's standards. In fact, many of the earliest computer games were written for UNIX. Such games used text-mode displays, using either prose to describe the player's game surroundings and actions (such as You are in a maze of twisty little passages, all alike, from the classic Adventure game) or crude text-based graphics—for instance, using vertical bars and dashes to mark out a maze.

You can find an assortment of text-based games in the games packages or ports section, but many of these games aren't clearly labeled as being text-based. Most people today are likely to be more interested in X-based games, which can display sophisticated graphics. One particular class of text-based game has survived and continues to see development, though: *adventure* games. This class of game, named after the classic Adventure, creates scenarios much like you'd find in a novel, and uses prose and storytelling techniques as a novel does. In an adventure game, though, you play the protagonist, and you give the game instructions. For instance, here's a short session from the commercial game *Planetfall*, as played with Frotz in FreeBSD:

```
Escape Pod
This is one of the Feinstein's primary escape pods, for use in
extreme emergencies. A mass of safety webbing, large enough to
hold several dozen people, fills half the pod. The controls are
entirely automated. The bulkhead leading out is open.

The ship shakes again. You hear, from close by, the sounds of
emergency bulkheads closing.

>wait
Time passes...
```

> Through the viewport of the pod you see the Feinstein dwindle as
> you head away. Bursts of light dot its hull. Suddenly, a huge
> explosion blows the Feinstein into tiny pieces, sending the escape
> pod tumbling away!
>
> You are thrown against the bulkhead, head first. It seems that
> getting in the safety webbing would have been a good idea.
>
>   **** You have died ****

Adventure games accept simple English commands, such as this example's **wait**. All but the most primitive games understand more complex syntax, though, such as **insert the gold coin into the vending machine**. When you play an adventure game, you should be prepared to "die" multiple times before completing the story— as the preceding example shows, even waiting can be a lethal course of action!

Most adventure games today use a gaming language known as *z-code*, which was used in the popular 1980s games by Infocom. Today, you can run old Infocom titles and new z-code games developed by a community of text adventure enthusiasts using any of several z-code interpreters, such as Frotz, Nitfol, `xinfocom`, `zip` (which is unrelated to the file archive utility of the same name), and Jzip. One particularly large archive of adventure games is `http://www.ifarchive.org/ indexes/ if-archiveXgamesXzcode.html`. This site houses mostly free games written by people around the world. If you can find a collection of Infocom games, you can run them, as well. (Various collections have been released over the years, but they're hard to find today.)

Another class of text-based game that's survived is based on an old UNIX standard called Rogue. This game was a text-based program in which players competed in exploring a maze, in the process collecting treasures and battling monsters. Rogue derivatives include NetHack, Angband, and Moria. Some of these derivatives sport more graphical interfaces or graphical subvariants than the original text-mode Rogue. In fact, many modern games on other platforms, such as Diablo and Quake, owe a lot to Rogue.

X-Based Games

Most games today use either X or SVGAlib to display graphics. These games range from simple computerized card games to very sophisticated first-person shoot-em-ups or strategy games. As with text-based games, you can find many of these games in the games packages or ports section. Many X-based games are labeled as such, but some are not. If something sounds interesting, you can try it; if you don't like it, you can uninstall it, as described in Chapter 11.

Both the GNOME and KDE environments ship with game collections, in the `gnomegames` and `kdegames` packages, respectively. Once you install these packages, you can reach the games from the GNOME or KDE menus, which makes it easy to find them. (One problem with the wide assortment of small FreeBSD games is that it's easy to forget what's installed, or even to be unaware that a particular game is available.) The GNOME and KDE games tend to be fairly basic programs—card games, puzzles, and so on.

Although most X-based games are fairly simple, some are more complex. Some of these include

- **GNU Chess**   As any regular player knows, chess is a complex game, although the core GNU Chess program isn't very flashy. There are several GUI front-ends to GNU Chess, such as GNOME Chess. These tools provide more elaborate but intuitive user interfaces.

- **FreeCiv**   This program is a strategy game similar to the commercial Civilization. Unlike the original, FreeCiv is network-enabled—it consists of a server package and a client package. To play the game on a single computer, you must install and run both packages. The server does the work of handling the game universe, and the client handles user interaction. This architecture enables you to easily support multiplayer games—somebody on another computer can install the client package alone and connect to your server.

- **LinCity**   This program is similar to the commercial SimCity program; it simulates a city that you must manage by placing virtual buildings, managing the city budget, and so on.

Summarizing how to operate games is fairly pointless because the games vary so much in user interfaces, goals, and so on. In a turn-taking game such as GNU Chess or FreeCiv, you generally select menu options or objects in the game window in order to effect changes in the game. Some turn-taking games require you to explicitly select an option to move to the next turn. Other games interact in real time, meaning that your actions are reflected nearly instantly on the screen. Such games include many shoot-em-ups such as `xasteroids`, and other games such as Jewel Box (aka `xjewel`).

Commercial Games

Unfortunately, you won't find many commercial FreeBSD games in your local computer superstore; the FreeBSD market is too small to support games. The Linux market is somewhat larger, though, and there have been several titles released for Linux, including Quake III Arena, Civilization: Call to Power, and SimCity 3000. Unfortunately, many commercial Linux games were ported by Loki, which has gone out of business. Thus, these games can be hard to find, but they may be available in some stores. There's also no guarantee that any particular game will work with

FreeBSD's Linux compatibility libraries. I recommend you do a web search or post to an appropriate Usenet newsgroup or FreeBSD mailing list before dropping money on a commercial Linux game.

Some Windows games can be run from FreeBSD using WINE, the Windows compatibility package for FreeBSD described in Chapter 4. In fact, gaming is one of the motivating forces behind the development of WINE, so some games run fairly well in WINE—better than some productivity tools, in fact. Nonetheless, WINE is far from perfect, and it can be a finicky package to configure. Before buying a Windows game for use with FreeBSD and WINE, you should check on compatibility at the WINE Application Database (`http://appdb.codeweavers.com`)—click one of the browse or search options on the left side of the page to find information on the game you want to run. If you can't find the information you want, try posting your query to the `comp.emulators.ms-windows.wine` newsgroup.

Summary

Multimedia applications are some of the most challenging for FreeBSD because FreeBSD's developers have traditionally favored more prosaic development efforts, such as optimizing the network stack, writing servers, and even creating business applications. Nonetheless, FreeBSD developers and users enjoy the benefits of multimedia tools, so FreeBSD provides a growing assortment of these programs. The FreeBSD multimedia tools range from simple command-line utilities to record or play back audio files to sophisticated audio editing and video playback programs. FreeBSD also sports a number of games. Most of these games are fairly simple by today's standards, but a few are moderately complex, and even the simple games can be enjoyable. It's also possible to run a few games written for other environments, such as Linux or Windows, from FreeBSD, although you're not likely to be able to run all the games you can find for such OSs.

The
Complete
Reference

FreeBSD

Part VI

System Maintenance

Chapter 28

Automated and Nonautomated Routine Maintenance

uch of this book is devoted to setting up a FreeBSD system or using it for day-to-day work. This chapter, though, begins Part VI, which describes how to keep a FreeBSD system working properly. The first topic at hand is routine maintenance—things you may need to do on a regular basis, such as daily or weekly. This chapter focuses upon four routine maintenance tasks: removing stray files, monitoring your system's CPU use, monitoring your system's memory use, and keeping your system software up-to-date. Watching these four items can help you head off problems such as disk-full errors that cause your users to lose work, or poor performance caused by a needlessly overloaded CPU or excessive memory use. It's far better to catch such problems early than to receive complaints from your users!

Cleaning Up Files

Computers are like houses, offices, cars, or anything else that sees human occupation or interaction: They collect clutter. Your house's clutter likely takes the form of old newspapers, junk mail, children's toys, tennis shoes, and so on. Your computer's clutter takes the form of old files. These files may be old log files, temporary files that haven't been deleted, unused program files, and user files of various sorts. Just as monitoring and controlling household clutter can make your life easier, monitoring and controlling FreeBSD file clutter can make your system administration easier. Fortunately, FreeBSD provides some tools to help in this respect, but some tasks still require your attention.

Log Files

It's sometimes important to be able to go back and review a program's activities in order to debug a problem, trace a potential system intrusion, or simply confirm that the computer is functioning correctly. For these reasons, many programs (particularly servers) record their activities in *log files*. Most FreeBSD log files reside in the `/var/log` directory. Important specific log files include `messages`, which holds generic system messages; `security`, which holds security-related messages; `auth.log`, which holds authentication messages; `sendmail.st` (a binary log file) and `maillog`, which hold information on the sendmail mail server's operations; and `cron`, which records the activities of the cron scheduling program. Other log files record information on particular servers or subsystems. You can peruse the `/var/log` directory's contents to see what's present. Some chapters of this book refer to particular log files and their contents, often as a debugging resource.

Unfortunately, recording information in log files means that the log files grow in size. In theory, this fact means that log files could eventually grow to consume all available disk space. To avoid this pitfall, it's necessary to periodically clean out log files. This task is most commonly handled by log file *rotation*, in which an active log file is retired and renamed, and possibly compressed to save disk space. A new file with the same name as the original is then opened. For instance, `/var/log/messages` may be retired, renamed, and compressed to create `/var/log/messages.0.gz`.

The computer then continues to record information in a new /var/log/messages file. On the next round, the system renames messages.0.gz to messages.1.gz, creates a new messages.0.gz from the old messages file, and creates a new messages file. Eventually, rather than renaming a compressed messages.#.gz file, the system deletes it.

This log rotation task is handled by a program called newsyslog, which is called from a system cron job (described in Chapter 6). The default configuration for FreeBSD works well for a typical installation, but you may need to tune this configuration. To do so, you must edit the /etc/newsyslog.conf file, which consists of comment lines that begin with pound signs (#) and one line for each log file to be rotated. The log file lines take the form:

```
/log/file/name   [owner:group]   mode   count   size   when   [flags] ⤶
[pid_file] [sig_num]
```

The meanings of these elements are

- **/log/file/name**   The first field is the complete path to the log file.
- **[owner:group]**   The second field is optional; you can omit it if you like. If you do specify it, the field contains the owner and group of the rotated files, such as root:wheel.
- **mode**   You must specify the permissions on the archived log files, as in 644 to enable anybody to read the files, or 600 to make the files readable only to the owner. (Chapter 8 describes file permissions in more detail.)
- **count**   This field is a number that specifies how many archived log files to retain.
- **size**   This field specifies the size threshold in kilobytes for archiving the original log file. For instance, if you set size to 100, newsyslog will archive the file after it exceeds 100KB in size. Setting this field to an asterisk (*) causes newsyslog to ignore the file size and rely upon the next field to decide when to archive a file.
- **when**   newsyslog is called once an hour by the standard FreeBSD system cron job, and ordinarily it uses the size field to determine when to archive a file. In such a configuration, the when field contains an asterisk. Alternatively, you can force a rotation at a particular time by placing an asterisk in the size field and entering a code in the when field. You can specify the time as an ISO 8601-format field by beginning the field with an at-sign (@); or you can lead the field with a dollar sign ($) and use the letters D, W, and M to specify the interval within a day, week, or month. For instance, $M1D6 specifies rotation at 6:00 A.M. on the first day of each month, and $W7D22 specifies rotation at 10:00 P.M. (D22) every Saturday (W7). These formats are more fully explained in the newsyslog man page.

- **[flags]**   This optional field serves a dual purpose. First, you can tell newsyslog to compress the archives using gzip or bzip2 by providing a Z or J character, respectively. Second, if a log file uses a binary format, you should provide a B character in this field. Ordinarily, newsyslog adds a plain-text notation to the file indicating when it was rotated; but such a notation is likely to cause problems in binary files, so the B flag tells newsyslog not to perform this action.

- **[pid_file]**   Some servers must be told when their log files are modified. To send such a message, newsyslog must know the process ID (PID) of the server. Many servers store their PIDs in files, and this optional field tells newsyslog what this filename is. Consult your server's documentation to learn where its PID is stored, if this option is necessary.

- **[sig_num]**   When you specify a PID file, you may also need to tell newsyslog what signal to send to the server. By default, newsyslog sends a SIGHUP, which causes most servers to reload their configurations and open a new log file, enabling newsyslog to back up the old one. Some servers don't respond appropriately to SIGHUP, though, in which case you can specify a signal number in the *sig_num* field. Consult your server's documentation to learn how it responds to SIGHUP.

In many cases, you won't need to touch the log file configuration; however, if you find that a particular log file is becoming very large, you may want to check /etc/newsyslog.conf to see if it's being rotated. If it's not, you may want to add it to the rotation, then check back to see that the rotation is proceeding correctly. On some systems, you may want to tweak the logging options—for instance, keeping fewer or more log files or changing the default log file size for your local needs.

Temporary Files

Many programs need to create temporary files. These files may contain data that are being processed, be backup files in case of program crashes, provide information on the running program, be files passed from one program to another in a processing chain, and so on. In theory, every temporary file created should be deleted by the process that created it or by a subsequent program in a processing chain. In practice, though, this doesn't always happen; factors such as program bugs, program crashes, or abnormal terminations (possibly even due to factors outside of a program's control, such as a power failure) may leave temporary files lying around. Given enough time, such problems can create a lot of clutter. On occasion, temporary files can cause another problem: They may grow to abnormal size, consuming all available disk space.

As one measure in controlling such problems, FreeBSD sets aside directories intended exclusively for use as community temporary space. The most important of these directories is /tmp, but other examples are /var/tmp and /usr/tmp.

Most programs that create temporary files do so in one of these directories. This fact has three important consequences:

- You can put temporary directories on their own partitions. This practice, described in Chapter 7, means that the damage caused by a program that creates an overly large temporary file is limited; it won't prevent users from saving files in their own directories, for instance. On the other hand, separating temporary files on their own partition means that a program might be more likely to exceed available temporary space.

- As a system administrator, you can readily search just a few directories for extremely old or overly-large temporary files.

- You can configure an automated process to help search for and deal with very old or large temporary files.

This last option is in fact enabled in a default FreeBSD installation. A cron job exists that calls the `periodic` utility to perform routine maintenance. This program, in turn, calls the `/etc/periodic/daily/100.clean-tmps` script to clean old files out of the `/tmp` directory tree. This script helps keep your system free of extraneous temporary files. It's not perfect, though. In particular, you may need to check `/var/tmp` and `/usr/tmp` yourself, particularly if you notice the `/var` or `/usr` partitions filling up. The `periodic` utility also sometimes misses stale files, even in `/tmp`, so checking that directory on occasion can be worthwhile. Finally, a few programs create temporary files in odd locations. For instance, the GIMP (described in Chapter 26) stores temporary files in the user's home directory. The upcoming section, "Keeping a Tab on Users' Files," provides information on tracking user file usage, including any temporary files that may reside in users' home directories.

If you find old or overly large temporary files, what should you do? First, check their dates. Recent files (say, less than a day old) may be in use, and so shouldn't be deleted on a routine basis unless they're causing serious problems. Files older than the last system boot (as determined by typing **uptime**) are usually stale and can be safely deleted. If you're uncertain about a file, find the file's owner (as reported by **ls -l**) and ask the owner if the file is important. If the file's owner isn't logged on (as reported by **who**), chances are the file isn't in use, but that's not certain—the file might have been created by a cron or `at` job.

Unused Programs

Unused programs consume disk space, and if you're short on disk space, this fact can be a problem. Furthermore, unused programs are a potential security risk; it's conceivable that a program contains a bug that could enable a miscreant to do things you'd rather not be done. This risk is increased for very complex programs and for those that run SUID `root`.

You may want to go through the main program storage directories (/usr/local/bin, /usr/local/sbin, and /usr/X11R6/bin) and check the status of every program. You can use pkg_info to determine what package owns a file, thus:

```
$ pkg_info -W /usr/X11R6/bin/xwave
/usr/X11R6/bin/xwave was installed by package xwave-2.2
$ pkg_info xwave-2.2
Information for xwave-2.2:

Comment:
Audio player/recorder/editor for the X Window System
```

Note   *Some program files, particularly in the /bin, /sbin, /usr/bin, and /usr/sbin directories, don't appear in the FreeBSD package database. Such programs were installed as part of the base FreeBSD system or by compiling a program from source code without the benefit of the FreeBSD ports system. You'll have to evaluate these programs in other ways.*

The second pkg_info command in the preceding example returns additional information you can use to evaluate whether or not you really need the program installed on the computer. If you don't, remove the program by using pkg_delete, as described further in Chapter 11:

```
# pkg_delete xwave-2.2
```

Although going through these directories shouldn't be necessary very frequently, doing so isn't a bad idea once you've become familiar with FreeBSD, in order to help identify and clean out unnecessary programs.

Keeping a Tab on Users' Files

Users sometimes consume excessive amounts of disk space. You can check on individual users' disk space usage with the du command, which displays the disk space consumed by every subdirectory of the one you specify. To learn how much disk space is used in a particular directory and all its subdirectories, add the -s option. For instance, to learn how much disk space sskinner is using, type the command

```
# du -s /home/sskinner
61034    /home/sskinner
```

This output indicates that sskinner's home directory contains 61,034 blocks of files. On most FreeBSD systems, each block is 1KB in size, so this value works out to 61,034KB. You can use this command to track who's using how much disk space.

 If your system's permissions enable users to store files in common areas, tracking that disk space usage may be tricky or impossible with du alone, although you can use du to find out how much space is consumed by the common file areas.

On small systems, using du to track users' disk usage can be reasonable; but on large systems, using du in this way can be quite tedious. For such systems, FreeBSD supports a feature known as *quotas* that enables FreeBSD itself to track users' disk usage, and to block creation of files beyond a limit that you specify. This feature can be quite worthwhile when you have many users, but you must enable it. This process can be a bit tedious, and some of the specific tasks have been covered in earlier chapters. In brief, enabling quotas requires performing these steps:

1. **Compile quota support into the kernel**   The standard FreeBSD kernel doesn't ship with quota support. You must recompile your kernel, as described in Chapter 12, but add the options QUOTA line to the kernel configuration file. You must then recompile the kernel.

2. **Enable quota support at boot time**   Add the following lines to the /etc/rc.conf file to tell the system to use the newly-compiled quota support:

   ```
   enable_quotas="YES"
   check_quotas="NO"
   ```

 The check_quotas line tells FreeBSD whether or not to perform checks of quota consistency at boot time. This check can be lengthy, so it's usually disabled by default; but you can enable it by setting the value to YES if you prefer.

3. **Mount partitions with quota support**   In /etc/fstab, you must add the userquota option to each filesystem you want mounted with user quota support, and groupquota to each filesystem in which you want to use group quotas. For instance, you might mount a /home filesystem using an entry such as this:

   ```
   /dev/ad4s3h    /home    ufs    rw,userquota,groupquota    2    2
   ```

4. **Build quota databases**   Type **quotacheck -a** to build the low-level quota databases on your quota-enabled filesystems.

5. **Start quota support**   Type **quotaon -a** to tell FreeBSD to begin using quotas for all the quota-enabled filesystems.

6. **Edit a typical user's quota settings**   Type **edquota -u *username*** to edit the quotas associated with *username*, or **edquota -g *groupname*** to edit quotas for the specified group. FreeBSD launches the editor specified by the EDITOR environment variable on a temporary file that specifies the user's quotas. You can then set the *hard limit*, which is the maximum disk space the user may consume; and the *soft limit*, which is the maximum disk space the user may consume over a long period. Both values are specified in blocks, which are usually 1024 bytes in size. For instance, if the hard limit is 100000 and the soft limit is 75000, the user may permanently store up to 75,000 blocks of files, and may temporarily exceed that limit to store up to 100,000 blocks of files. Precisely what "temporarily" means is defined in the kernel source code, or you can add -t to the edquota command to set the value you want. In addition to disk space, you can edit the number of *inodes* a user may consume. An inode is a data structure associated with a file, so the inode limit effectively caps the number of files a user may create. The quota file you edit resembles the following; you edit the hard and soft limits for both blocks and inodes:

```
Quotas for user sskinner:
/usr: blocks in use: 61034, limits (soft = 75000, hard = 100000)
        inodes in use: 6391, limits (soft = 7500, hard = 10000)
```

7. **Duplicate your typical user's settings**   Use the -p option to edquota to copy your quota limits to a range of users. For instance, **edquota -p sskinner 1001-9999** duplicates sskinner's quota limits to all users with UIDs between 1001 and 9999.

8. **Tweak quota settings for special cases**   If some users require different quotas than others, you can adjust their settings by performing Step 6 (and perhaps Step 7) to set the unique users' quotas.

I recommend you perform some tests to check that quotas are functioning as expected. Create a test account and attempt to go over quota in that account (say, by copying many large files to the account). If this doesn't work, or if the limits aren't what you expect them to be, review the preceding steps to be sure you've done everything correctly.

Monitoring CPU Use

CPU time is an odd resource. Some systems have far too much CPU power for their own good—for instance, a typical workstation used for word processing and other tasks for which the user is the bottleneck doesn't need anywhere near as much CPU power as a typical computer delivers in 2002. Other systems, though, are used in multiuser environments or to perform very CPU-intensive tasks, such as ray-tracing animation, engineering simulations, or scientific data analysis. Such computers often don't have enough CPU power for their users' desires. On such computers (especially multiuser systems), you may need to carefully track CPU use. If too many CPU-intensive jobs are run, the computer may become extremely sluggish. Indeed, such problems occasionally occur even on single-user computers because programs sometimes hang in such a way that they continue to consume CPU time, even though they aren't doing anything and their windows may even have closed. Knowing how to track CPU use, identify when CPU use is excessive, prevent problems, and correct problems can be a valuable set of skills for any FreeBSD administrator.

Tools for Checking CPU Use

One of the most basic tools for checking on CPU use is `uptime`. This program reports how long a system has been running, how many users are logged in, and three *load averages*, which are measures of demand for CPU time in the past minute, five minutes, and fifteen minutes. An example of this command in use is

```
# uptime
10:53AM  up 1 day, 20:17, 2 users, load averages: 0.06, 0.02, 0.01
```

In this example, the load averages are 0.06 for the last minute, 0.02 for the last five minutes, and 0.01 for the last fifteen minutes. A load average of 1.00 means that demand for CPU time exactly matches available CPU time. You're likely to see a load average of 1.00 or very close to it when you run a CPU-intensive program on a single-user workstation with no other CPU-intensive programs running. If you run two CPU-intensive programs on that computer, the load average will rise above 1.00. When this happens, programs can't get all the CPU time they request, and their performance degrades. Thus, the optimal load average for a computer is 1.00.

Note   *Most programs create brief spikes of heavy CPU use as they display windows, perform computations, and so on; then drop down to near nothing as they wait for user input or terminate. Thus, even if your CPU load is low, the computer can seem sluggish if the CPU is underpowered because these brief spikes of CPU use will last longer than they would on a faster CPU.*

If you use `uptime` and see that the load average is high, you may want to get a better idea of what's chewing up CPU time. You can do this with the `top` command, which displays a list of programs ordered according to CPU use. The program updates this list every few seconds so that you can monitor changes in CPU use. Figure 28-1 shows `top` in action. The `WCPU` and `CPU` columns show two measures of CPU use, and `top` sorts according to the `CPU` column. The `command` column provides the name of the program that's consuming CPU time. In Figure 28-1, the `x11amp` program is consuming close to half the CPU time, `Xvnc` is consuming about 10%, and the remaining programs are consuming trivial amounts of CPU time.

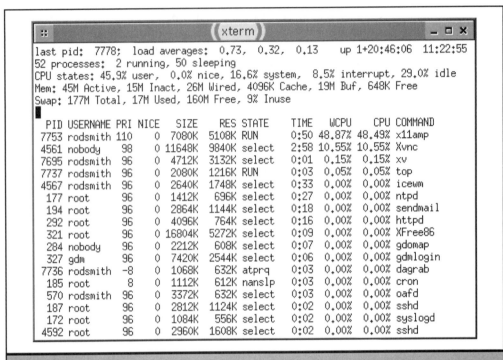

Figure 28-1.   The top utility enables you to locate CPU-hogging programs.

> **Note**   *The CPU times reported by top aren't directly comparable to uptime's load averages. The top percentages never exceed 100%; they're measures of actual CPU allocations, whereas uptime reports demand for CPU time, and so can exceed 1.0.*

Several other columns in top's output can be important in certain circumstances. The most important of these is the PID column, which shows the process ID of the program. You may need to use this information to kill or reprioritize a program that's consuming an inordinate amount of CPU time. The program's owner, as reported by the USERNAME column, may also be important in helping to identify users who regularly run CPU-intensive programs.

Knowing When CPU Use Is Excessive

Unfortunately, there's no simple rule to tell you when CPU use on any given computer is excessive. Although programs don't get the best possible performance on your hardware when the load average climbs above 1.0, using 1.0 as a cutoff for an acceptable CPU load may not be a reasonable criterion. If your FreeBSD computer functions as a remote login system for many users (via SSH, X, or VNC, for instance, as described in Chapter 21), chances are its load average will usually be above 1.0, as multiple people run programs simultaneously. Even a single-user system may end up running many CPU-intensive programs, and hence produce high load averages. Such a situation is to be expected on a multiuser computer, server, or heavily used workstation, and doesn't necessarily indicate a problem.

In the end, excessive CPU demands are those that cause unacceptable performance. Of course, performance problems may be caused by factors other than CPU demands, such as insufficient RAM, as described in the upcoming section, "Monitoring Memory Use." Thus, if your system isn't performing acceptably, you can check CPU use and see if it's high. If the load average is above 1.0, and especially if it's well in excess of that value, such as 5.0, you may want to look more closely into CPU issues.

If `top` shows that your CPU time is being consumed by strange processes or by programs that you didn't realize were running, then you must correct the problem. There are also steps you can take to make the system seem more responsive even when the load average is high. Doing so is sometimes tricky, but a few tips can help you in this task.

Correcting Problems

One CPU load problem that sometimes occurs involves *hung* processes. These are processes that have become unresponsive. Sometimes, hung processes do little harm, except for consuming memory. Other times, though, hung processes have hung because they've locked themselves into processing loops. Such processes consume CPU time, typically imposing a 1.0 load average on an otherwise unloaded system. You can easily spot such processes by using `top`; they typically appear at or near the top of the process list. Of course, you can't simply assume that any program consuming a lot of CPU time is a hung process, so you should try to figure out who owns the process (specified in the USERNAME column) and what it does before you terminate the process.

You can use the `kill` program (described in the "kill and killall" section of Chapter 5) to terminate a hung process. For instance, suppose you've concluded that process 7297 is hung. You could issue the following command to kill it:

```
# kill 7297
```

You can then check to see if the process is still running. Most hung processes won't respond to a simple `kill` command, so you must take a firmer hand and pass the KILL signal (signal number 9), which tells FreeBSD to terminate the program without giving it a chance to close itself down:

```
# kill -KILL 7297
```

You can also use `killall` *to kill a process by name rather than by number. Doing so can save you the bother of looking up a PID if you know a process is hung. On the down side,* `killall` *kills* all *processes of a given name, so if one process has hung but others of the same name are running normally, you'll terminate the processes that are not causing problems, as well as the troubled one.*

A less extreme problem involves a process that's running legitimately but that's consuming a lot of CPU time. Such a process can degrade performance, making the computer seem sluggish to users. You might want to run a CPU-intensive program that you know will take a long time to finish its work, but you might also want to run less CPU-intensive programs. For instance, distributed computing projects such as SETI@Home (http://setiathome.ssl.berkeley.edu) chew up lots of CPU cycles, but you probably don't want them to degrade your use of a computer for word processing, web browsing, or the like. You can use the `nice` command to launch another program with reduced priority, or use `renice` to change a process's priority. The "nice and renice" section of Chapter 5 describes these commands in more detail. As a problem-correcting tool, `renice` is more useful because it enables you to reduce the priority of a CPU-hogging process that's already running. For instance, suppose a small multiuser system normally has a load average of between 1 and 2, but it jumps to 3 one day because of one user's CPU-intensive program. Once you've identified that program as PID 7297 with `top`, you can issue the following command to reduce its priority:

```
# renice 10 7297
```

The first number in this command, `10`, is the process's new priority. Most FreeBSD processes have a priority of 0. Higher priority numbers indicate decreased priority, with the lowest-priority process having a value of 20. Thus, a value of 10, as in this example, is a good starting point for reducing a process's priority.

The disadvantage of reducing a process's priority is that the process is likely to finish its work later than it otherwise would because it gets less CPU time than competing processes. This situation is certainly likely to be true in the example of a CPU-intensive process running on a system that normally has a load average of 2.0. Reducing the priority of a CPU-intensive process on a computer that's otherwise lightly loaded (that is, with a load average of well under 1.0) is unlikely to have a great impact on the process's completion time because it will still get CPU cycles whenever other processes don't need them, which is most of the time.

Preventing Problems

You can take several steps to help prevent CPU load problems:

■ **Buy appropriate hardware**   If you know a system will support many users or CPU-intensive programs, be sure to equip it with a fast enough CPU. Unfortunately, it's hard to define precisely what "fast enough" is. As a hedge against CPU problems, you may want to buy a computer with a motherboard that supports a substantially faster CPU than the CPU that you buy; that way, if your CPU turns out to be inadequate, you can upgrade it without upgrading the motherboard.

■ **Run efficient programs**   Some programs run more efficiently than others. Compiling a program with optimizations for your particular CPU may gain a modest performance improvement, but sometimes more dramatic improvements can be gained by replacing an inefficient program with another program that uses more efficient algorithms. You'll have to research efficiency issues on a program-by-program basis.

■ **Run fewer programs**   Running many programs can degrade performance. For instance, Figure 28-1 reveals that x11amp (an MP3 player described in Chapter 27) consumes close to half of the CPU time on the target computer (which has a weak CPU by today's standards—a 233MHz AMD K6). Shutting down this program will free a lot of CPU time for potentially more important programs.

■ **Use `nice`**   You can launch CPU-intensive programs with `nice` to reduce their impact on more interactive programs. For instance, **`nice` *cpuhog*** launches the *cpuhog* program with a priority of 10, reducing its impact on other programs.

■ **Regularly check CPU load**   Particularly on multiuser systems, you should check the CPU load on a regular basis. If you notice a sudden increase in average load, you may be seeing the effect of a hung process. Although there's little you can do to actually prevent processes from hanging, killing them quickly can prevent users from becoming annoyed by reduced performance.

Monitoring Memory Use

FreeBSD is designed to hide details of memory use from the average user, and even from the average program. Every program is given its own memory space that's separate from the memory space of all other programs. The kernel manages all programs' allocated memory. When necessary, the kernel uses *swap space* (disk space that extends physical memory, as described in Chapter 7 and elsewhere) to run programs that won't fit in physical memory. Swap space, though, is much slower than physical memory, and if memory demands are too great, you can run out of swap space. These facts mean that if your system's memory demands are high enough, the system will slow down; and if they're higher still, programs may refuse to run or even crash. For these reasons, it's important to monitor the memory use of a FreeBSD system.

Tools for Checking Memory Use

To check on your system's memory use, it's important to know two things: How much memory your system has and how much memory your programs are demanding. You can then begin to evaluate whether memory use is excessive and take steps to correct the problem, if one exists.

Identifying Available Memory

One important memory use detail is how much memory your system has. You can learn about this with the `sysctl` program, which returns various important system statistics. You can use `sysctl` to learn how much RAM your system contains:

```
$ sysctl hw.physmem
hw.physmem: 96870400
$ sysctl hw.usermem
hw.usermem: 73068544
```

The `hw.physmem` value is the total physical memory installed in the computer, minus some reserved by the BIOS, hardware devices, and so on. The `hw.usermem` value is the total amount of memory available to user programs. This value is less than `hw.physmem` because the kernel needs some memory for its own uses. Both values are reported in bytes, so in these examples, the computer has 92MB of installed memory and 70MB of memory for user programs. These figures do not include swap space, though. You can discover your available swap space using the `top` command, as described in the next section.

Checking on Memory Demands

The `top` command, described earlier, in "Tools for Checking CPU Use," reports on memory use, as well as CPU use. Check Figure 28-1 again and examine the fourth and fifth lines in the `top` output. These lines report on the use of RAM and swap. The `Mem:` line reports on the allocation of memory (including both RAM and swap space) and the `Swap:` line reports on the use of swap space. The latter is easier to interpret because it presents clear information on how much swap space is used. For instance, Figure 28-1's figures are

```
Swap: 177M Total, 17M Used, 160M Free, 9% Inuse
```

This output indicates that 17MB of 177MB available swap space is in use. The 177MB figure is the total of all the swap partitions on your system. You created these swap partitions when you installed FreeBSD, whether you remember doing so or not.

The `Mem:` line is harder to interpret, and for a basic evaluation of whether you have enough memory, interpreting this line isn't necessary. FreeBSD dynamically allocates memory to various processes as required, including memory used to cache disk accesses. Thus, the amount of free memory is likely to be quite small, even on a lightly loaded system. Instead, you should rely upon the amount of total RAM reported by `sysctl`.

In this example, the computer has 92MB total available RAM, 70MB of which is for user programs. The computer has 177MB of swap space, 17MB of which is in use.

The `top` and `ps` programs both report on the memory demands of individual programs. The `SIZE` and `RES` columns in Figure 28-1 show memory allocated to specific programs. Typing **`ps -au`** creates a listing of all processes on the computer, including various statistics about them. The `VSZ` and `RSS` columns in this output display memory allocations. You can use this information to spot specific programs that are demanding too much memory—but of course, precisely what "too much" is depends on the program; some have very legitimate needs for lots of memory.

Knowing When Memory Use Is Excessive

As with CPU use, the real answer to the question of when memory use becomes excessive is that memory use is excessive when it begins to cause problems. These problems may be a slowdown of the system as it begins relying upon its swap space, or an inability of programs to launch or perform operations because total memory (RAM plus swap) is inadequate.

As a general rule, though, if the amount of swap space used begins to approach the total RAM on a regular basis, chances are you'll see performance problems. Thus, the example case of a 92MB system with 17MB of swap space in use doesn't constitute a memory shortage; the amount of swap space in use is small compared to the amount of memory available, so the system won't be greatly slowed down by swap activities. If this system regularly showed 90MB of swap space in use, though, the system could probably benefit by adding more RAM.

Another type of problem can occur if the swap space used approaches the total available swap space. For instance, if this example system had only 25MB of swap space, 17MB of swap space used might be a red flag because an additional swap space demand of only 8MB would reach the computer's swap space capacity. In such a system, it would be wise to add more swap space, as described in the upcoming section, "Adding Swap Space." Alternatively, adding more RAM can reduce the demands on swap space, accomplishing the same goal.

Note *Traditional advice is to give a computer roughly twice as much swap space as it has physical memory. Assuming typical loads use roughly as much memory as the computer has RAM, this practice gives the computer a good buffer to handle occasional atypical memory demands, as might happen during a particularly demanding period, such as the end of an academic term at a university or the end of an accounting period in a company's accounting department.*

You should be sure to monitor memory use over a period of time. Finding low system loads at 5:00 A.M. on Sunday morning, for instance, is to be expected for most systems; a better measure of typical memory demand is the load on a weekday afternoon.

If you suspect a single program is demanding too much memory, you may want to monitor its memory use over time using **ps -au**. If the program's memory demands increase over time and seldom decrease, it may have a *memory leak*, which is a condition in which a program requests memory and then "loses" it. Memory leaks are seldom serious in released versions of software, but they're more common in beta-test programs. Serious memory leaks can cause serious problems. Shutting down and restarting the offending program may help correct the problem on a short-term basis.

Preventing and Correcting Problems

Preventing and correcting memory problems consists of three main actions:

- **Installing enough RAM**   If a system has insufficient RAM for its duties, you'll see memory-related slowdowns or even program crashes. Most *x*86 computers available today accept hundreds of megabytes, if not gigabytes, of physical memory, and memory has been coming down in price for decades, so adding more memory is seldom a serious problem.

- **Configuring enough swap space**   Insufficient swap space is likely to cause problems when RAM is also inadequate or when a system experiences an unusual spike in memory demand. Prevention involves configuring the computer with enough swap space, as described in the next section, "Adding Swap Space."

- **Reducing memory demand**   If you can't add RAM or swap space to a computer, you can head off some problems by reducing the demand for memory. One potentially big step is to use a slim desktop environment rather than a large one such as KDE or GNOME. (Chapter 23 describes these environments in detail.) Other notorious memory hogs include the Mozilla web browser and the OpenOffice.org office suite. On a server, shutting down X can help reduce the memory load.

Adding Swap Space

If you didn't create enough swap space when you installed FreeBSD, or if your memory needs have gone up, you may want to add more swap space. Two practical ways to do this are to add a swap partition or add a swap file.

Adding a Swap Partition

Adding a swap partition is a tedious process when you've already partitioned and configured your computer because you must typically back up one or more partitions, delete those partitions, re-create them with new sizes, and restore your data. Chapter 7 describes partition management, so you should consult it for information on how to manipulate partitions. You can back up data to a tape device or another disk using `tar`, but chances are you'll need to boot an emergency system to restore the data. Overall, repartitioning a working system to add a swap partition is a process that's best avoided.

If you need to add disk space, though, you can easily add swap space at the same time; just create a swap partition along with the data partitions you want to create, as described in Chapter 7. You can then add an entry to `/etc/fstab` telling the system to use the new swap partition along with any existing swap partition. When you're done, use `top` to verify that FreeBSD has recognized your new swap space.

Because swap performance is so critical for overall system performance, you should place a swap partition where it can be accessed quickly. A location in the middle of the physical disk (between other partitions) is usually best because such a placement minimizes the time it takes to move the disk head to the swap partition.

Adding a Swap File

If you're not adding a new disk to your computer, it's possible to add swap space by using a swap file, which is a file that FreeBSD treats like a swap partition. The procedure for adding a swap file is different for FreeBSD 4.*x* and 5.0. A swap file is likely to be somewhat less efficient than a swap partition because the swap file may be fragmented, increasing head movements. Nonetheless, the simplicity of adding swap space in a file more than makes up for this minor performance hit in many cases. This procedure (especially in FreeBSD 5.0) is simple enough that it can be a good way to add swap space if you need an extraordinary amount of memory on a one-time basis—say, an unusually memory-hungry program that you want to run just once.

FreeBSD 4.x   To add a swap file, follow these steps:

1. Rebuild your kernel, as described in Chapter 12, and include the `vn` driver by using this line in your kernel configuration file:

   ```
   pseudo-device   vn  1  # vnode driver
   ```

2. Create a vnode device by typing these commands:

   ```
   # cd /dev
   # sh MAKEDEV vn0
   ```

3. Create a swap file by using `dd` to create an empty file of the desired size. For instance, to create a 100MB swap file in your root partition, you might type the following command:

   ```
   # dd if=/dev/zero of=/swap0 bs=1048576 count=100
   ```

4. Set the permissions on the swap file to 0600 by typing **chmod 0600 /swap0**, making any necessary adjustment to the file's name or location.

5. Configure FreeBSD to use the swap file at boot time by adding this line to your `/etc/rc.conf` file:

```
swapfile="/swap0"
```

6. Reboot the computer to use the kernel you compiled in Step 1, and use the swap file enabled in Steps 2–5.

FreeBSD 5.0   In FreeBSD 5.0, the vnode driver used to support swap files in FreeBSD 4.*x* has been replaced by the *memory disk* (md) driver. This driver is included in the standard kernel, so there should be no need to recompile the kernel to use a swap file. Follow these steps to enable swap file support in FreeBSD 5.0:

1. Create a swap file by using dd to create an empty file of the desired size. For instance, to create a 100MB swap file in your root partition, you might type the following command:

```
# dd if=/dev/zero of=/swap0 bs=1048576 count=100
```

2. Use the mdconfig utility to tell FreeBSD to create a device interface for the file you've just created. The following command will return the name of the device (probably md0, meaning it's accessible as `/dev/md0`):

```
# mdconfig -a -t vnode -f /swap0
```

3. Set the permissions on the swap file to 0600 by typing **chmod 0600 /swap0**, making any necessary adjustment to the file's name or location.

4. Type **swapon /dev/md0** to use this swap space. (Change `/dev/md0` if mdconfig returned a different device interface name.)

5. To enable the swap file automatically when you next reboot the computer, enter the following line in `/etc/rc.conf`, making whatever change is necessary to the name of the swap file:

```
swapfile="/swap0"
```

Keeping Software Up-To-Date

One aspect of routine maintenance that requires regular attention is keeping your software up-to-date. This task involves utilities and procedures described in Chapter 11, so you should review that chapter before proceeding, if you're not already familiar with FreeBSD's package and ports maintenance tools.

The Importance of Software Updates

Why should you bother updating software that you've already installed? There are three main benefits of doing so, two of which are closely related:

- **Improved features**   New versions of software often include new features that make the software easier to use, faster, or otherwise better than the previous version. Of course, you might or might not need or want these new features, but it's definitely worth checking what new features have been added when a new version of an important program appears.

- **Bug fixes**   Many software updates are issued to fix bugs. These bugs might cause the software to perform strangely, make computational errors, or crash, so some of these updates are quite important if you rely upon a program for any important operations.

- **Security fixes**   Some updates fix security problems. For instance, a server might contain a bug that enables outsiders to gain unauthorized entry to your computer, possibly even as `root`. When such an update appears, you should *always* upgrade your software as soon as possible.

The importance of a particular upgrade varies depending upon its nature. You might be willing to forego some feature improvements if you don't think they're important to yourself or your users, for instance. Even some bug fixes might not be worth applying if the bugs manifest themselves only in situations that don't apply to you, such as when hardware or software you don't have is installed.

Tools and Procedures for Checking Software Currency

Three methods for keeping your system up-to-date are common. In the first, you use ordinary package or port tools to upgrade individual packages on an as-needed basis. This approach requires that you track important updates for all of your programs, or at least for those that you think might require updates. The second approach is to use the `make world` process, which rebuilds every program on the computer from the latest source code. This approach is very time-consuming, but might be worthwhile if the computer requires a lot of upgrades. The final approach is to do a fresh reinstallation of FreeBSD. This approach can be disruptive because you must reconfigure everything, but it has the advantage of giving you a fresh start, which may be helpful if the system has collected a lot of configuration quirks you'd rather not have to untangle.

Knowing What To Update

Particularly in the case of per-package updates, it's sometimes hard to know precisely what packages require updating. The `portupgrade` program, described in the next section, "Per-Package Updates," can locate all the packages and ports for which updates are available. Likewise, the make world process upgrades everything. Sometimes you don't want to update every program, though. To perform a more selective update, you should evaluate what programs you want to update. The most important updates are those to fix security-related bugs, so you should keep abreast of security developments to learn what might need updating. FreeBSD maintains a list of security advisories at http://www .freebsd.org/security/, so checking this site on a regular basis (say, once a day) can help you learn of security problems. There are also dedicated security web pages and mailing lists, such as those maintained by the Computer Incident Advisory Capability (CIAC; http://www.ciac.org/ciac/) or the Computer Emergency Response Team Coordination Center (CERT/CC; http://www.cert.org). If you've installed packages from unusual sources, you should check back with those sources regularly to learn of important updates.

Nonsecurity updates are less critical, so you may simply want to periodically check for updates to important packages, particularly if you wish those packages were less buggy or had additional features. Installing or not installing such updates is a judgment call.

Per-Package Updates

The portupgrade program is an extremely useful tool for upgrading programs on a per-package (or per-port) basis. portupgrade may or may not be installed on your system; if not, you can install it from the sysutils packages or ports section. portupgrade supports many options, so you should consult its man page for details; but a simplified syntax is

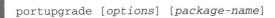

```
portupgrade [options] [package-name]
```

The meanings of these options are

- **-a or --all**   This option causes portupgrade to upgrade every package installed on the system.

- **-f or --force**   You can have portupgrade replace a package even if the "new" version is the same version number or older than the installed package. This option might be useful if you've upgraded to an experimental package but have problems with it, and so want to return to the last stable version of the package.

- **-g or --go-on**   Ordinarily, if a package depends upon other packages, portupgrade requires that the depended-upon packages be installed or upgraded successfully before the primary package is upgraded. This option tells the system to ignore failures to install or upgrade depended-upon packages. You might use this option if you've installed such dependencies in a way that doesn't use FreeBSD's package database.

- **-i or --interactive**   When you specify this option, `portupgrade` asks for confirmation before each installation or upgrade.

- **-n or --noexecute**   This option causes `portupgrade` to perform a "dry run" in which it reports what it would install, but doesn't actually install anything. The system still downloads a lot of data when you use this option, though, so it can be almost as time-consuming as a full upgrade.

- **-p or --package**   You can have `portupgrade` create a package for each port it builds by using this option. You might use this option if you want to upgrade several systems; you can then move the built packages from the first system to the other systems to save the time of compiling the ports on each system.

- **-P or --use-packages**   Ordinarily, `portupgrade` upgrades packages and ports using the FreeBSD ports system. This option tells `portupgrade` to use packages instead of ports whenever possible, which can save a lot of time. (Unfortunately, `portupgrade` sometimes has problems locating package repositories.) Packages are sometimes not as well optimized to your particular system, though.

- **-PP or --use-packages-only**   This option is like `--use-packages`, except that it tells `portupgrade` to *never* use ports; if a package isn't available, the upgrade isn't performed.

- **-r or --recursive**   This option causes all packages that depend upon the specified package to be upgraded.

- **-y or --yes**   Some packages or ports ask questions of you upon installation. This option forces the answer to these questions to be `yes`.

- **-R or --upward-recursive**   This option causes all packages upon which the specified package depends to be upgraded.

- ***package-name***   You can operate on a single package (such as `samba` to upgrade the Samba package) or a range of packages by using wildcards enclosed in quotes (such as `"*"` and `"?"`, much as in filenames) or extended regular expressions preceded by a colon (`:`).

Before running `portupgrade` it's a good idea to use `pkgdb` to ensure that your package database is in a consistent state. The following command does the job:

```
# /usr/local/sbin/pkgdb -F
```

This command can take a few minutes to run, particularly on a system with many installed packages or a slow CPU or hard disk. If it detects any inconsistencies, it will ask what to do about them. In most cases, a response of **yes** is appropriate because this response repairs the problems. Sometimes you'll be "flying blind," though; for instance, `pkgdb` may ask if it should replace one dependency with another, and you may have no way of knowing if such a substitution is appropriate. Your answers won't cause working programs to stop working, though; this process modifies only what FreeBSD believes to be true of dependencies between packages.

After installing `portupgrade` and using `pkgdb` to ensure your package database's consistency, you might want to try running it with the `-n` and `-P` options and a *package-name* of `"*"` to see what programs might need upgrading. You'll see a series of output lines relating to package updates. Most will report `No need to upgrade`, but some lines report on the upgrade process for specific packages or ports. It may take some time to study this output because it's quite long; in fact, you may want to redirect the output to a file so you can peruse it at your leisure:

```
# /usr/local/sbin/portupgrade -nP "*" 2> upgrade.txt
```

Even checking on available updates is likely to take quite some time because although this command doesn't actually install updates, it does download them. If you decide you want to upgrade everything, you can do so by omitting the `-n` option from the preceding command. If you want to upgrade just some programs, you can specify them all:

```
# /usr/local/sbin/portupgrade -P samba gplot apache pine
```

This command upgrades four packages: `samba`, `gplot`, `apache`, and `pine`.

Using make world

Many in the FreeBSD community are fond of building programs from source code. Doing so enables you to create binaries that are optimized for your computer, and some people feel safer building programs from source code than relying upon others to build the binaries. Thus, FreeBSD provides a special procedure that enables you to rebuild *everything* on the computer from source code: `make world`. This process upgrades your system not just to the latest stable programs, but to the latest versions that are under development. Thus, your system might conceivably be less stable after this upgrade than it had been before.

Although this procedure is referred to as `make world`, this specific command is deprecated. Instead, you type a series of commands to accomplish the job, as described shortly.

Upgrading your computer to the latest software using `make world` is not as simple as issuing a single command. In fact, the process can be downright tedious, not to mention dangerous. A failure at some critical step could leave your system unusable. It also requires rebooting the computer, so using `make world` is often not a good idea on production systems that must be up at all times. Finally, this process can take a very long time—probably several hours, even on a fast computer.

Do not *perform a* make world *on a whim or if you're not very experienced with FreeBSD! The following instructions are intentionally less explicit than many procedures in this book. If you can't work out the details on your own, you're far more likely to destroy your system trying to* make world *than you are to succeed. If you want more information, consult the FreeBSD Handbook,* `http://www.freebsd.org/doc/en_US .ISO8859-1/books/handbook/`.

These caveats aside, the basic process for performing a make world upgrade is

1. **Know what you're doing**   Before proceeding further, you should probably subscribe to the FreeBSD-STABLE or FreeBSD-CURRENT mailing list, depending upon the version of FreeBSD you want to upgrade. (The STABLE version is the latest in a regular FreeBSD release, but the CURRENT version is an experimental prerelease version of the OS.) Read these lists for a few days to get a feel for the types of issues you're likely to encounter. You can find instructions on subscribing to these mailing lists at `http://www.freebsd.org/support .html#mailing-list4`.

2. **Install system sources**   You can install source code for everything by using `sysinstall`. Go to the `Configure` menu, select `Distributions`, go to the `src` menu, and select `All`.

3. **Upgrade system sources**   You should use the `cvsup` process, described in Chapters 11 and 12 with respect to the ports system and the kernel source, to upgrade your system source code. The `/etc/cvsupfile` configuration file should include a line reading `src-all` to upgrade all your system's source code.

4. **Back up the computer**   Because of the dangers involved, I *strongly* advise you to back up your computer before proceeding further. In addition to a complete system backup, I recommend backing up all the files in the `/etc` and `/usr/ local/etc` directory trees, so that you can restore working configuration files if they're somehow overwritten.

5. **Read /usr/src/UPDATING**   This file contains information on the version of the software you're about to compile and install, including caveats and known bugs.

6. **Check and modify /etc/defaults/make.conf and /etc/make.conf**   These files contain defaults for the commands used to compile programs. You can change these defaults to customize the compilation for your system, such as adding CPU-specific optimizations. If you don't understand these files' contents, chances are you'll get yourself into trouble by trying to perform a make world.

7. **Update /etc/group and /etc/passwd** After running cvsup, you'll have two sets of configuration files—one in /etc and one in /usr/local/etc. The latter contains any changes required by updated software. One change you should tend to immediately is new groups or new users in the system's group and password files. If you update your system without adding these users, your system may behave strangely after the update, or perhaps not boot at all. You should compare your /etc/group and /etc/passwd files to /usr/src/ etc/group and /usr/src/etc/passwd, respectively. Add any users or groups you find in the latter files to the former ones, if they aren't already present.

8. **Enter single-user mode** Type **shutdown now** at the system console as root to enter a single-user mode. This process shuts down any running servers and logs off all other users so that you can perform the update.

9. **Type the following four commands** These commands ensure that your disk filesystems are in good order and properly mounted, and that your system is using swap space, in case it needs it.

```
# fsck -p
# mount -u /
# mount -a -t ufs
# swapon -a
```

10. **Set your clock** If your hardware clock is set to local time, type **adjkerntz -i** to tell the system to set the clock correctly. If you fail to do this, you may encounter some odd compilation errors on some files, depending upon your time zone and the time between downloading the updated sources and the time you compiled them.

11. **Change to the source directory** Type **cd /usr/src** to change to the main source code directory.

12. **Build the world** Type **make buildworld** to build all the programs. This process will probably take several hours.

13. **Build the kernel** Type **make buildkernel** to build the kernel. (Chapter 12 describes how to build a kernel with customizations for your system, which you should seriously consider doing instead of rebuilding the GENERIC kernel.)

14. **Install the world** Type **make installworld** to install the binary files you compiled in Step 12.

15. **Install the kernel** Type **make installkernel** to install the kernel you compiled in Step 13.

16. **Check for changed configuration files** You can use the mergemaster utility to check files in /etc against the new default files in /usr/src/etc. Typing

mergemaster creates a report of differences between the new default files and what you have installed. Each difference is reported using the diff file's output format. Some of these differences reflect changes you've made and that should still exist in the updated system; but others may reflect changes made by the FreeBSD maintainers to the new software. You should try to spot these changes and implement them yourself by copying the affected file or integrating the changes into your existing file.

17. **Reboot**   Typing **fastboot** at this point should reboot your computer into the new system.

If, after reading this procedure, you have a sinking feeling in the pit of your stomach, *do not perform the procedure*. Performing a make world is seldom, if ever, truly necessary. It's more of a tool for advanced FreeBSD administrators who want to squeeze a bit more performance out of a computer or otherwise customize it. I also recommend trying this process on a test system before you try it on a production computer; that will help familiarize you with the process, and perhaps help you identify potential problem areas and solutions, without risking the loss of a production system.

Reinstalling FreeBSD

In some ways, the most radical update procedure is to completely reinstall FreeBSD. This approach is useful if you're currently running a rather old version of the OS and you want to run something more up-to-date. It can also be useful if you've seriously mangled an installation and want to start over with a fresh installation.

Little can be said about reinstalling FreeBSD that's not in Chapter 2, so I refer you to that chapter for more information. You may, however, want to back up your /etc and /usr/local/etc directory trees for reference; these files can be invaluable in helping you recreate a configuration that you created on your first installation.

If you don't want to destroy user files, be sure *not* to delete and recreate the FreeBSD slice or the partition in which user files existed when you reinstall the OS. I also strongly recommend backing up any user files in case you make a mistake that destroys these files when you reinstall the OS.

Summary

FreeBSD includes tools to help handle certain aspects of routine maintenance, such as log file rotation and cleaning out temporary directories. Other aspects of routine maintenance require your attention. Specifically, you should keep an eye on overall disk use, CPU load, and memory load. If any of these system resources gets too low, you may need to examine your installed or running programs for the source of the problem or upgrade your hardware. Keeping your software up-to-date is also critically important; old software is often buggy, and some buggy software contains security flaws that can render your system vulnerable to attack. Some software update procedures are fairly painless, but others can be very time-consuming and even risky. Thus, upgrading software selectively can be an important procedure.

The Complete Reference

FreeBSD

Chapter 29

System Security Considerations

This book is filled with references to the security implications of particular programs, procedures, and practices. Thus, you probably already have some idea about good system security practices. Nonetheless, this topic is important enough that it deserves a chapter of its own. This chapter provides an overall context for computer security, including information on how computers are attacked, various important defenses you can take against attacks, and how to detect intrusions. This chapter is not the final word in FreeBSD security, though; far from it. As just noted, other chapters of this book include information relevant to specific programs and FreeBSD subsystems. For more detailed information on FreeBSD security, consult a book on UNIX or general networking security, such as Garfinkel and Spafford's *Practical UNIX and Internet Security, 2nd Edition* (O'Reilly, 1996) or McClure, Scambray, and Kurtz's *Hacking Exposed, 3rd Edition* (Osborne/McGraw-Hill, 2001).

An Overview of Methods of Attack

Computer crackers have many means of attack, which is part of the problem—fixing one or two potential security holes isn't enough because every nontrivial system has several areas that are at least potentially vulnerable to attack, making the task of protecting against attack quite complex. For purposes of this discussion, I've broken these methods into five broad categories: system probes, remote access attacks, local attacks, indirect attacks, and denial-of-service attacks. Each type of attack has its own characteristics and methods you can use to minimize the risks.

Hackers, Crackers, and Script Kiddies

The media generally uses the word *hacker* to refer to computer miscreants. Within the programming community, though, this term refers to people who enjoy programming or configuring computers and who use their skills to productive and legal ends. Many of FreeBSD's developers consider themselves hackers in this sense of the word. Thus, I don't use the word *hacker* as the media generally does; instead, I use the word *cracker* to refer to those who attempt to break into computers or otherwise disrupt their operation.

Another term that requires explanation is *script kiddie*. This term refers to crackers with little real skill who use well-known vulnerabilities and *root kits*—prepackaged software used to exploit a security flaw to gain `root` privileges. Some people prefer to relegate script kiddies to a category aside from that used to refer to "real" crackers, but I consider script kiddies to be the least-skilled category of cracker.

System Probes

The first step in attacking a system over a network is usually to *probe* it in some way. As a general rule, crackers engage in two types of probes:

- **System detection probes**   Crackers may know of a vulnerability and probe large numbers of computers in an effort to locate affected systems. For instance, if somebody discovers a bug in the popular Apache server, crackers may scan entire blocks of computers for systems that show the vulnerable fingerprint.

- **In-depth system probes**   If a cracker wants to break into a particular computer, the cracker may perform more in-depth probes of the target computer. These probes are designed to locate many potential vulnerabilities. Indeed, crackers may probe other systems on the same network as the target system in hopes of breaking into the ancillary computers and using them to attack the target system.

System probes are extremely common. If your computer is connected to the Internet at all times, chances are it will be probed several times a day. You may not be aware of these probes unless you set up detection tools, such as firewall rules (described in Chapter 17). You might detect some probes if you examine log files for servers you run on your system, too.

Although probes often signal hostile intent, it's seldom worth following up on them. You can't be sure that a probe really is an indication of cracker activity. An attempt to access a port on your computer might be an innocent mistake—somebody might have believed that a publicly-accessible server was running on your computer, or might have mistyped a hostname or IP address. Without evidence of hostile intent (such as probes from the same IP address of many computers, or probes of multiple ports on your computer), you're likely to just cause annoyance by reporting such probes. If you believe a probing system is up to no good, though, you might want to report it to the administrator of the network in question. You can use the `whois` utility to locate the people in charge of an IP address; for instance:

```
$ whois 172.19.20.21
```

This command returns information on the owner of the specified IP address. Formatting details differ substantially from one network to another, but with any luck you'll see a contact e-mail address. Try to find an "administrative" or "technical" contact address. If you send e-mail, be sure to include whatever log file entries or other evidence points to the offending IP address, and tell the other network's administrator what your time zone is and whether or not you're using NTP to set your server's time to a veridical source. Phrase your message politely because there's a good chance that the system probing yours has itself been compromised; the person you contact is probably more of a victim than you are.

Aside from being able to report a probe, monitoring probes can be useful because it can let you know what sorts of attacks are popular. A sudden upsurge in probes on UDP port 53, for instance, might be an indication that a bug has been found in a DNS server because UDP port 53 is used by DNS. If you have a DNS server, you should investigate this issue, and if you discover a vulnerability in the software you use, upgrade it.

Remote Access Attacks

The most stereotypical attack is a remote access attack—a cracker sitting in a room miles from the target breaks into a computer with the goal of stealing credit card numbers, defacing a web page, or otherwise doing no good. Such attacks certainly do happen, but certain aspects of the stereotype don't always apply. Most importantly, you can be targeted for attack even if the cracker isn't particularly interested in your computer *per se*. Typically, crackers use several computers as "stepping stones" between themselves and their ultimate targets. This practice makes it harder to trace the attack back to the source; if you're the ultimate target and discover the break-in attempt, you can trace it back to the last victim in the chain, but possibly no further.

Crackers may also break into computers with the exclusive goal of turning them into tools for attacking other computers in an automated way. Such computers are often referred to as *zombies* or *bots* (short for *robots*), and they're generally used to launch *distributed denial-of-service (DDoS)* attacks against other computers, as described in the upcoming section, "Denial-of-Service Attacks."

Another set of motivations for intrusion relates to the thrill of it or obtaining bragging rights among other crackers. Such motivations are particularly common among script kiddies. Such crackers may or may not do anything to deliberately damage your computer, but even an intruder who doesn't intend harm may do it through incompetence.

In any event, remote access attacks are usually accomplished by exploiting a bug in a server. (The method of using such a bug is often called an *exploit*.) One common class of bugs is the *buffer overflow* bug, in which the attacker sends a string that's larger than the server has allocated for the data. The result can be that the attacker's string overwrites other data stored by the program, or possibly even program code. When planned carefully, a buffer overflow attack can cause a server to execute any code that the attacker desires. The attacker might use this feature to launch another server through which the attacker can enter to gain more complete control of the computer.

 Recall that X is a server. As such, it is potentially vulnerable to attack. You can use firewall rules, described in Chapter 17, to limit access to X servers, which typically run on port 6000 for the first X session, 6001 for the second, and so on. Running X as `root` *increases the risk because a compromised X server running as* `root` *can do more damage than the same server running as an ordinary user.*

Another class of remote attacks doesn't rely upon servers at all; instead, the attacker exploits vulnerabilities in client software. For instance, most web browsers today support Java and JavaScript, which are programming environments. Web pages can include Java or JavaScript, and the web browser runs this code. A miscreant can put up a web page that includes Java or JavaScript that installs a `root` kit or does something else you might not like. Of course, there are safeguards in place to minimize the risk of malicious Java or JavaScript, but the risks aren't zero. Crackers can also exploit buffer overflow bugs in clients, much as they can exploit such bugs in servers. One benefit of FreeBSD is that its account and security system means that a compromised client is unlikely to enable the attacker to gain full control of the computer; the attacker will have ordinary user privileges, not `root` privileges. Client-based attacks are very common on Microsoft Windows; the worms and viruses that are running rampant through e-mail in 2002 are examples of this type of attack.

 The greater potential for damage should an attacker break in through a bug in a client is one of the reasons you shouldn't generally use network clients as `root`.

A final class of remote access attack involves *social engineering*. A cracker who uses this method attempts to trick individuals (usually ordinary users, but sometimes system administrators) into revealing sensitive information or reconfiguring the system in some unsafe way. A common social engineering attack involves an e-mail that claims to be from a system administrator asking users to reveal their passwords. You should be sure to tell your users that any such request is bogus—after all, as you know from Chapters 3 and 10, with superuser privileges you don't need any user's password except your own. Even system administrators can fall victim to social engineering, though. One example is a *Trojan horse*—a program that claims to do one thing but that does another. If you install a Trojan horse on your system, it can in principle do anything at all. Trojan horses are a major risk when installing software from any but well-trusted sources.

Local Attacks

Although many people think of attacks on our computers as originating from outside the local system or local network, many attacks come from disturbingly close to home. There are two ways that this can happen. First, you might have a "bad apple" in your organization—a *local* cracker. Naturally, this risk is very high when you have many users, but much lower on tiny systems. Second, an external cracker might have gained local access to a computer using an ordinary user account—say, through a successful social engineering attack or a buffer overflow bug in a server that was running as an ordinary user. This second class of attack is not local in all senses, but from the point of view of the methods the attacker can use to do damage, it might as well be local.

What, then, can a local cracker do? Such a miscreant can do several things:

- **Downstream attacks** A local cracker might use your system as nothing more than a launch pad for attacks upon other computers. In fact, depending upon the type of attack and the nature of your own security, you might not know that anything is wrong unless and until a remote system administrator contacts you about the problem.

- **Theft of service**   A local cracker might use your computer as a way to do things that aren't illegal, except insofar as they represent unauthorized use of your computer and network connection. Applied to truly local users, such activities don't really qualify as cracking, but it's possible a cracker has broken into your computer using a regular account to do nothing more than steal your CPU time.

- **Data theft**   Just as with remote attacks, local crackers might want to steal your data. This risk is particularly high if you're in a competitive industry in which industrial espionage is a real possibility.

- **Packet sniffing**   A local cracker might set up a *packet sniffer*, which is a program that monitors low-level network traffic. If you use protocols that don't encrypt passwords, a packet sniffer can easily recover these passwords. If your local protocols don't encrypt their data, a packet sniffer can recover the bulk of documents sent over the local network. Using switches rather than hubs can help protect against the problems of packet sniffers, but even the use of switches can't protect data if the cracker has installed the sniffer on the source or destination system.

- **Rooting the computer**   A local cracker might want to acquire root privileges on the computer, usually as a means to some other end, such as data theft or packet sniffing.

Many of the techniques described in upcoming sections, such as removing unnecessary software and creating secure passwords, are as effective against local crackers as they are against remote crackers. You must be more concerned with software available to local users when protecting against local crackers, though. One additional challenge is that local attackers often have physical access to your network, and perhaps even to the target computer. If the attacker can have an hour alone with the computer, chances are the attacker can steal any desired data from the computer, acquire root privileges, or do just about anything else. If nothing else, an attacker can open the computer and copy data to or from the hard disk. Physical security measures, such as locking the room in which the computer operates, locking the computer's case closed, chaining the computer to a floor or wall, and using BIOS passwords to prevent unauthorized individuals from booting the computer, can help reduce such risks.

Indirect Attacks

Indirect attacks don't involve the ultimate target computer directly. For instance, you might operate a web site using an Apache server you run locally, but suppose you rely upon your domain registrar to provide DNS service to the outside world. A cracker who wanted to deface your web site might do so indirectly, by breaking into your domain registrar's DNS server and changing it to point to another computer's web server. This cracker-operated (or cracker-compromised) computer might host modified versions of your web site. Thus, to the outside world it would appear that your web site had been defaced, even though your own computers had not been compromised.

Indirect attacks can also be used as a way to gain more direct entry to your computers. For instance, suppose you run an NFS server, as described in Chapter 18. NFS uses a trusted-hosts security model, in which access is granted based on the calling computer's IP address or hostname. If you use a hostname, an attacker might break into your DNS server, thus effectively giving the cracker control over who may access your NFS server.

As a general rule, you should always be wary of configurations that rely upon other computers—even those under your direct control—for authentication. Such configurations are becoming increasingly common as the need to centralize authentication for multiple computers becomes greater, but these configurations make the computers that control authentication enticing targets for crackers.

Denial-of-Service Attacks

A final type of attack is the *denial-of-service (DoS)* attack. A DoS attack is designed to deprive the victim of the use of the attacked computer, or at least of its network connectivity. The attacker need not break into the computer, as in a remote access attack, to accomplish this goal. Instead, the attacker abuses some vulnerability in the victim's software, or in the Internet at large, to do the damage. Some methods that have been used for DoS attacks include

- **Massive numbers of server connections** An attacker might initiate a large number of connections to a server without actually using these connections. This practice ties up local resources (memory and CPU time), preventing their use in serving legitimate users.

- **Log file attacks** If an attacker knows that the victim logs particular types of activity, the attacker might generate activity that meets the logging profile in order to create overly large log files and consume disk input/output time in the process.

- **Network bandwidth attacks** If the attacker has more network bandwidth than the victim, then the attacker can flood the victim's network connection, thus preventing its use in communicating with legitimate outside parties. There are even techniques to get the victim to consume network bandwidth in response to a relatively small amount of bandwidth used by the attacker. Attackers may also hijack other computers to do the dirty work—this practice is the DDoS attack mentioned earlier, in "Remote Access Attacks."

Some DoS attacks are impossible to defend against, at least through local configurations alone. A typical DDoS attack, for instance, does harm no matter how you configure your computer; the incoming packets consume bandwidth whether or not you want them to do so. If you come under DDoS attack, your best course of action is to contact your ISP. They may be able to block the incoming packets at their end.

Standard FreeBSD configurations help protect against some other types of DoS attacks. For instance, FreeBSD's log file rotation policy (described in Chapter 28) is based on file size, so an attack would have to generate a very large log file very quickly to cause problems. Isolation of log files on a separate /var partition also helps to minimize the impact of such attacks. Some servers include tuning parameters that limit the number of simultaneous connections they'll accept from a single remote site or in total, thus limiting the severity of problems caused by server connection attacks.

As a general rule, DoS attacks are targeted at high-profile sites or at individuals who annoy the miscreants who typically launch such attacks. Thus, a small installation is unlikely to fall under a DoS attack. A more likely occurrence is that your computer will be cracked and used as a zombie (described earlier in the section "Remote Access Attacks") in a DDoS attack. The local security issue in this case is one of remote access, so you should try to prevent it as such.

Eliminating Unnecessary Software

Most methods of attack, including the important remote access and local attacks, rely upon bugs in or misconfigurations of software installed on your computer. If you really need a particular type of software, you must take the risk that it contains a bug— although of course you can and should take steps to ensure that your software is up to date, as described in Chapters 11 and 28. Often, though, more software is installed on a computer than is strictly necessary. The risk associated with unnecessary local packages is small for each individual package, but the collective risk is not negligible. Worse is the case of unnecessary servers, which may be accessible to anybody on the Internet, depending upon your network configuration. Using a firewall, as described in Chapter 17, can help minimize this risk, but removing unnecessary software can also be an effective strategy. Although actually removing the software is the safest approach, related options include restricting who may use software and deactivating it but leaving it installed on the computer.

 Security is best applied in layers. You shouldn't think of running a firewall and removing unnecessary servers as being mutually exclusive alternatives. Instead, think of them as being two locks on your computer's figurative door. If one lock fails, the other may prevent a break-in.

Identifying Unused Software

One of the trickiest aspects of removing unnecessary software is identifying that software. The "Unused Programs" section of Chapter 28 describes one method of locating such programs—brute force. Briefly, you can examine all the files in common software directories, such as /usr/local/bin, /usr/local/sbin, and /usr/X11R6/bin. Once you've identified a program, you can evaluate whether you need it installed on the computer. Unfortunately, this process is quite tedious.

Another approach is to use the FreeBSD package database. Typing **pkg_info -a > packages.txt** creates a file called packages.txt that contains information on all the packages installed via the FreeBSD packages and ports systems. This file is likely to be at least a megabyte in size, so it can take a while to browse through it, but it contains a sentence or two describing most packages, making it easier to evaluate whether a program is worth keeping installed.

One of the greatest security risks involves servers you don't know are running. The preceding approaches may locate such software, but they won't tell you if a server is actually accessible. One method of locating such servers is to use the `netstat` command, described in Chapter 16. Specifically, the following command creates a list of all the processes that are listening for connections—that is, those that are servers:

```
$ netstat -aA | grep -E "Proto|LISTEN"
Socket     Proto Recv-Q Send-Q Local Address    Foreign Address  (state)
c7bc3700   tcp4     0      0    *.x11            *.*              LISTEN
c7bc3b40   tcp4     0      0    *.submission     *.*              LISTEN
c7bc3d60   tcp4     0      0    *.smtp           *.*              LISTEN
c7bc21c0   tcp4     0      0    *.ssh            *.*              LISTEN
c7bc2e80   tcp4     0      0    *.telnet         *.*              LISTEN
c7bc1d80   tcp4     0      0    *.ftp            *.*              LISTEN
```

This example shows six server ports in use—x11, submission, smtp, ssh, telnet, and ftp, according to the names listed under the Local Address column. These names appear in the /etc/services file, and if a server uses a port that's not listed in that file, the port number appears rather than the name. If you're unsure if a server should be running on a particular port, you should investigate it further. You can do so by using the fstat command, which returns information on open files and sockets. Use grep to filter this command's output so that it shows information on only the socket identified in netstat's Socket column. For instance, to investigate the submission server from the preceding example, you might type the following command:

```
$ fstat | grep -E "CMD|c7bc3b40"
USER     CMD         PID    FD MOUNT      INUM MODE        SZ|DV R/W
root     sendmail    194    5* internet stream tcp c7bc3b40
```

The important information in this output comes in the first three columns, which list the user, the command, and the process ID (PID) of the program connected to this port. In this case, sendmail uses this port, in addition to port 25 (smtp). Thus, there's nothing fishy about this example—assuming you intend the computer to be running all of these servers. If you believe the computer isn't running a Telnet server, for instance, you should investigate its configuration, as described in Chapter 21.

Note *The submission port isn't used much in 2002, but it may be used in the future. The idea is to provide separate ports for e-mail clients than for SMTP servers in order to better control how clients and other servers use a mail-server system. Thus, you might want to close off the submission port to outsiders using a firewall, but enable local users to access it.*

In the case of servers launched through a super server, the `fstat` command reveals the super server command (`inetd` on a typical FreeBSD installation). If you see this output, you should study your `/etc/inetd.conf` file to see which server is associated with a port.

Restricting Access to Software

Sometimes a computer must run software, but only certain users should have access to it. As a general rule, you use different techniques to control access to programs used by ordinary users as opposed to servers. The upcoming section, "Restricting Access to Servers," describes methods you can use to control who can access your servers; this section describes controlling access to local software.

Suppose some of your users should be able to use a particular program or class of programs, but others shouldn't have this sort of access. For instance, you might want to enable some users to run the Mozilla web browser, but prevent others from using this program. (You might do this on some remote-login servers to encourage users to run a web browser on their local computers in order to reduce the load on the server, but provide exceptions for users who log in from X terminals or other anemic computers.)

The simplest method of restricting access to software is to use FreeBSD's normal file-access controls. For instance, to enable only some users to run Mozilla, you can follow these steps:

1. Create a group for authorized Mozilla users. Chapter 10 describes the group creation process. Alternatively, you can use an existing group, if its membership exactly matches what you want to use for the Mozilla users and you expect these memberships to always exactly overlap. This example assumes the Mozilla users' group is called `mozusers`.

2. Add the users who should be able to run Mozilla to the `mozusers` group.

3. Change the group ownership of the Mozilla binary to the `mozusers` group. For instance, you might type **chgrp mozusers /usr/X11R6/bin/mozilla**.

4. Change the permissions on the Mozilla binary so that only the owner and members of the `mozusers` group can read or execute the file. In practice, this means removing world read and execute permission from the file. You can do this by typing **chmod o-rx /usr/X11R6/bin/mozilla**. Note that read permissions are just as important as execute permissions because if a user can read the file, the user can copy the file, change its permissions, and run the copy.

After you follow this procedure, users won't be able to run Mozilla unless they're in the `mozusers` group. There are certain caveats, though. Most importantly, as noted in Step 4, if a user can copy the file, the user can run it. A corollary of this fact is that users can copy a binary from another FreeBSD system and run it. Thus, in practice this procedure is very limited. One way to restrict users' ability to work around your limitation by copying a binary is to use the `noexec` mount option on the partitions to which they can write. With this option enabled, FreeBSD won't execute files even if they have their execute bits set. This practice, though, requires that all directories to which users can write exist on partitions that should never hold executable files. This practice also restricts users' ability to perform independent software development, which isn't an acceptable restriction in some cases, such as on workstations in a university's computer science department software development lab.

Deactivating Software

Another approach to restricting access to software is to completely deactivate it. In the case of most servers, the software can be deactivated by killing the process, ensuring that it doesn't start when FreeBSD boots, and ensuring that it's not listed in a super server configuration file. You'll then be able to run the server on an as-needed basis, even if it's not constantly running. For instance, if you want to enable a Secure Shell (SSH) server for a single night so you can log in to a computer at work from home one evening, you can do so by running the server manually before leaving work, even if the computer doesn't normally run SSH.

The simplest and safest method of deactivating nonserver software is to uninstall it, as described in the next section, "Removing Software." Short of that, you can effectively deactivate most software by removing its execute permissions. This process is essentially the same as restricting access, as described in the preceding section, "Restricting Access to Software," except that you remove *all* read and execute permissions from a program file. For instance, in Step 4, instead of typing **chmod o-rx /usr/X11R6/bin/mozilla**, type **chmod a-rx /usr/X11R6/bin/mozilla**. To reactivate the software, type **chmod a+rx /usr/X11R6/bin/mozilla**.

Deactivating software can be useful as a temporary measure when you learn of a potential problem. For instance, if you notice a program is consuming too much CPU time, you might deactivate it until you can track down the cause. (You could instead restrict access to a group containing only yourself so that you can debug the problem.)

Removing Software

The best way to deactivate software is to remove it completely. If you installed the software from a package, you can remove it using the `pkg_delete` command, but you'll need to know the exact package name, including the version number. You can obtain this information from `pkg_info` if you know the name of even one file in a package. For instance:

```
# pkg_info -W /usr/X11R6/bin/mozilla
/usr/X11R6/bin/mozilla was installed by package mozilla-0.9.9_3,1
# pkg_delete mozilla-0.9.9_3,1
delete mozilla-0.9.9_3,1? y
```

These commands will work for removing programs installed from ports, as well, but they won't do precisely the correct job. To remove a port, it's better to move into the original port subdirectory in /usr/ports and then type the following command:

```
# make deinstall
```

This process removes the port, much as pkg_delete does, but it handles the few port-specific details properly. Both of these options are described in more detail in Chapter 11.

If you install a program from source code without the benefit of using a FreeBSD package or port, as described in Chapter 30, removing it can be trickier because there's no installation database. In such a situation, you'll have to track down all the program's files. In practice, the most important file is usually the primary executable program, but some programs ship with support executables, scripts, configuration files, documentation, and so on. Although configuration files and documentation aren't likely to be security risks if left installed, they might be confusing to users and they do consume disk space.

Many programs' installation scripts display lists of files they install as they do so. Thus, you may want to try rerunning the installation script and using the list of installed files to locate and remove all of a program's files when you remove the program.

Limitations of Eliminating Software

One major limitation of eliminating software is that a determined user can typically add the software back by copying it from another computer or even compiling it from scratch, and then installing the software in a directory to which the user has write access. As noted earlier, in "Restricting Access to Software," you might be able to restrict users' ability to do this by using the noexec mount option on users' home partitions and other partitions to which users can write, such as /tmp; but unless you plan your installation very carefully from the start, it's likely you'll miss a directory in which users can hide their programs. This approach is also useless if users should be able to develop their own programs. On the other hand, some of the riskiest programs must be installed SUID root, and ordinary users can't create those permissions unless the computer's already been compromised. Thus, removing or restricting access to SUID root programs can be a worthwhile endeavor.

Eliminating and restricting access to software are useful techniques for managing the risk of running servers or a multiuser computer. These techniques won't protect you from system probes, indirect attacks, or many DoS attacks, though. You can eliminate all the software you like and your network connection will still become useless if you come under a DDoS attack, for instance.

Restricting Access to Servers

Servers are important, high profile, and all too frequently vulnerable to attack. Most local programs, such as text editors, compilers, e-mail clients, and so on, can run with no special privileges. They're also normally accessible only to local users, so the chance of abuse even if they contain security flaws is minimal, particularly on small systems. Servers, though, are by their very nature accessible to a much larger population. They frequently must be run as `root`, so a security flaw can have much more devastating consequences than a bug in a typical local user program. For these reasons, servers require special attention when it comes to security. Fortunately, many tools exist to help you protect servers. These include passwords, server-specific protections, TCP Wrappers, and firewalls.

Protecting Servers with Passwords

One of the most important protections for many server types is to use appropriate passwords. In fact, passwords are useful beyond their use by servers, and they're important enough that the upcoming section, "Creating Secure Passwords," describes the creation of passwords in more detail. Not all servers use passwords, though; for instance, most web servers enable anybody to retrieve web pages, and most SMTP mail servers accept mail without requiring passwords. Servers that deliver sensitive data or that provide users with unusual control of the computer, though, typically use passwords. For instance, POP and IMAP mail servers and most login servers use passwords.

Most password-using servers rely upon the underlying FreeBSD authentication system, which in turn uses the Pluggable Authentication Module (PAM, described in Chapter 6) to do the job. This fact means that a bug in PAM can cause problems for most servers that rely upon passwords. On the other hand, it also means that servers are less susceptible to bugs and quirks related to authentication because so much of the code is standardized in PAM, and the PAM code is well tested for security problems.

A few servers that use passwords don't use PAM, or use it only under certain circumstances. The most notable of these servers is Samba (described in Chapter 20), which can optionally accept passwords encrypted in a way that's compatible with the Server Message Block/Common Internet File System (SMB/CIFS) protocols that Samba speaks. Unfortunately, SMB/CIFS password encryption is incompatible with FreeBSD password encryption, so Samba cannot use PAM for authentication of encrypted passwords. Thus, Samba optionally maintains its own encrypted password file, as described in Chapter 20, which you must maintain independently of the main FreeBSD password file. If you configure Samba to accept unencrypted passwords, though, the server uses PAM authentication, just like most password-using servers.

One password issue that's particularly relevant for servers is that of encryption. Many protocols, including the standard forms of Telnet, FTP, POP, and IMAP, send their passwords in cleartext, meaning they're unencrypted. If a cracker has installed a sniffer on the sending, receiving, or sometimes even other local computers, the cracker can then record the password and use it to gain entry to the computer on which the server runs. If users employ the same passwords on multiple computers, the cracker can use one password to gain entry to many computers. Thus, unencrypted passwords are a serious problem. Whenever possible, you should use an encrypted password scheme, particularly if your local network wires are difficult to secure. SSH is a popular tool for encryption, and it encrypts *all* data it transfers, not just the password. As described in Chapter 21, SSH can be used in place of Telnet and FTP. With some more work, which is beyond the scope of this book for most protocols, SSH can be used to tunnel other protocols, lending its encryption advantages to almost any other protocol. Some protocols provide explicit support for encryption of passwords. Samba is one of these, but Samba's encryption method requires it to use a non-PAM password database. VNC is another protocol that encrypts its passwords. Neither Samba nor VNC encrypts nonpassword data, though.

Using Server-Specific Protections

Many servers, and especially many complex servers, provide protections that are unique to the servers themselves. You should consult the servers' documentation for information on how to use such protections. Examples include

- **IP address restrictions** Servers may allow or disallow connections from computers based on specific IP addresses. In fact, some servers, such as NFS and `rlogind`, use this method instead of usernames and passwords as the primary access-control method. Others use such protections as a secondary security tool. Some servers enable you to specify hostnames instead of or in addition to IP addresses, but doing so opens your system up to an indirect attack should your DNS server be compromised.

- **Network restrictions** You can often restrict access based on network addresses, much as you can restrict access based on IP addresses. Potentially more interesting, though, are restrictions based on network *interfaces*. For instance, you might set up an SSH server on a router so that you can administer the router; but to minimize abuse, you might configure SSH to respond to connection requests only from the network interface connected to the local network, not to the interface connected to the Internet.

- **Temporal restrictions** Some servers can be configured to accept accesses at some times of day but not at others. The `xinetd` (http://www.xinetd.org) super server, for instance, supports such restrictions. (`xinetd` can replace both `inetd` and TCP Wrappers.)

- **Local filesystem restrictions** Most file servers and login servers use the FreeBSD ownership and permissions system to restrict who may access what files. If the server requires a username and password, the user typically has the same permissions as when logged in at the console. (Some servers, though, such as Samba, provide overrides that can be quite complex.) Other servers run as a fixed user, and so provide access based on that account, not the ultimate user's login account.

■ **"Strike-out" protections** Many servers disconnect from the client or take special actions after some number of authentication errors or suspicious commands. For instance, some mail servers impose increasing delays whenever a sender tries to send to an unauthorized address. This measure helps make your system unappealing to would-be spammers.

■ **Remote username logging** Most servers log some of their activities to /var/log/ messages or other log files. Some servers can be configured to include information on the client's username, if the remote system is running an ident (aka auth) server. This information doesn't directly protect the server or your system, but it may be useful in tracking abuse. If you have this information in your log and contact the remote system's administrator, that administrator can more easily track the abusive individual and take appropriate action.

Some of these features can be added with tools outside of the server. For instance, you could use cron jobs (described in Chapter 6) to alter a system's firewall rules (described in Chapter 17) so as to enable or disable access to specific ports at specific times, creating temporal restrictions even for servers that don't normally support this feature. Firewall rules alone can impose restrictions based on IP addresses.

Using TCP Wrappers

TCP Wrappers is a standard security tool in UNIX and UNIX-like OSs, including FreeBSD. TCP Wrappers is an access-control tool. It's most commonly called by the inetd super server as a preliminary step in launching a server in response to a connection request. For instance, suppose a computer is running an FTP server via inetd, and an FTP connection request comes in. inetd answers this request, but immediately hands it off to TCP Wrappers, which examines the nature of the request—most importantly, the originating IP address. If this request meets the criteria in TCP Wrappers' configuration file, the program then launches the FTP server and tells it to handle the request. Ordinarily, all of this takes a fraction of a second, so it's not noticeable to the person using the client. If the incoming request doesn't match TCP Wrappers' criteria, the connection can be terminated before it's passed on to the target server.

Using TCP Wrappers enables you to apply consistent access controls to all the servers mediated by inetd. (Some servers also call TCP Wrappers directly, and so can be protected by TCP Wrappers even if the server isn't launched by inetd.) You can also configure TCP Wrappers to apply different criteria to different servers. This combination means that servers intended to be launched from inetd can simplify themselves by omitting code to explicitly support features such as restrictions based on IP addresses because TCP Wrappers handles the job.

When you launch `inetd` with the `-W` or `-w` option, it automatically uses TCP Wrappers for internal (`inetd`-provided) or external services, respectively. The default startup method for `inetd` uses both of these options, so unless you reconfigure it, FreeBSD uses TCP Wrappers for all `inetd`-mediated servers by default. You can verify that this is the case by typing the following command:

```
$ ps ax | grep inetd
  183  ??  Is     0:00.10 /usr/sbin/inetd -wW
```

This command shows the `inetd` process, including the `-wW` options. If you don't see these options, or don't see an `inetd` process at all, consult Chapter 16 for more information on starting and using `inetd`.

The `/etc/hosts.allow` file controls TCP Wrappers. Like many configuration files, this file uses a pound sign (#) as a comment indicator. Other lines take the following format:

```
daemon-list : client-list : option [: option ...]
```

> **Note** *Some early versions of FreeBSD and some non-FreeBSD systems use two files to control TCP Wrappers, `hosts.allow` and `hosts.deny`. The method described here adds the specification of whether to allow or deny access to the single configuration file. Earlier systems left this information in the name of the file.*

The elements in each control line have specific meanings:

- **daemon-list** The *daemon-list* is a list of one or more servers. You can specify the servers by their names in `/etc/services` or by various keywords, such as `ALL` (which matches all servers). TCP Wrappers also accepts the names of certain specific servers, such as `sendmail`. When listing multiple servers, separate their names by commas or spaces.

- **client-list** The *client-list* is a list of one or more clients. You can specify clients by hostname, IP address, patterns, or wildcards, as described shortly. As with *daemon-list*, you can specify several clients separated by commas or spaces, and certain keywords apply, including `ALL` to match any client.

- **option** In most cases, *option* will be `allow` or `deny` to grant or block access, respectively. It's possible to provide several colon-separated *option* fields, though, in which case options before the final one specify extra commands to be run or tests to be performed. Such advanced configurations are beyond the scope of this chapter.

Both the *daemon-list* and the *client-list* support the `EXCEPT` keyword, which enables you to specify an exception to some other rule. For instance, a *daemon-list* of `ALL EXCEPT telnet` creates a rule that applies to all protected servers except for the Telnet server; and a *client-list* of .luna.edu EXCEPT werner.luna.edu applies to all computers in the luna.edu domain except for werner.luna.edu. This last example makes use of a pattern—namely, the use of a leading dot to indicate a match to all computers within a domain. Possible patterns for specifying computers include

- **Individual hostnames**   You can specify a computer by hostname, as in werner.luna.edu. Such a specification matches a single computer, as determined by a DNS lookup.

- **Individual IP addresses**   You can specify a computer by IP address, as in 172.21.102.67.

- **Leading dots**   A domain name can be specified by a leading dot, as in .luna.edu for the entire luna.edu domain. All subdomains are matched as well, so .luna.edu matches tranquility.psych.luna.edu, among many other possibilities.

- **Trailing dots**   A numeric address with fewer than four dot-separated elements and a trailing dot matches all addresses that begin with the specified numbers. For instance, 172.21. matches all computers with addresses between 172.21.0.0 and 172.21.255.255.

- **NIS netgroup names**   A name that begins with a leading at-sign (@) is a Network Information Services (NIS) netgroup name. Of course, your system must be configured to use NIS for this form to work.

- **IPv4 netmasks**   You can specify a range of IP addresses with an IP address and its associated 8-byte netmask. For instance, 172.21.0.0/255.255.0.0 matches the specified network block.

- **IPv6 netmasks**   You can specify a range of IPv6 addresses with an IP address and its associated prefix length. For instance, [3ffe:505:2:1::]/64 matches all addresses between 3ffe:505:2:1:: and 3ffe:505:2:1:ffff:ffff:ffff:ffff. Because IPv6 is still rare in 2002, you're unlikely to need this format.

- **Filenames**   You can place patterns in a file and use the filename, preceded by a slash (/), as the *client-list*. For instance, you might specify /etc/badclients and place a list of blacklisted clients in that file— one hostname, IP address, or other specification per line.

It may be helpful to consider some example rules at this point. Here are a few:

```
ALL : ALL : allow
ssh : ALL : allow
ftp vnc : tranquility.psych.luna.edu, .threeroomco.com : allow
ALL EXCEPT sendmail : ALL EXCEPT 172.21. : deny
```

The first of these rules appears at the top of the default FreeBSD `hosts.allow` file. In that location, the rule effectively disables TCP Wrappers because it allows all accesses from all clients to all servers. If you want to use TCP Wrappers to control access, you must comment out or remove this line.

The second line also allows any computer to connect, but only to one server—SSH. You might use this line to let any caller from any network connect to a service that's well secured and that should be accessible to the world.

The third line reflects a more restrictive policy. It applies to the FTP and VNC servers, and grants access only to the `tranquility.psych.luna.edu` computer and the `threeroomco.com` domain. Other computers may match other rules elsewhere in the file.

The final example makes heavy use of the `EXCEPT` keyword, which can make it difficult to parse. This line applies to all servers except for sendmail, and denies access to all computers except those with IP addresses that begin with 172.21. In other words, it denies most accesses to most servers—for FTP, Telnet, SSH, or anything else, only computers in the 172.21.0.0 network can connect. Sendmail is excepted from this rule, but it might be handled by another rule.

Typically, you'll include a series of rules in the file, and then end the file with a rule that sets the default policy for any access attempt that doesn't match other rules. The default file includes the following default rule:

```
ALL : ALL \
        : severity auth.info \
        : twist /bin/echo "You are not welcome to use %d from %h."
```

This rule uses some advanced options, but it basically amounts to a sophisticated `deny` option. Thus, if you remove the `ALL : ALL : allow` line near the start of the default file, TCP Wrappers will deny all accesses except for those that are explicitly allowed in the default configuration. This is a good starting point; as with firewalls, a default-deny TCP Wrappers configuration can help protect against accidental misconfigurations in which a server is running without your knowledge.

TCP Wrappers is more complex than I can describe in this chapter. To learn more, read the `hosts_options` man page, which describes the format of the `/etc/hosts.allow` file in more detail, including information on some of the more advanced options.

Using a Firewall

Chapter 17 describes firewalls in more detail, so you should read it to learn about the mechanics of configuring these powerful tools. For now, you should know that firewalls are powerful tools for restricting access to a computer. They work on criteria similar to those employed by TCP Wrappers—IP addresses, at the core, along with server port numbers. You can use a router with firewall tools to protect an entire network, though, and you can use firewall rules to protect servers that don't use TCP Wrappers and even nonserver programs.

Indeed, you may wonder why you should bother with TCP Wrappers if you configure a good firewall. There are three main reasons. First, your firewall rules may contain a flaw that wouldn't be duplicated by your TCP Wrappers rules. In such a situation, TCP Wrappers becomes a second line of defense. Second, the FreeBSD firewall code may contain a bug that would enable an attacker to gain access. Again, TCP Wrappers serves as a second line of defense. Finally, TCP Wrappers offers some advanced options (not described in this chapter) that aren't duplicated by FreeBSD's firewall rules.

Creating Secure Passwords

Passwords are an extraordinarily important security tool, for both local and remote access to a computer. For this reason, you should know how to create good passwords. Just as important, your users should know how to create good passwords. Thus, you should relay the information in the next few pages to your users in order to help them generate passwords that won't come back to haunt them—and you—in the months and years to come. (As a practical matter, not everybody will bother to create good passwords, but some will.) Because the root account has such extraordinary power, you must be particularly careful with its password.

The Importance of Password Security

Passwords are like keys to your computer. Just as you don't want the keys to your home, car, or office to fall into strangers' hands, you don't want your passwords to fall into the wrong hands. This unfortunate event can happen in several different ways:

- **Lax user practices**   Somebody may willingly give a password to somebody else—a friend, co-worker, classmate, or what have you. Using appropriate permission schemes should normally obviate the need for such password trading, but some users may not understand how to accomplish their goals in simpler ways. Another lax user practice is writing a password down; a passerby could find the password, or if the paper on which the password is written is stolen, it may fall into the wrong hands. A final lax user practice is using the same password on several computers. If some other computer is compromised, the cracker may try the password on other computers, and some of these attempts may succeed.

- **Social engineering**   As noted earlier, in "Remote Access Attacks," crackers sometimes try to trick users into giving up their passwords, often successfully.

■ **Packet sniffing**   As noted earlier, in "Local Attacks," crackers sometimes employ packet sniffers in an effort to steal passwords. This practice is sometimes successful, particularly if you use protocols that don't encrypt passwords.

■ **Theft of password files**   Crackers may be able to steal your `/etc/master` `.passwd` file, in which passwords are stored. This file encrypts the passwords, so in theory they'll do the attacker no good; however, password cracking techniques enable crackers to discover some passwords. These techniques work by passing a large dictionary of words and word variants through the encryption techniques that FreeBSD uses. If any word matches an encrypted password, that word will function as a password for the account in question. The procedure described in the next section, "Password Creation," is designed to create passwords that aren't likely to be in crackers' dictionaries.

■ **Blind attacks**   Crackers may try attacking a computer by trying passwords randomly. This approach is unlikely to succeed, but could in some cases. For instance, a distressing number of users use their own usernames as their passwords.

■ **Shoulder surfing**   In public areas, such as university computer labs or even corporate cubicle farms, crackers may be able to discern a user's password by watching the user type it in. Users can protect against this practice to some extent by being vigilant and by using terminals in the least well-trafficked areas whenever possible, but the risk isn't nonexistent.

■ **Trojan horse login programs**   In some public environments, crackers may leave fake login screens running on public terminals. These login Trojans exactly mimic the behavior of a normal login screen when a user mistypes a password, but store the password in the cracker's account. The login Trojan then exits, causing the real login screen to appear. The result is that users believe they've mistyped their passwords, when in fact the cracker has stolen them.

You can reduce the likelihood of some of these attacks succeeding by administrative fiat; for instance, you can completely remove or disable a Telnet server, replacing it completely with SSH, thus making packet sniffing an unlikely means of acquiring a password from remote text-mode users. (You may need to reconfigure or eliminate other servers, too, such as POP or XDMCP servers, to completely eliminate this risk.) Other attacks are much more difficult to protect against. Even perfect passwords can be stolen, through shoulder surfing for instance.

Password file theft, although difficult on a properly configured computer, has been known to happen. A cracker who manages to acquire this file on a large multiuser system can probably break into any of several user accounts within a few hours. Network protocols' password encryption is not always entirely effective, either; the encrypted password can sometimes be isolated and attacked in much the same way passwords in a password file can be attacked. The severity of these problems therefore demands that users be particularly careful in designing their passwords.

Password Creation

The best passwords, from the point of view of being unbreakable should a password database fall into the wrong hands, are random collections of letters, digits, and punctuation. Unfortunately, such passwords are not very memorable to mere mortals. Administrators who force their users to cope with such passwords discover that this requirement backfires: Users write down their difficult-to-remember passwords. Once on paper, the passwords can be misplaced or a miscreant might find a password in a desk or even read it over a user's shoulder. Thus, truly random passwords, although theoretically a good idea, in practice are not so great.

A good compromise is to perform a two-step process. First, begin with a password *base*, which is memorable and might by itself make a poor password. Second, modify that base in various ways to turn it into something that won't be likely to appear in any cracker's dictionary. Two common types of bases are unrelated word pairs and acronyms that are personally relevant. For instance, a two-word base might be `bunpen` (*bun* and *pen*). A personal acronym might be `yiwttd` (for *yesterday I went to the dentist*). Neither combination is likely to appear in a dictionary, although a two-word base might be found by a procedure of combining short words.

These examples use fairly short (six-letter) bases because some systems impose eight-character limits on password length, and subsequent modifications expand the length by two or more characters. FreeBSD, however, takes longer passwords, and the longer a password, the better. As a general rule, eight characters should be considered the minimum safe size for a password.

Caution

Do not *use the example bases presented here. As they've been published, they may well already appear in crackers' dictionaries. Create your own personal base from two words or an acronym.*

Once you've generated a base, you should apply modifications to the base to increase its size and make it less likely that it will be discovered through a dictionary attack. Possible modifications include, but are not limited to

- **Adding characters**   Add numbers or punctuation to the password, preferably at random locations. For instance, `bunpen` might become `b#un7pen`, and `yiwttd` might become `yi0wtt<d`.

- **Mixing case**   You can randomize the case of letters, such as `b#Un7pEN` or `YI0wtT<d`. Some systems use case-insensitive passwords, so this technique isn't always effective. FreeBSD's normal PAM-mediated passwords are case-sensitive, but SMB/CIFS encrypted passwords are not.

- **Reversing letter order**   If you use a two-word base, reverse the order of one word. For instance, `b#Un7pEN` might become `b#Un7NEp`.

The idea behind these modifications is to move the base further away from words that might be in a cracker's dictionary. For instance, a cracker might use a dictionary that includes combinations of common words, such as `bunpen`; but the cracker's dictionary is less likely to include every possible variation on case, letter order reversals, and inserted random punctuation. Thus, the final password of `b#Un7NEp` is unlikely to be in a cracker's dictionary.

Of the modifications, the first (adding numbers and punctuation) is arguably the most important because it creates the largest number of variants. In fact, some password-changing tools on some systems require that passwords use at least one or two letters or symbols. (FreeBSD's standard `passwd` tool does not impose this requirement, though.)

Special Comments for the root Account

The `root` account is extraordinarily important, and thus its password is unusually sensitive. On some systems, more than one user needs the `root` password—for instance, a multiuser system that has several administrators. You should take special care in generating the `root` password, and if the system has several administrators, make sure that each one understands the importance of `root` password security. Never send the `root` password over a network connection that's not encrypted. For instance, you should never use `su` to acquire `root` privileges from a Telnet login or when using a system remotely via X or VNC (unless the session is tunneled through SSH). You should also be diligent about changing your `root` password on a regular basis, so that if it is compromised, the intruder will have a limited window of opportunity in which to use the `root` password.

Of course, some of the same caveats about passwords apply to system administrators as to ordinary users—a typical system administrator will find it difficult to remember a truly random password, for instance. Nonetheless, because the number of system administrators is typically small (often just one), and because it's the system administrator's job to secure the system, the `root` password may reasonably be less memorable than most ordinary user passwords.

Detecting Intrusion

Precautions such as those described up to this point in this chapter are very important, but a 100 percent secure computer is about as real as a unicorn. No matter how much work you do and how skilled you are, there's always some chance that somebody can break in. Possible methods of entry include unknown (to you, but not to an attacker) bugs in servers or other software, misconfigurations of servers or other programs, stolen passwords, and attacks based on physical access to the computer. Because you can't absolutely rule out the possibility of intrusion, you should develop a plan to detect intrusion. There are several steps you can take to improve your chances of quickly detecting an intruder. These include general vigilance, monitoring log files, and using intrusion-detection tools such as Tripwire. If you do detect an intrusion, knowing how to handle it can be very important.

General Warning Signs

Fortunately, most crackers aren't very skilled. Script kiddies commonly invade poorly secured computers, and the `root` kits they use frequently leave traces behind. These traces may include modified utilities that don't work quite like the originals, modified configuration files that damage normal functionality, and so on. You should be on the lookout for certain warning signs that sometimes indicate an intrusion:

- **Broken programs**   If a program suddenly stops working, investigate the matter. For instance, if a common program such as `ls` or `cat` suddenly starts crashing, it could be that the program has been replaced with one written or modified by a cracker.

- **Odd program behavior**   Less serious problems than out-and-out crashes may signal an intrusion. In the UNIX world generally, programs such as `ifconfig`, `grep`, and `netstat` work differently on different platforms. Even in FreeBSD alone, these programs also change over time; options in FreeBSD 5.0 may be slightly different than those in FreeBSD 4.6, for instance. A cracker might have replaced one of these tools with a modified version derived from a non-FreeBSD source or from an earlier or later version of FreeBSD than you're using. If so, the program's output or options may suddenly change, from your point of view.

- **Changes in resource use**   Sometimes crackers break in to steal your CPU time, network bandwidth, or other resources. Chapter 28 describes how to monitor many of these resources. If you notice a sudden change in these factors, you should investigate the cause to be sure it's not malicious activity.

- **Forgotten passwords**   If a user comes to you and claims to have forgotten a password, investigate further. Ask the user when the account was last used, then check `/var/log/auth.log` to see if there were any logins after that date. If there were, it could be the password hasn't been forgotten, but has been changed by a cracker.

- **Suspicious account activity**   You may notice that a user is logged in at a peculiar time (say, as listed in the output of `ps` or `who`). For instance, if you know a particular person is on vacation with no network access, but you see that user logged in using a local terminal, it could be that a cracker has broken into the user's account.

- **Gaps in log files**   Crackers sometimes delete lines from log files, or even entire log files, to mask their activity. If you notice such gaps, you may want to investigate further. For instance, you can use the `find` command (described in Chapter 8) to locate files that were created or modified within the gap period. Be very suspicious if any critical system binaries or configuration files were modified at that time.

If you notice any of these warning signs, or anything else unusual about the operation of your FreeBSD system, it *might* be an indication of a compromised system. That word deserves emphasis again: *might*. All of these warning signs can be indicators of perfectly innocent happenings, as well as more sinister occurrences. For instance, you might have upgraded a program and so changed its operation, a user might be legitimately using a system resource to a greater extent than usual, a forgotten password might be precisely that, a user on vacation might have accidentally left a terminal running in a locked office, or there might be a gap in a log file because nothing worth logging has happened during that period. The key is to look into these problem signs to determine their true causes. If further investigation reveals more troubling news, such as a person caught logged into another person's account at a public terminal or strange servers consuming network bandwidth on ports you've never heard of, then it might be time to take stronger measures, as described in the upcoming section, "What To Do After an Intrusion."

Using Tripwire

FreeBSD is a very complex OS, and completely monitoring it yourself is a full-time job—indeed, it's probably a full-time job for several people. It's also an extremely tedious and repetitive job—precisely the sort of job computers were invented to perform. Thus, it shouldn't be surprising that tools exist to help watch your system for intrusion. One of the most popular of these tools is Tripwire (`http://www.tripwire.org`), which is available in the `security` section of the FreeBSD ports system. The upcoming section, "Miscellaneous Intrusion-Detection Programs," covers some additional tools, most of which are less powerful than Tripwire, but all of which can be useful in specific situations.

Tripwire Basic Principles

Tripwire operates by storing various checksums on critical system files. After installing Tripwire, you run it periodically and the program recomputes its checksums. If any don't match, or if Tripwire encounters missing files, it reports the problem. Thus, if a cracker breaks into your computer and alters system files, Tripwire should detect this intrusion on its next run. As described in the upcoming section, "Using Tripwire to Detect Intrusions," it's common to run Tripwire from a daily cron job and configure it to e-mail reports of problems to you.

If you make changes to your system, such as updating any software or monitored configuration files, you must update the Tripwire database so that the program doesn't raise a false alarm about the change.

As just described, Tripwire could be overcome by an alert cracker—such a person could alter the Tripwire database to avoid an alert over modified files or programs. Recent versions of Tripwire, though, encrypt their databases and configuration files to prevent such modification. If you want to be extra-cautious, though, you can copy the Tripwire database file, described in the next section, to a removable medium. (The databases on most systems are too large for a single floppy, but a Zip disk or the like should do nicely.) You can then compare this backup to the original file from time to time to be sure you haven't been compromised. If you do this, though, be sure to do this comparison before updating the Tripwire database, then replace the backed-up file with the new one after making the update.

Tripwire is a useful intrusion detection tool, but it's most useful if it's installed immediately after installing and configuring FreeBSD itself. In fact, it's best to install FreeBSD, configure the system *without* connecting it to the Internet, install and configure Tripwire, and only then connect the computer to the Internet. This procedure minimizes the risk of compromise before Tripwire's database is initialized. Unfortunately, Tripwire is most easily installed in FreeBSD as a port, which requires Internet connectivity, so as a practical matter, your best course of action is to make Tripwire installation the first order of business after connecting the system to the Internet. Should you install Tripwire after your computer has been cracked, Tripwire will happily record the compromised files' checksums and report no problems.

Installing Tripwire

When you type **make install** in the Tripwire port directory, in addition to the usual processes, the installer tells you where it will install various binaries, asks for two passphrases for the checksum database (a site passphrase and a local passphrase), and generates an initial checksum database file. Some of these operations can take quite a few minutes, so don't be alarmed if the computer doesn't seem to do anything for a while. A large part of this process involves Tripwire's reading a large number of system files and generating various types of checksums from these files.

 A passphrase is like a password, but is longer—typically several words. Tripwire uses two passphrases, one to encrypt the policy database file and a second to encrypt the checksum database file.

When it's done installing, the Tripwire checksum database resides in the `/var/db/tripwire` directory and is named after the computer on which it runs, such as `werner.luna.edu.twd`. This file is encrypted and compressed, so it's unintelligible if viewed with a text editor or file viewer. There are several Tripwire configuration files, all stored in `/usr/local/etc/tripwire`:

- **twcfg.txt** This file sets overall options, such as the locations of database files and the method used to send e-mail.

- **tw.cfg** Tripwire doesn't read the `twcfg.txt` file directly; instead, it relies upon a cryptographically signed version of the file, known as `tw.cfg`. This file is encrypted with the site passphrase.

- **twpol.txt** Tripwire works by computing several different types of checksums on critical system files and comparing them with stored checksums. The `twpol.txt` *policy file* describes the files that Tripwire should check and the types of checksums it should compute for each file.

■ **tw.pol** This file is the encrypted form of the twpol.txt policy file. It's the file that Tripwire actually uses in operation.

The default configuration when you install Tripwire is a reasonable starting point; however, it may need some fine-tuning for your system.

Changing the Tripwire Configuration

The file you're most likely to modify as you configure Tripwire is twpol.txt. When you configured Tripwire initially (as part of the **make install** process), you may have noticed several error messages relating to files or directories that didn't exist. You'll see similar messages every time you run Tripwire unless you comment out the lines that refer to these files or directories from the twpol.txt file. Pound signs (#) denote comments, so adding these symbols to the start of the relevant lines will do the trick.

If you remove a Tripwire configuration file reference to a file or directory and then subsequently add that file or directory, Tripwire won't monitor the relevant files unless you add the files or directories back to the configuration file.

Tripwire's configuration file format is fairly complex. To fully understand it, consult the Tripwire Policy Guide, which is installed at /usr/local/share/doc/tripwire/policyguide.txt. In brief, the file consists of several parts. The first couple of parts set environment variables; for instance, the following line tells Tripwire where to find its checksum database file:

```
TWDB="/var/db/tripwire";
```

Other assignments set up file classes, which are used to tell Tripwire what type of files reside in a given directory. Tripwire performs different types of checks depending upon the file type. For instance, the following line sets up a name for binary files:

```
SEC_BIN     = $(ReadOnly) ;      # Binaries that should not change
```

Subsequent definitions can use $SEC_BIN to refer to binaries. These definitions tell Tripwire about individual files or entire directories. For instance, these lines tell Tripwire how to handle its own binaries:

```
# Tripwire Binaries
(
  rulename = "Tripwire Binaries",
  severity = $(SIG_HI)
)
```

```
{
    $(TWBIN)/siggen                        -> $(SEC_BIN) ;
    $(TWBIN)/tripwire                      -> $(SEC_BIN) ;
    $(TWBIN)/twadmin                       -> $(SEC_BIN) ;
    $(TWBIN)/twprint                       -> $(SEC_BIN) ;
}
```

This definition consists of two parts. The first part is enclosed by ordinary parentheses and includes assignments of a rule name and a severity level. The second part is enclosed in curly braces ({ }) and uses an unusual assignment operator (->) to tell Tripwire how to handle specific directories or files. Although not used in this example, a configuration line may be preceded by an exclamation mark (!) to indicate a *stop*—Tripwire isn't to check the files in the specified subdirectory. You can use this feature to exclude sub-directories from directory trees that should otherwise be checked.

Initializing and Updating the Database

Tripwire automatically initialized its database when you installed it via the FreeBSD port. If you make extensive changes to the program, you might conceivably want to completely reinitialize it. If so, you can do so by typing

```
# /usr/local/sbin/tripwire --init
```

This command runs Tripwire through its entire initialization process, in which it computes various checksums on all the files specified in its configuration file and creates the checksum database file. In order to accomplish these tasks, you must type both the site and local passphrases.

Tripwire supports two distinct update operations. These functions update the database file alone or the database file and the entire Tripwire configuration. You would update the database file alone after updating or installing a FreeBSD package, port, or monitored configuration file. To do so, type the following command:

```
# /usr/local/sbin/tripwire --update
```

If you make changes to the Tripwire configuration itself, you need to use another command. This command takes the text-mode twcfg.txt and twpol.txt files and converts them to their encrypted binary forms. This command also updates the data in the configuration file itself, just as the --update option alone does. The command to do all these things is

```
# /usr/local/sbin/tripwire --update-policy /usr/local/etc/tripwire/twpol.txt
```

As with the initialization command, you must type both the site and local passphrases to use this command. Unfortunately, this command alone may fail; if it detects any changes to files aside from the configuration files, it refuses to change the checksum database file. To override this behavior and force Tripwire to implement changes to the database file, add the `--secure-mode low` option.

All three of these commands are likely to take several minutes to complete.

Using Tripwire to Detect Intrusions

Once Tripwire is configured with an accurate database, you can use its `--check` option to check the current state of the system against the state recorded in its database:

```
# /usr/local/sbin/tripwire --check
```

One common approach is to create a cron job (described in Chapter 6) to perform a Tripwire check on a daily basis—say, at 3:00 A.M., when system load is likely to be low. Tripwire generates a report on `stdout`, and cron normally e-mails such output to the caller, so `root` should receive a Tripwire report on a daily basis in this configuration.

Miscellaneous Intrusion-Detection Programs

Tripwire is one of the most powerful intrusion-detection tools available for FreeBSD, but others have their place, as well. Space limitations prevent a full discussion of these tools, but you may want to investigate some of these programs, particularly in certain situations:

- **AIDE**   The Advanced Intrusion Detection Environment (AIDE) program fills a role similar to that of Tripwire, but it's installable from the FreeBSD packages system, as well as from the ports system.

- **chkrootkit**   This program checks your computer for known `root` kits. You might run this program if you haven't previously installed Tripwire or a similar tool but you suspect you may have been cracked.

- **clog**   This program logs information that's not normally logged on network connections. It's not really an intrusion detection tool *per se*, but you can use it, particularly in conjunction with log-monitoring tools such as `logcheck` or SWATCH, to help detect suspicious activity.

- **Doctor Web**   This program, installed from the `drweb` package or port, is a virus scanner for FreeBSD. It's most useful in detecting Windows viruses that may have infected files stored on a FreeBSD Samba server. A companion program, `drweb-sendmail`, helps monitor incoming mail messages for viruses.

- **fwlogwatch**   Monitoring log files for suspicious activity can be a tedious proposition. This tool helps by summarizing log file entries generated by firewall logging options (described in Chapter 17).

- **logcheck**   Like `fwlogwatch`, `logcheck` is a log file monitoring tool; but `logcheck` summarizes more than just firewall activity.

- **Snort**   This program is a souped-up packet sniffer. Although packet sniffers can be used by crackers, they're also useful network diagnostics, and Snort is designed to help detect suspicious network activity. As such, it can detect intrusions on computers other than the one to which it's attached. Using switches locally can reduce Snort's effectiveness, though, unless you run it on your firewall computer.

- **SWATCH**   The Simple Watcher (SWATCH) is a program that monitors log files. You can use it to e-mail reports when something interesting happens, or to create a meta-log file that contains only suspicious log file entries.

- **YAFIC**   This program is Yet Another File Integrity Checker (YAFIC), and its full name is quite descriptive.

All of these tools can be installed from the `security` section of the FreeBSD packages and ports systems. Indeed, you may want to browse that section to see what else is available; there are dozens of programs to test programs for security flaws, check the quality of passwords, add new PAM authentication methods, and so on.

Caution   *Some security tools, although legitimate in that role, can also be used by crackers. Thus, using these tools can sometimes lead you into trouble because you might be accused of cracking activity. In particular, if you use packet sniffers such as Snort, password-cracking programs, or port scanners (often called auditing tools), you may find yourself in hot water, possibly without a job, or conceivably even charged with a crime. These tools* are *worth using, but before doing so, obtain permission in writing from your supervisor.*

What to Do After an Intrusion

System intrusions are not inevitable, but neither are they as uncommon as they should be. Thus, the question arises: What should you do if and when you discover your system has been compromised? In brief, the procedure is

1. **Disconnect from the Internet**   If your system has been compromised, it may be used as a base of attack against others. Therefore, it's important that you remove it from the Internet *immediately*.

2. **Back up**   You should probably back up the computer. At the very least, back up your users' data. Backing up everything else is a good idea, too; such a backup could conceivably become evidence in legal proceedings, and if you have a chance to study the intrusion, the backup may be quite informative. (Chapter 8 describes backup procedures.)

3. **Investigate the cause**   Try to discover how the cracker got into your computer. This task is usually easier said than done, unfortunately, because many intrusion methods leave few definitive traces. You may be able to correlate something in a log file to information on security web sites, though, or otherwise get lucky. Failing discovery of a definitive cause, you should familiarize yourself with security updates that have been released since you installed FreeBSD and study security issues generally.

4. **Wipe it clean**   Delete FreeBSD from the computer. Depending upon your partitioning scheme, you may be able to do this during the next step by reformatting the installation partitions, leaving user data unaffected. If your /home directory isn't on a separate partition, though, you'll probably have to set up entirely fresh partitions. Unfortunately, it's not completely safe to simply eliminate files the intruder changed. The cracker may have changed other files you haven't discovered, in which case trying to clean only affected files is likely to leave you with a still-compromised system. The safest procedure is to assume that no system file is clean and wipe them all out.

5. **Reinstall**   Reinstall FreeBSD from its original CD-ROM. This action should guarantee that your system is clean, assuming you completely reformat your FreeBSD partitions (with the possible exception of /home) during reinstallation.

6. **Apply updates and security patches**   To prevent future infection, correct whatever problem you identified in Step 3. You should also tighten security generally, especially if you couldn't identify the specific vulnerability the intruder used. For instance, you might install and configure Tripwire if you hadn't used it before, and switch from Telnet to SSH. The safest way to apply updates is to download the packages using another computer, then transfer them to the compromised system via floppy disks or other removable media.

7. **Check user files**   It's conceivable that a cracker might leave a surprise in users' files—say, a hacked SUID root program for reinvading the system. You can use the find command to locate executable files in /home, as in **find /home -perm +111**.

8. **Change user passwords**   Wiping out the /etc directory should make this step unnecessary, but in case you tried saving user accounts by copying the user database files, be sure to change the passwords. It's possible that the intruder got in via a stolen user password, in which case restoring the same old passwords will be like leaving a welcome mat out for the intruder.

9. **Restore full functionality**   *After* making all the changes and improvements, you can restore the computer to full Internet functionality. Some packages and improvements are best installed after restoring Internet functionality. If possible, take the hard route and install everything by copying files from another computer. If you really must bring the system online before completely cleaning and updating it, try to put the system behind a tough firewall, and install the improvements as soon as possible after restoring connectivity.

In one case this set of steps isn't necessary: If you use a virus scanner and detect a non-FreeBSD virus, such as a Windows virus on a Samba share, you don't need to tear down and rebuild your FreeBSD system. Instead, use the virus scanner to remove the virus from the share, or delete and re-install the files.

Following these steps will minimize the risk of problems should your unwelcome guest pay you a visit during or soon after your restoration is complete. You should maintain a high degree of vigilance for some period after restoring the system. It's possible you'll notice a break-in attempt from your unwelcome former guest. If so, you may be able to track the individual. Unfortunately, computer crime is fairly common in 2002, and although cracking activities are illegal in the United States and most other countries, law enforcement agencies lack the resources to follow up on every complaint. Thus, you may not be able to get much help in shutting down the cracker unless you've suffered substantial financial losses (several thousand dollars) as a result of the cracking.

Caution *Do not, under any circumstances, attempt to retaliate in kind for a break-in, DoS attack, or other disruption. Such vigilante activities are easily misdirected and only make the Internet a more hostile place. A counterattack might end up costing you your job, or even landing you in jail if you manage to cause the sort of disruption that will draw the attention of law enforcement agencies.*

Summary

System security is an extremely important topic for FreeBSD administration. Several methods of attacking FreeBSD systems exist, ranging from DoS attacks to actual break-ins. Each method of attack has several variants, and protecting against all these methods of attack can be tricky. Fortunately, a few simple rules, such as removing unnecessary software and keeping your software (especially your servers) up to date, can go a long way towards securing your system. Configuring your software appropriately for your needs and creating secure passwords are also important preventive measures. Unfortunately, even diligent administrators sometimes find that their computers have been compromised. Knowing the signs of a compromised system and knowing how to respond are important final defenses. Acting swiftly in the event of an intrusion can prevent a cracker from using your system in unwanted ways.

Chapter 30

Compiling Software

731

Chapter 11 describes the process of installing software in FreeBSD. That chapter emphasizes two methods of software installation: FreeBSD *packages* and *ports*. Packages are precompiled binaries, which are quick to install. Installing a port requires running a script that downloads the source code, applies FreeBSD-specific patches, compiles the software, and installs it using the FreeBSD package database. Thus, ports take much longer to install than packages, but they're sometimes preferable because the software is compiled using *your* system's specific support programs, which occasionally produces a modest performance or reliability boost.

On occasion, though, you may want to install a program that's not available as either a package or a port, or which doesn't compile properly as a port. In such cases, you may need to resort to compiling and installing the software "raw," without the help of the FreeBSD port system. This chapter describes this process, beginning with a discussion of when you might want to do this and moving on to the tools you need and a description of the compilation and installation process.

When to Compile Software

The vast majority of the software you install on a FreeBSD system is available as a package, a port, or both. Thus, chances are you won't need to resort to a "plain vanilla" software compilation process very often. The primary reason to do so is if the software you want to use isn't available as either a package or as a port, or if the version you want to use hasn't yet been made available in these forms. Another reason to compile a program in this way is if you want to modify it. Such modifications require at least a minimal understanding of programming, though.

Understanding the Compilation Process

Programmers write most software in so-called *high-level programming languages*, such as C, C++, Pascal, Modula-2, and FORTRAN. The FreeBSD kernel is written largely in C, and most FreeBSD software is written in C or C++. All of these languages are complex enough that describing their use is well beyond the scope of this book; you should consult a programming book, such as Schildt's *C: The Complete Reference* (Osborne/McGraw-Hill, 2000) or Schildt's *C++: The Complete Reference* (Osborne/McGraw-Hill, 1998) for information on programming. To create complex GUI programs, you may also need references for the toolkit you use, such as Dalheimer's *Programming with Qt, 2nd Edition* (O'Reilly, 2002) or Sheets' *Writing GNOME Applications* (Addison-Wesley, 2000).

Unfortunately, computer CPUs don't understand C, C++, or other high-level programming languages. Instead, CPUs understand *machine language*, aka *machine code* or *binary code*. (Some people make subtle distinctions between these terms based on the form in which the code is presented.) Binary code is a series of numbers that tells the CPU to perform various operations. The binary code for one CPU family (say, Intel's *x86* line and compatible models from AMD, VIA, or Transmeta) is incompatible with the binary code for another CPU family (say, the PowerPC line from Motorola, IBM, and Apple). Even within a family, there can be variations; for instance, Pentium CPUs support features that weren't present in the earlier 80486 CPU. For all of these reasons, high-level programs must be converted into low-level binary code for particular CPUs or CPU families. This process is known as *compiling* the program.

Typically, the compilation process involves two or three main steps:

1. Each source code file is converted from the source language into *assembly language*, which is a representation of binary code that's slightly more intelligible to humans. Instead of raw numbers to represent CPU operations, assembly language uses mnemonic codes.

2. Each assembly language file is converted into an *object code file*, which is a file that contains binary code. The object code file alone isn't a complete program, though.

3. All of the object code files are combined together and tied to a set of *libraries*, which provide common functions useful to many programs. This process is known as *linking* the program. The result is an executable program.

Some compilers convert source code directly into an object file, effectively combining the first two steps. There are also many variants on each of these steps. For instance, libraries can be linked *statically*, meaning that they're combined into the final program file; or they can be linked *dynamically*, meaning that the libraries are stored in separate files on the computer. Dynamic linking produces smaller binaries and can reduce the memory demands of programs if many programs use the same libraries; but such a configuration requires that any program that uses a library have the appropriate libraries installed. Upgrading a program may require upgrading its libraries, and upgrading the libraries may require upgrading the programs that depend upon them. One of the advantages of the FreeBSD packages and ports systems is that they help manage these dependencies, but upgrading individual programs or libraries can still cause a cascade of problems with dependencies.

Most programs today consist of several source code files. Writing a program as dozens, hundreds, or even thousands of files simplifies collaboration and minimizes the effort involved in recompiling the software during development; when a programmer makes a change, only the changed files need to be recompiled into object files. Programmers use special tools to help track what files have changed and automate the compilation process. One of the more popular of these tools is `make`, and in fact the FreeBSD ports system uses `make`—you type this command to build a port, as described in Chapter 11. Many source code packages come with a file called `Makefile`, which controls the compilation process. More complex programs frequently come with a script called `configure`, which creates a `Makefile` based upon examination of your system.

Pros and Cons of Compiling Your Own Software

Compiling your own software provides certain opportunities and advantages, including

- **Available software**   A few programs aren't available in the FreeBSD packages or ports systems, but are available as source code. Such programs may or may not compile easily on FreeBSD.

- **System optimization**   When you compile software, you can usually edit the `Makefile` or pass parameters to `configure` or `make` to optimize the compilation process for your specific CPU, producing a modest performance boost.

- **Modifications**   Once you've obtained the source code, you can make changes. Some changes, such as altering the text in prompts or menus, take almost no programming knowledge to pull off. Others, such as adding major new features, require extensive programming skill.

- **Trust**   You can examine the source code in detail if you so desire, to help ensure that a program isn't a Trojan horse. You don't stand much chance of doing this with all the software on FreeBSD, but if security is important to you, you might consider doing it with a few critical but small programs. Compiling the software yourself ensures that a package hasn't been built with changes that aren't included in the official source code.

Some of these advantages require you to have extensive programming knowledge. Others require you to have information on specific packages; for instance, system optimization procedures vary somewhat from one package to another, so consult the program's documentation for details.

Compiling your own software has certain important disadvantages, too:

- **Time requirement**   Even compiling software via the FreeBSD ports system takes time. The extra time required by compiling everything from the original maintainer's files can be substantial, particularly if the software requires patches to compile or install in FreeBSD. For most single installations, this time demand far outweighs any small speed increase you'll get by optimizing the compilation for your CPU.

- **Lack of package database information**   When you compile and install a program yourself, your system will lack all package database information on that program. This shortcoming can make removing or upgrading the software more difficult. This disadvantage does *not* apply to using the FreeBSD ports system, though.

Ultimately, these drawbacks far outweigh the advantages of performing a custom compilation for most programs, most systems, and most administrators. Thus, I recommend compiling from raw source code only when a package or port doesn't exist, or when it doesn't work to your satisfaction.

If you write your own software, chances are you'll do so using procedures similar to those described in this chapter. Of course, you'll need to know a lot more about programming, too.

Tools Needed to Compile Software

You need certain software installed in order to compile programs. If you've used the FreeBSD ports system, chances are most or all of these tools are already installed on your system. If not, you can install most of them from the FreeBSD packages or ports systems.

Language Compilers

The most obvious tool needed to compile software is a *compiler*—the program that converts high-level language code to assembly code or machine code. Each language has its own compiler, so you'll need different tools to compile, say, Pascal than C. FreeBSD uses the GNU Compiler Collection (GCC) for certain important languages, including C and C++. GCC is installed by default on most FreeBSD systems. Some other compilers may require installing appropriate additional packages.

Although in some sense separate from the compiler, an *assembler*, which converts assembly language into object code, may also be needed to compile programs. When required, an assembler is a dependency of a compiler, so if you install from the `sysinstall` packages handler, the system should install any necessary assembler along with the compiler.

You need a linker to combine object files into a coherent executable file. FreeBSD uses `ld` as its linker. This program is part of GCC, and so is installed on most FreeBSD systems.

If you're uncertain what compiler you need to compile a given program, consult its documentation. If the documentation doesn't say, chances are it's written in C, which is the most common language for FreeBSD development. You can also examine the source code filenames. If those filenames have `.c` and `.h` extensions, they're C files. Other languages use other extensions. For instance, `.cxx`, `.c++`, and `.cpp` are common C++ extensions; and `.p` and `.pas` are common Pascal extensions. You can also examine the `Makefile` to see what program it's calling to do the compiling work—`gcc` is for C, `cpp` is for C++, and so on.

Support Libraries and Development Headers

Most programs rely upon one or more libraries. In order to compile the software, you must have the matching libraries installed. If the software uses a `configure` script, it checks for the presence of the required libraries and complains if any aren't found. You can then track down the libraries (probably using `sysinstall`) to install them. If the program doesn't use a `configure` script, the first you'll know of a missing library is when the program fails to link, or possibly even when it fails to run after having been linked. (The latter is most common if you compile on one system but move the program to another system to run it.) The error messages in these cases are likely to be fairly cryptic, so I recommend carefully reviewing the program's documentation to learn what libraries it requires.

Closely related to the issue of libraries is that of development *headers*. These are files that are associated with libraries, but that provide information to programs on how to interface with the libraries. In order to compile a program that uses a library, your system must contain the appropriate headers for the library. If your system lacks these headers, you'll see a file not found error during compilation. This error probably complains about the lack of a file with a .h extension. If you're lucky, the name may contain a clue about what library headers are missing. Again, you should review the program's documentation for additional clues. Check to be sure that the appropriate library headers are installed. In most cases, the headers install along with their matching libraries, but sometimes you may need to install a separate development package to get the libraries.

In some cases, headers are installed but the compiler can't find them because the compiler is looking for them in the wrong place. In such cases, often a quick workaround is to create a symbolic link in the location where the compiler is looking for the header to the location where the header actually exists.

General-Purpose Development Tools

As noted earlier, in "Understanding the Compilation Process," compiling software usually requires a program called make, which controls the compilation process. This program checks for the existence of object files and, if they're not present or if they're older than the source code files from which they're built, make builds new object files. The program then links these files together into an executable. The details of this process are controlled through the Makefile. As with many tools, make is installed by default on most FreeBSD systems, so you shouldn't need to go looking for it. Some variants exist, though, such as gmake. If the program you want to compile requires one of these, you may need to install it from the FreeBSD packages or ports system.

If you want to modify the software in any way, you'll need a text editor. Any plain-text editor, such as Emacs, vi, or NEdit, should work fine. Some editors include features that help you edit files associated with specific languages. For instance, *syntax highlighting* displays particular parts of program files in different fonts or colors, such as italic comments and green keywords.

A *debugger* is a program that helps run a program in a controlled manner, enabling you to watch what happens to variables as a program runs. Debuggers are extremely useful in tracking down and correcting bugs, but an explanation of their use is beyond the scope of this book. The gdb program is a common debugger for FreeBSD. GUI front-ends to gdb, such as the Data Display Debugger (ddd) and kdbg, can simplify debugger use, particularly if you're not intimately familiar with gdb commands.

The *Concurrent Versioning System (CVS)* is a tool for collaboration in a programming environment. CVS enables multiple programmers to "check out" and "check in" individual files for development work. Even nonprogrammers can use CVS to obtain the very latest source code for a program, and in fact FreeBSD uses this tool to help manage the kernel source tree and the ports tree, as described in Chapters 11 and 12. Many individual programs use CVS, and it's possible for you to use CVS to obtain the software. Read the instructions on the programs' web pages for details.

An *integrated development environment (IDE*; not to be confused with the disk interface hardware with the same acronym) is a tool that ties together many other development tools, such as a compiler, a debugger, `make`, and a text editor. Examples of IDEs for FreeBSD include Anjuta (shown in Figure 30-1), gIDE, KDevelop, Moonshine, MOTOR, Qt Designer, QtEZ, and `xwpe`. Most of these IDEs are X-based tools, and many (including Anjuta, gIDE, KDevelop, Qt Designer, and QtEZ) are built with special support for particular GUI environments or widget sets. Some IDEs work with only one or two programming languages; others work with many. A few other tools provide IDE-like features. Emacs, in particular, can be used to control the compilation process, much like an IDE. If you just want to compile and install a program that already exists, chances are you don't need a full IDE. If you plan to make extensive changes to the program or

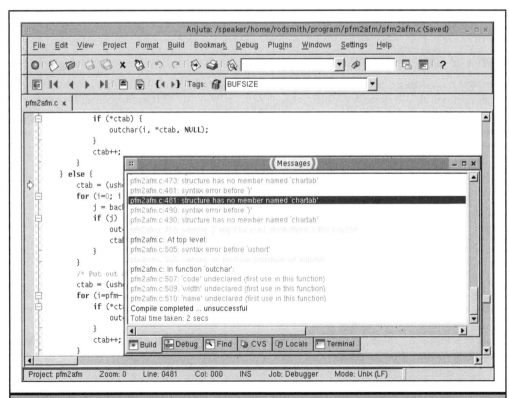

Figure 30-1. *An IDE provides point-and-click access to common development tools such as editors and debuggers.*

join its development team, an IDE might prove useful because you're far more likely to need to make changes to many source code files and use debugging features.

A Typical Software Compilation Session

The details of software compilation differ substantially from one package to another; nonetheless, certain steps are common to most or all packages. This section presents these steps, broken into four parts: obtaining the software, reading the documentation, configuring the software, and compiling the software. Of course, you must also install the software, but this step marks a turning point; before you install the software, you can easily abandon the attempt to build a program from scratch. After you install the software, it becomes more difficult to track down the installed files, particularly if any of these files overwrite existing files on your system.

This section describes compiling a program without making changes to it. If you want or need to change the software, you'll use a text editor to alter the source code files. For extensive changes, using an IDE can be very helpful.

Obtaining the Software

The first step you must take is to obtain the software. Typically, you'll acquire the software from the developer's official web site or from an FTP archive site. Most open source program web sites include one or more download links. This description uses the Macintosh-Like Virtual Window Manager (MLVWM; http://www2u.biglobe .ne.jp/~y-miyata/mlvwm.html) 0.9.1 as a sample program. This program is large enough to require configuration but small enough that it compiles quickly, even on fairly old computers. MLVWM is a window manager that's modeled after older Macintosh systems.

MLVWM is available as a FreeBSD package and as a port, so installing it as described here is normally not necessary.

You can download MLVWM source code from a link on the software's main page. This action creates a file called mlvwm091.tar.gz. You can examine the names of the files contained in the tarball by typing **tar tvfz mlvwm091.tar.gz | less**. This action reveals that all the files install in a directory called mlvwm091. Source tarballs usually include all their files in a subdirectory named after the program, so MLVWM is quite typical in this respect.

After examining the tarball's contents, change to a directory in which you want to store the source code. Many administrators use /usr/src for this purpose. If you want to keep source you download yourself separate from the usual FreeBSD /usr/src directory tree, you may want to use a directory in your ordinary user home directory, or perhaps /usr/local/src. You can perform most compilation steps as an ordinary user, assuming that account has write permission in the directory you select, but you must be root to perform the installation steps. When you've changed to the target directory, type **tar xvfz /path/to/mlvwm091.tar.gz** to extract the files, where /path/to is the path to the directory in which the tarball resides. This command creates a subdirectory called mlvwm091.

 Always *use the* --list *(or* -t*) option to* tar *to examine the tarball's contents before extracting the files with* --extract *(or –x). If a developer creates a tarball without the "carrier" subdirectory, extracting files directly could create quite a mess.*

Reading the Documentation

Once you've extracted the source code, change into the source directory and type ls to examine the names of the files in that directory. Look for documentation files, which usually have filenames that are in all uppercase or that end in .txt. In the case of MLVWM, three files meet these criteria: CHANGELOG, CONFIGURATION, and README. (There are also files of the same name that end in .jp; these are Japanese equivalents of the English files.) Many projects include a CHANGELOG file that describes changes. You may want to read this file if you're updating an existing package. When you read the remaining two files, you'll find that CONFIGURATION describes the format for the MLVWM user configuration file, ~/.mlvwmrc. As such, you can ignore it for the moment, although you'll need to come back to it to learn how to use the program. README, though, contains information on how to compile and install the software. Some programs include files with other names, such as INSTALL, that describe this procedure. A few programs include a separate documentation directory that contains compilation and installation instructions. For some, you can find this information on the program's web page in addition to or instead of with the source code tarball.

Although source code packages are increasingly using standardized configuration, compilation, and installation methods, it's important to read the documentation. Some programs do things a bit differently than others, and some include important caveats in their documentation. Still other programs provide information on how to optimize a program in a particular way—for instance, complex programs often include compile-time options. These may enable you to add or remove features, change installation locations, or optimize the program for your CPU. MLVWM is fairly simple; it includes no special options.

Configuring the Software

All but the smallest projects today require you to run a command to create the Makefile for the project. Many projects use a script called configure for this purpose; you would type **./configure** to run the script, perhaps followed by options to tell the system to compile for a particular CPU, build a binary with a particular set of features, or set other options. MLVWM uses a different approach, though: It uses the xmkmf utility to create a Makefile. In FreeBSD, this program is installed with the imake package or port. The MLVWM documentation specifies typing **xmkmf -a** to perform the configuration. This job will take a few seconds as xmkmf checks the files on your system and creates an appropriate Makefile. The configure script that's used by many projects often takes a bit longer to run because these scripts frequently check more details about your system.

If the program's documentation describes configuration options, you may want to try applying them to your project. If you're not sure what an option does, do a web search using your favorite search engine, or try to find a more elaborate description in the documentation. MLVWM offers no configuration options.

If you know enough about the compilers used by the program, you can edit the Makefile directly to optimize compilation for your CPU or to achieve other effects. Such changes require a fairly high level of expertise, though, so I don't describe them here.

Compiling the Software

Typically, compiling the program requires issuing a single command: **make**. The make program examines the Makefile and uses it as a guide to calling compilers, assemblers, and linkers to create an executable program. Depending upon the size of the project and the speed of your computer, you may find a completed executable just a second or two or many hours after you type **make**. You'll see a line displayed for each operation that make performs—that is, each file that it compiles. These lines typically begin with cc, gcc, or the name of some other compiler, and include a large number of options. In fact, each line has so many options that it probably occupies two or three lines on a standard 80-column display.

Chances are you'll see occasional compiler warnings, such as the following:

```
borders.c:729: warning: `win' might be uninitialized in this function
```

Warnings are usually harmless; they tell the programmer about a condition that doesn't prevent the program from compiling or running, but that might have unintended consequences. Usually the programmer knows better than the compiler what the code actually does, so you shouldn't be concerned about warnings in program compilation. Errors, on the other hand, cause the compilation process to terminate:

```
borders.c: In function `SetUpFrame':
borders.c:254: `lcp' undeclared (first use in this function)
```

The output continues with several warnings, then displays the following:

```
*** Error code 1

Stop in /home/rodsmith/Projects/mlvwm091/mlvwm.
*** Error code 1
```

These error messages indicate a problem that halts the compilation of the program. If you know nothing about programming, this is the end of your attempt to install a program from source code. If you know a bit about programming, though, or if you're willing to learn, you can investigate this error. In this case, line 254 of the `borders.c` file contains a variable that's not been defined before: `lcp`. This can be your starting point for debugging the program, but this task is one that's well beyond the scope of this book. (In this particular case, I deliberately changed a variable name—`lp` became `lcp`—in order to generate an error.)

Sometimes a perfectly functional program generates an error message during compilation. This can happen because you don't have an appropriate library installed, so you may want to review the software's library requirements. The code may also rely upon features that aren't supported by your compiler or by FreeBSD itself. Such system dependencies are harder to overcome, and they're one of the reasons the FreeBSD ports system exists—ports include *patches* to programs, which modify the program so that it will compile properly on FreeBSD.

Installing Compiled Software

If the program compiles successfully—that is, if you don't see any error messages in the last few lines of the `make` output—you can try installing the software. The package documentation usually specifies a simple command to accomplish this task, but I recommend performing some initial checks first. These reduce the chance that you'll damage some existing software when installing the new package. After you install the program, you can check that it's working correctly.

Checking for Conflicting Packages

FreeBSD's package maintenance tools, described in Chapter 11, maintain a database of installed files and packages. This database enables the package tools to provide automated update commands, such as `pkg_update`, which clean out old files when performing an upgrade. These checks don't occur, though, when you install a package from source code without the benefit of the FreeBSD ports system. Worse, it's possible for a program installed from source to overwrite program files installed via the packages or ports systems. When this happens, the FreeBSD package database will contain inaccurate information. If you're lucky, you may install a program over an older version of the same one, so that the package information may still be somewhat relevant, if not completely accurate. If you're unlucky, you might install one program over another program that's unrelated except for some unfortunate file naming conflicts.

In theory, you can examine the `Makefile` to determine what files it will install and where. In practice, doing so isn't likely to be very enlightening unless you're familiar with `Makefile` structures; the file tends to be filled with layers of variable references and even calls to `Makefiles` in subdirectories.

In practice, you're likely to obtain good results by searching for executable files within the build directory tree and then checking your system to be sure it doesn't contain any files of the same name. For instance, you might type the following command to find all executable files, and receive the specified output in the case of MLVWM:

```
$ find ./ -perm +0111 ! -type d
./man/mlvwm.man
./man/mlvwm._man
./mlvwm/mlvwm
```

This command returns the path to the MLVWM executable (`mlvwm/mlvwm`), which was recently built, and to the MLVWM man page, which happens to have its execute bit set in this case. You can then search for an executable file called `mlvwm`. If you find nothing, you know that installing the program at least won't overwrite any existing binaries.

You may want to check for man pages or other documentation that an install command might copy to system directories and check that they don't already exist on your system, as well. Check subdirectories called `man`, `doc`, `documentation`, or anything similar in the new program's source directory, and then check `/usr/local/man` and `/usr/X11R6/man` for duplicate files.

Chances are good that you won't find any duplicates unless you've already installed the software via the FreeBSD packages or ports system or from a prior source code release. In the case of a prior source code release, installing over the old files isn't a problem, but there are two other potential problems:

- **Duplicate files**   Sometimes a developer changes the location in which files install themselves. If this happens, you may end up with two copies of the executable—say, one in `/usr/X11R6/bin` and another in `/usr/local/bin`. If this happens, you may end up using the old program at least some of the time, which can be confusing. The solution is to manually delete the old program files and any support files that might cause problems.

- **Stale files**   If a new version of a program consolidates two files into one, installing the new version from source will probably leave an old file in place. Chances are this file won't do any harm except for wasted disk space, but if you know about it, you might as well delete it.

Avoiding problems such as these is one of the primary reasons for using the FreeBSD packages or ports systems. In the long run, they can be real headache deterrents. Managing one or two programs through raw source code usually isn't too much of a problem, though.

If you're not positive you want to install the program, you may be able to run it from the compilation directory to test it. If you don't like the program, don't install it, and remove the compilation directory.

Performing an Installation

As suggested in the previous section, the `Makefile` usually controls the installation process through a target called `install`. As with compiling the program, this configuration mirrors that used by the FreeBSD ports system, but a raw source code installation doesn't take advantage of the FreeBSD package database. Typically, you install the program using a command such as the following:

```
# make install
installing in ./mlvwm...
/usr/bin/install -c -s  mlvwm /usr/X11R6/bin/mlvwm
install in mlvwm done
installing in ./sample_rc...
install in sample_rc done
installing in ./man...
install in man done
```

Because this installation process usually writes to system directories such as `/usr/local/bin` or (as in the preceding example) `/usr/X11R6/bin`, you *must* type this command as `root`. Most programs display information on what they're doing—possibly just from what directories they're installing files, or possibly all the files they're installing. This information can be very helpful for debugging purposes.

Tip *You can make a note of what files are installed for future reference. If you subsequently decide to delete the program, you can use these notes to help track down and delete the package's files. One good way to take these notes is to use the `script` program—type* **script record.txt** *to store a copy of everything run in your shell to `record.txt`. When you're done, type* **exit** *to terminate `script`.*

Although most source code tarballs respond to the **make install** command, a few don't. Some smaller packages require you to manually copy particular files to locations on your path, such as `/usr/local/bin`, and a few larger packages include scripts called `install` or something similar. Consult the program's documentation for details.

Checking the Installed Package

The most important check of an installed package is to see if it runs; type its name or launch it in whatever way is appropriate. For MLVWM, you'd replace the call to your window manager with `mlvwm` in your `.xinitrc`, `.xsession`, or other X startup file, and then restart X. If the program runs, you can celebrate. If not, you're in for a potentially tough debugging task. Most programs that compile correctly also run fine, but those that don't usually fail because of a subtle bug or FreeBSD incompatibility, and these usually take a fair amount of debugging skill to track down and correct.

In the case of MLVWM run on FreeBSD 5.0, the window manager runs, but unless you create an appropriate `.mlvwmrc` file in your home directory, it will function only minimally. You can copy `sample_rc/Mlvwmrc` to `~/.mlvwmrc` to obtain this functionality, then edit the configuration file as described in the `CONFIGURATION` file. The `.mlvwmrc` file in turn refers to several graphics files, many of which are stored in the `pixmap` subdirectory of the MLVWM source directory. You must copy those files to an appropriate place on your disk, such as `/usr/local/include/X11/pixmaps` (which may not exist on your system, so you may need to create it). Of course, any similar fine-tuning for other packages will be highly package-specific, so you may need to pay attention to error messages or other strange behavior as you run the program initially, and then check the source directory tree or do a web search to try to figure out what extra steps you may need to take to get the program working optimally.

In some cases, you may want to check some details of the configuration. For instance, you might want to check the owner and group of the program file, as well as its permissions. Some programs must be installed SUID `root`, but if you want to limit who can run such programs, you may need to change the program's group ownership and permissions, as described in Chapter 29.

Summary

FreeBSD's packages and ports systems provide a huge array of software in easy-to-install forms. Sometimes, though, these systems are inadequate. A few programs aren't available as packages or ports, or you may want to customize or modify the software in ways that neither packages nor ports allow. In such cases, installing software from the developer's original source code can be desirable. FreeBSD enables you to do this, but you must take the time to read compilation and installation instructions, which differ from one package to another. Installing "raw" packages in this way also loses the benefits of FreeBSD package management. Thus, although all FreeBSD system administrators should know how to install a source package, most FreeBSD systems are better served by use of packages or ports whenever possible.

Chapter 31

Writing Scripts

T his book is filled with references to *scripts* or *shell scripts*. For instance, Chapter 6 describes a particularly important class of scripts: those that help control the startup of the computer. Scripts are a type of program written in what's known as an *interpreted language*, as described in the section "Bridging the Gap." Shell scripts are scripts written in the scripting language of a particular user shell. Although you don't need to be a scripting guru to administer a FreeBSD system, a basic understanding of scripting can help you immensely, for two reasons. First, knowing something about scripting can help you to modify existing scripts on the computer; and second, knowing about scripting enables you to create scripts to help automate tedious tasks you might otherwise be forced to perform manually on a regular basis.

This chapter begins with a look at what scripts are and how they compare to compiled programs. It then moves on to an overview of common scripting languages. From there, some critical scripting features are examined, including using external commands, variables, conditional expressions, and loops. These sections will help you understand (and, if necessary, modify) existing scripts as well as create new ones.

If you want to become truly proficient at scripting, you should consult a book on the topic. Most such books focus on just one scripting language, so you should decide what language you want to learn and locate a book for it. Example titles include Wyke and Thomas's *Perl: A Beginner's Guide* (Osborne/McGraw-Hill, 2000), Brown's *Python: The Complete Reference* (Osborne/McGraw-Hill, 2001), and Newham and Rosenblatt's *Learning the Bash Shell* (O'Reilly, 1998).

Compiled and Interpreted Programs

It's important to understand where scripts fit into the range of FreeBSD programs. Scripts are different from most executable FreeBSD programs in that you can examine a script with a text editor and figure out what it does—at least, assuming you know the scripting language! If you try to do this with most FreeBSD executables, you'll see something that looks a lot like gibberish because most FreeBSD programs have been compiled, as described in Chapter 30.

Machine Code and Human-Readable Code

Computer CPUs understand numbers. To tell a CPU to perform an operation such as adding two numbers, you must feed it the numbers you want to add and another number that stands for the addition operation. The act of delivering the numbers to the CPU and storing the addition result in memory may require additional numeric operators. Thus, the code a CPU understands looks like gibberish when shown to a human. This code is referred to by several names, including *machine code*, *machine language*, and *binary code*.

Humans find it difficult to understand, much less directly create, machine code. Instead, humans prefer to work in a higher-level programming language. Such programming languages can be roughly ordered according to how far removed their constructs are from the features of a typical CPU. *Assembly language* is the lowest-level language in common use; it supports a one-to-one correspondence of language codes (called *mnemonics*) and machine code instructions. Assembly language is not portable across CPU types, so if you have (say) a PowerPC assembly language program, you cannot use it on (say) an *x*86 computer. A bit higher up the scale is the popular C language, which provides many fairly low-level constructs but is far enough removed from machine language that it must be *compiled* for a specific CPU—that is, converted in a fairly complex way from C into a given CPU's machine language, as described in Chapter 30. C is generally considered one of the lowest-level of the high-level languages. Many other languages are higher-level than C, including Pascal, FORTRAN, and the scripting languages described in this chapter.

In 2002, computer languages are very precise and specialized compared to natural human languages such as English or Swahili. Computer languages are, after all, designed as a means of controlling a machine, not exchanging general information or gossip. Thus, you won't find an English compiler for FreeBSD, although many computer languages use certain words from English to communicate certain specific tasks. To use a computer language, you must learn its vocabulary, syntax, and grammar.

Bridging the Gap

As noted in the last section, one common approach to converting between a high-level language such as C or Pascal and the low-level machine language is to compile a program. This process, described in Chapter 30, creates a program file that contains machine language from one or more high-level language files. Most large programs for FreeBSD, including the FreeBSD kernel, are written in high-level languages and compiled. This isn't the only way to bridge the gap between high-level and machine languages, though. A second approach is to *interpret* the program—to have the CPU work out the meanings of each keyword and variable in the high-level language on the fly. This task requires the use of an *interpreter* rather than a compiler. The interpreter is a program (which is usually itself compiled) that reads a program file and executes the equivalent machine language instructions immediately. Essentially, the interpreter converts the program source code into machine language as the interpreter runs. This arrangement and its contrast to compiling a program are illustrated in Figure 31-1.

Scripting languages are typically interpreted, although scripting isn't synonymous with interpreted languages. Some high-level languages are available in both compiled and interpreted forms, and such languages aren't usually referred to as scripting languages, even when they're run via an interpreter. Scripting languages are typically designed for quickly creating solutions to problems. Historically, the term derives from interactive utilities to help automate tasks, but it's now commonly applied to a broad range of interpreted languages. In FreeBSD, as in other UNIX-like OSs, scripts typically begin with a line such as

```
#!/bin/sh
```

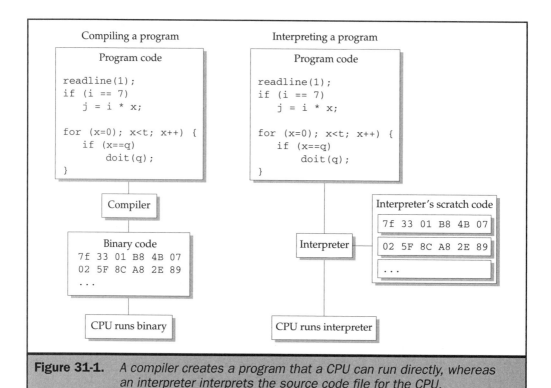

Figure 31-1. *A compiler creates a program that a CPU can run directly, whereas an interpreter interprets the source code file for the CPU.*

The first two characters of this line are a code that the kernel recognizes as indicating a script. Most scripting languages use a pound sign (#) as a comment character, so the interpreter itself ignores the line. The rest of the line after the first two characters points to the interpreter that's to execute the program, so in this case, /bin/sh handles the job.

Some languages fall in between the compiled and interpreted cases. In such a language, the program code is converted into a form that's not fully compiled. This intermediary form is difficult for both humans and CPUs to understand, but the job of interpreting this code is easier than is the job of interpreting the original code. Thus, this code executes more quickly than would the same code run by a traditional interpreter.

Pros and Cons of Compiled and Interpreted Code

The main difference between compiled and interpreted languages is one of where CPU time is invested. In a compiled program, the compiler spends considerable CPU time creating a binary file, which the CPU can then execute. If the compiler and coding practices are efficient, the CPU can run the program very efficiently. With an interpreted language, by contrast, no CPU time is spent compiling the program, but the interpreter spends considerable time handling each line of the program file. Thus, the program executes more slowly than does a compiled program.

As a general rule, using an interpreter is good for development because you can test a change to a program without bothering to recompile it, which can save a lot of development time; but interpreters are bad for execution speed of the final program. This set of tradeoffs makes interpreters good for creating "quick and dirty" programs to handle a task, or to create programs that are likely to be changed frequently. The former makes interpreted scripting languages good for system administrators, and the latter is why startup scripts are written in interpreted scripting languages.

Common Scripting Languages

Dozens of programming languages are in common use in 2002. The primary reason for the proliferation of languages is that each language has its own strong points. For instance, assembly language enables a proficient assembly programmer to write extremely efficient code, which can be important when writing time-critical software; the popular C language provides a middle ground between assembly and higher-level compiled languages such as Pascal or FORTRAN; and Perl provides extensive support for manipulating *strings* (that is, collections of text). Even within the realm of scripting languages alone, there's substantial variability. Some of the more common scripting languages include

- **Shell scripting languages**   Most shells that you use to type commands in an xterm or a text-mode login support scripting. You can create a file that contains a series of commands and use the shell to run those commands. The shells themselves also include programming control features, as described in the rest of this chapter. Many FreeBSD startup scripts are written as shell scripts.

- **Perl**   The *Practical Extraction and Reporting Language (Perl)* is a popular scripting language on FreeBSD. It borrows from many other scripting and nonscripting languages and is well known for its commands for manipulating strings.

- **Python**   This language, named after the Monty Python comedy troupe, includes strong string-handling features and is often used as a "glue" between unrelated programs to get them to work together.

- **Tcl**   The *Tool Command Language (Tcl*; pronounced *tickle)* is a language that's designed to interact with other programs. The Tcl libraries may also be called by other programs, enabling other programs to use Tcl as their built-in command languages. A Tcl extension (*Tk*, pronounced *tick)* provides X interfaces, enabling Tcl/Tk scripts to provide GUI interfaces.

- **awk**   This scripting language, named after its first three authors (Alfred V. Aho, Peter J. Weinberger, and Brian W. Kernighan), is often used in pattern-scanning applications and in conjunction with the *stream editor*, sed, which enables programs to make changes to text files. Perl borrows heavily from awk, but Perl is the more powerful language, so many people now use Perl instead of awk.

Some programmers prefer not to refer to some or all of these languages as scripting languages. Indeed, compilers for some of these languages are available.

Each of these scripting languages has its adherents, some of whom can be quite adamant that their chosen language is the One True Programming Language. I don't intend to debate this point, but for practical purposes, I must choose one language to use for examples in the rest of this chapter. Because it's available on all FreeBSD systems and because it's used by so many startup scripts, I use shell scripting for examples.

As you might guess, each shell provides its own shell scripting language. These languages implement the features of the shell in question, and thus differ somewhat from one shell to another. Thus, it's possible to write a `tcsh` shell script that won't work in the Korn shell, to name just one possible conflict. As a general rule, though, you should try to write shell scripts that don't rely upon specific shells' features. Indeed, many shell scripts will work when run from any common FreeBSD shell. As described earlier, in "Bridging the Gap," you can and should use the first line of the script to specify the shell you're using if you use features of a particular shell. Most scripts specify `/bin/sh` as their scripting language, so that's what I use as an example in this chapter.

 In FreeBSD, `/bin/sh` is a basic Bourne shell. On some other UNIX-like systems, though, `/bin/sh` may be something else. For instance, on most Linux systems, `/bin/sh` is a symbolic link to the Bourne Again Shell (Bash), which is an expanded relative of the Bourne shell. Thus, it's possible to run into scripting feature problems when transferring a script from one UNIX-like OS to another. Writing for a "plain" Bourne shell referred to as `/bin/sh` seldom causes problems. A Linux script that uses Bash-specific features may not work correctly on FreeBSD, though, unless you modify the script to point to Bash (`/usr/local/bin/bash` in FreeBSD).

Starting and Ending a Script

In addition to the codes in the first two bytes of a file identifying the file as a script, shell scripts normally have their execute permission bits set, as described in Chapter 8. Doing this enables you to type the name of the script to launch it. If you don't include execute permission, you can usually still run the script, but only by explicitly passing it to the shell in question. If you create a new script, therefore, you should set it to be executable with a command such as

```
$ chmod a+x myscript.sh
```

Many scripts end unceremoniously; they just stop. The most proper way to end a shell script, though, is with the `exit` command:

```
exit 0
```

This command tells the shell script interpreter that the script has ended; even if other commands follow this one, they're ignored. More important, the `exit` command takes a parameter, which is the *exit code* for the script. You can use this code to communicate the success of the script to other programs or scripts that may call it. A program that completes successfully should return an exit code of 0. Higher values denote errors. If you like, you can assign different exit codes to different types of error. Actually creating unique exit codes requires programming techniques described later in this chapter, such as conditional expressions (see "Using Conditional Expressions"). You can use the exit code from one script to guide another script via its own conditional expressions, as well, or as a test condition in a loop (see "Using Loops").

Using External Commands

One of the most basic uses of a script is to launch external programs. For instance, you might create a script that launches half a dozen programs at once, or that launches programs with some complex set of parameters you frequently need. Indeed, your system's login scripts, such as /etc/rc, and your account login scripts, such as ~/.shrc, are basically just ways to launch programs, although they may use additional scripting features to do more than just blindly launch external commands.

In addition to launching programs, you can use redirection and pipes (described in Chapter 5) to string together multiple external programs or redirect their input or output. These features alone enable you to create a simple script that does the jobs of half a dozen or more individual commands.

Launching External Programs

Launching an external program is extremely simple: You need only include the name of the program on a line in the script, optionally followed by any parameters you want to pass to the program. For example, Listing 31-1 constitutes a complete shell script.

Listing 31-1
Simple But Complete Shell Script

```
#!/bin/sh
/bin/ls -l
exit 0
```

If you type these lines into a file called (say) `ls1`, make the file executable, and then type **./ls1**, you'll see the same output you'd see if you'd typed **ls -l** directly. If you copy the `ls1` script to somewhere on your path, such as /usr/local/bin, you can then call it as you would any other command, by typing its name alone. (The path is set via the $PATH environment variable, as described in Chapter 6.)

This example calls `/bin/ls` *by specifying its complete path. In most cases, scripts work even if you don't include the complete path to the programs they call, but it's good practice to include the complete path, for two reasons. First, doing so minimizes the risk that a script's behavior could be changed if duplicate programs are added elsewhere in the path. Second, specifying the complete path guarantees the script will work even for users whose paths don't include the target directory. On the other hand, including the complete path may reduce the portability of the script because the same program may reside in different locations on different systems.*

One problem with this approach is that the script won't pass on any parameters you give it. For instance, if you type `./lsl a*` and expect to see only files whose names begin with a, you'll be disappointed—the script drops the a* parameter, so you'll see all the files. The upcoming section, "Using Command-Line Arguments as Variables," describes how to work around this limitation.

A script can call more than a single external program. Place each program call on a line by itself and the script will call them all in sequence, waiting for each program call to complete before moving on to the next. If you follow a program call with an ampersand (&), the program launches in the background, just as when you type a program name followed by an ampersand at a shell prompt. For instance, consider Listing 31-2.

Listing 31-2
A Sample
Script to
Launch
Several
Programs

```
#!/bin/sh
/usr/X11R6/bin/xterm &
/usr/X11R6/bin/xclock &
/usr/X11R6/bin/xload &
exit 0
```

This script launches three programs—an xterm window, the `xclock` program, and the `xload` program. Because these are X-based programs that you probably want to use concurrently, each one's name is followed by an ampersand. When you run this script, you'll see three new windows open on your screen, one for each program called.

Piping Programs and Redirecting Input and Output

Chapter 5 introduced the use of pipes and redirection in the context of commands typed at a shell prompt. These features work in precisely the same way within a shell script. For instance, suppose you want to create a script that displays the names of all the active network interfaces on a computer. Listing 31-3 accomplishes this goal.

Listing 31-3
An Example
of Pipelining
in a Script

```
#!/bin/sh
ifconfig | grep flags | cut -f 1 -d ":"
exit 0
```

Note	*For readability, Listing 31-3 and most subsequent listings do not provide complete paths to external programs. You can add them if you like; use* whereis, *as in* **whereis ifconfig**, *to locate these program files.*

Listing 31-3 calls three programs in a pipeline. The first, ifconfig, displays information on the computer's network interfaces, as described in Chapter 14. This information is too verbose, though. For instance, here's some typical output of ifconfig:

```
$ ifconfig
vr0: flags=8843<UP,BROADCAST,RUNNING,SIMPLEX,MULTICAST> mtu 1500
        inet 192.168.1.6 netmask 0xffffff00 broadcast 192.168.1.255
        ether 00:80:c8:fa:3b:0a
        media: Ethernet autoselect (100baseTX)
        status: active
lp0: flags=8810<POINTTOPOINT,SIMPLEX,MULTICAST> mtu 1500
lo0: flags=8049<UP,LOOPBACK,RUNNING,MULTICAST> mtu 16384
        inet 127.0.0.1 netmask 0xff000000
ppp0: flags=8010<POINTTOPOINT,MULTICAST> mtu 1500
```

The four interfaces in this example are vr0, lp0, lo0, and ppp0, but extracting them and discarding everything else requires trimming the output. The second command, grep, searches for the lines that contain interface names. These lines all contain the word flags, so that's what grep searches for. The third command, cut, trims all but the first field of the output. The -f 1 option tells cut to cut everything except the first field, and the -d ":" option tells cut to use a colon as a field delimiter. Running Listing 31-3 creates output such as this:

```
$ ./ifinfo
vr0
lp0
lo0
ppp0
```

Although Listing 31-3 isn't likely to be a critically important program, you might use techniques such as this to generate a list of options for users of the script. Later examples also build upon Listing 31-3 to perform more interesting tasks. You might also want to record this information to a file. To do this, you might use redirection to send the output to a temporary or permanent file. For instance, you might change the second line in Listing 31-3 to this:

```
ifconfig | grep flags | cut -f 1 -d ":" > /tmp/if-info.txt
```

You can then examine the output after the script has run, load it into another program, or even read it into another program using the same script that created the file by using input redirection. You can combine these techniques with the use of command-line arguments (described in the upcoming section, "Using Command-Line Arguments as Variables") to have a script read or write a file that you specify as an argument to the script.

Using Variables

Variables are an important part of any programming language, and scripting languages are no exception to this rule. Shell script variables are closely related to environment variables, which were introduced in Chapter 6. In fact, you can treat environment variables in shell scripts just like other variables. Conventionally, environment variable names appear entirely in uppercase, whereas script variable names appear in lowercase, or occasionally in mixed case. In a shell script, variables work much as they do at a command shell prompt, but there are certain important extensions when dealing with command-line arguments. It's common to manipulate variables in a script more than you would at a shell's command prompt.

Assigning Values to Variables

Chapter 6 described how to assign values to variables from a shell's prompt, and the same procedure works in a shell script. The most basic case in a Bourne shell looks like this:

```
export color=red
```

This example sets the value of the $color variable to red. The value can be a string, such as red, or a number, such as 12. If the value is a string that includes a space, you should enclose it in quotation marks (" "). When you assign a value to a variable, you don't include a leading dollar sign ($), but you must include this symbol when you subsequently refer to the variable.

In fact, it's possible—and usually desirable—to do away with the export command entirely because that command is used to export a variable as an environment variable. Thus, the preceding command is better expressed as

```
color=red
```

Do not place a space between the equal sign and either the variable name or its value. If you do, the shell will either try to interpret the variable name as a command or assign a null value to the variable and then try to interpret your intended value as a command.

Using Command-Line Arguments as Variables

One common use for variables in scripts is to pass command-line arguments to the script. For instance, you might want to pass the name of a file or directory. Consider Listing 31-1 once again. This script displays the contents of the current directory in a long directory listing, but if you type the script name followed by another directory name, the script ignores the directory name you provide. Fortunately, there's a straightforward way to recover parameters passed to a shell script: You can refer to them as numbered variables, from $0 to $9. (You can use the shift command to access parameters beyond the ninth.) $0 is the name of the shell script itself, $1 is the first parameter passed to the script, $2 is the second parameter, and so on. If you need to know how many parameters are passed to a script, the $# variable holds this information. Listing 31-1 rewritten to pass a single parameter on to its command is shown in Listing 31-4.

Listing 31-4
An Example of a Parameter Used in a Shell Script

```
#!/bin/sh
ls -l $1
exit 0
```

There's no need to explicitly define the parameter variable; it's defined implicitly by the shell itself. If this script is called ls1, then typing **./ls1** produces a long listing of the current directory, but adding a directory name (such as **./ls1 /tmp**) produces a long listing of the specified directory. One limitation with this approach, at least if the purpose is to pass a file or directory name to the script, is in the handling of wildcards. FreeBSD shells *expand* wildcards—that is, they convert the wildcards into a list of files that may span multiple parameters—before calling the program whose name a user types. Thus, if you type **./ls1 ***, Listing 31-4 receives the name of the first file or directory in the current directory as the value of $1. You can force the issue by enclosing the parameter in quotes. For instance, typing **./ls1 "*"** passes an asterisk (*) as the value of $1, which is then expanded in the call to ls within the script.

You can pass information other than filenames as parameters. For instance, you might create a script that manipulates user information, in which case you might pass a username as a parameter. You could then use a parameter variable such as $1 in place of a username when the script calls account manipulation programs such as passwd or adduser.

Displaying and Using Variables

Listing 31-4 illustrates one possible use of variables—you can pass them on to external commands. You can do other things with variables, though. For one thing, as the name implies, variables can change. It's also useful to be able to display the value of a variable, and to set a variable to a value based upon the user's input.

Displaying a Variable's Value

Scripts must frequently display information. You can do so with the echo command. (This command is actually an external program, so passing a variable to echo is really the same thing as passing a variable to ls or any other external command.) Consider Listing 31-5, which is a template for experimenting with variables.

Listing 31-5
A Skeletal
Variable
Manipulation
Script

```
#!/bin/sh
echo "The input variable is" $1
# Assign to a local variable
myvar=$1
# Perform some manipulation
# (To be filled in)
echo "The transformed variable is" $myvar
```

Suppose you call this script scratch. You might run it as follows:

```
$ ./scratch FreeBSD
The input variable is FreeBSD
The transformed variable is FreeBSD
```

The echo command echoes to the display any and all parameters it's given. Thus, this command echoes both the information strings, such as The input variable is, and the value of the $1 variable. Because Listing 31-5 is a simple skeleton that doesn't actually manipulate the variable in any way, that variable is unchanged.

Setting a Variable to a User's Input

So far, this chapter has shown extremely short scripts as examples. Scripts can be quite complex, though. Such complex scripts may ask a user for input—say, to prompt for a series of usernames or information that's to be used in processing. Prompting for input in this way often creates a more user-friendly script than would result if the script required all its inputs as parameters. To obtain such input, you can use the read command, which accepts input from the user, who terminates input by pressing ENTER. For instance, consider Listing 31-6, which shows read in action.

Listing 31-6
A Script
Demonstrating
the Use of
read

```
#!/bin/sh
echo "Please enter some information:"
read info
echo "You typed " $info
exit 0
```

A typical run of this script looks something like this:

```
$ ./input-info
Please enter some information:
Shakespeare was a great writer of scripts!
You typed Shakespeare was a great writer of scripts!
```

The variable is set to anything the user types, including an entire sentence; spaces don't bother the read command. You can use this technique to prompt users for their own names, filenames, URLs, or anything else you might need to collect in the script.

Modifying String Variables

Broadly speaking, there are two types of variables: *strings*, which contain any combination of letters and numbers; and *numeric variables*, which contain just numbers. You may want to manipulate these two types of variables in different ways.

Modifying a string variable is essentially a variant on assigning a value to the variable. For instance, suppose you want to add information to the beginning and end of a variable. You can do so as illustrated in Listing 31-7, which is a variant on Listing 31-5.

Listing 31-7
Adding Data to a String Variable

```
#!/bin/sh
echo "The input variable is" $1
# Assign to a local variable
myvar=$1
myvar="Lions, "$myvar", and bears."
echo "The transformed variable is" $myvar
```

Running this program creates output such as this:

```
$ ./add-data tigers
The input variable is tigers
The transformed variable is Lions, tigers, and bears.
```

One caveat is that such transformations don't work with parameter variables. This is the reason for assigning the value of the parameter variable to a local variable ($myvar); the local variable can be manipulated. As Listing 31-7 illustrates, adding information to the variable is a matter of surrounding the variable name with the information to be added. There should be no spaces between the variable name and the information to be added.

To perform more complex string manipulations, you must normally call external programs, at least when programming using a shell script language. (Perl, Python, and some other languages provide extensive built-in string-handling tools.) Some common commands for performing operations on strings include

- **grep** This command finds text within a file. It's described more fully in Chapter 8.

- **cut** This command trims a line of text. You can cut based on character positions (say, leaving the first ten characters) or by symbols you know are present in the input string.

- **sed** This is an extremely powerful command that enables performing all sorts of text manipulations.

- **sort** This command is usually applied to entire files; it sorts them according to some criterion you specify, which can be very useful if you want to summarize information.

Consult these commands' man pages for more detail. As a general rule, for simple scripts, you can accomplish a great deal with just grep and cut, as illustrated by Listing 31-3.

Modifying Numeric Variables

Sometimes you want to perform mathematical operations on variables. For instance, you might want to write a short script that converts gigabytes as reported by hard disk manufacturers (10^9 bytes) into gigabytes as used in most other computer measurements (2^{30} bytes). Listing 31-8 presents such a script. It uses the bc command, which evaluates a mathematical or logical expression and returns the result.

Listing 31-8
A Script That
Performs
Mathematical
Computations

```
#!/bin/sh
gib=`echo "($1 * 1000000000) / 1073741824" | bc -l`
echo $1 "disk gigabytes is" $gib "computer gigabytes."
exit 0
```

Listing 31-8's assignment to the $gib variable looks confusing. This is in part because bc is itself a powerful tool for performing computations. It's designed to work on files, so Listing 31-8 uses it in a pipe—the echo command prepares output in a form that bc will accept as a file and pipes it to bc, which can then treat the input as if it were a file. You can't simply place the expression to be evaluated as a parameter to bc. The echo command prepares the equation that performs the conversion. The entire computation command, from echo through bc -l, is enclosed in back quotes (`). These symbols appear to the left of the 1 key on most keyboards, and they have the effect of telling the shell that the text they enclose should be treated like a command, its value to be assigned to the $gib variable. The result of this work can be seen in a run of the conversion script:

```
$ ./gb2gib 65
65 disk gigabytes is 60.53596735000610351562 computer gigabytes
```

Using Conditional Expressions

Frequently, you may not know when writing a script precisely what sort of input it will receive, and thus whether it makes sense to perform some operation based on the input. When this happens, it's time to bring out another programming tool: *conditional expressions*. These are tools that enable you to tell the computer to execute certain lines of the script only if the specified expression is true. Conditional expressions support the development of considerably larger and less trivial scripts than I've presented thus far in this chapter.

Basic Logic Tools

Conditional expressions (particularly the `if` and `elif` statements, described in the next section) rely upon a logical test—some expression must be either true or false. These expressions can test for the existence of a file, check whether two strings are identical, and so on. Table 31-1 summarizes common shell script expressions.

Conditional Expression	Meaning
-a *file*	True if *file* exists
-b *file*	True if *file* is a block file
-c *file*	True if *file* is a character file
-d *file*	True if *file* is a directory
-e *file*	True if *file* exists
-f *file*	True if *file* is a regular file
-g *file*	True if *file*'s SGID bit is set
-h *file*	True if *file* is a symbolic link
-k *file*	True if *file*'s "sticky" bit is set
-p *file*	True if *file* is a named pipe
-r *file*	True if *file* is readable
-s *file*	True if *file*'s size is greater than 0
-t *fd*	True if the *fd* file descriptor is open and points to a terminal
-u *file*	True if *file*'s SUID bit is set
-w *file*	True if *file* is writeable

Table 31-1. *Conditional Expression Logic Tests*

Conditional Expression	Meaning
-x *file*	True if *file* is executable
-O *file*	True if *file* is owned by the user who runs the script
-G *file*	True if *file*'s group is the same as the user who runs the script
-L *file*	True if *file* is a symbolic link
-S *file*	True if *file* is a socket
-N *file*	True if *file* has been modified since it was last read
file1 -nt *file2*	True if *file1*'s modification date is more recent than *file2*'s modification date
file1 -ot *file2*	True if *file1*'s modification date is less recent than *file2*'s modification date
file1 -ef *file2*	True if *file1* and *file2* have the same device and inode numbers (that is, if they're hard links to the same file)
-o *optname*	True if the *optname* shell option is enabled
-z *string*	True if *string*'s length is 0
-n *string*	True if *string*'s length is greater than 0
string1 = *string2*	True if the strings are equal
string1 != *string2*	True if the strings are not equal
string1 < *string2*	True if *string1* sorts before *string2*
string1 > *string2*	True if *string1* sorts after *string2*
arg1 -eq *arg2*	True if the integers *arg1* and *arg2* are equal
arg1 -ne *arg2*	True if the integers *arg1* and *arg2* are not equal
arg1 -lt *arg2*	True if integer *arg1* is less than integer *arg2*
arg1 -le *arg2*	True if integer *arg1* is less than or equal to integer *arg2*
arg1 -gt *arg2*	True if integer *arg1* is greater than integer *arg2*
arg1 -ge *arg2*	True if integer *arg1* is greater than or equal to integer *arg2*

Table 31-1. *Conditional Expression Logic Tests* (continued)

Because shell scripts are often used to operate on files, they support many conditional expressions that relate to the existence of files and various characteristics of the files, such as modification dates, sizes, and so on. Whether the expressions relate to files or to other features, such as string or numeric comparisons, you must use the expression within an if or elif statement.

if, elif, and else Statements

Binary (that is, two-state) logic tests are implemented in the if statement. In its most basic form, this statement looks something like this:

```
if [ $configfile -ot $oldconfigfile ]
then
    echo "Warning!"
    echo "New configuration file appears to be old!"
fi
```

This code snippet tests the ages of two configuration files, whose names should have already been stored in the $configfile and $oldconfigfile variables. Some features you should note about this example are

- **Brackets around the expression** The logical test is enclosed within square brackets ([ ]) following the keyword if.

- **Spacing around the expression** You *must* include spaces on both sides of the opening bracket and a space before the closing bracket. The shell will become confused if you don't include these spaces.

- **Indentation** Indentation on the third and fourth lines of this example is optional. In this example, the statements that are executed only if the expression is true are indented to help you identify them visually.

- **if clause termination** An if statement terminates with the fi keyword (if spelled backwards). Everything between the then keyword and fi executes if and only if the conditional expression evaluates as true. (The else keyword modifies this rule, though, as described shortly.)

As you might imagine, an if statement is a good way to specify a block of code that you might or might not want to execute, depending upon some condition. You can extend this block's capabilities in a couple of ways, with the elif and else statements.

You can provide a second conditional after the first with elif. For instance, you might want to test to see if one file is older than another, as in the preceding example. If that test fails, you might want to perform another test, such as for the presence of a third file. The elif statement is structured just like the if statement, but the two statements share a single closing fi statement (there is no separate closing for elif).

The `elif` statement enables you to nest tests one after another within an overarching `if` statement. If all of those tests fail, you may want to provide some fallback code. This code is specified by starting a block with the `else` statement. Commands after `else` but before `fi` execute only if the `if` statement and any intervening `elif` statements evaluate to false.

To illustrate `if`, `elif`, and `else` in action, consider Listing 31-9. This script attempts to identify the chipset used by an Ethernet card based on its assigned device name, as reported by `ifconfig`. To do so, this script first isolates the names of all the Ethernet cards, using `ifconfig`, `grep`, and `cut`, much as Listing 31-3 does. The resulting `$iface` value, however, includes *all* the interfaces, so another use of `echo` and `cut` isolates just the first of these interface names. `$iface` then contains a string that can be compared using `if` operators. In this particular case, the order of the comparisons is unimportant. The main `if` statement compares `$iface` to the string `fxp0`, which identifies Intel EtherExpress Pro 100B boards. If a match is obtained, the script prints this information and skips the rest of the comparisons. If a match isn't found, the script goes on to the next comparison, which identifies DEC/Intel Tulip chipsets via an `elif` statement. The second `elif` identifies boards that use VIA Rhine chipsets. If none of these comparisons matches, the script uses the `else` clause to give up, notify the user of that fact, and tell the user what the device name is.

Listing 31-9
A Script
Demonstrating
the Use of `if`,
`elif`, and
`else`

```
#!/bin/sh

# Get all interface names
iface=`ifconfig | grep flags | cut -f 1 -d ":"`

# Isolate the first interface (normally the first Ethernet device)
iface=`echo $iface | cut -f 1 -d " "`

# Identify the hardware
if [ $iface = "fxp0" ]
then
    echo "This computer has an Intel EtherExpress board."
elif [ $iface = "de0" ]
then
    echo "This computer as a DEC/Intel Tulip chipset."
elif [ $iface = "vr0" ]
then
    echo "This computer has a VIA Rhine chipset."
else
    echo "I can't identify this computer's primary network card."
    echo "The unidentified interface name is" $iface
fi
exit 0
```

For brevity's sake, Listing 31-9 includes only three comparisons. A complete script would include dozens of comparisons, one for each Ethernet device driver in FreeBSD.

When Listing 31-9 is run, it will either announce the name of your Ethernet chipset or tell you that it can't determine this information. For instance, your output might look like this:

```
$ ./identify
This computer has a VIA Rhine chipset.
```

Listing 31-9 could be modified in various ways. If you wanted to identify only one Ethernet chipset, for instance, you could eliminate both `elif` statements, including the `then` and `echo` lines associated with each. If you didn't care about the inability to identify an interface, you could eliminate the `else` clause and its following two `echo` lines. If you wanted to do more than print a single message about the interface, you could include additional code to do something else, such as issue networking commands that operate on specific devices—say, to optimize the network settings differently depending upon the installed hardware.

case Statements

The `if` statement and its `else` extension are useful for making binary distinctions—those between two conditions. As Listing 31-9 illustrates, the use of `elif` helps to extend the capability to distinguishing between several states—Listing 31-9 identifies three distinct Ethernet chipsets using one `if` and two `elif` statements, and includes a fallback condition signified by `else`. This procedure is effective, but a bit awkward when you have many possible conditions—you might mistype one of the comparisons, for instance. Thus, shell scripting supports another conditional tool: `case`. This statement executes one of an arbitrary number of statement blocks depending upon the value of a variable you supply. The basic format of a `case` statement is

```
case varname in
    option1) commands1
            ;;
    option2) commands2
            ;;
    [...]
esac
```

The *varname* is a variable (including its leading dollar sign), and each option is a possible value for the variable. If the variable has that value, the associated commands are executed and the remaining options are skipped. Each option block ends with a double semicolon (`;;`). You can have as many options as you like. Certain options have special meanings. You can use wildcards, such as an asterisk (*) or question mark (?), much as you would to specify multiple filenames. It's common practice, but isn't required, to make a final option an asterisk as a default; this option matches if no other option matches, making it similar to the `if` structure's `else` clause. The entire structure ends with the `esac` statement. Listing 31-10 illustrates the use of `case`; it's functionally equivalent to Listing 31-9.

Listing 31-10
A Script
Demonstrating
the Use of
case

```
#!/bin/sh

# Get all interface names
iface=`ifconfig | grep flags | cut -f 1 -d ":"`

# Isolate the first interface
iface=`echo $iface | cut -f 1 -d " "`

# Identify the hardware
case $iface in
   fxp0) echo "This computer has an Intel board."
        ;;
   de0) echo "This computer has a DEC/Intel Tulip chipset."
        ;;
   vr0) echo "This computer has a VIA Rhine chipset."
        ;;
   *) echo "I can't identify the primary network interface."
      echo "The unidentified interface name is" $iface
        ;;
esac
exit 0
```

Because you don't need to type the name of the variable many times, and because there's less typing generally for features such as equal signs and brackets, a `case` statement is often easier to use than a series of `if` and `elif` statements. The `if` and `elif` statements are more flexible, though. For instance, you can more easily test a series of conditions related to a file's status (whether it exists, when it was last accessed, and so on) with `if` and `elif`.

Conditional Command Execution

One shorthand you're likely to see in ready-made scripts, and eventually use in your own scripts, is the use of conditional command execution. An example looks like this:

```
tar cvz payroll-backup.tgz /home/payroll/ && rm -r /home/payroll/*
```

Recall that many programs and scripts return a success code—0 for a normal exit and higher values for errors. The `&&` operator, when placed between two commands, tells the shell to look at the success code of the first command and execute the second command if and only if the first command returns a normal exit code. Thus, the preceding example removes the files in the `/home/payroll` directory tree only if the previous `tar` command has successfully backed up the directory. If `tar` runs into problems, the directory won't be deleted.

A related operator is `| |` (two vertical bars). This operator works much like `&&`, but the meaning is effectively reversed—the second command executes only if the first fails. You might use this feature to display an error message in the event a command runs into problems.

Using Loops

Another important scripting feature is loops. You might want a script to perform the same series of actions many times—for instance, play every sound file in a directory or update every user's account expiration date. Loops were created for such tasks; they tell the computer to execute a block of code multiple times. There are several different types of loops, which vary in their exit conditions—what circumstances cause them to break out of the loop.

for Loops

The `for` loop executes a fixed number of times. Specifically, the loop executes once for each argument in a list it is passed. This list could be a prepared string containing a series of filenames, device names, usernames, or other data. Frequently, though, the list is created within the `for` statement itself by enclosing a command that creates a list in back quotes (`` ` ``). The basic form of the `for` statement is

```
for varname in list
do
    commands
done
```

In this case, `varname` is a variable name, which might not have been used before in the script. If it has been used before, its value will be overwritten by each item in `list`, which is a variable or expression that contains or produces a list of elements. The looping variable takes on each of these elements in turn. The `commands` between the `do` and `done` statements can be any normal scripting commands. To illustrate `for` in action, consider Listing 31-11. This script is a modification of Listing 31-10. One problem with this earlier script is that it identifies only the first interface. This is normally your Ethernet interface, but it might not be. Listing 31-11 corrects this problem by using a `for` loop to scan each element in the list of network interfaces. This configuration also enables the script to identify non-Ethernet devices, such as PPP and loopback interfaces. Because the `for` loop automatically assigns each element to the `$iface` value in turn, there's no need for a line to isolate the first interface name; instead, the command to generate the list of interfaces is integrated into the `for` command itself.

Listing 31-11
A Script
Demonstrating
the Use of
`for`

```
#!/bin/sh

for iface in `ifconfig | grep flags | cut -f 1 -d ":"`
do
    case $iface in
        lo0) echo "This computer has a loopback interface."
            ;;
        fxp0) echo "This computer has an Intel board."
            ;;
        de0) echo "This computer has a DEC/Intel Tulip chipset."
            ;;
        vr0) echo "This computer has a VIA Rhine chipset."
            ;;
        ppp0) echo "This computer has a PPP interface."
            ;;
        *) echo "I can't identify an interface:" $iface
            ;;
    esac
done
exit 0
```

Listing 31-11 generates a series of output lines, one for each interface. The result looks something like this:

```
$ ./identify3
This computer has a VIA Rhine chipset.
I can't identify an interface: lp0
This computer has a loopback interface.
This computer has a PPP interface.
```

As with Listings 31-9 and 31-10, the list of interfaces is incomplete, for brevity's sake. Nonetheless, this script has identified three of the four interfaces on the test computer.

while Loops

A second type of loop uses the keyword `while`. These loops continue to execute while a specified condition remains true. The basic form for this loop type is

```
while [ condition ]
do
    commands
done
```

For instance, you might use a structure such as this to perform some operation so long as a file continues to exist, while two variables continue to be equal to each other, or until a user decides to stop an operation. Listing 31-12 illustrates a `while` loop in action. This script calls `passwd` for multiple users, enabling you to change many users' passwords without typing **passwd** for each one. (You must still type the password twice for each user, though.)

sting 31-12
A Script
monstrating
the Use of
while

```
#!/bin/sh
echo "This script changes multiple user passwords."
echo "Enter a username ('n' to exit):"
read username
while [ $username != "n" ]
do
    passwd $username
    echo "Enter a username ('n' to exit):"
    read username
done
exit 0
```

Note *Listing 31-12 must be run as `root`; only `root` may change passwords for arbitrary users.*

In operation, Listing 31-12 prompts you for a username, then calls `passwd` for that username. The `passwd` program in turn asks for the password twice. (The password you type doesn't echo to the screen.) The result looks like this:

```
# ./multipasswd
This script changes multiple user passwords.
Enter a username ('n' to exit):
```

```
tennyson
Changing local password for tennyson.
New password:
Retype new password:
passwd: updating the database...
passwd: done
Enter a username ('n' to exit):
wilder
Changing local password for wilder.
New password:
Retype new password:
passwd: updating the database...
passwd: done
Enter a username ('n' to exit):
n
```

One point to note about Listing 31-12 is that it's necessary to initialize the $username variable prior to entry to the loop. Thus, it's not uncommon with while loops to see some of the code within the loop duplicated before the loop starts, and in fact Listing 31-12 does this—it prompts for and reads the first username before the loop starts, but all the rest of the usernames are acquired within the while loop.

until Loops

A third type of loop uses the keyword until. These loops continue to execute until a specified condition becomes true. The basic form for this loop type is:

```
until [ condition ]
do
    commands
done
```

In practice, until loops are extremely similar to while loops, and they can usually be used interchangeably. For instance, Listing 31-12 can be modified to use an until loop merely by changing the while keyword to until and changing the conditional expression to read $username = "n". Listing 31-13 illustrates a somewhat greater departure from Listing 31-12. Instead of duplicating the prompt for the username outside of the loop, that prompt is relocated to the beginning of the loop and the call to passwd is placed within an if statement to prevent the password from being changed when it shouldn't be. This approach requires assigning a "dummy" value to $username before the loop is entered, though. (This basic approach can be used with while loops, as well as with until loops.) In the case of the scripts in Listing 31-12 and 31-13, these changes actually increase the script's length and make it more difficult to follow. In some cases, though, this approach can be worthwhile. For instance, if it takes several lines of code to create the variable that's tested, it's probably simpler to place the code only once in the loop.

ting 31-13
A Script
nonstrating
the Use of
    until

```
#!/bin/sh
echo "This script changes multiple user passwords."
username="scratch"
until [ $username = "n" ]
do
    echo "Enter a username ('n' to exit):"
    read username
    if [ $username != "n" ]
    then
        passwd $username
    fi
done
exit 0
```

Using Functions

A final important feature of shell scripts is *functions*. These are program subsets that can be called by other parts of a program. For instance, instead of performing some lengthy operation in one big block, you can break it down into logical pieces, place each piece in a function, and call the functions in turn. This approach may sound pointless at first, but it has several advantages over writing one massive block of code:

- **Mentally grasping an operation** Human cognitive limitations makes it difficult to comprehend what a very large series of code lines does. Breaking it down into smaller chunks can make it much easier to follow a script's operations.

- **Readability** Sometimes a segment of code may become difficult to read because it's deeply nested within loops or conditionals or because a tedious multiline procedure separates lines that are really closely related. Moving the heavily nested or tedious multiline code into a function can improve the readability of the script as a whole.

- **Debugging** Breaking an operation down into functions can help in debugging. You can write a "dummy" program that calls each function individually to better observe what it does, simplifying the debugging task.

- **Code duplication** Sometimes a script has to perform the same task at many different points. Rather than duplicate code, you can place that code in a function and call the function. This produces a smaller script and makes errors from typos less likely. This feature also makes changes easier to implement; rather than change the same code at several points, you need only change the one function.

The basic syntax for use of a function is

```
functionname() {
    commands
}
...
functionname
```

This syntax means that a function definition begins with a name for the function, followed immediately by an open and close parentheses, a space, and an open curly brace ({). The function body consists of one or more commands that follow the opening line, and the function ends with a close curly brace (}). There are likely to be intervening lines of code in the program before the function is called. You call the function just like an external program, by name.

Listing 31-14 illustrates the use of functions. This script is a modification of Listing 31-11, which placed a `case` statement within a `for` loop. Although Listing 31-11 isn't very deeply nested, a similar approach with a more deeply-nested series of commands could reduce nesting and therefore improve readability. One point to note about Listing 31-14 is that the function has access to the `$iface` variable defined in the main body of the script. This feature is actually necessary for Listing 31-14 to work.

Listing 31-14
A Script Demonstrating the Use of Functions

```
#!/bin/sh

identify() {
    case $iface in
        lo0) echo "This computer has a loopback interface."
            ;;
        fxp0) echo "This computer has an Intel board."
            ;;
        de0) echo "This computer has a DEC/Intel Tulip chipset."
            ;;
        vr0) echo "This computer has a VIA Rhine chipset."
            ;;
        ppp0) echo "This computer has a PPP interface."
            ;;
        *) echo "I can't identify an interface:" $iface
            ;;
    esac
}
```

```
for iface in `ifconfig | grep flags | cut -f 1 -d ":"`
do
    identify
done
exit 0
```

When should you use functions? As a general rule, functions are most useful when you write a script that's more than a few screenfulls in length, and when that script uses many conditionals and loops to send the script on paths that you can't fully predict when writing the script. For instance, if you write a script that presents a menu of options to the user, you might write a function for each option, then call these functions from a `case` statement. Functions are less useful when the script performs a fairly direct set of actions, such as launching a fixed set of programs. Another rule of thumb is that if you can't simultaneously see the start and end of a script in your editor, you should break it up into functions, each of which fits entirely on one page of your editor. This practice can help you keep a logical block of code in mind, but you shouldn't adhere to it too strictly—sometimes it's necessary to create an extra-long function to display a lot of text, set a lot of variables, or perform some other lengthy but linear task.

Summary

Scripting is a key FreeBSD skill for advanced system administration and even for normal user operations. Writing scripts enables you to automate otherwise tedious tasks by linking together unrelated programs and even providing control logic to enable the script to make decisions, perform one task multiple times, and so on. You can choose to write scripts in any of several different scripting languages, each of which has its strong points and adherents. For purposes of system administration, shell scripting is arguably the most important type because many of FreeBSD's startup scripts are shell scripts. Thus, understanding shell scripting enables you to better understand and modify these important scripts.

No matter what language you employ, you should know how to use several important scripting features—external commands, variables, conditional expressions, loops, and functions. Together, these features enable you to write some very complex programs, even in a modest shell scripting language.

The Complete Reference

Chapter 32

Troubleshooting

This book describes how FreeBSD works—or more precisely, how it *should* work. Although I've tried to anticipate certain common problems in writing each chapter, I can't predict every problem you might encounter. Even if I could, writing about every possible problem in the appropriate chapter would at least double the size of the book. Thus, this chapter emphasizes general troubleshooting skills—diagnosing and correcting your FreeBSD problems. This chapter begins with an overview of some resources you can use to locate information and obtain advice. It then moves on to one of the broadest aspects of troubleshooting: isolating a problem to the realm of hardware or software. Once you've done that, you should try to further localize the problem, so this chapter describes some procedures you can use to do so, along with information on some common problem causes. Testing a solution is next up. Finally, the chapter concludes with a look at emergency boot systems, which are very useful for correcting extremely serious problems that prevent your system from booting at all.

Getting Help

Before embarking on any troubleshooting quest, it's useful to know about some resources for getting help. For purposes of this discussion, I've divided these resources into three categories: those that come with FreeBSD, printed resources, and online resources. Each has its strengths, and you may want to avail yourself of several resources when solving a problem. You should also remember personal local resources, such as friends, family members, local office "gurus," user groups, and even paid consultants. If you use FreeBSD for anything more than a trivial period of time, chances are you'll use all of these resource types.

All of these help resources provide information about FreeBSD, so they're useful for discovering how the system *should* be operating. (Some "problems" are the result of misunderstandings about how a feature is supposed to work.) Some resources can help you learn about problem symptoms and their likely causes, so they're extremely valuable in helping to diagnose problems. Others can help you find workarounds or fixes once you've diagnosed a problem.

Help Resources That Come with FreeBSD

The first class of help resources is those that come with FreeBSD itself. These resources are mostly documentation, which varies in focus and quality from one form and program to another. Important FreeBSD documentation resources include

- **FreeBSD release notes**   If you installed FreeBSD from CD-ROM, you should check the disc for files whose names are in uppercase with extensions of .TXT and .HTM. Specific files (in plain-text form) are likely to include ERRATA.TXT, HARDWARE.TXT, INSTALL.TXT, README.TXT, and RELNOTES.TXT. These files all contain useful general information about FreeBSD. The HARDWARE.TXT file is most likely to be useful in determining whether your hardware is supported, and the `INSTALL.TXT` file may help you handle installation problems. You can find all of these files on the FreeBSD web site if you didn't install the OS from a CD-ROM.

- **System documentation**   Check the `/usr/share/doc` directory tree for a great deal of information about FreeBSD. For English documentation, check `/usr/share/doc/en`. This directory contains two subdirectories: `articles` and `books`, each of which has several subdirectories of its own. The `articles` subdirectory contains articles of a few pages (when printed) detailing how to accomplish particular tasks or use certain tools, such as configuring a multiboot system or using Zip disks. The `books` subdirectory contains larger documents, such as the FreeBSD Handbook and the FreeBSD FAQ, which cover more ground. The articles and books in these subdirectories are available in plain text, HTML, and sometimes PostScript formats. If you upgrade your system, you may need to update the documentation via `cvsup` and then type **make install** in the `/usr/share/doc` directory to update the documentation.

> **Tip**   *Try creating bookmarks in your web browser that point to `file:///usr/share/doc/en/books/` and `file:///usr/share/doc/en/articles/`. When you select these bookmarks, you'll see listings of the books and articles, respectively, so you can quickly find help.*

- **Package documentation**   Many FreeBSD packages and ports ship with documentation files. Most of these files reside in subdirectories of `/usr/local/share/doc`. The format of these documentation files varies from one package to another; some come in plain text, others in HTML, others in PostScript, and so on. Some packages ship with minimal documentation—perhaps just a license file. Others come with extensive book-sized documentation.

- **Man pages**   The traditional primary documentation utility for FreeBSD is `man`, whose name is short for *manual*. Documentation files in this form are known as *man pages*, and most commands, configuration files, and procedures have associated man pages. Typing **man *subject*** produces the man page for *subject*, where *subject* is a command, filename (without its leading path), or topic. Man pages tend to be written in a fairly terse style; they're intended more as references than as tutorials.

- **Info pages**   In recent years, the `info` utility has come to supplement and, in some cases, supplant `man` as the FreeBSD documentation system. It's used much like `man` and usually provides similar or identical information. The `tkinfo` utility provides a GUI front-end to `info`. A similar front-end is available in Emacs.

- **In-program help**   Many programs—particularly GUI programs—provide help tools, usually from a Help menu option or button. These tools may open a small help window or launch a web browser on a documentation file (perhaps one stored in `/usr/local/share/doc`).

Don't underestimate the FreeBSD help resources. Although they're somewhat obscure and hard to find if you're not familiar with FreeBSD (or UNIX generally), this documentation is often extremely useful. The FreeBSD system documentation in `/usr/share/doc`, in particular, is unusually well written and complete, unlike the documentation that comes with many OSs. Once you're familiar with FreeBSD, man and info pages can be extremely helpful if you need to refresh your memory about how to use a specific command or configuration file. For the most part, though, these resources aren't designed as troubleshooting resources. In most cases, they'll provide only minimal clues about what might be going wrong. They're best used as a way to learn how to work around a problem by using alternative tools or commands.

Printed Help Resources

Printed documentation can help provide static information, much like the files that ship with FreeBSD or web pages devoted to the OS. Of course, you're holding a printed resource, so you should use it to the fullest. Check this book's table of contents and index to help find information, and do the same with any other books you have on the topics at hand. Many of this book's chapters provide pointers to other books with more in-depth coverage of specific topics, and these other books can be valuable guides. You may also find it helpful to go to a local book store and browse through several books on whatever subsystem is giving you problems, then buy whichever one seems to provide the best information.

In addition to books, there are various magazines that can be helpful. The most important of these are probably *Daemon News*, which also operates a web site (`http://www.daemonnews.org`), and *Sys Admin Magazine*, which also has a companion web site (`http://www.sysadminmag.com`). *Daemon News* is devoted to the BSD operating systems, including FreeBSD, whereas *Sys Admin Magazine* is devoted to professional system administration more generally, with a focus on UNIX systems but some coverage of Windows NT/2000 and other OSs. Both are valuable learning resources, and if you have a subscription and keep back issues, they may be important troubleshooting resources. These magazines' web sites may also contain information, including back issues' articles, that can be valuable when troubleshooting. Overall, though, they're best viewed as general learning resources, which can pay off in future troubleshooting efforts.

Printed resources have one huge advantage over FreeBSD's standard documentation and online resources: You can use them even if your computer is completely nonfunctional and you have no alternative computer or OS.

Online Help Resources

Assuming your system is working well enough to provide Internet access, or if you've got Internet access through another computer, you can avail yourself of several online help resources. Many of these resources are more interactive than the ones that come with FreeBSD—you can ask a question and obtain an answer from a real person, often soon after asking the question. Other online resources are more static in nature, and some duplicate the information that ships with FreeBSD. The online versions may be more up-to-date, though. Some of the most important online help resources include

- **FreeBSD web site**   The main FreeBSD web site, `http://www.freebsd.org`, is a good starting point for obtaining lots of information about FreeBSD. This site provides much of the same documentation you can find on a running FreeBSD system. One particularly important resource is the FreeBSD Security Information page, `http://www.freebsd.org/security/`, which you should consult from another computer if you believe your system has been compromised. (Chapter 29 of this book also covers security issues, including what to do in the event of a break-in.)

- **Supplemental FreeBSD web sites**   Some web sites are devoted to FreeBSD but aren't officially part of the FreeBSD project. These sites can provide useful information. Examples include the BSD Vault (`http://www.bsdvault.net`), Fresh Ports (`http://www.freshports.org`), and FreeBSD Diary (`http://www.freebsddiary.org`).

- **Security web sites**   Many web sites today are devoted to security issues, and may be consulted from another system if you believe your FreeBSD computer has been compromised. Two of the most important are the Computer Incident Advisory Capability (CIAC; `http://www.ciac.org/ciac/`) page and the Computer Emergency Response Team Control Center (CERT/CC; `http://www.cert.org`) page.

- **Usenet newsgroups**   Usenet newsgroups are global discussion forums that are open to the public. To use Usenet news, you need a *news reader* program, such as `tin`, KNode, or Pan, all of which come with FreeBSD. You must also know the hostname of your ISP's news server computer. When you point your news reader at the news server, the news reader gives you access to Usenet newsgroups, which are arranged in a hierarchical system similar to directories on a computer. Of particular interest for FreeBSD issues are the `comp.unix.bsd.freebsd` groups. There are also groups devoted to specific programs and computing topics, such as `comp.security.ssh` (devoted to the Secure Shell, or SSH, login server) and `comp.periphs.printers` (devoted to discussion of printers). Before posting a question to a newsgroup, try using the Google Groups Usenet archives at `http://groups.google.com`. Enter search keywords, such as **FreeBSD SSH starting** if you can't get SSH to start. If you can't find an answer, post a message to the relevant newsgroup. With any luck, you'll get a response within minutes or hours. A response isn't guaranteed, though; Usenet is a collection of interested individuals, not (for the most part) people paid to provide a service. Nonetheless, it's an extremely useful help resource.

- **Mailing lists**   Mailing lists operate much like Usenet newsgroups, but they use e-mail as a medium rather than the Usenet news protocols. You subscribe to a mailing list by sending mail to a specific address. Thereafter, you'll receive mail messages addressed to the group, and you'll be able to send messages to the group. A list of FreeBSD mailing lists, as well as instructions on subscribing to the lists, is available at `http://www.freebsd.org/doc/en_US.ISO8859-1/ books/handbook/eresources.html#ERESOURCES-MAIL`. The most useful mailing list for new users is probably `freebsd-questions`, but it's a very high-traffic group. There are more FreeBSD-specific mailing lists than newsgroups, and many of the FreeBSD mailing lists are quite active, so the mailing lists can be an extremely valuable troubleshooting resource. Posting etiquette is similar to that for newsgroups. In particular, try a newsgroup search or a search in the mailing list archives before posting a new question.

■ **IRC** *Internet Relay Chat* is a medium for real-time communication among groups of people. You can think of it as a real-time version of Usenet news. As such, it can be a valuable resource for solving problems in real time—a helpful person might be willing to help guide you through a tricky configuration task, for instance. You need an IRC client, such as `ircii` or `xchat`, both of which come with FreeBSD (in the `irc` packages or ports section). You must then select an IRC network and connect to one of its nodes. Check `http://www.irchelp .org/irchelp/networks/` for information on IRC networks. You'll also need to locate an appropriate *channel* within a network. The channel is similar to a Usenet newsgroup, but channels aren't organized hierarchically.

Online resources can be a good way to get personalized help from other people. Web sites typically provide static documentation, but Usenet newsgroups, mailing lists, and IRC channels can all put you in touch with literally thousands of other FreeBSD users. The collective experience of these individuals can be a real boon in solving problems. Try to give back, though—once you know enough (which may be soon after you begin using FreeBSD), begin answering questions that you can answer. Such activity helps ensure the continued viability of these valuable online resources.

Identifying Hardware and Software Problems

One of the first tasks in solving a problem is diagnosis, and the first issue in computer problem diagnosis is determining whether a problem's cause lies in hardware or software. Sometimes this determination is hard to make because the two types of problems sometimes present similar symptoms. Problems with drivers can be particularly difficult to distinguish from hardware problems—but fortunately, driver problems are fairly rare in FreeBSD, and are most common with very new hardware for which the drivers are not yet fully mature.

Common Symptoms of Hardware Problems

Hardware problems can be some of the most difficult to diagnose and fix. These problems are often sporadic in nature, and complete diagnosis often requires swapping out hardware components. If you're working in an environment with lots of spare computer parts, or even a computer that can be taken down for a while for a temporary component swap, exchanging parts may not be too difficult. For smaller installations, though, this is a costly proposition. (For instance, while writing this book, one of my computers' motherboards went south, but I couldn't determine whether it was the motherboard or the CPU until after I replaced the CPU, so I ended up replacing both the CPU and the motherboard—as well as the RAM because the new motherboard required newer RAM than had the older motherboard.)

The first trick in diagnosing a hardware problem is in determining that it *is* a hardware problem. Typical characteristics of hardware problems include

- **Unpredictable operation**   Some hardware problems manifest as random events—random system crashes, random video glitches, and so on. Software problems are usually a bit more predictable, although this isn't universally true.

- **Hard crashes**   FreeBSD has a reputation as a highly reliable OS; it seldom crashes. Thus, if your computer crashes or reboots very often (meaning more than once a year at the outside), there's a good chance that you've got a hardware problem. The other likely alternative is a very buggy driver, which might be fixed by a kernel upgrade (described in Chapter 12).

- **Problems related to hardware devices, not programs**   Most hardware can be used by multiple programs, so hardware problems tend to cause difficulties for many programs. A bad Ethernet adapter will cause problems for web browsers, e-mail clients, Samba, and other programs, for instance.

- **Unbootable computer**   Severe hardware problems may stop a computer from booting. Severe system misconfiguration can do the same, but the symptoms will be somewhat different. Typically, a hardware problem bad enough to stop the boot process manifests before the FreeBSD boot loader appears on the screen, or possibly during the kernel boot messages. If the FreeBSD kernel messages appear and complete, and the system at least starts displaying messages associated with the `/etc/rc` script, chances are it's not a hardware problem.

- **Problem confined to one computer**   If FreeBSD is installed on multiple computers, and is configured identically on all of them, then a problem that appears on just one is likely to be hardware-related. This diagnosis isn't certain, though; a configuration problem unique to one computer could be the cause of the difficulties.

- **Problems across OSs**   If your FreeBSD system multiboots into another OS, you may want to check operation in the other OS. If the problem appears in both OSs, it's most probably a hardware issue. If the problem doesn't appear in the other OS, it's more likely a software issue, although this isn't certain. (Occasionally one OS's drivers won't trigger a problem that really is hardware related.)

If your system isn't configured to multiboot, you might try a CD-bootable demo OS. Some demo versions of Linux are available at `http://www.linuxiso.org` *and can be useful for this purpose. DemoLinux and the SuSE Live Evaluation versions should both do well. FreeDOS (`http://www.freedos.org`) may also be useful. This is an open source implementation of the old standard DOS, and it can be booted and run entirely from floppy disk.*

You should realize that these problems are *typical* of hardware problems, but not all hardware problems produce these symptoms. Some hardware problems can be quite deceptive, in fact, and produce *none* of these symptoms. The more of these symptoms a problem exhibits, though, the more likely that problem is hardware-related.

Common Symptoms of Software Problems

Sadly, software problems exist, even in FreeBSD. These problems include software bugs, software that doesn't perform adequately (is too slow, for instance), and configuration problems. Some software problems aren't easily solved because the problem is related to the fundamental design of a program—there's no easy way to speed up a program that's sluggish because it's written inefficiently, for instance. (Upgrading your CPU may help, though—a solution that illustrates the interconnectedness of hardware and software.) Typically, solutions to software problems involve upgrading a problem program or modifying your computer's configuration.

Software problems can produce a wide array of symptoms. Some common characteristics of software problems include

- **Problems are repeatable** It's often possible to get a software problem to appear on cue—say, loading a particular file to get a spreadsheet to crash, or using a particular server configuration to make the server disconnect from clients too soon.

- **Problems related to programs, not hardware devices** Most software problems are related to specific programs or logical FreeBSD subsystems, rather than specific hardware devices. For instance, if a specific sound editor crashes but other audio tools work fine, chances are the problem is with the crashing sound editor, not your sound card.

- **Problems recur on multiple computers** If you have multiple FreeBSD systems, the problem is likely to occur on all of them, at least once they're configured similarly. One possible exception to this rule is if the computers have identical hardware and if the hardware design itself is flawed. Such a problem can be hard to distinguish from driver problems, though.

- **Problems restricted to FreeBSD** If your system boots into another OS and the problem doesn't occur there, then the problem is most likely caused by FreeBSD's software, drivers, or configuration. This isn't certain, though; sometimes hardware is broken in a way that manifests differently in different OSs, or sometimes not at all in one OS.

■ **Problems restricted to one program or software system**   Many software problems are caused by bugs in individual programs, and so show up in just one program. Others may affect several closely-related programs because those programs all rely upon a single library or underlying configuration. For instance, misconfiguration of your network interface will affect all your network programs. Sometimes the problem is in a subsystem that's so important it has wide effects, though, which can make diagnosis more difficult.

■ **Problems restricted to one user or set of users**   Some configuration problems occur for just some users. Such a problem may be related to account configuration details, to directory permissions, or to permissions on program or device files. Sometimes configuration files in users' accounts become corrupt, so it may be worth creating a test account with fresh configuration files to attempt to reproduce a problem.

As with characteristics of hardware problems, these software symptoms aren't perfect predictors; a software problem might exhibit few or none of these features. The more a problem does conform to this pattern, though, the more likely it is to be a software problem.

Procedures for Localizing a Problem

Diagnosing a problem, be it hardware or software, requires narrowing down the field of possible problems. You can apply general problem-solving techniques to any problem, but sooner or later you'll run into the need for domain-specific expertise. For instance, if you don't know that fluorescent lights and other magnetic sources can cause cathode ray tube (CRT) monitors to flicker, you may not be able to fix a flickering display that's caused by a fluorescent light too close to the monitor. The body of knowledge required for complete diagnosis of all problems is huge, so this chapter can present only a few pointers, along with general tips on localizing the problem. With luck, localizing the problem will enable you to discover the fix, either through random experimentation or by consulting one of the resources described earlier, in "Getting Help."

General Localization Procedures

Troubleshooting a computer problem is similar to a scientific undertaking. A scientist conducts experiments in order to test two or more competing hypotheses. The hypotheses should make divergent predictions, and the experiment tests these predictions. In just such a way, you can create a small experiment to test differing hypotheses about the cause of a problem you're experiencing. For instance, you might not know if a problem is caused by defective RAM or by an overheating CPU. Two possible tests of these hypothesis might be to replace the RAM or install a more powerful heat sink and fan on the CPU. These tests also happen to correspond to possible fixes of the problem, but some tests need not double as fixes. For instance, if your RAM comes in the form of two dual inline memory modules (DIMMs), you could temporarily remove one DIMM and then the other. If just one DIMM is defective, the problem should go away when you remove the defective DIMM.

One rule of thumb when conducting experiments is to change only one variable at a time. For instance, you shouldn't replace both the RAM and the CPU fan at once—at least, not if you want to know the cause of the problem. If you replace both components at once, the problem may disappear, but then you won't know if the RAM you've removed is defective or if the CPU and fan were inadequate for the computer. This knowledge could be important—say, if you want to use the RAM to upgrade other computers. On the other hand, sometimes you might want to make several changes at once. You might suspect one of four components of being defective. Replacing two at a time should enable you to narrow the field to just two components, whereupon a second test should reveal the culprit. Replacing a single component, on the other hand, could take up to four tests to find the problem.

Another important procedure in troubleshooting is to take careful notes of your activities. If you write down what you do and what the results of each test are, you'll stand a better chance of discovering the problem than if you dig in and start making changes without taking notes. If you take the latter approach, a difficult problem will, sooner or later, leave you wondering if you've made a particular test or not. You might even believe that you had tested something when in fact you had not, which can greatly extend the time it can take to solve a problem. Unfortunately, problems that seem initially to be simple sometimes balloon into real monsters. You might decide initially that it's not worth taking notes. If you don't take notes and a problem begins to expand on you, jot down whatever you remember doing as soon as it becomes clear that the problem is more complex than you'd at first thought, while your memory of what you've already done is still clear.

When diagnosing a software problem, try to reproduce the problem using several accounts, if possible. Software problems are often related to individual users' configurations, so if you find differences by account, tracking down those differences can be very important.

One tool that's sometimes extraordinarily helpful in debugging problems is the computer's log files. These files are usually located in the /var/log directory, and they hold information on the activities of various programs and subsystems. The single most important log file is /var/log/messages, but other files are devoted to sendmail, Samba, cron, and other tools. Immediately after a problem manifests itself, try examining the end of a relevant log file. The tail command can be very useful in doing so. This command displays the last few lines of a file, so you can see the latest entries in a log file by using tail.

Hardware Diagnostics

Hardware problems can be frustrating to track down because they're often sporadic in nature. A computer might crash randomly twice a week, for instance. Debugging such a problem can be extraordinarily difficult because changes you make to try to uncover the problem may not have any obvious impact for several days. Knowing some common symptoms of problems can help immensely in tracking down the problem in such cases.

One issue you should investigate across many different hardware types is the quality of the physical connection between components. CPUs, memory modules, and various expansion cards all plug into motherboards; and cables for external devices all plug into connectors on motherboards or expansion cards. If these connections are weak, hardware may work unreliably or not at all. These connections are particularly likely to be weakened after a computer is shipped.

CPU Problems

If you're lucky, a defective CPU will manifest itself in an inability to boot the computer. You may not even see the BIOS screen appear if this is the issue. Such a problem is hard to miss, and if you have spare parts, you can swap them out fairly easily, leading quickly to a solution.

If a computer won't boot, try removing all extraneous hardware, such as sound cards, Ethernet cards, CD-ROM drives, and so on. If the computer still won't boot, swap out vital components, such as memory, the CPU, and if it's a separate board, the hard disk controller. When you swap in a good replacement for the broken component, the system should boot. If all of these steps fail, chances are your motherboard is defective.

A more common CPU problem is related to overheating. All modern *x*86 CPUs generate enough heat to destroy themselves in a matter of seconds. To avoid such an ignominious end for their creations, computer designers place large heat sink and fan assemblies atop their CPUs, as shown in Figure 32-1. The heat sink alone dissipates a lot of heat by conducting heat away from the CPU and enabling air to cool their radiating fins. The fans improve matters by moving air over these fins. Sometimes, though, a heat sink works loose and must be reattached to the CPU using clips on two sides of the heat sink. Other times a fan stops spinning, its rate of spinning slows due to age and the buildup of dust, or dust accumulation causes the assembly's cooling efficiency to drop. In all of these cases, the computer may experience random crashes. Similar symptoms can result if the room in which the computer resides becomes too hot. (What "too hot" is varies depending upon the computer, but as a general rule of thumb, if you're uncomfortably warm, your computer may be suffering, too.) Sometimes you can alleviate problems by removing the cover from the computer's case—but sometimes this action actually makes matters worse. (The effects of removing the cover depend upon the air flow characteristics of the case.) In the long run, an overheating CPU is best dealt with by upgrading the heat sink and its fan. If the computer's case is crowded with lots of hard disks and add-in cards, adding an extra fan for the case itself may help, too. Consult your CPU manufacturer's web page for recommended models. If a heat sink and fan have been dislodged or working improperly for long enough, you may need to replace the CPU because it may have been irreparably damaged by its own waste heat.

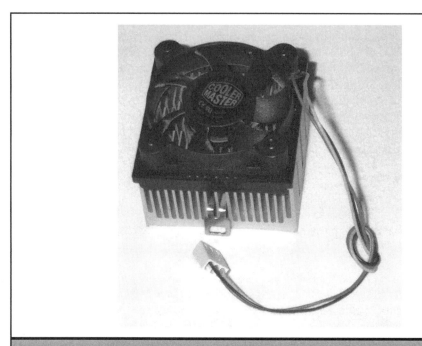

Figure 32-1. *CPU heat sink and fan assemblies dissipate heat generated by modern CPUs via cooling fins and a fan to move more air over the fins.*

Another, and thankfully rarer, class of CPU problems is related to CPU bugs. Modern CPUs are complex enough that they always contain design flaws. These flaws are usually minor, or at least well enough understood that they're readily worked around by modern compilers. Occasionally, though, a serious bug crops up, such as the infamous Pentium floating-point bug from the mid-1990s, or problems that caused the GNU Compiler Collection (GCC) to crash on early AMD K6 CPUs. Chances are you'll quickly run across talk of such a bug if you perform minimal web, Usenet, or mailing list research of a problem. Replacing the CPU may fix the problem, or you may need to upgrade your compiler and perhaps recompile everything on your system.

Motherboard Problems

The motherboard is the heart of the computer, so motherboard problems are likely to have profound effects upon system reliability. There are three broad classes of motherboard problems:

- **Too-new motherboards** Some motherboards cause problems for FreeBSD simply because they're too new. Such motherboards use chipsets for which FreeBSD drivers don't yet exist. The usual symptom of using such a board is an inability to use its on-board interfaces, such as its EIDE disk interface, its sound hardware, or its video hardware. Sometimes you can use these components, but they produce suboptimal performance. If a newer version of FreeBSD is available, try using it. If not, you can usually use add-on boards to replace the problem components—for instance, you can use a PCI EIDE controller and disable the EIDE controller on the motherboard.

- **Defective motherboard designs** Like CPU flaws, motherboard designs often contain flaws. As with CPU design problems, motherboard design flaws can often be worked around in drivers, but if the motherboard design is new, you may need to wait for a workaround to appear. Such problems frequently manifest in flaky behavior when accessing on-board interfaces.

- **Broken motherboards** Motherboards may be damaged by static electricity, power surges, or physically clumsy handling. In most cases, a motherboard so damaged simply won't boot at all, and such a symptom can be almost impossible to distinguish from a damaged CPU. In some cases, the damage may be restricted to one subsystem, such as the disk controller, in which case you may be able to bypass it by adding a replacement component. Such problems, unlike design defects and too-new designs, may manifest themselves on a previously working computer.

As a general rule, motherboard problems cause either an inability to boot at all or problems with specific subsystems, such as disk access. Replacing a motherboard is one of the more tedious hardware repairs, so you should try this operation after trying other measures, unless you're fairly certain that the culprit is the motherboard.

Memory Problems

Defective RAM can cause no end of problems. Symptoms include random program crashes and system reboots. On rare occasion, a document in memory may become corrupted. Severely defective RAM may be spotted by the motherboard during its power-on self-test (POST); if your computer freezes partway through the POST, displaying a value of less than the amount of RAM you've installed, chances are your RAM is defective.

 Many computers offer an option in their BIOS configuration screens to enable or disable a "fast POST" or words to that effect. If you suspect memory problems, disable the fast POST and reboot; the computer will then perform a somewhat more complete test of its memory before booting.

FreeBSD offers a program called `memtest` that performs various tests of memory. These tests are necessarily incomplete, but if `memtest` tells you your memory is bad, it probably is bad. Most computer dealers also have dedicated memory-testing hardware, so taking your memory modules to a dealer for testing may be worthwhile.

When transporting memory or other computer components, try to do so only in antistatic bags. Most computer components ship in these bags, which resemble thick sandwich bags. The plastic from which they're made has antistatic properties that minimizes the risk of the component being damaged by an electrostatic discharge.

Disk Problems

The two main sources of problems related to hard disks (or other disk-type devices, such as CD-ROMs or Zip disks) are

- **The disk controller** The EIDE disk controller or SCSI host adapter may be defective. Such problems often manifest across all devices the controller handles, although this isn't always the case. Such problems can sometimes be overcome by updating the FreeBSD kernel, if the problem is with a buggy driver or a design flaw in the device itself.

- **The disk itself** Hard disks and other disk devices occasionally fail. You can sometimes work around the problem by performing a low-level format on the device, but more often replacing it is in order.

Disk device problems manifest as slow disk performance, unexpected read or write errors, corrupt files, an inability to launch certain programs, or sometimes even an inability to boot the computer. (Boot failures usually manifest late in the boot process, after the kernel has finished loading.) If a corrupt disk sector exists in the swap partition, problems may more closely resemble those of bad RAM.

Many disk manufacturers offer disk-test programs that give their drives workouts and report the results. Unfortunately, these programs usually run under DOS or Windows. You may be able to run a DOS disk-test program from FreeDOS (`http://www.freedos.org`). If necessary, you can temporarily move a FreeBSD system's disk to a Windows computer to use a Windows disk-test tool.

 Some disk-test utilities offer both destructive and non-destructive tests. The destructive tests overwrite data on a disk, so be sure not to use a destructive test on a disk that holds important data, including your FreeBSD installation.

Video Problems

The most common FreeBSD video problems relate to basic XFree86 configuration. You might not be able to get X working at all, or it may work, but only at a suboptimal resolution or refresh rate. Chapter 13 describes X configuration, so you should first review that chapter for information on getting X to work properly. Many problems are caused by an attempt to use a video chipset that's too new for your XFree86 version. Consult the XFree86 web page (`http://www.xfree86.org`) to learn what version of XFree86 is latest and what version is required to support your video card. If necessary, upgrade your XFree86 installation. You might also find a more up-to-date driver on your video card manufacturer's web site or on the web site for the chipset used on your video card.

If X suddenly stops working or if your video signal disappears altogether, visually check your video card. Modern video cards often have processors so fast that they require heat sinks, and sometimes even fans, similar to those used by CPUs (see Figure 32-1). If a fan has stopped spinning, turn off the computer and don't turn it on again until the matter is fixed.

Monitors can go bad, just as can video cards. Monitors aren't easily fixed by end users, so if your monitor is dead, take it to a repair shop. Fortunately, there's no FreeBSD-specific information you need to provide to the repair person.

CRT monitors contain components that can retain large charges for long periods of time. Thus, you can seriously injure yourself by opening a monitor and poking around inside if you don't know what you're doing. Don't try it; leave monitor repair to professionals.

One common monitor problem that *is* easily fixed by end users is related to magnetic fields. Fluorescent lights, unshielded speakers (most computer speakers are shielded), telephones, and various other devices produce magnetic fields that can distort a CRT monitor's picture or cause it to shake. Moving the offending device or the computer usually fixes the problem. LCD monitors aren't as bothered by magnetic fields, so in an extreme case, replacing a CRT monitor with an LCD model can be a useful fix.

Sound Problems

Fortunately, sound cards aren't necessary for basic FreeBSD operation, so chances are you can leave sound card debugging to whenever you have time for the job. Most FreeBSD sound problems boil down to a complete inability to use sound utilities, which are described in Chapter 27. In most cases, these problems are issues of driver support; you may need to use `kldload` to load a driver, or even recompile your kernel with support for your sound hardware.

One problem with sound under FreeBSD is that most sound cards' sound hardware is inherently single-tasking—that is, if Program A is using the sound card, Program B can't use the sound card. Thus, one problem that can occur is that the sound card may be tied up by an "impolite" program, or even by a program that's crashed. If sound works for a while but then stops working until you reboot, chances are good this is what's happening. There are efforts underway to provide interfaces to moderate this problem, but in 2002 they're still not completely functional. (In fact, the version of GNOME released with some beta-test versions of FreeBSD 5.0 includes one such solution that causes more problems than it solves.)

Another audio problem is corrupt sound. Most often, you hear this as harsh buzzing instead of an expected audio stream. This problem can sometimes be corrected by updating your kernel audio drivers. It's often caused by trying to play back one type of sound file as if it were another sound type. Try adjusting parameters to `play`, or whatever program you're using to play the sound file.

External Input/Output Problems

External input/output is a fairly broad category, including such interfaces as the parallel port, RS-232 serial ports, and universal serial bus (USB) ports. FreeBSD drivers for these common interfaces are quite mature (USB less so than most others), so drivers aren't often a problem. Likely problem causes include

- **Defective cables**   Cabling can be a serious problem in some cases. Some printers require bidirectional parallel cables, so you should be sure you have the correct type of printer cables. RS-232 serial port problems can sometimes be caused by using a null-modem cable instead of a straight-through cable or vice-versa. Some RS-232 cables are marked as to type, but others aren't, so you may need to swap cables. Plain old worn out or defective cables can also cause problems.

- **Defective connectors**   The connectors for external interfaces can sometimes be defective or damaged, particularly if the system's seen a lot of connecting and disconnecting of devices to the port in question. The easiest workaround if this is the case is usually to add a replacement port to the computer. Defective connectors on external devices usually require replacing or repairing the device itself.

- **Incorrect parameters**   RS-232 devices, in particular, provide adjustments for various parameters, such as the bit rate. You must be sure these parameters are set correctly in whatever program you use—a terminal program or a printer queue, most likely.

- **Device-specific USB drivers**   Although FreeBSD includes a general-purpose USB driver, specific USB devices also require drivers. As of FreeBSD 5.0, few USB devices are supported. Check `http://www.etla.net/~n_hibma/usb/` for information on USB drivers for specific devices.

Networking Hardware Problems

Networking problems can be difficult to track down because so much can go wrong. Some issues you may want to look into include

- **Physical connections**   Network cabling can be defective or go bad, just as can any external cabling. Many network types also use hubs or switches to interconnect computers, and these devices can fail. Replacing a cable is an important, simple, and inexpensive test you can perform should a network connection die completely.

- **Link lights**   Most network cards, hubs, and switches feature LEDs that light up when a connection is detected, and often when traffic is transmitted. These LEDs are diagnostic treasure troves. They can help you spot problems with physical connections (typically, the LEDs will all be dead) or determine whether data are being transmitted (via the transmit LED, if it's present). If data are being transmitted, it's still possible that a problem is caused by hardware, but odds are it's a software issue.

■ **Driver compatibility** At the border of hardware and software is the issue of driver compatibility with specific devices. This issue is particularly serious for certain types of Ethernet cards, such as those based upon the DEC/Intel "Tulip" chipset and its clones. The core of the problem lies in this last phrase—"and its clones." There are so many variants on the Tulip chipset that it's hard for the FreeBSD developers to keep up. Ethernet cards are inexpensive enough that it may be simpler to replace the card than to try to get the driver to work.

Many networking problems are software issues—incorrect parameters passed to `ifconfig`, client/server incompatibilities, and so on. These issues are described in the upcoming section, "Networking Software Problems." One test you can perform is to type **ifconfig** alone, or followed by the name of your network interface. This command returns information on your network interface:

```
# ifconfig vr0
vr0: flags=8843<UP,BROADCAST,RUNNING,SIMPLEX,MULTICAST> mtu 1500
        inet 192.168.1.6 netmask 0xffffff00 broadcast 192.168.1.255
        ether 00:80:c8:fa:3b:0a
        media: Ethernet autoselect (100baseTX)
        status: active
```

This output demonstrates the fact that FreeBSD has found the hardware and has configured it in what appears to be a reasonable way. If you don't see any output for your Ethernet card at all, it might not be properly inserted in its slot, it may be completely defective, or it may not have been recognized by the kernel for some reason (for instance, it may be a new model with no FreeBSD drivers). If there's an entry for the card but there's no IP address and netmask assigned to it, then there may be a software problem, or the card might have a subtle hardware problem. If you're using DHCP to obtain an IP address, it could be that a cable, hub, or switch is bad.

Printer Problems

Printer problems frequently boil down to issues of Ghostscript compatibility. As described in Chapter 9, FreeBSD relies upon Ghostscript and a properly functioning printer queue to convert the PostScript generated by most FreeBSD applications into a form that a non-PostScript printer can understand. Consult the database at `http://www.linuxprinting.org` to discover what printers work with Ghostscript.

Some printing problems are related to the external interfaces or cables, as described earlier in "External Input/Output Problems." You can often spot such problems by checking the activity LEDs on the printer, which should normally blink when you send data to a printer, even if the file doesn't print correctly. If the LEDs don't blink, then the problem is most likely one of cabling or basic interface functionality.

Software Diagnostics

Diagnosing software problems often involves tracing through configuration or startup files. Problems are often the result of software bugs, so the final diagnosis and the fix are more or less synonymous, and involve upgrading the software in question. (In some cases, the buggy software is a library, which can affect many programs.)

System Startup Problems

A default FreeBSD installation should boot correctly, although it's possible that a problem will cause parts of the system to not work. For instance, your network configuration might not work, so networking might be disabled immediately after you boot. Three main areas can cause system startup problems:

- **Boot loader**   The boot loader, described in Chapters 3 and 4, enables you to select which OS to boot. Even on a FreeBSD-only computer, you must have a boot loader, but in that case it boots directly into FreeBSD. Boot loader problems manifest themselves after the computer has finished its BIOS POST but before the kernel begins its checklist. The computer may freeze up with a blank screen or after displaying an error message. These problems usually occur immediately after installing FreeBSD or after you alter the boot loader configuration. You may also have boot loader problems immediately after installing another OS (Microsoft OSs are notorious for damaging other OSs' boot loader configurations).

- **Kernel**   If the FreeBSD kernel is buggy, misconfigured, or lacks necessary drivers, the computer may not boot or some hardware devices may not work. A boot failure is likely to occur when the kernel is running through its device checklist, described in the "Interpreting Boot Messages" section of Chapter 3. If problems occur with a default FreeBSD kernel, you may need to look into upgrading the kernel or replacing the hardware that causes the problems. Another common scenario is a problem that occurs after you begin using a custom kernel. In that case, revert to the default kernel while you fix the problem, which was most likely caused by a failure to include a necessary driver in the new kernel. Chapter 12 describes kernel configuration in more detail.

- **Startup script**   Startup scripts can be incomplete or buggy. The default scripts are a good starting point in most cases, but they may be set with incorrect options. Startup script problems manifest after the kernel has completed its device checks, when FreeBSD displays messages stating that it's starting particular programs, such as sendmail or `cron`. Some startup script problems may not be obvious until the system has finished booting, at which point some subsystem simply won't work as you expect. Various chapters of this book describe modifications to startup scripts to enable many features, especially network servers. Review the relevant instructions and be sure there are no typos if a server doesn't start. The upcoming section, "Networking Software Problems," provides additional information on networking problems.

Startup problems can be particularly troublesome because they leave you with a nonfunctional FreeBSD system, or at best, one that works suboptimally. In many cases, using an emergency startup system, as described in the upcoming section, "Using an Emergency Boot System," can help you correct the problem by providing a minimally functional FreeBSD system. In a few cases, using another OS can also help; for instance, you might be able to install another OS's boot loader to replace a damaged or misbehaving FreeBSD Stage 0 boot loader.

Device Driver Problems

Some device driver problems prevent the computer from booting. For instance, if a system with a SCSI hard disk and no EIDE disk lacks drivers for the computer's SCSI host adapter, FreeBSD won't be able to boot. It may get partway through the kernel boot messages, but it will fail before being able to run any boot scripts. Such problems are likely to manifest themselves at system installation or when using a newly compiled kernel for the first time.

Less extreme driver problems produce more subtle symptoms—but "more subtle" in this context includes some pretty nasty happenings, such as random system crashes. Other problems include an inability to use devices that aren't critical for the system to boot, such as a sound card or Ethernet interface; odd errors when using such devices, such as distortion when playing sound files; and poor performance, such as sluggish disk accesses. In sum, driver problems produce symptoms that are very similar to those produced by defective hardware.

Much of the task of diagnosing driver problems relates to isolating the problem as being hardware or software. You can use techniques such as hardware swapping between computers and tests in multiple OSs to help make this diagnosis—but remember that these tests can sometimes lead you astray. For instance, two OSs might have similar bugs in their device drivers, particularly if the OSs are closely related; and it's always possible you'll have two defective boards.

Fixing device driver problems requires upgrading the kernel to a version that includes fixed drivers, or recompiling a kernel so that it includes a driver that was originally omitted. In a few cases, using `kldload` to load a driver module is all that's required. Chapter 12 describes all these topics.

Networking Software Problems

Networking problems can be difficult to track down because the networking subsystem is quite complex. Some networking problems are related to network hardware or drivers, but many problems are related to software or configuration. Common problem areas include

■ **Network hardware and drivers**   Network hardware can be defective, and network drivers can be buggy. If your network connection seems to be flaky overall, you should investigate these issues.

- **Network startup scripts**   The `/etc/network` startup script controls the network startup process. This script relies upon settings in other scripts, most notably `/etc/rc.conf`. The basic network interface configuration is defined here, as is the startup of many common servers. Chapter 14 and other chapters of Part III describe these issues in detail. Typos or more severe misconfiguration can cause problems ranging from a complete inability to use the network to subtle errors on the part of servers.

- **Server configuration files**   Most servers use their own configuration files to set server-specific options. If a single server isn't functioning as you expect, these files are a good place to start looking for answers, in conjunction with appropriate documentation and log files. Configuration errors can produce a wide range of symptoms, ranging from a complete lack of response by the server to subtle misbehaviors.

- **Firewalls**   If you configure a firewall, as described in Chapter 17, that firewall might interfere with the normal functioning of both clients and servers. The typical symptom is a complete inability to contact outside systems using a client, or of a server to respond to requests sent from outside systems. Even a firewall that's not located on your own computer can cause problems; routers sometimes include firewalls that block access to particular ports for security reasons. Consult whoever operates your local router if you suspect this to be the case.

- **DNS problems**   The Internet relies heavily upon the Domain Name System (DNS) to convert hostnames into IP addresses and vice-versa. One common network configuration problem is a mis-setting of the DNS computer. The `/etc/resolv.conf` file sets from one to three DNS computers, specified by IP address on `nameserver` lines. If these computers' IP addresses are set incorrectly, or if the DNS servers have crashed, you won't be able to access remote computers by name, but IP addresses will still work.

- **Program-specific bugs**   Both clients and servers can suffer from bugs. These bugs produce program-specific symptoms ranging from program crashes to subtle quirks. The usual solution is to upgrade the program to a fixed version.

One key to network diagnostics is to try to reproduce the problem on multiple computers. For instance, if you can't reach particular outside web sites on any computer on your network, chances are good that the problem is on the external computers, in firewall blocks, or with similar issues, rather than problems on the web browser systems. If the problems occur only on some systems, look for commonalities. For instance, perhaps all the problem systems are running a particular version of the web browser, or they're all on a single subnet. These commonalities can be important clues to the cause of the problem.

User Program Problems

Programs run by ordinary users can be buggy. Unfortunately, the range of possible bugs in such programs is extremely wide. Fortunately, it's usually fairly obvious that the problem is isolated to just one program because it's the only one that exhibits any odd behavior. Buggy libraries can cause problems in many programs, though.

As a general rule, a good place to begin when investigating reports of problems from users is to attempt to reproduce the problem in a new account. Some problems are caused by errors in the user's own configuration files. In such a case, testing the software in a new account may turn up no problems, which narrows the range of possible causes to configuration issues, including the user's own configuration files and issues such as permissions on the user's or common files or directories and configuration problems related to the user's group. You can use `diff` to compare the user's configuration files to those in a fresh account and investigate possible configuration issues.

If you run into the same problems in a new account that an existing user reports, you may want to investigate the software itself. It may be buggy or have a misconfiguration in a global configuration file. Bug fixes for user programs are not uncommon, so you may want to look for an updated version of the software.

Some problems with user programs are related to permissions. For instance, audio software needs access to the sound card devices. A default FreeBSD installation enables ordinary users to write to the sound card device files, as described in Chapter 27, but you may have changed this configuration. Such access might not exist for all software; for instance, tape backup and CD-R packages require access to the tape and CD-R devices, respectively, but normally only `root` may access these devices. You may need to change this configuration if ordinary users should be able to use these devices.

It's possible that you're the first person to encounter a bug. If your bug seems fairly exotic—say, if it happens only under a very particular and odd set of circumstances—you may need to contact the program's author. Consult the program's official web page for details. Sometimes you can submit a bug report via e-mail. Other times (particularly for large projects) you may need to use a web-based bug report system. If you know enough about the programming language and relevant toolkits used by the program, you can try debugging it yourself and then submitting the fix to the author. In fact, this can be an excellent way to give back to the open source community that created FreeBSD.

Testing a Solution

In many cases, identifying a problem and solving the problem go hand in hand; diagnostic techniques involve making changes that, if successful in identifying the problem, also solve the problem. Once you've solved a problem, though, you may want to further test the affected subsystem. For instance, if a program has been crashing frequently and you've upgraded the program to a version that seems more stable, you may want to test the program more extensively—say, by running it for a long period of time or with input designed to stress the program. Such tests can help reassure you that the problem really is solved and won't recur.

Some problems can be difficult to diagnose and solve because they're sporadic. Such problems may require extensive testing after you've made a change that you believe will solve the problem. Sometimes these tests can be as simple as leaving the computer running in a normal manner and hoping it doesn't crash. Other times you may need to monitor log files, CPU load, or other system performance metrics. You may want to create a cron job or use a tool such as the Simple Watcher (SWATCH), which monitors log files for patterns you specify, to help in this process.

If a solution doesn't work out as you expect, you may have to return to the starting point. Of course, you'll have learned something in the process, but tracking down another solution can still be a daunting process. Occasionally your original solution really was the correct one but it didn't work because it wasn't extreme enough. For instance, if you replace the fan on an overheating CPU with a model that's better than the original but still not good enough, your system crashes may drop in frequency but not disappear completely. A still more powerful heat sink or fan may finally solve the problem. Similarly, an update might be available for a buggy program, but if that update doesn't fix the bug in question, it won't do you much good.

Using an Emergency Boot System

Some problems are so extreme that they prevent FreeBSD from booting at all, or they require editing files in a way that's not possible when FreeBSD is running normally. In such cases, an emergency boot system comes in handy. Such a system gives you access to the FreeBSD system without booting it. Emergency boot systems can also be useful in performing certain types of upgrades and maintenance, such as resizing your system's root partition. Such a system can take any of several different forms:

- **Alternative OS installation** For some functions, an OS other than FreeBSD can be useful for emergency recovery. You can use a disk partitioning tool in just about any OS to check the *x86* partition table, for instance. (Few non-UNIX OSs can understand FreeBSD's partitions within the FreeBSD slice, though.) If your Stage 0 boot loader is damaged, you can replace it with various non-FreeBSD boot loaders, such as Linux's LILO or the commercial BootMagic from PowerQuest (http://www.powerquest.com).

A few OSs, such as Linux, provide support for FreeBSD's filesystems. You should be cautious about using this support to write to a FreeBSD partition, though. Linux's FFS/UFS support, in particular, is immature and may damage the filesystem.

■ **Alternative FreeBSD installation** You can install FreeBSD twice on a single computer. Make one installation small, containing only the minimal set of tools, and use the second installation as your main system. You can then boot the first system for emergency or low-level maintenance work.

■ **Second hard disk installation** You can install FreeBSD on a second hard disk and use it to perform maintenance on the main hard disk. If the second hard disk is permanently installed, this is just a variant of the previous option; but you can install FreeBSD on a second disk installed for emergency purposes even if you don't prepare this configuration from the start.

■ **Removable disk installation** A variant of the preceding option is to install FreeBSD on a high-capacity removable disk device, such as a Zip, LS-120, or Jaz disk. You can prepare and test such a system, then remove the disk and store it for emergencies. One difficulty with this approach is that these devices may not be bootable, so you may need to play games with boot loaders to get it to work.

■ **FreeBSD recovery CD-ROM** In a multi-CD-ROM version of FreeBSD, the second CD-ROM is usually a bootable recovery CD-ROM. The system boots into what looks like a normal FreeBSD installation, but if you select the Fixit option, you can launch a full FreeBSD system that's based on a custom set of tools on a floppy disk or the standard tools included on the CD-ROM. You'll need to mount your normal system, whereupon you can edit files, run testing utilities, and so on.

As a general rule, this last option is a good one for general use. The FreeBSD recovery CD-ROM contains a small but useable system, including the vi and ee editors, standard disk tools and commands such as mount and fsck, and archiving and backup tools such as tar. After you mount your normal FreeBSD installation, you can use at least some programs from it, although programs that load libraries may pose problems because they may not be able to find them.

Unless you install a full FreeBSD system with all your favorite tools to use as an emergency system, chances are you'll find an emergency system to be rather spare. Nonetheless, if you're familiar with the basic command-line tools you should be able to get by well enough to perform emergency repairs.

Tip *Become familiar with whatever emergency system is available to you. Try booting it and using it to read and alter a few noncritical files on your system (or for added safety, on a test system). Familiarity with emergency tools will speed recovery and make it less likely that you'll do more damage when a real emergency presents itself.*

Summary

Troubleshooting is largely synonymous with problem-solving. As such, various heuristics and rules of thumb can help guide you through the process. The number of specific problems and solutions is so large that this chapter is only long enough to present a few guiding principles and symptoms of some of the more common problems and problem classes. If you run into a real stumper, you can avail yourself of various resources to get help, including books, web pages, and Usenet newsgroups.

The Complete Reference

Glossary

account   A set of data structures that enable a person to use a FreeBSD system.

AGP bus   A hardware standard for connecting video cards to motherboards. Most *x*86 motherboards sold in 2002 have precisely one AGP bus, but some include video hardware on the motherboard itself, which uses an internal AGP bus. Older motherboards used the *PCI bus* or the *ISA bus* for video hardware.

anti-aliasing   A technique for font display in which curves and diagonal lines use gray pixels in addition to the usual black and white. Some people find that anti-aliasing can improve the readability of some fonts at certain sizes, but other people dislike the effect. Also known as *font smoothing*.

ASCII   The *American Standard Code for Information Interchange* is the standard mapping of alphanumeric characters, punctuation characters, and certain control characters into numbers understandable by computers.

assembler   A program that converts assembly language into machine language.

assembly language   A representation of *machine language* using mnemonic codes for the benefit of humans. Programmers can write software in assembly language and produce machine code using an *assembler* program. Assembly language is a lower-level language than the more popular high-level languages such as C, Pascal, and Perl.

ATA   The *Advanced Technology Attachment* standard, a hardware standard for connecting hard disks and similar devices to their controller cards or motherboards. Also known as *EIDE*.

ATAPI   The *ATA Packet Interface*, a standard used by CD-ROMs, tape drives, and some other devices that use the ATA standard. See also *EIDE*.

binary   A base-2 numbering system; each digit may be either 0 or 1. Computers operate on base-2 arithmetic. (2) A file format that holds raw nontextual data, such as graphics or sound files. (3) A binary data file format for programs. *Source code* is turned into binary code by being compiled.

binary code   See *machine language*. (*Binary code* is a synonym because the CPU operates on base-2 numbers, although in practice machine language is often represented in base-16 for human consumption.)

bit   A binary digit—that is, 1 or 0—used in a base-2 number system.

bitmap   A method of representing data in which individual bits map onto specific pieces of binary information. Bitmaps are frequently used for graphical data, in which the bits map onto pixels on the display. In the case of color graphics, multiple bits define each pixel, so the term *bitmap* is something of a misnomer, but it's still used. See also *vector graphics*.

bitmap font   A *font* file format that describes each letter in a font as a bitmap. Bitmaps require little CPU power to display, but they don't scale well, so to support multiple sizes or output devices of multiple resolutions, many font files are required for each font family.

boot loader   A program that directs the boot process. Some boot loaders allow booting multiple computers, or can direct the boot process to a *secondary* boot loader, which further directs the boot process.

broadcast   In networking, a type of traffic that's directed at all computers on a network segment. Computers use broadcasts to help locate other computers, and certain protocols (such as *DHCP*) also use broadcasts in normal operation.

BSD   *Berkeley Software Distribution* is the name of patches to the original AT&T UNIX, and subsequently a complete OS in its own right, from which FreeBSD is derived. The acronym *BSD* is also applied to various features found in the BSD OS, such as its startup script system and license.

BSD license   The software license under which much of FreeBSD is distributed. This license allows modifications to be distributed under the BSD license or any other license. See also *open source* and *GPL*.

bus topology   A type of network configuration in which one computer is tied to another, which is tied to another, and so on, creating a logical "line" of computers. The old thin and thick coaxial Ethernet hardware used a bus topology.

child   In the context of FreeBSD processes, *child* is a relative term that refers to a program that was launched by another program. One program can have multiple child processes. See also *parent*.

CHS geometry   The *cylinder/head/sector geometry* is a triplet of numbers used to uniquely identify a sector (typically 512 bytes) of data on a hard disk. EIDE disks and *x*86 partition data structures use CHS geometries. In modern hard disks, the numbers used are convenient fictions; they bear no resemblance to the true hard disk geometry. This system contrasts with *LBA mode*.

CIFS   The *Common Internet File System*. See *SMB/CIFS*.

client   A program that initiates requests for network data transfer. Examples include FTP clients, mail readers, and web browsers. (2) A computer that runs network client programs but few or no network server programs.

compiler   A program that converts *source code* into a *binary* (definition 3) representation for use on a computer.

console   A keyboard, monitor, and possibly a mouse attached to a computer. Most frequently, this word refers to the set of user input/output devices that are connected *directly* to the computer, as opposed to remote terminals.

cooperative multitasking   A multitasking method in which each process uses CPU time until it needs no more. The program then relinquishes control of the computer to other processes. This is simpler than the *preemptive multitasking* method used by FreeBSD.

cracker   A person who breaks into or otherwise disrupts the operation of a computer. Crackers may be motivated by many factors, including curiosity, greed, or revenge. The popular media typically refers to crackers as *hackers*, but that term's meaning is more ambiguous. See also *script kiddie*.

CSS   The *Content Scrambling System* is a data encryption method used on commercial video DVDs.

daemon   A program that runs in the background to provide necessary services. Most server programs run as daemons.

data structure   A definition of how data should be arranged (structured) in a file or in memory for a particular purpose. It's often possible to design multiple data structures to solve the same problems, but programs must be written to understand any data structures they're to use.

DDoS attack   A *distributed DoS attack* is a type of DoS attack in which the attacker uses many computers (possibly compromised systems themselves) to attack another one.

default route   A specification of what to do with network traffic that doesn't have a more explicit route defined in the computer's routing table. Normally, the default route points to the *router* for the local network.

device file   A special type of file that provides user-mode programs with access to a computer's hardware. These files are conventionally located in the /dev directory.

DHCP   The *Dynamic Host Configuration Protocol* enables a server to provide TCP/IP configuration information to DHCP clients, thus simplifying TCP/IP configuration on the client computers.

domain name   A name that identifies a part of the Internet, typically owned or operated by a single organization or individual. See also *hostname* and *machine name*.

DoS attack   A *denial-of-service attack* is a type of computerized attack that's designed to deprive victims of the use of their computers or of their network connections.

dot file   A program whose filename begins with a dot (.). Such files don't appear in file listings created via ls or many other tools, unless an option to show dot files (such as the -a option to ls) is used. Many user configuration files are dot files, to keep them from cluttering ordinary directory listings.

dumb terminal   A keyboard and monitor linked to a computer through a serial port or similar means. In the 1970s and 1980s, dumb terminals were a common method for accessing UNIX systems, and FreeBSD still supports their use. See also *terminal program*.

EIDE   The *Enhanced Integrated Drive Electronics* standard. See *ATA*.

environment variable   A setting that's readable from any program. Frequently used to set a path of directories to search for runnable programs or to set global options used by specific programs.

Ethernet   A common type of local network hardware, capable of top speeds ranging from 10 Mbps to 1 Gbps, depending upon the variety.

exploit   Used as a noun in the context of security, this word refers to a specific bug or method of attack used by crackers to break into a computer, as in "the cracker used a well-known exploit to break into the ISP's web server."

filesystem   A set of low-level data structures stored on a partition or hard disk, enabling an operating system to store data on the disk. (2) A directory structure, consisting of files and subdirectories.

firewall   A computer, program, or configuration that restricts incoming and/or outgoing network access based on IP addresses, packet types, or other criteria. See also *packet filter* and *proxy server*.

font   A collection of characters (typically an alphabet, numbers, and punctuation) in a particular style.

font smoothing   See *anti-aliasing*.

FQDN   A *fully-qualified domain name* is a hostname complete with its domain name, such as www.whitehouse.gov.

gateway   See *router*.

Ghostscript   A program that converts *PostScript* into various other graphics file formats, including those used by many common printers. Ghostscript is commonly called by filters as part of a FreeBSD *print queue*.

GID   A *Group ID* is a number that identifies a group of users. Group names are linked to GIDs.

GNOME   The *GNU Network Object Model Environment*, a popular desktop environment for FreeBSD. See also *KDE*.

GPL   The GNU *General Public License* is a software license used by some software that ships with FreeBSD. The GPL requires that derived works also be distributed under the GPL. See also *BSD license* and *open source*.

group   A collection of accounts. Every account belongs to at least one group. Groups can be used to provide a collection of users with access to certain files while excluding other users.

hacker   An individual who is skilled with and enjoys working with computers, and particularly with computer programming, and who uses those skills to productive purposes. Many of the individuals who created FreeBSD are hackers in this sense. (2) A *cracker*. This use is common in the popular media, but is unpopular with much of the open source community, who used the first meaning of *hacker* long before the popular media redefined the term.

hard link   A type of *link* in which two files' directory entries point to a single *inode*. In some sense, neither file links to the other; both point directly to the same file.

hash   A type of encryption that can be worked in only one direction. Hashes are often used to store passwords because decrypting a password from the hashed value is theoretically impossible. (In practice, though, encrypting random or targeted possible passwords and comparing them to the hashed value can sometimes yield the password.)

hostname   An alphanumeric name assigned to a computer. In TCP/IP, the hostname consists of two parts: the *machine name* and the *domain name*.

HTML   The *Hypertext Markup Language* is a method of providing formatting to a plain-text file that's to be displayed in an HTML-aware program. HTML is most commonly used as a file format for web pages.

HTTP   The *Hypertext Transfer Protocol* is the protocol used by web browsers and web servers to deliver web pages.

hub   A network device that ties together multiple computers. A hub differs from a *switch* in that a hub echoes packets to all the attached devices, whereas a switch sends data only to the destination. If two devices send data at the same time with a hub, this design causes a "collision," in which the two packets corrupt each other. The result is degraded performance when the senders have to pause and try to send again.

ICMP   The *Internet Control Message Protocol* is a way to send very simple control and error packets between computers on a TCP/IP network.

inode   A disk structure used on FFS and some other filesystems. Inodes are associated with files, one inode per file. Directory entries point to inodes, and inodes contain information on the file's size, where the file is stored on the disk, and so on.

internet/Internet   When not capitalized, refers to any network of networks, typically linked by routers. (2) When capitalized, refers to the globe-spanning network that expanded very rapidly in the 1990s, and which enables individuals to send e-mail globally, read web pages from around the world, and so on.

interpreter   A program that interprets a *source code* file on a line-by-line basis. Interpreters run programs slowly, but interpreted languages are easy to use because they require no compilation process. *Scripts* are programs written in interpreted languages.

IP address   A 4-byte (32-bit) address for computers on a TCP/IP network. The IP address is usually expressed as four base-10 numbers separated by dots, as in *172.19.65.11*.

IRC   *Internet Relay Chat* is a protocol used for real-time communication among groups of people. It's used for recreation and to obtain or provide help in performing computer problem solving.

ISA bus   A hardware standard for connecting add-on cards such as modems and sound cards to motherboards. The ISA bus is becoming rare, having been largely displaced by the *PCI bus*.

KDE   The *K Desktop Environment*, a popular desktop environment for FreeBSD. See also *GNOME*.

Kerberos   A network authentication and security protocol. Kerberos enables users to enter a password once for a session, and use services on any Kerberos-enabled server on an entire network. Its web page is `http://web.mit.edu/kerberos/www/`.

kernel   The core software component of an operating system. The kernel controls hardware access, disk filesystems, memory access, and so on.

kernel mode   A term describing a process that runs as part of the kernel. Such processes have privileged access to hardware and other kernel-mode processes, and are thus potentially dangerous if they contain bugs. See also *user mode*.

LAN   A *local area network* is a network that covers a small physical area, such as an office, a single building, or a small cluster of buildings. LANs can be linked to other LANs or to the Internet at large.

LBA mode   *Linear* (or *Logical*) *Block Addressing* is a mode of addressing a hard disk that uses a single linear number to uniquely identify a sector (usually 512 bytes) of data. SCSI disks have always used LBA mode, and modern EIDE disks also support this mode. This system contrasts with *CHS geometry* addressing, used on older disks and in some low-level disk data structures.

link   A directory entry that points to a file associated with another file. There are two types of links: *hard links* and *symbolic links* (also called *soft links*).

load average   A measure of CPU use. A load average of 1.0 represents demand for 100 percent of a CPU's time. Higher load averages indicate demand from more programs than the CPU can service, so most processes must make do with less CPU time than is optimal.

log file   A file in which servers and other system processes record information on their activities for future reference. Most FreeBSD log files reside in the /var/log directory, and /var/log/messages is the most commonly accessed log file.

machine code   See *machine language*.

machine language   The low-level codes that a computer understands. Machine language looks like gibberish to most people, including most computer programmers.

machine name   The portion of a *hostname* that uniquely identifies a computer within a domain (see *domain name*).

mail relay   A computer that accepts mail from one system for delivery to another system. If configured too loosely, a mail relay is known as an *open mail relay*, which can be abused to deliver *spam*.

MBR   The *Master Boot Record*, which is the first sector on an *x*86 hard disk. The MBR includes boot loader code and the primary partition table.

memory leak   A bug that causes a program to request memory it doesn't need, often repeatedly. A serious memory leak can cause available memory on a computer to shrink until the entire computer experiences problems.

MIME   The *Multipurpose Internet Mail Extension* is a code that can be used to identify a file type—for instance, an AbiWord document or a particular audio file type. MIME types are encoded with certain types of mail attachments, web page retrievals, and file browsers.

mount point   A directory that's used as an interface point for a filesystem (definition 2). Files and directories on the filesystem can be accessed as if they existed within the mount point directory.

netmask   See *network mask*.

network mask   A number that specifies the portion of an IP address that represents the network and the portion that represents the machine on the network. Also called the *netmask*.

network stack   A set of protocols that allow computers to communicate with one another on a network. The most common network stack in 2002 is TCP/IP.

NIC   A *network interface card* plugs into a computer to add a network interface (typically an *Ethernet* interface) to the computer.

office suite   A collection of programs that perform common office computing tasks. Office suites typically include at least three or more from the following program categories: word processor, spreadsheet, database, presentation, and business graphics.

open mail relay   A *mail relay* that's configured to allow any computer to relay mail, or at least many more computers than it should.

open source   A software development and distribution philosophy that calls for the release of source code, freedom to modify and redistribute that code, and various other ideals. FreeBSD is one of the major open source OSs in 2002.

outline font   See *scaleable font*.

packet filter   A type of *firewall* that operates on individual TCP/IP packets. Such firewalls allow or deny traffic based on source and destination IP addresses, port numbers, interfaces, and similar low-level criteria.

packet sniffer   A program that monitors and optionally records low-level network traffic (data packets). A packet sniffer can be a useful network diagnostic tool or a weapon used by crackers to steal passwords or other sensitive data.

pager   A type of program that displays a text file one screenful at a time. Two common pagers in FreeBSD are `more` and `less`.

PAM   The *Pluggable Authentication Module* is a system for handling usernames and passwords on FreeBSD. Rather than have each program read `/etc/passwd` directly to verify that a user's password is valid, the program calls the PAM tools, which do the job in a standardized way.

parent   In the context of FreeBSD processes, *parent* is a relative term that refers to the process that launched the subject process. Each process has precisely one parent process. See also *child*.

partition   A region of a hard disk that's accessed separately from other areas. Partitions generally hold filesystems, but they may hold other partitions or swap space. (2) Used as a verb, the act of creating a partition.

partition table   A data structure that describes the layout of partitions on a hard disk. In the *x86* world, the main partition table is part of the *MBR*, but supplemental partition information is associated with extended partitions and FreeBSD slices.

PCI bus   A hardware standard for connecting add-on cards such as SCSI host adapters and network cards to motherboards. The PCI bus is very popular in 2002. See also *ISA bus* and *AGP bus*.

PID   *Process ID.* This is a number that uniquely identifies a single process. Certain administrative commands operate on PIDs.

piping   Linking programs together in a virtual chain; each one runs, processing the output of the preceding program in the chain, and sending output to the next program in the chain. See also *redirection*.

playlist   A list of audio files or audio CD tracks you want to play in one session. Playlists are often maintained by MP3 players and CD players.

port   A translation of a program from one OS to another. (2) In networking, a resource created by the network stack, to which a network-enabled program attaches itself in order to send or receive data independently of other programs.

ports system   A collection of files that provide information on obtaining and compiling a wide variety of programs for FreeBSD. The ports system provides for semiautomated installation of many programs for FreeBSD.

PostScript   A page description language developed by Adobe. PostScript is commonly used on high-end printers (particularly laser printers, image setters, and so on). It's the *de facto* printing command language for UNIX (and hence FreeBSD) programs. See also *Ghostscript*.

preemptive multitasking   A method of multitasking in which the OS controls how much CPU time each program receives. This system contrasts with *cooperative multitasking*.

print queue   A virtual holding area for files waiting to be printed.

process   A running program. See also *PID*.

proxy server   A type of *firewall* that uses a server that partially processes a request, generates a new request to the original target, and delivers the returned data to the original client. Proxy servers can cache or modify data, resulting in speed improvements and the ability to filter data, such as removing ads or adult content from web sites.

public-key cryptography   A method of encoding data in which one participant makes a key available to anybody. This key may be used to encrypt data that can be decrypted only by the recipient's "private" key, or to decrypt data encrypted with the private key.

pull protocol   A protocol in which the client retrieves a message or document. This term is frequently used in reference to e-mail protocols such as POP or IMAP.

push protocol   A protocol in which the client sends a message or document. This term is frequently used in reference to e-mail protocols such as SMTP.

redirection   Sending output from a program to a file or through another program, or sending a file's contents or another program's output to a program as its input. Commonly used to let programs work together.

resolve   Translate a hostname into an IP address or vice versa, as in "to what address does `www.threeromco.com` resolve?"

`root`   The username associated with the system administrator. (In practice, this person should also have a non-`root` account.)

router   A computer that receives network traffic from one network and relays that traffic to another network.

Samba   A file and print server that uses the *SMB/CIFS* protocols, which are most commonly used by Windows file and print sharing. Samba allows a FreeBSD system to function as a file or print server for Windows systems.

scaleable font   A *font* that's described in mathematical terms, with each letter defined as a series of lines and curves. These descriptions can be scaled to display properly at any size on a device with any resolution, so they're quite flexible compared to the simpler *bitmap font* technologies.

script   A type of program written in a computer language that's designed to not require compilation. Scripts are often simple compared to compiled programs, and they're often used for configuration or to combine several compiled programs into a more flexible whole.

script kiddie   A relatively unskilled cracker, who works almost exclusively from intrusion kits (*scripts*) written by others. Some people prefer to reserve the term *cracker* for individuals with greater skills than those exhibited by script kiddies.

SCSI   The *Small Computer System Interface*, a hardware standard for connecting hard disks and similar devices to a computer. Less popular, more expensive, and more capable than the competing *ATA* standard.

server   A program that responds to network requests for data transfer. Examples include web servers, mail servers, and file servers. (2) A computer whose main purpose is to run one or more server programs.

shell   A program that accepts commands from the user. Typically used to refer to a text-mode program in which you type program filenames to launch those programs, among other things. Many FreeBSD shells include scripting features to help you automate routine or tedious tasks.

shell script   A script written in a shell language, such as sh, bash, or tcsh. Shell scripts are commonly used as system startup scripts and to perform various administrative tasks. See also *script*.

signal   A code that can be sent to a process to affect how it runs. Some common types of signals are used to terminate processes that cannot be terminated in other ways.

slice   A FreeBSD primary *x*86 partition.

SMB/CIFS   The *Server Message Block* (aka *Common Internet File System*) protocols, used by Windows systems for file and print sharing. See *Samba*.

social engineering   A type of attack on a computer in which an individual is tricked into revealing sensitive information such as a password.

soft link   See *symbolic link*.

source code   The form of a computer program that was written by, and is most easily modified by, a computer programmer. Source code files must be either processed directly by the computer using an *interpreter* program, or converted into *binary* format and run directly.

spam   Unsolicited bulk e-mail.

stage *n* boot loader   FreeBSD uses a three-stage boot loader process. The first stage resides in the hard disk's Master Boot Record (MBR) and allows you to choose the OS to boot. The second and third stages reside in the FreeBSD slice and allow you to enter kernel parameters or boot FreeBSD.

star topology   A network topology in which all the computers are tied together at a central point (a *hub* or *switch*). Modern 100 Mbps Ethernet uses a star topology.

sticky bit   A special permission bit that's commonly used on shared user directories, such as /tmp. This bit indicates that only a file's owner may delete a file in the directory.

super server   A server that listens for connections directed at several other servers, and that launches the appropriate server when a connection appears. Super servers can provide a degree of added security by applying uniform security checks to all the servers they handle, and they can reduce memory consumption in some situations. The standard FreeBSD super server is known as inetd.

superuser   See *system administrator*.

swap space   Disk space that FreeBSD treats as an extension to RAM. Swap space enables a computer to run more programs than it otherwise could, but slower than it would with an equivalent amount of additional RAM.

switch   A network device that ties together multiple computers. A switch differs from a *hub* in that a switch attempts to echo data packets from a source only to the addressee and not to other attached computers. This characteristic can help improve performance.

symbolic link   A type of *link* in which the link points to another file's directory entry. These links can point across different partitions, but are slightly slower to access than *hard links*.

system administration   Actions relating to the installation or maintenance of the operating system as a whole, or the hardware on which it runs. Typical system administration tasks include adding, updating, or removing programs; adding or deleting user accounts; and changing the options for servers.

system administrator   The individual responsible for configuring a computer, including adding or removing programs, creating user accounts, and so on. Also known as the *superuser*, the system administrator uses the root account.

tag   A code embedded in a file or data structure to carry special meaning. For instance, tags in *HTML* files indicate where links, bold text, headings, and so on begin and end.

tarball   A tar file, typically compressed with gzip. Tarballs have filenames that end in .tar.gz, or .tgz.

TCP   The *Transmission Control Protocol* is a type of network protocol that's a major component of the common *TCP/IP stack*. TCP packets encapsulate data in a larger data transfer. Most common Internet protocols, such as SMTP, HTTP, Telnet, and FTP, use TCP packets.

TCP/IP stack   The *Transmission Control Protocol/Internet Protocol stack* is the most popular set of network protocols in 2002. Two computers that use the TCP/IP stack can communicate with one another over a network, provided they have compatible high-level programs (such as a Telnet server and a Telnet client).

terminal program   A program that allows a computer to emulate a *dumb terminal*. Frequently used as a lowest-common-denominator method of access to UNIX or FreeBSD systems via serial ports or modems.

Trojan horse   A program that's advertised to do one thing, but that does something malicious instead of or in addition to the claimed function. Trojan horses are one of several methods that miscreants use to gain access to others' computers.

UDP   The *User Datagram Protocol* is a way to exchange data on a *TCP/IP* network. UDP packets are more complex than *ICMP* packets, but less complex than *TCP* packets. They're used by some simple TCP/IP protocols such as DNS and *DHCP*, and a few more complex ones, such as NFS.

UID   A *User ID* is a number that identifies a particular account. The usernames we use as humans are linked to UIDs.

USB   The *Universal Serial Bus*, a hardware standard for connecting modems, mice, keyboards, printers, scanners, and other low-speed external devices to computers. FreeBSD includes limited USB support, which is improving in scope and quality.

user mode   A term describing a process that's run outside of kernel mode. Such processes are managed by the kernel; they rely upon the kernel for access to memory, hardware, and other resources.

vector graphics   A method of describing an image in terms of lines, curves, and other shapes. Vector graphics scale well to output devices at any resolution, unlike *bitmap* graphics.

virtual console   A console session maintained independently of others, using a single console. You can switch between virtual console sessions in FreeBSD by pressing one of the function keys (F1 through F8; press these in conjunction with ALT if you're running X). This feature allows you to run multiple programs and easily switch between them.

virtual desktop   One of several displays operated by a window manager or desktop environment, each of which can host its own set of windows. You can switch between virtual desktops by clicking buttons or picking options from a menu. Virtual desktops help reduce clutter when you work with many X-based programs.

VNC   *Virtual Network Computing* is a client/server package that enables remote GUI access to a computer running XFree86, Windows, Mac OS, or other environments.

X Window System   FreeBSD's GUI environment, often referred to as X.

zombie   A computer that's been compromised to perform *DDoS attacks*. (2) A process on a FreeBSD system that's not been properly shut down.

Index

I

L

N

T

X

INTERNATIONAL CONTACT INFORMATION

AUSTRALIA
McGraw-Hill Book Company Australia Pty. Ltd.
TEL +61-2-9900-1800
FAX +61-2-9878-8881
http://www.mcgraw-hill.com.au
books-it_sydney@mcgraw-hill.com

CANADA
McGraw-Hill Ryerson Ltd.
TEL +905-430-5000
FAX +905-430-5020
http://www.mcgraw-hill.ca

**GREECE, MIDDLE EAST, & AFRICA
(Excluding South Africa)**
McGraw-Hill Hellas
TEL +30-210-6560-990
TEL +30-210-6560-993
TEL +30-210-6560-994
FAX +30-210-6545-525

MEXICO (Also serving Latin America)
McGraw-Hill Interamericana Editores S.A. de C.V.
TEL +525-117-1583
FAX +525-117-1589
http://www.mcgraw-hill.com.mx
fernando_castellanos@mcgraw-hill.com

SINGAPORE (Serving Asia)
McGraw-Hill Book Company
TEL +65-863-1580
FAX +65-862-3354
http://www.mcgraw-hill.com.sg
mghasia@mcgraw-hill.com

SOUTH AFRICA
McGraw-Hill South Africa
TEL +27-11-622-7512
FAX +27-11-622-9045
robyn_swanepoel@mcgraw-hill.com

SPAIN
McGraw-Hill/Interamericana de España, S.A.U.
TEL +34-91-180-3000
FAX +34-91-372-8513
http://www.mcgraw-hill.es
professional@mcgraw-hill.es

**UNITED KINGDOM, NORTHERN,
EASTERN, & CENTRAL EUROPE**
McGraw-Hill Education Europe
TEL +44-1-628-502500
FAX +44-1-628-770224
http://www.mcgraw-hill.co.uk
computing_neurope@mcgraw-hill.com

ALL OTHER INQUIRIES Contact:
Osborne/McGraw-Hill
TEL +1-510-549-6600
FAX +1-510-883-7600
http://www.osborne.com
omg_international@mcgraw-hill.com

LICENSE AGREEMENT

THIS PRODUCT (THE "PRODUCT") CONTAINS PROPRIETARY SOFTWARE, DATA AND INFORMATION (INCLUDING DOCUMENTATION) OWNED BY THE McGRAW-HILL COMPANIES, INC. ("McGRAW-HILL") AND ITS LICENSORS. YOUR RIGHT TO USE THE PRODUCT IS GOVERNED BY THE TERMS AND CONDITIONS OF THIS AGREEMENT.

LICENSE: Throughout this License Agreement, "you" shall mean either the individual or the entity whose agent opens this package. You are granted a non-exclusive and non-transferable license to use the Product subject to the following terms:
(i) If you have licensed a single user version of the Product, the Product may only be used on a single computer (i.e., a single CPU). If you licensed and paid the fee applicable to a local area network or wide area network version of the Product, you are subject to the terms of the following subparagraph (ii).
(ii) If you have licensed a local area network version, you may use the Product on unlimited workstations located in one single building selected by you that is served by such local area network. If you have licensed a wide area network version, you may use the Product on unlimited workstations located in multiple buildings on the same site selected by you that is served by such wide area network; provided, however, that any building will not be considered located in the same site if it is more than five (5) miles away from any building included in such site. In addition, you may only use a local area or wide area network version of the Product on one single server. If you wish to use the Product on more than one server, you must obtain written authorization from McGraw-Hill and pay additional fees.
(iii) You may make one copy of the Product for back-up purposes only and you must maintain an accurate record as to the location of the back-up at all times.

COPYRIGHT; RESTRICTIONS ON USE AND TRANSFER: All rights (including copyright) in and to the Product are owned by McGraw-Hill and its licensors. You are the owner of the enclosed disc on which the Product is recorded. You may not use, copy, decompile, disassemble, reverse engineer, modify, reproduce, create derivative works, transmit, distribute, sublicense, store in a database or retrieval system of any kind, rent or transfer the Product, or any portion thereof, in any form or by any means (including electronically or otherwise) except as expressly provided for in this License Agreement. You must reproduce the copyright notices, trademark notices, legends and logos of McGraw-Hill and its licensors that appear on the Product on the back-up copy of the Product which you are permitted to make hereunder. All rights in the Product not expressly granted herein are reserved by McGraw-Hill and its licensors.

TERM: This License Agreement is effective until terminated. It will terminate if you fail to comply with any term or condition of this License Agreement. Upon termination, you are obligated to return to McGraw-Hill the Product together with all copies thereof and to purge all copies of the Product included in any and all servers and computer facilities.

DISCLAIMER OF WARRANTY: THE PRODUCT AND THE BACK-UP COPY ARE LICENSED "AS IS." McGRAW-HILL, ITS LICENSORS AND THE AUTHORS MAKE NO WARRANTIES, EXPRESS OR IMPLIED, AS TO THE RESULTS TO BE OBTAINED BY ANY PERSON OR ENTITY FROM USE OF THE PRODUCT, ANY INFORMATION OR DATA INCLUDED THEREIN AND/OR ANY TECHNICAL SUPPORT SERVICES PROVIDED HEREUNDER, IF ANY ("TECHNICAL SUPPORT SERVICES"). McGRAW-HILL, ITS LICENSORS AND THE AUTHORS MAKE NO EXPRESS OR IMPLIED WARRANTIES OF MERCHANTABILITY OR FITNESS FOR A PARTICULAR PURPOSE OR USE WITH RESPECT TO THE PRODUCT. McGRAW-HILL, ITS LICENSORS, AND THE AUTHORS MAKE NO GUARANTEE THAT YOU WILL PASS ANY CERTIFICATION EXAM WHATSOEVER BY USING THIS PRODUCT. NEITHER McGRAW-HILL, ANY OF ITS LICENSORS NOR THE AUTHORS WARRANT THAT THE FUNCTIONS CONTAINED IN THE PRODUCT WILL MEET YOUR REQUIREMENTS OR THAT THE OPERATION OF THE PRODUCT WILL BE UNINTERRUPTED OR ERROR FREE. YOU ASSUME THE ENTIRE RISK WITH RESPECT TO THE QUALITY AND PERFORMANCE OF THE PRODUCT.

LIMITED WARRANTY FOR DISC: To the original licensee only, McGraw-Hill warrants that the enclosed disc on which the Product is recorded is free from defects in materials and workmanship under normal use and service for a period of ninety (90) days from the date of purchase. In the event of a defect in the disc covered by the foregoing warranty, McGraw-Hill will replace the disc.

LIMITATION OF LIABILITY: NEITHER McGRAW-HILL, ITS LICENSORS NOR THE AUTHORS SHALL BE LIABLE FOR ANY INDIRECT, SPECIAL OR CONSEQUENTIAL DAMAGES, SUCH AS BUT NOT LIMITED TO, LOSS OF ANTICIPATED PROFITS OR BENEFITS, RESULTING FROM THE USE OR INABILITY TO USE THE PRODUCT EVEN IF ANY OF THEM HAS BEEN ADVISED OF THE POSSIBILITY OF SUCH DAMAGES. THIS LIMITATION OF LIABILITY SHALL APPLY TO ANY CLAIM OR CAUSE WHATSOEVER WHETHER SUCH CLAIM OR CAUSE ARISES IN CONTRACT, TORT, OR OTHERWISE. Some states do not allow the exclusion or limitation of indirect, special or consequential damages, so the above limitation may not apply to you.

U.S. GOVERNMENT RESTRICTED RIGHTS: Any software included in the Product is provided with restricted rights subject to subparagraphs (c), (1) and (2) of the Commercial Computer Software-Restricted Rights clause at 48 C.F.R. 52.227-19. The terms of this Agreement applicable to the use of the data in the Product are those under which the data are generally made available to the general public by McGraw-Hill. Except as provided herein, no reproduction, use, or disclosure rights are granted with respect to the data included in the Product and no right to modify or create derivative works from any such data is hereby granted.

GENERAL: This License Agreement constitutes the entire agreement between the parties relating to the Product. The terms of any Purchase Order shall have no effect on the terms of this License Agreement. Failure of McGraw-Hill to insist at any time on strict compliance with this License Agreement shall not constitute a waiver of any rights under this License Agreement. This License Agreement shall be construed and governed in accordance with the laws of the State of New York. If any provision of this License Agreement is held to be contrary to law, that provision will be enforced to the maximum extent permissible and the remaining provisions will remain in full force and effect.

GNU GENERAL PUBLIC LICENSE
Version 2, June 1991

Copyright (C) 1989, 1991 Free Software Foundation, Inc.

675 Mass Ave, Cambridge, MA 02139, USA

Everyone is permitted to copy and distribute verbatim copies of this license document, but changing it is not allowed.

Preamble

The licenses for most software are designed to take away your freedom to share and change it. By contrast, the GNU General Public License is intended to guarantee your freedom to share and change free software—to make sure the software is free for all its users. This General Public License applies to most of the Free Software Foundation's software and to any other program whose authors commit to using it. (Some other Free Software Foundation software is covered by the GNU Library General Public License instead.) You can apply it to your programs, too.

When we speak of free software, we are referring to freedom, not price. Our General Public Licenses are designed to make sure that you have the freedom to distribute copies of free software (and charge for this service if you wish), that you receive source code or can get it if you want it, that you can change the software or use pieces of it in new free programs; and that you know you can do these things.

To protect your rights, we need to make restrictions that forbid anyone to deny you these rights or to ask you to surrender the rights. These restrictions translate to certain responsibilities for you if you distribute copies of the software, or if you modify it.

For example, if you distribute copies of such a program, whether gratis or for a fee, you must give the recipients all the rights that you have. You must make sure that they, too, receive or can get the source code. And you must show them these terms so they know their rights.

We protect your rights with two steps: (1) copyright the software, and (2) offer you this license which gives you legal permission to copy, distribute and/or modify the software.

Also, for each author's protection and ours, we want to make certain that everyone understands that there is no warranty for this free software. If the software is modified by someone else and passed on, we want its recipients to know that what they have is not the original, so that any problems introduced by others will not reflect on the original authors' reputations.

Finally, any free program is threatened constantly by software patents. We wish to avoid the danger that redistributors of a free program will individually obtain patent licenses, in effect making the program proprietary. To prevent this, we have made it clear that any patent must be licensed for everyone's free use or not licensed at all.

The precise terms and conditions for copying, distribution and modification follow.

GNU GENERAL PUBLIC LICENSE TERMS AND CONDITIONS FOR COPYING,
DISTRIBUTION AND MODIFICATION

0. This License applies to any program or other work which contains a notice placed by the copyright holder saying it may be distributed under the terms of this General Public License. The "Program", below, refers to any such program or work, and a "work based on the Program" means either the Program or any derivative work under copyright law: that is to say, a work containing the Program or a portion of it, either verbatim or with modifications and/or translated into another language. (Hereinafter, translation is included without limitation in the term "modification".) Each licensee is addressed as "you".

Activities other than copying, distribution and modification are not covered by this License; they are outside its scope. The act of running the Program is not restricted, and the output from the Program is covered only if its contents constitute a work based on the Program (independent of having been made by running the Program). Whether that is true depends on what the Program does.

1. You may copy and distribute verbatim copies of the Program's source code as you receive it, in any medium, provided that you conspicuously and appropriately publish on each copy an appropriate copyright notice and disclaimer of warranty; keep intact all the notices that refer to this License and to the absence of any warranty; and give any other recipients of the Program a copy of this License along with the Program.

You may charge a fee for the physical act of transferring a copy, and you may at your option offer warranty protection in exchange for a fee.

2. You may modify your copy or copies of the Program or any portion of it, thus forming a work based on the Program, and copy and distribute such modifications or work under the terms of Section 1 above, provided that you also meet all of these conditions:

a) You must cause the modified files to carry prominent notices stating that you changed the files and the date of any change.

b) You must cause any work that you distribute or publish, that in whole or in part contains or is derived from the Program or any part thereof, to be licensed as a whole at no charge to all third parties under the terms of this License.

c) If the modified program normally reads commands interactively when run, you must cause it, when started running for such interactive use in the most ordinary way, to print or display an announcement including an appropriate copyright notice and a notice that there is no warranty (or else, saying that you provide a warranty) and that users may redistribute the program under these conditions, and telling the user how to view a copy of this License. (Exception: if the Program itself is interactive but does not normally print such an announcement, your work based on the Program is not required to print an announcement.)

These requirements apply to the modified work as a whole. If identifiable sections of that work are not derived from the Program, and can be reasonably considered independent and separate works in themselves, then this License, and its terms, do not apply to those sections when you distribute them as separate works. But when you distribute the same sections as part of a whole which is a work based on the Program, the distribution of the whole must be on the terms of this License, whose permissions for other licensees extend to the entire whole, and thus to each and every part regardless of who wrote it. Thus, it is not the intent of this section to claim rights or contest your rights to work written entirely by you; rather, the intent is to exercise the right to control the distribution of derivative or collective works based on the Program.

In addition, mere aggregation of another work not based on the Program with the Program (or with a work based on the Program) on a volume of a storage or distribution medium does not bring the other work under the scope of this License.

3. You may copy and distribute the Program (or a work based on it, under Section 2) in object code or executable form under the terms of Sections 1 and 2 above provided that you also do one of the following:

a) Accompany it with the complete corresponding machine-readable source code, which must be distributed under the terms of Sections 1 and 2 above on a medium customarily used for software interchange; or,

b) Accompany it with a written offer, valid for at least three years, to give any third party, for a charge no more than your cost of physically performing source distribution, a complete machine-readable copy of the corresponding source code, to be distributed under the terms of Sections 1 and 2 above on a medium customarily used for software interchange; or,

c) Accompany it with the information you received as to the offer to distribute corresponding source code. (This alternative is allowed only for noncommercial distribution and only if you received the program in object code or executable form with such an offer, in accord with Subsection b above.)

The source code for a work means the preferred form of the work for making modifications to it. For an executable work, complete source code means all the source code for all modules it contains, plus any associated interface definition files, plus the scripts used to control compilation and installation of the executable. However, as a special exception, the source code distributed need not include anything that is normally distributed (in either source or binary form) with the major components (compiler, kernel, and so on) of the operating system on which the executable runs, unless that component itself accompanies the executable.

If distribution of executable or object code is made by offering access to copy from a designated place, then offering equivalent access to copy the source code from the same place counts as distribution of the source code, even though third parties are not compelled to copy the source along with the object code.

4. You may not copy, modify, sublicense, or distribute the Program except as expressly provided under this License. Any attempt otherwise to copy, modify, sublicense or distribute the Program is void, and will automatically terminate your rights under this License. However, parties who have received copies, or rights, from you under this License will not have their licenses terminated so long as such parties remain in full compliance.

5. You are not required to accept this License, since you have not signed it. However, nothing else grants you permission to modify or distribute the Program or its derivative works. These actions are prohibited by law if you do not accept this License. Therefore, by modifying or distributing the Program (or any work based on the Program), you indicate your acceptance of this License to do so, and all its terms and conditions for copying, distributing or modifying the Program or works based on it.

6. Each time you redistribute the Program (or any work based on the Program), the recipient automatically receives a license from the original licensor to copy, distribute or modify the Program subject to these terms and conditions. You may not impose any further restrictions on the recipients' exercise of the rights granted herein. You are not responsible for enforcing compliance by third parties to this License.

7. If, as a consequence of a court judgment or allegation of patent infringement or for any other reason (not limited to patent issues), conditions are imposed on you (whether by court order, agreement or otherwise) that contradict the conditions of this License, they do not excuse you from the conditions of this License. If you cannot distribute so as to satisfy simultaneously your obligations under this License and any other pertinent obligations, then as a consequence you may not distribute the Program at all. For example, if a patent license would not permit royalty-free redistribution of the Program by all those who receive copies directly or indirectly through you, then the only way you could satisfy both it and this License would be to refrain entirely from distribution of the Program.

If any portion of this section is held invalid or unenforceable under any particular circumstance, the balance of the section is intended to apply and the section as a whole is intended to apply in other circumstances.

It is not the purpose of this section to induce you to infringe any patents or other property right claims or to contest validity of any such claims; this section has the sole purpose of protecting the integrity of the free software distribution system, which is implemented by public license practices. Many people have made generous contributions to the wide range of software distributed through that system in reliance on consistent application of that system; it is up to the author/donor to decide if he or she is willing to distribute software through any other system and a licensee cannot impose that choice.

This section is intended to make thoroughly clear what is believed to be a consequence of the rest of this License.

8. If the distribution and/or use of the Program is restricted in certain countries either by patents or by copyrighted interfaces, the original copyright holder who places the Program under this License may add an explicit geographical distribution limitation excluding those countries, so that distribution is permitted only in or among countries not thus excluded. In such case, this License incorporates the limitation as if written in the body of this License.

9. The Free Software Foundation may publish revised and/or new versions of the General Public License from time to time. Such new versions will be similar in spirit to the present version, but may differ in detail to address new problems or concerns.

Each version is given a distinguishing version number. If the Program specifies a version number of this License which applies to it and "any later version", you have the option of following the terms and conditions either of that version or of any later version published by the Free Software Foundation. If the Program does not specify a version number of this License, you may choose any version ever published by the Free Software Foundation.

10. If you wish to incorporate parts of the Program into other free programs whose distribution conditions are different, write to the author to ask for permission. For software which is copyrighted by the Free Software Foundation, write to the Free Software Foundation; we sometimes make exceptions for this. Our decision will be guided by the two goals of preserving the free status of all derivatives of our free software and of promoting the sharing and reuse of software generally.

NO WARRANTY

11. BECAUSE THE PROGRAM IS LICENSED FREE OF CHARGE, THERE IS NO WARRANTY FOR THE PROGRAM, TO THE EXTENT PERMITTED BY APPLICABLE LAW. EXCEPT WHEN OTHERWISE STATED IN WRITING THE COPYRIGHT HOLDERS AND/OR OTHER PARTIES PROVIDE THE PROGRAM "AS IS" WITHOUT WARRANTY OF ANY KIND, EITHER EXPRESSED OR IMPLIED, INCLUDING, BUT NOT LIMITED TO, THE IMPLIED WARRANTIES OF MERCHANTABILITY AND FITNESS FOR A PARTICULAR PURPOSE. THE ENTIRE RISK AS TO THE QUALITY AND PERFORMANCE OF THE PROGRAM IS WITH YOU. SHOULD THE PROGRAM PROVE DEFECTIVE, YOU ASSUME THE COST OF ALL NECESSARY SERVICING, REPAIR OR CORRECTION.

12. IN NO EVENT UNLESS REQUIRED BY APPLICABLE LAW OR AGREED TO IN WRITING WILL ANY COPYRIGHT HOLDER, OR ANY OTHER PARTY WHO MAY MODIFY AND/OR REDISTRIBUTE THE PROGRAM AS PERMITTED ABOVE, BE LIABLE TO YOU FOR DAMAGES, INCLUDING ANY GENERAL, SPECIAL, INCIDENTAL OR CONSEQUENTIAL DAMAGES ARISING OUT OF THE USE OR INABILITY TO USE THE PROGRAM (INCLUDING BUT NOT LIMITED TO LOSS OF DATA OR DATA BEING RENDERED INACCURATE OR LOSSES SUSTAINED BY YOU OR THIRD PARTIES OR A FAILURE OF THE PROGRAM TO OPERATE WITH ANY OTHER PROGRAMS), EVEN IF SUCH HOLDER OR OTHER PARTY HAS BEEN ADVISED OF THE POSSIBILITY OF SUCH DAMAGES.

END OF TERMS AND CONDITIONS

Appendix: How to Apply These Terms to Your New Programs

If you develop a new program, and you want it to be of the greatest possible use to the public, the best way to achieve this is to make it free software which everyone can redistribute and change under these terms.

To do so, attach the following notices to the program. It is safest to attach them to the start of each source file to most effectively convey the exclusion of warranty; and each file should have at least the "copyright" line and a pointer to where the full notice is found.

<one line to give the program's name and a brief idea of what it does.> Copyright (C) 19yy <name of author>

This program is free software; you can redistribute it and/or modify it under the terms of the GNU General Public License as published by the Free Software Foundation; either version 2 of the License, or (at your option) any later version.

This program is distributed in the hope that it will be useful, but WITHOUT ANY WARRANTY; without even the implied warranty of MERCHANTABILITY or FITNESS FOR A PARTICULAR PURPOSE. See the GNU General Public License for more details.

You should have received a copy of the GNU General Public License along with this program; if not, write to the Free Software Foundation, Inc., 675 Mass Ave, Cambridge, MA 02139, USA.

Also add information on how to contact you by electronic and paper mail.

If the program is interactive, make it output a short notice like this when it starts in an interactive mode:

Gnomovision version 69, Copyright (C) 19yy name of author Gnomovision comes with ABSOLUTELY NO WARRANTY; for details type `show w'. This is free software, and you are welcome to redistribute it under certain conditions; type `show c' for details.

The hypothetical commands `show w' and `show c' should show the appropriate parts of the General Public License. Of course, the commands you use may be called something other than `show w' and `show c'; they could even be mouse-clicks or menu items—whatever suits your program.

You should also get your employer (if you work as a programmer) or your school, if any, to sign a "copyright disclaimer" for the program, if necessary. Here is a sample; alter the names:

Yoyodyne, Inc., hereby disclaims all copyright interest in the program `Gnomovision' (which makes passes at compilers) written by James Hacker.

<signature of Ty Coon>, 1 April 1989
Ty Coon, President of Vice

This General Public License does not permit incorporating your program into proprietary programs. If your program is a subroutine library, you may consider it more useful to permit linking proprietary applications with the library. If this is what you want to do, use the GNU Library General Public License instead of this License.

BSD LICENSE AGREEMENT

All of the documentation and software included in the 4.4BSD and 4.4BSD-Lite Releases is copyrighted by The Regents of the University of California.

Copyright 1979, 1980, 1983, 1986, 1988, 1989, 1991, 1992, 1993, 1994

The Regents of the University of California. All rights reserved.

Redistribution and use in source and binary forms, with or without modification, are permitted provided that the following conditions are met:

1. Redistributions of source code must retain the above copyright notice, this list of conditions and the following disclaimer.

2. Redistributions in binary form must reproduce the above copyright notice, this list of conditions and the following disclaimer in the documentation and/or other materials provided with the distribution.

3. Neither the name of the University nor the names of its contributors may be used to endorse or promote products derived from this software without specific prior written permission.